D1824750

INTRODUCTION TO BLUECOAT WEB SECURITY

BlueCoat Proxy SG, Caching, Proxy AV, BCWF, K9 and Reporter

JOE ANTONY

ISBN: 0615582931
ISBN 13: 9780615582931

Library of Congress Control Number: 2012930077
CreateSpace, North Charleston, SC

ABOUT THE AUTHOR:

Joe Antony Sebastin (BTPSP #5) has 8 years of experience in Information Security field. To make a great contribution to his BlueCoat folks, friends, vendors, engineers/ administrators, and partners, he wrote his first official book for BlueCoat technology. This book makes everyone easily to understand how BlueCoat technology functions and gain more insight about it. He holds an esteemed and prestigious BTPSP certification in both the Web Security and Acceleration (WAN Optimization) pillars from BlueCoat called Blue Touch Professional Services Partner (BTPSP). He works for Dimension Data one of the top five best companies for providing IT support and services. The author provides sales, support, architect services and best practices solutions for BlueCoat technology. He has consulting and deployment experience in BlueCoat technologies for many fortune 100 companies includes financial industries, government agencies, data centers, health care, security consulting firms, consumer market companies, telecommunications, technology infrastructure, energy industries and etc... He has overall knowledge, experience, and certified in many vendor products and technologies like Checkpoint, Juniper, Cisco, RedHat, McAfee and IBM.

You could always reach the author for any review, comments and ideas about this book to joe.antony@bluecoatweb.com . You could also visit the website www.bluecoatweb.com for any additional information, blogs and news/events about BlueCoat technologies. We sincerely appreciate all your inputs and support on this project, without you, this book would not be a great success.

ACKNOWLEDGEMENT

I would first like devotionally thank the Lord Jehovah and Jesus, who showered me with the infinite wisdom to write my first book and my mother and brother Oliver Frank. My great credits and honor go to for my philosophical mentors Edward Hanus and David Soltesz, who thought and guided me to this new world of publishing and made me a good writer. Always I want to thank to my friends who inspired and supported on this project the credits goes to Latchoumi Narayanan, Vincent Price, Heather Garber, Shantanu Mehrotra, Mohamed Idris, Cindy Sizemore, Kris/Ryan/John Craig, Fredrick Selby, Kodi Krishnan, Daisy Ramos, Trilok Budathoki, Amy Matlock, Eva (Enesh),Petar Miskovic, Alice Norkeen, Kurt Krautheim, Brenda Evans, David Abraham, Divnaduke, Donald Lefft, Gary Armstrong, Nathan Alex, Heath Jones / Ama Blackwood, Mehran, Pete Spinel and all friends at Tokubei(Mucho and Tak-ya).

I'd like to thank everyone in Dimension Data and especially Gregory Truex, Mark Behan, Dean Ferraro, John Addeo, Jason Howland, Richard Szkodzinski, Joshua Fedor, Kerrie Corrigan, Ingrid Barchat, Paul Ayars, Frank Jones, Douglas Concepcion, Crystal Soles, Jeanne Malone, Michael Thuroff and Darryl Eady.

I would always extend my thanks to my BlueCoat friends Steven Watkins, Glenn Medina, Shannon Buggie, Mark Pray, Pam, Kerry, Ritesh, Jerry Ducasse, Kevin Keithan, Keith Chomentowski, Jerry Archer and all the BlueCoat employees who I missed to include here.

And finally word of thanks to my Macfee friends Larry Pfeifer and Joseph_Fiorella for their support. And my best people and friends in Morgan Stanley for all their contribution Istvan Lodor, Chris Kozlowski, Maryam Arakelian, Richard Vianna, William Goeren, Michael Lo, Andrew Dumaresq, Thuy Nguyen, Jeff Ehrenkrantz, Choy William, Elliott Kang, Yongning Shao, Tamika, and Eric Medina.

TABLE OF CONTENTS   PAGE

Chapter 1- Introduction to Bluecoat   *1*

1.1 Benefits of Proxy server   *1*
1.2 Introduction to BlueCoat   *3*
1.3 Bluecoats security products list   *4*
1.3.1 BlueCoat Proxy SG   *5*
1.3.2 BlueCoat AV   *6*
1.3.3 BlueCoat WebFilter   *8*
1.3.4 BlueCoat Proxy Client   *10*
1.3.5 BlueCoat K9 Web Protection   *12*
1.3.6 BlueCoat Reporter   *13*
1.3.7 BlueCoat Director   *14*
1.5 Threat Pulse   *15*
1.6 Test Yourself   *17*

Chapter 2 - Caching and Optimization   *19*

2.1 Caching and paging methods   *19*
2.2 Caching Terminology   *22*
2.3 Caching Algorithm   *24*
2.3.1 On-line algorithm   *24*
2.3.2 Off-line algorithm   *26*
2.3.3. Competitive Ratio   *29*
2.4 Different caching Replacement Algorithms   *29*
2.4.1 Belady's Algorithm   *30*
2.4.2 Least Recently Used   *30*
2.4.3 Most Recently Used   *31*
2.4.4 Least-Frequently Used   *32*
2.4.5 Pseudo-LRU   *32*
2.4.6 Adaptive Replacement Cache   *33*
2.4.7 Random Replacement   *34*
2.4.8 First in First Out (FIFO)   *35*
2.4.9 Simple Time based   *36*
2.4.10 Extended time-based expiration   *36*

2.4.1 Sliding time-based expiration   *37*

2.5. Caching and optimization in Blue Coat   *38*

2.6 MACH5   *38*

2.7 What is Object?   *39*

2.7.1 Object caching   *41*

2.7.1 Object pipelining   *41*

2.7.2 Adaptive refresh   *45*

2.7.3 SSL optimization   *45*

2.8 Byte Caching   *45*

2.9 Bandwidth management   *47*

2.10 Protocol optimization   *48*

2.11 Compression and methods   *49*

2.11.1 HTTP method   *50*

2.11.2 Point-to-Point method   *52*

2.12 Text Yourself   *53*

Chapter 3 - Bluecoat SG Proxy Deployment   *55*

3.1 Brief description of Proxy Deployment   *55*

3.2 Transparent proxy deployment   *56*

3.2.1 Virtual Inline deployment   *58*

3.2.1.1 Transparent : Layer 4 switch – Virtually Inline   *58*

3.2.1.2 Transparent: Cisco WCCP – Virtual Inline   *61*

3.2.2 Inline deployment   *63*

3.2.2.1 Transparent : Bridging Inline   *63*

3.2.2.2 Transparent: Default router - Inline   *64*

3.2.2.3 IP forwarding   *65*

3.3 Explicit proxy deployment   *66*

3.4 Reverse Proxy Deployment   *69*

3.5 Forward Proxy Deployment   *71*

3.6 Test yourself   *73*

Chapter 4 - Configuring Blue Coat Proxy SG   *77*

4.1 Initial setup of Proxy SG   *77*

4.1.1 Setup via Serial console   *78*

4.1.2 Setup via LCD panel   *83*

4.1.3 Setup via network TCP / IP   *88*

4.2 Management console   *88*

4.3 Configuring hostname   *90*

4.4 Configuring time and time zone   *91*

4.5 Configuring Adapters/Network interfaces/VLAN   *94*

4.5.1 Configuring IP routing and gateway   *102*

4.5.1.1 Load Balancing   *104*

4.5.1.2 Failover   *106*

4.6 Configuring DNS and DNS imputing   *109*

4.7 Creating Private Networks and Private Domains   *115*

4.8 Configuring Proxy Services   *117*

4.9 Test Yourself   *123*

Chapter 5 - Content filtering and WebPulse   *127*

5.1 What is Content Filtering   *127*

5.2 Content Filtering Categories and Databases   *128*

5.3 Content filtering vendors   *131*

5.4 On-Box Versus Off-Box Content filtering Solutions   *132*

5.5 BlueCoat Web Filter (BCWF) and categories   *137*

5.6 Configuring BCWF database   *147*

5.7 WebPulse   *150*

5.7.1 DRTR   *151*

5.7.1.1 Real time mode   *151*

5.7.1.2 Background mode   *155*

5.7.2 Configuring DRTR dynamic categorization   *156*

5.7.3 WebPulse cloud service deployment   *159*

5.7.2 Malware Feedback or Proactive threat detection   *160*

5.8 IWF (Internet Watch Foundation)   *164*

5.9 Local Database   *166*

5.10 Test Yourself   *172*

Chapter 6 -Visual Policy Manager   *175*

6.1 What is VPM   *175*

6.2 CPL files and VPM files   *176*

6.3 Policy Evaluation options and Global Policy   *179*

6.4 Visual Policy Manager (VPM)   *181*

6.5 Creating Administrator Accounts   *182*

6.6 VPM Dashboard   *190*

6.7 Policy Evaluation Order   *196*

6.8 Policy Translation and VPM Objects   *200*

6.9 Web Content filtering   *201*

6.10 Combined objects   *207*

6.11 Deny and Force Deny   *210*

6.12 Local Database   *214*

6.12 Caching configuration   *216*

6.12.1 Always Verify   *217*

6.12.2 Do not cache   *217*

6.12.3 *Force Cache*   218
6.13 *Test Yourself*   219

Chapter 7 – Authentication   223

7.1 *Introduction to Authentication*   223
7.2 *Authentications types in BlueCoat*   223
7.3 *Authorization*   224
7.4 *Authentication in Bluecoat*   225
7.4.1 *Authentication for managing Proxy SG*   225
7.4.2 *Authentication for OCS*   232
7.4.3 *Authentication for accessing Proxy SG services*   233
7.4.3.1 *Explicit authentication*   233
7.4.3.2 *Transparent authentication*   234
7.5 *Transparent Authentication using cookie surrogate*   237
7.6 *Transparent authentication using IP surrogate*   241
7.7 *Enabling Cookie/IP authentication for Transparent proxy*   243
7.8 *Configuring authentication servers*   244
7.9 *Configuring the VPM policies for authentication*   248
7.10 *Test Yourself*

Chapter 8- WCCP   253

8.1 *What is WCCP?*   253
8.2 *Benefits of WCCP*   254
8.3 *Service group*   255
8.3.1 *Router with multiple service groups with BlueCoat SG*   255
8.3.2 *BlueCoat SG with multiple service groups with router*   257
8.4 *Service group types*   258
8.5 *Service group IP addressing*   258
8.6 *GRE forwarding and return method*   260
8.6.1 *Cached object*   260
8.6.2 *Non-cached object*   262
8.7 *L2 forwarding and return method*   265
8.7.1 *Cached object*   265
8.7.2 *Non-cached object*   267
8.8 *Router Affinity*   268
8.9 *Load Balancing Methods*   268
8.9.1 *Equal load balancing*   268
8.9.2 *Unequal load balancing*   269
8.10 *Designated cache*   270
8.11 *Load balancing algorithm*   270
8.11.1 *Hash Assignment*   271

8.11.2 Mask assignment   272
8.12 Configuring WCCP in BlueCoat SG   273
8.13 Test Yourself   277

Chapter 9 - Proxy Anti Virus   281

9.1. What is BlueCoat Proxy AV?   281
9.2. Protocols scanned by BlueCoat Proxy AV   282
9.3 What is Malware?   283
9.4 ICAP Protocol   283
9.5 Scanning modes in ICAP   284
9.5. 1 REQMOD mode   284
9.5.1 RESPMOD mode   286
9.6 ISTag   288
9.7 Proxy AV deployment   289
9.7.1 One Proxy SG And One Proxy AV   290
9.7.2 Multiple Proxy SG and One Proxy AV   291
9.7.3 Multiple Proxy AV and One Proxy SG   292
9.7.4 Multiple Proxy SG and Multiple Proxy AV   293
9.8 Initial Configuration of BlueCoat Proxy AV   294
9.9 Adding Proxy AV in VPM policies   300
9.10 Update the license and upgrade the Proxy AV   301
9.11 Anti-virus signature and Firmware update   305
9.11.1 Anti-virus Signature update   305
9.11.2 Firmware update   305
9.12 Integrating Proxy SG and Proxy AV   306
9.13 Testing the Proxy AV   319
9.14 Scanning file types   329
9.15 Deferred Scanning   322
9.16 ICTM (Intelligent Connection Traffic Monitoring)   322
9.17 Test Yourself   323

Chapter 10 - BlueCoat Reporter   327

10.1 BlueCoat Reporter Network Architecture   328
10.2 BlueCoat Reporter Internal Architecture   329
10.3 Types of logs in BlueCoat   332
10.4 BlueCoat Reporter installation   333
10.5 Configuring the BlueCoat Proxy for access logs   329
10.6 Creating databases in the BlueCoat Reporter   344
10.7 Log source and Dashboard   351
10.8 Generating Reports   353
10.9 Test Yourself   357

Chapter 11 - K9 Web Protection   *359*

11.1 What K9 Web Protection   *359*
11.2 Rrequirements for installing BlueCoat K9 protection   *361*
11.3 Registration with BlueCoat K9 Webprotection   *362*
11.4 Installing BlueCoat K9 protection   *362*
11.5 Configuring the Web categories   *368*
11.6 Configuring Time restrictions and Night Guard   *370*
11.7 Web Site exceptions   *372*
11.8 Blocking effects   *373*
11.9 URL Keywords   *376*
11.10 Advance Options   *376*
11.10 .1 Update to Beta   *376*
11. 10.2 Force Safe Search   *377*
11. 10.3 Filtering Secure Traffic   *378*
11.10.4 Supervisor Mode   *379*
11.10.5 Reset to Initial Settings   *380*
11.11 Internet activity   *380*
11.12 Test Yourself   *382*

Chapter 12- Trouble-Shooting and Maintenance   *385*

12.1 Trouble-shooting Proxy SG   *385*
12.2 Trouble-shooting Proxy AV   *402*
12.3 Trouble-shooting BlueCoat Reporter   *408*
12.4 Test Yourself   *416*

Question and Answers   *419*

Appendix A   *437*

Index   *439*

C H A P T E R 1

....

INTRODUCTION TO BLUECOAT

INTRODUCTION TO PROXIES:

In this chapter we will give a brief introduction to proxies, how they evolved in technology, and their benefits compared to other security devices. We will also explain the different security products that are available in BlueCoat and how they all make the Blue Coat Secure Web Gateway, which is a combination of all the BlueCoat products like Proxy SG, Proxy AV, BlueCoat Director, K9 Web protection, BCWF, Web Pulse, and Threat Protection.

The best definition we can give for "What is a Proxy?"
"A 'proxy' is a device, server, or appliance that serves to allow clients to make in-direct network connections or acts as an intermediary system to connect other network services."
The above was a basic definition when proxy first evolved in the IT industry. As time went on, many new features were added to it, like URL filtering, ICAP (Internet Content Adaption Protocol) scanning, caching, logging (Access and Event), authentication, IP access-list, bandwidth management, inbox virus scanning, etc.

So what are the benefits of proxy server?

1. I have firewall. Do I need a proxy server?

A firewall is network device, which inspects on Layer 3 and 4 in TCP/IP layer, but all modern firewalls have features of ALG (Application Layer Gateways) also known as proxies which support HTTP, FTP, Telnet, SMB, CIFS etc... but could handle only the basic known TCP functions, but it is not completely aware of the application layer functions. This doesn't mean a proxy shouldn't be used; the traffic is distributed and forwarded to do a detailed analysis application engine which is the proxy, specially built for applications, for example. HTTP, HTTPS, SMB, CIFS, RTMP, RTSP, MMS, etc.

URL filtering can be done, scanning both inbox and outbox in the firewall, but the load is off-loaded on the firewall to an application security device like the proxies, so that it can process the network traffic efficiently, avoid false-positives, and avoid single-point-failures.

2. Which applications can be proxied?

Any application in the IT industry could be proxied, but the question is, "What proxy am I using to do it, and on what application?" or, "Will the proxy support that application?" The proxy technologies and products that are available on the market, like Blue Coat®, WebWasher from MacAfee, Web Sense, and Riverbed, are focused on widely distributed applications that are used in a network such as HTTP, HTTPS, RTMP, RTSP, MMS, or IM. But there are application-specific proxies that have been developed by the vendors themselves for their products; for example, Oracle uses its own Oracle proxy server for the Oracle database and application. Will the same Oracle database and application proxy feature be supported in Blue Coat®, Mcafee WebWasher, Websense, or RiverBed, etc? The answer will be no, since their application can only be supported if the vendor is able to understand the protocol and how it works.

In Blue Coat®, applications like HTTP, HTTPS, RTMP, RTSP, MMS, IM (AOL, MSN, Yahoo), DNS, FTP, SOCKS, Telnet, or CIFS can usually be proxied.

3. Caching saves bandwidth and money!

Generally a "cache" refers to a component that transparently stores data so that future requests for that data can be served faster. Here the cache is stored locally, so the round-trip time to the server to fetch the data is saved. The data that is stored within a cache might be values that have been computed earlier or duplicates of original values that are stored elsewhere.

A cache is not as same as a proxy, but it is one of the features that is built into the proxy. The first request is proxied and the subsequent requests are served from the cache. Some technology works by only proxying and not caching, such as antivirus software or DLP (Data loss prevention).

Caching is used in different hardwares and technologies like CPU, disk, protocols (DNS, web), database, etc. Blue Coat® offers caching solutions for applications like HTTP, HTTPS, RTMP, RTSP, MMS, FTP, SMB, and CIFS.

4. Antivirus scanning

For most networks, web application traffic is mission-critical, representing 80% of the total Internet traffic. Web traffic includes HTTP, FTP, IM, peer-to-peer (P2P), and streaming. Viruses, malware, and Trojans can be scanned and stopped at the gateway. Inbox scanning can be done on the proxy itself, but the scanning is off-loaded to AV engines on explicit servers; this increases the performance. To integrate the AV solution, ICAP protocol is used.

5. URL filtering

As we are aware, 70% of malware attacks are web-based. URL filtering provides a way to categorize the sites into categories and allows the administrator to access based on categorizes. Examples of categorizes are Shopping, News/Media, Hacking, Pornography, and Spyware/Malware sources. Usually a group of users is assigned using LDAP to certain set of categories and allow or deny as per the business requirement of the company. In this way there is control and visibility in the network of the sites that have been accessed by the users in the network.

6. Authentication

Modern proxies have capabilities of integrating with authentication databases like LDAP, Single Sign-on, RADIUS, Siteminder, etc. Authentication can be based on IPs or users. For more granular-based access control and security best practices, we go for user-based authentication. This gives visibility of all the users' access and surfing habits, and tracks users on using the Internet for business reasons and accountability for legal issues.

7. Access logs and Reporting

In a corporation, analysis is needed of the web traffic that users surf, to fulfill the compliance requirements on a weekly or monthly basis. Modern proxies have the capability of generating access logs for the users that can be collected in reporter servers such as Blue Coat® Reporter, SNARE, Arcsight, Websense log server, or AWstats.

8. Data Loss Prevention (DLP)

Data Loss Prevention (DLP) is used to protect the data that is exchanged between the internal and external network. Say, for example, that you don't want the employees to send the company's confidential documents to their personal email addresses and do a data theft. The Proxy SG can be integrated with DLP solutions to stop all these activities. There are many vendors that provide DLP solutions, such as BlueCoat, MacAfee, Symantec, and Sophos. The DLP products can be included with BlueCoat SG with the ICAP protocol.

What is Blue Coat®? And Why Use it?

Blue Coat Systems, Inc., previously known as CacheFlow, founded in 1996, is a network security and network management company based in Sunnyvale, California. Blue Coat®

is a leader in web security gateway (proxies), ADN (Application Delivery Networks), and WAN optimization products. They have products for a wide variety of other security technologies like DLP, Antivirus, URL filtering, host-based WAN optimization products,lLog reporters, and network visibility tools.

We all are here in the world of the web, and you are with us, the Blue Coat® family, the #1 product for web security technologies. As we say to all our clients, vendors, and partners, "Grow with the leaders."

Blue Coat® produces a family of both intelligent, powerful appliances and powerful software applications that all work together in both small and large enterprises, with the ability to protect against all the latest security threats and enhance network performance.

Blue Coat® identifies itself as an Application Delivery Network (ADN) specialist, and Blue Coat® SG proxies are the center of the product family. The Blue Coat® Product Suite provides security, acceleration, and visibility to networks, users, and traffic.

Blue Coat Secure Web Gateway solution is a collection of different products and technologies such as BlueCoat Proxy SG, BlueCoat Proxy AV, BlueCoat Director, BlueCoat Reporter, BlueCoat DLP, BCWF (BlueCoat Web Filter), Web Pulse protection, Threat Protection, and K9 protection.

BLUE COAT® PRODUCT SUITE:

Product list

Hardware-Based/Appliance	Software-Based
Blue Coat® SG Appliance	Blue Coat® WebFilter
BlueCoat Proxy One Appliance	Blue Coat® Reporter
DLP (Data Loss Prevention) Appliance	Proxy Client
PacketShaper Appliance	Blue Coat PolicyCenter
Blue Coat® Proxy AV Appliance	K9 Web protection
Blue Coat® ProxyRA Appliance	
Blue Coat® Director Appliance	
Blue Coat® IntelligenceCenter Appliance	
Blue Coat CacheFlow Appliance	

Of the above list, Blue Coat® also provides cloud service as SaaS (Software as a Service), and IaaS (Infrastructure as a Service).

In this book we will be explaining about the products like Blue Coat® SG proxy, Blue Coat® AV, Blue Coat® Webfilter, Web Pulse, K9 Web Protection, and Blue Coat® Reporter.

Here is a brief introduction to Bluecoat products Blue Coat® SG proxy, Blue Coat® AV, Blue Coat® WebFilter, Proxy Client, K9 Web Protection, Blue Coat® Reporter, and Blue Coat® Director.

1. Blue Coat® Proxy SG Appliance

Blue Coat® SG appliance provides Secure Web Gateway solution and advanced WAN Optimization feature sets. The same SG appliance supports both proxy and WAN optimization features, which means that when the system is booted there is an option to either to install a Proxy Edition SGOS (Security Gateway Operating System) or a MACH5 (Multiprotocol Accelerated Caching Hierarchy) Edition; for example, in a computer you could have Windows Vista and Windows 7 or Windows or Linux. These two operating systems are installed in any default SG appliance.

MACH5 is used for WAN acceleration and optimization, widely known as ADN (Application Delivery Networks). In this book we will focus on proxy features, but we will give an introduction to WAN acceleration techniques in the later chapters.

When SGOS is installed, there are features from the MACH5; but conversely, when MACH5 is installed, there are only limited proxy features.

 The terms Secure Web Gateway, Web Application Gateway, Blue Coat® SG appliance, or Blue Coat® SG gateway all refer to the proxy technology and are used interchangeably.

The benefits of the Blue Coat® SG proxy are as follows:

1. Blue Coat® SGOS provides a complete proxy protocol support for HTTP, HTTPS, DNS, SOCKS, FTP, telnet, RTMP, RTSP, MMS, streaming media (Real Player, QuickTime, Microsoft), and IM (Yahoo, AOL, MSN).
2. It can install web filter software for URL categorization.
3. It can scan on-box for traffic and protect against spyware, malware, viruses, and Trojans.
4. The integrated caching technology can be used for object and byte caching.
5. Bandwidth management techniques can be used to optimize and improve the performance of the network.
6. Blue Coat®'s patented Plicy Processing Engine helps administrators to create granular policies via CLI, policy files, and Visual Policy Manager (VPM).
7. It can integrate with authentication for both users and administrators.
8. It can use the access log to monitor the network web traffic.
9. It can integrate with third-party AV solutions.

BLUE COAT® SG PRODUCT FAMILY:

Blue Coat ProxySG 210 Full Proxy Edition

- 30 to Unlimited User License Capacity
- 80 to 250 GB Storage
- WAN Optimization and Application Acceleration

Blue Coat ProxySG 510 Full Proxy Edition

- 200 to Unlimited User License Capacity
- 160 GB to 640 GB Storage
- WAN Optimization and Application Acceleration

Blue Coat ProxySG 810 Full Proxy Edition

- 2,500 to Unlimited User License Capacity
- 146 GB to 1.2 TB Storage
- WAN Optimization and Application Acceleration

Blue Coat ProxySG 8100 Full Proxy Edition

- Unlimited User License Capacity
- 600 GB to 2.4 TB Storage
- WAN Optimization and Application Acceleration

Blue Coat ProxySG 9000 Full Proxy Edition

- Unlimited User License Capacity
- 2 TB to 5 TB Storage
- WAN Optimization and Application Acceleration

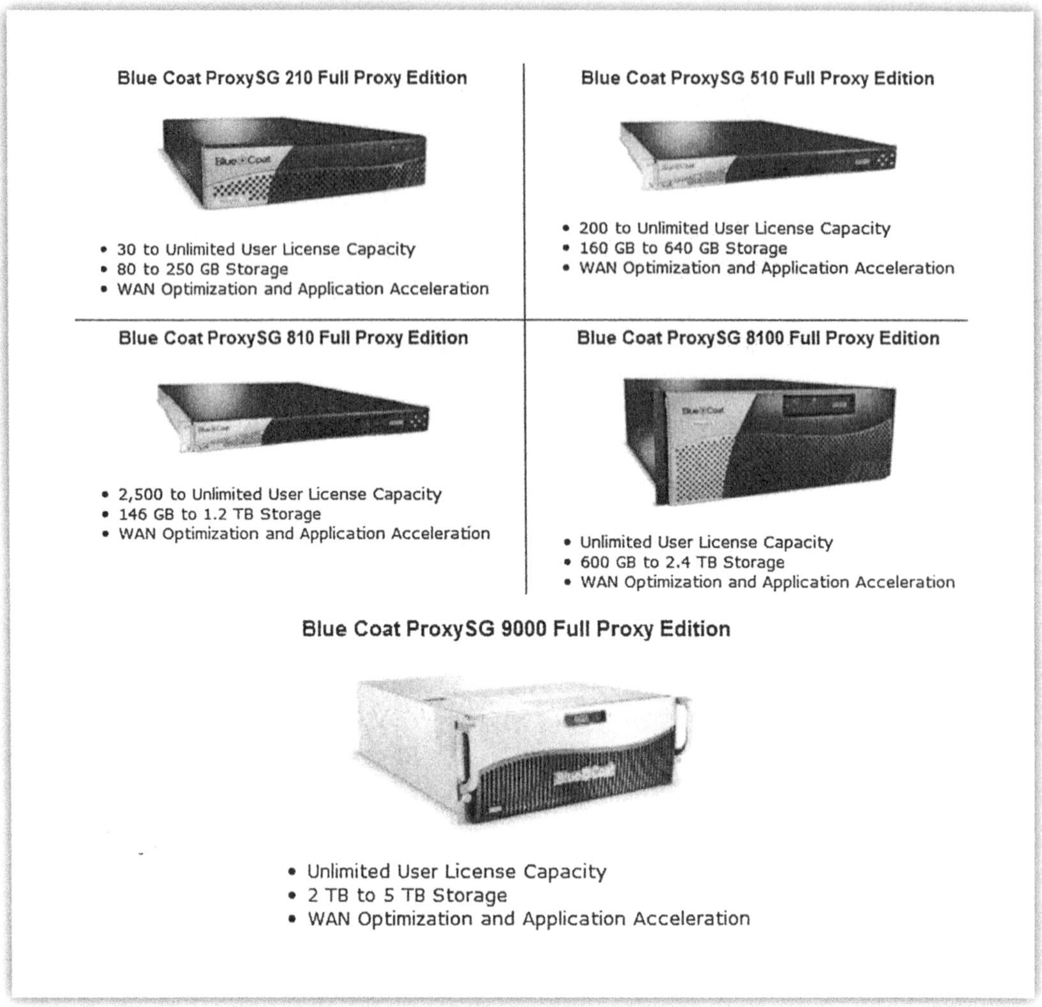

Figure 1.1: BlueCoat SG product family

2. Blue Coat® AV Appliance

In the real world, 70% of the malware attacks are propagated by the web. This includes web-based applications and email, which bring and spread malware, viruses, Trojans, worms, rootkits, etc. into the corporate networks, leading to loss of data, data theft, system damage, and production outages and thus cause the company to lose its reputation.

Blue Coat ProxyAV™ appliance delivers advanced malware detection at the web gateway, with high performance, integrating with the Blue Coat® Proxy SG appliance to provide inline threat protection and malware scanning of web content. Since scanning happens at the gateway, Blue Coat® establishes a security model know as "Blue Coat's layered security framework," which enhances and helps the other security components in the network like IDS, IPS, DLP, desktop AV, and firewall.

Deploying this unified framework helps us to gain visibility to the network. ProxyAV supports leading malware engines from Panda, Sophos, McAfee, and Kaspersky with updates as frequently as every five minutes. ProxyAV communicates with ProxySG via ICAP(S)(Internet Content Adapation Protocol) a lightweight HTTP-like protocol specified in RFC 3507 used for high-performance and standards-based protocol.

Key benefits of using the Proxy AV:

1. Both key points of Security and Performance are achieved without compromise and delays.
2. It extends protection to users who are not running antivirus software.
3. It is more reliable than the desktop AV solutions since the updates happens every five minutes at the gateways, making the network clean and safe against zero-day attacks.
4. BluCoat provides a mechanism called deferred scanning, which removes long load objects like live streaming, web radio, and other media from processing threads and consuming the AV resources, and increases the Web Gateway performance.
5. ProxyAV can be configured to analyze both inbound and outbound traffic, thus having complete control in the network for both Request and Response queries.
6. ACL can be configured for file extensions to scanned and their timeout values, file size limits, and trusted sites that can be excluded from scanning such as Microsoft, Cisco, IBM, and Intel, since it uses the "Trusted Base" security model and save scanning loads on the Proxy AV.
7. ProxyAV supports four modes of content analysis, including traditional object analysis, trickle first or last stream analysis, and deferred scan.
8. ProxyAV can scan files up to 2 GB in size and analyze compressed archives up to 99 layers deep.
9. ProxyAV integrates with multiple threat awareness clouds, including Blue Coat WebPulse and third-party clouds (over 70 million users are protected), providing multi-vendor cloud protection at the gateway.
10. ProxyAV protects against web-email, web spam, email-spam, and browser-based file downloads, where most attacks come in.

BLUE COAT® AV PRODUCT FAMILY:

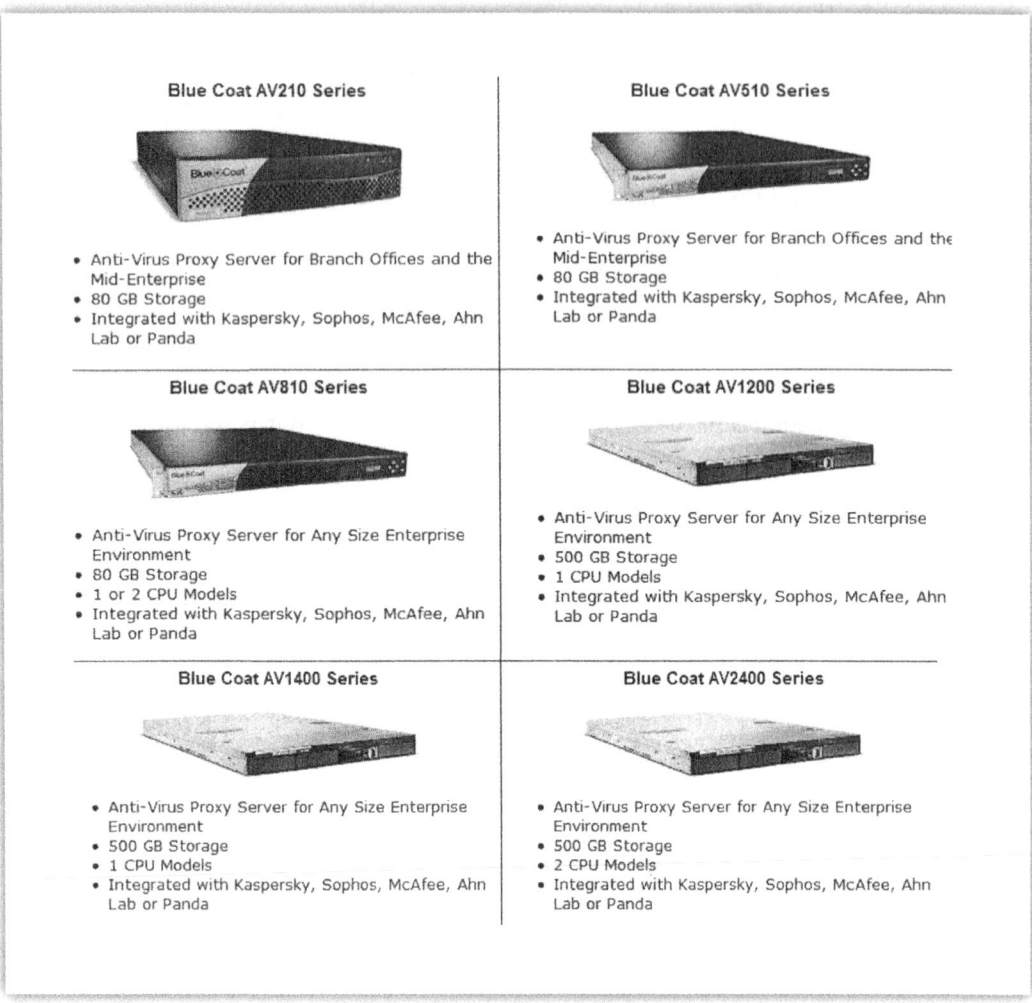

Figure 1.2: BlueCoat AV product Family

3. Blue Coat® WebFilter

"Blue Coat® WebFilter (BCWF)," WebFilter, or content filtering, terms that are used interchangeably, refer to software that is installed on-box in the ProxySG which provides web filtering solutions that help corporations to allow or deny categories based upon their business classifications of access. This helps an enterprise to protect the network against spyware, malware, and phishing attacks. The ProxySG supports Blue Coat WebFilter as well as other third-party databases, such as Proventia, SmartFilter, Optenet, Websense, Surfcontrol, I-Filter, Intersafe, or Webwasher.

Blue Coat WebFilter in conjunction with the WebPulse service offers a comprehensive URL-filtering solution. Blue Coat WebFilter provides an on-box content filtering database and WebPulse provides the off-box dynamic categorization service for real-time categorization of URLs that are not available in the on-box database. WebPulse services are offered to all customers using Blue Coat® WebFilter. The WebPulse is a cloud service that allows inputs from multiple enterprise gateways and clients and creates a computing grid. This grid consists of Blue Coat WebFilter, K9, and ProxyClient customers, who provide a large sample of Web content requests for popular and unrated sites.

The key benefits of using Blue Coat® WebFilter(BCWF):

1. BCWF is performed as on-box filtering so the performance of the Proxy SG is increased.
2. There are almost more than 80 categories available for the BCWF, which helps the administrator to classify the site in the appropriate category.
3. Nearly 50 languages are supported by the BCWF database.
4. BCWF provides a hybrid model of both on-box and off-box solutions of dynamic categorization of the sites. On-box categorization is done by BCWF and off-box categorization is done by Webpulse, a could computing service.
5. BCWF provides a hybrid way of analyzing the site via web crawling and looking for keywords in the site and a team manually checking the site contents and categorizes. This makes the database its most powerful and reliable.
6. The BCWF provides deeper analysis and traverses 50 sections in a URL. For example. google.com is categorized as Search Engine/Portals, but translate.google.com is Translation and google.com/translate is Reference, since the database contains website ratings representing billions of web pages.
7. Since WebPulse is cloud service, the processing by Proxy SG is off-loaded, and WebPulse requires a smaller bandwidth for DRTR (Dynamic Real-Time rating) technology.
8. WebFilter provides over 7 billion ratings per day for over 75 million users located in the largest enterprises, corporations and service provider networks around the world.
9. WebPulse cloud analysis uses Dynamic Link Analysis (DLA) to define the next generation of URL filtering for Web 2.0 content and dynamic links.

BLUE COAT® WEB FILTERING (BCWF) CLOUD ARCHITECTURE.

Figure 3 below shows how the BCWF cloud architecture is built and gets web rating from different sources like the Proxy SG that has Web Filter, Proxy Client, K9 Web protection, Proxy AV, and BlueCoat Reporter.

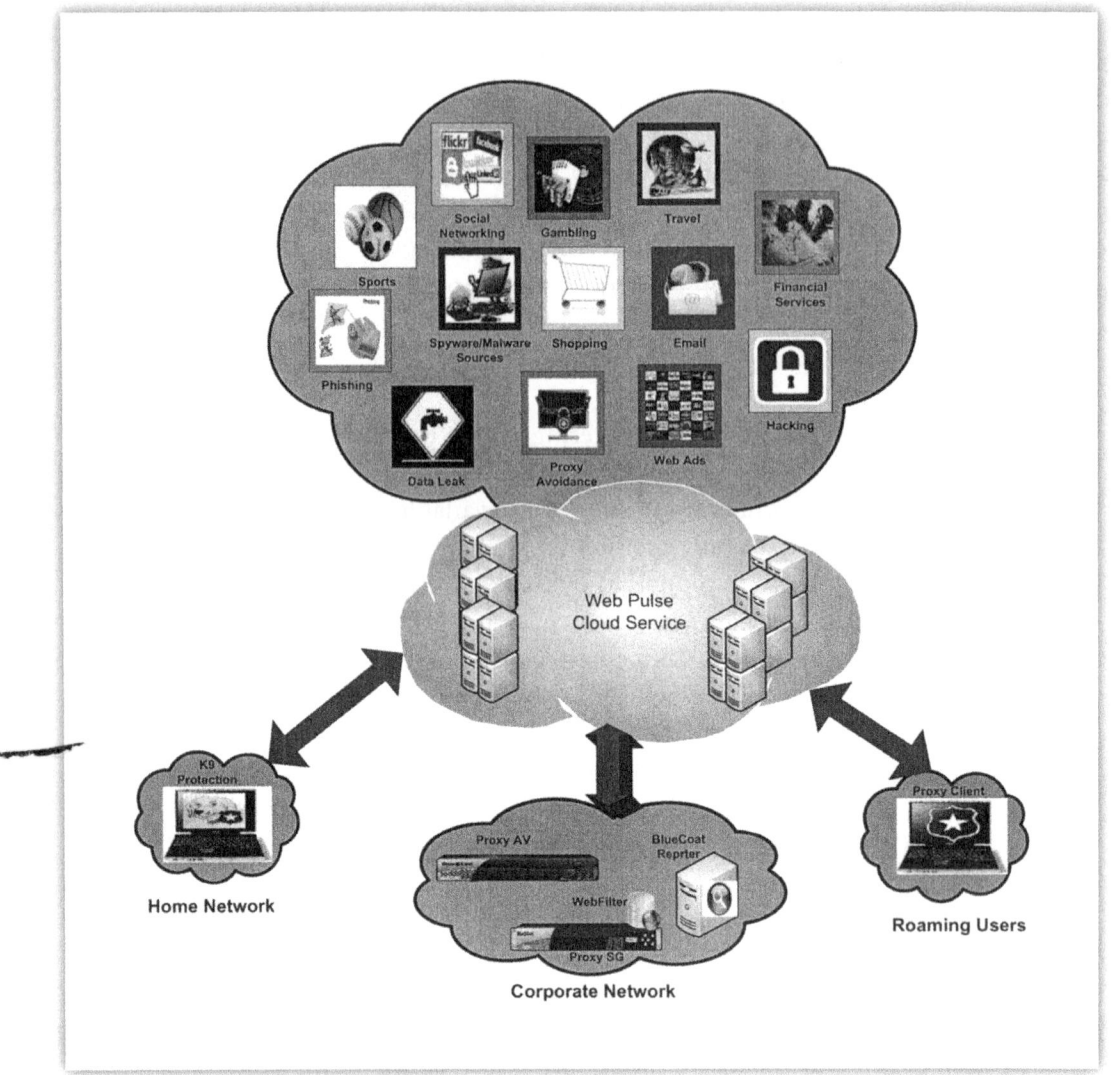

Figure 1.3: BlueCoat BCWF cloud architecture

4. Blue Coat® Proxy Client

As roaming users and mobile technology are expanding, users and employees working from home, fields, and small offices via VPN (Virtual Private Network) require the same performance that is achieved when in the corporate network environment. This is done via ProxyClient, a software that is installed in users' PC, laptops, or mobile devices.

The Blue Coat® Proxy client is installed on all client machines and managed by the Blue Coat® Proxy Manager, which is a feature that is available to Proxy SG. ProxyClient can be managed with the ProxySG management console for easy provisioning, configuration, and maintenance. Blue Coat ProxyClient™ secures remote users and small branch offices from today's rapidly evolving web threats, while accelerating network applications by up to 35 times for greater productivity. ProxyClient works with Blue Coat WebPulse™ cloud service to mitigate threats from malicious web content like viruses, Trojans, malware, social networking (Facebook, Twitter, MySpace), manipulated search engine results (SEO), or other attacks.

Key benefits of using Blue Coat® ProxyClient:

1. It reduces the cost of deploying the ProxySG in small offices with few users, by replacing ProxySG solutions with installing ProxyClient on users machines.
2. It continuously analyzes background web content for hidden malware and rates new web content using both Webpulse and on-box scanning.
3. Blue Coat ProxyClient delivers the WAN optimization feature which helps the users to accelerate the business traffic in low-speed Internet connections and deliver the applications faster.
4. It provides Remote Acceleration such as Byte Caching, Object Caching, Protocol Optimization, and compression.
5. ProxyClient provides remote web filtering both via BCWF and WebPulse.
6. It can deploy, manage, and update Blue Coat® ProxyClient from any Blue Coat ProxySG without any additional licenses, management appliances, or overhead costs.
7. The ProxyClient logs can be encrypted and sent to the Client Manager. It can collect traces for troubleshooting problems from the client.
8. The ProxyClient can configure location awareness, which enables the client to detect the network and use the Proxy client feature. For example, if you are in the local corporate network, the ProxyClient can be configured to use the Proxy SG in the network to use web filtering and WAN optimization features, thus reducing the overhead on the client.
9. The Client Manager provides centralized policy management that makes unified acceptable Internet policies for remote users and provides endpoint control over the machines of the users.

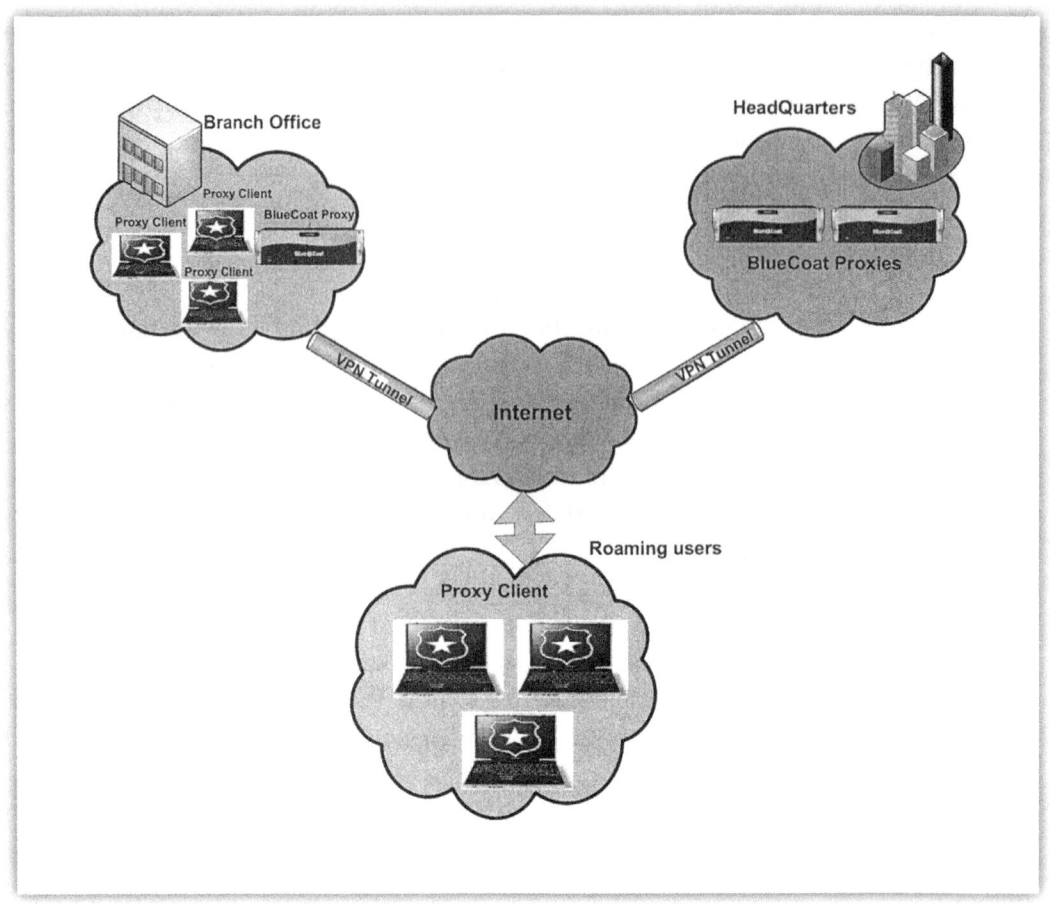

Figure 1.4: Blue Coat® Proxy Client network architecture

5. Blue Coat® K9 Web Protection

Blue Coat® K9 Web Protection, a free product for home users, is mostly an Internet filter and parental control software for your home Windows or Macintosh computer. It enables parents to monitor and control what sites their children access and enables them to block offensive or potentially dangerous sites. K9 Web Protection also uses the same best of breed web-filtering technology, WebPulse™ service, to update the database continuously and protect from all new threats.

Key benefits of using Blue Coat® K9 Web protection:

1. The web filter is same as BCWF and has 75 categories to let parents to control access to their children's web surfing from potentially dangerous sites.
2. It is integrated with the WebPulse cloud service so that a real-time site categorization is done.

3. It is free software that Blue Coat® offers to provide web parental control for their children.
4. K9 web protection software can be installed in both Windows and Mac machines.
5. K9 uses enhanced anti-tampering technology that makes it very difficult for children to break in and circumvent the system.
6. It also provides "Safe Search" for all major and popular search engines (e.g. Google, Yahoo, MSN Bing).
7. It enables parents to log all the internet activities, generate reports, and monitor the surfing habits of their children.
8. K9 Web protection can be installed on the iPhone, iPod, and iPad.

6. Blue Coat® Reporter

Blue Coat® Reporter provides an intelligent dashboard to have a complete visibility of users' activity on the web. This helps an organization to meet its needs for compliance of security standards, security best practices, monitoring the network for suspicious activities, and bandwidth management. Proxy SG, Proxy Client can forward the access logs(Internet activity) to Blue Coat® Reporter, which processes the raw log files and produces the reports about traffic access in the network.

Blue Coat® Reporter is software that can be installed in Windows or Linux servers. Blue Coat® Reporter processes by log lines, so if the network traffic and the access logs are huge, it needs to get the license depending upon the data. Usually, retaining six months of data is the security best practice and fulfills thestandard security compliance. It can log all the access, and log formats that are supported are HTTP, HTTPS, CIFS, Endpoint Mapper, FTP, Instant Messaging, telnet, Windows Media, Real Media/Quick Time, HTTPS Reverse/Forward proxy, SOCKS, Flash, Peer-to-Peer, and MAPI.

Key benefits of using Blue Coat® Reporter:

1. It gives complete visibility of network web traffic and users' surfing habits.
2. It gives a dashboard which gives an quick overview of the network.
3. It gives visibility of web traffic performance, security threats, bandwidth management, streaming traffic levels, top domains accessed/blocked .
4. Blue Coat® Reporter uses a custom database so that large access log files can be compressed and stored.
5. Real-time logs can be fed into the Blue Coat® Reporter for analysis.
6. It can integrate with SIEM tools like ArcSight and forward logs, for log correlation.
7. It can role-based access to the reports and dashboard to different teams in the organization.
8. It can produce predefined reports and easy custom report creation for all data trends.

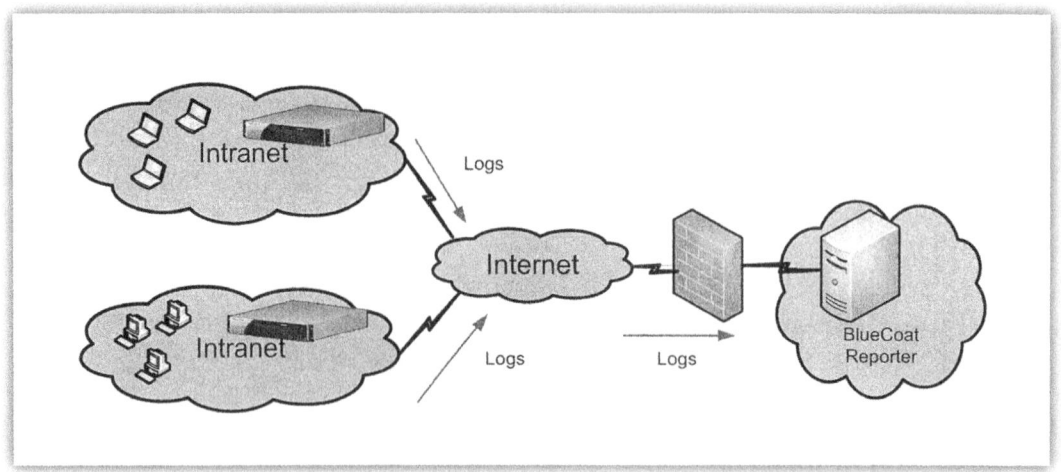

Figure 1:5 Blue Coat® Reporter network architecture.

7. Blue Coat® Director

Blue Coat® Director centrally manages and monitors multiple Blue Coat ProxySG appliances simultaneously. Blue Coat Director is the single point of administration, monitoring, configuration, and policy management for one or more ProxySG appliances in the network. With Blue Coat® Director Proxy SG appliance configurations can be centrally managed, validated, backed-up, license managed, monitored for health and performance, and upgraded.

Blue Coat® Director helps to configure policies for a large corporation that needs to manage up to 100 proxies. It saves administrative time: say there is a virus outbreak and a policy has to be configured to stop access to certain site; if the environment has 100 devices, logging into each device and configuring is a cumbersome way to do it. Here where the Blue Coat Director helps in these situations.

Key benefits of using Blue Coat Director:

1. You can configure groups of Proxy SGs based on geographic locations, applications, device types, etc.
2. You can schedule policies for Proxy SG based on time and reduces the administration overhead.
3. You can back up the Proxy SG, compare the different backups, and restore configuration backup, if the policy fails, and rever to the old stable and running policy.
4. You can monitor ProxySG appliance status, statistics, configurations, and system health.
5. You can upgrade Proxy SG simultaneously and reduce maintenance time.

6. You can build a failover system which helps the Director system always stay up.

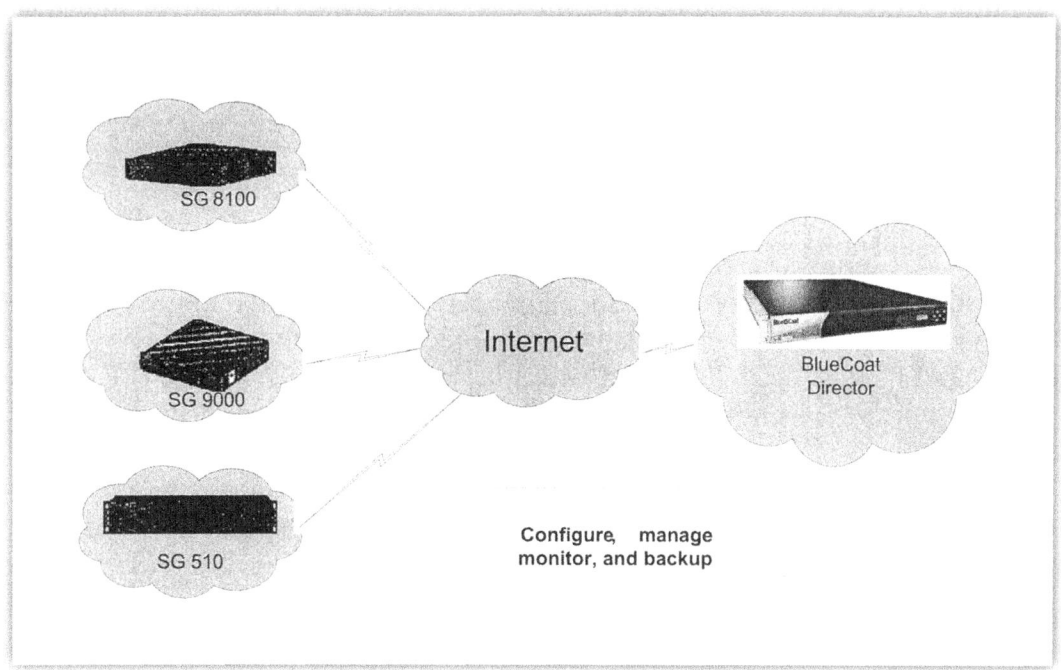

Figure 1:6 BlueCoat Director network architecture.

Threat Pulse

The modern emerging technology is Cloud Computing. Most of the market technology leaders have started cloud computing for business with their customers and vendors. So what is cloud computing? Cloud computing is the delivery of computing as a service rather than a product; a service may be email, the web, a database service, storage, URL filtering, etc. So Threat Pulse is an Internet-delivered service that leverages the cloud and uses BlueCoat web technology for real-time web threat protection for all types of users, in any location. "All types of users" means anyone from corporate users to home users and even mobile users.

So Threat Pulse scans all the traffic that the user is accessing in the Internet cloud, without any external hardware in the company, for proxy, Reporter, web filtering and enhanced malware detection, which ultimatley minimizes the cost and administartion burden. So to simplify, Threat Pulse is a combination of BlueCoat Secure Web Gateway, Reporter, and Web Pulse. BlueCoat offers Threat Pulse as a Security-as-a-Service (SAAS), which is Cloud Computing technology.

Threat Pulse can be very easily deployed by any users or corporations by using any of the four following methods.

1. IPSec VPN

Site-to-site VPN needs to be configured with the Threat Pulse cloud service, so that all the web traffic from the firewall or VPN device is transparently forwarded to the cloud. So just the firewall needs to be in place and the proxying and web security is applied in the cloud. This method is used when the web traffic contains sensitive data of the company which needs to be encrypted.

2. Proxy Chaining

The existing Proxy SG can be used in the corporation to just forward traffic to the Threat Pulse cloud web gateways. Remember: only non-internal web traffic should be forwarded; all the internal traffic should be routed inside the network.

3. Explicit Proxy

The user's browser is configured with the proxy settings; this is very granlaur for mobile users, since all browsers can be configured for using the proxy.

4. Client Connector

A desktop agent, which is installed in the mobile user's system, forwards the traffic to the Threat Pulse cloud transparently.

If you're not familiar with concepts like proxy chaining, explicit, etc., that's fine—these will be covered in later chapters in detail.

Key benefits of Threat Pusle:

1. It reduces cost, complexity, and maintanence.
2. It does a real-time analysis and protects against all web threats and provides dynamic malware protection.
3. It can scale from smaller to larger corporations.
4. It provides BCWF web filtering using WebPulse cloud technology.

What other proxy products are available in the market?

There are many products available in the market apart from Blue Coat, but Blue Coat is the best and the number one product in the industry and rated in the first rank from Gartner journal reports. The other products are:

1. Microsoft ISA
2. Websense
3. Juniper Proxy Networks
4. Linux Squid
5. Oracle IPlanet
6. Riverbed *Optimization System*
7. Mcafee Web Wahser
8. Cisco IronPort

Test Yourself:

1. If you have the world's best firewall in your network and it can also do proxy and AV scanning with high performance, do you still need BlueCoat in your network?

   a. Yes
   b. No

2. How many websites are being rated per day by BlueCoat BCWF?

   a. 2 Million
   b. 2 Billion
   c. 7 Billion
   d. 4 Billion

3. What is BlueCoat Reporter?

   a. A software product
   b. An Appliance

4. Which is not a Secure Web gateway solution product?

   a. BlueCoat Proxy SG
   b. K9 Web Protection

   c. BCWF

   d. Blue Coat® Intelligence Center Appliance

5. What is K9 web protection?

   a. A browser

   b. A software product

6. Which of the following products does BlueCoat Director not manage? (Choose three.)

   a. BlueCoat Proxy AV

   b. BlueCoat Proxy SG

   c. BlueCoat Reporter

   d. K9 Web Protection

7. Is BCWF installed on Proxy Client?

   a. Yes

   b. No

8. Which company has the best products for both Secure Web Gateway and WAN optimization and is rated as the as number one product in the industry in Gartner?

   a. Websense

   b. RiverBed

   c. BlueCoat

   d. Cisco

9. Which application does the BlueCoat ProxySG does not provide complete proxy functionality(Application level) and can only do a TCP tunnel?

   a. BlackBerry

   b. RTSP

   c. EndPoint Mapper

   d. Yahoo IM

10. What protocol could be Antivirus and DLP could be integrated with BlueCoat ProxySG?

   a. HTTP

   b. HTTPS

   c. TCP tunnel

   d. ICAP

CHAPTER 2

....

CACHING AND OPTIMIZATION

CACHING AND OPTIMIZATION

Before moving into how to configure Blue Coat and different options that can be used to fine-tune and troubleshoot, we will start looking at the basics of caching and various optimization techniques in general and how Blue Coat focuses and implements in the IT market for the best of caching and optimization techniques.

What is caching?

The caching concept was first introduced by IBM in 1960. It is a fundamental metaphor that is used in modern computing, and it finds wide application in web servers, storage systems, runtime compilers, databases, operating systems, distributed systems, network applications, middleware, processors, file systems, disk drives, disks controllers, network card interfaces, etc. It is widely used in everywhere in today's IT world.

The basic definition of caching or cache is "the temporary location where the data is stored, as the original data is expensive to be fetched, so it can be retrieved faster." Usually memory is arranged in a hierarchy of levels: very small, fast, and expensive registers in the CPU to small, fast cache memory; larger DRAM; very large hard disks; and slow and inexpensive nonvolatile backup storage. Say in a two-level memory hierarchy, a cache performs faster than auxiliary storage but is more expensive. Cost concerns thus usually limit cache size to a fraction of the auxiliary memory's size, which is usually big.

The terms "auxiliary storage", "auxiliary memory", and "secondary memory" refer to storage devices that include hard disks, floppy disks, CD-ROMs, and tape backup systems. In BlueCoat or proxy server it is called OCS (Origin Content Server), which is a server in the network. This book is focused on fetching data from remote servers, in other words, web servers and application servers.

What is paging?

Paging is one of the memory-management methods by which a system can store and retrieve data from secondary storage for use in main memory, but the object or data first goes into cache. In the paging memory-management method, the operating system retrieves data from secondary storage in same-size blocks or uniform-sized items called pages.

CACHE HIT:

When a client invokes a request to the system (web application), it first checks the cache, and if the data or the page is found in the cache then it is called a cache hit. A cache hit is the primary measurement for the effectiveness of the caching that the system is using. The percentage of accesses that result in cache hits is known as the hit rate or hit ratio of the cache.

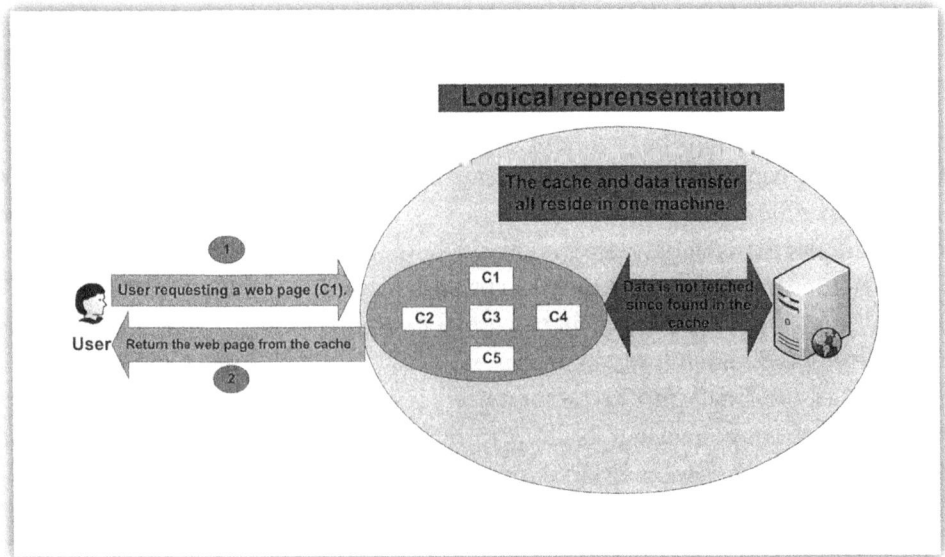

Figure 2:1 Cache Hit

CACHE MISS:

When a client invokes a request to the system (web application), it first checks the cache, and if the data or the page (technically called) is not found in the cache then it is called a cache miss. Then the request is forwarded to the OCS (Origin Content Server) and the request is fetched and sent back to the user and stored in the cache for further requests that are served from the cache.

OCS stands for Origin Content Server where the client actually tries to contact server. It can be also called the real/actual destination server (e.g. google.com, yahoo.com, etc.).

There are two different scenarios in which this mechanism works.

1. First scenario (when cache is empty):

If there is free space in the cache (the cache space didn't reach its limit), the request that caused the cache miss will be retrieved from the OCS and get inserted in to the cache.

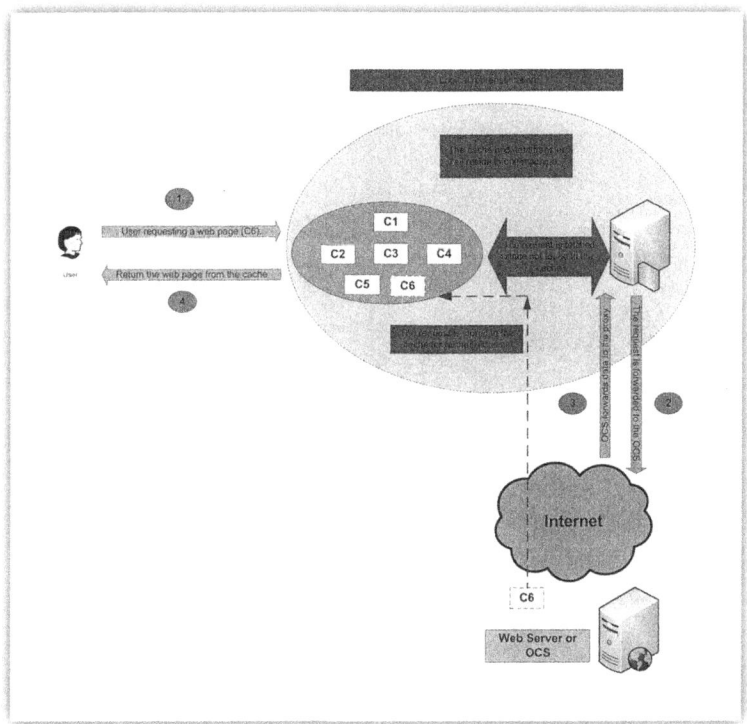

Figure 2:2 Cache Miss (When cache is empty)

2. Second scenario (when the cache is full):

If there is no free space in the cache (the cache has reached its limit), the object that caused the cache miss will be fetched from OCS and then it will have to be decided which data or objects in the cache need to be purged or moved out in order to place the newly fetched data (the new data that was just retrieved from the OCS) to store in the cache. This is done by a replacement policy (caching algorithms) that decide which entry will be removed to make space of new data.

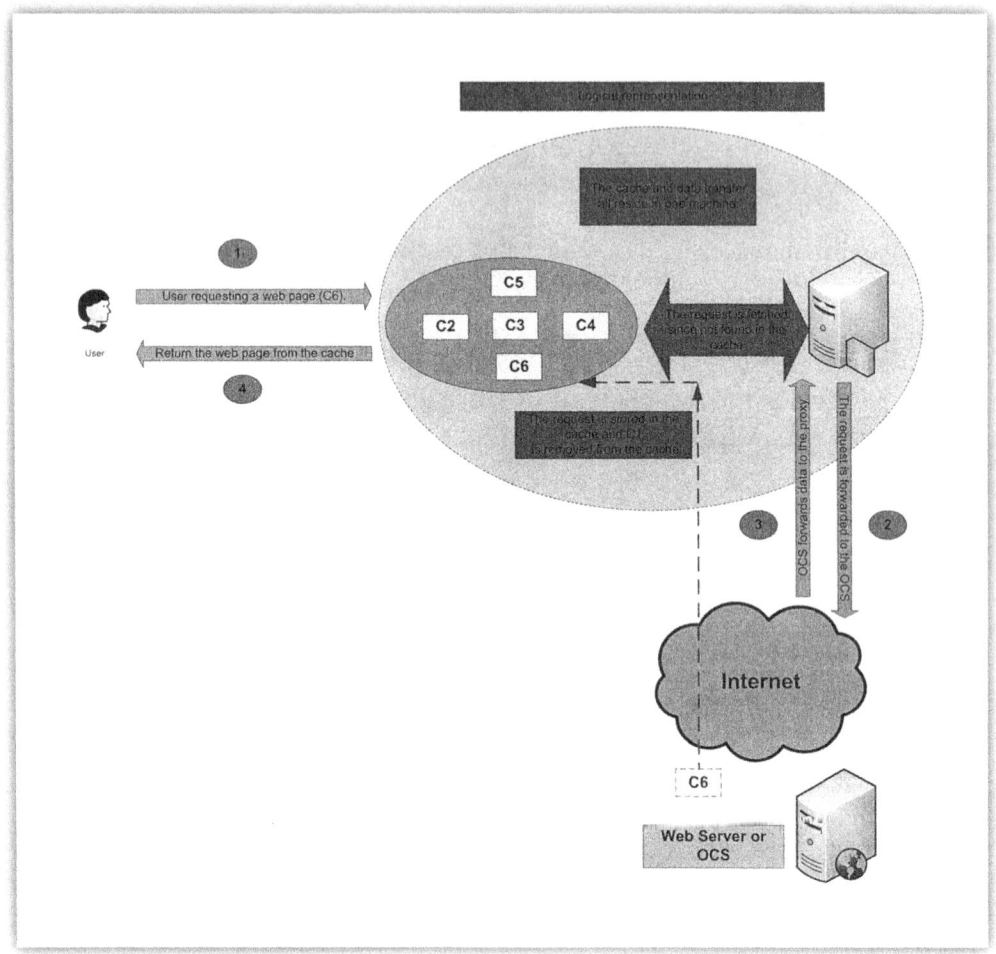

Figure 2:3 Cache Miss (When cache is full)

Caching Terminology

There are different terms that are used in caching technology. Let us briefly discuss each one before we discuss the various caching algorithms used in the industry and the Blue Coat–patented caching techniques.

1. Storage Cost

When a cache miss occurs, data will be fetched from the OCS, loaded, and placed in the cache. But how much space will the data that was fetched occupy in the cache memory? This is called storage cost.

2. Retrieval Cost

When a cache miss occurs, the data must be loaded. How much time will it take to load the data? This is known as the retrieval cost.

3. Invalidation

The data or objects that reside in the cache need to be refreshed. Since it is invalid or not fresh, the process of data being fetched from the OCS to keep the cache up to date is known as invalidation.

4. Replacement Policy or Algorithm

When a cache miss happens and assuming the cache space is full, the cache needs to delete or eject some data or object in order to make space for the newly fetched uncached data. This is known as the replacement policy.

5. Hit Rate

The hit rate of a cache describes how often a searched-for item is actually found in the cache. More efficient replacement policies keep track of more usage information in order to improve the hit rate (for a given cache size).

6. Latency

The latency of a cache describes how long after requesting a desired item from the cache can return that item (when there is a cache hit). The faster replacement strategies typically keep track of less usage information—or, in the case of a direct-mapped cache, no information—to reduce the amount of time required to update that information.

 Each replacement policy or algorithm is a compromise between hit rate and latency.

When it comes to caching algorithms, there are two different sets of algorithm: one is the caching algorithm and the other is the replacement algorithm. First we will discuss the caching algorithm and its types and the advantage of each type.

CACHING ALGORITHM

A caching algorithm, also called replacement algorithm or replacement policy,(subset function of caching algorithm) is mainly used by a cache engine to maintain its efficiency and processing speed. There are two other algorithms for caching that can be used in conjunction with caching algorithms or replacement algorithms, which is a way do some analysis of the data that it needs to be processed. The analysis-caching algorithms can be divided into two types.

1. On-line algorithm

The on-line algorithm processes input in a serial way, one-by-one or chunk-by-chunk. Sothe processt only knows the current and past requests in the sequence. This works fine for static content, such as a web page, but it will be a problem when this algorithm is used for streaming content where the data is infinite. At this point since it knows the current and past events, if the algorithm is forced to make decisions on the data, later the decision will not be useful or optimal. So competitive analysis is used to analyze an online algorithm and make a decision based upon the competitive analysis. The competitive analysis used here is the dynamic algorithm or dynamic caching for a dynamic problem.

On-line algorithms arise in any situation where decisions must be made and resources allocated without knowledge of the future.

For example, the first factor is that this analysis is used in streaming video or multimedia streams, since the file size is extremely large. This means that the entire stream has to fit in the cache and the maximum number of simultaneous cache misses rather than the total number of cache misses. The second factor is to reduce the bandwidth in the network. BWe need to balance both the factors, so there was a dynamic caching framework proposed by Dan and Sitaram or Hofmann et al is used.

• Streams to fit in the cache

It restricts only to a single cache that can access streams from a single server. Say that user A requests a data stream at time T1 and user B requests the same data stream at time T2.
So time for $T2 = T1 + \Delta,$

Δ Is the temporal distance between the two requests. So if there is space for the Δ stream then it is cached. The requests of User A and User B can both be served by using only one connection to the server. The last Δ time difference units of the stream that were seen by the first request are cached. The second request can always obtain from the cache the current stream data that it needs.

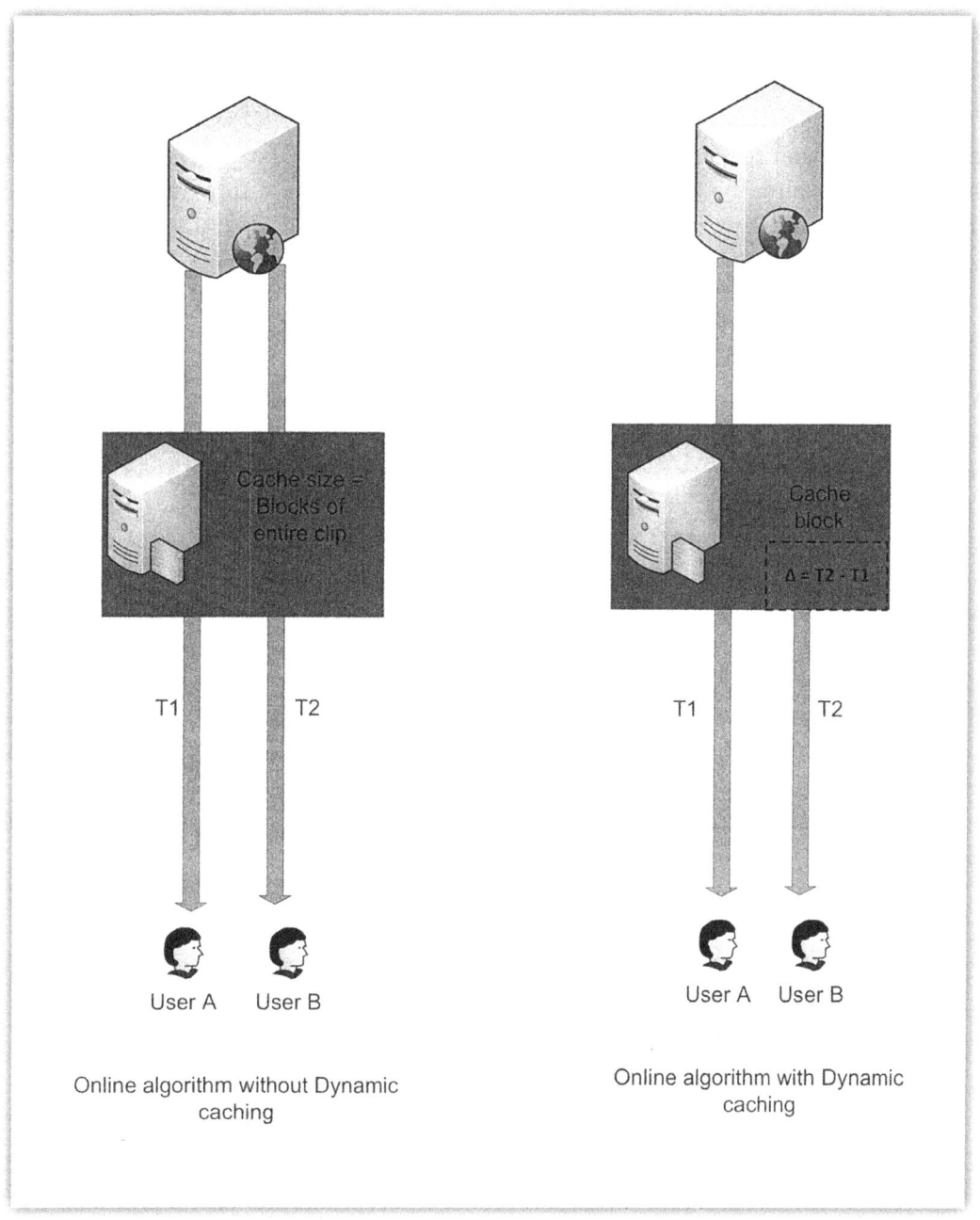

Figure 2:4 Online algorithm with/without Dynamic caching

In this section the example was for a cache connection to a single server with single link and two users, but for multiple users, various links, and multiple cache units, the logic will a be little different where cost and various other factors are involved. Mathematical and probability functions will not be introduced in this book, since we want to help you understand the basics very well. Various advanced techniques will be focused on in our future books.

- ## b. Bandwidth problem

The cache always maintain the last Δ time units of the stream that were seen by the first request, the second request always obtain the stream from the cache. So the challenge is always in determining which part of the streams to maintain to reduce the number of simultaneous connections to the server and hence to reduce the bandwidth of the network.

2. Off-line algorithm

An algorithm for the problem which assumes prior knowledge of the complete request sequence is called an off-line algorithm. In other words, if an algorithm is given the entire sequence of service requests in advance, it is said to be an offline algorithm. This means there is all the required information to make decision.

Let us say there is a single OCS, n number of caches, and m number of users. And the whole cache has been refreshed and is up-to-date; imagine that by refreshing it there may be a slight increase in the cache size, which the disk should have enough space to afford. So here all the data for computation is there and the analysis can be done without any failures. The same rule applies for several OCSs, with n number of caches and m number of users, but here another factor will add to the analysis apart from the cache size, which is the cost. This refers to the time taken by the caching engine to reach different OCSs in the network, as the round-trip time in the network varies for each OCS and the computational speed in the OCS itself. The basic idea is that for an off-line algorithm, the knowledge is in place to do analysis and make decisions.

The n number of caches to the same server means different files, objects, web pages, and videos in the single server; in the previous diagram and example it was the same stream for two different users.

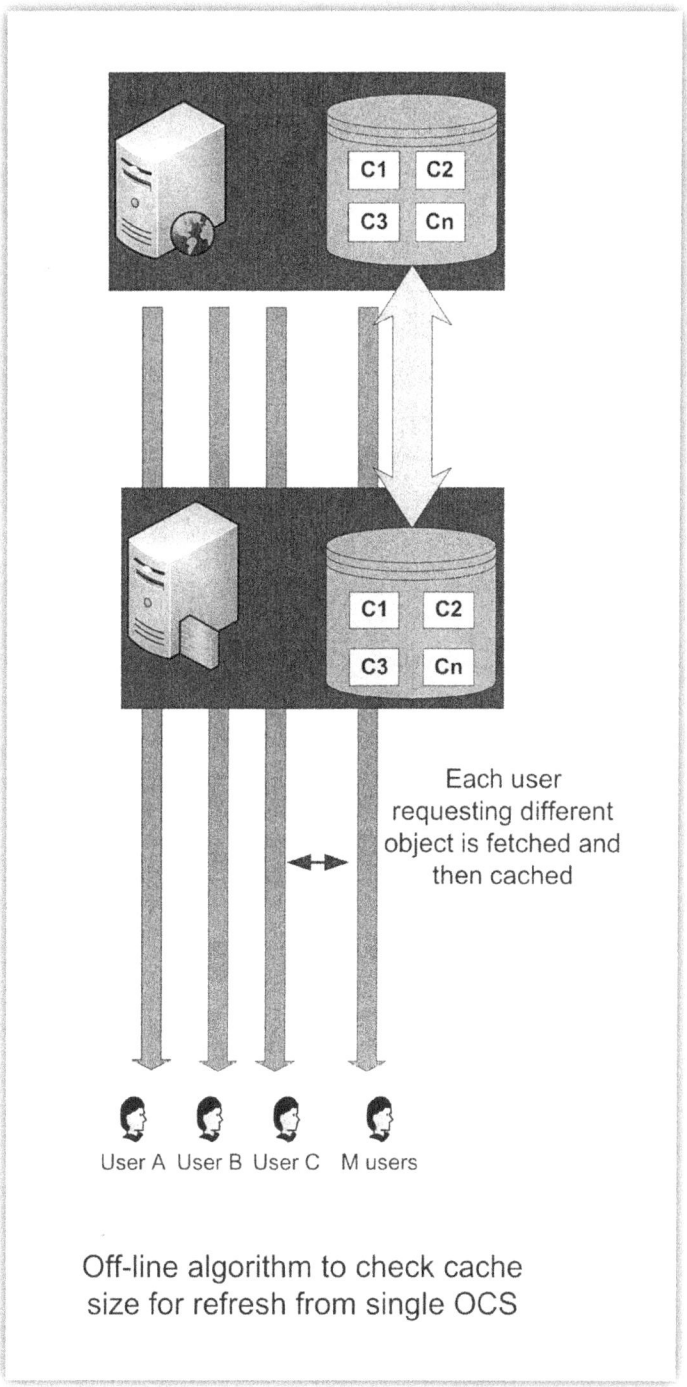

Figure 2:5 Offline algorithm with single OCS with m users and n cache objects

The above diagram is for a single OCS with m users and n cache objects that should be refreshed.

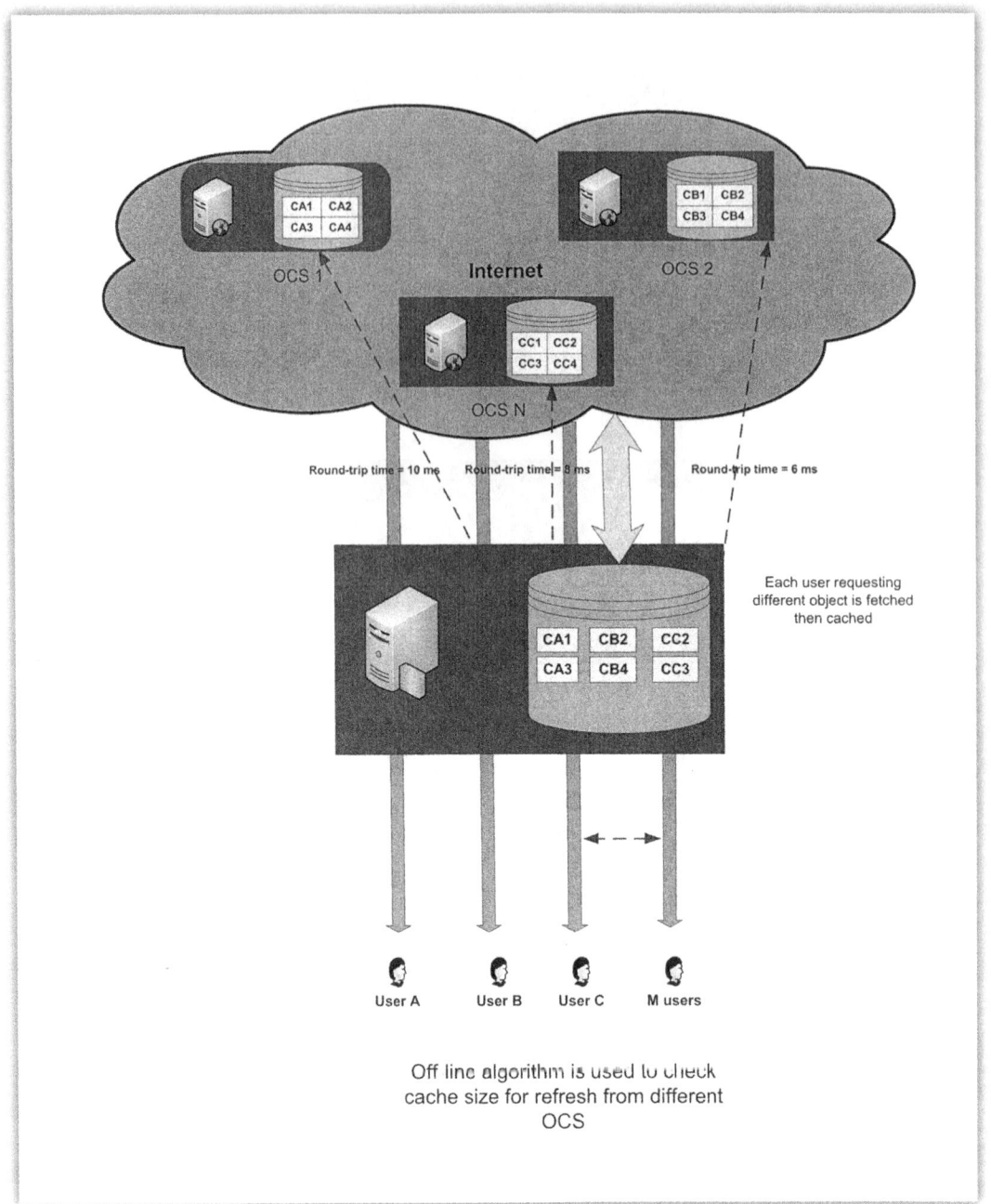

Figure 2:6 Offline algorithm with N OCS with M users and multiple cache objects

The above diagram is for N OCS with M users and multiple cache objects that should be refreshed.

At times an off-line algorithm can be converted to an on-line algorithm; also, if one wants to increase the cache size of an object say to 16 KB, as the default is 4 KB. The analysis is done to increase every 4 KB when the cache needs to be increased and for each cache the first 4KB blocks of the stream are stored, but when a request comes for the same object it served from the cache with the smallest computed value, until a new optimum value is calculated.

What is the competitive ratio?

The effectiveness of an On-line algorithm is measured by its "competitive ratio," defined as the worst-case ratio between its cost and that of a hypothetical off-line algorithm which knows the entire sequence of requests in advance and chooses its actions optimally. Since an On-line receives a sequence of requests and performs an immediate action in response to each request and always perform worse than an Off-line algorithm, competitive analysis is very important for On-line algorithms.

Now let's look the various replacement algorithms that affects the cachet and the advantages and disadvantages of each method.

Direct-Mapped cache, 2-Way Set Associative, and Segmented LRU alogrithms as they are not related to the caching used on the web.

The different replacement algorithms are listed below:

1. Belady's Algorithm
2. Least-Recently Used
3. Most-Recently Used
4. Least-Frequently Used
5. Pseudo-LRU
6. Adaptive Replacement Cache
7. Random Replacement
8. Direct-Mapped Cache
9. 2-Way Set Associative
10. Segmented LRU
11. First in, First out (FIFO)
12. Simple Time-Based
13. Extended Time-Based Expiration
14. Sliding Time-Based Expiration

1. Belady's Algorithm:

Alias: Optimal page replacement policy OPT or Belady's OPT or Clairvoyant algorithm.

Principle of working:

Always discard or replace the cache that will not be needed for the longest time in the future. E.g. When a cache entry that is not going to be used for the next 10 seconds will be replaced by an entry that is going to be used within the next 5 seconds.

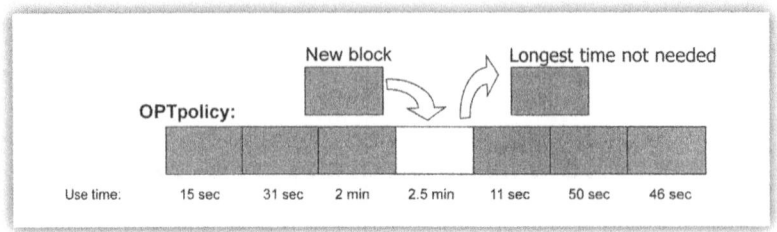

Figure 2:7 Belady's algorithm

Advantage:

Belady's algorithm is the best algorithm of any caching algorithm, when the analysis is accurate.

Disadvantage:

It is a heuristics-based algorithm and OPT is impossible to achieve, but most algorithms do it.

2. Least-Recently Used (LRU or Last Used):

Principle of working:

The LRU discards the least-recently used items first or removes the ones that haven't been used for the longest time. It needs to have a clock or timer or age bits for the whole cache and needs to keep track of what is used and not used; the timer reflects when any cache is accessed. New items are placed into the top of the cache and when the cache exceeds its size limit, it will discard the objects from the bottom of the cache. The trick is that whenever an object is accessed, it is placed at the top.

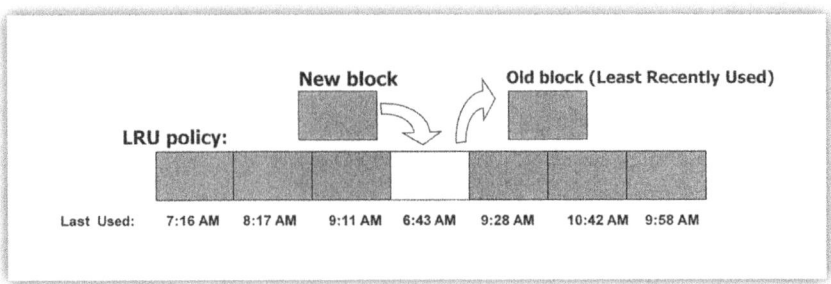

Figure 2:8 LRU Algorithm

Advantages:

1. LRU can be used as a full statistical analysis of recently used pages, since the policy takes advantage of the heuristic search that pages which have been accessed recently are more likely to be accessed again.
2. LRU can be employed in RAM, web browsers/web proxies, RAID, databases, data compression, and applications.

Disadvantages:

1. Since LRU is implemented with double-linked lists, it is expensive to implement in practice, and if implemented with the best algorithm, performance is a problem.
2. LRU supports just the fundamental locality principle and is problematic when the object is huge.

Fundamental locality principle: The fundamental locality principle claims that if a process visits a location in the memory, it will probably revisit the location and its neighborhood soon.

Advanced locality principle: The advanced locality principle claims that the probability of revisiting will increase as the number of the visits increases.

3. Most-Recently Used (MRU):

In contrast to LRU, MRU discards recently used items. When an item is repeatedly accessed in a looping sequence and high time-complexity operation, MRU is the best replacement algorithm. MRU uses the advanced locality principle. It is commonly used in a database memory cache whenever a cache record is used or the cache has no space.It will replace the entry at the top of the stack.

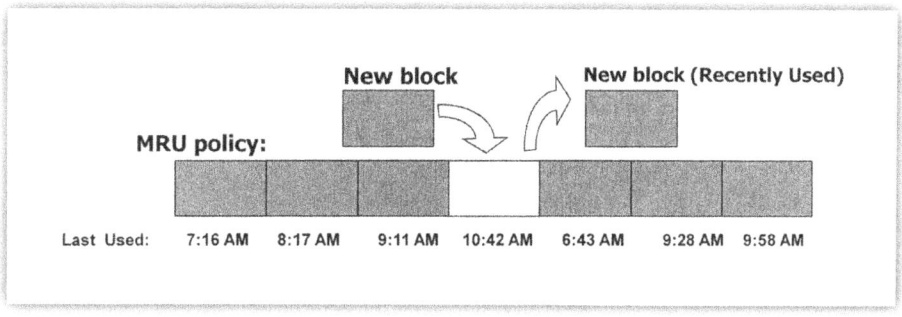

Figure 2:9 MRU algorithm

Advantages:

1. MRU can scan objects or records with huge datasets and repeated patterns with more hits than LRU; It can be used in database memory cache systems.
2. MRU algorithms are most useful in situations where the older an item is, the more likely it is to be accessed.

Disadvantage:

It cannot be used in a wide variety of applications, as the nature of MRU is more inclined toward older items, while in certain applications the outcome is the opposite.

4. Least-Frequently Used (LFU):

LFU adds a counter of how often an entry is needed by incrementing a counter associated with that entry. If the use frequency of each entity is the same, then they are expired by the Least-Recently Used (LRU) algorithm. There are variations of the LFU algorithm: LFU*, LFU-Aging, LFU*-Aging, and Windows-LFU.

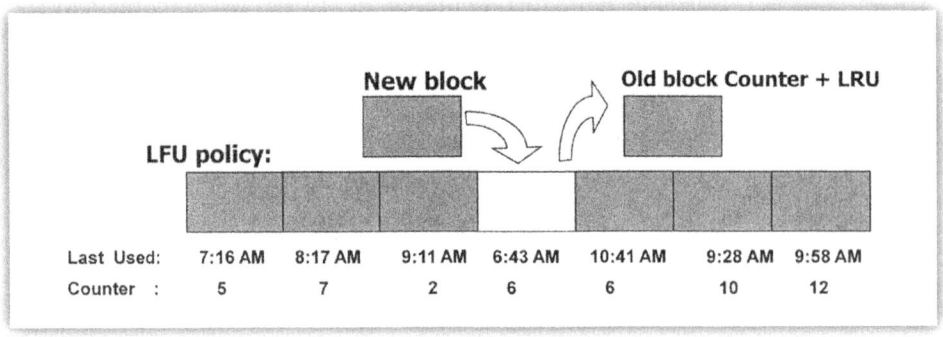

Figure 2:10 LFU algorithm

Advantages:

Since the LFU manages and keeps track of all the records, the OS uses it in memory management and file system management..

Disadvantages:

Since it needs to maintain the counters in the table, it is a heavily loaded algorithm, and it has a cache pollution problem which can be overcome by aging policy.

5. Pseudo-LRU:

Pseudo-LRU or Tree-LRU algorithm involves using a binary search tree. A binary search tree is a binary tree in which each internal node x stores an element such that the element stored in the left subtree of x are less than or equal to x and elements stored in the right subtree of x are greater than or equal to x.

6. Adaptive Replacement Cache (ARC):

ARC constantly balances between LRU and LFU to improve their combined results, but it is actually two LRU lists: one list, L1, contains recently used entries, and the other, L2, contains frequently referenced entries. It also contains ghost lists B1 and B2. *Ghost* lists act as scorecards by keeping track of the history of recently evicted cache entries, and the algorithm uses *ghost* hits to adapt to recent change in resource usage. Note that the *ghost* lists only contain metadata (keys for the entries) and not the resource data itself; in other words, as an entry is evicted into a *ghost* list, its data is discarded.

Advantages:

1. ARC performs better in applications like storage controllers, OS, file systems, disks, RAID, databases, web caching, web search query caching, processors, data compression etc.
2. You can scan huge objects with scan-resistant cache and offers low overhead.
3. It increases the effective cache capacity by reducing the number of copies of data in the caches and using access pattern aware adaptive replacement policies.
4. It reduces access latency by bringing both data and metadata as close to the access as possible.

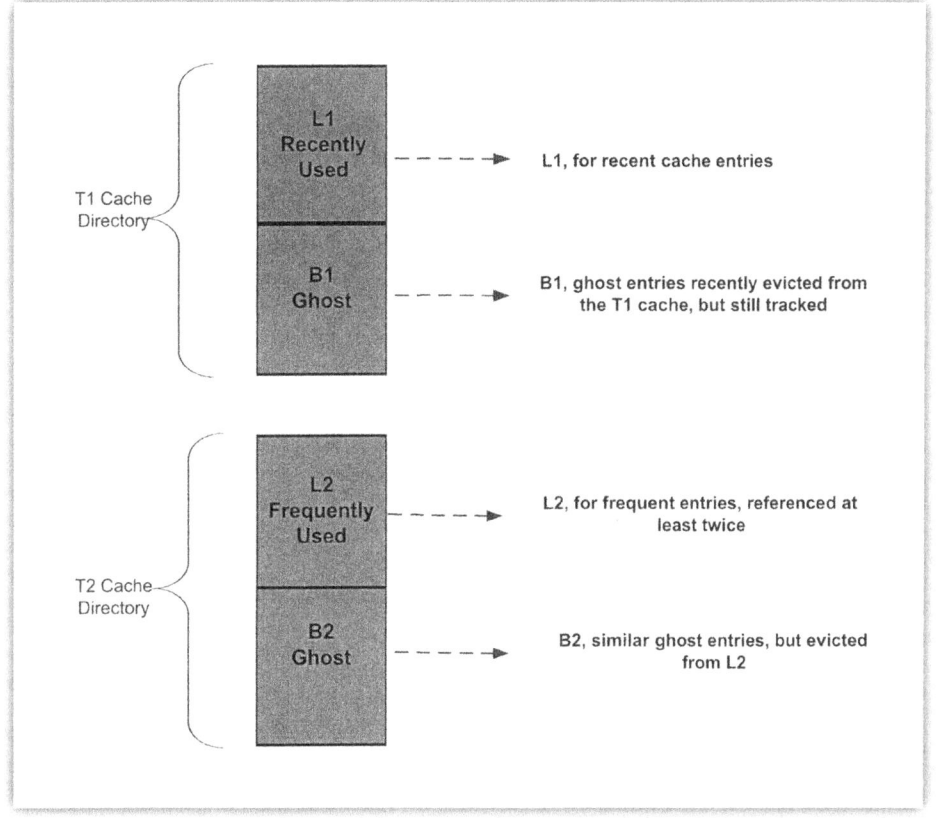

Figure 2:11 ARC algorithm

7. Random Replacement:

Also known as Random Cache, Random Replacement randomly selects an entry and discards it to make space when necessary. The key concept for this algorithm is that it does not require keeping any information about the access history or tracking references.

Advantages:

1. Random Replacement is better than other algorithm, since there is no overhead to track any references.
2. It is simple to deploy.

Disadvantage:

It has a high miss rate.

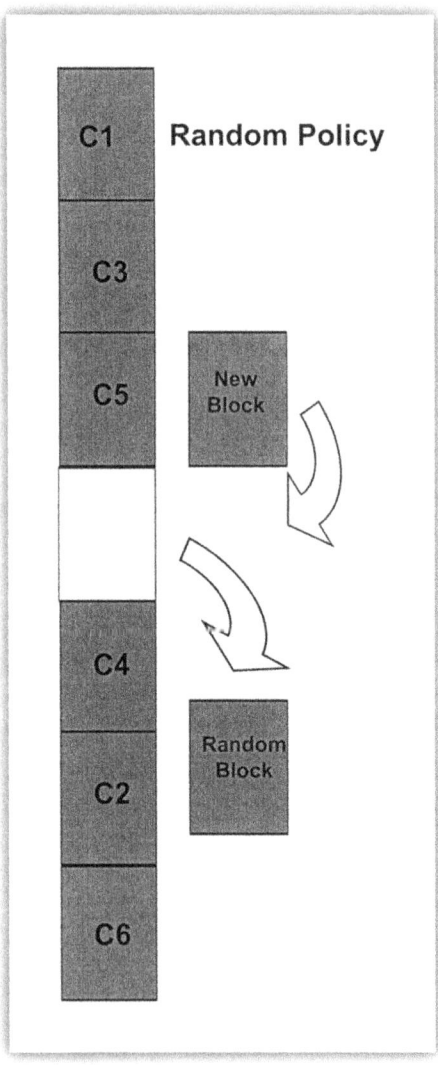

Figure 2:13 Random Replacement

8. First in First Out (FIFO):

FIFO is the simplest and low-overhead algorithm which requires less resources to maintain the cache entries. The only entries that it keeps track of are the most recently used entry in the back and oldest-used entry in the front. When the cache size is full and it is time to apply a replacement policy, an entry from the front (the oldest entry) is removed and replaced with the newly fetched entry into the cache.

Advantage:

The algorithm is easy to implement and there is less overhead in resource utilization.

Disadvantage:

The algorithm is fast but not adaptive.

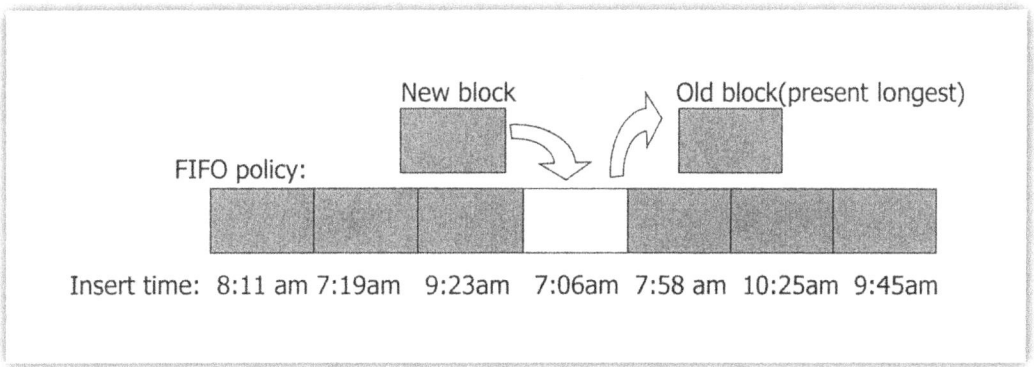

Figure 2:14 First in First Out (FIFO)

There are other variations of the FIFO algorithm which certainly have advantage over the FIFO. They are,

1. Second chance, or Second Chance Replacement (SCR) algorithm:

The stack or cache arrangement is same as the FIFO—the oldest entry in the front and the recently accessed entry in the back, but when a replacement policy needs to be applied when a newly fetched cache entry has to stored,second chance checks if the reference bits are set (a bit that tracks whether the entry has been used or requested before or not). If they are not set, it will replace the entry. If they are set, it will clear the referenced bit and then insert this entry at the back of the queue (as if it were a new entry); this process repeats in a continuous fashion like a circular queue. The second time it encounters the same entry which second entry cleared the reference bit before, it will replace the entry now as if its reference bit cleared.

*2.*Clock:

The clock is the other modified version of FIFO, and it has better performance than either FIFO or Second Chance. It functions the same as Second Chance, but instead of moving the cache entry to the back it keeps the "hand" (iterator) pointing to the oldest page in the list. Say if a cache miss occurs and the cache is full, then the R (referenced) bit is inspected at the hand's location. If R is "0", the new page is put in the place of the page the "hand" points to; otherwise the R bit is cleared. Then, the clock hand is incremented and the process is repeated until a page is replaced.

There are other variants of F Clock they are Clock-Pro, WSclock, and CAR.

9. Simple Time-Based:

In a simple time-based cache, the cache entries are invalidated based on the concept of "absolute time periods". Time-based invalidation of cached content is defined inside the caching rule, where an "expiry" field value is specified (in seconds). This is the time after the response is cached, when the cache expires. When a cache miss happens and a cache is full, the replacement happens with the cache that is expired, which means its value is zero.

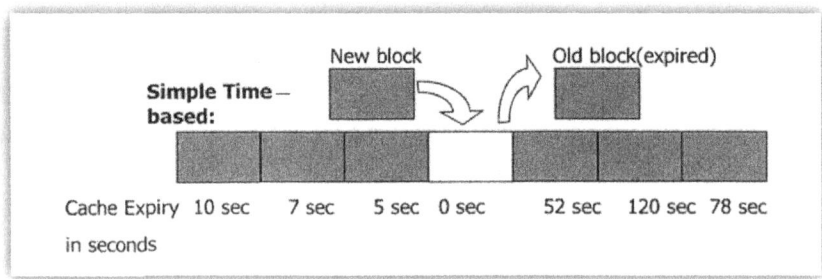

Figure 2:15 Simple Time-Based

The disadvantage is that it is not really adaptive for access patterns and not scan-resistant.

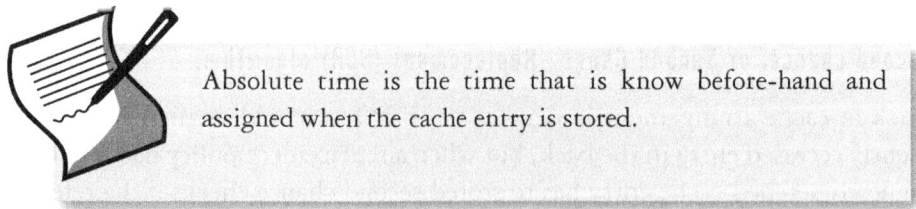

Absolute time is the time that is know before-hand and assigned when the cache entry is stored.

10. Extended Time-Based Expiration:

In extended Time-Based Expiration, the data in the cache is invalidated based on relative time periods. Items are added to the cache and remain there until the cache or replacement algorithm invalidates at certain points in time, such as every five minutes, 1 hour, each day at midnight, etc.

Advantage:

It is fast in accessing the cache.

Disadvanatge:

It is not really adaptive for access patterns and not scan resistant.

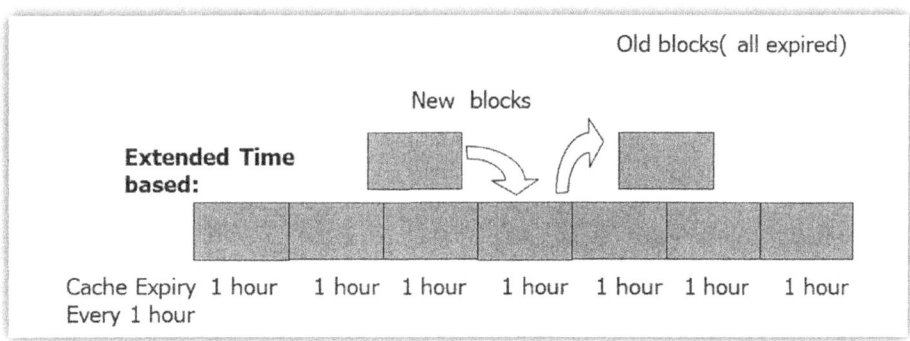

Figure 2:16 Extended Time-Based Expiration

11. Sliding time-based expiration:

In Sliding time-based expiration, the data in the cache is invalidated by specifying the amount of time the item is allowed to be idle in the cache after the last access time.

Advantage:

It is fast in accessing the cache.

Disadvantage:

It is not really adaptive for access patterns and not scan resistant.

What Caching and optimization technique does BlueCoat use?

We have discussed many different algorithms so that you could get a good understanding about the caching algorithm. BlueCoat uses patent-pending algorithm and it is propriety algorithm which applies all the algorithms best feature more efficiently and gets the best performance and security in the market for caching.

Blue Coat uses only two typesof caching: object caching and byte caching. But caching is not only the only mechanism that is used to speed transactions; here what we mean is when a new object is fetched and the cache is full, the different algorithms shown above are used to discard the unused or old cache entry. Is there a mechanism to decide which object the proxy should fetch and under what circumstances should it do it? How fast can I fetch the object and reduce the network latency? To provide an answer to all these questions "optimization techniques" are used to enhance the caching process. Both caching and WAN optimization techniques work hand-in-hand to give the maximum benefits of Blue Coat products and technology.

 Always remember that the Blue Coat OS is SGOS (Secure Gateway Operating System), a patent-pending embedded operating system architected entirely by Blue Coat Systems. The SGOS contains no general-purpose code and does not reuse code from other systems.

But in the Proxy SGOS there are always two frameworks that exist:

1. Proxy Edition
2. MACH5 Edition

The framework helps in building the policy and deciding what technology should be used. Say you want to deploy web, streaming, and FTP proxy—then you will use the Proxy Edition. If you want to accelerate all our applications in the WAN, due to faster performance or maybe due to having a slower link, to help out in this situation, you will use the MACH 5 Edition. Always remember that both are different frameworks but can be used together as well. This means that any Proxy SG products purchased , contains either "Full Proxy Edition" or Acceleration Edition," but has the same hardware specifications; the difference comes when you boot the system and it asks you which framework you want to choose: "Proxy Edition" or "MACH5 Edition". Even Proxy Editionwe could use both proxy and for acceleration functions, but for best practices on a large network separate the both functionality, so that you will get the full benefit and power of Blue Coat technology.

What is MACH5?

MACH5 (Multiprotocol Accelerated Caching Hierarchy) is a framework providing a multilayered approach to accelerating applications. MACH5 technology accelerates enterprise applications and enhances users performance. It is not a single solution, as it has different modules or technology it uses to achieve this. There are five basic technologies it uses: bandwidth management, protocol optimization, object caching, byte caching, and compression. Each of these has its own purpose for improving the speed of the application, reducing bandwidth, and optimizating the network.

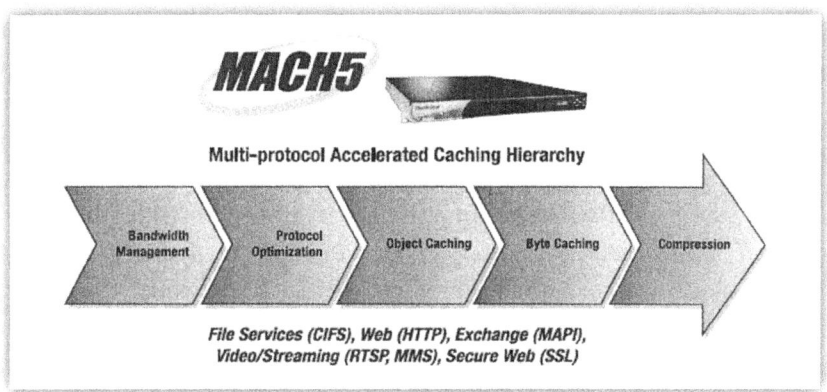

Figure 2:17 MACH5 Framework

The above diagram shows the order in which the techniques could be applied step-by-step, starting from the left with bandwidth management, then applying protocol optimization, etc. This is a layered approach, similar to that used in the OSI model for TCP/IP: the sender sends data and TCP/IP flow is from the Application layer to the Physical layer and the receiver receives the data in vice-versa. But in this book we have reordered for helps in easily understanding the concepts.

Remember that any of the five technologies could be used as per their business requirements. This means the Proxy SG could either be used for object caching and bandwidth management for our web access, and/or byte caching and compression for all TCP traffic. When all five are implemented, the processor flow of execution goes from left to right. It is just a schema of how the flow order is and howdifferent application could be benefited to get the best optimization and performance from Blue Coat technology.

Before we begin explaining the various proxy-caching technologies, we will cover some basic terminology that we use in this book; which will help us to understand Blue Coat products and technology easily.

What is an object?

An object is anything that can be stored in the object store, which can be a hardware or software cache. Objects can be text files, HTML,XML, audio, pictures, JavaScript, etc. For example, when you go to http://www.google.com, this is called the URL, but you are actually downloading different objects from the main page—all the pictures, the search engine, the logo, and certain JavaScript that runs behind the page.

This example shows how different objects are fetched from the server via an HTTP GET request and that each have unique Uniform Resource Identifier (URI) where the images or files reside in the server. It has been noted that the objects could be static or dynamic. Static objects is defined as the size of the object is known and it can be decided beforehand whether or not the object can be stored in the cache. The maximum object size can be specified in Blue Coat so that if an object is greater than the maximum size, it can be directly served to the client without caching. On the other hand, a dynamic object is defined when the object size is not known, where the size always varies from time to time: e.g. video streams like live streaming, flash objects like newsstickers, stock sticker, online radio, etc. In this case there are different ways of configuring the Proxy SG to determine whether to cache or not; this will be discussed in the later part of the book in Chapter 6.

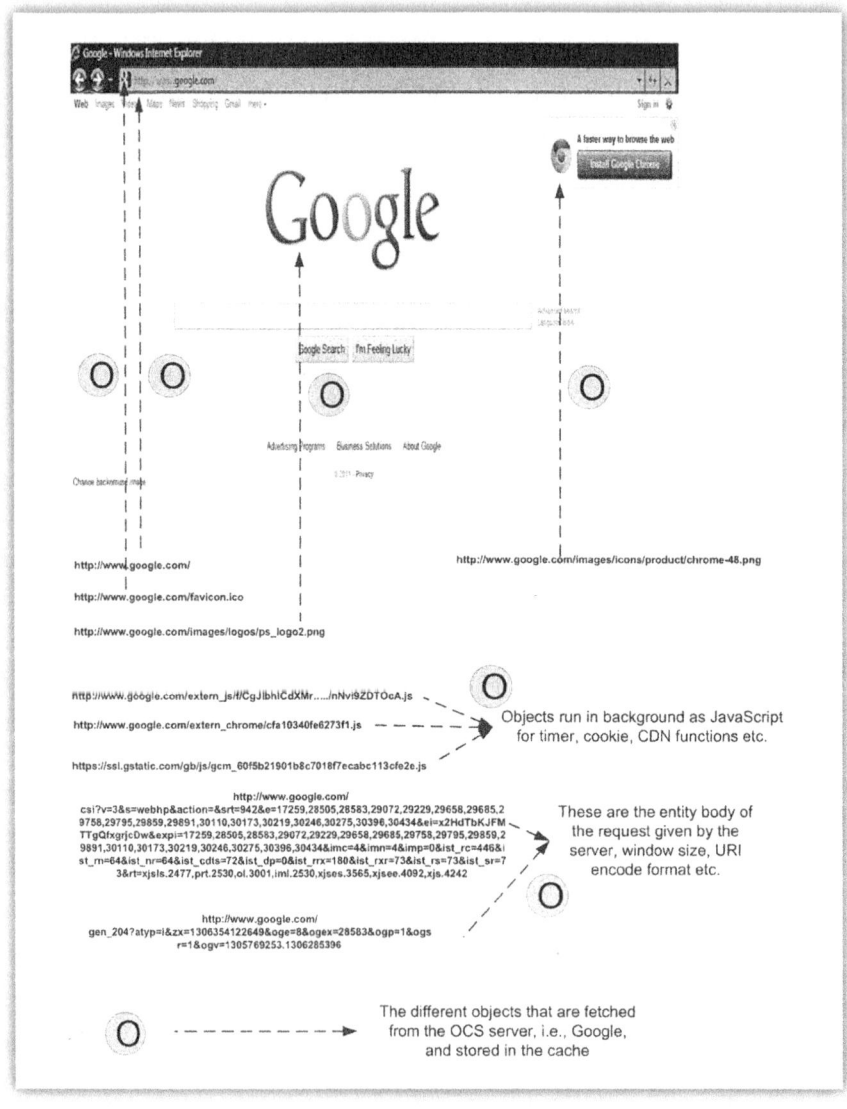

Figure 2:18 Objects from OCS (Google)

1. Object caching:

Storing an object in a cache is known as **object caching**. This is done to reduce the bandwidth, network resources, and also OCS performance. When objects are cached, the only traffic that crosses the WAN is permissions checks (when required), and verification checks that ensure that the copy of the object in the cache is still "fresh" or "current". When the user tries to access the site for the first time, the proxy does not have any cache objects for this site; it then contacts the OCS server and gives it to the user, and all future requests for the same object can be served directly from the cache.

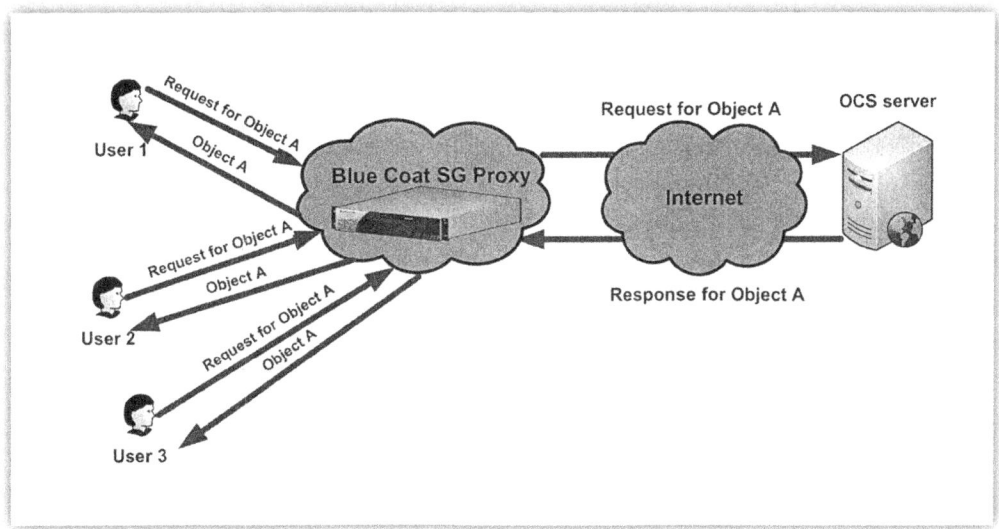

Figure 2:19 Object caching

In conjunction with object caching, there are other technologies that help optimize the traffic efficiently, which improves the object caching. They are

    a. Object pipelining,
    b. Adaptive refresh, and
    c. SSL optimization.

a. Object pipelining:

Pipelining is a common feature that is used in every browser. The terms "pipelining" and "object pipelining" are used interchangeably, but technically pipelining should be used when talking about browsers (IE, Firefox, Safari, etc.). Object pipelining is the term that is used in Blue Coat SGOS Proxy.

So what is pipelining?

Pipelining, also know HTTP pipelining, is a feature or technique using one TCP/IP handshake to pull or fetch multiple objects. That is, using one three-way handshake, multiple HTTP requests are used, but as per HTTP RFC spec, only two keep-alive packets can be used for one connection s per server. For example, when you visit any site at www.cnn.com, there many images, text, videos etc. The browser uses one TCP/IP handshake and pulls two images or two text files or two videos from www.cnn.com. In this way, the latency and network round-trip time are reduced. The important point to note here is that normally HTTP requests are issued sequentially, with the next request being issued only after the response to the current request has been completely received. There are two Request for Comments (RFC) standards for HTTP: HTTP 1.0 and HTTP 1.1, but pipelining is only supported in HTTP 1.1, not in 1.0. This means the server should handle HTTP 1.1 connections to make pipelining work.

In the following diagram, we see that using two TCP/IP handshakes four objects are pulled using pipelining; without pipelining, three handshakes are used and three objects pulled. Using the pipelining feature helps to gain better performance.

A browser can make two connections to the server and in each connection there can be 2 HTTP requests. Only GET and HEAD requests should be pipelined, and not POST and PUT requests.

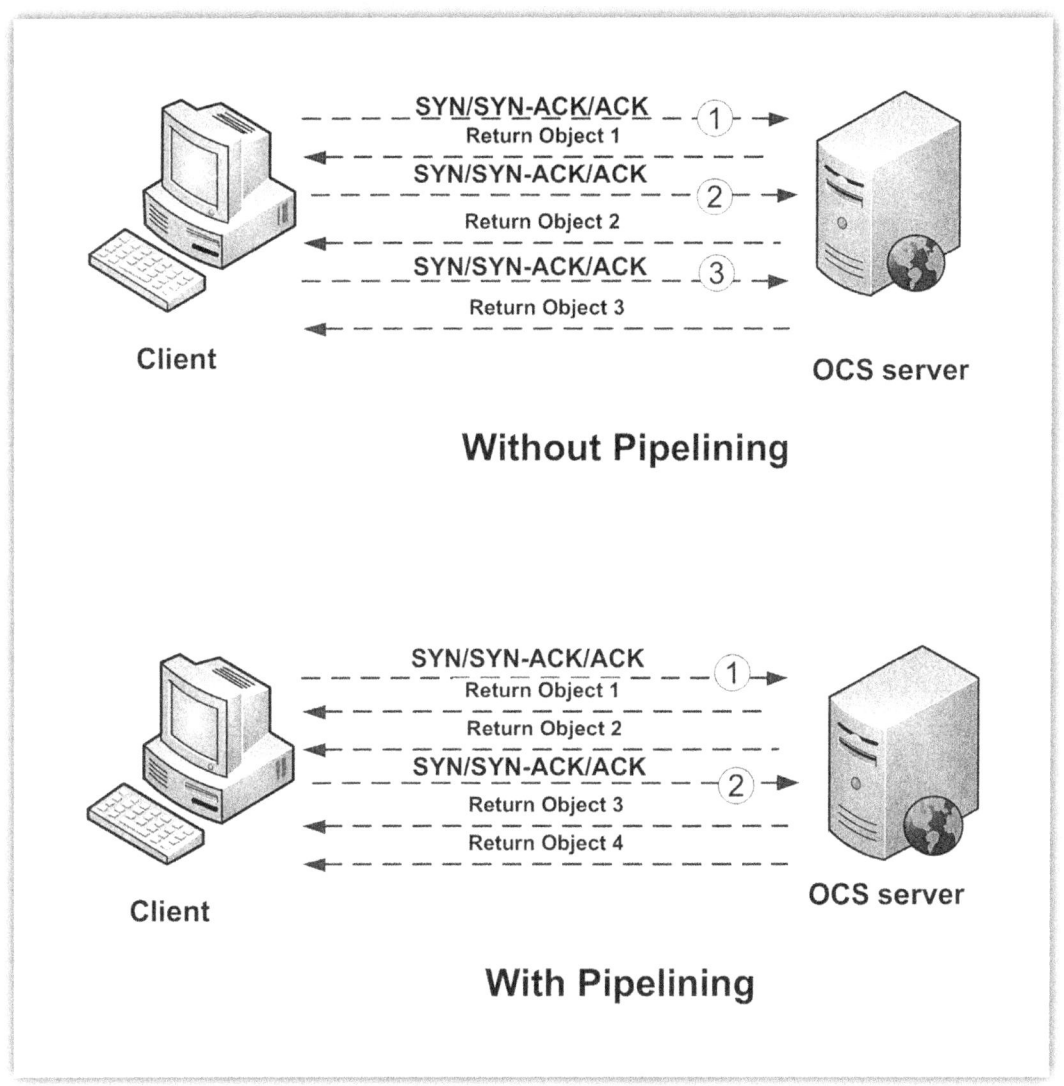

Figure 2:20 Object Pipelining

So what is object pipelining?

In object pipelining, which is used Blue Coat, the objects are requested parallely instead of serially. Object pipelining is defined as feature in which the embedded objects in a container page are requested in parallel.

For example, when a user requests a web page from www.yahoo.com, as the Blue Coat Proxy SG returns the content it simultaneously requests the embedded object from the server side so that by the time the client browser requests the objects in the page, they are already in cache. This means the proxy doesn't need to wait until the user explicitly requests the other objects from that object. ProxySG will open many connections to the server to retrieve objects before the browser asks for them.

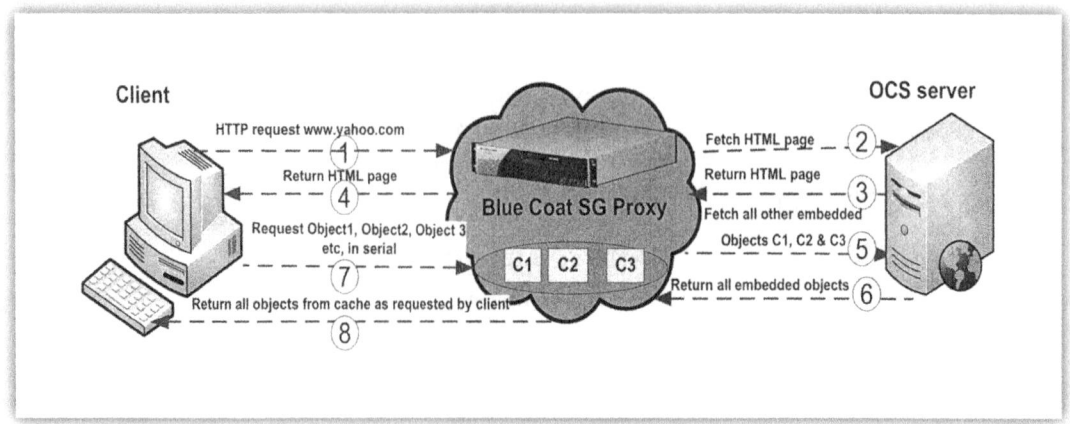

Figure 2:21 BlueCoat Object Pipelining traffic flow

You can see in the above figure 2.21 how objects have been fetched from the server and how object pipelining works for application layer, in this case it is HTTP. But how does the TCP handshake happens between the client, the proxy, and the server? Is it just one handshake for the whole process of connection between the client, proxy, and OCS? Or do many TCP handshakes happen?

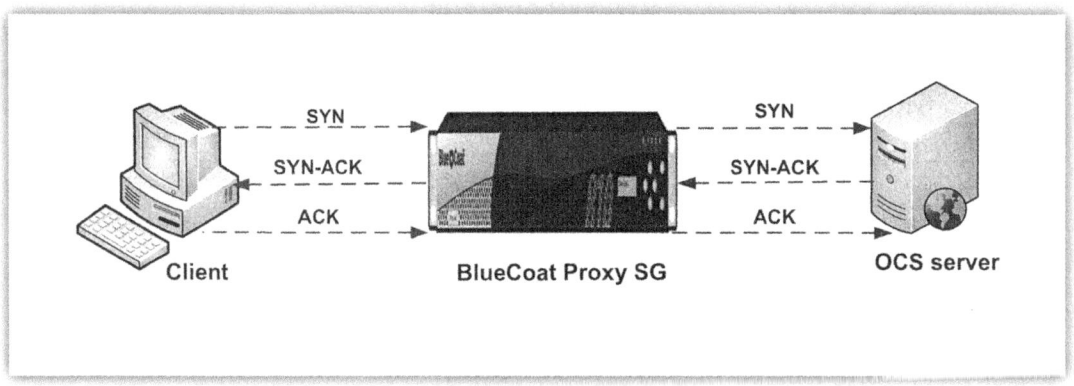

Figure 2:22 TCP handshake between client, proxy, and OCS server

As you can see in the above Figure 2:22, the client makes a TCP handshake with the proxy and the proxy in turn makes a TCP handshake with the OCS server. So here there are two TCP handshakes involved. But if a client packet traverses through a router/ firewall/VPN/load balancer, it will be just one TCP handshake between the client and the peer device (e.g., web server). But if you come across someone saying that firewall or load balancer does a full proxy connection, this basically means that two sets of handshake are involved, one from the client to the firewall/load balancer and the other from the firewall/load balancer to the server—the same as what the proxy does—rather than just forwarding the traffic.

b. Adaptive Refresh

Two terms that are used interchangeably are "adaptive refresh" and "Asynchronous Adaptive Refresh" (AAR). This is one more latency-attacking algorithm. The AAR allows the ProxySG to keep cached objects as fresh as possible, thus reducing response times. It does this by automatically refreshing the objects that are stored in the cache without the user requesting it. If it refreshes the content after the user requests the content then there will be round-trip time delays. this refresh is done by the traditional proxies; to deliver content to the end user with the proxy being confidence that the data is fresh, tradational proxies must send a "refresh check" to the OCS. The AAR algorithm allows the HTTP proxy to manage cached objects based on their rate of change and popularity: an object that changes frequently and/or is requested frequently will be more eligible for asynchronous refresh than an object with a lower rate of change and/or popularity.

The only method for delivering web pages quickly and accurately is for the refreshing activity to be uncoupled from the actual end-user requests. This refreshing activity occurs asynchronously to actual user requests, so as to not impact response times. The Adaptive Refresh algorithm is integral to Blue Coat SGOS and is the only technology in the industry that develops a "model of change" for every web object in its cache store.

Blue Coat Object Caching is so effective that it can reduce latency of first-time requests by 50%. After objects are cached, it can reduce latency by 90%.

c. SSL optimization

You can accelerate and optimize both internal and external SSL applications with object caching. With secure (https) web applications on the rise, SSL Optimization has become a key requirement in any enterprise WAN Optimization project. This benefit can be achieved if you have enabled SSL interception, which can decrypt the packets and apply HTTP object caching algorithm.

2. Byte Caching

Byte Caching is also known as dictionary compression, network sequence caching, and transparent data reduction. Byte caching is a very low-level WAN optimization technique for replacing repetitive streams of raw application data with shorter "tokens" prior to transmission over the network. Byte caching slices the objects into bits and then sends only the updated bits over the network. It is not application-specific, so any TCP traffic could be used with) -Bbyte Caching technique such as email, FTP, file shares, backup applications, datacenter-to-datacenter disk synchronization, etc.

Byte Caching works very well where the same content or dynamic content is stored in multiple locations.

How exactly does byte caching work?

1. Two Proxy SGOSs are needed to perform this—say branch office to branch office or to a head office.
2. As objects are stored in a cache store, the byte caching stores tokens in byte cache dictionary. These tokens, also called identifiers, can replace up to 64 KB of data each.
3. When new data is intercepted, it creates a token and compresses the data into gzip format and sends only the data to the other Proxy SG so that Byte Caching can build the same byte cache dictionary. This process takes place until Byte Caching populates all the data that is flowing in the network.
4. When Byte caching encounters the same data sequence, the Proxy SG sends the token representing that data instead of the bulky traffic.
5. The other Proxy SG device then takes the token and using its own byte cache dictionary, identifies the corresponding data pattern. It then reconstitutes the data into its original form before transmitting it to the application (or user).

Since byte caching is bidirectional, once the byte cache dictionary has been populated on both Blue Coat Proxy SGs, the same byte cache dictionary tokens can be used for data requested, as well as data posted or saved.

The diagram below shows how byte caching works. In this example, the user wants to access a Microsoft Word or Excel document that is on the file server across a WAN. The first time the user fetches the document, the byte dictionary is populated; then when the user edits the file and saves it, the Proxy SG recognizes the file and transmits tokens to represent the data that seen earlier and only the saved portion of the file is sent as tokens. So there two sets of tokens: one to identify which data the other Proxy SG should check in its own byte cache dictionary, and the other is changed or edited portion of the data as tokens. All subsequent requests for the file such as edit, delete, both Proxy SGs will use the tokens to represent most of the document.

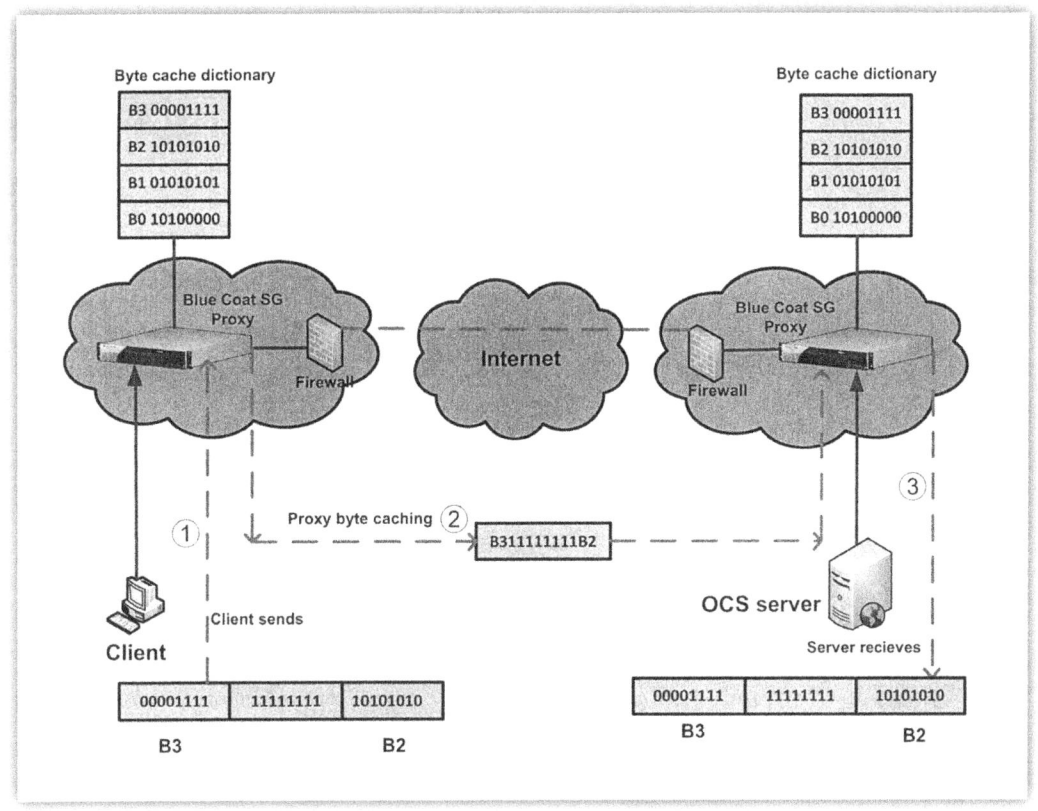

Figure 2:23 BlueCoat Byte Caching traffic flow

Byte caching can be used in different types of applications—that is, say the same document is accessed via email (MAPI protocol), fileserver (CIFS or Samba), web server (HTTP), or FTP server, byte caching could be applied, as it inspects the raw data that makes up the object. Byte caching could be applied to SSL traffic; SSL interception is enabled on the Blue Coat SG MACH5.

Blue Coat's byte caching feature is stream-based (versus packet-based). This allows for more compression than packet-based byte caching.

3. Bandwidth management

The term "bandwidth management" is also known as traffic shaping. Bandwidth management is the process or technique of measuring, controlling, and monitoring the network traffic on a link, to avoid "throttle"in the link's capacity, which would result in network congestion and poor network performance. The priority for applications has an effect both on the order the traffic is sent in, and on the amount of guaranteed bandwidth the application is allocated, regardless of other traffic on the network. This means the network is always available for highest-priority or business-critical applications and less-important applications are assigned a limited bandwidth. This ensures that all business-related applications are performed efficently and with lowlatency.

The Proxy SG can be configured by assigning priority to applications, creating different classes, and allocating maximum and minimum bandwidth for each class. The bandwidth management can be controlled for applications based, website, URL category, users/groups/IP address/Subnet, and time.

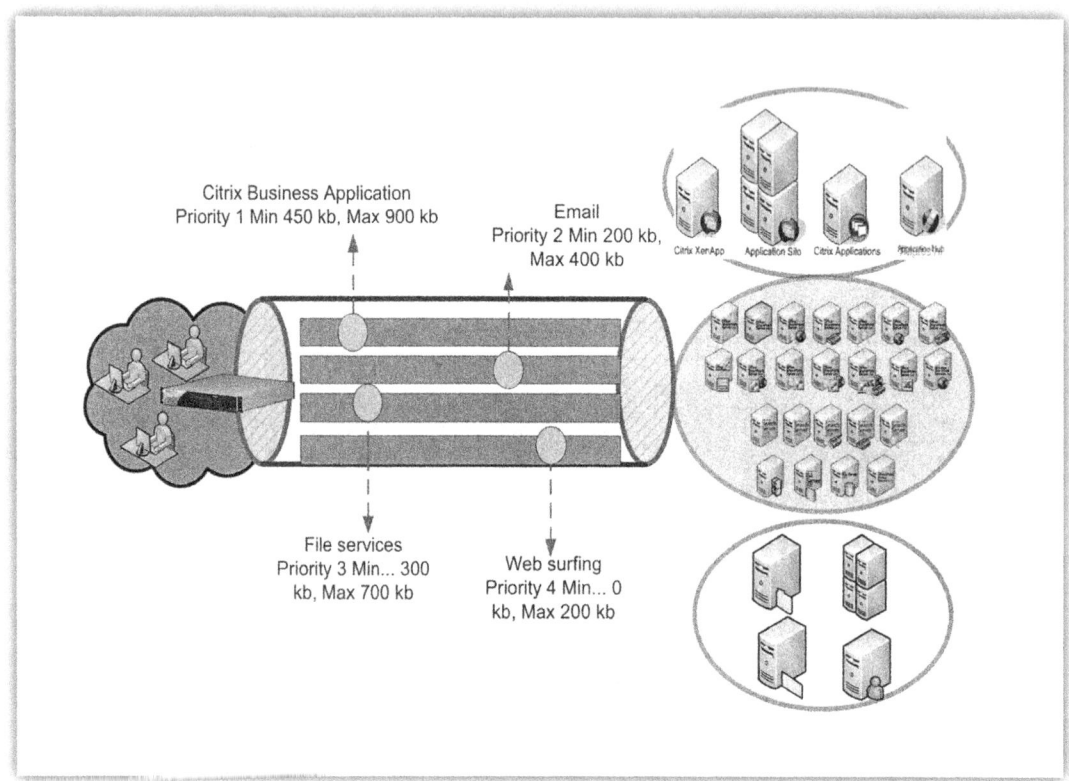

Figure 2:24   BlueCoat Bandwidth Management

4. Protocol optimization

Protocol optimization does not reduce the amount bandwidth that an application consumes, but it can greatly accelerate delivery of applications and reduce latency in the process. The fundamental concept behind protocol optimization is that many protocols, such as DNS, CIFS˙ built to work in LAN, where the round-trip time and number of handshakes are not an issue. When running the same services on the WAN, the factors of round-trip time and number of handshakes come into consideration. Because even to perform a simple operation, these WAN protocols have to run into many process to accomplish it. A great example is the object pipelining that we discussed earlier: with one TCP/IP handshake, two objects can be fetched; this reduces the second TCP/IP handshake and gets the data in a simpler fashion. So we could say that object pipelining is one of the protocol optimization types.

There are different types of protocol, such as object pipelining, CIFS optimization, running non-standard applications on standard port, DNS caching, local authentication (BCAAA), Exchange MAPI optimization, TCP, video/streaming (RTSP, MMS), HTTP, and HTTPS optimization.

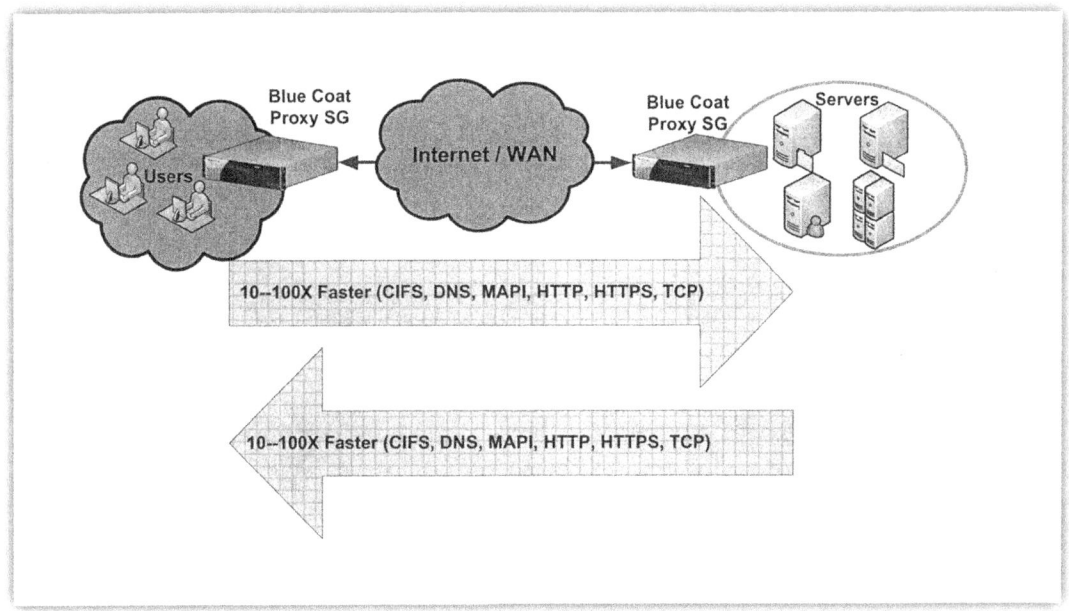

Figure 2:25 Protocol Management

5. Compression

Compression is a technique used to remove extraneous/predictable/duplicated data in the traffic before it is transmitted and reconstructed at the destination using the same technique. The compression can be done by either the client browser or the Proxy SG itself. This means that if the client browser doesn't support the compression method, the Proxy SG will decompress the data it fetched from the OCS and give it to the client. Compression reduces the size of the content transferred over the network, enabling optimized bandwidth usage and faster response times.

Blue Coat SG supports two types of compression methodologies:

1. HTTP and
2. Point-to-Point.

1. HTTP method

The HTTP method was first proposed in HTTP version 1.1 for improved page download time. It requires a compression feature implemented at the web server and a decompression feature implemented at the browser.

The content that needs to be compressed can be either

1. Static content, or
2. Dynamic content.

a. Static content

Static content is files that are compressed once and stored in the OCS server. After that, when the server receives a request it will return the compressed data. In a static content file (HTML, CSS, XHTML, or JavaScript), the compression is improved to reduce the file size to $1/4^{th}$—that is, it is reduced by 60% to 85%, depending on how redundant the code is.

b. Dynamic content

Dynamic content compresses every time a client requests one specific file, such as a large CSV file-generating engine located on the server back-end. The applications used to generate dynamic content include Java Servlet, Java Server Pages (JSP), Personal Home Pages (PHP), Perl Scripts, Active Server Pages (ASP), Net applications, etc.

The static and dynamic contentcan be either HTML or text file, then we can compress it, could the other formats that can be compressed are XML and JSON for Ajax

The algorithms used for compression/decompression are Gzip and Deflate. These are both used on browsers, but ideally GZIP is used in the Proxy SG for better performance, as recommended by many experts. In the HTTP method, the decompression can be done either by the Proxy SG or the browser.

By Proxy SG:

The Proxy SG does the compression and decompression in either of the following situations as shown below:

a. If the browser doesn't supports decompression, (but most modern browsers support), the decompression is done by the Proxy SG.

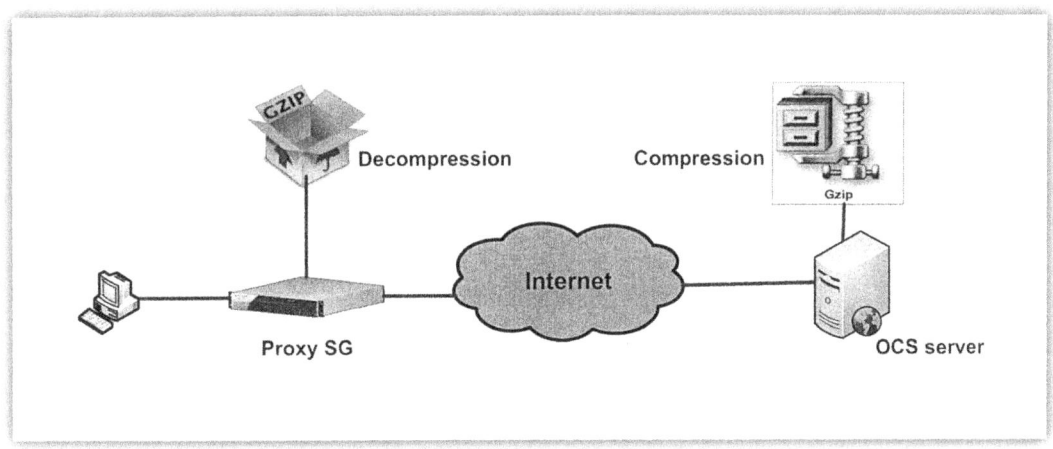

Figure 2:26 Compression/Decompression between Proxy SG and OCS

b. In certain cases the module or third-party software to support compression is not installed in the web server (OCS); again the Proxy SG does the compression, which greatly improves the performance of the web server.

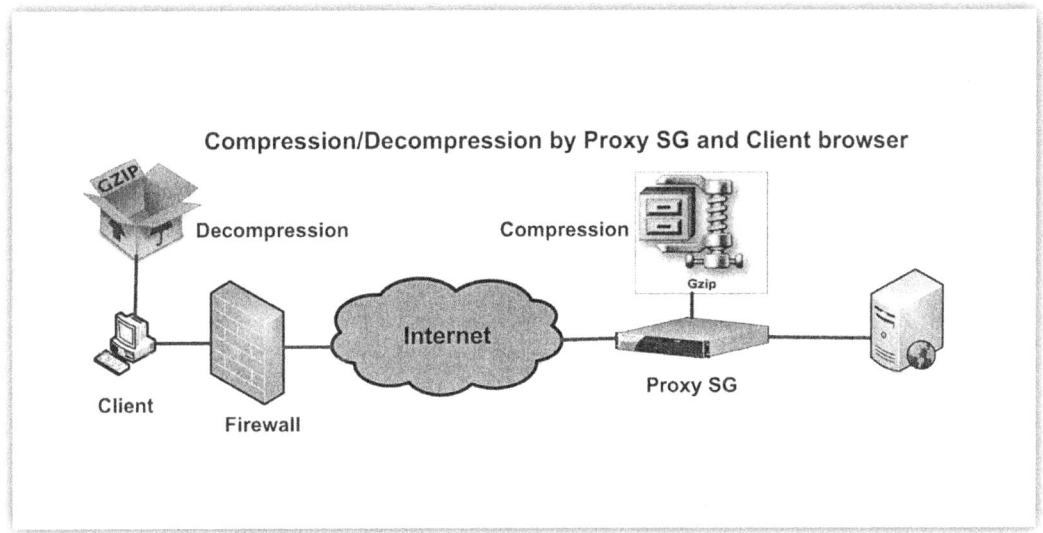

Figure 2:27 Compression/Decompression between Proxy SG and client

By Browser:

This is the usual method, where the OCS performs the compression and the browser performs the decompression of the web page.

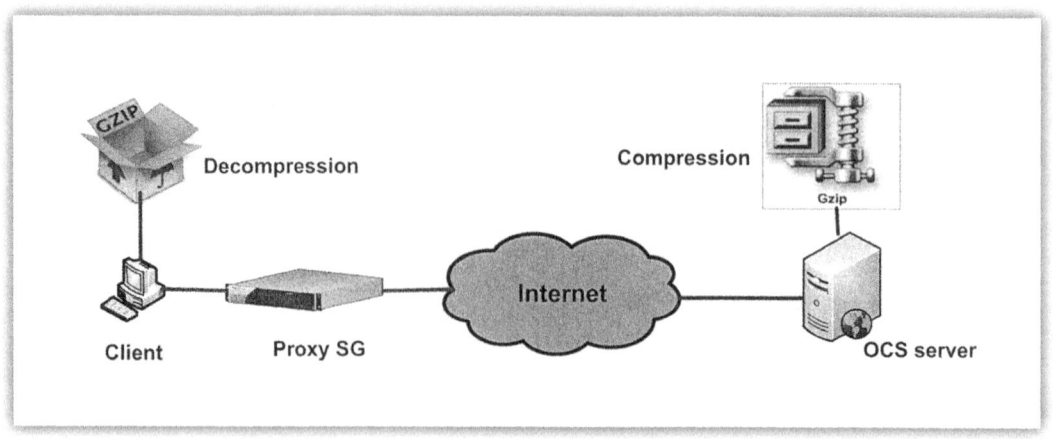

Figure 2:28 Compression/Decompression between Client and OCS

2. Point-to-Point method

This method is used for any protocol and used by Proxy SG. It creates compressed tunnels between proxies, so the Proxy SG compresses the traffic before sending it, and the other Proxy SG decompresses it and forwards the requests to the peer.

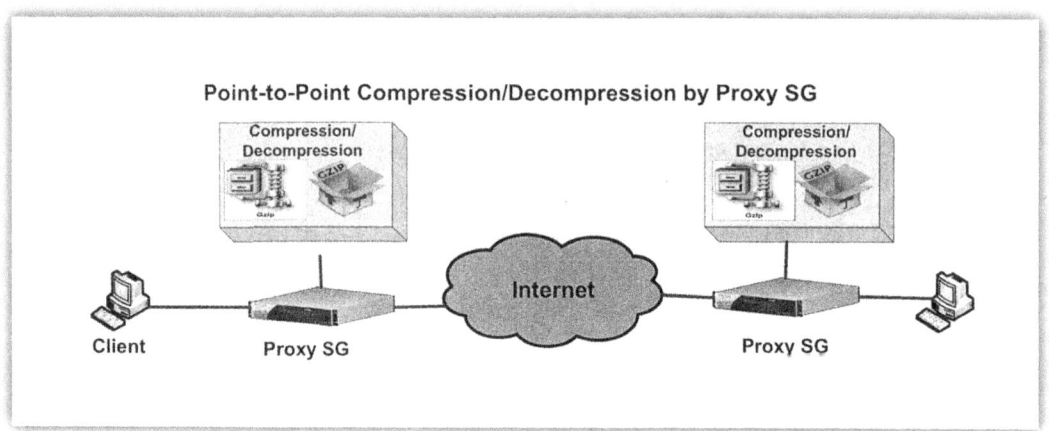

Figure 2:29 Compression/Decompression between Proxy SG and Proxy SG

The features that Proxy SG support in compression are as follows:

1. It uses GZIP as a standard for the best performance and it can compress any protocol or traffic.
2. Proxy SG can cache both compressed and decompressed objects.
3. When compression is applied with object caching and byte caching, bandwidth savings is optimized and performance is enhanced.

4. Proxy SG can be used to compress dynamic content "on-the-fly" with better performance and accuracy.

Do not compress images and PDF files since they are already compressed; if they are compressed again, either size of the file can increase or the file cannot be accessed by the client and sometimes gets corrupted.

Test Yourself:

1. If you are using BlueCoat Proxy SG as a caching engine for your organization, which is the best decision you could conclude that the cache engine is working at best performance based on Cache Hits and Cache Misses?

    a. More Cache Misses
    b. More Cache Hits
    c. Less Cache Misses
    d. Less Cache Hits

2. If John started watching a video at 10:00 a.m., and Sam wants to watch the video and requests the video at 10:10 a.m., how much of the video is stored in the cache?

    a. The Full video
    b. 1 hour
    c. 5 minutes
    d. 10 minutes

3. The ARC (Adaptive Replacement Cache) constantly balances between two algorithms (choose two):

    a. LRU
    b. MRU
    c. Pseudo-LRU
    d. LFU

4. Does MACH5 (Multiprotocol Accelerated Caching Hierarchy) provide encryption features?

    a. Yes
    b. No

5. In web and proxy terminology, which of the following is not an object?

    a. XHTML

    b. JSON/AJAX

    c. FLV

    d. User-Agent

6. How does the Asynchronous Adaptive Refresh (AAR) feature work in BlueCoat?

    a. A user requests an object and if the object in the cache is expired, then BlueCoat fetches a fresh object from the OCS.

    b. A user requests an object, and BlueCoat has a copy of the object in the cache that is not expired, then BlueCoat sends a "Refresh request" to the OCS to confirm the freshness of the cached response.

    c. Without the user's request, all the cached objects are automatically refreshed based on their rate of change and their popularity.

    d. Without the user's request, all cached objects are automatically refreshed.

7. With object pipelining, how many objects are requested for one TCP connection?

    a. 2

    b. 1

    c. 4

    d. 3

8. If you are deploying the MACH 5 solution in your company, you want make sure that the web traffic used by different groups in the organization is controlled so that the IT team uses 25% of the web traffic, 25% is used by the Sales and Marketing team, and senior management uses the remaining 50%. Which MACH 5 feature will you implement to achieve this?

    a. Protocol Optimization

    b. Bandwidth management

    c. Byte caching

    d. Compression

9. What are the compression/decompression methods supported by Proxy SG?

    a. GZIP

    b. WinRAR

    c. Deflate

    d. ASCII encoding

C H A P T E R   3

BLUECOAT SG PROXY DEPLOYMENT

BLUECOAT SG PROXY DEPLOYMENT:

Let us look first at how Blue Coat SG proxy is deployed in the network and the different security architecture models that could be installed in the real world. We will provide an overview in this book; a future book will cover the best security practices and configurations for any enterprise or corporate environment.

There are different ways to install Blue Coat SG in the network; it all depends on the network architecture and business requirements. This ultimately depends upon the management's decision regarding which method to deploy, but as Blue Coat professional service engineers, it is our responsibilities to highlight the different pros and cons of each method.

The methods we will discuss here about the designs are the same for other proprietary and open-source products. In other words, the design principles are the same for any proxy technology, which lays a fundamental idea for all enterprises in how they deploy proxies. It is the same even for the big networks like Google, Facebook, Twitter, Amazon etc., but all these companies go for open source technology, which we will discuss in detail in the advance book. The reason we are shedding light in this track about other products and technology is to gain more confidence and knowledge about the Blue Coat products and really understand the fundamentals of proxy technology, which will make us the leader in the market, competing better with others.

So to start, how is Blue Coat deployed in the real world, and we will discussthe different architectures that any enterprise could design the BlueCoat proxy for their business and users?

There are four types of proxy deployment:

1. Transparent proxy
2. Explicit proxy
3. Reverse proxy
4. Forwarding proxy

Each of the methods has its own pros and cons, and understanding Blue Coat's technology and recommendations for the best practices to the customers totally comes from its extensive knowledge and understanding about web security technology and how deeply we are involved and updated of every change that happens in the Internet about the web.

We will discuss in detail about each method and show concepts like how the packet flow looks and how the proxy is installed in the network with architecture diagrams.

1. Transparent proxy deployment

The quick definition of "transparent proxy deployment" is "Clients or users don't 'KNOW' there is a proxy in the path." Although the term "transparent" is confusing and contradicts the basic definition of "transparency," which means the insight knowledge, the true meaning of transparent proxy is that "the transparent proxy server shouldn't alter data." But this is not the case as you modify the data when you authenticate, suppress HTTP headers, redirects etc. So transparent is assumed here to mean it is for the client that doesn't alters that data when it communicates with server as you don't do any changes in the client request until you need to do it and the client assumes that is talking to the peer server; thus from the client's view it is sees the real server and assumes that there is no proxy in the path.

The reason to choose transparent deployment is that no changes are made in the client's machine. This may be due network reasons, or a mixed environment where the remote client's machines is not managed by the domain controller, or the desire to have flat systems and networks and to limit any client changes; it always depends on the dynamic nature of the network to handle the request, and this absolutely is the work culture of the organizations or their methods and philosophical ways of of implementing proxy solutions.

In transparent mode the client will do a DNS lookup of the destination; for example, when the client wants to connect to www.yaho.com, it resolves the destination address www.yahoo.com and then connects to it..

There are many challenges involved in deploying a transparent proxy in the network. The first question that always comes from customers is, "Does it involve additional costs?" The answer is both "Yes" and "No." There needs to be a Layer 4 switch or firewall that supports Cisco WCCP (Web Cache Communication Protocol), or Blue Coat SG bridging. So if the answer is "Yes," it includes additional costs. It means if you are deploying a new Internet for the customer, thatthe customer should buy additional switches or routers that support Layer 4 switching, or routers or firewalls that support WCCP. If the answer is "No," it means that there is already a well-defined network with complete traffic-flow control and this features Layer 4 switching or WCCP protocol support in its modules, which only involves a few configuration changes in the network. But again, even if the network is designed perfectly and it has multiple data centers and distributed networks, then transparent proxy is a complicated and complex deployment.

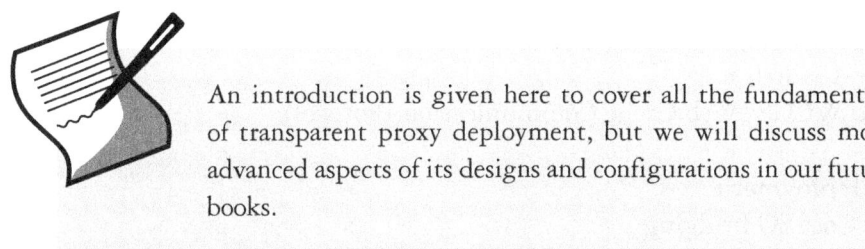

An introduction is given here to cover all the fundamentals of transparent proxy deployment, but we will discuss more advanced aspects of its designs and configurations in our future books.

There are two methodologies to deploy Proxy SG in a transparent deployment.

1. **Inline deployment**
   In an inline deployment, the ProxySG appliance is physically inserted into the path of the clients, and all traffic must pass through the Proxy SG appliance.

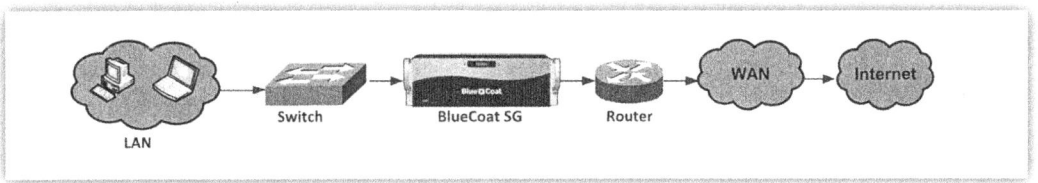

Figure 3:1 Inline deployment

2. **Virtual inline deployment**
   In a virtual inline deployment, the Proxy SG appliance is not in the physical path of clients and servers, but depends on an external device (a switch or router) to redirect traffic to the Proxy SG.

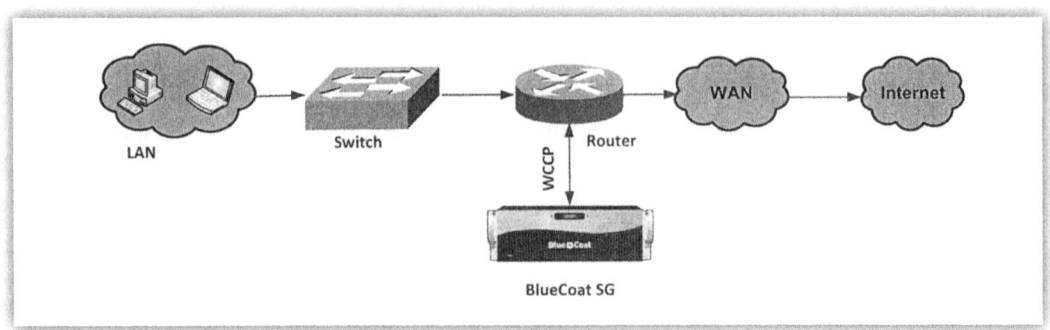

Figure 3:2 Virtual Inline deployment

So transparent deployment can be done in four different ways:

1. **Virtual Inline deployment**
   a. Layer 4 switch
   b. Cisco WCCP (Web Cache Communication Protocol)

2 . **Inline deployment**
   a. Blue Coat SG bridging
   b. Blue Coat as the default router

We will explain each method with architecture diagrams with pros and cons about the each setup; this will allow you to get a feel about the proxies in Internet and web security.

1. Virtual inline deployment

a. Transparent: Layer 4 switch—Virtually Inline deplyment.

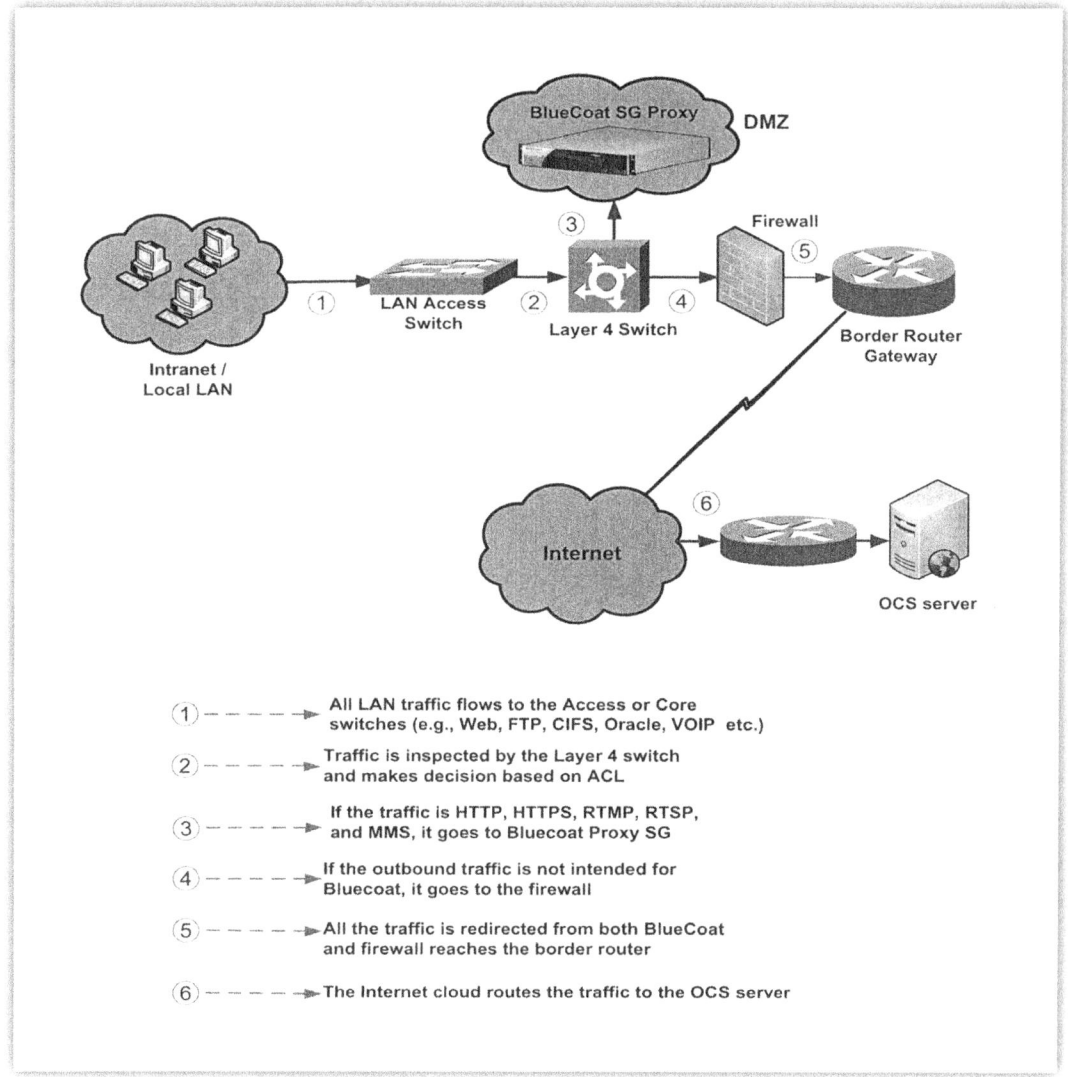

Figure 3:3 Transparent: Layer 4 switch—Virtually Inline

In a transparent deployment, a Layer 4 device or a switch receives and inspects all outbound traffic, making decisions of forwarding the traffic to either Bluecoat Proxy SG or the firewall, depending upon the policies that are set on the switch. This can be implemented with PBR (Policy-Based Routing), which can inspect any fields in the TCP/IP layer source/destination address, protocols, ports, etc. With PBR which makes the routing decision and the respective traffic flows based on the ACL that have been setup.

Oftentimes, administrators or even architects get a little confused by what exactly a Layer 4 switch is. The ideal definition of a "Layer 4 switch" is that when a switch wants to make Layer 2 switching and to do that depends on the upper layers (say Layers 3 and 4) to make decision, then we call it a Layer 4 switch. The term so called a Layer 4 switch in the market for vendors like Cisco or Juniper, the only term when you recommend a customer to install with a Layer 4 switch is that on router do the PBR, and this function is a router not switching. So if the router could do Layer 3 and 4 then you could do PBR, if they need URL hashing and functions like that then it is not the router or switch or so called Layer 4 switching that comes into picture, it is the load-balancer which does Layer 4 to Layer 7 switching, say e.g. Cisco ACE, F5, Net Scaler etc...

So it all depends upon the needs and requirements of the customer and what features each routing and switching module supports.

A normal router or switch or Layer 4 switch should have the following attributes to make routing decisions:

1. Source IP/Destination IP
2. Source port/Destination port
3. Protocol number
4. NAT techniques
5. Load-balancing method (it is CEF [Cisco Express Forwarding] or IP CEF), not the real load balancing method.
6. Fault tolerance and redundancy with advance features (HSRP, link failures, hardware failures etc.)

When advanced application-level features are needed, layer 4 to layer 7 switchings are used, which are the load balancers and should have the following features to support this transparent deployment:

1. Load balancing techniques
2. URL hashing for server monitoring
3. Application rules to forward traffic (IRules in F5)
4. NAT techniques
5. Intelligent DNS load balancing
6. Application persistence connections
7. Handling cookies
8. SSL termination

The main drawback of this deployment is the cost of the Layer 4 switch, and this depends upon the size of the network or features needed. For a smaller network, the existing routers and switches could be used to do implement transparent depolyments. If the network is big or needs more functionality then it will need Layer 4 to 7 switches or load balancer modules, and a redesign of the network may also be required depending upon customer needs.

Blue Coat should always be in the DMZ and behind the firewall.

b. Transparent: Cisco WCCP—Virtual Inline deployment

The WCCP (Web Cache Communication Protocol) is a Cisco proprietary protocol and it is content-routing technology which enables WCCP enabled routers, switches, or firewalls to redirect requests to one or more web cache servers. It has built-in load balancing, scaling, fault tolerance, and service-assurance (failsafe) mechanisms.

The latest version of WCCP is Version 2 and it is a transparent redirection mechanism that a router or switch or even firewall could do. All Cisco firewalls and VPN devices can support the WCCP feature. So for this deployment, all that is needed is a WCCP-enabled device which can act as the WCCP master, and Blue Coat SG as the peer device which can join in the web cache groups.

By default when WCCP is enabled, the HTTP traffic can be forwarded to Blue Coat devices; in order to forward to other protocols like HTTPS, RTMP, RTSP, MMS, FTP, etc., service groups should be used. This deployment is pretty straightforward and simple; you just need to make sure that the Internet traffic should reach the WCCP-enabled device, which can decide to forward the traffic either to the Proxy SG or to the outbound firewall. The biggest advantage of using WCCP is that there is less load on the WCCP-enabled device and the group of Proxy SG in the cluster,because WCCP has a load mechanism to eventually distribute the traffic to the Proxy SG than compared to the default CEF method which Cisco uses, which loads the one web cache more than the other. The new IP CEF load-balancing mechanism is same as the WCCP; this load distribution technique reduce load on the web cache.

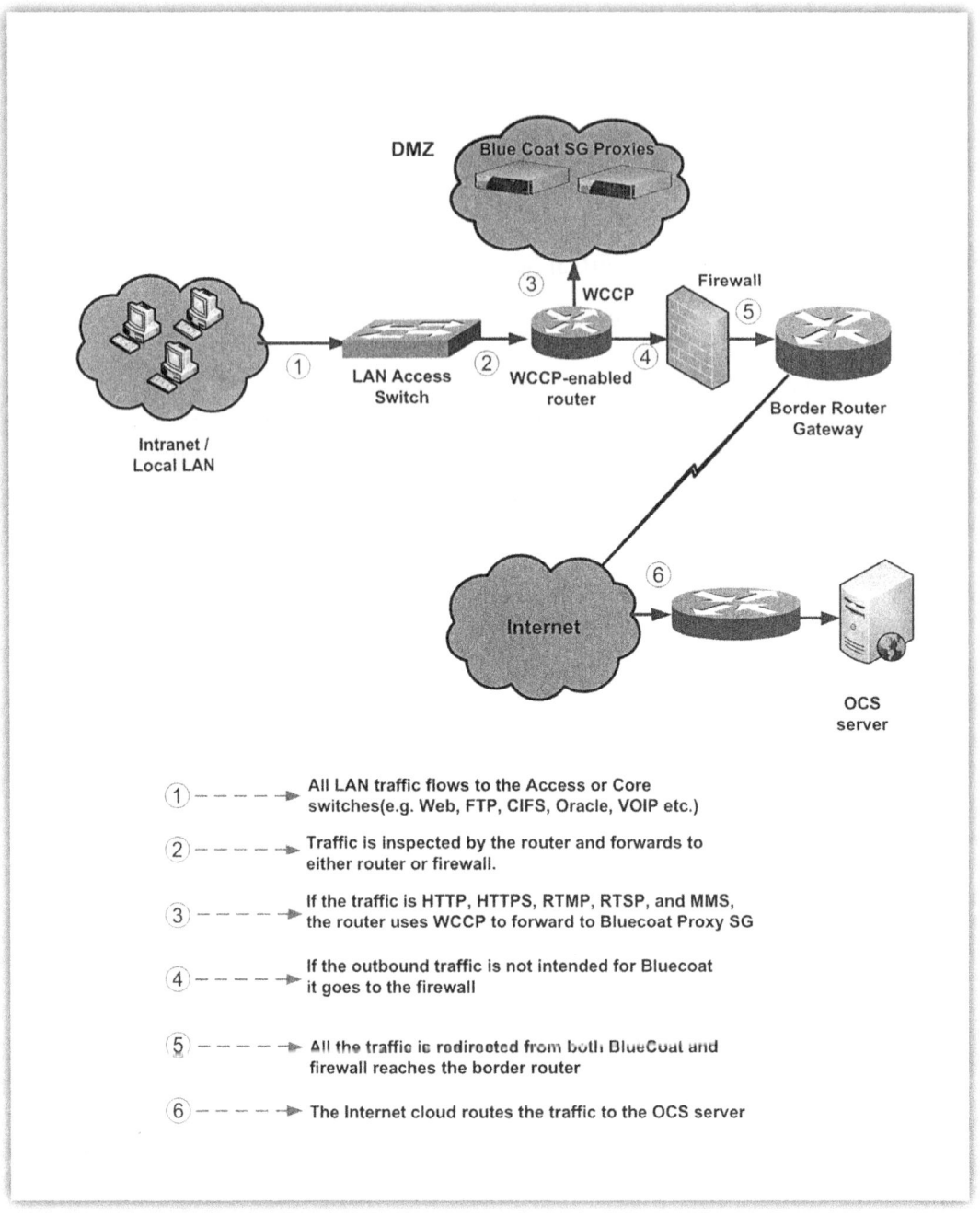

Figure 3:4 Transparent: Cisco WCCP—Virtual Inline

2. Inline deployment

a. Transparent: Blue Coat SG Bridging—Inline.

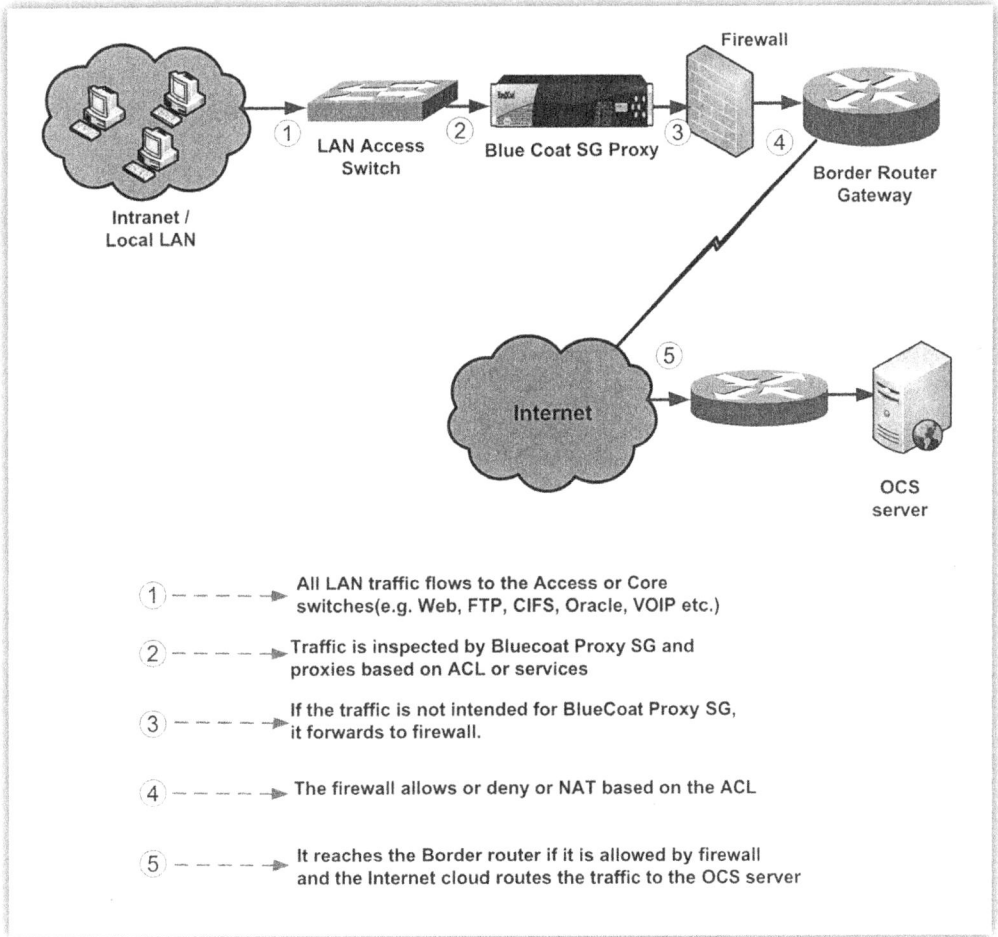

Figure 3:5 Transparent: Blue Coat SG bridging—Inline

The other method of deployment is that Blue Coat SG could be installed in bridge mode. A bridge is a network device that interconnects multiple networks. Bridges are also known as Layer 2 devices. This type of deployment can be done for small networks where the network has less than 250 hosts. This type of solution is not recommended for medium or large deployments.

All the network traffic must pass through the Blue Coat, which inspects the traffic to determine whether it needs to either allow, deny, redirect, or cache what is configured on the proxy. This means that even the traffic that is not intended for Blue Coat should also be inspected; when too many hosts are added in the network or user traffic increases, there is overloading on the Blue Coat proxy, making user access gets slower and experiencing delays..

The advantage of this method is that there's no need to buy any additional L4 switches or WCCP-enabled products, which reduces the cost for customers. This is a feasible solution for small customers; when talking about redundancy and fault tolerance, it is guaranteed to a certain extent that the network will be stable, since again there are several modes of deployment—either via parallel failover or serial failover mechanisms. Both these mechanisms are in-line mode.

b. Transparent: Blue Coat Proxy SG default router—Inline:

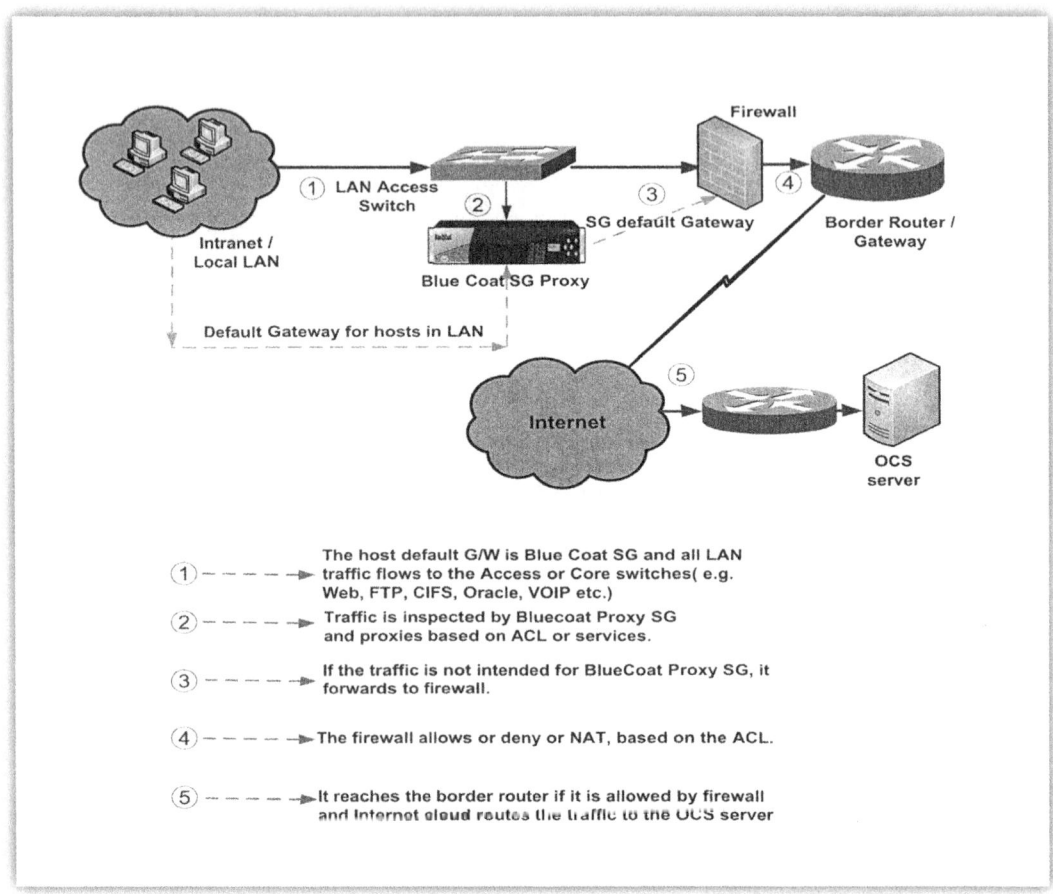

Figure 3:6   Transparent: Blue Coat Proxy SG default router—Inline

This is an inline deployment mode, where the Proxy SG acts as a default gateway for the network and users in the LAN. Ideally, in network either the Layer 4 switch or a router or firewall should be the default gateway. An alternative design could be to add Blue Coat Proxy SG as a default gateway, thus implementing Blue Coat security solutions in a new, fashionable way rather than a traditional way. The advantage of this method of deployment is that if the customer needs the LAN to point to a default gateway   to be a security device and the proxy also wants to be behind the firewall that is in the DMZ. So the questions here becomes: why isn't the LAN point the default gateway to the firewall? But the major disadvantage of this is that the firewall is already in stress by protecting the Internet traffic and adding the LAN segment as well puts an additional load on the firewall. This isn't necessarily the methodology that should be followed, but a way to implement Blue Coat security solutions with minimum cost.

 This is designed for small-sized business network with less than 250 hosts. And every packet has to go through the Proxy SG, which is always a load on it.

When the client wants to access Internet services, the client desktop default gateway is pointed to BlueCoat Proxy SG and when the packet reaches Blue Coat, it looks for the destination port; if the, port service is allowed able to be intercepted. If yes it processes the request and proxies it, otherwise it forwards the request to the firewall. For this to happen you need to enable the feature "IP forwarding" in the Proxy SG.

What is IP forwarding?

"IP forwarding" is a process that enables the server to sit on two LANs and to act as a gateway. forwarding IP packets from one LAN to another. IP forwarding is also referred to as "bridging" networks.

To deploy this setup, two settings must be configured, to act as a default router:

1. All the hosts in the network should configure the TCP/IP setting of the client hosts are set Blue Coat Proxy SG as the default gateway.
2. IP forwarding should be enabled in the Blue Coat Proxy SG. This makes the Blue Coat SG capable of routing any kind of traffic—UDP, TCP, unicast, multicast, etc., so that internal networks are reached with the destination Mac and external networks are forwarded to the router or the firewall. If IP forwarding is not enabled, the packets will be rejected by Blue Coat Proxy SG.

It is very simple design, but it will introduce a single point of failure, which can be overcome by introducing redundancy by adding more Proxy SG.

2. Explicit proxy deployment:

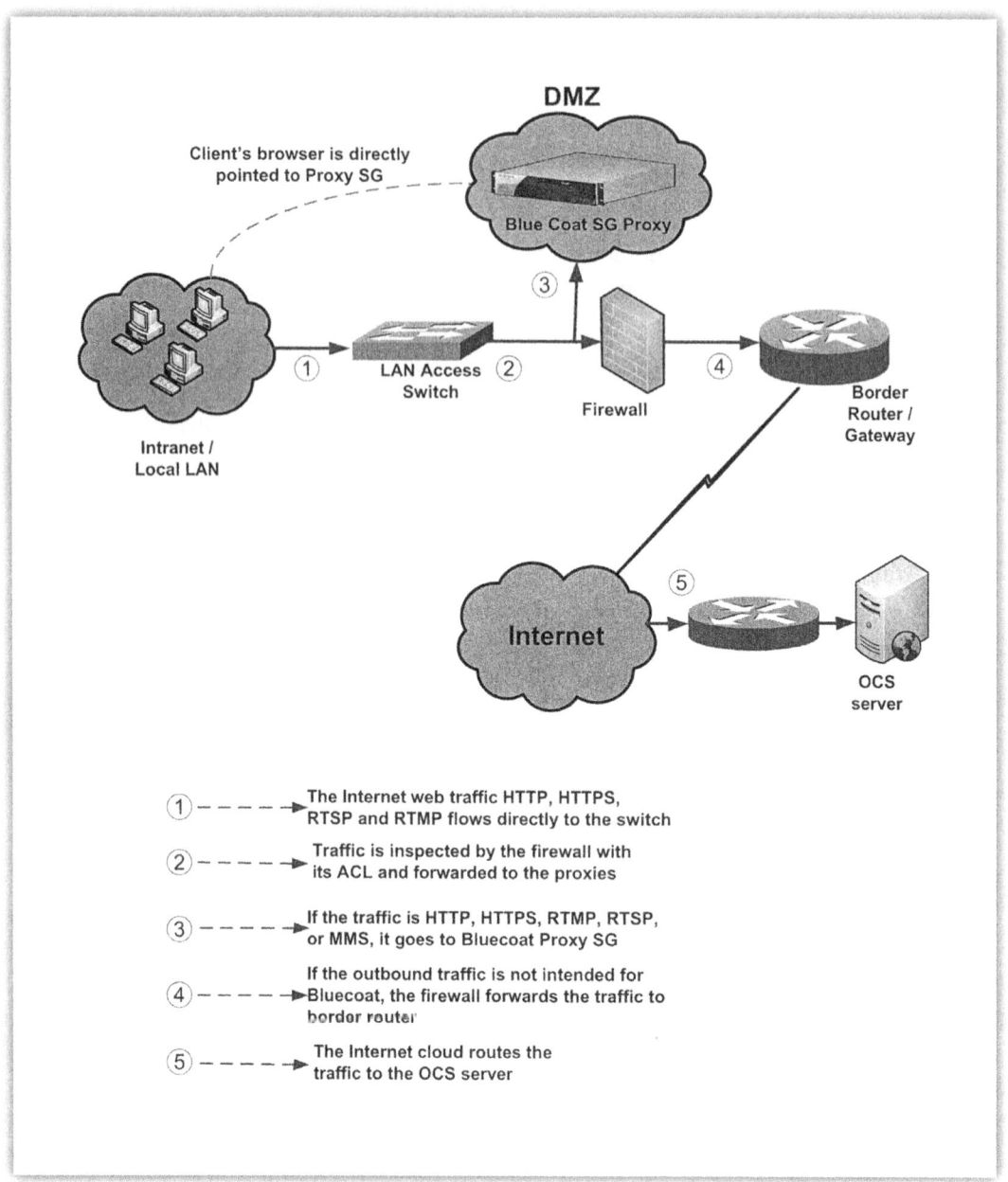

Figure 3:7 Explicit proxy deployment

This is the other way of deploying a Proxy SG in the network. In an explicit proxy deployment, every client browser and application should be configured to forward traffic specifically to Blue Coat. This makes the client aware that the browser is communicating to the proxy, and all requests are directly forwarded to the client.

In explicit mode, the BlueCoat Proxy SG will do a DNS lookup for the destination and not the client who connects to it.

These proxy settings must be manually added to Firefox, IE, Safari, and Chrome.

a. Firefox

Open Firefox. On the top of the screen, go to Tool → Advanced → Network → Settings, "Select Manual Proxy Configuration:" and enter the IP address and the port information of the proxy.

◉ Manual proxy configuration:		
HTTP Proxy: 172.16.10.100	Port:	8080 ⬍
☐ Use this proxy server for all protocols		
SSL Proxy: 172.16.10.100	Port:	8080 ⬍

Figure 3:8 Firefox settings

b. Internet Explorer

Open Internet Explorer (IE). At the top of the screen, go to Tools → Internet Options → Connections → LAN Settings. In the Proxy server section, select the option "Use a proxy server for your LAN…"

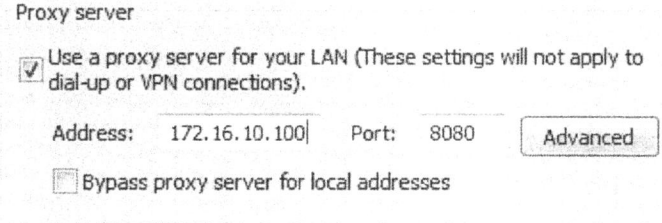

Figure 3:9 Internet Explorer settings

c. Safari

Open Safari, click the drop-down in top right-hand corner of the page. Go to Preferences → Advanced, then click on the button "Change Settings" in the Proxies section as shown below:

Figure 3:10 Safari settings

This will open the Internet Explorer (IE) settingssince Safari browser uses it.

d. Chrome

Open Chrome, click the drop-down in top right-hand corner of the page Go to Options → Under the Hood, and click "Change proxy settings" as shown below.

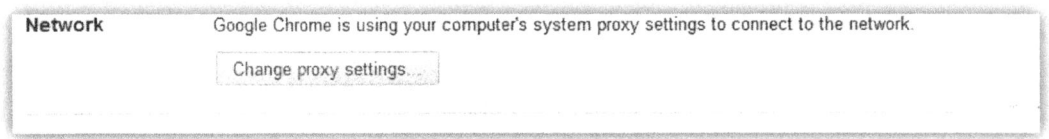

Figure 3:11 Chrome settings

This will open the internet Explorer (IE) settings, since Chrome browser uses it.

   The downside to Explicit Proxy Deployment is that it involves more system administration involved in pushing the setting for the browsers from the Windows/Linux Domain Controller, and if the network is distributed and mixed, where there is not one common place for managing the nodes or hosts from the Domain Controller, the process become tedious. The other downsides of explicit deployment are redundancy required when the proxy goes down, and it involves configuring intelligent load balancing, virtual IP, PAC files, etc. And the major security issues are that the proxy IP could be footprinted and hackers could very easily break or circumvent this explicit deployment.

3. Reverse Proxy Deployment

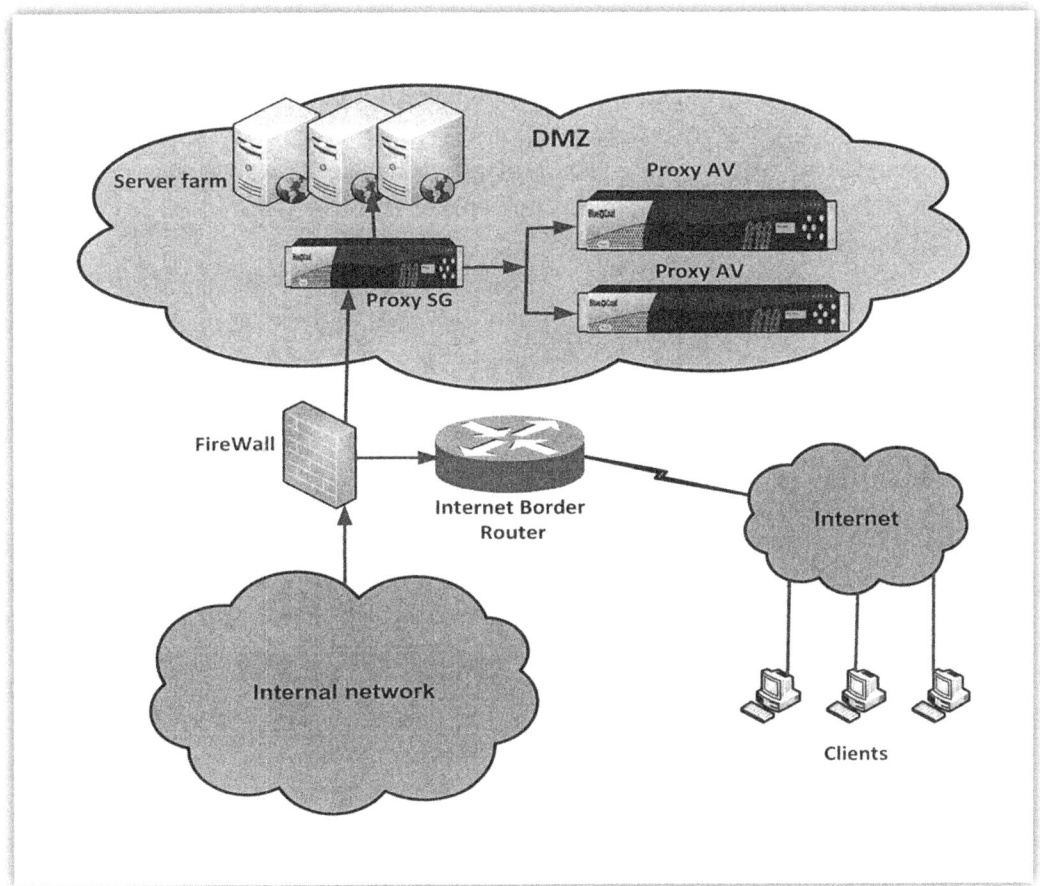

Figure 3:12 Reverse Proxy Deployment

Is a reverse proxy the same thing as a load balancer? We can correlate the basic principles of how they work, but reverse proxy is not a load balancer. A load balancer only load balances the traffic to the backend servers, but it doesn't offers any caching of data. So reverse proxy is still a proxy server, but it is installed inside the network, and stands before the web servers or server farm, and proxies requests on behalf of the internal or backend HTTP servers. So a reverse proxy acts a "man in the middle" for the web servers, protects them, and offload the processing capacity from servers. To the end-user it still looks like it is communicating to a web server, but the reverse server is the one that serves the requests.

What are the benefits of using a reverse proxy server?

1. It is the only point of contact with the HTTP service; this hides the real servers and adds one more layer of defense in web security.

2. SSL encryption can be offloaded from the servers to the reverse proxy.

3. The load on the servers can be reduced by caching both static and dynamic objects.

4. The backend HTTP servers can be in any flavor of OS or web applications and the traffic is still accelerated for the content and objects.

5. Backend servers can be replaced when they crash, upgrade transparently, and apply changes without impacting the production time, as other servers in the farm can handle the request while you do maintenance on the web servers.

6. The web traffic can be optimized by compressing the data, so read, write, and load times are drastically improved.

These are benefits of using a reverse proxy server, but there are downsides to this design as well:

1. The reverse proxy becomes the single point of contact; if it is down, the complete HTTP service goes offline.

2. It's necessary to patch the reverse proxy server and the web servers frequently, because if the reverse proxy is compromised, you could complete footprint all the web servers behind the reverse proxy, and if any of the servers are in the internal network, then the whole network is compromised. So for this reason we make sure all reside in the DMZ.

3. Since ports 80 and 443 are opened to the reverse server, sophisticated HTTP vector attacks could be carried out. For this reason, additional content filtering, scanning, or WAF module integrated with the reverse proxy, which slows down the responses.

4. We cannot generate web access report do analysis for forensics reporting, when web servers are breached, since the all the HHTP hits are from the reverse proxy.

Several hardware and software modules are available for reverse proxy, such as Apache HTTP server module, Sun Java system web server, Squid, F5, nignx, varnish cache, etc. But the question here is: why do we use Blue Coat SG to perform this? The reasons are as follows:

1. Blue Coat SG appliances are built on a proven architecture, both in hardware and software, to handle huge amounts of traffic.

2. The TCP/IP stack is very stable and powerful, which makes the system faster because the dynamic content Ajax, Javacript, CGI, and ASP pages cannot be cached, so BlueCoat reverse proxy fetches the dynamic content from the web servers with minimum TCP handshakes, optimizing the performance of the network.

3. The above dynamic content optimization is done by Blue Coat "Object Pipelining." We will discuss this later in the book.

4. The objects that are cached are refreshed automatically without the user's request, thus improving the speed for content serving. Blue Coat uses a patented feature called "Adaptive Refresh Algorithms".

5. BlueCoat Proxy SG can be integrated with with Proxy AV for the scanning of HTTP objects and to ensure that no malware attacks are carried out when serving web content and makes our network protected from all latest internet malware threats.

4. Forward Proxy Deployment:

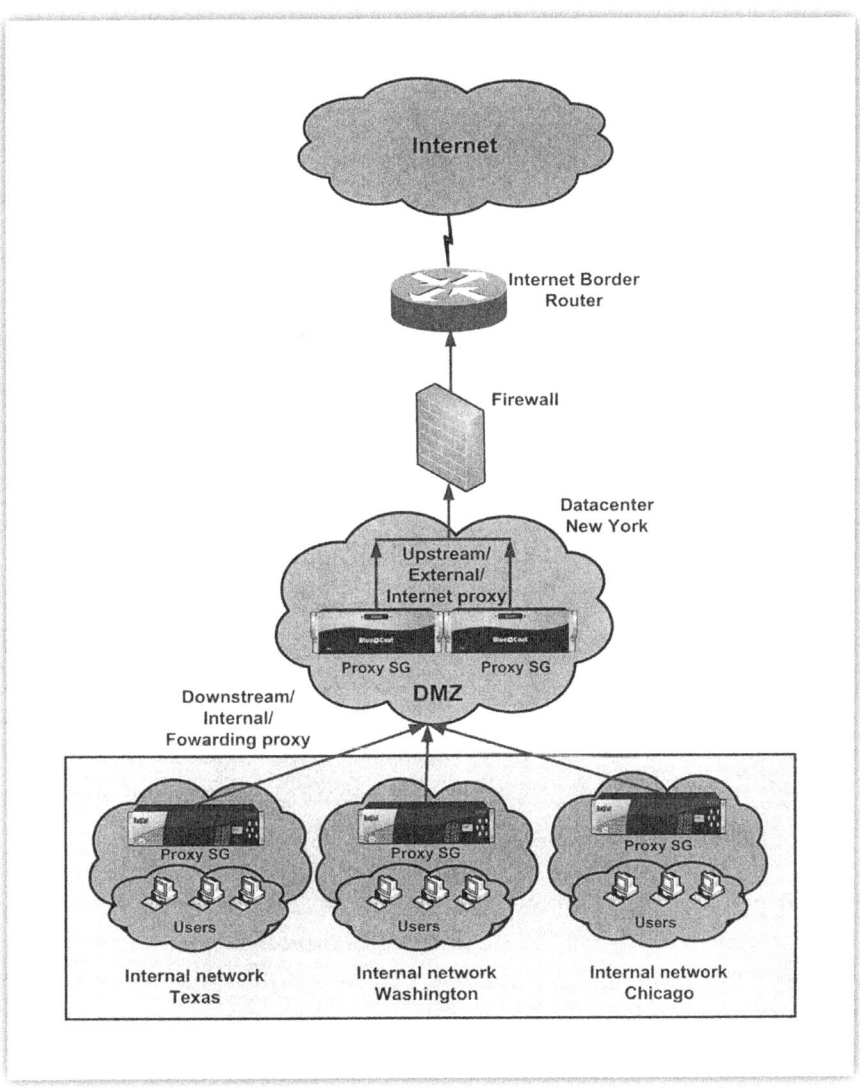

Figure 3:13 Forward Proxy Deployment

A forwarding proxy is also well known as proxy parenting, the proxy which does the forwarding is called the child proxy, internal proxy, intranet proxy, or downstream proxy, is used for both internal and external services. The proxy that is listening to the forwarding proxy is called the parent proxy, external proxy, upstream proxy, or Internet proxy. This type of deployment is used in highly advanced networks where the volume of traffic is high, splitting the client from directly reaching the Internet proxies. All the hosts in the LAN will be connected either explicitly or transparently to the BlueCoat Proxy SG, and in turn these internal BlueCoat Proxies connect to the upstream proxies to access the Internet. For example, as shown in the above figure, a company has its branch offices in Texas, Washington, Chicago. All the users in the LAN in the branch offices will be explicitly or transparently pointed to the proxies in their corresponding branch offices to access the Internet. The users in the Texas branch office will connect to the proxy in Texas, the users in Washington will connect to the proxy in Washington, the users in Chicago will connect to the proxy in Chicago, and so on. And in turn, all these branch offices' proxies will connect to the Headquarters at the New York data center. All the requests from the branch offices are forwarded to the New York HQ, which is the proxy that contacts the OCS and fetches the information. In this way the users and clients are masked from directly contacting the Internet proxies.

Advantages of using a forwarding proxy:

1. Since all the web requests are forwarded to the internal proxy, the internal proxy forwards only the Internet traffic to the upstream proxy, and the local intranet web traffic to the local network.
2. Content filtering is included in the downstream proxy, so that all traffic need not go through the Internet proxies to get blocked, and the bandwidth of the traffic is reduced.
3. The internal proxy acts as the caching proxy and the external proxy as content filtering proxy, so all cached content is available from the internal proxies for the LAN users, and all URL-based content is denied on the external proxies.
4. One more layer is added to hide the internal network, by using proxy parenting. This improves security in the network.
5. By using internal proxies, caching is improved for all internal sites, and there is a great bandwidth gain in the network.

The forwarding proxy deployment can be used for any specific needs for the customers. This means that content filtering can be added on both internal and external proxies, or caching can be applied on both child proxy and parent proxy; it all depends upon the requirements of the applications and services.

Disadvantages of using a forwarding proxy:

1. Since the internal proxy serves both internal and external web access if the proxy fails, all access to both internal and external services are lost. This can avoided by using VIP for two internal proxies. In other words, virtual IP (VIP) will be used for e.g. users in Texas to access the Texas proxy when it is active, and if it fails

they can access the proxy in Washington. These can all be done by using either a PAC file intelligent DNS services, routing or load balancing.

2. If caching is enabled, the cache is shared between internal and external sites, which is not a good security practice.

3. Again, if the parent proxy goes down, all the local sites in the branch office are affected, since all the branch offices depend upon one Internet outlet.

4. There is a delay in milliseconds by forwarding the request back and forth between internal and external proxies.

5. The local database of allowed or denied sites should be maintained if URL filtering is used on both internal and external proxies.

Test Yourself:

. . . .

1. Which is the most challenging deployment for BlueCoat Engineers in terms of authentication, web filtering, security, networking, etc.?

   a. Transparent proxy
   b. Explicit proxy
   c. Reverse proxy
   d. Forwarding proxy

2. In transparent mode, if a user tries to access the website http://www.bluecoatweb.com, what will be the source IP, destination IP, and GET request when originating from the user?

   a. Source IP: User's machine IP; Destination IP: Proxy IP; GET request: "GET index. html HTTP/1.1"

   b. Source IP: User's machine IP; Destination IP: Proxy IP; GET request: "GET http:// www.bluecoatweb.com/index.html HTTP/1.1"

   c. Source IP: User's machine IP; Destination IP: BlueCoatWeb.com (IP address); GET request: "GET index.html HTTP/1.1"

   d. Source IP: User's machine IP; Destination IP: BlueCoatWeb.com (IP address); GET request: "GET http://www.bluecoatweb.com/index.html HTTP/1.1"

3. You have a customer who wants to deploy the BlueCoat Proxy SG solution for Internet access for all users. All nodes in the company are not managed by the Domain Controller; they allow external DNS queries in the internal network. What is the best deployment method you would recommend for this customer?

   a. Explicit proxy
   b. Transparent proxy
   c. Reverse proxy

d. Forwarding proxy

4. If you decided to use transparent deployment for a large network, which would be the most efficient and reliable method of implementing the solution?

   a. Inline method
   b. Forward Proxy deployment
   c. Reverse Proxy deployment
   d. Virtually inline method

5. In which method do all client computers' default gateways point to the BlueCoat Proxy SG?

   a. Explicit—BlueCoat Proxy SG bridging mode
   b. Transparent—BlueCoat Proxy SG default router mode
   c. Explicit—BlueCoat Proxy SG default router mode
   d. Transparent—BlueCoat Proxy SG bridging mode

6. In explicit mode, if a user tries to access the website www.bluecoatweb.com, what will be the source IP, destination IP, and GET request when originating from the user?

   a. Source IP: User's machine IP; Destination IP: Proxy IP; GET request: "GET http://www.bluecoatweb.com/index.html HTTP/1.1"
   b. Source IP: User's machine IP; Destination IP: Proxy IP; GET request: "GET index.html HTTP/1.1"
   c. Source IP: User's machine IP; Destination IP: BlueCoatWeb.com (IP address); GET request: "GET index.html HTTP/1.1"
   d. Source IP: User's machine IP; Destination IP: BlueCoatWeb.com (IP address); GET request: "GET http://www.bluecoatweb.com/index.html HTTP/1.1"

7. If you are a BlueCoat engineer, a customer wants to implement BlueCoat solution for Internet access to the users, and the customer doesn't want to buy any extra hardware like an L4 switch or router and doesn't wants to change any network design to implement BlueCoat Proxy SG. Which BlueCoat Proxy SG method would you recommend to the customer?

   a. Transparent proxy
   b. Explicit proxy
   c. Reverse proxy
   d. Forwarding proxy

8. You work for a BlueCoat consulting firm. A customer has four web servers which need to be hosted on the Internet. The customer requirements for their web servers are malware protection, load balancing, caching , Av scanning for web traffic and handle

heavy amount of web traffic. Which is the BlueCoat deployment mode you would recommend?

a. Transparent proxy
b. Explicit proxy
c. Reverse proxy
d. Forwarding proxy

9. What are the advantages of the BlueCoat Proxy SG reverse proxy deployment method over the traditional load balancers?

a. Security, scalability, virus scanning, performance, and caching
b. Security, scalability, virus scanning, and caching
c. Security, scalability, and caching
d. Scalability, virus scanning, performance, and caching

10. You are consulting for a BlueCoat customer who has high volume of Internet traffic in the network and wants to implement a BlueCoat web security solution for users' Internet and intranet access, such as high caching of contents, users could only access intranet Proxy SG for both internal and external web access, masquerade the internal network traffic few times, and separate internal and external cache data. Which deployment would you recommend?

a. Transparent proxy
b. Explicit proxy
c. Reverse proxy
d. Forwarding proxy

CHAPTER 4

CONFIGURING BLUE COAT PROXY SG

Before we discuss how to configure the Blue Coat Proxy SG, apply policies, integrate AV and LDAP, etc., we will look at how to perform a Blue Coat Proxy SG initial setup, what different license types need to be purchased, and different features that are supported by licenses. This will include an overview of configuring the new Blue Coat Proxy SG, how to manage Blue Coat boxes, how to secure Blue Coat Proxy SG, different methods to implement policies, and how to create administrator accounts.

There are different ways to do an initial setup of Blue Coat SG after purchasing a new SG box and making it active in the network, so that you can configure the policies remotely and administer it. To register the box online with Blue Coat requires a web power account to manage the license of the box. For this please contact the sales and support team; they will help you in getting this created.

There are three ways to configure the Proxy SG for initial setup access:

1. Serial Console
2. LCD panel
3. Over the network (TCP/IP)

There are various models in Blue Coat Porxy: SG 210, SG 510, SG 810, SG 8100, and SG 9000, but the same methods and procedures are followed for the initial installation and configuration of a new box or to do factory settings.

To do this there are two requirements for the console connection:

1. A computer with a 9-pin port and a rollover or console cable (DB9 connector) with serial port pin or USB port.
2. To do this remotely, a terminal server or jump box with the same connection above.

Use a 9-pin console cable to connect to the serial console on the ProxySG and to your laptop or desktop, and use tools like Secure CRT, Putty, or any HyperTerminal. In this section we are using Putty which is a free tool. You can download Putty from http://www.chiark.greenend.org.uk/~sgtatham/putty/download.html.

1. Launch Putty and configure the settings.

Just double-click the "Putty" icon and it will launch. Then go to Connection → SSH → Serial and fill in the following settings in the screen below:

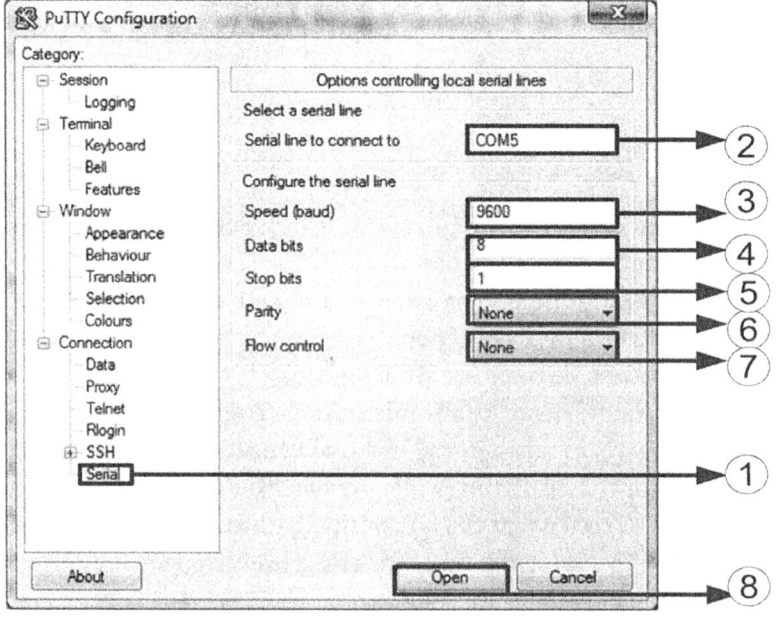

Figure 4:1 Putty configuration

The settings are as follows:
* Bits per second (bps): 9600
* Data bit: 8
* Parity: None
* Stop bits: 1
* Flow control: None
* Serial line to connect to: COM5 (Depends upon the computer or laptop).

To check which COM port the laptop uses, go to Control Panel → Device Manager → Ports (COM & LPT) and check which COM port the laptop or computer uses.

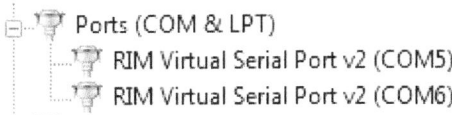

Ports (COM & LPT)
    RIM Virtual Serial Port v2 (COM5)
    RIM Virtual Serial Port v2 (COM6)

Figure 4:2 Device Manager

Once connected via the serial port, press the "Enter" key three times to activate the serial console.

the text is bold that needs to be inputted into the console.

A menu similar to the following will appear:

```
------------------------Output Begin---------------------

Welcome to the SG Appliance Serial Console

        Version: SGOS 6.1.2.1, Release id: 54104

----------------------- MENU ----------------------------

1) Command Line Interface
2) Setup Console

---------------------------------------------------------

Enter option: 2     [Press 2]

Welcome to the Blue Coat ProxySG 8100-20 configuration wizard.
This appliance's serial number: 1234567890

    ---------------------------------------------------------------
    You can get field help by entering a question mark ? in the fields.
    You can move backwards through the steps by pressing the UP arrow.
    You can exit the wizard without saving your entries by pressing ESC.
    ---------------------------------------------------------------
```

Step 1: How do you plan to configure this appliance?
    a) Through a manual setup
    b) Through a Director-managed setup

      Your choice: [a] **a**   **[Type a]**

Step 2: Which solution would you like to implement?
    a) Acceleration
    b) Other solution

      Your choice: [b] **b**   **[Type b]**

 Welcome to the SG Appliance Setup Console

--------------------- (page 1 of 4) ---------------------

    Press <ESC> at any time to return to the main menu
Setup mode: Manual

DIRECTIONS:

    Please enter the IP addresses for the SG Appliance.
    The following interface will be configured:
        1. Bridge passthru-0 (WAN: link, LAN: link)

Is the IP address to be configured on a non-native VLAN? (Y/N) [No]
No
IP address [0.0.0.0]: 192.168.10.101   **[Type]**

IP subnet mask [0.0.0.0]: **255.255.255.0[Type]**

IP gateway [0.0.0.0]: **192.168.10.100**   **[Type]**

DNS server [0.0.0.0]:**192.168.10.50**   **[Type]**

You have entered the following IP addresses:

IP address: 192.168.10.101
IP subnet mask: 255.255.255.0
IP gateway: 192.168.10.100
DNS server: 192.168.10.50

Would you like to change any of them? Y/N [No] **No**   **[Type No]**

--------------------- (page 2 of 4) ---------------------

Press <ESC> at any time to return to the main menu

DIRECTIONS:

The console username, password, and enable password are special administrative credentials which can be used to log in to the command line interface or web management interface.

Would you like to change the console user account now? Y/N [No] **Yes** **[Type yes]**

Enter console username [admin]: **admin**   **[Type]**

Enter console password: **bluecoat123**   **[Type]**

Verify console password:**bluecoat123**   **[Type]**

Enter enable password:**bluecoat123**   **[Type]**

Verify enable password:**bluecoat123**   **[Type]**

DIRECTIONS:

When the serial port is secured, access via the serial port must be authenticated.

A setup password is required to gain access to the Setup Console and administrative credentials are required to access the command line interface.

Do you want to secure the serial port? Y/N [Yes] **No**   **[Type]**

Note: Enter the password in the above console and make sure that you don't lose it. Recover the password by calling Blue Coat support; otherwise the box will have to be reset.

--------------------- (page 3 of 4) ---------------------

Press <ESC> at any time to return to the main menu

DIRECTIONS:

The console username and password are special:they can be used to log in to the CLI or web management interface even in circumstances where this is denied by VPM or CPL policy.

This makes the console account useful in emergencies, as a way to log in when policy is broken, but it may also create a security hole.

To close the security hole, we recommend that you restrict the use of the console account to specific workstations, identified by their IP address.

This dialog allows you to add one IP address to the list of work-stations that are authorized to use the console account.

(This same list is also used to restrict which workstations can use SSH with RSA authentication.)

Additional workstations may be configured later, from the command line interface or the web interface.

The console account can currently be used only from authorized workstations.

Would you like to add another authorized workstation? Y/N [No] No [Type No]
--------------------- (page 4 of 4) ---------------------

DIRECTIONS:

The SG Appliance has been successfully configured to use IP address: "**192.168.10.101**"

You can connect to the command line interface or web interface to perform additional management tasks.

To connect to the command line interface, open the following location from your SSH application: 192.168.10.100

To connect to the web management interface, go to the following location with your web browser: **https:// 192.168.10.101:8082/**

---------------- CONFIGURATION COMPLETE -------------------

Press "enter" three times to activate the serial console

----------------------------------Output End----------------------------------

The important points to be considered when configuring the Blue Coat for initial setup are:

1. Gather all the information about the IP address settings, DNS server, password, etc. before configuring the SG, in order to implement the policies faster.

2. Please do not set a password to protect the serial access to the Blue Coat Proxy SG, unless physical security is required. Losing the password will require having the box reset or returned to Blue Coat for replacement.

3. Make sure the ARP request is is recordedin switch or router. Sometimes GARP is not generated, making Blue Coat not reachable in the network.

4. Next make sure the default gateway can be reached, so there is connectivity to the network.

5. Make sure the DNS server is working fine and responding to all queries.

6. Please check to make sure there isn't a duplicate IP address in the network for the SG box which will cause intermittent problems. To do this, please send a ping to the IP, check the switch and router for the ARP entries for the IP address, and check with MAC address of the Blue Coat Proxy SG.

2. LCD Panel

The other method of configuring Blue Coat SG is to use the LCD panel. This method is the quickest and easiest way to do a first-time configuration. The previous method is a legacy way of doing, but it is the best way when remotely configuring the box and in times when the box crashes. If it is connected to the console, it is easy to work remotely and configure the box.

The LCD can be found in the front panel. The display varies for different models, but the concept is the same.

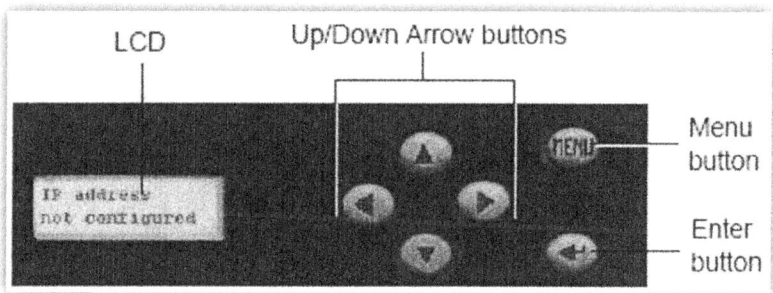

Figure 4:3 LCD Panel

Before configuring using the LCD panel, let us understand the three modes that are found in the LCD panel.

1. Status mode

This is the default mode in the LCD for the SG, before the SG is configured. The LCD in Status mode displays "IP address not configured". After initial configuration, the LCD in Status mode displays CPU utilization and proxied traffic statistics.

Before configuration:

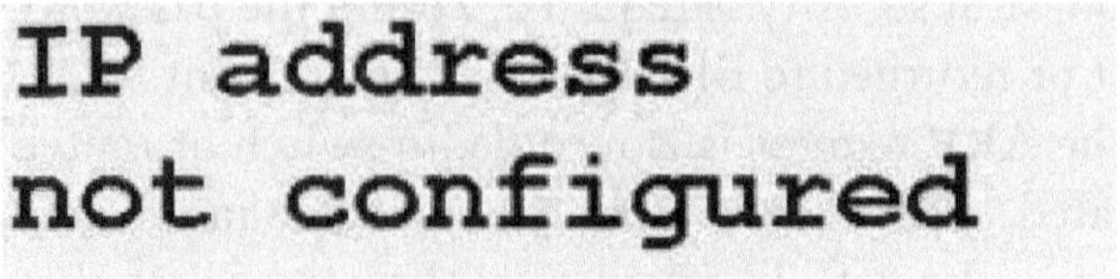

IP address
not configured

Figure 4:4 LCD Panel without configuration

After configuration:

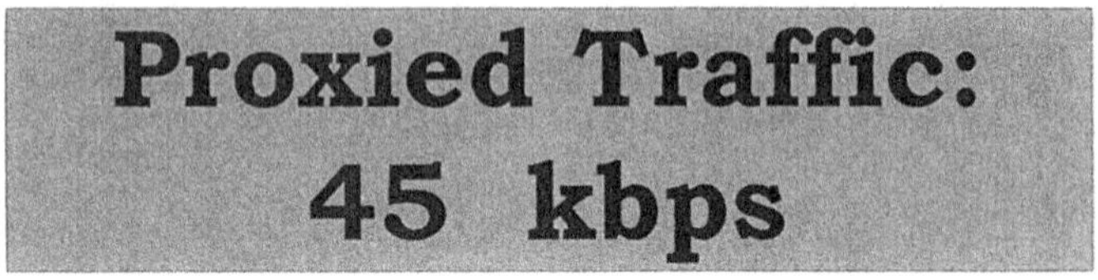

Proxied Traffic:
45 kbps

Figure 4:5 LCD Panel with configuration

In Status mode, there is no cursor in the LCD.

2. Configuration mode:

In Configuration mode, you can use the **Up** and **Down** arrow buttons to move the LCD through the following six networking parameters:

1. IP Address
2. Subnet mask
3. Gateway address
4. DNS address
5. Console Password and
6. Enable Password

From Status mode, to go to Configuration mode by pushing the Enter button.

IP address :
192.168.10.101

Figure 4:6 LCD Panel with IP Address in configuration mode

In Configuration mode, the cursor is an underscore in the LCD.

3. Edit Mode:

From the Configuration mode, use the Up or Down arrow button until the parameter you want to configure is displayed, then press the Enter button to go to Edit mode for that parameter (for a first-time configuration, you must begin with the first displayed parameter—IP address). To configure any of the six parameters, use the Left and Right arrow buttons to position the cursor over a character you want to change, then use the Up and Down arrow buttons to move through the characters. When the parameter is configured correctly, press the Enter button to save the setting and return to Configuration mode.

Tip: If no activity is detected for 20 seconds, the SG will automatically exit Edit mode without saving parameter configurations.

In Edit mode, the cursor is a blinking box in the LCD.

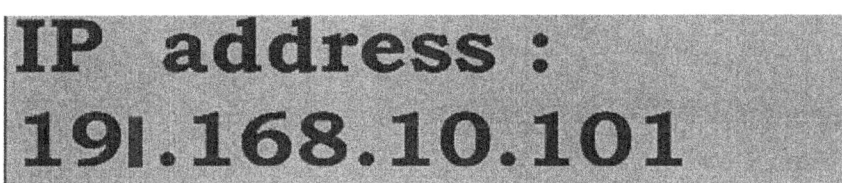

Figure 4:7 LCD Panel with IP Address in Edit mode

The button functions in the LCD panel are as follows:

1. The Enter button

When you push the Enter button Proxy SG cycles as follows:

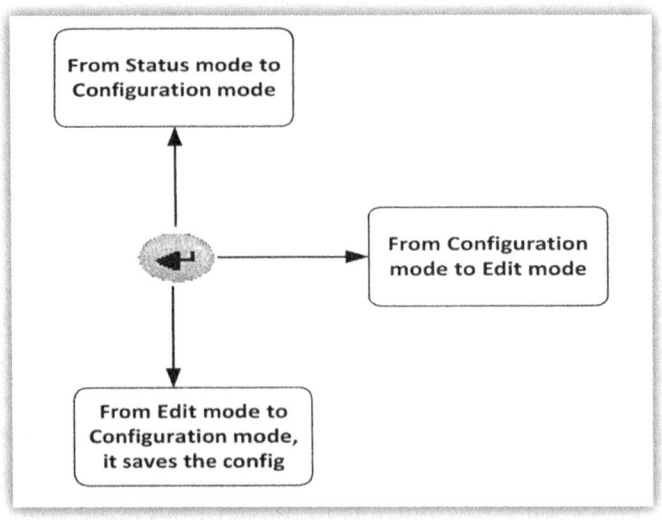

Figure 4:8 Enter button in different modes

2. The Menu button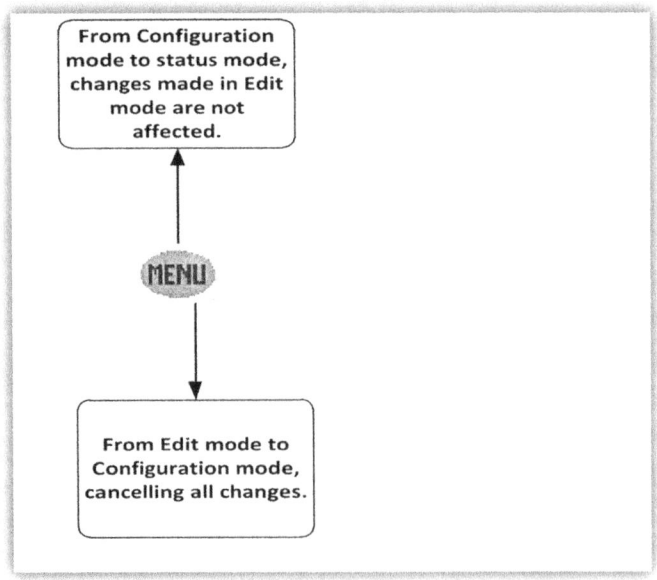

When you push the Menu button, it cycles as follows:

Figure 4:9 Menu button in different modes

The Menu button functions like an Escape key.

3. Left and Right arrow buttons

When you push the Left and Right arrow buttons in Edit mode, the cursor moves back and forth over the configurable settings of the parameter displayed.

4. Up and Down arrow buttons

When you push the Up and Down arrow buttons in Configuration mode, the SG 8100 goes through the six configurable parameters, as we discussed in the previous section.

When you push the Up and Down arrow buttons in Edit mode, the SG 8100 goes through the characters available for the selected setting of the parameter (the selected setting is the character that the cursor is over when you push the arrow buttons).

So with the information above, you can configure the network settings using the front panel.

Using the front-panel components, you can do a first-time configuration of the following six networking parameters on Adapter 0:

1. When the LCD reads, "IP address not configured", press the Enter button to enter Configure mode. The IP address parameter appears in the LCD, and the cursor appears as an underscore.
2. Press the Enter button again to enter Edit mode. The cursor changes to a blinking box. Now press the Left or Right arrow buttons to position the cursor over the characters you want to change; press the Up or Down arrow buttons to change them.
3. When you have all the characters of the parameter entered correctly, press the Enter button to save the changes and return to Configure mode.
4. Now press the Down arrow button to move to the next parameter; press the Enter button to enter Edit mode.
5. Repeat Steps 3 through 5 for the Subnet mask, Gateway address, and DNS address parameters. When the LCD reads, "Console password: Push to set", go to Step 7.

3. Over the network (TCP/IP):

After the initial setup, you need to configure a few basic settings to make the Proxy SG completely accessible and configurable. The parameters that you will configure are the hostname, DNS settings, setting time, license registration, routing, and back-up.

Before configuring the settings, we will cover how to log in to the box and configure the initial settings.

There are three ways to access the box:

1. Web console access or Management console (HTTP, HTTPS)
2. Command line interface (SSH)
3. Console port access

MANAGEMENT CONSOLE

You can log in to the web console using the browser (IE, Firefox, or Safari). This is Blue Coat GUI's way of doing it, and it is an easy and efficient method. You can access the management console using the IP address that you configured the first time when you configured it using the serial console and then use the port 8082 the default port for logging to the management console. So you can log in using https://192.168.10.101:8082 with the username as "admin" as the default and the password that you set when you configured the Blue Coat Proxy SG via serial console access.

When you log in you will see three tabs:

1. Configuration tab
2. Maintenance tab
3. Statistics tab

1. Configuration tab

In the Configuration tab, you can configure the policies using CPL, network settings, authentication, integrate AV,adding web filtering, accessing VPM, etc.

2. Maintenance tab

In the Maintenance tab you can manage disks, perform maintenance/upgrades, generate core images, configure SNMP, manage Health Monitoring, applying license, doing packet capture.

3. Statistics tab

In the Statistics tab, you can monitor the health and status of the Blue Coat Proxy SG. You can also monitor the sessions, access log, ICAP, traffic flow, etc.

Now in this section we will only discuss Configuration tab and different options in it, the Maintenance and Statistics tab will be discussed in the later chapters. So when you log in to the Blue Coat Proxy SG, by defaultyou get the Statistics Tab, then click the Configuration tab; here you can configure all the basic settings that are needed to be on the network.

The Configuration tab has many sections; we will briefly describe each section below and then discuss how to configure the basic settings.

General: You can configure the hostname and time, and archive the system.

Network: You can configure the adapters, interface settings, software/hardware settings, gateways, routing information, WCCP, failovers settings, and private network settings.

ADN (Application delivery Network): You can configure the Blue Coat SG Proxy box for WAN optimization technology for tunneling, byte caching, routing, ADN manager settings, and the tunneling feature.

Services : Here you can configure the proxy services that can be configured on the Proxy SG, like HTTP, HTTPS, CIFS, FTP, IM, MAPI, SOCKS, TCP-tunnel, etc. You can even configure the static bypass list, restricted intercept list, and management services access to the console and CLI.

Proxy Client: You can manage the Proxy Client products, like the Client Manager, Proxy Client software, Acceleration settings for the Proxy Client, and web filtering for the Proxy Client.

SSL: Here you can configure and manage SSL technology by creating keyrings, importing and creating certificates, checking the validity of certificates and device profiles settings, and managing appliance certificates and OCSP settings.

Proxy settings: You can configure the proxy settings for the CIFS, FTP, HTTP, IM, MAPI, Shell, SOCKS, SSL, and streaming proxies.

Bandwidth management: You can control the bandwidth used by different classes of network traffic, by setting priority for bandwidth classes for different classes.

Authentication: Here you can define realms for IWA, Windows SSO, LDAP, Novell SSO, RADIUS, Certificate, CA eTrust SiteMinder, Oracle COREid, XML, and forms. You can also configure the local authentication settings and assign sequence for all realms.

Content filtering: You can configure the Blue Coat SG to integrate with BCWF and IWF or third-party filtering tools like Websense, Smart filter, Proventia, or Optenet.

Threat Protection: You can configure the Web Pulse and Malware scanning settings.

External services: Here you configure ICAP settings for Blue Coat AV or Websense off-box service.

Forwarding: You can configure the forwarding settings and all their properties and SOCKS gateways.

Health Checks: You can configure the Health Check settings for different services and notifications settings and background DNS.

Access logging: Here the access logs can be configured for different formats, and forwarded to servers like FTP, HTTP, or BlueCoat Reporter Client software for log storage and to generate reports.

Policy: The different policies like VPM or CPL are the places where you can compile and build access list for the proxy. Here you can configure the different exceptions pages to manage for notifying the client about access information such denied pages and error messages.

Here in this chapter we will show the basic and essential configuration that is needed to run the proxy. We will also discuss the administration portion of the proxy such as monitoring, backup, etc.

CONFIGURING THE PROXY NAME:

Log in to the proxy with the GUI interface at https://ipaddressoftheprocess:8082, or https://192.168.10.101:8082, and go to Configuration à General à Identification. Enter the Proxy name next to the "**Appliance name**" field.

The name should be unique and easily identified by you. Select a name that is meaningful, so that the same name can be used for authentication, DNS, etc. While it could be different, maintaining consistency is very important.

Enter the name as below and click "Apply".

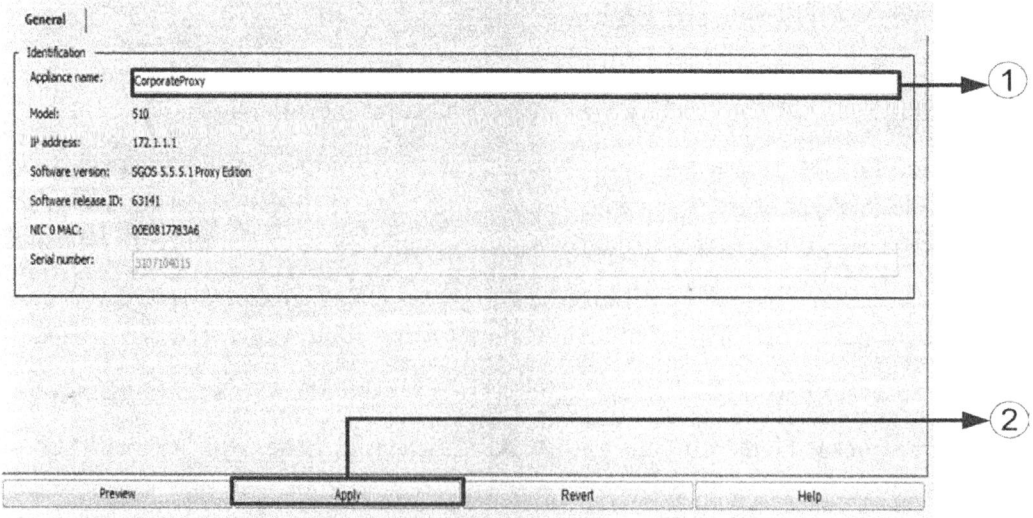

Figure 4:10 Appliance name configuration

The reason the name should be consistent is that, say for example your appliance as shown above is CorporateProxy and you configure a DNS entry of the proxy as Proxy-1, which resolves to the IP address of the proxy. Technically it works fine having different names, but it creates a lots of difficulties when there are large number of proxies to manage.

CONFIGURING TIME AND TIME ZONE:

Configuring time is very important in the proxy and is the most critical step. This is because the cookies, time-based ACL, logs, cache expiration time, authentication timeouts, and what not all are based on the clock of the proxy. So make sure you understand the importance of it. This could break the whole proxy infrastructure if not properly configured and maintained. The default time zone that is configured in Proxy SG is UTC. UTC stands for Coordinated Universal Time and is the international time standard based upon 24 hours. By default, Proxy SG connects to the NTP servers (ntp. bluecoat.com and ntp1.bluecoat.com) in the NTP tab, to acquire and sync the UTC time. The figure below shows the default time zone:

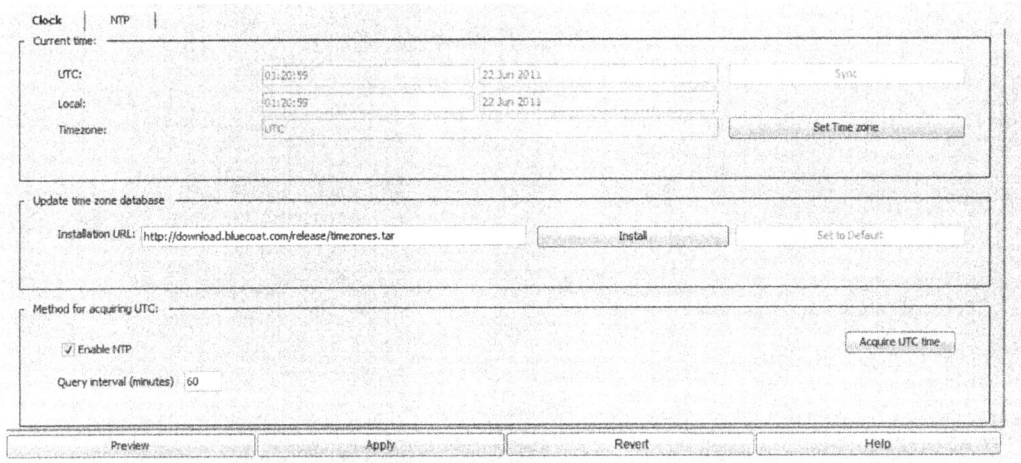

Figure 4:11 Time and Time Zone configuration

To change the time zone, log in to the proxy via GUI, and go to Configuration → General → Clock → Clock and click "Set Time Zone" in the "**Current time**" section. Select the time zone as shown below and click "OK".

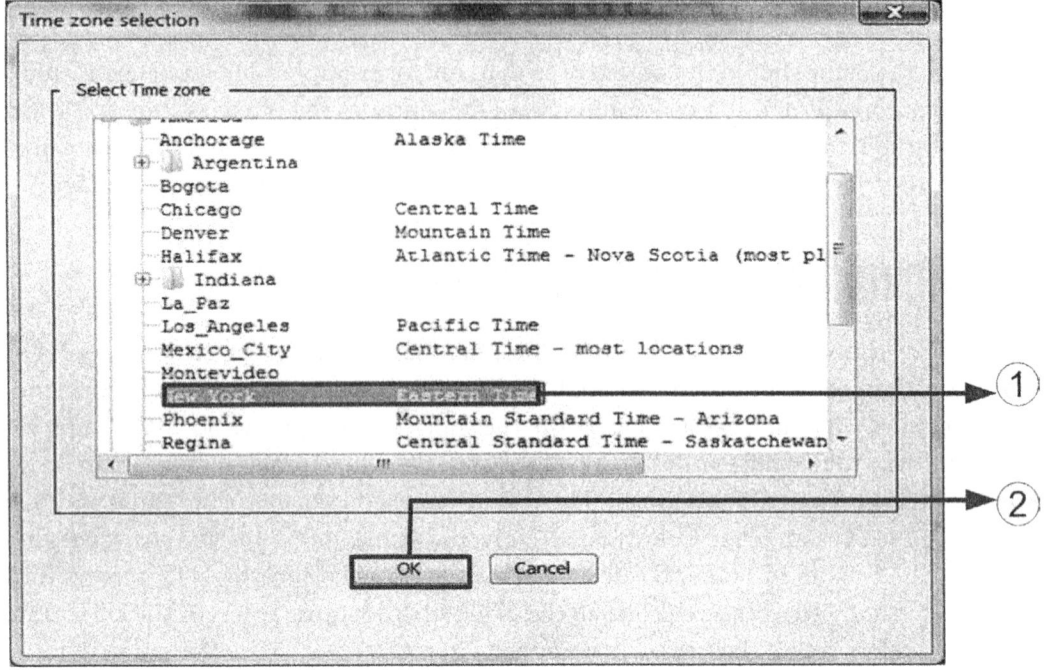

Figure 4:12 Changing time zone

You will see the time zone changed to your local time as shown below.

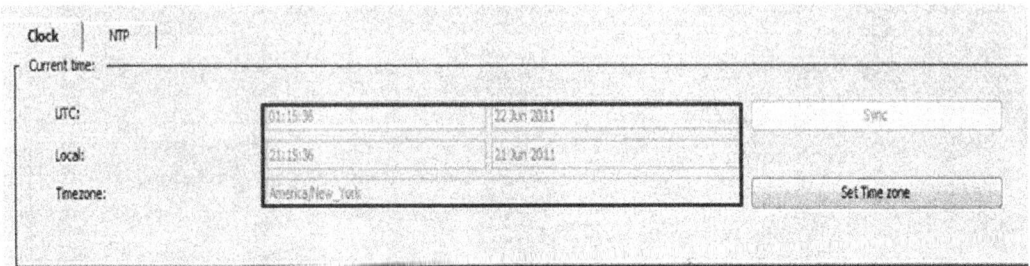

Figure 4:13 After changing the time zone

 If a specific time zone is not available from the list, the list can be updated by downloading the full time zone database from http://download.bluecoat.com/release/timezones.tar.

Updating the time zone database can be done in the same Clock page as shown in the figure 4.11 at the bottom of this section called "Update time zone database" and click the

Install button, if the proxy is internal and could be reached via the Internet then download the file and upload in a local web server, and point the address to in the "Installation URL" to the web server where the file is located.

The NTP server can also be configured; by default it is enabled, as shown in the figure 4.11 , at the very bottom as "**Enable NTP**". To change the NTP servers, in the case that you need to point to the Corporate NTP server rather than the BlueCoat NTP server, go to NTP tab, and delete the both the entries by clicking each one and hitting the delete button. Then click the "New" button and enter either the domain name or IP address as shown below:

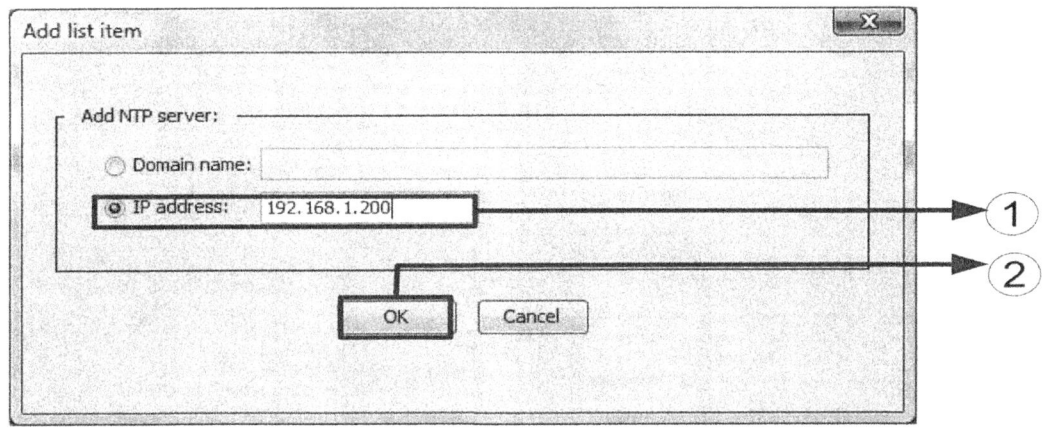

Figure 4:14 Configuring the NTP server

Then click "OK" and add all the NTP servers; confirm the changes clicking "Apply".

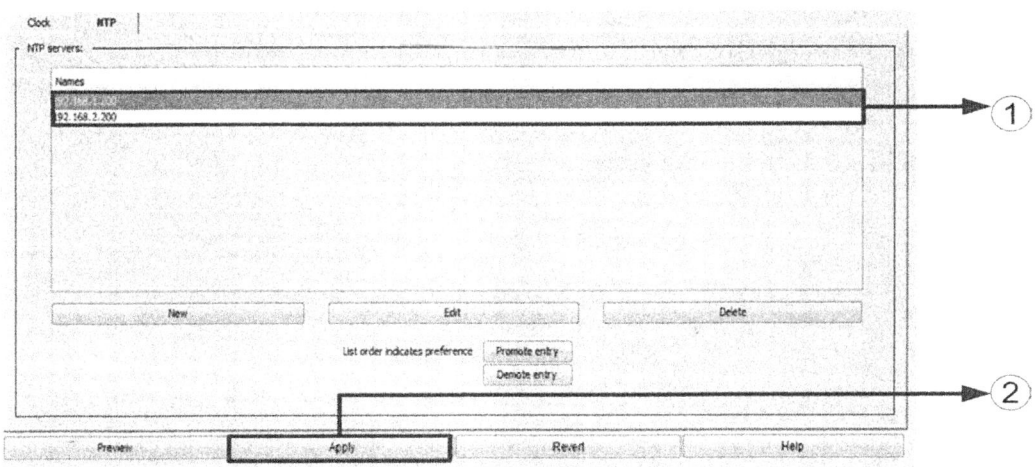

Figure 4:15 Apply the NTP server setting

CONFIGURING ADAPTERS/NETWORK INTERFACES

BlueCoat Proxy SG has one or more adapters, which you can think of as slots, and one or more interfaces in it. This usually varies beween different hardware models of the Proxy SG. All the recent Proxies come with the labeled name on the interface such as LAN or WAN. Some small Proxy SG has only on interface which you could either for LAN or WAN. Here we are showing how to configure the proxy either in Transparent or Explicit mode, but the concept of configuring is the same.

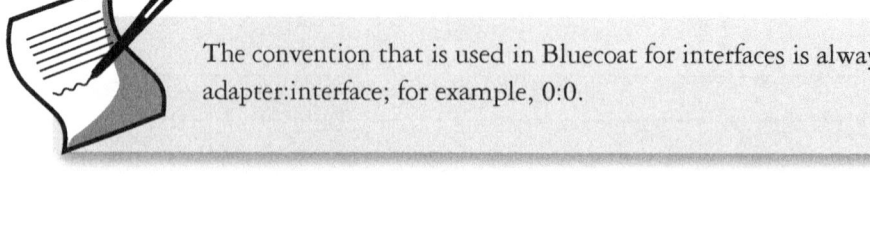

The convention that is used in Bluecoat for interfaces is always adapter:interface; for example, 0:0.

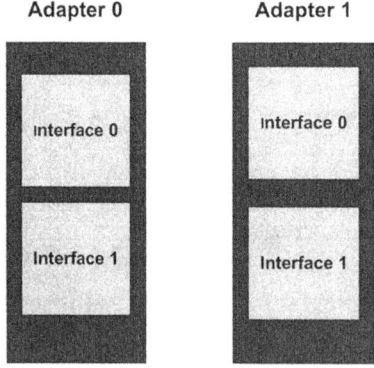

Figure 4:16 BlueCoat adapter schema

To configure the network interface, follow the steps as shown below:

1. Log in to the GUI and go to Configuration → Network → Adapters, and you should see the following screen:

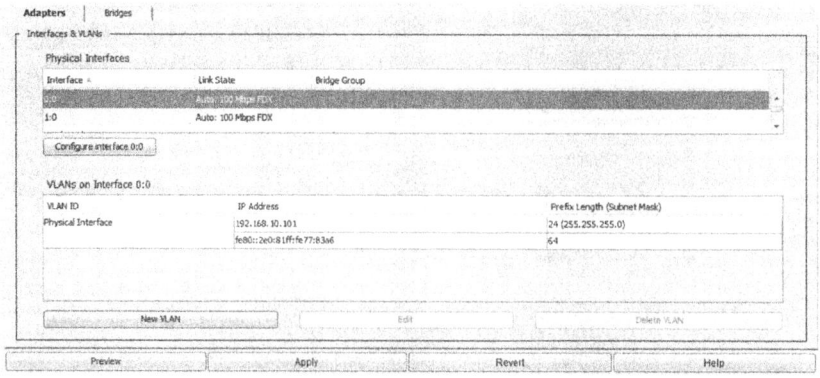

Figure 4:17 Adapter and interface settings

2. Click on the interface 0:0 and click "Configure interface 0:0". You will see the interface properties screen as shown below:

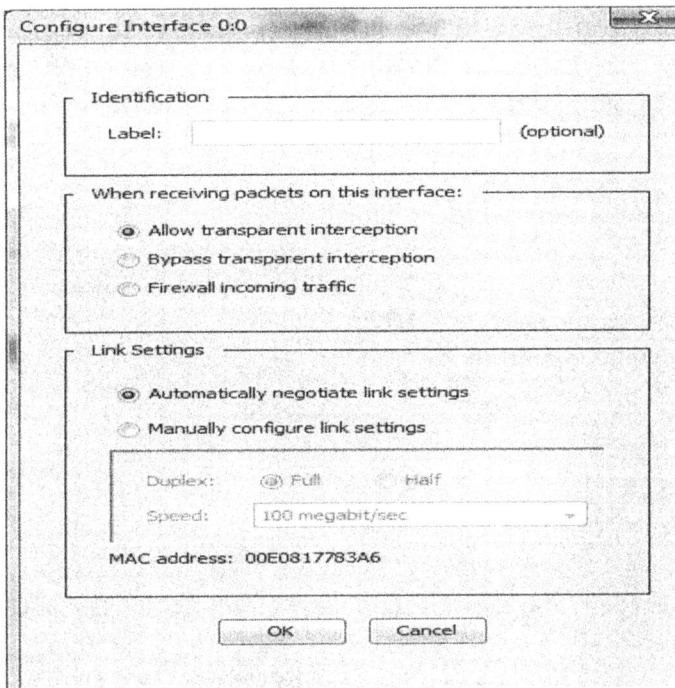

Figure 4:18 Interface settings

We will explain each option as shown below:Label section: The "Label" is an optional section and it is user-defined.

Interception section : Moving to the next configuration section, "When receiving packets on this interface:".

Allow transparent interception: This is the default option enabled, and it varies from version to version of the Proxy SG. It intercepts the required traffic that you allow for the services in the Proxy SG. Other traffic which is not configured to intercept is bridged or forwarded based upon the rules that you configure in the services. This is the first place to enable the interface to listen for the traffic, (preparing the network layer in the TCP/IP stack), then ports or services that needs to intercepted will be configured in the Configuration → Services section.

Bypass transparent interception: The Proxy SG bridges or forwards all inbound traffic on this interface for transparent connections, not explicit connections, regardless the configuration in the Configuration → Services section. The idea is simple: you block the traffic at the network layer (in TCP/IP), but services or port numbers (Transport layer in TCP/IP) are still enabled, the Network layer is passive, so packet will not go above it.

So only transparent interception is bypassed, meaning it will perform network functions like forwarding and bridging.

Firewall incoming traffic: The Proxy SG drops silently or drops all inbound connections on this interface. The proxy interface is completely turned off; even services that are enabled in the Configuration → Services will not do anything, because the network layer is off.

The table below summarizes the different options and their corresponding processes

Interception Options	ProxySG Management and Console Connections (GUI, SSH)	Explicit Proxy Service Traffic	Transparent Proxy Service Traffic	Other Traffic
Allow	Intercepted	Intercepted	Intercepted	Forwarded
Bypass	Intercepted	Intercepted	Forwarded	Forwarded
Firewall	Dropped silently	Dropped silently	Dropped silently	Dropped silently

Table 4:1 Allow, bypass, and firewall traffic flowLink Section: The next section is "Link Section" . Link section is where the interface speed and duplex settings are configured. By default, Proxy SG auto-negotiates with any device it is connected to, it may be a switch, router, or firewall.The

Speed: The Proxy SG comes with different speeds in the interface, like 10 megabit/second, 100 mega/bit/second, and 1 gigabits/second. So the speed is the maximum transfer rate an interface can support. The interface card speed type depends upon the hardware purchased; for a high-speed environment, 1 Gigabits/Second is used.

Duplex: Duplex is defined as the ways in which traffic flows in an interface . There are two types of Duplex settings that you can configure the Proxy SG with: Full Duplex and Half Duplex. In Full Duplex, both devices will transfer to and from each other simultaneously, allowing each direction to use the maximum transfer speed without affecting the other direction of the communication. In Half Duplex mode, only one device will transmit at any one given time, effectively sharing the maximum transfer speed of the interface.

Blue Coat always recommends using the auto-negotiate feature which is the default option in Proxy SG. In some situations you'll need to set manually; if all the interfaces are 100 Mbps connected to Giga interface of the switch or router, then manual configuration is the best option.

There is no hard and fast rule, but if the auto-negotiation is not working, then try with the manual setting and also check with routers and switch to functionality that supports these settings, because certain auto-negotiation settings may change with different vendors.

In the same interface section, you have the link settings portion at the bottom of the figure 4:19 as shown below:

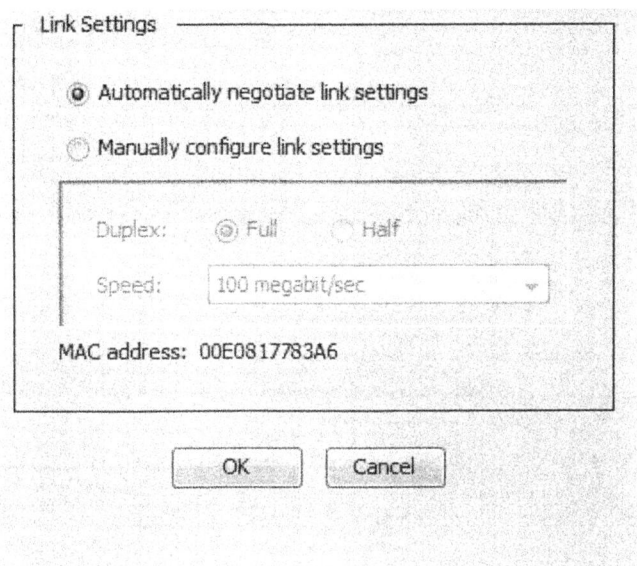

Figure 4:19 Link settings

By default the interface is Auto-Negotiated. If you want to manually configure settings then select the radio button "Manually configure link settings". Then you'll have a choice of what the Duplex could be: either Full or Half, and a Speed of either 10, 100, or 1000 megabit/sec as shown in the figure below.

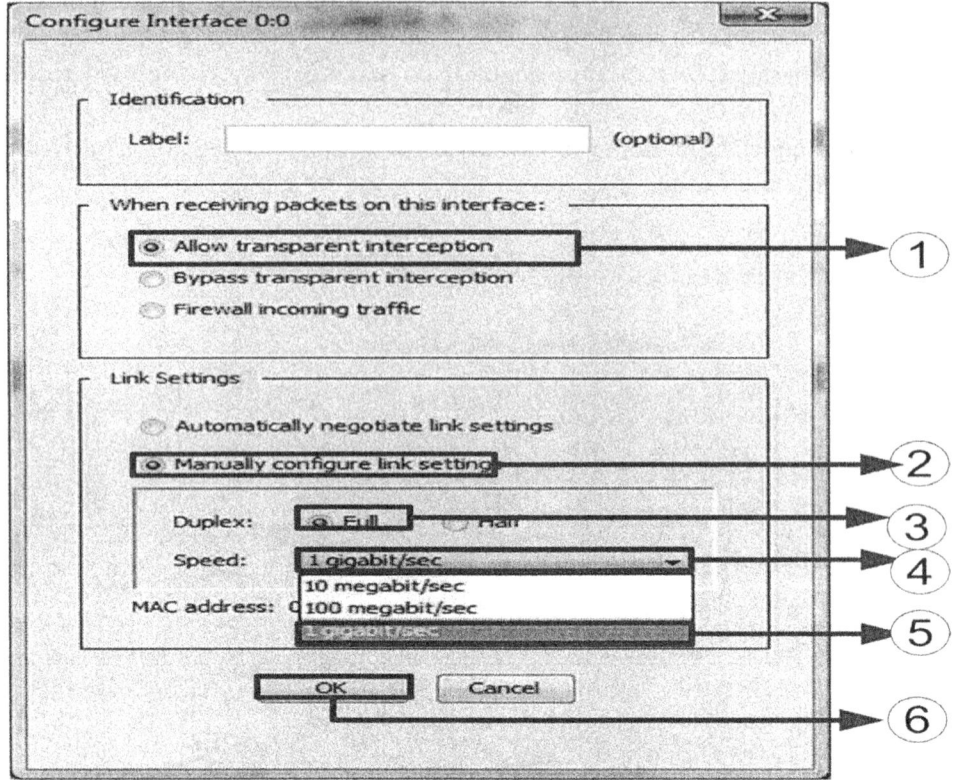

Figure 4:20 Manual link settings configuration

Select the required speed and click "OK" and then "Apply" in the main screen to confirm the changes.

3. VLAN

As we know, VLAN (Virtual LAN) is used to make networks looks logical, so that all hosts in the network can communicate. By default all networking devices and BlueCoat are in the Native VLAN. Native VLAN has a tag ID 1, which is attached to the L2 layer of the TCP/IP, so traffic in native VLAN is not tagged by = BlueCoat or the switch. BlueCoat accepts any packets regardless of the VLAN tag, and passes them from one interface to another by preserving the original VLAN tag. If the packet is untagged and the destination interface is not a Native VLAN, the Proxy adds a VLAN tag to ensure that the VLAN ID is maintained. And remember, Proxy SG always strips the Native VLAN tag on all outgoing traffic. There is one more concept called Trunk ports, which are used to connect between switches and routers, and which carry tag packets with VLAN ID and pass traffic between them.

In the main screen of the Adapters section, the bottom portion is the VLAN settings. When you have to create VLAN, click "New VLAN", enter any VLAN ID between 1 to

4094 (but the native VLAN ID is 1) in the "Identification" section, then under the section "When receiving packets on this VLAN", select any option that you want for your network of all these options we have discussed in section Configuring Adapters/Network interfaces . You can assign the corresponding IP address for the VLAN in the "IP Addresses" section by clicking "Add IP" and entering the IP address and subnet as shown below:

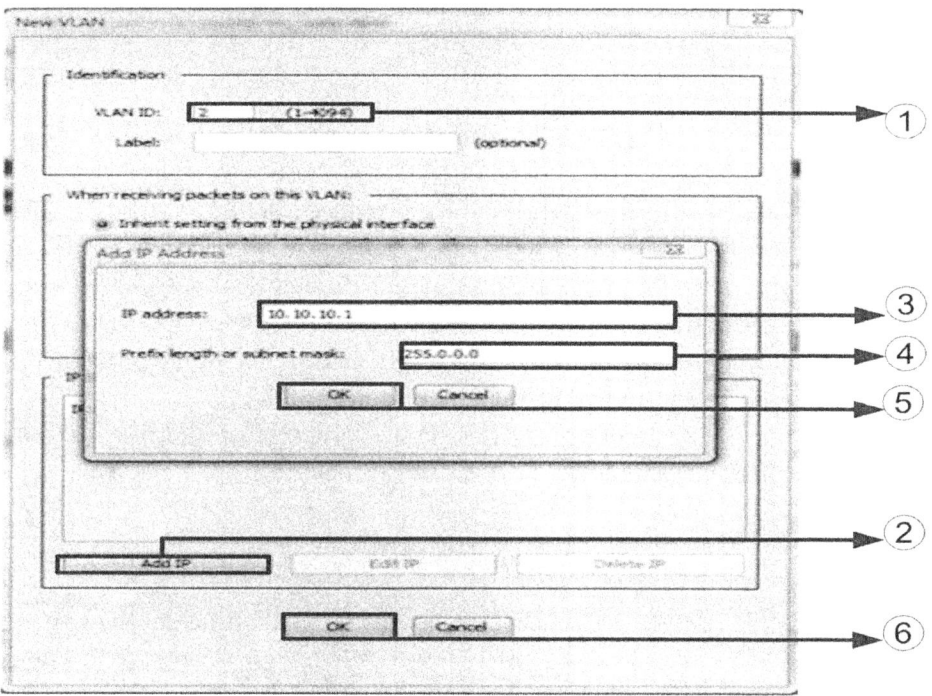

Figure 4:21 Configuring VLAN

Then click "OK".

While the TCP/IP settings in the Proxy get updated your connection to will be lost; you can open a new console and get connected . To confirm. click "OK" in the pop-up as shown below:

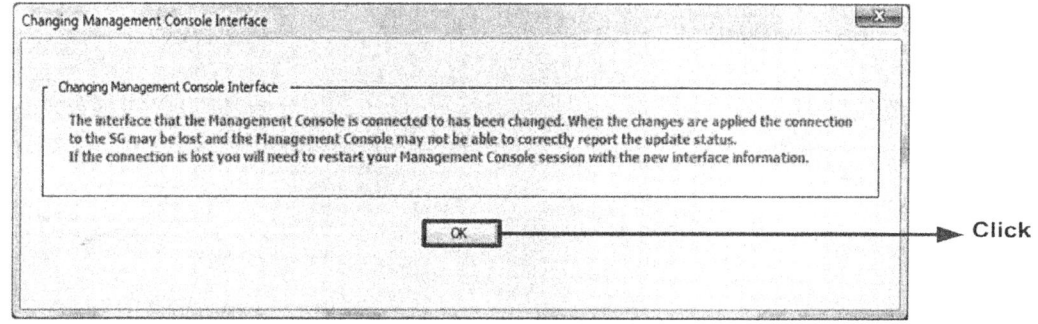

Figure 4:22 Interface alert pop-up

Then settings will looks as follows:

VLANs on Interface 0:0		
VLAN ID	IP Address	Prefix Length (Subnet Mask)
Physical Interface	192.168.10.101	24 (255.255.255.0)
	fe80::2e0:81ff:fe77:83a6	64
2	10.10.10.1	8 (255.0.0.0)

New VLAN	Edit	Delete VLAN

Figure 4:23 VLAN settings for Interface

The above figure clearly tells us that the physical interface is VLAN 1, the IP is 172.1.1.1, and the sub-interface IP is 10.10.10.1 with VLAN ID 2. You can add multiple IP addresses to an interface, which can be in the same subnet or different subnet. When assigned in the same subnet, you can allow one interface for managing one service (HTTP) under a specific IP and another service under a different IP (FTP). For different subnets, again, different services can be configured across different networks.

To assign multiple IP address to an interface, select the interface section under "VLANs on interface 0:0" and click "Edit" as shown below:

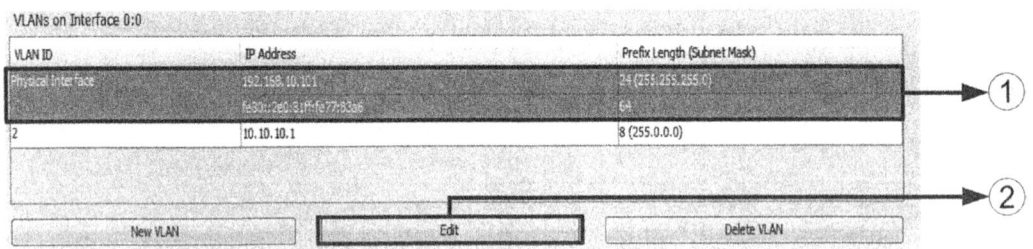

Figure 4:24 Adding multiple IP address to an interface

Then click the "Add IP" and enter the IP address and subnet mask details and click "OK", as shown below:

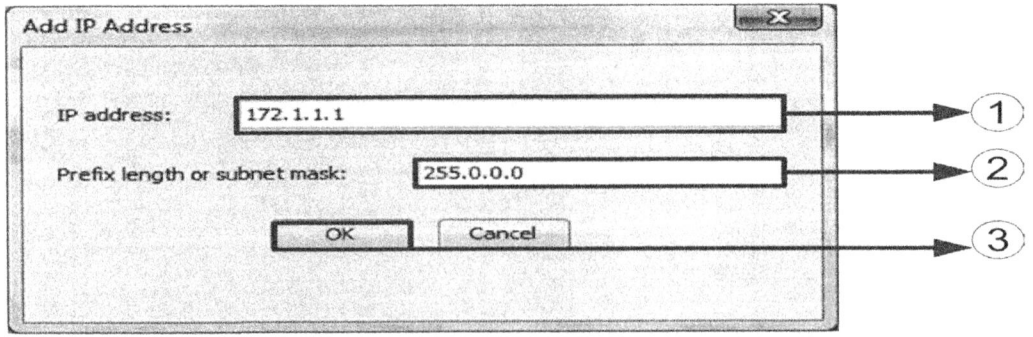

Figure 4:25 IP details for the sub-interface

To add IP addresses in a different subnet as shown below, click "Add IP" and enter the IP address and subnet mask details and click "OK", as shown below:

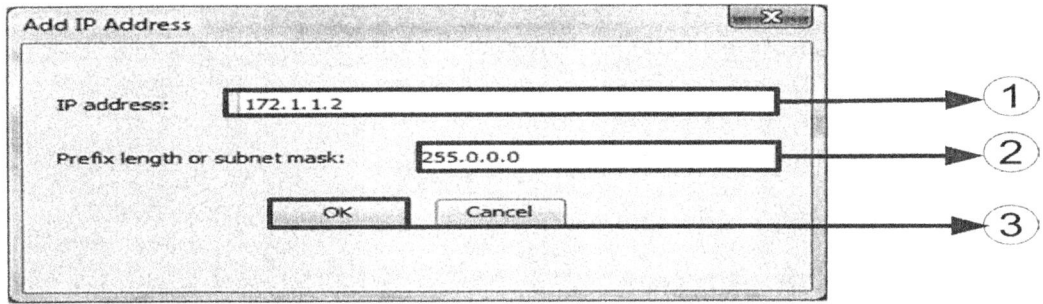

Figure 4:26 IP details for additional sub-interfaces

Then click "OK" on the main screen. You will have the pop-up for the management console as a lost message for resetting the TCP/IP setting. Just click "OK" and if logged out, log in again to the management console.

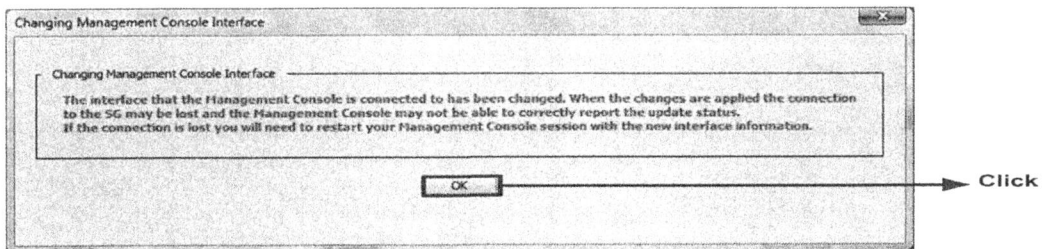

Figure 4:27 Interface alert pop-up

All the settings for the VLAN that you created and the multiple IP addresses that we discussed and that you configured for the interface 0:0 will be as shown below:

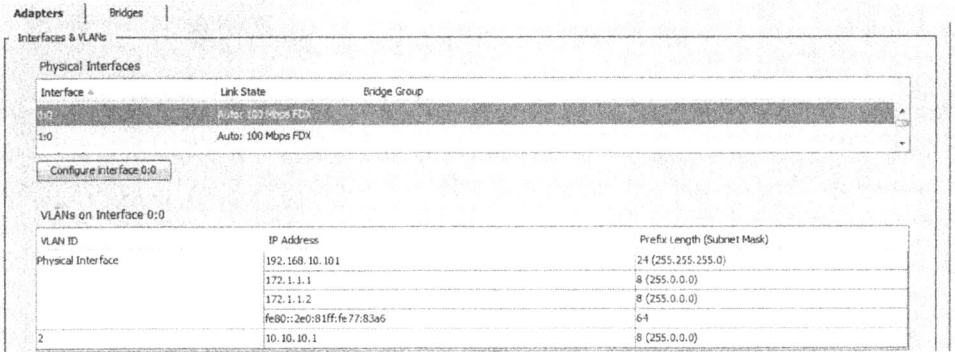

Figure 4:28 Adapters with interface and sub-interface settings

If you have only the IP in the Proxy SG and use it to log in to the Management Console, please do not edit and change the IP to a network IP that will not be reachable in your network, and make sure you don't doing it in a production network or it will cause outages. If this happens accidentally, always make sure that you have console access to the BlueCoat Proxy box.

CONFIGURING IP ROUTING:

You'll need to configure the default gateway, as the Proxy SG needs to forward the traffic after processing it to either the intranet or the Internet. The ProxySG sends all traffic to the default gateway unless another specific route is configured. As we have shown, initially when configuring the proxy through the serial console, you will be providing the default gateway. If you had configured the default gateway then check in the Management Console by going to Configuration → Routing → Gateways, as shown below:

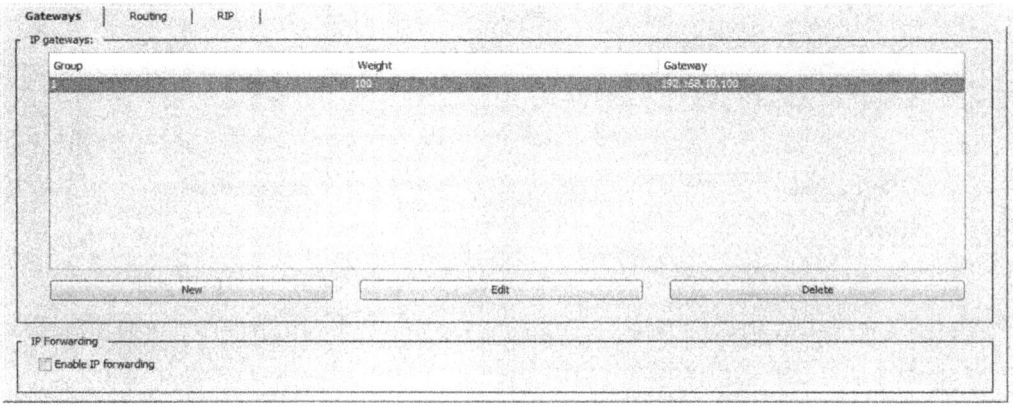

Figure 4:29 BlueCoat Proxy SG default gateway

As you see in the above Figure, the Gateway is specified as 192.168.10.100. There two additional fields in the settings: one is Group and the other is weight; these are used for load balancing. The Group field has an group ID range between 1 and 10 and the weight range is between 1 and 100. Ideally when you have only one gateway, the Group can be any ID between 1 and 10, and weight can be any between 1 and 100. By default when you have only one gateway added during during installation, the Group ID will be 1 and the weight 100. This is equivalent to having one gateway with any value for Group and weight; this doesn't makes any difference—the default routing condition will be the same, meaning that all the traffic which doesn't have any static routes will be forwarded to the default gateway, as shown below:

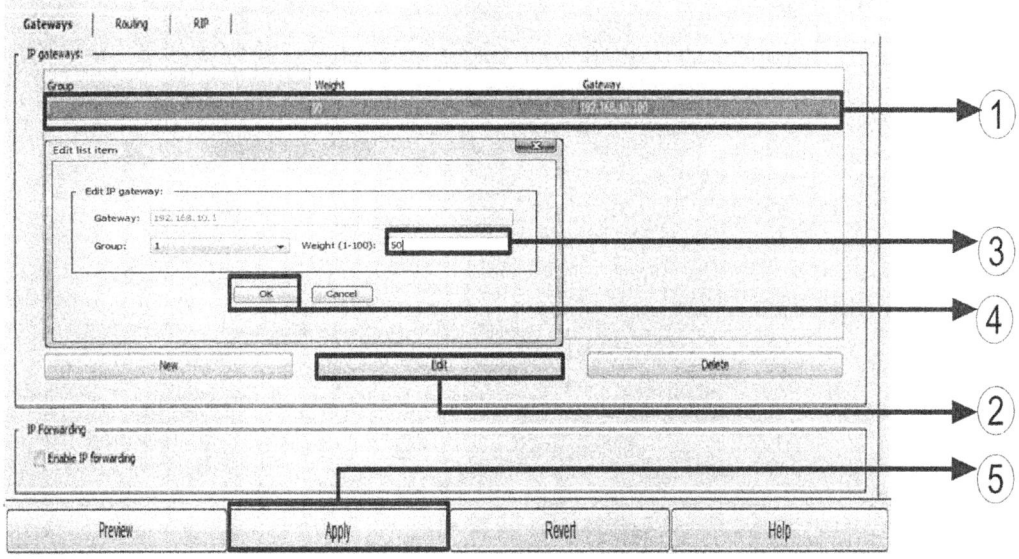

Figure 4:30   BlueCoat Proxy SG default gateway with weight of 50

1. Load Balancing:

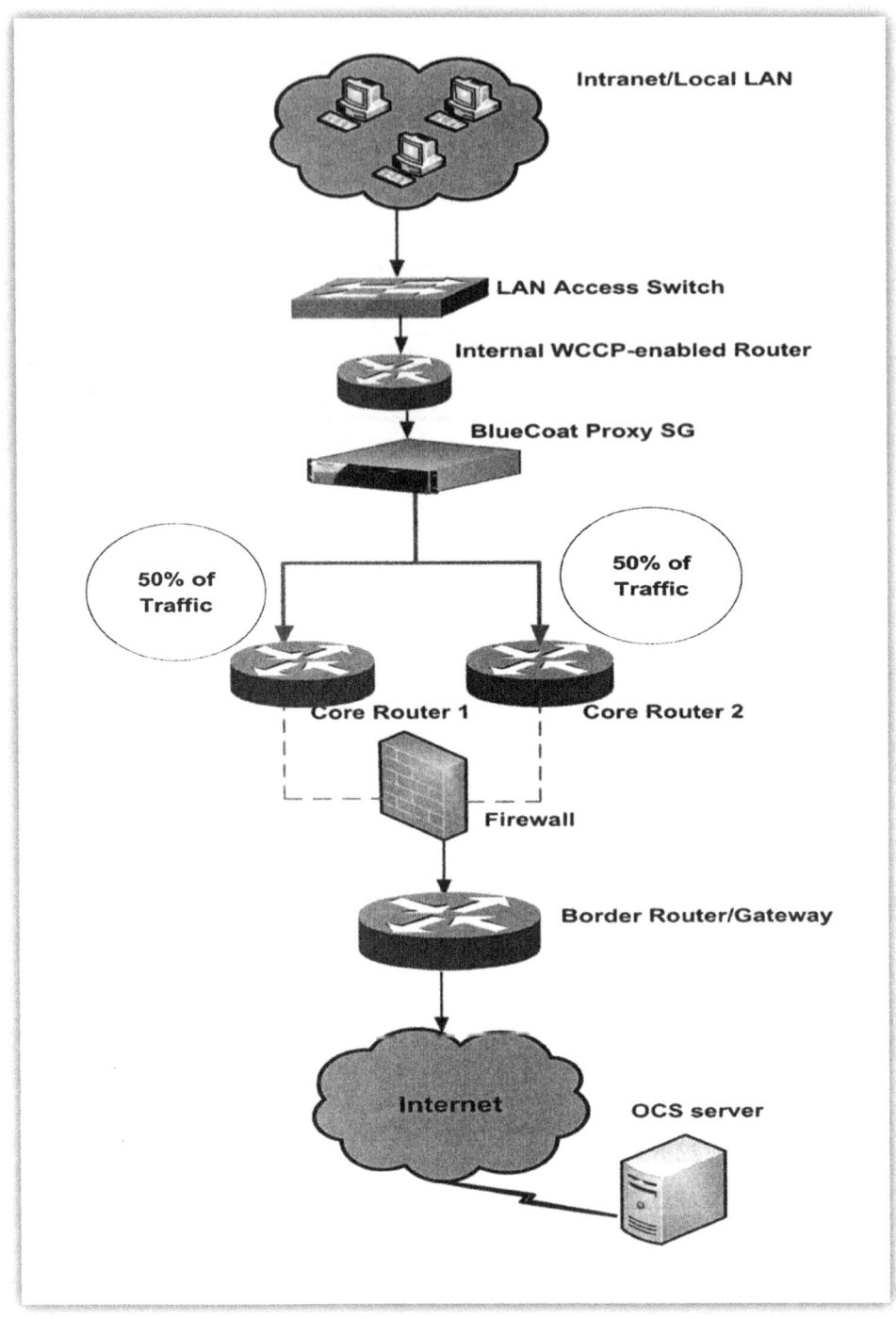

Figure 4:31 BlueCoat Proxy SG load balancing with two routers

Let's take the following scenario: you have two gateways where the traffic needs to be load balanced between them. So you should configure the two gateways with the same group ID (could be any value between 1 and 10), and the weight should be the same (and could be any value between 1 and 100). To configure load balancing, please do the following:

Go to Configuration → Network → Routing → Gateways. Click "New" and enter the values and click "OK".

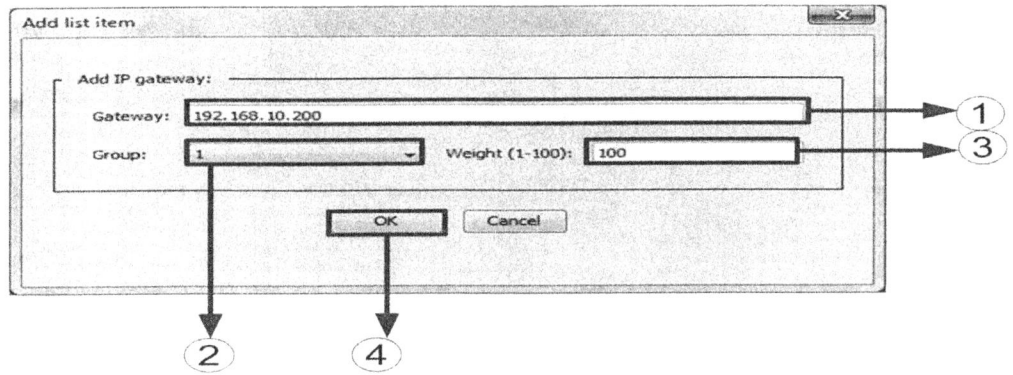

Figure 4:32 Configuring the new gateway

And "Apply" changes.

Then Gateway configuration will be as shown below:

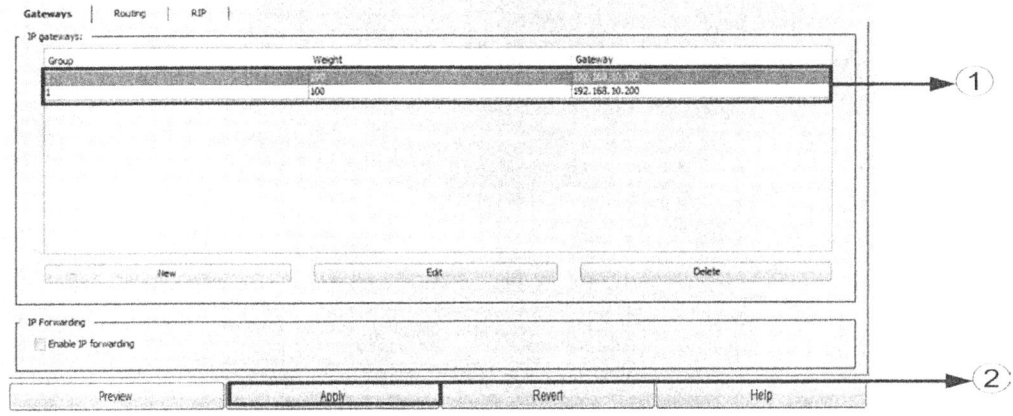

Figure 4:33 Applying the change

You can use any gateway in the group for load balancing, provided the interface IP is the same as for the gateway subnet that is specified in the adapters on any interfaces.

2. Failover:

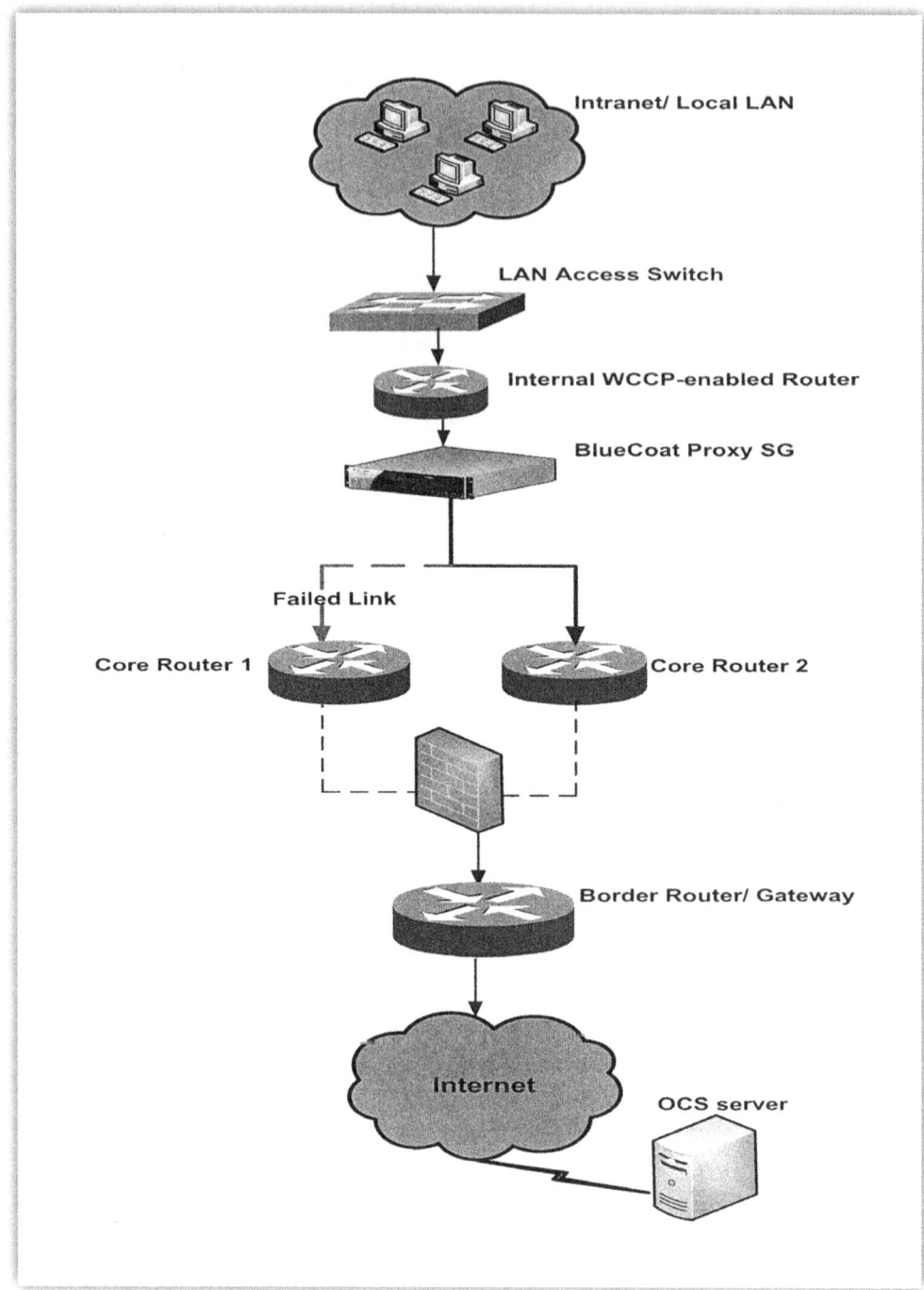

Figure 4:34 Failover with two default gateways

Consider the following scenario: if one of the link or the gateway fails, and you need to route the traffic to the secondary gateway, you should configure a gateway failover setting in the Proxy SG. For this the group ID should be different. All gateways in the lowest preference group ID are considered to be active until one of them becomes unreachable and is dropped from the active gateway list, but any remaining gateways within the group will be continued to be used. If all gateways in the lowest preference group ID become unreachable and fail, the gateways with the next lowest preference group ID will become the active gateways (unless one of the gateways in a lower preference group becomes reachable again).

Go to Configuration → Network → Routing → Gateways and click "New" and enter the values (create 172.1.1.100 and 172.1.1.200 new gateway with Group ID as 2). Confirm by clicking "OK" and "Apply" changes. Repeat the same for all the gateways that need to be added and it should look as follows.

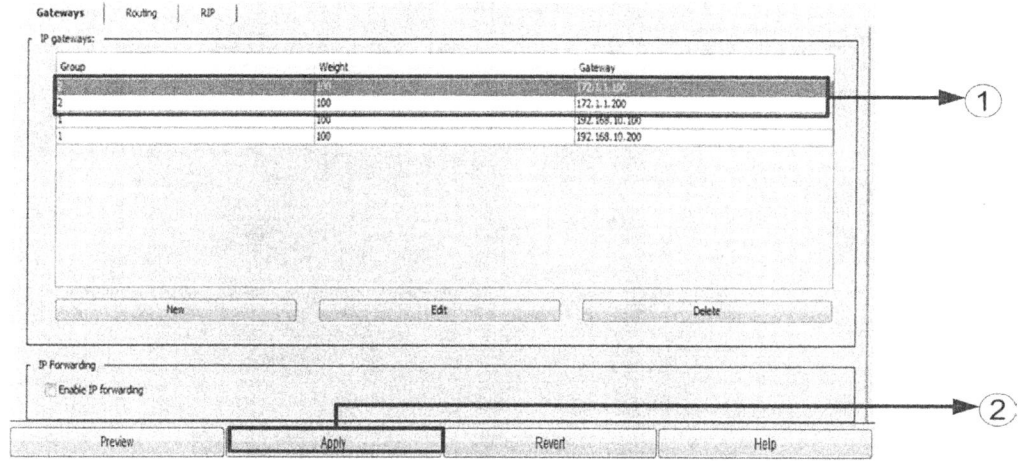

Figure 4:35 Creating two gateways for failover

In the above failover setting, for the Group preference ID 1, the traffic is load balanced for the gateways 192.168.10.100 and 192.168.10.200. Say for instance the gateway 192.168.20.100 fails; the other gateway in the group preference ID 1 will still work; that is, 192.168.10.200. If 192.168.10.200 also fails, then the lower preference group ID 2 will become active and the traffic will be load balanced between 172.1.1.100 and 172.1.1.200. Remember, the failover is detected within 20 seconds, and if the primary Group preference Group 1 any of the gateway is active again, e.g. 192.168.10.100 or 192.168.10.200, the Blue Coat Proxy SG failover back to the Primary, that is Group preference ID 1.

STATIC ROUTES:

Static routes are the specific routes that the Proxy SG can be configured to so that for a particular destination, the Proxy SG will forward the traffic to the specific gateway that is configured in the proxy rather than forwarding to the default gateway.

The static routes have the following syntax:

IP-Address   **Subnet Mask**   **Gateway**

IP-Address : The IP address field specifies the destination of the traffic that should be forwarded; it can be either a specific destination or a network address.

Subnet Mask: The Subnet Mask represents the network mask of the destination. For one specific address it will be 255.255.255.255; for a class C network it will be 255.255.255.0.

Gateway: The gateway that the Proxy SG should forward the traffic can be either the router or firewall or any server. The address should be in range of the adapter's interface IP address.

The static address can be configured with any of the following three methods:

Go to Configuration → Network → Routing → Routing and click the drop-down next to the "Install" button:

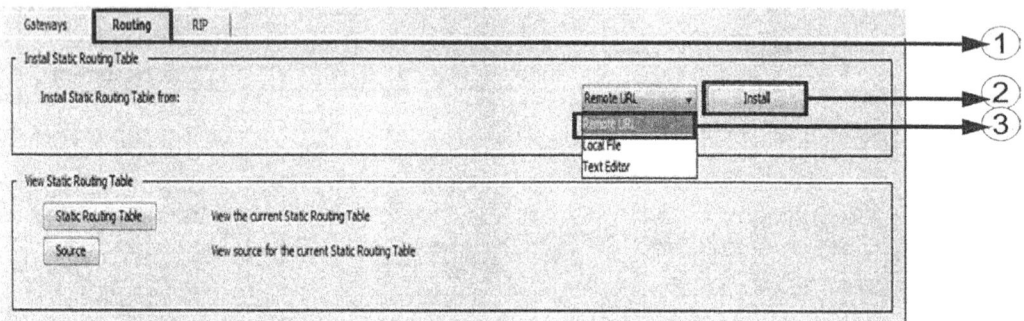

Figure 4:36 Configuring static routes

a. **Remote URL:** → You can find the file in the remote web server and download it. To configure the remote web server path, select "Remote URL" and click "Install", as shown below:

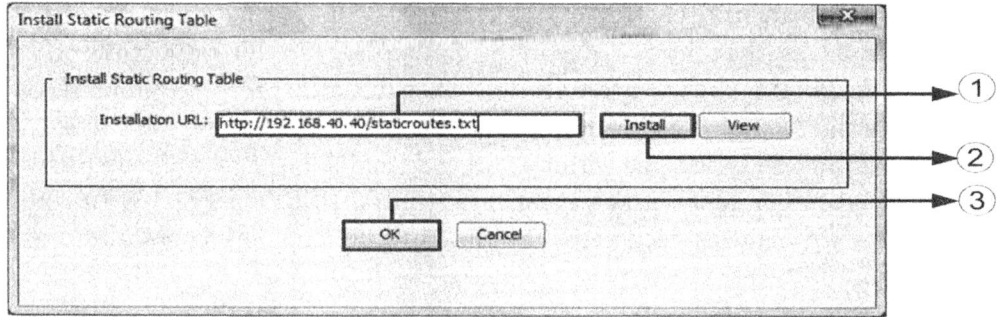

Figure 4:37 Installing static routes from web server

Then enter the path of the web server as shown above.

b. **Local file:** You could find the file in the local system or on a shared drive and upload it.

c. **Text Editor:** Select "Text Editor" from the drop-down and enter the static route information as shown below and confirm by clicking "Install".

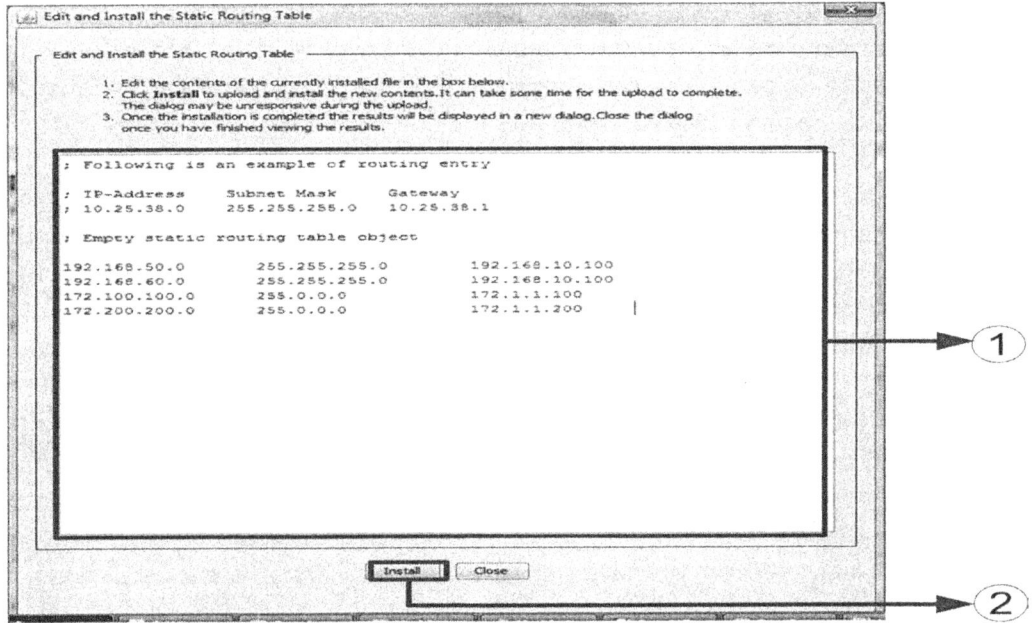

Figure 4:38 Installing static routes in Text Editor

CONFIGURING DNS:

The Proxy SG uses the DNS for name resolution of the websites to the IP address and vice-versa. This is a very important functionality of the Proxy SG, since Proxy SG will only forward the traffic if it knows the IP address of the destination. So the ProxySG is not a DNS server; it is just a DNS client, performing DNS queries for the Proxy SG to perform its function for content filtering, policies, proxy services, etc.

There are many DNS record types, but two DNS record types which are used in Proxy SG in most situations, are the A record in which for a forward DNS query is from domain name to IP address, say it resolves domain www.yahoo.com to 204.232.137.207 and the PTR record is a reverse DNS query in which IP address to domain name vice-versa.

Broadly classifying DNS queries is divided into two types,

1. **Non-recursive queries:**

The non-recursive query means the DNS server can provide a full answer or a partial answer, or return an error to the Proxy SG.

Full answer : A full answer has been received by the DNS server, to the DNS request that the Proxy SG has requested, such as IP address to domain name or domain name or IP address.

Partial answer → The DNS server requests the Proxy SG to try contacting other DNS servers, since it doesn't have the answer to the Proxy SG request, but the Proxy SG doesn't honors the request. Instead, it queries the other DNS servers in the list that you configured in the list in the Proxy SG.

Error answer → The DNS server states that there is an error in the domain name or any general error in the DNS request that has been requested by the Proxy SG. In this case the Proxy SG also tries the whole list and then reports the error to the user or client who initiated request.

So by default, the Proxy SG has two groups created and they cannot be deleted, as shown below:

Go to **Configuration** → Network → DNS → Groups → the "DNS Group" section.

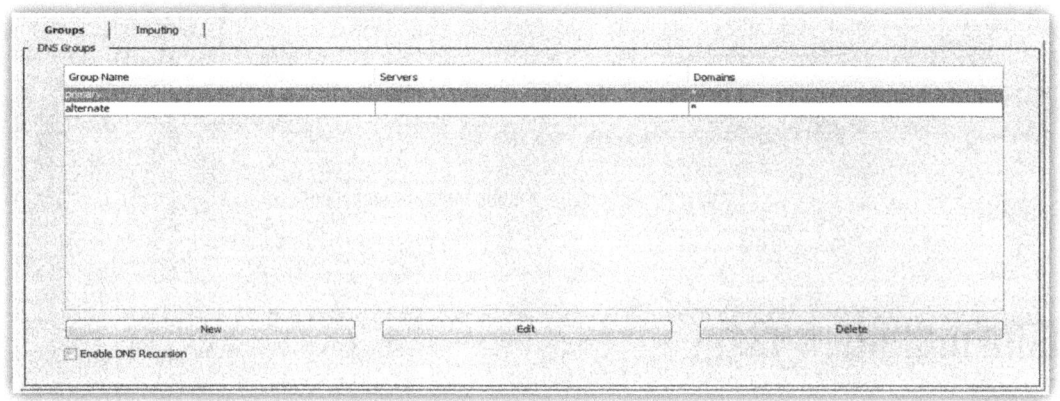

Figure 4:39 DNS server settings

So first you will add the whole DNS server list and will explain later, so it will be easier for you to understand.

ADDING PRIMARY DNS SERVER

Usually the primary DNS server should be the Corporate DNS server or your company DNS server; this is not a rule but can help you for faster DNS queries. And if you are using Proxy SG for internal web servers as well, then the local internal address space gets resolved here. If the Proxy SG is an external proxy and your internal DNS server doesn't want to handle external queries, then add all the ISP DNS servers that you ISP have provided.

The "Domains" column is grayed out and has * in it, as shown below, All DNS queries are done here if your DNS servers can handle both internal and external DNS queries.

Select Primary and select "Edit", and enter the DNS list, one per line as shown below, and click "OK" and to apply the changes.

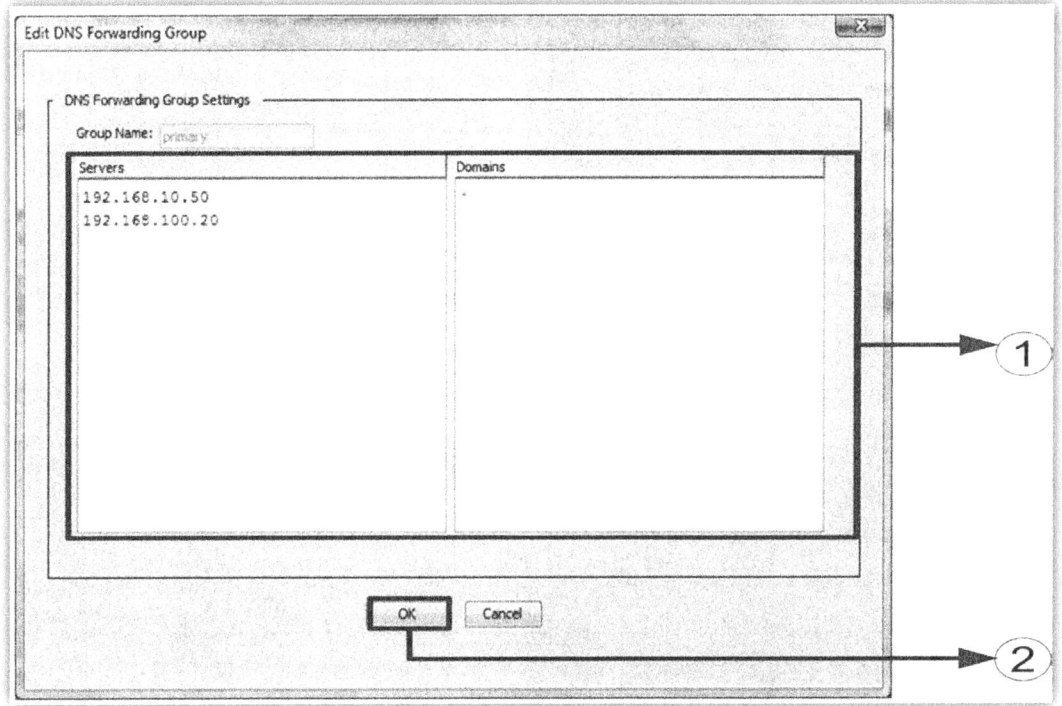

Figure 4:40 Configuring DNS server

Assuming the DNS servers 192.168.10.50 and 192.168.100.20 can handle both internal and external DNS queries for the users request or Proxy SG DNSqueries.

ADDING ALTERNATE DNS SERVERS

It is the same logic, but if the query couldn't be completed by the Primary group, then the Proxy SG will look for an answer in the Alternate DNS group. Usually we define either the ISP DNS servers or the Open DNS servers. For clarity we add one ISP DNS server and one Open DNS server from Verzion.

The "Domains" column is grayed out and has * in it, as shown below. All DNS queries are done here, if your DNS servers can handle both internal and external DNS queries.

Select Alternate and select "Edit", and enter the DNS list, one per line as shown below, and click OK and to apply the changes.

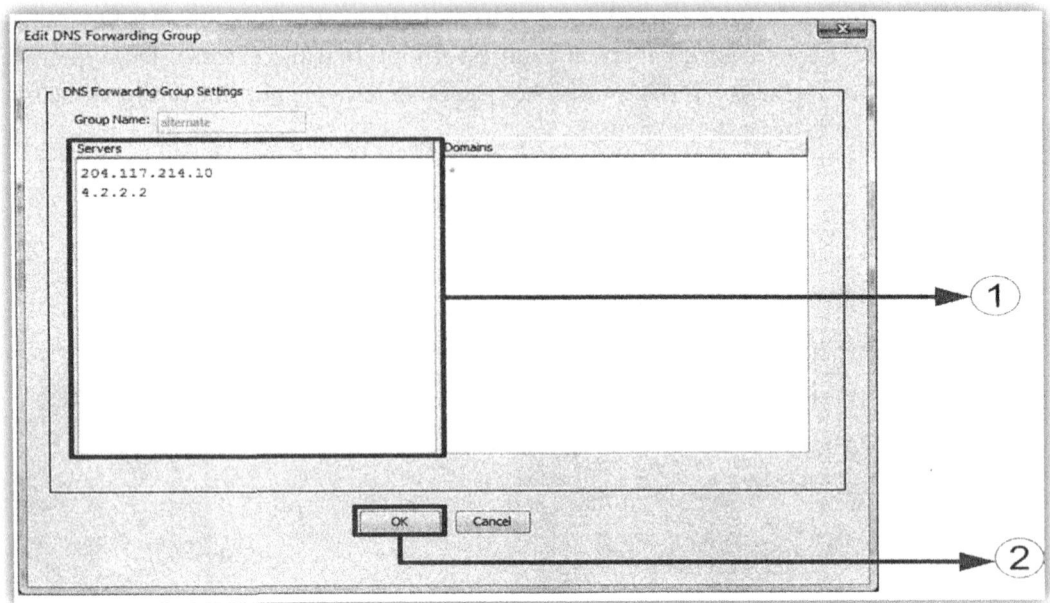

Figure 4:41 Configuring the DNS server

So the final list should be as shown below:

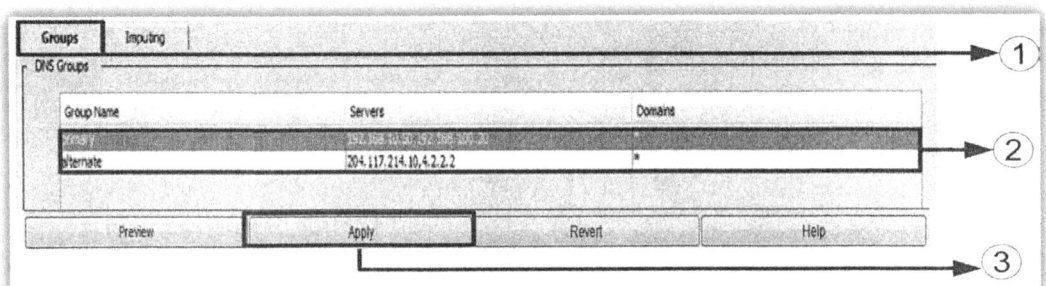

Figure 4:42 Applying the DNS change settings

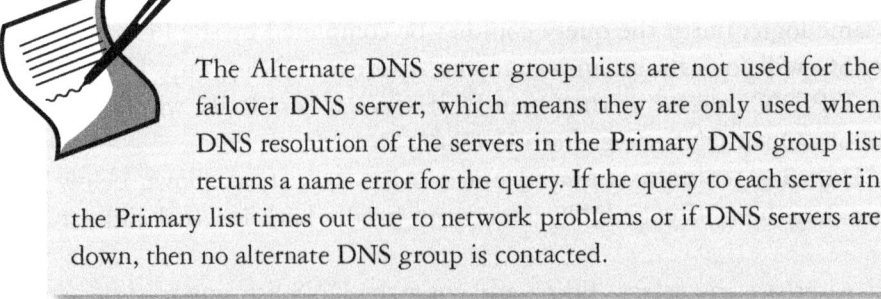

The Alternate DNS server group lists are not used for the failover DNS server, which means they are only used when DNS resolution of the servers in the Primary DNS group list returns a name error for the query. If the query to each server in the Primary list times out due to network problems or if DNS servers are down, then no alternate DNS group is contacted.

The Proxy SG uses the following mechanism to resolve a DNS query:

1. The Proxy SG checks the domain suffix (e.g. google.com) in all the DNS groups (Primary and Secondary). If matched, the DNS servers in the group list are queried; if not, it selects the Primary DNS group. In our configuration above, since we have *, the first DNS group is matched that is the Primary group and the Proxy SG selects this DNS group.

2. The Proxy SG sends DNS requests to the DNS servers in the Primary group list, in the order they appear. If it gets a response from the first DNS server 192.168.10.50, then it stops processing and no attempt is made to contact any of the list in the Primary DNS group; if no response, then the second DNS server 192.168.100.20 is tried and if there is a response, it stops processing or else it moves to the second DNS server in the Alternate group.

3. The Proxy SG sends DNS requests to the DNS servers in the Alternate group list, in the order they appear. Say it gets a response from the first DNS server 204.117.214.10. Then it stops processing and no attempt is made to contact any of the list in the Alternate DNS group. If no response, the second DNS server 4.2.2.2 is tried. If there is a response then it stops processing, or if it is unable to resolve the host name, an error is returned to the client, and no attempt is made to contact any other DNS servers.

2. **Recursive queries:**

Recursive queries are also known as referral queries. Say the Proxy SG sends a DNS query for either the A record or PTR record; the DNS server replies that it has no answers, but that it could give information of the authoritative DNS server, so that DNS server could query the authoritative DNS server and follow all referrals given by other DNS servers and so on. By default it is disabled; you can enable it by going to in the same page where you configured the DNS servers list at the bottom of the screen, as shown below:

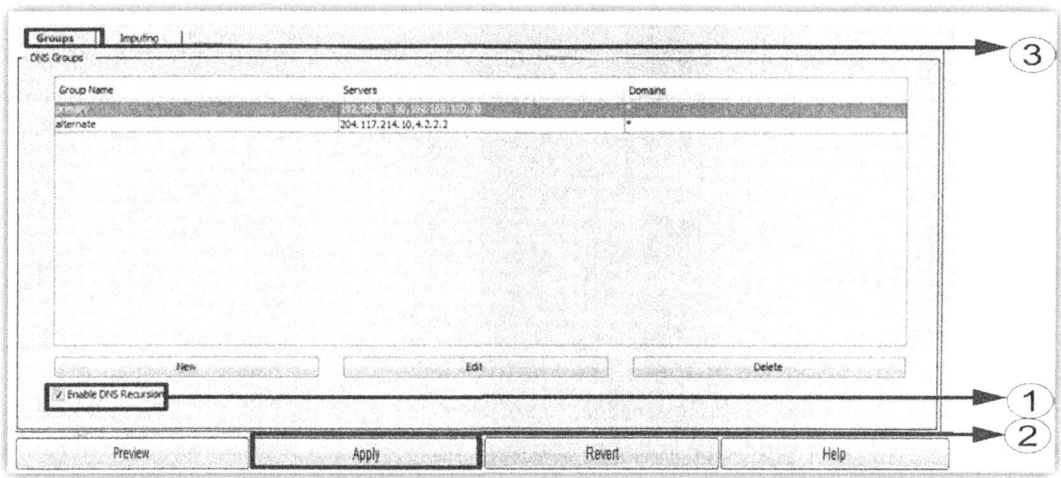

Figure 4:43 Enabling DNS Recursion

CUSTOM DNS GROUP LIST:

As stated earlier, you cannot add or delete the default Primary or Alternate DNS groups and you cannot even add a domain suffix in it. To get around this limitation, you can create custom groups and add a domain suffix. The reason for creating custom groups is that you can make the Proxy SG query certain DNS servers for certain domain suffixes and the query depends upon the Primary and Alternate DNS group settings. Say you want the Proxy SG to query internal domains; only the internal DNS servers, such as internaldomain.com, should be queried by the internal DNS servers; that is, all top-level domains matching internaldomain.com will be queried by these servers.

Go to Configuration → DNS → Groups and click "New", and enter the Group name as "InternalDomain". Enter the server list and the domain names as follows:

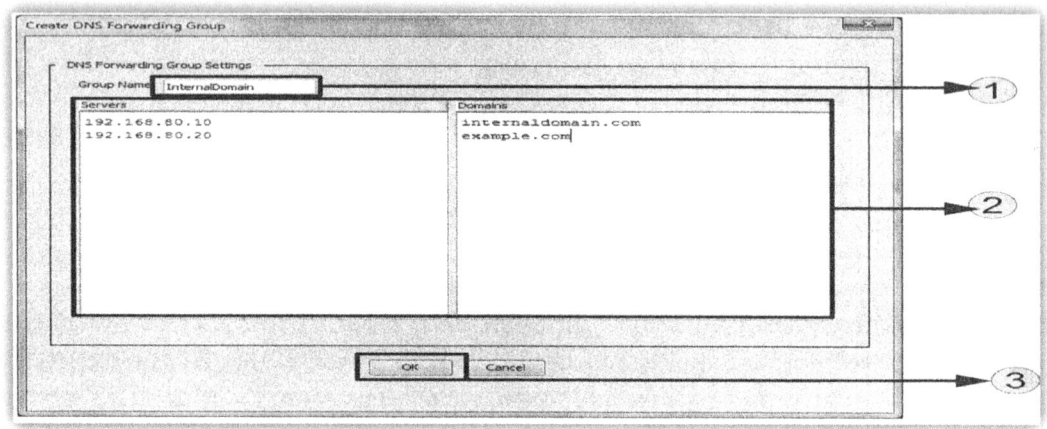

Figure 4:44 Adding the domain suffix

The limitations of custom group DNS setting are that the maximum you can create is 8 custom groups, and each custom group can contain a maximum of four DNS servers and eight domains. The other limitation is that it cannot accept wildcards (e.g. *.internaldomain.com) and cannot pattern match (internal.com will not match internaldomain.com).

DNS IMPUTING

DNS imputing is used in accessing the internal domain. Say the user just types http://payroll. The Proxy SG queries the original hostname before checking imputing suffixes, unless there is no period in the hostname, in which case imputing is applied first. Here in our example, the DNS adds the suffix to the user query and it makes a complete domain name as payroll.internaldomain.com and then forwards the request to the DNS server to resolve the IP address of the server.

To create the DNS imputing suffix, go to Configuration → Network → DNS → Imputing and click "New" and add the imputing suffix as shown below:

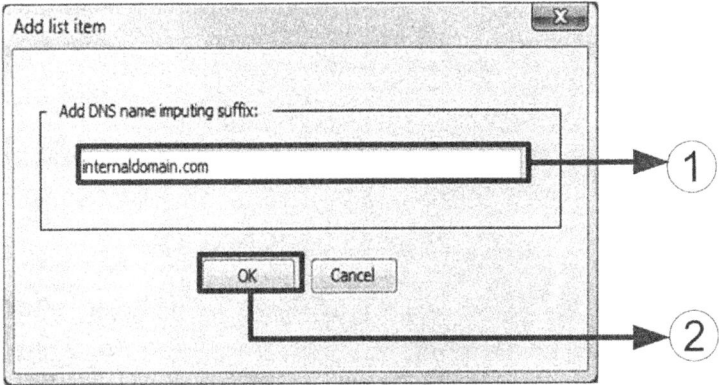

Figure 4:45 Adding DNS imputing suffix

And apply changes.

PRIVATE NETWORKS AND PRIVATE DOMAINS:

A private network is a network which you assume is private for the corporation.. But the definition for a private network is an internal network that uses private IP addresses, which are usually not routed over the public Internet. But if your DMZ has private addresses, and a certain subnet range you bought from the IANA for your company etc., all are considered to be private. By default, Proxy SG has the list of the whole IEEE RFC specified private addresses configured in it.

By configuring the private domain information, as we see in chapter 5, "Content Filtering," any private information is not sent to the DRTR servers for dynamic categorization. And even sensitive HTTP headers like Referer are removed. This makes the Proxy SG well aware of the internal networks and adds more protection and security to it. If you have Proxy AV engines, you can ignore all the scanning of the file extensions used by the internal web servers and streaming traffic from internal streaming servers, as you know these are trusted sources, and you add less load in the Proxy AV engines and improve the performance of both the Proxy SG and the Proxy AV.

The same logic as above applies to the Private section in the Proxy SG. Instead of having the IP address, you could add the domain name in the Proxy SG. By default this section is empty and you could add all internal domain names for the web servers, FTP servers, streaming servers, etc.

 All the entries in both the Private Network and Private Domain are treated as private by the Proxy SG and policies are applied as required.

For both Private Networks and Private domains, go to Configuration → Network → Private Networks → Private Network and you will see the list as shown below:

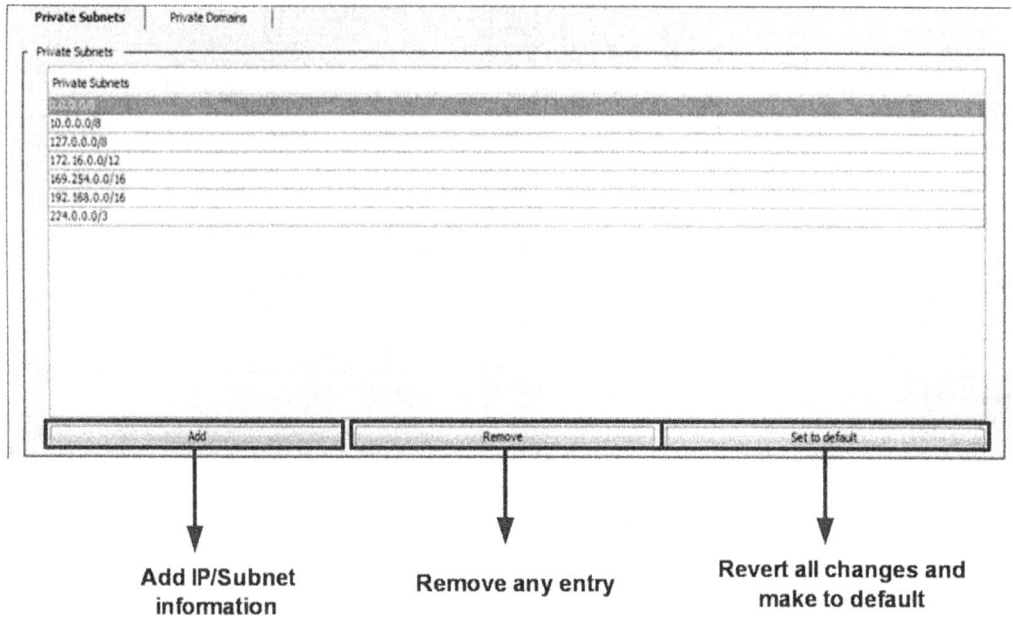

Add IP/Subnet information

Remove any entry

Revert all changes and make to default

Figure 4:46 Adding/Removing/Setting to default for Private Subnets

Select the Private domain section in the above screen and add entries, one entry in each line, and configure as shown below:

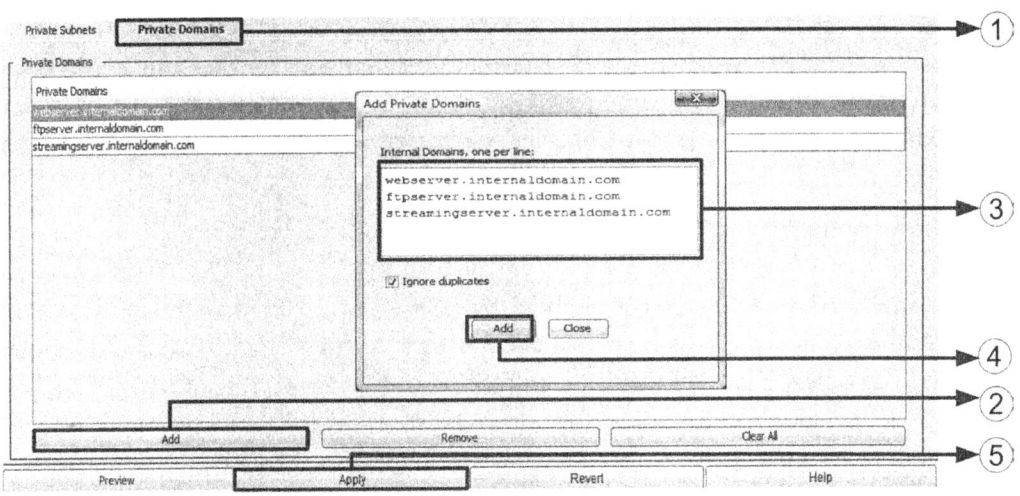

Figure 4:47 Adding a private domain list

CONFIGURING PROXY SERVICES:

A service or protocol refers to how the traffic will be handled by BlueCoat SG: it will either allow, manage, intercept, forward, deny, or route it. Here "service" means the Layer 4 in TCP/IP stack; in other words, you configure the port numbers and assign several attributes to them.

Usually, services in BlueCoat are broadly classified into two services:

a. Console services:

Console services are used to manage or administer BlueCoat SG itself. Administration involves configuring policies, back-up, troubleshooting, auditing, collecting logs, etc. There are five console services that are used to manage the box.

1. **HTTP**:
It is allowed to manage the BlueCoat SG via the Management console, and it is a GUI interface. It is a non-encrypted and disabled by default. BlueCoat recommends against HTTP to manage the Management Console. A browser is used for this service. The port used is 8081.

2. HTTPS:

It is allowed to manage the BlueCoat SG via the Management console, and it is a GUI interface. It is encrypted and enabled by default. BlueCoat recommends to only use HTTPS to manage the Management Console. A browser is used for this service. The port used is 8082.

3. SSH:

The box is managed via CLI. SSH is enabled by default, and BlueCoat recommends to use this SSH service when accessing across the network, since it is encrypted. SSH client tools are used to access it, such Putty. The port used is 22.

4. Telnet:

The box is managed via CLI. Telnet is disabled by default, since it is non-encrypted in nature. BlueCoat discourages the use of this protocol across the network. You can use command shell or any telnet client to access it. The port used is 23.

5. Serial:

This is the OOB interface that is connected to the Proxy SG. This service is used for the first-time installation or when the box gets hung.

You can configure the settings in the management console. Go to Configuration → Services → Management Services → Management Services, as shown below:

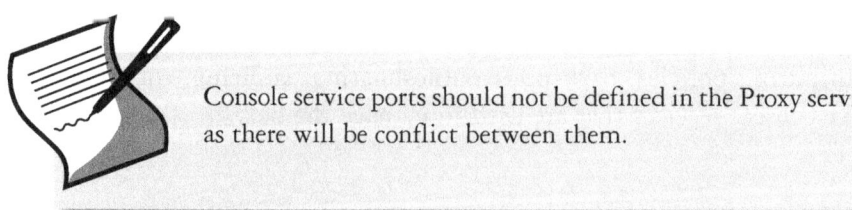

Figure 4:48 Management Services for BlueCoat Proxy SG

> Console service ports should not be defined in the Proxy service, as there will be conflict between them.

b. Proxy Services:

Proxy services are the services that enable the Proxy SG to listen for traffic and intercept, forward, proxy, or deny the traffic depending on the policies configured on the box. Here you define the destination port numbers for the services on the Proxy that should listen to perform proxy functionality. Here you also define whether the Proxy for a particular service should be explicit or transparent, and you can specify which source IP address can use certain services.

By default there is an HTTP listener service group that is enabled for Interception(depends upon SG version) , which has two services or protocols enabled and allowed for interception: they are ports 80 and 8080. The ports can be used for both transparent and explicit deployments, but port 8080 is only used for explicit mode. These are configurable and can be changed as per your requirements.

Go to Management Console → Configuration → Services → Proxy Services → Proxy services → Expand the Standard Group, and you will find the HTTP service group as shown below:

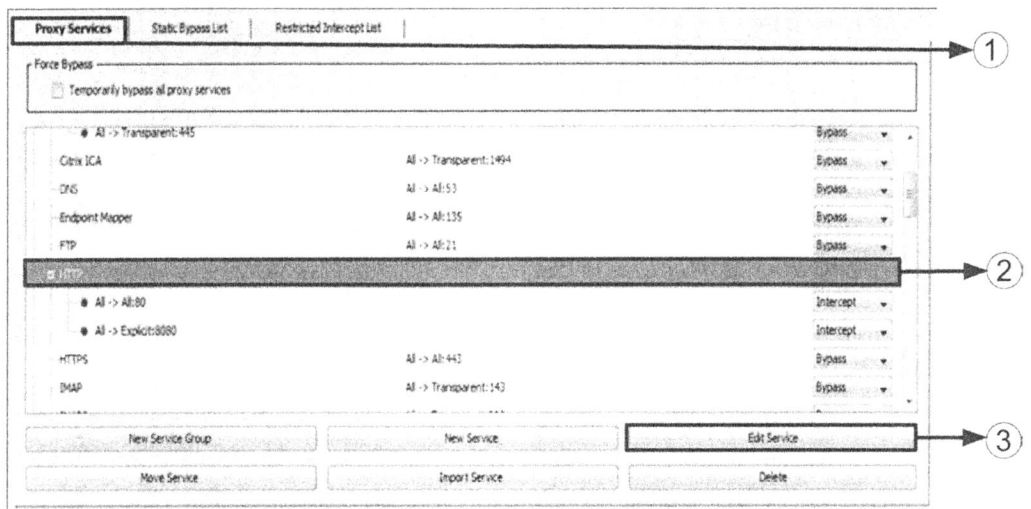

Figure 4:49 Management Services for BlueCoat Proxy SG

Click on the HTTP service group and click "Edit Service" as shown above.

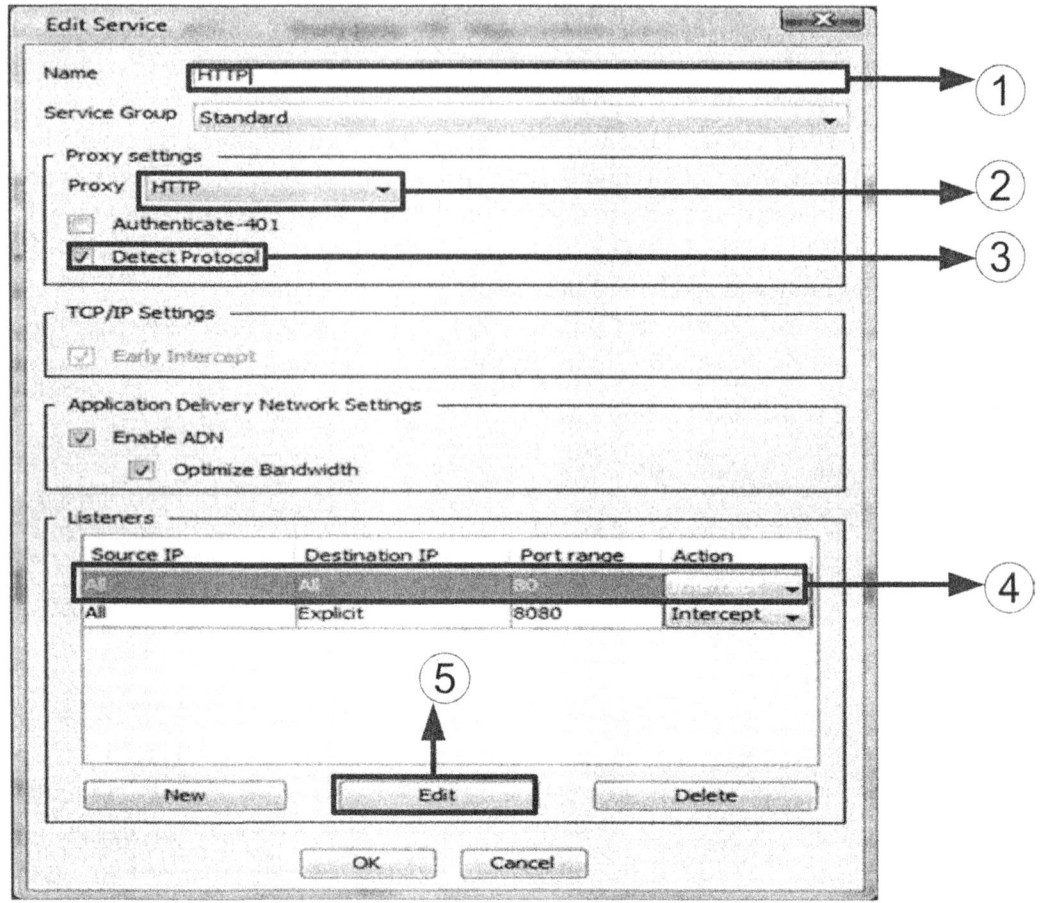

Figure 4:50 Editing services in BlueCoat Proxy SG

Each section is described as follows:

1. **Name:** Name of the service. Here it is HTTP; this is a user-defined name and can any alphanumeric characters.

2. **Service Group:** By default there are three service groups created: Standard, Bypass recommended and Tunnel recommended. Only Standard has all the services in it; the other two are empty.

3. **Proxy:** Under Proxy when you select the drop-down, you can see the different proxy services or protocols that are available. Here you intercept only HTTP protocol, so you select HTTP. The other available options are MMS, RTSP, CIFS, FTP, SOCKS, Telnet, etc.

4. **Authenticate-401:** All the traffic received by the Proxy SG in either Transparent or Explicit mode always uses transparent authentication HTTP 401 code. This setting is used in proxy-chaining mode.

5. **Detect Protocol:** You can detect the protocol type for the port that has been intercepted. If the protocol doesn't match the RFC for that specific protocol, Proxy SG holds the connections up to 30 seconds to find what nature of protocol it is and then transfers the traffic to the respected services for interception, such as sending FTP traffic through HTTP protocol.

6. **Enable ADN:** This is for WAN optimization for the ADN tunnels.

In the above **Figure 4:49 Editing services in BlueCoat Proxy SG**, select the first section and click "Edit" and the Listener section appears as shown below:

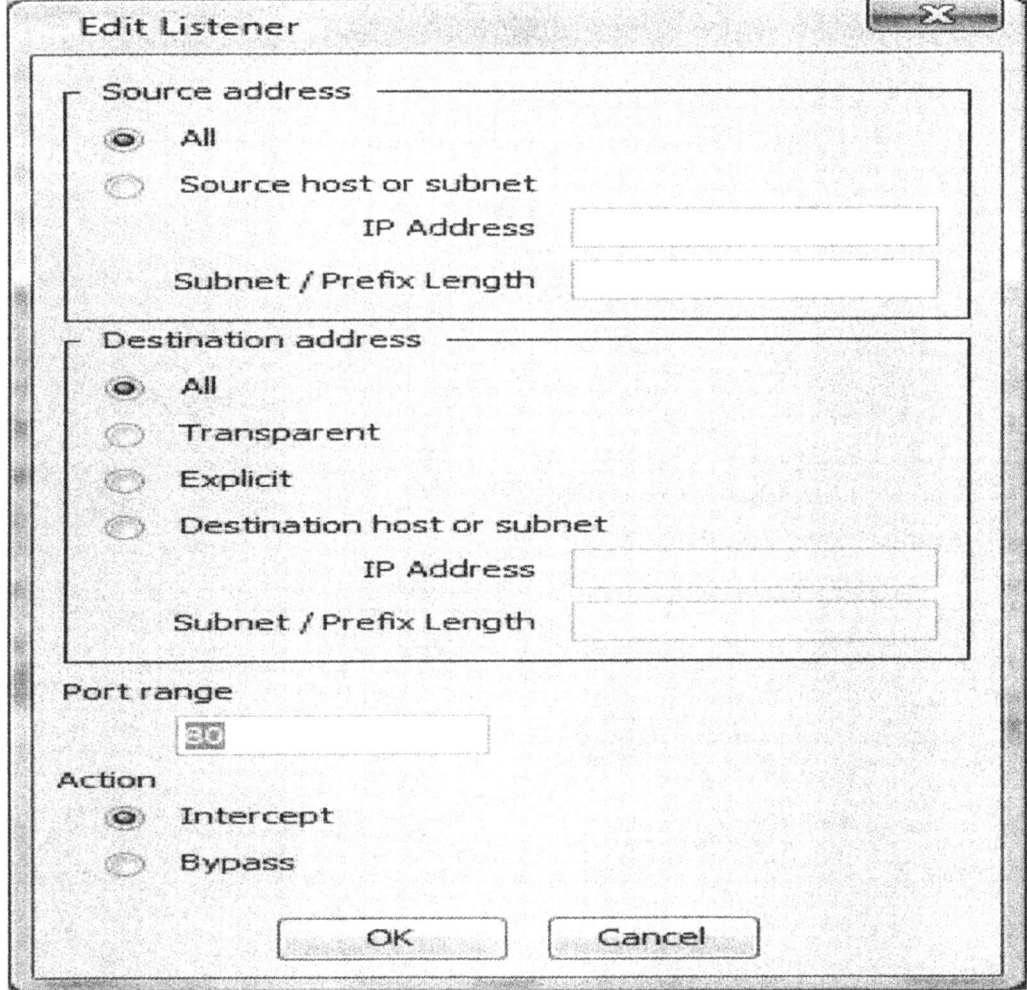

Figure 4:51 Listener service for port 80 in BlueCoat Proxy SG

As we see in the above figure, you can specify the IP address of the source that needs to use this Proxy Services, and in the Destination portion you can specify whether our can be explicit or transparent mode, but here it can be used for both mode. At the very bottom you can specify the port number that the service will listen; you can make the Proxy to listen to the traffic by selecting Intercept (the default for HTTP), or if you want to Bypass the traffic you can select the Bypass the button. The port number 80 is used when you deploy transparent interception; otherwise port 8080 should be used for explicit deployments.

Please make sure not to use port 80 for users to connect directly to the proxy in explicit mode, as it is not a good security practice.

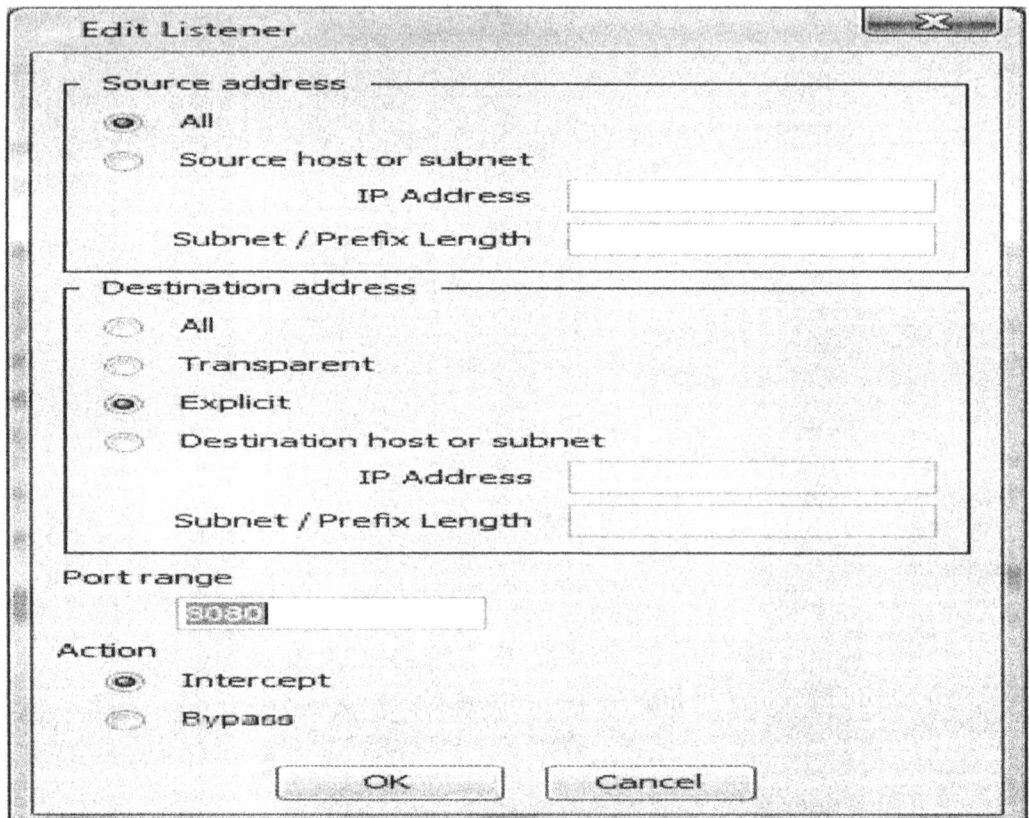

Figure 4:52   Listener service for port 8080 in BlueCoat Proxy SG

You can see that the other listener in the HTTP service group is in Explicit mode for port 8080. The above default configuration intercepts traffic for HTTP and HTTPS.

There are many pre-configured services in BlueCoat, as you can see in the standard drop-down. They include CIFS, DNS, Citrix ICA, FTP, IMAP, POP3, LDAP, Kerbros, MySQL, NFS, Oracle, RTSP, SMTP, SOCKS, IM, etc. You can intercept any of these protocols; all you have to do is change the Bypass mode to Intercept mode in the Standard group and "Apply" changes. In addition, you can also create custom groups and create the port number that the application is using and set to Intercept mode and then the proxy will start proxying the application for the configured port.

BYPASSING PROXY SERVICES

While you are troubleshooting, you can bypass individual services to check the problem or you can disable all the Proxy services (not recommended), to find if there is any problem with the application or Proxy SG, by going to Configuration → Services → Proxy Services, and checking the option "Temporarily bypass all proxy services" as shown below:

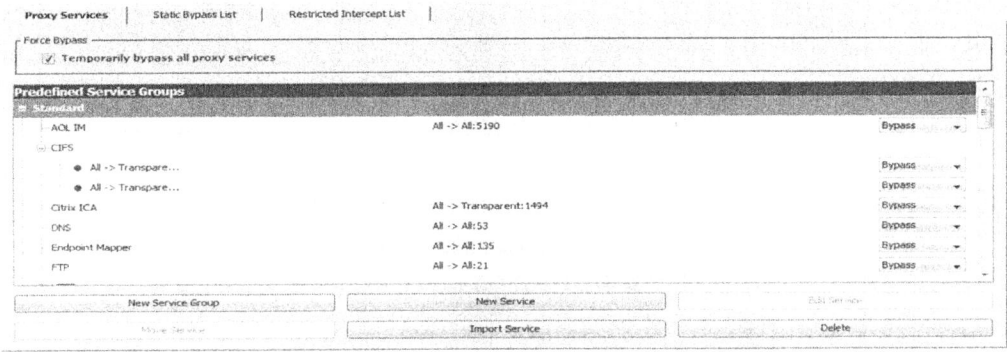

Figure 4:53 Bypassing proxy services in BlueCoat Proxy SG

Test Yourself

1. Which serial console cable do you use to connect to the BlueCoat Proxy SG and configure the initial settings?

   a. CAT6 cable
   b. Serial console cable
   c. RJ-45 cable
   d. Null modem cable

2. What are the different ways you can configure settings on a BlueCoat Proxy SG?

   a. Serial console, LCD panel, SSH, HTTPS GUI
   b. SSH, HTTPS GUI
   c. Serial console, SSH, HTTPS GUI
   d. Serial console, SSH

3. When viewing the rear portion of the Proxy SG, you see an Ethernet naming convention as 1:0. What does it infer?

   a. Adapter 0: Interface 1
   b. Adapter 1: Interface 0
   c. Interface 1: Adapter 0
   d. Interface 0: Adapter 1

4. There are two gateways, 10.10.10.100 and 10.10.10.200, configured in the Proxy SG with Group ID as 5 and weight as 5. What would be traffic between Proxy SG and the two gateways?

   a. The traffic is load balanced between the two gateways 10.10.10.100 and 10.10.10.200 from the Proxy SG.
   b. The traffic is sent to gateway 10.10.10.200 and if it is down, the traffic is forwarded to gateway 10.10.10.100 from the Proxy SG.
   c. There cannot be two gateways in the Proxy SG.
   d. The IP address with the lowest octet, 10.10.10.100, is chosen as the only default gateway, and all other configured gateways are ignored.

5. There are four gateways configured in the Proxy SG: Gateway 1, Gateway 2, Gateway 3 with Group 5 and weight 100, and Gateway 4 with Group 10 and weight 50. When will Gateway 4 activate in processing traffic?

   a. When any of the gateways 1, 2, or 3 are down, the traffic is failover to Gateway 4.
   b. When Gateway 3 is slow, the traffic is failover to Gateway 4.
   c. When all Gateway 1, Gateway 2, and Gateway 3 are all down, the traffic is failover to Gateway 4.
   d. When Gateway 1, Gateway 2, and Gateway 3 cannot handle the throughput, the traffic is failover to Gateway 4.

6. You have Internet facing-Proxy SG and you have configured only two Primary DNS servers, 4.2.2.2 and 8.8.8.8, in the same order. No Alternate DNS servers are configured, and 4.2.2.2 DNS server is down and is failing to respond DNS queries. Will the users in your network will be able to access the Internet?

   a. Yes, all my users will be able to access the Internet, as the other Primary DNS server 8.8.8.8 will be used by Proxy SG.
   b. It doesn't matter. All the users in the network can do an external query in our network, and Proxy SG DNS is not of major importance.
   c. This configuration is not correct since the Proxy SG needs to have both Primary and Alternate DNS servers configured.

    d. No, the Internet will be down. If the first DNS server in the Primary group is down, it will not failover to the second DNS in the Primary; it will only failover if there is a DNS server configured in the Alternate group.

7. **What is the default time zone in the Proxy SG?**

    a. EST
    b. GMT
    c. UTC
    d. PST

8. **You have configured DNS imputing in the proxy as corporate.com. The user tries accessing an internal website at http://perks. How will Proxy SG apply DNS imputing to it?**

    a. The user needs to type in the full URL as http://perks.corporate.com, or the user will not be able to access the site.
    b. The Proxy SG will append .corporate.com to the user's request as http://perks.corporate.com and will query the DNS server for the IP address.
    c. The Proxy SG will append .corporate.com to the user's request such as http://perks.corporate.com and forward the request to the web server.
    d. When the Proxy SG sees such request, it will query the Root DNS for the zone owner.

9. **In the interface setting, you configure the interface as "Bypass transparent interception". How will BlueCoat Proxy handle the explicit traffic?**

    a. The Proxy SG will bridge or forward all inbound traffic on this interface for transparent connections, not for explicit connections.
    b. The Proxy SG will bypass both explicit and transparent connections.
    c. The Proxy SG will bridge or forward all inbound traffic on this interface for explicit connections, not for transparent connections.
    d. The Proxy SG will allow both explicit and transparent connections.

CHAPTER 5

CONTENT FILTERING AND WEBPULSE

In this chapter we will discuss content filtering and WebPulse technology. These are some of the key features in Blue Coat, since they are the technologies used to block malicious content and are the first point of defense. They are also dynamic in nature: and they protect from all zero-day attacks, and real-time threats are updated frequently. These features reduce administrator maintenance of the box and give you ave complete control over the network and users. Content filtering and WebPulse are different technologies that are used in conjunction to provide comprehensive URL filtering.

What is Content Filtering?

Content filtering is the technique used to scan or do analysis and then allow or block the content based upon the results. In general, the term is used for email content filtering/ email filtering and web content filtering/webfiltering. email filtering is where the email gateway filters out SPAM email based on the body of the email, subject, sender, etc. Web filtering is also known as URL filtering, where access to websites are based on which category the site belongs to (categories are a collection of websites with similar characteristics; e.g., http://www.google.com is categorized as Search/Engine Portals). The term content filtering is also used in Antivirus terms since it also filters email attachments, downloads of viruses, etc.

Content Filtering terminology depends upon where the content is filtered for the traffic in the OSI model and the application type, such as email, web, virus, DOS/DDOS, worms, Trojans, Adware, Spyware, Bots, Malware, etc.

In this book when we say content filtering, we are referring to URL filtering, web filtering, or web content filtering, as Blue Coat offers webcontent filtering as a rich URL filtering for categorizing and analyzing webcontent.

About Content-Filtering Categories and Databases

A content-filtering database is a collection of predefined sets of categories provided by the content filtering vendor. We can interchangeably use the terms content filtering database or database. Here, screening refers to what websites that you can allow or deny, as per the corporation's or organization's policies. As stated earlier, a category is the collection of URL of sites, and the number of categories depends upon the vendor. The different vendors are Blue Coat Web Filter, IWF, Optenet, Proventia, SmartFilter, Websense , SurfControl, I-Filter, InterSafe, and WebWasher.

Only Websense is supported by on-box methods, as we will discuss in the later chapter.

So we know that content filtering is a method for screening access to webcontent. We will provide a simple example. In the illustration below, the site is denied by the BlueCoat proxy as per the policy:

1. Blocking Web content:

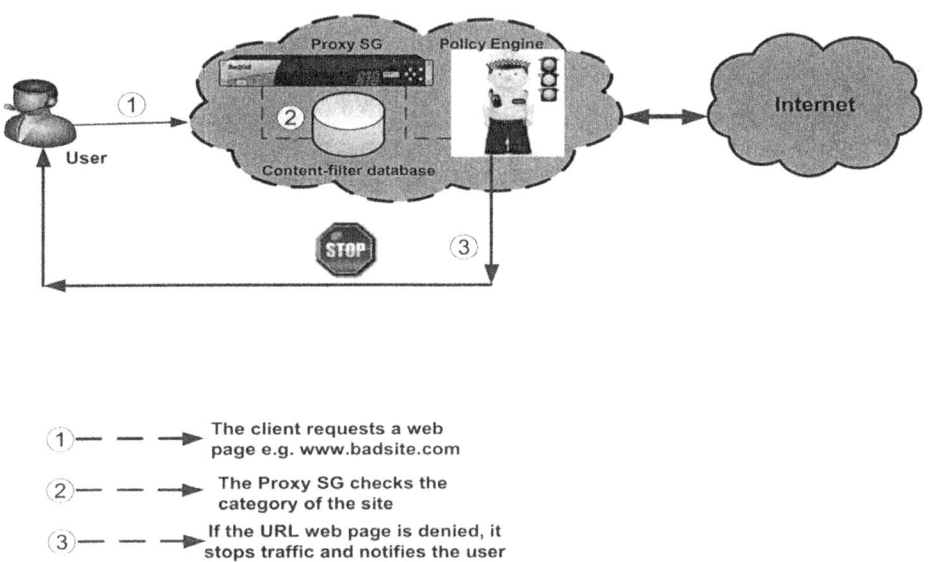

①— — — → The client requests a web
page e.g. www.badsite.com

②— — — → The Proxy SG checks the
category of the site

③— — — → If the URL web page is denied, it
stops traffic and notifies the user

Figure 5.1 Blocking Web content with Web Filters

In the above diagram, the flow of the traffic is as follows:

1. The user requests a site that is not allowed by the organization; in this case we'll say an adult content website, such as http://www.badsite.com.
2. The Proxy SG receives the request and checks the site in the content-filtering database to determine the category. Once the category is found for that site, the URL is categorized; in this case, say the category is "Pornography".
3. Then the Proxy SG checks the request in the "Policy Engine," whether this site should be allowed or blocked for the user. In this example it is blocked, since the organization blocks all "pornography content". The decision is now made only by the BlueCoat Policy Engine, not the content-filtering database, and the content is denied.
4. A notification of the denied web page is sent to the user, saying the content is blocked since the web page is in the "Pornography" category.

In the above example, only the Policy Engine makes the decision, not the content-filtering database, so the content-filtering database just lies inside the Proxy SG. Policies uses content-filtering database to filter the traffic.

One example is that, say the category "Brokage/Trading" is blocked in a corporation, since it doesn't want its employees to spend time on stockexchange. In this case w the category "Brokage/Trading" is blocked. Imagine you are working in financial organization and your job role is to compare all the stocks from different kinds of financial firms and do a statistical analysis. In this case your company policy will allow access to the "Brokage/ Trading" category for the financial and trading department. Why not for the all the users in the company? There are several different departments like sales, IT, and accounting, where for these departments you could block access to the "Brokage/Trading" category, as their job roles are not the same as for the financial and trading department. So you could go by user-based roles (very efficient) or IP-based solutions. The logic is that the database exists, but we use policies in BlueCoat to allow or deny requests.

2. Allowing Web content

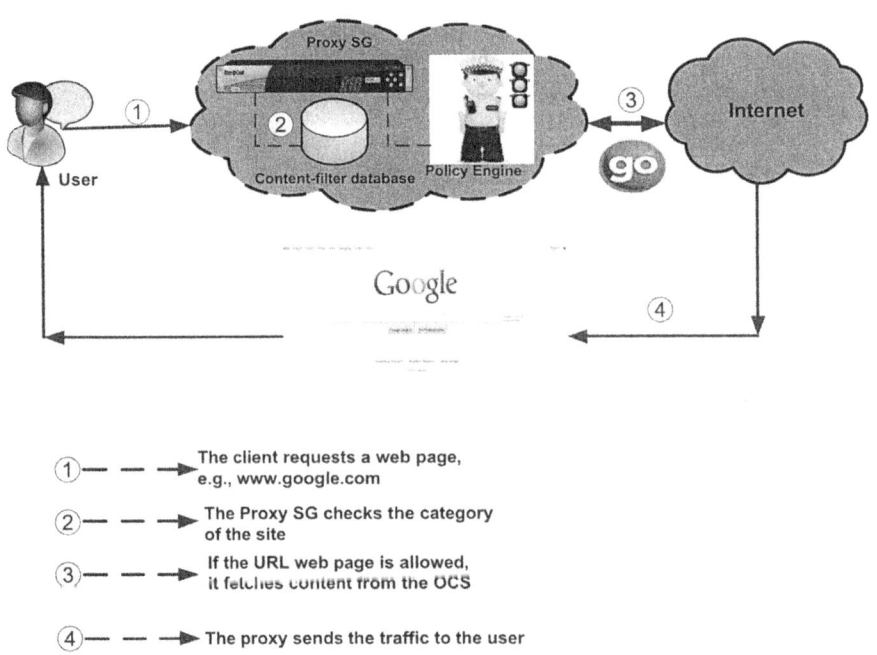

① - - → The client requests a web page, e.g., www.google.com

② - - → The Proxy SG checks the category of the site

③ - - → If the URL web page is allowed, it fetches content from the OCS

④ - - → The proxy sends the traffic to the user

Figure 5.2 Allowing Web content with Web Filters

In the above diagram, the flow of the traffic is as follows:

1. The user requests a site that is allowed by the organization; in this case let's say it's a search engine website, such as http://www.google.com.

2. The Proxy SG receives the request and checks the site in the content-filtering database to determine the category. Once the category is found for that site, the URL is categorized; in this case let's say it is "Search Engines/Portals".

3. Then the Proxy SG checks the request in the "Policy Engine," whether this www.google.com should be allowed or blocked for the user. In this example it is allowed.

4. If the object is in the cache, it serves contents from the cache or it fetches the web page from the OCS and serves back to the client. As discussed earlier, the decision is made as the cache algorithm.

Content-filtering vendors

As stated earlier, there are different vendors for content filtering. They are Blue Coat Web Filter (BCWF), IWF, Optenet, Proventia, SmartFilter, Websense , SurfControl, I-Filter, InterSafe, and WebWasher. The Proxy SG supports all the content-filter providers. In this book we will discuss BCWF and IWF. The rest we will discuss in a future book. Apart from the vendor providing the content-filtering database, you can create your own database in the Proxy SG. This means that you can override the content-filtering database and allow or deny certain sites based upon the company policies.

For example, and this is just an example, but the polices and corporate culture vary from organization to organization. Say "Sports/Recreation" is blocked, but ESPN and foxsports.com is allowed during a big event or between the lunch hours of 12:00 to 2:00 p.m. Though "Sports/Recreation" is blocked as a category, to override this you can create a local database and maintain the explicitly allowed sites. The same rule applies for the "Blocked" category. In this example, say "Audio/Video Clips" is allowed in an organization, but the policy is so strict that they need to block YouTube (which is "Audios/Video Clips" and "Open/Mixed Content"). Then they could create a local database explicitly to block YouTube.

Which content-filtering vendor should I use?

The answer totally depends upon the decision and different administrators' understanding of the content-filtering vendors technology that they use. The best of the products that are available on the market is the BCWF. This is because it has an extensive list of all the websites, dynamic categorization, real-time analysis, greater frequency of updates, and a wide variety of categories.

But you are not limited to any content filtering solutions and integration that BlueCoat provides. You can use any three content-filtering combinations that BlueCoat Proxy SG provide.

1. Vendor Content-filtering Database:

You can use any of the content-filtering databases that different vendors provide, including BCWF, which supports different third-party vendors like Proventia, SmartFilter, Optenet, Websense, Surfcontrol, I-Filter, Intersafe, or Webwasher.

2. IWF (Internet Watch Foundation):

IWF is a content-filtering database that is provided by Internet Watch Foundation (IWF), which is a non-governmental charitable body based in the United Kingdom. Its goal is to minimize the availability of "potentially criminal" Internet content, specifically images of child sexual abuse hosted anywhere, and criminally obscene adult content in the United Kingdom.

3. Local Database:

You can create your own custom content-filtering database and upload it to the Proxy SG appliance. This custom local database is just a simple text file.

As stated earlier, you could use any combination of the three or all the three; it depends on the requirement of the organization. This means, for example, that you could use BCWF, IWF, and local database; or Websense, IWF and local database; or SmartFilter and the local database, etc. But the best combination to use the full power of content-filtering is to use BCWF, IWF, and the local database.

You cannot use two vendor content-filtering databases at the same time, such as using BCWF and SmartFilter in the same Proxy SG appliance; it will not work.

On-Box Versus Off-Box
Content-filtering Solutions

There are three different ways the content filtering solutions work on the BlueCoat Proxy SG appliance.

1. On-Box content filtering solutions:

With On-Box content-filtering solutions, the content-filtering database exists on the Proxy SG appliance. Since the database resides locally inside the box, it has the best performance because the Proxy SG does not need to retrieve information from the other server in the network, which adds bandwidth and latency to all requests. There are two types of On-Box filtering:

a. Content filtering offered by the vendors:

The On-Box options offered by the vendors are Blue Coat Web Filter, IWF, Optenet, Proventia, SmartFilter, Websense (on-box), Surfcontrol, I-Filter, Intersafe, and Webwasher. All these databases reside locally in the Proxy SG appliance, and this database gets updated periodically and depends upon the configuration that you set on the box.

Only database gets updated from all vendor in the Internet for new updates, but the policy using the database that is locally will be always checked for all requests.

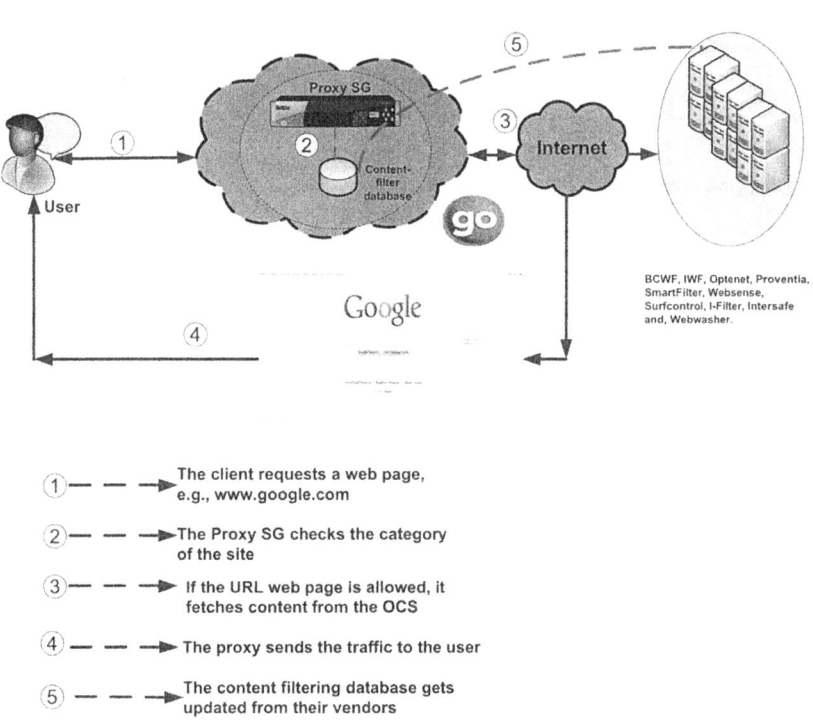

1— — → The client requests a web page,
e.g., www.google.com

2— — → The Proxy SG checks the category
of the site

3— — → If the URL web page is allowed, it
fetches content from the OCS

4— — → The proxy sends the traffic to the user

5— — → The content filtering database gets
updated from their vendors

Figure 5.3 On-Box content filtering

b. Custom-built local database

The custom-built local database that every administrator can configure which resides locally in the Proxy SG. The custom local database can be built locally inside in the Proxy SG with policy files or downloaded from a web server. It can be stored locally and the freshness of database can be updated frequently based on the configuration that you set from the local web server.

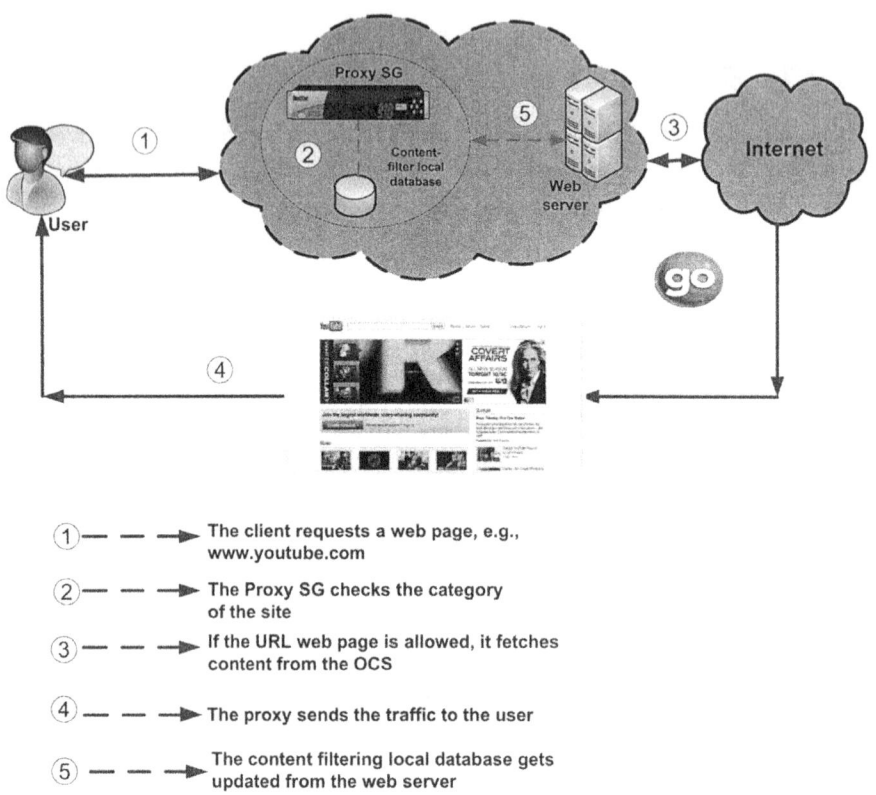

1 — — → The client requests a web page, e.g., www.youtube.com

2 — — → The Proxy SG checks the category of the site

3 — — → If the URL web page is allowed, it fetches content from the OCS

4 — — → The proxy sends the traffic to the user

5 — — → The content filtering local database gets updated from the web server

Figure 5.4 Custom-built local database

2. Off-Box content-filtering solutions:

In off-box content-filtering solutions, the content-filtering database does not exist on the Proxy SG appliance. The Proxy SG contacts servers in the intranet or in the Internet, to provide URL filtering. The vendors use different methods or protocols to communicate with vendors like Websense (WISP protocol), WebWasher (ICAP), and BlueCoat WebPulse protocol (DRTR service). As this solution introduces more latency and bandwidth into the network, it is not a recommended method by BlueCoat as a regular content-filtering solution. For example, if BlueCoat Proxy SG needs to allow www.google.com, you know it is a search engine and the policy allows it. But imagine if the URL is not categorized, Blue Coat needs to contact every time contact the server in the LAN/Internet for URL categorization, and thereby a lot of delay is introduced. But for a real-time analysis Off-Box is the best mechanism, it is a very good approach. Imagine that a URL is not categorized and needs to be categorized before it is allowed. In this scenario BlueCoat uses a technology for real-time cloud technology called WebPulse, where all the new websites that are not categorized and that come everyday get categorized using BlueCoat WebPulse services. This is the best method for real-time analysis, but not for regular content categorization. We will discuss WebPulse later in this chapter.

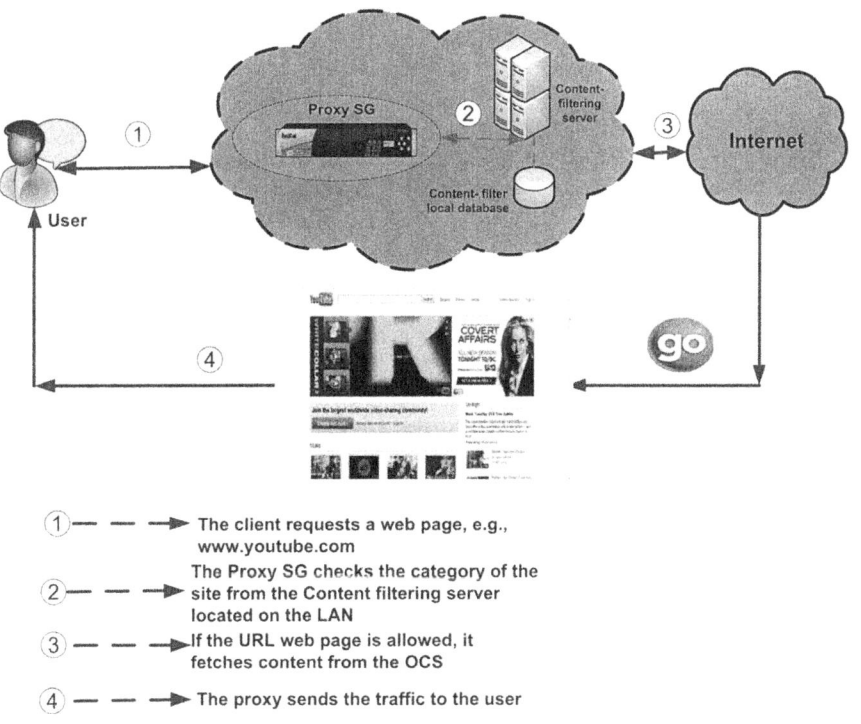

① — — → The client requests a web page, e.g., www.youtube.com

② — — → The Proxy SG checks the category of the site from the Content filtering server located on the LAN

③ — — → If the URL web page is allowed, it fetches content from the OCS

④ — — → The proxy sends the traffic to the user

Figure 5.5 Off-Box content filtering

3. Hybrid solutions:

As the name states, these are a combination of On-Box solutions and Off-Box solutions. The content-filtering database exists on the BlueCoat ProxySG appliance, and an off-box real-time rating service is available for URLs that are not included in the on-box database. This hybrid solution is available with Blue Coat Web Filter and the WebPulse service. While Blue Coat Web Filter provides the on-box database, the WebPulse service provides real-time/dynamic categorization of new or lesser-known websites.

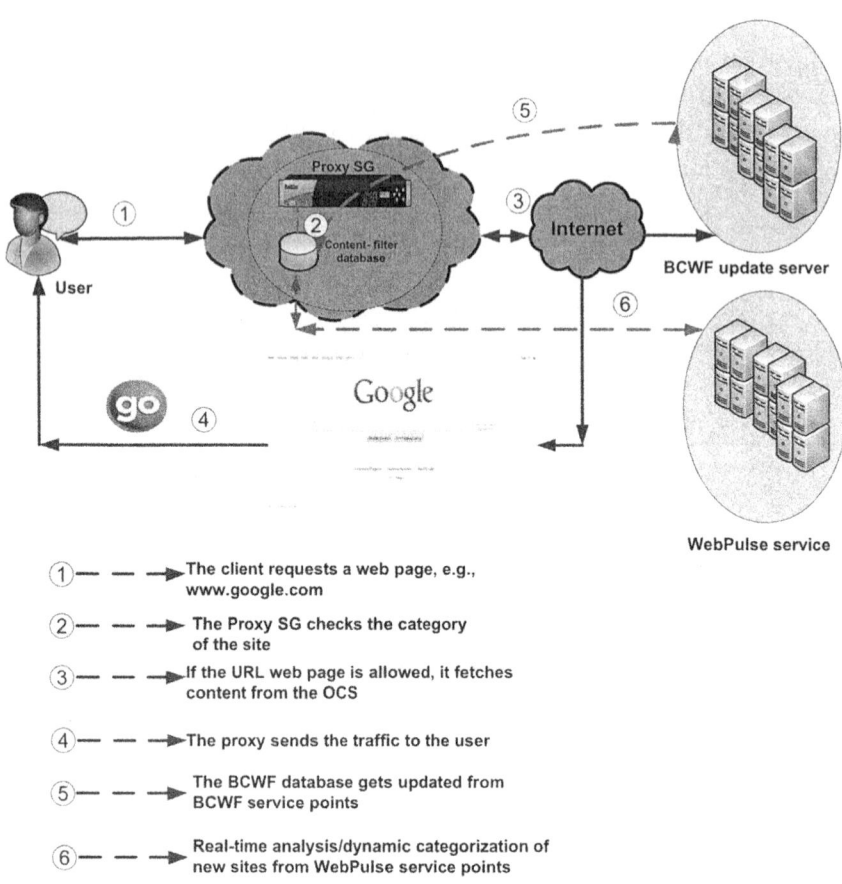

The client requests a web page, e.g., www.google.com

① — — → The client requests a web page, e.g., www.google.com

② — — → The Proxy SG checks the category of the site

③ — — → If the URL web page is allowed, it fetches content from the OCS

④ — — → The proxy sends the traffic to the user

⑤ — — → The BCWF database gets updated from BCWF service points

⑥ — — → Real-time analysis/dynamic categorization of new sites from WebPulse service points

Figure 5.6 Hybrid solutions

In this chapter we will discuss only BCWF, IWF, WebPulse, and the local database, as this is the best combination for deploying content filtering in any network and the best security practice.

BlueCoat Web Filter (BCWF)

So what is BCWF? BCWF is the web or URL solution offered by BlueCoat systems which works in conjunction with WebPulse (cloud service/off-box filtering) to offer a versatile URL-filtering solution. Some folks say that BCWF takes a hybrid approach in providing its content-filtering solution. In a way this is true, but remember that BCWF and Web Pulse are two different technologies that work together to provide full comprehensive URL filtering, as Web Pulse is cloud service and DRTR is the service that is used to rate the sites in real time.

BCWF provides a On-Box filtering solution, which a software or component that is installed in the BlueCoat proxy appliance. The administrators could write policies to allow or deny the traffic based on categories that are provided by the BCWF.

What is so special about BCWF?

BCWF has almost 80 categories, supports 50 + languages, rates almost 7 billion rating requests per day, has a user community of 75 million, and has 10,000 new or unique URLs per day. The data could be summarized as follows:

Features	Quantity
Categories	80+
Languages	50+
User community	75 million
Categorization per day	10,000 URL /day
Rating requests	7 billion ratings per day
URL list	100 million

Table 5.1 BCWF features

There are almost 80 categories in BCWF, listed below with explanations:

CATEGORIES	EXPLANATION
Abortion	Sites that provide information or arguments in favor of or against abortion, describe abortion procedures, offer help in obtaining or avoiding abortion, or provide information on the effects, or lack thereof, of abortion.
Adult/Mature Content	Sites that contain material of adult nature that do not necessarily contain excessive violence, sexual content, or nudity. These sites include very profane or vulgar content and sites that are not appropriate for children.

Alcohol	Sites that offer for sale, promote, glorify, review or in any way advocate the use or creation of alcoholic beverages, including but not limited to beer, wine, and hard liquors. This does not include sites that sell alcohol as a subset of other products such as restaurants or grocery stores.
Alternative Sexuality/ Lifestyles	Sites that provide information, promote, or cater to alternative sexual expressions in their myriad forms. Includes but is not limited to the full range of nontraditional sexual practices, interests, orientations or fetishes. This category does not include sites that are sexually gratuitous in nature which would typically fall under the Pornography category, nor does it include lesbian, gay, bisexual, transgender or any sites that speak to one's sexual identity.
Alternative Spirituality/ Belief	Sites that promote and provide information on alternative spiritual and nonreligious beliefs such as atheism, agnosticism, witchcraft, and Satanism. Occult practices, voodoo rituals, or any other form of mysticism are represented here. This includes sites that endorse or offer methods, means of instruction, or other resources to affect or influence real events through the use of spells, incantations, curses, or magic powers. This category includes sites that discuss or deal with paranormal or unexplained events.
Art/Culture	Sites that nurture and promote cultural understanding of fine art including but not limited to sculpture, paintings, and other visual art forms, literature, music, dance, ballet, and performance art, and the venues or foundations that support, foster, or house them such as museums, galleries, symphonies, and the like. Sites that provide a learning environment or cultural awareness outside of the strictures of formalized education, such as planetariums, are included under this heading.
Auctions	Sites that support the offering and purchasing of goods between individuals. This does not include classified advertisements.
Audio/Video Clips	Sites that provide streams or downloads of audio or video clips—typically 15 minutes or less in length. This also includes sites that provide downloaders and players for audio and video clips.
Blogs/Personal Pages	Sites that primarily offer access to personal pages and blogs. This classification includes but is not limited to content that shares a common domain such as web space made available by an ISP or some other hosting service. Personal home pages and blogs tend to be dynamic in nature and their content may vary from innocuous to extreme.
Brokerage/Trading	Sites that provide or advertise trading of securities and management of investment assets (online or offline). This also includes insurance sites as well as sites that offer financial investment strategies, quotes, and news.

Business/Economy	Sites devoted to business firms, business information, economics, marketing, business management, and entrepreneurship. This does not include sites that perform services defined in another category (such as information technology companies, or companies that sell travel services). This also does not include shopping sites.
Charitable Organizations	Sites that foster volunteerism for charitable causes. This also encompasses nonprofit associations that cultivate philanthropic or relief efforts. Does not include organizations that attempt to influence legislation as a significant portion of their activities or organizations that campaign for, contribute to, or affiliate with political organizations or candidates.
Chat/Instant Messaging	Sites that provide chat, text messaging (SMS), or instant messaging capabilities or client downloads.
Computers/Internet	Sites that sponsor or provide information on computers, technology, the Internet, and technology-related organizations and companies.
Content Servers	Servers that provide commercial hosting for a variety of content such as images and media files. These servers are typically used in conjunction with other webservers to optimize content retrieval speeds.
Education	Sites that offer educational information, distance learning, or trade school information or programs. This also includes sites that are sponsored by schools, educational facilities, faculty, or alumni groups.
Email	Sites offering web-based email services, such as online email reading and mailing list services.
Entertainment	Sites that provide information on or promote mass entertainment media including but not limited to film, film trailers, television, home entertainment, music, comics, entertainment-oriented periodicals, reviews, interviews, fan clubs, and celebrity gossip. This also includes wedding or other photography sites of a non-adult nature.

Extreme	Sites that are extreme in nature and are not suitable for general consumption. This includes sites that revel and glorify in gore, human or animal suffering, scatological or other aberrant behaviors, perversities or debaucheries. It includes visual or written depictions deemed to be of an unusually horrific nature. These are salacious sites bereft of historical context, educational value or artistic merit created solely to debase, dehumanize or shock. Examples would include necrophilia, cannibalism, scat, and amputee fetish sites.

Financial Services	Sites that provide or advertise banking services (online or offline) or other types of financial information, such as loans. This does not include sites that offer market information, brokerage or trading services.
For Kids	Sites designed specifically for children. This category is typically used in conjunction with other categories—it is not a stand-alone category.
Gambling	Sites where a user can place a bet or participate in a betting pool, participate in a lottery, or receive information, assistance, recommendations, or training in such activities. This category does not include sites that sell gambling-related products/ machines or sites for offline casinos and hotels, unless they meet one of the above requirements.
Games	Sites that support playing or downloading video games, computer games, or electronic games. This includes sites with information, tips, or advice on such games or how to obtain cheat codes, and also includes magazines dedicated to computerized games and sites that support or host online sweepstakes and giveaways.
Government/Legal	Sites sponsored by or that provide information on government, government agencies, and government services such as taxation and emergency services. This includes sites that discuss or explain laws of various governmental entities. This also includes sites that advertise legal services, lawyers for hire, adoption services, information about adoption, immigration information, and immigration services.
Greeting Cards	Sites that facilitate the sending of electronic greeting cards, animated cards, or similar electronic messages typically used to mark an event or occasion.
Hacking	Sites that distribute, promote, or provide hacking tools and/ or information which may help gain unauthorized access to computer systems and/or computerized communication systems. Hacking encompasses instructions on illegal or questionable tactics, such as creating viruses, distributing cracked or pirated software, or distributing other protected intellectual property.

Health	Sites that provide advice and information on general health such as fitness and well-being, personal health or medical services, drugs, alternative and complementary therapies, medical information about ailments, dentistry, optometry, general psychiatry, self-help, and support organizations dedicated to a disease or condition.

Humor/Jokes	Sites that primarily focus on comedy, jokes, fun, etc. This may include sites containing jokes of adult or mature nature. Sites containing humorous Adult/Mature content also have an Adult/Mature category rating.
Illegal Drugs	Sites that promote, offer, sell, supply, encourage, or otherwise advocate the illegal use, cultivation, manufacture, or distribution of drugs, pharmaceuticals, intoxicating plants or chemicals, and their related paraphernalia.
Illegal/Questionable	Sites that advocate or give advice on performing acts that are illegal or of questionable legality such as service theft, evading law enforcement, fraud, burglary techniques, and plagiarism. This also includes sites that promote scams or that provide or sell legally questionable educational materials such as term papers.
Internet Telephony	Sites that facilitate Internet telephony or provide Internet telephony services such as voice over IP (VOIP).
Intimate Apparel/ Swimsuit	Sites that contain images or offer the sale of swimsuits or intimate apparel or other types of suggestive clothing. This does not include sites selling undergarments as a subsection of other products offered.
Job Search/Careers	Sites that provide assistance in finding employment and tools for locating prospective employers.
LGBT	Sites that provide information regarding, support, promote, or cater to one's sexual orientation or gender identity including but not limited to lesbian, gay, bisexual, and transgender sites. This category does not include sites considered sexually gratuitous in nature that would typically fall under the Pornography category.
Media Sharing	Sites that allow sharing of media (e.g., photo sharing) and have a low risk of including objectionable content such as adult or pornographic material.
Military	Sites that promote or provide information on military branches or armed services.

News/Media	Sites that primarily report information or comments on current events or contemporary issues of the day. This category also includes news radio stations and news magazines but does not include sites that can be rated in other categories.
Newsgroups/Forums	Sites that primarily offer access to newsgroups, messaging or bulletin board systems, or group blogs where participants can post comments, hold discussions, or seek opinions or expertise on a variety of topics.

Non-viewable	Servers with non-malicious, non-offensive content or resources used by applications, but not directly viewable by web browsers. Includes but is not limited to web analytics sites (such as visitor tracking and ranking sites) and content filtering systems.
Nudity	Sites containing nude or seminude depictions of the human body. These depictions are not necessarily sexual in intent or effect but may include sites containing nude paintings or photo galleries of artistic nature. This category also includes nudist or naturist sites that contain pictures of nude individuals.
Online Meetings	Sites that facilitate online meetings or provide online meeting, conferencing, or training services.
Online Storage	Sites that provide secure, encrypted, off-site backup and restoration of personal data. These online repositories are typically used to store, organize and share videos, music, movies, photos, documents, and other electronically formatted information. Sites that fit this criteria essentially act as your personal hard drive on the Internet.
Open/Mixed Content	Sites with generally non-offensive content but that also have potentially objectionable content such as adult or pornographic material that is not organized so that it can be classified separately. Sites that explicitly exclude offensive content are not included in this category.
Pay to Surf	Sites that pay users in the form of cash or prizes for clicking on or reading specific links, email, or webpages.
Peer-to-Peer (P2P)	Sites that distribute software to facilitate the direct exchange of files between users. P2P includes software that enables file search and sharing across a network without dependence on a central server.
Personals/Dating	Sites that promote interpersonal relationships.

Phishing	Sites that are designed to appear as a legitimate bank or retailer with the intent to fraudulently capture sensitive data (e.g., credit card numbers, PIN numbers).
Placeholders	Sites that are under construction, parked domains, search-bait or otherwise generally have no useful value.
Political/Activist Groups	Sites sponsored by or that provide information on political parties, special interest groups, or any organization that promotes change or reform in public policy, public opinion, social practice, or economic activities.
Pornography	Sites that contain sexually explicit material for the purpose of arousing a sexual or prurient interest.
Potentially Unwanted Software	Sites that distribute software that is not malicious but may be unwanted within an organization such as intrusive adware and hoaxes.
Proxy Avoidance	Sites that provide information on how to bypass proxy server features or gain access to URLs in any way that bypasses the proxy server. This category includes any service which will allow a person to bypass the Blue Coat filtering system, such as anonymous surfing services.

Radio/Audio Streams	Sites that provide streams or downloads of radio, music, or other audio content—typically more than 15 minutes in length.
Real Estate	Sites that provide information on renting, buying, or selling real estate or properties. This also includes vacation property rentals such as time-shares and vacation condos.
Reference	Sites containing personal, professional, or educational reference, including online dictionaries, maps, censuses, almanacs, library catalogues, genealogy-related sites, and scientific information.
Religion	Sites that promote and provide information on conventional or unconventional religious or quasi-religious subjects, as well as churches, synagogues, or other houses of worship. This does not include sites about alternative forms of spirituality or ideology such as witchcraft or atheist beliefs (Alternative Spirituality/Belief).
Remote Access Tools	Sites that primarily focus on providing information about and/or methods that enable authorized remote access to and use of a desktop computer or private network.

Restaurants/Dining/Food	Sites that list, review, discuss, advertise, and promote food, catering, dining services, cooking, and recipes.
Search Engines/Portals	Sites that support searching the Internet, indices, and directories.
Sex Education	Sites that provide information (sometimes graphic) on reproduction, sexual development, safe sex practices, sexuality, birth control, tips for better sex, and sexual enhancement products.
Shopping	Sites that provide or advertise the means to obtain goods or services with either prices listed or a clear way to order. This does not include sites that can be classified in other categories (such as vehicles or weapons).
Social Networking	Sites that enable people to connect with others to form an online community. Typically members describe themselves in personal webpage profiles and form interactive networks, linking them with other members based on common interests or acquaintances. Instant messaging, file sharing and weblogs (blogs) are common features of Social Networking sites. Note: These sites may contain offensive material in the community-created content. Sites in this category are also referred to as "virtual communities" or "online communities." **This category does not include more narrowly** focused sites, like those that specifically match descriptions for Personals/Dating sites or Business sites.

Society/Daily Living	Sites that provide information on matters of daily life. This includes but is not limited to pet care, home improvement, fashion/beauty tips, hobbies, and other tasks that comprise everyday life. It does not include sites relating to entertainment, sports, jobs, personal pages, or other topics that already have a specific category.
Software Downloads	Sites that are dedicated to the electronic download of software for any type of computer or mobile device, whether for payment or at no charge.
Sports/Recreation	Sites that promote or provide information about spectator sports or recreational activities. This does not include sites dedicated to hobbies such as gardening, collecting, board games, scrapbooking, quilting, etc.
Spyware Effects/Privacy Concerns	Sites to which spyware (as defined in the Spyware/Malware Sources category) reports its findings or from which it alone downloads advertisements. This does not contain sites that serve advertisements Spyware/Malware Sources for other webpages in addition to spyware advertisements; only those sites uniquely used by spyware. Includes sites that contain serious privacy issues, such as "phone home" sites to which software can connect and send user information; and sites to which browser hijackers redirect users. This usually does not include sites that can be categorized as Spyware/Malware Sources.

Spyware/Malware Sources	Sites that host or distribute spyware and other malware or whose purpose for existence is as part of the spyware and malware ecosystem. Spyware and malware are defined as software that takes control of a computer, modifies computer settings, or collects or reports personal information without the permission of the end user. This includes software that misrepresents itself by tricking users to download or install it, or to enter personal information. This includes sites that perform drive-by downloads; browser hijackers; dialers; any program that modifies your browser homepage, bookmarks, or security settings; and keyloggers. This also includes any software that bundles spyware (as defined above) as part of its offering. Information collected or reported is "personal" if it contains uniquely identifying data, such as email addresses, name, social security number, IP address, etc. A site is not classified as spyware if the user is reasonably notified that the software will perform these actions (e.g., it alerts that it will send personal information, be installed, or thatit will log keystrokes).
Spyware/Malware Sources	Sites that host or distribute spyware and other malware or whose purpose for existence is as part of the spyware and malware ecosystem. Spyware and malware are defined as software that takes control of a computer, modifies computer settings, or collects or reports personal information without the permission of the end user. This includes software that misrepresents itself by tricking users to download or install it, or to enter personal information. This includes sites that perform drive-by downloads; browser hijackers; dialers; any program that modifies your browser homepage, bookmarks, or security settings; and keyloggers. This also includes any software that bundles spyware (as defined above) as part of its offering. Information collected or reported is "personal" if it contains uniquely identifying data, such as email addresses, name, social security number, IP address, etc. A site is not classified as spyware if the user is reasonably notified that the software will perform these actions (e.g., it alerts that it will send personal information, be installed, or that it will log keystrokes).
Suspicious	Sites considered to have suspicious content and/or intent that poses an elevated security or privacy risk. This categorization is determined by analysis of web reputation factors. This also includes sites that are part of the weband email spam ecosystem. If a site is determined to be clearly malicious or benign, it will be placed in a different category.
Tobacco	Sites that offer for sale, promote, glorify, review or in any way advocate the use or creation of tobacco or tobacco-related products including but not limited to cigarettes, pipes, cigars and chewing tobacco. This does not include sites that sell tobacco as a subset of other products such as grocery stores.

Translation	Sites that allow translation of text (words, phrases, webpages, etc.) between various languages or that can be used to identify a language.
Travel	Sites that promote or provide opportunity for travel planning, including finding and making travel reservations, sharing of travel experiences (pro or con), vehicle rentals, descriptions of travel destinations, or promotions for hotels/casinos or other travel related accommodations. Mass transit information including but not limited to posting of schedules, fares, or any other public transportation-related data are also included in this category.
TV/Video Streams	Sites that provide streams or downloads of television, movie, or other video content—typically more than 15 minutes in length.
Vehicles	Sites that provide information on or promote vehicles, boats, or aircraft, including sites that support online purchase of vehicles or parts.

Violence/Hate/Racism	Sites that depict extreme physical harm to people, animals, or property, or that advocate or provide instructions on how to cause such harm. This also includes sites that advocate or depict hostility or aggression toward, or denigrate an individual or group on the basis of race, religion, gender, nationality, ethnic origin, or other involuntary characteristics, and includes content that glorifies self-mutilation or suicide.
Weapons	Sites that sell, review, or describe weapons such as guns, knives, or martial arts devices, or provide information on their use, accessories, or other modifications. This does not include sites providing information on BB guns, paintball guns, black powder rifles, target shooting, or bows and arrows, unless the site also meets one of the above requirements. Also does not include sites that promote collecting weapons, or groups that either support or oppose weapons use.
Web Advertisements	Sites that provide online advertisements or banners. This does not include advertising servers that serve adult-oriented advertisements.
Web Applications	Sites with interactive, Web-based office/business applications. This excludes email, chat/IM or other sites that have a specific content category.
Web Hosting	Sites of organizations that provide top-level domain pages, as well as webcommunities or hosting services.

Table 5.2 BCWF categories

In the future the following three categories will be renamed for clarity:

1. "Illegal/Questionable" will become "Scam/Questionable/Illegal".
2. "Spyware Effects/Privacy Concerns" will become "Malicious Outbound Data/Botnets".
3. "Spyware/Malware Sources" will become "Malicious Sources".

And there four new categories will be added in the future:

1. "Spam"
2. "Dynamic DNS Host"
3. "Child Pornography"
4. "Informational"

> If you find a category that is mis-categorized, you can go to http://sitereview.bluecoat.com/ and change the category. Just fill in the form and you will be able send a review to the BlueCoat team and they will manually check and categorize the site appropriately.

CONFIGURING BCWF DATABASE:

The steps to configure the Proxy SG for installing the Proxy SG of BCWF database are as follows:

1. Log in to the management console of the Proxy SG, via https://ipaddressofthcproxy:8082.
2. Go to Configuration → Content filtering → General, check the box next to BlueCoat WebFilter, and select the Radio button for "Llookup mode" Always (Default), else you could select the "Uncategorized" radio buttonnext to it.

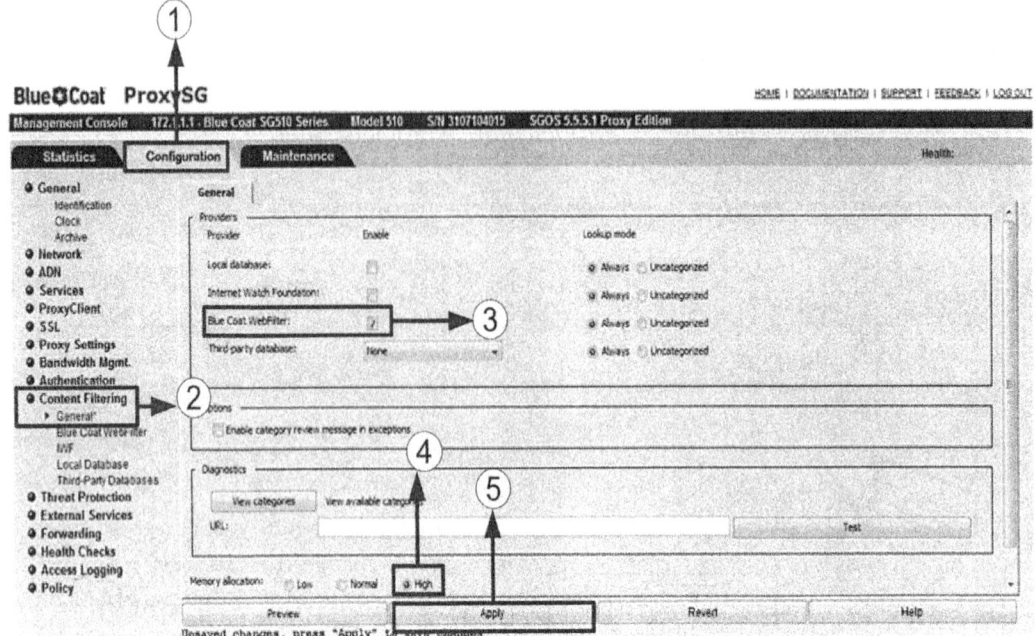

Figure 5.7 Enabling BCWF in BlueCoat Proxy SG

3. At the very bottom of the screen, there is a portion named "Memory allocation". Make sure "High" is selected here, because if you use content filtering for a high transaction rate, this option will allow you to run content filtering efficiently.

4. Apply changes.

5. Then go to Configuration → Content Filtering → BlueCoat WebFilter and enter the username and password that was given by BlueCoat while registering or purchasing the BCWF. If it is the first time you are configuring the BCWF database on a new Proxy SG, hit the "Download Now" button. The Proxy SG will start downloading the BCWF database from the BlueCoat BUFF database.

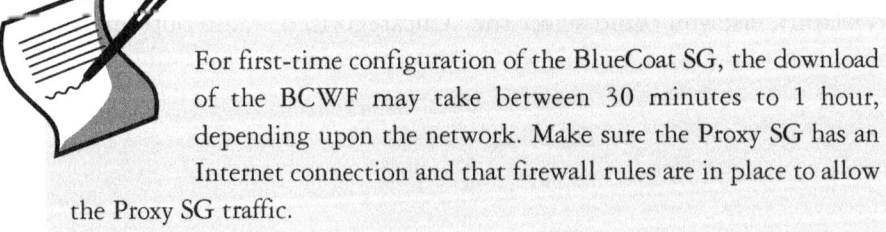

For first-time configuration of the BlueCoat SG, the download of the BCWF may take between 30 minutes to 1 hour, depending upon the network. Make sure the Proxy SG has an Internet connection and that firewall rules are in place to allow the Proxy SG traffic.

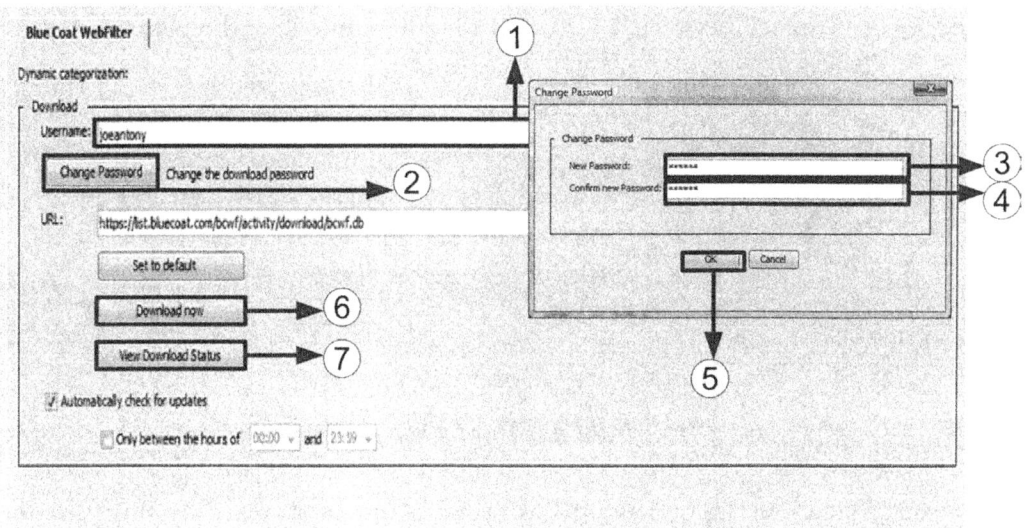

Figure 5.8 Credentials and database download for BCWF

In the above figure, the URL is set to the default location where the local BCWF database can download the updated BCWF database. This is the default; don't change it, unless if you have you proxy to be internal and doen't hasInternet access, you can point it to the local web server, where the updated BCWF database is located.

6. Select the update interval in the very bottom of the screen. The default is five minutes, which is ideal for security purposes, as you always have total control of all sites that is accessed by the users in the Internet, because the sites are always categorized correctly and then policies is applied dynamically frequently. Select "Automatic check for updates", which is the default option. There are situations where the network traffic and bandwidth are a problem, so you can change the automatic updates settings to off hours, where the traffic in the network is minimum, so that you can download the updated BCWF from BlueCoat. To change the default, check the option "Only between the hours of", enter the time, and "Apply" changes as shown below:

Figure 5.9 Time interval for BCWF download

The updates are checked between 12:00 a.m. to 2:00 a.m., when the network traffic is low.

Here we have discussed how to download the database, license it, set update intervals, etc. We have applied policies for this, and we will discuss how to apply different categories to users in the VPM chapter.

WebPulse

WebPulse is a cloud service and an off-box solution that is provided by BlueCoat for a real-time analysis for the websites that are categorized as unrated or when malicious event is found. When we say a site is unrated, it refers to the fact that there are many new sites launched every day. Web Pulse tries to categorize all these sites every day. Let's say a popular site, such as http://www.microsoft .com/downloads/tools/IE7, is categorized as "Computers/Internet", and someone hacks it and replaces the original file with a malicious one. The Proxy SG then sends this information about the malicious URL, which was detected by the Proxy AV, to Web Pulse (it sends it to Proxy SG after flagging). This information comes from various customers throughout the globe and is categorized as "Spyware/Malware Sources". Remember that the primary domain http://www.microsoft. com is still "Computers/Internet", but the download path is flagged as malicious.

WebPulse gets inputs from multiple enterprise gateways and client systems and then creates a powerful computing grid. The computing grid consists of BlueCoat Webfilter installed on Proxy SG, Cache Flow appliance, Proxy One, K9, and Proxy Client, which provide a large input data about websites that are not categorized, virus detected in websites, unrated websites etc... to the grid for computation. WebPulse analyzses all these inputs and then categorizes and updates the BCWF master database, which then gets pushed to all the clients and gateways periodically, making the URL filtering from BlueCoat more powerful and robust.

By default, WebPulse or DRTR service is enabled to dynamically categorize unrated and new webcontent for immediate enforcement of policy. You could run DRTR in the background if there is a response/performance problem; but if you disable DRTR, it disables proactive threat detection, and content and reputation ratings.

WebPulse offers two services to the customers:

1. DRTR
2. Malware feedback or Proactive Threat detection

All the above configurations and settings are applicable to BlueCoat SG Ver. 5.5.5.1. The versions before that have a separate menu of configurations.

1. DRTR or Dynamic Categorization

The dynamic categorization service analyzes and categorizes new or previously unknown URLs which are not in the on-box Blue Coat WebFilter database. The terms DRTR and dynamic categorization are used interchangeably, but DRTR is the technology that is used while dynamic categorization is the methodology of how you achieve this. So using the terms interchangeably is not a mistake, but try understanding the difference will help in reading this chapter and applying the right terms.

DRTR can be in processed in two modes:

a. Real time mode
b. Background mode.

a. Real-ime mode

In real-time mode, for the URL that is not categorized, WebPulse can offer a real-time analysis via DRTR technology to categorize the sites. After WebPulse sends the category, BlueCoat makes the decision based upon the policies that are implemented.

In real-time mode there will be a small fractional delay in serving the URL, since it has to go through the WebPulse cloud in the Internet and get a reply from the query. But in a real scenario, 95% of the sites are categorized. So of the traffic that is served by the Proxy SG, 95% is served without any delay. Only 5% of the sites are uncategorized or unknown sites that go through the DRTR process, and usually the maximum time taken to serve the site is 6 seconds when using the DRTR. But if you find there is a performance problem in the network due to DRTR and you want to disable the real-time rating, you could always run the deamon in Background mode.

In DRTR, when a site is not categorized, it can be any of the following not rated categories :

1. None
2. Pending
3. a. Unavailable
    b. Unlicensed

1. None

When a site categorizedas "None", it could be due to any of the following:

a. DRTR is disabled.

b. DRTR is enabled; the ProxySG appliance did not get a response from the WebPulse service.

c. DRTR is enabled; the WebPulse service was unable to retrieve the requested URL in a timely manner.

d. DRTR is enabled; the WebPulse service cannot categorize the request with high confidence.

2. Pending

When a site categorizedas "Pending", it could be due to either of the following:

1. If DRTR runs in background, the ProxySG appliance continues to service the URL request without waiting for a response from WebPulse.

2. If DRTR runs in background, if a response is not received in a timely manner or the request results cannot be categorized, nothing is added to the rating cache.

3.a. Unavailable

There is a problem in the local BCWF database due to software corruption or network problems for accessing the WebPulse service.

3.b. Unlicensed

There is a problem with the BCWF license, due to temporary license or expiration issues.

Remember, when the DRTR returns "None", that is, it cannot categorize the site at the moment, the Proxy SG could allow or deny the access; this is based upon the policies built into the system. In the next chapter when we discuss VPM, we will show how this could be implemented through policies.

DRTR dynamic categorization has three states:

1. Enabled : By default, this state attempts to categorize sites.

2. Disabled: If disabled, the Proxy SG does not contact WebPulse service, regardless of the policy installed.

3. Suspended: The categorization from the database continues, but the service is no longer employed. This mainly occurs when the installed database is over 30 days old due to the expiration of BCWF download credentials or network problems. After credentials are renewed or network problems are resolved, the service returns to Enabled.

1. Real-time rating:

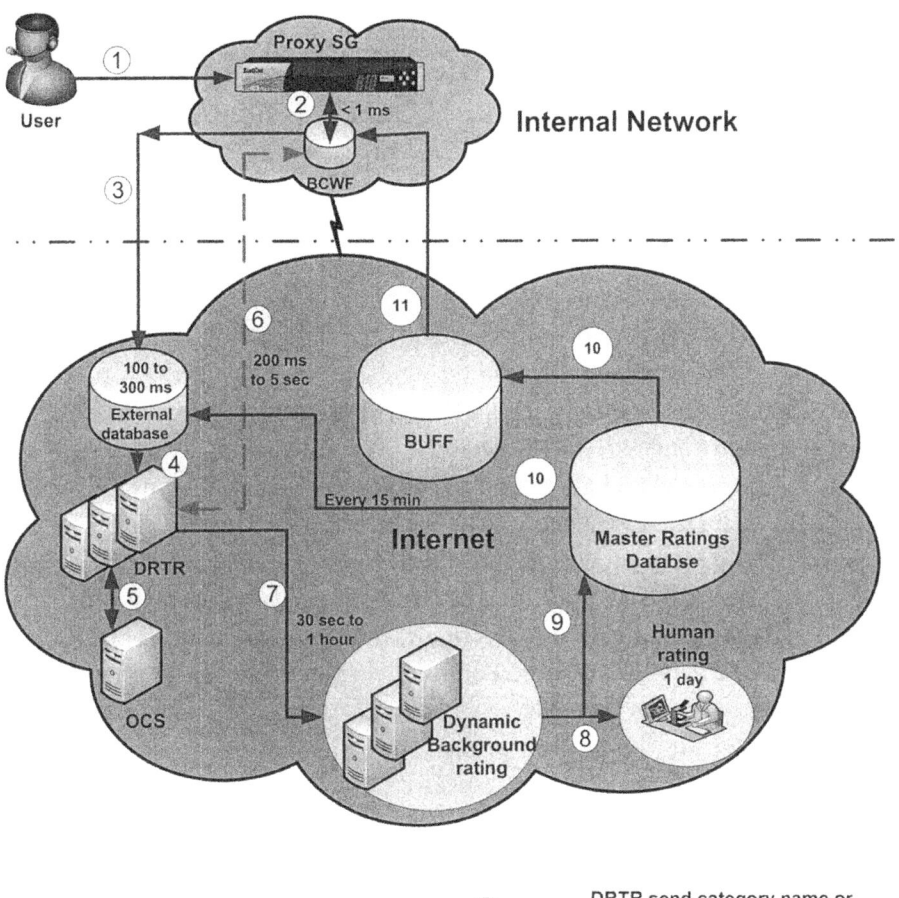

Figure 5.10 DRTR Real-time rating

We will explain the step-by-step how WebPulse DRTR real-time rating works, and how websites get categorized.

The steps are as follows:

1. The user requests a web page from a site. BlueCoat checks its local BCWF database. Usually it is < 1 ms; the request has 95% success rate since most users visit the popular sites, which will usually be categorized. If the site category is found, the site is then allowed or denied based upon the policies built in the Proxy SG.

2. If the site URL is not found in the content-filtering database, the BCWF will query the external database. This database contains the most up-to-date list of websites including the newly updated list for the following day. It is updated every 15 minutes by the MRB (Master Rating database). This lookup for the query takes between 100 to 300 milliseconds; it returns the query if it has the category for the site that is requested and also some additional categorized sites. The updated list gets stored in the rating cache of the proxy. All future requests are checked in the local BCWF and then the rating cache; if the category not found it sends to the external database.

3. When the external database does not have the category of a site, it forwards the request to the DRTR (Dynamic Real Time Rating) server. This DRTR server requests the web page from the OCS server as the same user's request. It tries to analyze the site only for really unacceptable content for the following 13 categories like Adult/Mature Content, Extreme, Gambling, Hacking, LGBT, Pornography, Proxy Avoidance, Potential unwanted Software, Spyware Effects/ Privacy Concerns, Spyware/Malware Sources, Suspicious, and Translation. This is because these are the highest-priority categories of sites that corporations and cannot accept.

   The DRTR can correctly categorize up to 95% of the requests. If it receives these kinds of sites, this behavior reduces the overall number of positive matches for DRTR requests to 12%. Say, for example, DRTR gets 100 requests for porn content. It will correctly categorize 95% accurately and correctly. If DRTR gets 100 requests for a non-pornographic sites, DRTR will only return a 12% correct positive match. This usually takes between 200 milliseconds to 5 seconds.

 There are two possible replies that DRTR could returnto the Proxy SG: either as Categorized or Unrated category.

4. If the DRTR server couldn't categorize the site, it forwards it to Dynamic Background Rating (DBR) for additional review. This process is considered little more intensive than the previous lookup, since it takes up to an hour. Since this service runs in the background, it has no committed respond to any of the Proxy

SG queries. It does a deeper analysis to categorize the site. If the URL is categorized, it is uploaded into the Master Rating Database (MRD).

5. Master Rating Database (MRD) is the database where the sites are rated based upon their popularity. From here categries get uploads to the BUFF database and External database (Step 2). The BUFF database is used to create download lists available daily to all BCWF customers. By default it is 24 hours time period configured on the Proxy SG to download an updated list every day.

6. If the MRD couldn't categorize the site, it sends it to a BlueCoat multilingual team of content researchers for manually reviewing the site. This usually takes a day and once done, it is uploaded to both the External database and BUFF.

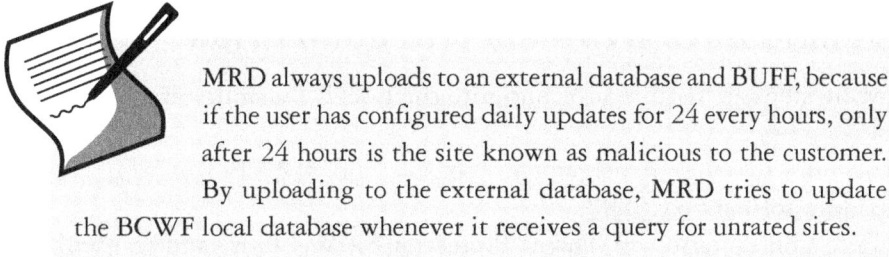

MRD always uploads to an external database and BUFF, because if the user has configured daily updates for 24 every hours, only after 24 hours is the site known as malicious to the customer. By uploading to the external database, MRD tries to update the BCWF local database whenever it receives a query for unrated sites.

The process seems to be lengthy, but it is a state-of-the-art design which is an accurate, fast, reliable, and secure way for organizations to protect against all the web attacks and inappropriate web surfing from users. You could always turn off DRTR, but BlueCoat doesn't recommend it.

2. Background mode.

In background mode, when a client requests a URL, and Proxy SG checks its local BCWF database and rating cache and cannot find the category, it allows the request and then queries the WebPulse cloud. But here DRTR runs in the background; it serves the client request without waiting the response from the WebPulse.

If a response is received, it is added to the rating cache, so all future requests for that same URL will have the appropriate list of categories, and Proxy SG can serve the request based on the policies configured. If a response is not received in a timely manner, or the request results cannot be categorized, nothing is added to the rating cache. References to the site from other sites are recorded for future categorization in the BCWF database, either through automated background URL analysis or human analysis.

If the external database or DRTR server couldn't categorize a site, it goes through the same process as we discussed in the Real-time mode, but the difference here is that the client requests is allowed. It is categorized as Pending until it is able to be categorized. Proxy requests are not blocked while DRTR is consulted. If an object or URL is categorized as Pending, it means Proxy SG has consulted or forwarded the request to DRTR.

CONFIGURING DRTR DYNAMIC CATEGORIZATION:

The following steps are required to configure the DRTR dynamic categorization:

1. Log in to the management console of the Proxy SG, via https://ipaddressoftheproxy:8082.
2. Go to Configuration → Threat Protection → WebPulse and you will see screen below:

By default the WebPulse is enabled in the Proxy SG. BlueCoat recommends using WebPulse services to avoid all of the latest web attacks.

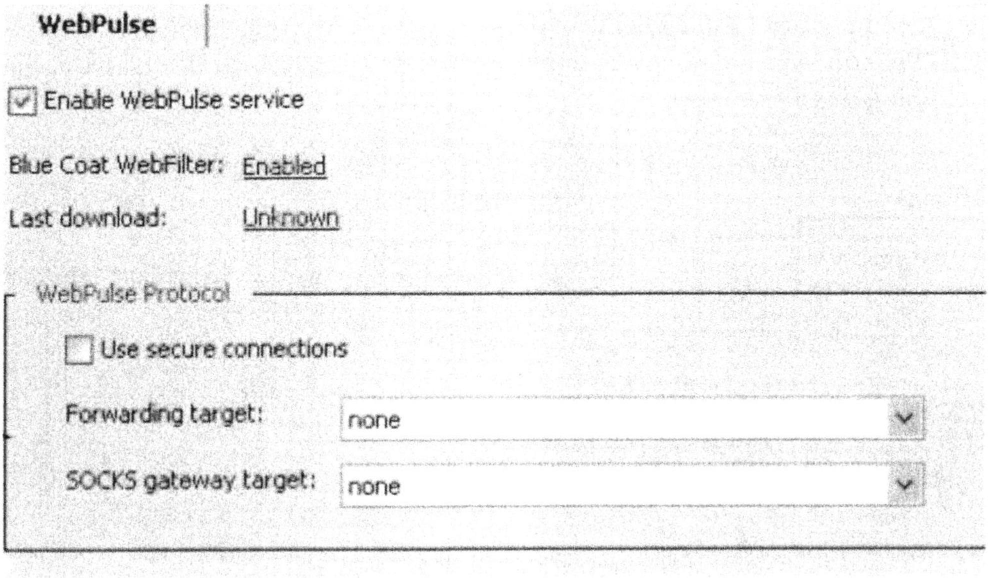

WebPulse

☑ Enable WebPulse service

Blue Coat WebFilter: Enabled

Last download: Unknown

WebPulse Protocol

   ☐ Use secure connections

   Forwarding target: none ▾

   SOCKS gateway target: none ▾

Figure 5.11 Enabling Web Pulse

3. If you want to select DRTR to be real time or in the background, in the same page of WebPulse select the option at the section called "Dynamic Categorization". By default real time analysis is performed as we the see the option "Immediately" is selected as shown:

Dynamic Categorization
☑ Perform dynamic categorization
   ◉ Immediately
      Categorize the request in real-time and wait for the result.
   ○ In the background
      Categorize the request but do not wait for the result,
      returning the category as "pending" on the initial access.

Figure 5.12 Enabling Dynamic Categorization

If you wantDRTR to be perfomed in the background in the same page of WebPulse as shown above figure select the radio button "In the background" and "Apply" changes, as show below:

Dynamic Categorization
☑ Perform dynamic categorization
   ○ Immediately
      Categorize the request in real-time and wait for the result.
   ◉ In the background
      Categorize the request but do not wait for the result,
      returning the category as "pending" on the initial access.

Figure 5.13 Enabling Dynamic Categorization in background

4. If you want to disable DRTR in the same page of WebPulse, uncheck the option "Perform dynamic categorization" as shown below. BlueCoat doesn't recommend doing this.

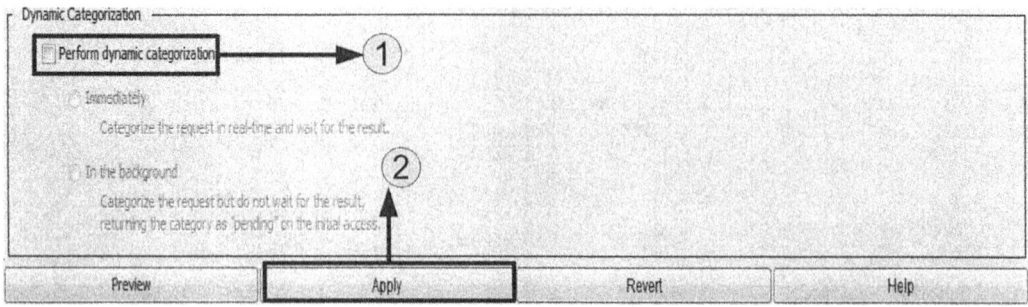

Figure 5.14 Disabling Dynamic Categorization

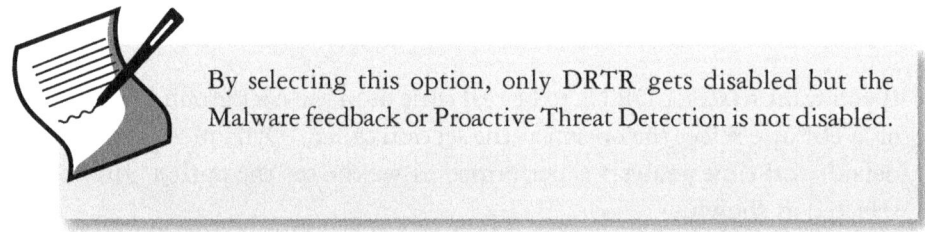

By selecting this option, only DRTR gets disabled but the Malware feedback or Proactive Threat Detection is not disabled.

In the figure 5:11, there is an option to select DRTR to forward the DRTR requests either to Proxy chaining or a SOCKS gateway.

Proxy Chaining:

Proxy chaining is a method for routing client requests through a chain of ProxySG appliances until the requested information is either found in the cache or is serviced by the OCS.

SOCKS Gateway:

If proxy chaining is used for load balancing or for forwarding the dynamic categorization request through an upstream SOCKS gateway, the SOCKS gateway should be configured before configuring the WebPulse service.

The above two options are used when deploying upstream proxy design, which will be discussed in great detail in a future book.

How is the WebPulse cloud service deployed?

We have shown above how DRTR works in categorizing URLs. The next fact to note is how this cloud technology is deployed. WebPulse is deployed throughout the globe in four different data centers. These datacenters are called service points. Proxy SG uses 3-DNS load balancing entry for sp.cwfservice.net to find out the response times, and forwards the requests to the DRTR server that is nearest or the one that responds fastest.

So if you did an nslookup for sp.cwfservice.net, you would get multiple IP addresses as follows:
C:\Users\thejoe>nslookup
Default Server: UnKnown
Address: 192.168.1.1
> sp.cwfservice.net
Server: UnKnown
Address: 192.168.1.1
Non-authoritative answer:
Name: sp.cwfservice.net
Addresses: 8.21.4.203
    8.28.16.201
    8.28.16.203
    119.27.62.201
    199.19.249.201
    199.19.249.203
    203.12.2.160
    8.21.4.201

Blue Coat rarely updates and changes the IP addresses of its services.

The Proxy SG uses the service point by using Health Check. By default, the ProxySG checks the health of the service point every 10 seconds. In a healthy state, the ProxySG checks WebPulse every 10,800 seconds. Both values for service point and WebPulse time periods are configurable. The ProxySG will only change the selected service point after a failed health check. Say N failures will cause an early health check to "Trigger." Default N value is 1 (N=1). If we are in our long 10,800-second healthy window, a WebPulse failure will trigger an immediate health check. This may cause the Proxy SG to select a new service point to use the DRTR service.

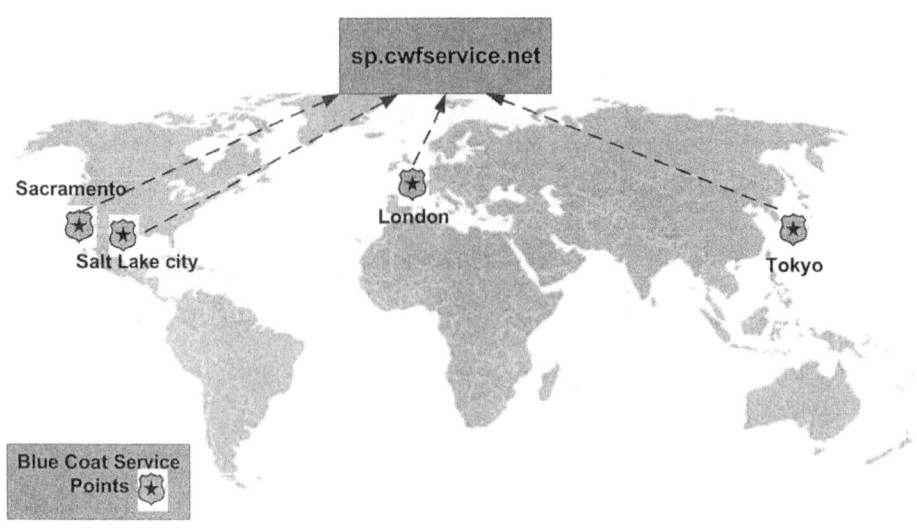

Figure 5.15 WebPulse service points

As we see in the above diagram, there are four service points in different geographic locations across the globe providing DRTR service to worldwide customers. Their service includes BCWF database downloads and also Malware feedback or Proactive Threat Detection. Currently these services are in Europe, Japan, and the United States. These servers are designed with high bandwidth, load balancing, fault-tolerance, and highly secured environments.

2. Malware feedback or Proactive Threat Detection

As we know, the Internet is big. Interactive Proxy AV provides a multi-layered approach for cohesive solutions that provide protection from existing and emerging web threats. In a highly secured environment, Proxy SG is integrated with Proxy AV for the scanning of objects. If Proxy AV detects the requested object to be a Malware, it notifies the Proxy SG and sends a "Denied" message to the client who initiated the request. The ProxySG monitors the results of the ProxyAV scan and notifies the WebPulse service when a new virus or malware is found. Then WebPulse analyzes the URL, categorizes the site, and sends an update to the external and BUFF databases, so that all the BlueCoat customers throughout the world get notified and their local BCWF databases get updated. The site and all further requests to the site are now blocked. Thus BlueCoat is chaining the security from users and organizations to prevent all zero-day attacks from penetrating into any network.

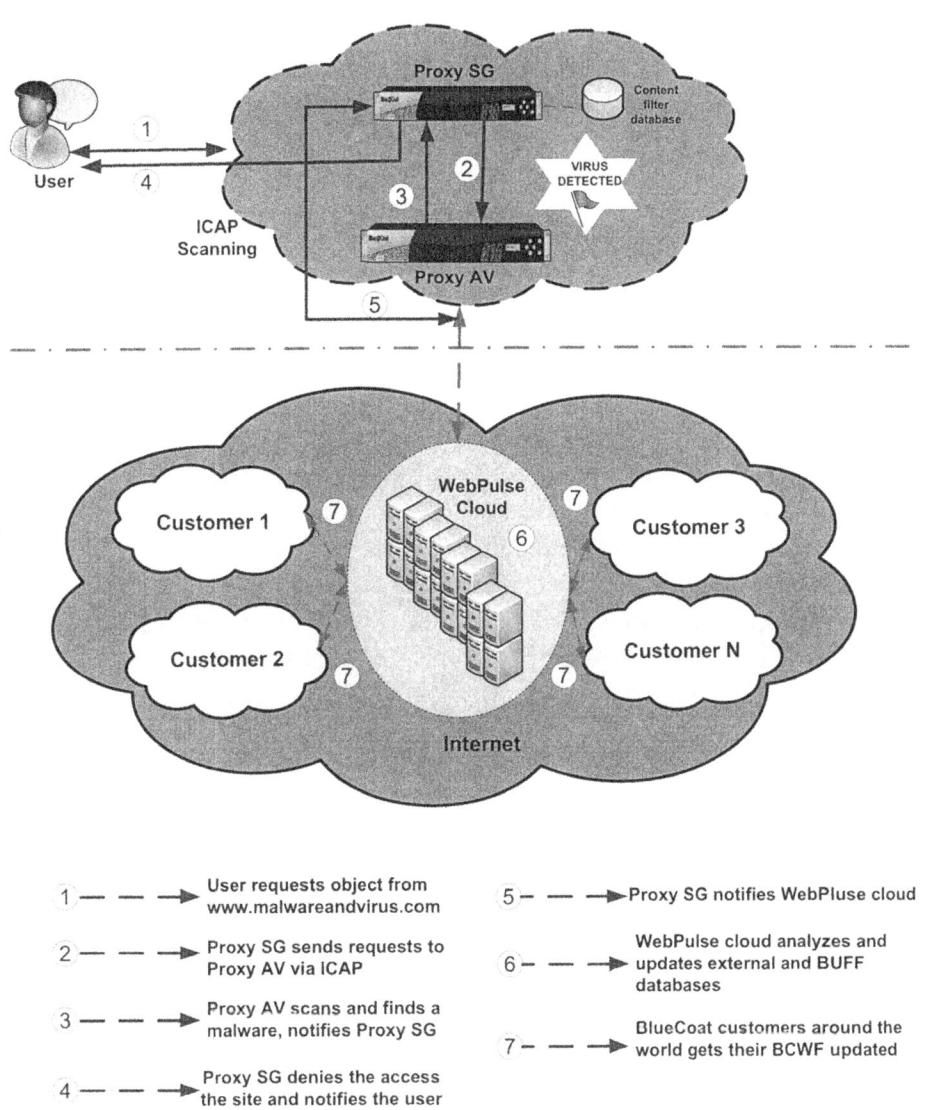

Figure 5.16 WebPulse Threat Protection

BlueCoat's best practice recommends to protect from all malware and virus threats, it is required to enable the WebPulse service in the Proxy SG for both DRTR and Malware protection.

Key considerations that should be noted when using the BlueCoat WebPulse service:

1. A question that is generally asked by users and customers is "what information is sent to BlueCoat WebPulse?"

The answer is that prior to Proxy SGOS V5.4.1, the information sent to WebPulse could not be modified, but from V5.5 on, information regarding the private network, domain names, and IP subnets can be user-defined.

But the information sent could be configurable for both DRTR and Malware protection starting from Proxy SGOS 5.5.5.1. The table below shows the information that is sent to BlueCoat WebPulse on a default Proxy SGOS installation:

Information sent to WebPulse	SGOS < V5.4.1	SGOS > V5.4.1
Customer License Key	Yes	Yes
Scheme (e.g.,HTTP, FTP,RTSP)	Yes	Yes
Method (e.g.,GET, POST, PUT)	Yes	Yes
URL Host (e.g.,http://www.cnn.com)	Yes	Yes
URL Port (e.g.,21,80,443)	Yes	Yes
URL Path(e.g.,download/d1.html)	Yes	Yes
URL Query String(e.g.,search?hl=en& ...)	Yes	No
Referer Header(e.g.,http://www.yahoo.com)	Yes	Controllable via Policy
User-Agent Header (e.g.,Mozilla/5.0 (compatible; MSIE 9.0;Windows NT 6.1; Trident/5.0)	No	Controllable via Policy
URL for malware found by ProxyAV	No	Controllable via Policy
Private Network (e.g.,10.0.0.0/8, 172.16.0.0/16, 192.168.0.0/24)	No	Controllable via Policy
Domain names (e.g.,All inside domain suffixes)	No	Controllable via Policy

Table 5.3 Information sent to WebPulse

2. Can I use SOCKS and proxy chaining for WebPulse?

Yes, you can use SOCKS and Proxy chaining to forward WebPulse traffic to the \ upstream HTTP proxy. For this you need to configure forwarding proxy for Proxy chaining, and SOCKS gateway for the SOCKS proxy. When both SOCKS and forwarding are configured, the ProxySG appliance connects to the SOCKS gateway first, then to the forwarding host, and then to the WebPulse service.

3. Is HTTPS traffic forwarded to the WebPulse cloud and can I send my request to WebPulse encrypted?

Yes. if HTTPS traffic is intercepted, the information is forwarded to the WebPulse cloud. You could send the rating query to Webpulse encrypted,to enable encrypted option in the Proxy SG goto Configuration → Threat Protection → WebPulse at bottom of the screen.

4. Is there any information such as private domains or private network/ subnet that is configured or access logs about private domain/networks is sent to WebPulse cloud?

No. Before the Proxy SG sends the information for content rating, it checks whether it is a private domain or a private network/subnet. If yes, the rating is not sent to the WebPulse cloud. From SGOS V5.4.1 on, these options are user-defined.

By default, service send-request-info is enabled in the Proxy SG. This means that all customer information, including URL Query string, Referrer Header, and User-Agent, is sent to the WebPulse cloud.

If the service send-request-info is disabled, only the customer license key, URL scheme, method, host, port, and path are sent to the WebPulse cloud.

Log in to the CLI using SSH, and go to Enable mode and type the commands as shown in bold letters below

    #(config) **content-filter**
    #(config content-filter) **bluecoat**
    #(config bluecoat) **service send-request-info enable**
    Or
    #(config bluecoat) **service send-request-info disable**

 Both HTTP and HTTPS requests that are part of the private network are not sent to the WebPulse cloud.

IWF (Internet Watch Foundation)

The Internet Watch Foundation (IWF) is a nonprofit organization that provides enterprises with a list of known child pornography URLs.

IWF history from its website

In 1996 the Metropolitan Police Opens in New Window notified the Internet Service Providers Association Opens in New Window (ISPA) that some newsgroup content being carried by UK Internet service providers (ISPs) were indecent images of children. The police believed this may have constituted a publication offence under the Protection of Children Act 1978 (England and Wales) by the ISPs. Efforts were then undertaken to find a way to combat the hosting of such content in the UK whilst protecting the Internet industry from being held criminally liable for providing access to the content.

Following discussions between the former Department of Trade and Industry (DTI), the Home Office Opens in New Window, the Metropolitan Police, some ISPs, and the Safety Net Foundation (formed by the Dawe Charitable Trust), an R3 Safety Net Agreement regarding rating, reporting, and responsibility was created by ISPA, the London Internet Exchange Opens in New Window (LINX), and the Safety Net Foundation. A key outcome of the Agreement was the formation of the Internet Watch Foundation (IWF).

The IWF was established to fulfill an independent role in receiving, assessing, and tracing public complaints about child sexual abuse content on the Internet and to support the development of website rating systems. Since its formation the IWF has been actively engaged in operating this Hotline service for the public to report potentially criminal content and providing a 'notice and takedown' service to advise ISPs in partnership with the Police Services in the UK to effect its removal.

For more information regarding IWF, you can visit its website at http://www.iwf.org.uk.

The key point in the IWF is that it only has one category called "IWF-Restricted" and the only URL filtering that could exist in combination with other vendor's URL filtering. BCWF and IWF can exist together, but not BCWF and Websense or any other third-party web filtering.

To configure the IWF, please follow the steps below:

1. Log in to https://ipaddressoftheproxy:8082, and enter the Username/Password.
Got to Configuration → Content Filtering → General and enable the IWF service and "Apply" the changes as shown below:

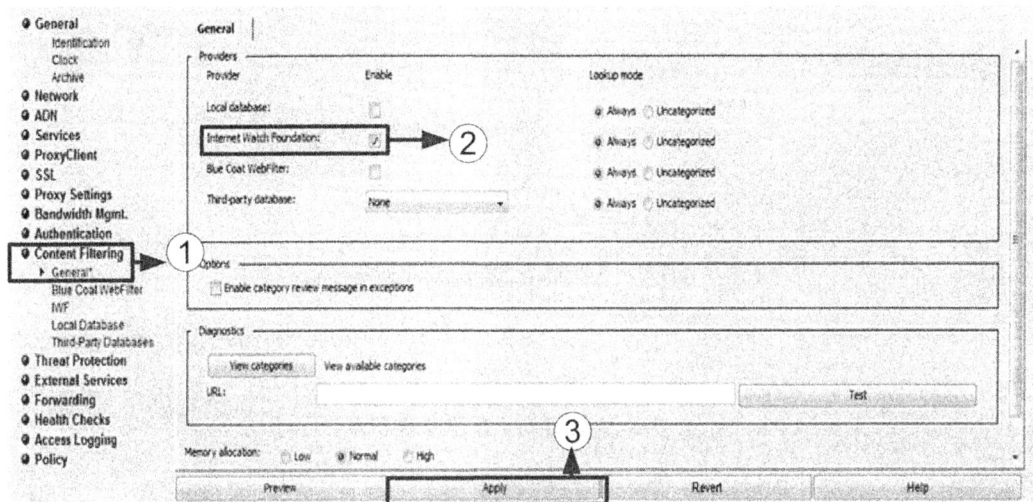

Figure 5.17 Enabling the IWF database

2. Go to Configuration → Content Filtering → IWF. For IWF you don't need the download credentials (since it a free database); just hit the "Download Now" button, and the IWF database will be downloaded, as shown in the diagram below:

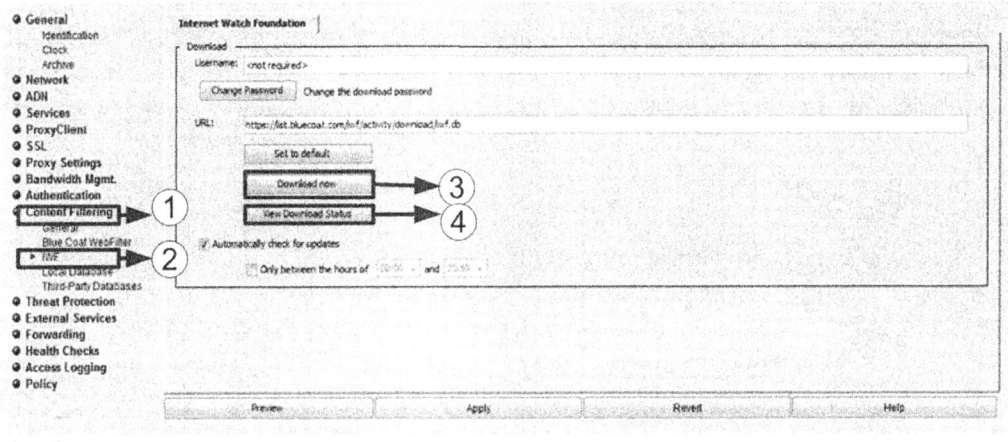

Figure 5.18 Downloading the IWF database

Always use "View Download Status" button as shown in the above figure 5:18 to check the download status of the IWF database.

3. By default, the download frequency is every five minutes. This can be changed by checking the option "Only between the hours of" in the same screen, as shown below.

Figure 5.19 Automatic updates for IWF database

Local database:

Apart from loading filtering database from different vendors, you can create your own database file and download it to the BlueCoat SG. The reason for using the cutom user-defined database is to create your own database and populate it with all the URLs that need to be allowed as per your organization's needs. Say for instance that the category "Financial Services" is blocked in the organization, but there is corporate policy to allow Citibank to all the employees because their paychecks are deposited into Citibank. You could block the "Financial Services" category and only allow Citibank; this is done via a local database file. This is just an example of how important it is to only allow specific sites for business needs when the main category is blocked. The list of exceptions could be huge, as there are thousands of sites that will be needed for business reasons.

This can be done in many ways, by using the Policy file, VPM, and a database file from the web server. But as per BlueCoat best practices, use the database file, the reasons for doing this are highlighted below.

In this chapter we will show how to configure local database in a Policy file. In the next chapter we will show to implement the local database in VPM. The main reasons for keeping the local database separate from, the Policy file and VPM include the following:

1. A local database is more efficient than the policy file and VPM if there is a large number of URLs, because the URLs are not loaded along with the CPL for execution, so the CPL becomes thin and only needs to refer to the local database when it is required.

2. The local database separates administration of categories and policy, which makes things easy in the time of troubleshooting, as the traces and captures will be focused on policy and URL filtering..

3. The same local database can be shared among many proxies when it is centrally maintained, and in-turn each proxy can have its own policies and just download the database.

4. The policy file looks clear and easy to understan for administrators to know it works. When the local database in introduced into it, it becomes cluttered.

The restrictions of the local database are as follows:

1. In the local database file, there can be no more than 200 separate categories.
2. Any URL pattern can appear in no more than four category definitions.

 Blue Coat recommends locating your local database on the same server as any central or local policy files you are using.

The local database is just a text file that can be located in the web server and should be downloaded from the proxy. The syntax of the local database is the same even if you have in "Policy files" (not recommended), we will show how to create local database in a local file in the proxy, which is not recommended as explained above. We will show this as an example, but always make sure to put the file in the web server.

Configuring the local database:

1. Log in to https://ipaddressoftheproxy:8082 and enter the username and password.
2. Go to Configuration → Content Filtering → General and enable "Local database" as shown below:

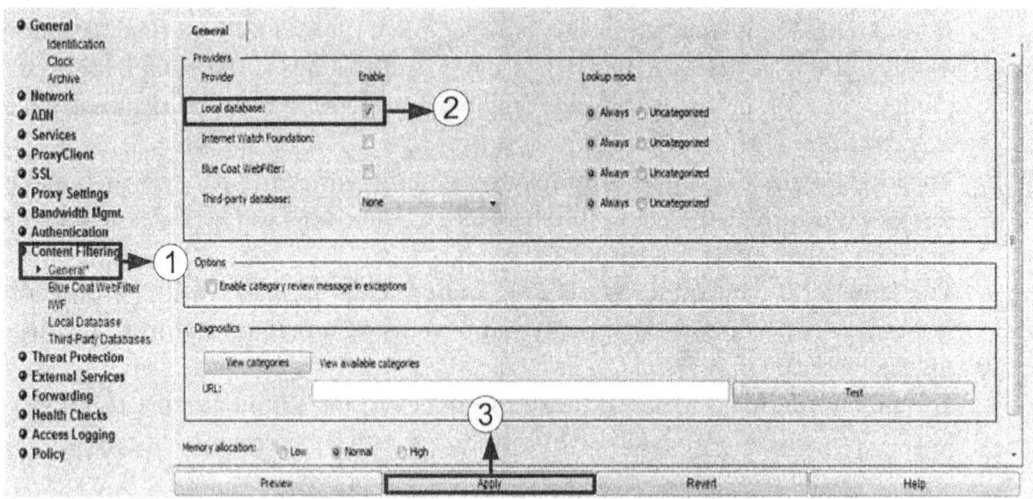

Figure 5.20 Enabling the Local Database

3. Then create a text file and save the file with the following syntax (this is just an example):

define category Allowed_Sites
  google.com
  yahoo.com
  cnn.com
end

define category Denied_Sites
  sex.com
  gambling.com
  mail.yahoo.com
end

The above syntax is as follows:

define category user-defined name
      list of URL each in a line
end

The saved file should be uploaded to a web server where the proxy server can download.

Then go to Configuration → Content Filtering → Local database, and in the URL section enter the IP address or domain name and the full path of the web server for example, http://10.8.1.100/Download/Contentfiltering/localdb.txt, and click "Apply" changes, as shown below:

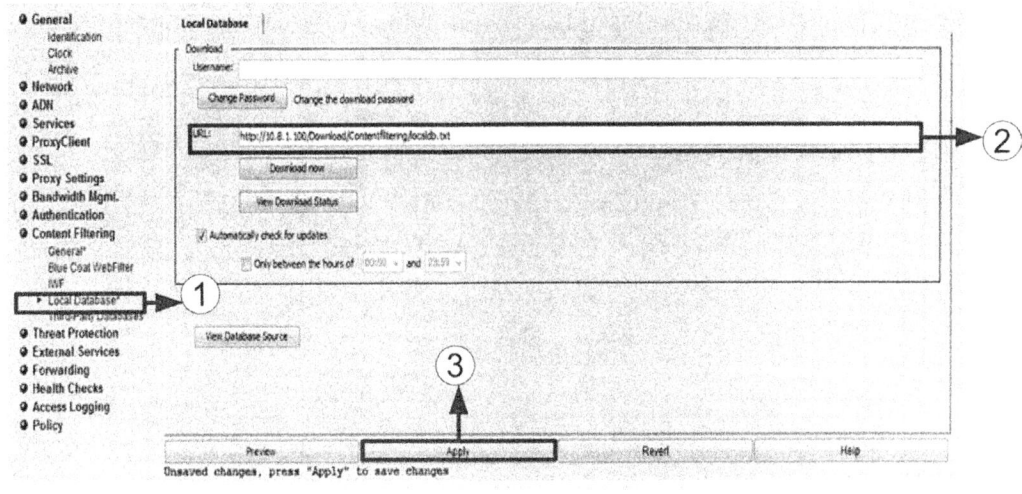

Figure 5.21 Configuring the Local Database

4. This method is not recommended, but for demonstration purposes we are show-ing how to do it in policy files. The best method is to put the file in the central-ized web server where BlueCoat Proxy SG can download it.

Go to Configuration → Policy → Policy Files. Click the drop-down next to "Install Local File from:" and select "Text Editor" and click "Install". You will have the editor opened as shown below. Paste the content that you created in step 3 and click "Install".

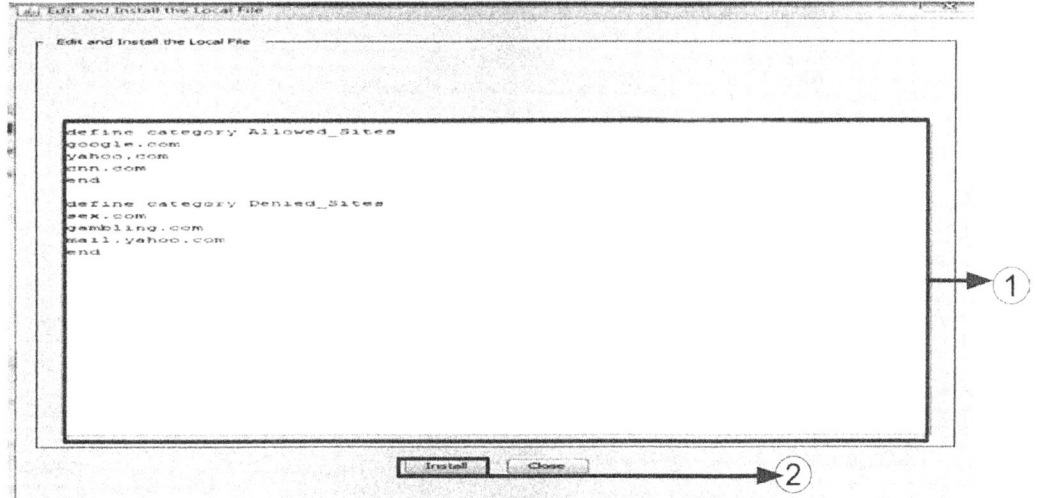

Figure 5.22 Adding sites to the Local Database

Confirm the changes of the local database by clicking "OK" in the pop-up as shown below:

Figure 5.23 Installation confirmation for the Local Database

5. Now that the local database is installed in the Proxy SG, you should use VPM or CPL to implement policies. But you can check the category that you created for the local database in the GUI or CLI.

Now go to Configuration → Content Filtering → General. In the bottom portion where you have Diagnostics, enter the URL as www.google.com in the URL section, you will get a page saying "Search Engine Portal; Allowed_Sites". if don't have any of the URL filtering installed you will just get "Allowed_Sites".

The above step is used to check the URL of sites locally in the Proxy SG.

Most of the troubleshooting can be checked in the GUI, but there are some situations where you will need CLI for viewing the configuration or status. They are as follows:

Use Putty and log in to CLI via SSH and go to Enable mode.

1. Tto display the content filter status that is installed type the commands that is blod letters as shown below; here in this case it is BCWF.

SGOS#conf t
SGOS#(config) show content-filter status

Provider: Blue Coat
Status: Updated
Download URL:
https://list.bluecoat.com/bcwf/activity/download/bcwf.db
Download Username:
Automatic download: Enabled
Download time of day (UTC): 0
Download on: sun, mon, tue, wed, thu, fri, sat
Category review message: Disabled

Dynamic Categorization Service: Enabled
Dynamic Categorization Mode: Real-time
Download log:
Blue Coat download at: Mon, 20 Jun 2011 02:43:24 UTC
Downloading from https://list.bluecoat.com/bcwf/activity/download/bcwf.db
Requesting differential update
Differential update applied successfully
Download size: 84103448
Database date: Wed, 25 Jul 2011 09:12:11 UTC
Database expires: Sat, 25 Aug 2011 09:12:11 UTC
Database version: 2011060

2. If you are using a forward proxy or upstream proxy, run the following command for the BCWF and WebPulse to work through the upstream proxy.

SGOS#conf t
SGOS#(config)forwarding
SGOS#(config forwarding) download-via-forwarding enable

3. You can view the status of each content-filtering database as we discussed in this chapter by using the "View" command as shown below:

For BCWF,

SGOS#**conf t**
SGOS# **content-filter**
SGOS# (config content-filter) **bluecoat**
SGOS #(config bluecoat)view

For IWF,

SGOS#conf t
SGOS# content-filter
SGOS# (config content-filter) iwf
SGOS #(config iwf)view

For local,

SGOS#conf t
SGOS# content-filter
SGOS# (config content-filter) local
SGOS #(config iwf)view

4. We could test the category of the sites using t he CLI also, remember the file that we created in step 5 of configuring the local database, just run the command as follows:

SGOS#conf t
SGOS# content-filter
SGOS# test-url gambling.com
Testing URL 'http://gambling.com/'
category: Denied_Sites

 Always you could use a ? mark in the prompt which will easily drive you all the options that is available for the commands.

Test Yourself

1. If you consider performance and security, which one will you recommend to your customer: On-box content filtering or Off-box filtering solutions?

   a. On-box filtering
   b. Off-box filtering
   c. Both
   d. Neither

2. Which is the state-of-art design in the content-filtering solutions provided by Blue Coat?

   a. On-box filtering
   b. Off-box filtering
   c. Hybrid filtering
   d. None

3. Blue Coat offers a hybrid content-filtering solutions which is a combination of On-Box content filtering and Off-Box content filtering. What is the technology called On-Box and the Off-Box content filtering solution?

   a. On-Box is BCWF and Off-Box is WebPulse DRTR
   b. On-Box is BCWF and Off-Box is WebPulse DRTR, Threat Protection
   c. On-Box is BCWF and Off-Box is WebPulse Threat Protection
   d. On-Box is BCWF and Off-Box cloud service

4. You are a Blue Coat customer and you would like to participate contribute and check content filtering database porgram by recommending domain names for categorization. Which is the online site portal where BlueCoat offers this service?

    a. http://sitereview.bluecoat.com
    b. http://www.siteadvisor.com/
    c. http://www.siterating.com
    d. http://www.sitereview.com

5. What is the WebPulse service point provided by BlueCoat?

    a. www.bluecoat.com
    b. www.webpulse.bluecoat.com
    c. 8.21.4.203
    d. sp.cwfservice.net

6. Which of the following content-filtering combinations is feasible for installing in a BlueCoat Proxy SG?

    a. Websense + IWF + BCWF + Local Database
    b. SmartFilter + Websense + Local Database
    c. BCWF +IWF + Local database
    d. SurfControl + Proventia

7. Which is the best design for the local database that could store sites and categories so that all BlueCoat Proxy SGs in the network can download it?

    a. Create a local database in the Proxy SG using Policy Files.
    b. Create the local database in a webserver or FTP server so that all Proxy SG can download it.
    c. Create a local database in third party database such as MySql.
    d. Create the local database FTP server so that only one Proxy SG can download it.

8. From which database does the BCWF gets the daily update from the WebPulse cloud?

    a. BUFF database
    b. External database
    c. Master Rating database
    d. Human rating

9. Are the information regarding the Private Networks and Private Domain from the BlueCoat Proxy SG sent to the WebPulse cloud?

    a. Yes

    b. No

10. Can a domain be in multiple categories in BCWF?

    a. Yes

    b. No

CHAPTER 6

....

VISUAL POLICY MANAGER

VISUAL POLICY MANAGER (VPM)

In this chapter we will discuss Visual Policy Manager (VPM), which is an important portion of configuring BlueCoat Proxy SG. We will see policy flow, configure administrator access such as R/O or R/W for different administrators, add content filtering groups, and configure different caching options, proxy parenting, DNS settings, and acceleration settings.

Before we start with configuring administrator access to the BlueCoat Proxy SG, we will discuss what Blue Coat policies are and how we define them, and how these policies constitute the ACL that enables BlueCoat SG to inspect the traffic and apply correct filtering rules.

What are policies in BlueCoat Proxy SG?

The Blue Coat policies are fundamental building blocks for the BlueCoat Proxy SG. These are the configuration values and ACL or rules that apply to all users requests which the Proxy SG intercepts in order to make decisions of either allowing or denying using content filtering, authentication, scanning using AV, content transformation, applying caching techniques, logging requests and responses, etc. There are two possible methods of building the Blue Coat policy that both achieve the same goals:

1. VPM (Visual Policy Manager)
2. CPL (Content Policy Language)

BlueCoat CPL is a programming language which is used for writing, installing, and enforcing the policies to all the requests and responses of the traffic that flows via

BlueCoat. When you use VPM, the GUI creates and installs policies automatically for you. Otherwise, instead of using GUI, you manually use the CPL programming language to write, install, and enforce policies. This is totally dependent on the administrators' and the corporation's business requirements of how they are going to manage the policies in their environment. BlueCoat recommends whichever way you are comfortable with in writing policies; both work for the same goal, except, most of configuration are found in both VPM GUI and manual CPL, but certain very few polices cannot be written in VPM GUI, in such cases you should write CPL codes. It's very easy to write CPL codes, and you should practice doing it. In this book we are focused on VPM GUI, as it is the easiest way for the beginners to understand the concepts and implement policies quickly.

Before moving to VPM, we will give an overview of where you can find CPL and VPM CPL files and some related options that help you have a strong understanding how different portions work together and enforce policies.

1. CPL files:

Log in to the Management Console via https://ipaddressoftheproxy:8082 and go to Configuration→ Policy → Policy Files. You will the following screen:

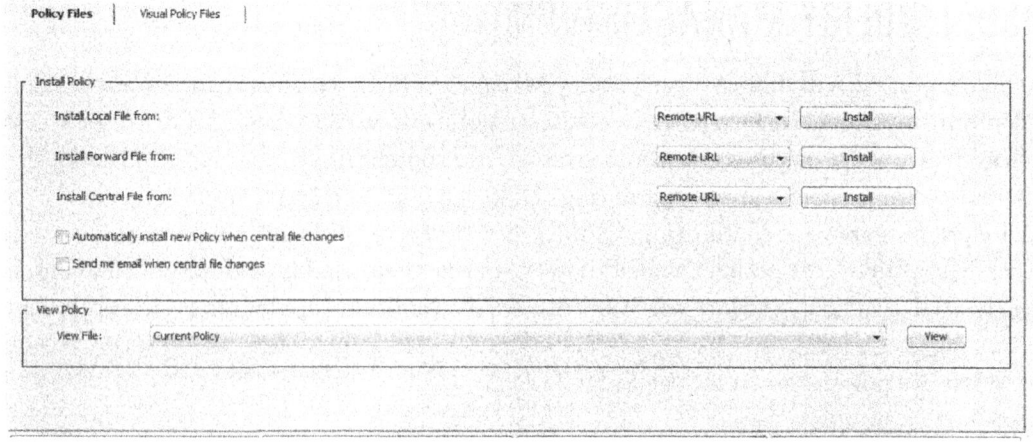

Figure 6:1 Policy Files

The Policy Files tab, as seen above, is the place to write CPL. In the chapter "Content Filtering and Webpulse," simple code was written for a static database—yes, it was CPL programming code! You can write the code either in the "Local file or Central file". But as you can see in the above figure, there is also a Forward file, so let's examine these three types of Policy File options.

1. Local file:
The local file can be used to write your own CPL code, but it can also be used in either of the following situations: when you use both VPM and CPL (some policy options are not

available in VPM) or as per BlueCoat recommends, when you use BlueCoat support for troubleshooting or diagnostic purposes. The second option doesn't mean you should not use the Local file option; if you decide to use this, the BlueCoat team can use the Central file as a choice. So it's all your administration's decision of how to use Policy files.

2. Forward file:

We could use a forward file as a supplement for the other files VPM file, local and central. In some older versions SG 2.0 it contained the forwarding hosts when upgrading. But after SGOS 4 this file is a supplement file. Always spare this file in case if you need for some additional emergency purposes.

3. Central file:

As per BlueCoat best practice recommendations, the Central file could be used for configuring the global settings in Proxy SG when there is a performance problem(bugs in SGOS) and filters (new emerging virus, worms, etc..). So BlueCoat uses the following URL for SGOS 4, 5, and 6: https://download.bluecoat.com/release/SG4/files/CentralPolicy.txt for the latest update that all the customers around the globe can load. As in the figure below, you can click "Install" in the "Install Central file from:" and the option is selected as "Remote URL", and you will see the same path to BlueCoat's site.

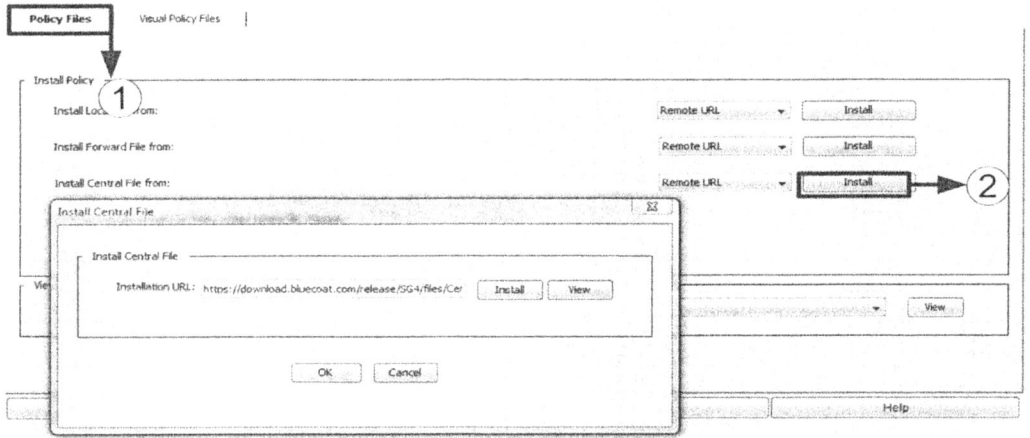

Figure 6:2 Central Policy File

You can change the path if you are using the central internal web server for all central policy files.

Remember that in all the three policy files, you have three ways of installing the file. As you click the drop-down next to the policy options "Install Local file from:", "Install Forward file from:", or "Install Central File from:", you will see the options as shown below:

Figure 6:3 Install options for the Policy File

Remote URL: A valid and reachable web server, either internal or external (such as BlueCoat). For Local and Forward files, the entry is empty by default, but for Central files there is the BlueCoat web server for central updates by default.

Local file: A simple text with the codes saved in your local computer or a remote shared drive and uploaded to the Proxy SG.

Text editor: You can edit the file that is uploaded or downloaded from the web server and add policies and save them. If you are downloading or loading the file, the additional contents that were added manually will be erased. So always make a backup of whatever modifications you do.

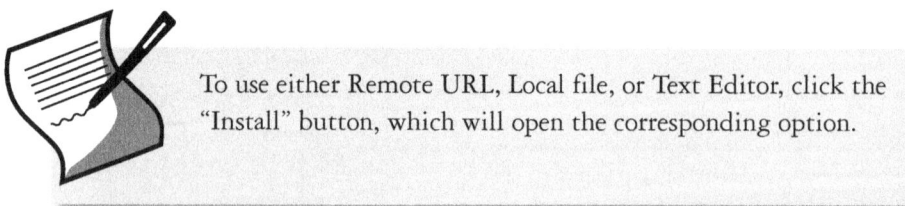

To use either Remote URL, Local file, or Text Editor, click the "Install" button, which will open the corresponding option.

In the above figure 6.3, you can see an option "Automatically install new Policy when central file changes" with a check box next to it. Enable this option by checking the option, which enables the central policy get installed with the new policy when the file changes in the server, the default is 24 hours.

2. VPM files:

In the figure below, you can see the tab "Visual Policy Files". Click it and you will see the screen below:

| Policy Files | **Visual Policy Files** | |

Install Visual Policy

Install VPM-CPL from: Remote URL   ▼   [Install]

Install VPM-XML from: Remote URL   ▼   [Install]

Be careful when using this feature.
This will overwrite the existing files on the system.

View Visual Policy Files

[VPM-CPL]   View the source for the current VPM policy
[VPM-XML]   View the current VPM-XML file

Figure 6:4 Visual Policy Files

We have **VPMCPL** file here, which is one that is automatically created by the Proxy SG when you create policies using the GUI. Here there two files: the VPM-CPL file and the VPM-XML file. The VPM-CPL file is the actual file or code that enforces the policy, and the VPM-XML file is the one which helps to build the GUI objects or VPM objects. But handling this Policy file it is not the same way as CPL Policy file when it comes to editing and applying changes. Please do not edit this file; if you do, the next time you install the policy, all changes are deleted. And when loading from the central file, always remember to load both files—the VPM-CPL and VPM-XML.

You can view both the files, as shown in the above figure under the section "View Visual Policy Files". Click the button "VPM-CPL" to view the CPL file that is automatically generated by the Proxy SG, and click the button "VPM-XML" to view the VPM objects in the XML file format.

Even if you write policies in **VPM** when it is complied it is converted into CPL policy, but instead of writing CPL directly you will use the **GUI** tool, which automatically generates Policy file.

POLICY EVALUATION OPTIONS:

Imagine you have policies in all places, such as VPM, Central file, Forward file, and Local file. Which policy will be enforced? The answer is that you can have policies in all these places, but the Proxy SG follows an evaluation order which can be configured as per your convenience. Log in to the Management console and go to Configuration → Policy → Policy Options → Policy Options tab.

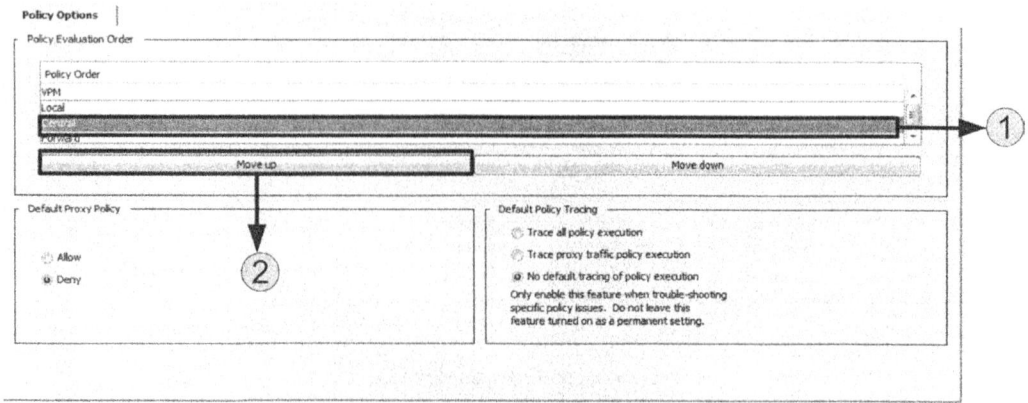

Figure 6:5 Changing Policy evaluation order

In the Policy Evaluation Order section you could change the order, so as per the above figure, the policy is executed in the following order: first is VPM, second is Local, third is Central, and last is the Forward file. You could change this order as per your requirement. To change the order, say for example you want to move the Central Policy to the top of the order, select the option "Central" as shown above, and click the "Move up" button and then "Apply" changes. The order now looks as shown below:

Figure 6:6 Policy evaluation order

GLOBAL DENIED ACCESS:

Let's say that a user tries accessing a site. The access doesn't match any of the rules in VPM, central file, Local file, or Forward file. What happens to the users request—is it allowed or denied? By default, Proxy SG has "Deny" as the Proxy Policy, which you can see in the figure 6.5 at the bottom portion of the screen in the "Default Proxy Policy", section, the option as "Deny". BlueCoat recommends this global policy to be in Denied mode, but you can "Allow" this then override it by creating policies in the VPM. Such policies are called the manual deny or clean-up rule.

Visual Policy Manager (VPM)

VPM, or Visual Policy Manager, is the GUI interface for BlueCoat Proxy SG for creating policies which automatically gets translated to CPL codes, which the actual code that gets complied by the Proxy SG and gets installed in the proxy and the code performs policy enforcement to all the traffic. Before moving on to how to configure policies in a VPM, let's first discuss some terminology used in VPM. There are four terms you need to know while creating VPM policies:

1. Objects:

Objects, also know as rule objects, are the variables or properties defining an element. For example, Source IP address, username, URL, and time are all objects needed to write a complete rule. Objects are again divided into two types:

a. Static objects:

Static objects are self-contained objects which cannot be edited or removed. For example, Allow is an object and it predefined by the Proxy SG so that you can use it, but you cannot modify or delete it.

b. Configurable objects:

Configurable objects, also know non-static objects, can be created by the administrator and used in rules. Say you create a non-static object for the source network 192.168.10.80/24 to access certain websites. Here the network 192.168.10.80/24 is created as a configurable object, which can edited or modified later.

2. Rule:

A rule, also known as an access-list, is a set of variables or objects defining a method of action. A rule is created to trigger an action. There could be hundreds of rules in the VPM to enforce policies. A rule defines "Who needs access (source entity), What type of access (level), When do they access (time), Where do they access (destination entity), and how to access (service entity).

3. Layer:

A layer consists of a group of rules that have same functions and which belong to the same policy set. A policy layer contains multiple rules. For example, a webaccess Layer consists of a group of rules for allowing site access. Admin Access Layer is used for allowing different Administrators to manage and configure the BlueCoat Proxy SG.

4. Policy:

A policy is a statement which is the aggregation of all the variables that define a particular business rule. Say, for example, the company policy is that it needs to authenticate all users who access the Internet. For this, the corresponding rule is created in the Web Authentication layer. So policies very often depend upon a combination of different layers. For example, the Admin/Web Authentication Layer is used for authenticating the administrators/users, and the Admin/Web Access layer is used to determine what the admin/user should after authentication.

How do you access VPM?

To access VPM, log in to the Management console via https://ipaddressofthe proxy:8082. Go to Configuration → Policy → Visual Policy Manager and click the "Launch" button.

Since there is no policy configured, the VPM should look as follows:

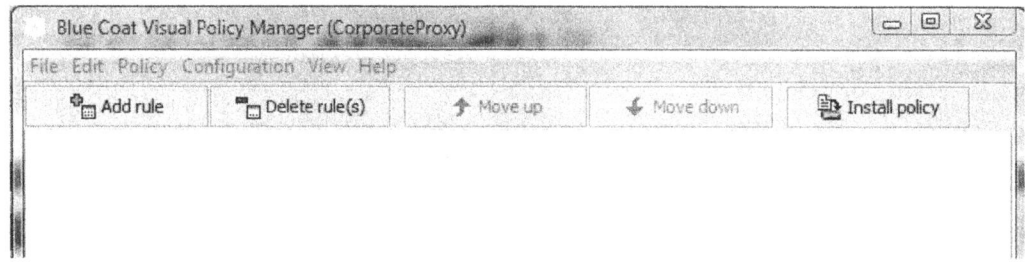

Figure 6:7 VPM initial policy

Before explaining the different types of objects, layers, evaluation orders, etc., we will quickly explain how to create administrator accounts for R/O and R/W access, so you will get a feel for how different pieces works in BlueCoat. Later each portion will be explained in detail

CREATING ADMINISTRATOR ACCOUNTS:

By default there is only one account configured in BlueCoat. That account is the administrator account called "admin". As you may recall, you created this when you where configuring the new BlueCoat Proxy SG box. To change this, go to Configuration

→ Authentication → Console Access, as shown below.

Console Account | Console Access | SSH Host | SSH Client |

Console account

User name: admin

[Change Password] Change the console password

Console realm name:

☑ Enforce Web auto-logout

Web auto-logout (minutes): 15

☑ Enforce CLI auto-logout

CLI auto-logout (minutes): 5

Figure 6:8 Administrator console

As just shown in the above figure, change the "admin" account name to any name you like, but remember that this is the super account. You can add more administrators to the BlueCoat SG for managing the configuration and policy; the purpose for creating different administrator accounts is for auditing and security purposes. Let's consider the following example as shown below:

User	Access Type
Jane	RO (Readonly)
James	RO (Readonly)
Katty	RW (ReadWrite)
Jack	RW (ReadWrite)

Table 6:1 User and Access Type

 We are showing an example of quickly building the initial VPM policy, then we will explain what the different components are in VPM and how it works, etc. This will help you understand the policy layout in VPM more easily.

Readonly administrators can only view the settings and cannot edit, add, or remove any options in the BlueCoat Proxy SG, while ReadWrite administrators can edit, add, and remove any options and also create other administrators in the BlueCoat ProxySG.

In the following example, we are using a group of administartors, so that it will be easier for administration and so all the usernames belong to the local database (inside the ProxySG). Jane, James, Katty, and Jack will belong to the group called "corporateproxy-admin". In BlueCoat administrators group is configured as database or called as local database.

To create a local database and add users to the list, please follow the steps below:

1. Log in to the Proxy SG via SSH through a Putty client and go to Enable mode as shown below:

   Log in as: admin

   admin@192.168.10.101's password:

   CorporateProxy>en

   Enable Password:

   CorporateProxy#

2. Go to configuration mode, add the group corporateproxyadmin, and execute the commands as below:

   CorporateProxy#conf t

   CorporateProxy#(config) security local-user-list create corporate proxy admin

   ok

3. Now you need to add the users Jane, James, Katty, and Jack to the corporateproxy-admin group, so please execute the following commands:

   CorporateProxy#(config)security local-user-list edit corporateproxyadmin

   CorporateProxy#(config local-user-list corporateproxyadmin)user create jane

   Ok

   CorporateProxy#(config local-user-list corporateproxyadmin)user edit jane

   CorporateProxy#(config local-user-list corporateproxyadmin)password

   Enter password: *******

   Confirm password: *******

   ok

   CorporateProxy#(config local-user-list corporateproxyadmin jane) exit

   Follow the same step to create the users James, Katty, and Jack, and now all the users will belong to the corporateproxyadmin group.

4. Now you need to create a realm for the local database, so log in to the management console and go to Configuration → Authentication → Local → Local Realm. Click "New" and add the realm name as "CorporateAuthProxyAdminRealm".

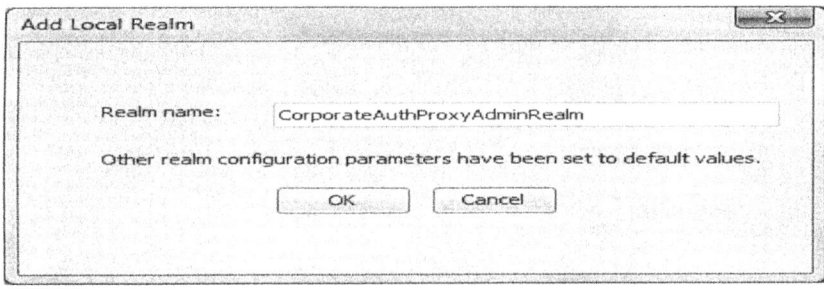

Figure 6:9 Adding the Local Realm

The group namecorporateproxyadmin and Realm name "CorporateAuthProxyAdminRealm" are user-defined, so you can name itwhatever you like and click "OK".

> A Realm is defined as a database that contains usernames and passwords, timeouts for credentials, inactivity, logout attributes, roles associated to user, etc.

5. Now go to the Local Main tab next to the Local Realms tab. You will see the following settings:

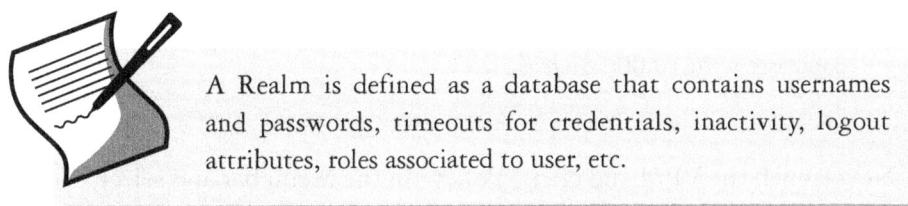

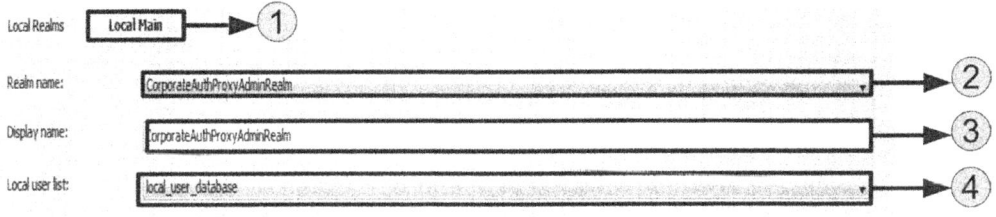

Figure 6:10 Assigning the Realm to the database

So now you need to change the database for the CorporateAuthProxyAdminRealm Realm. To do this, hit the drop-down menu in the "Local user list" as shown above and change the selection to corporateproxyadmin and "Apply" changes. The realm page will be as shown below:

Figure 6:11 CorporateAuthProxyAdminRealm Realm with corporateproxyadmin database

You can see in the "Local user list" a default database called
local_user_database. You could use the same, but to show how
you could have multiple user-lists (also knows as local databases
or just databases) and add users to them, which would be an
elegant way of assigning access to administrators, you could create 50
databases with 10,000 users each.

6. Now launch the VPM and click "Policy" in the Menu bar and select "Add Admin
   Authentication Layer". Then enter the layer name; it is user-defined—let's name
   it as "Corporate Admin Authentication Layer". Then click "OK", as shown below.

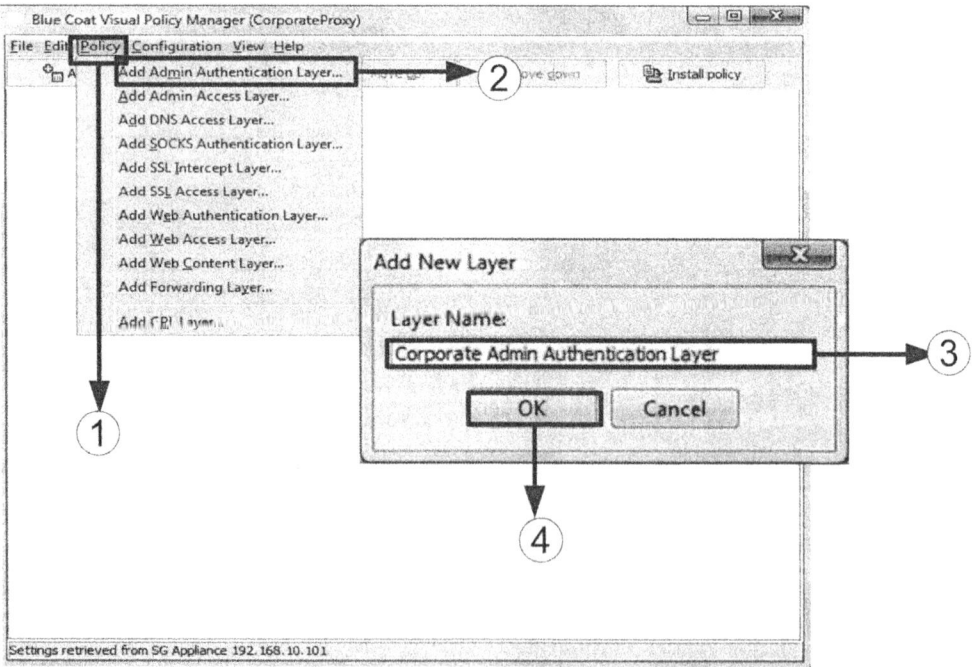

Figure 6:12 Adding the Admin Authentication Layer

7. The "Corporate Admin Authentication Layer" gets created, then right-click on the "Action" tab and select "Set" as shown below:

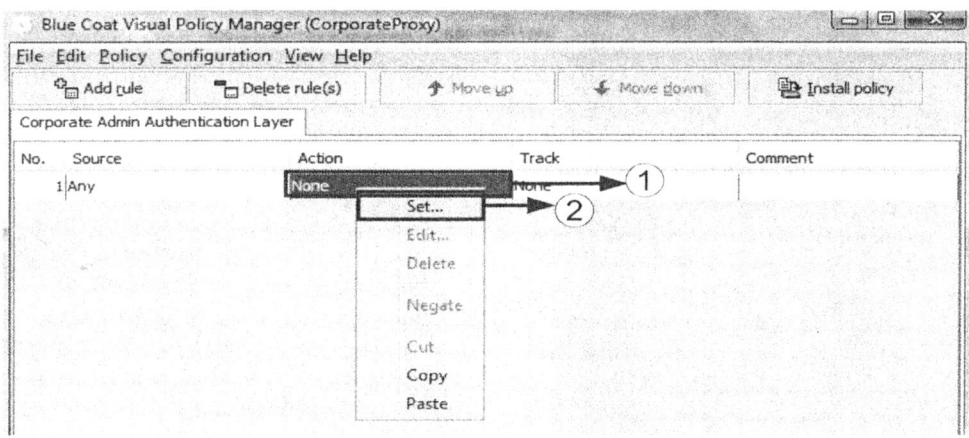

Figure 6:13 Adding the Action Object

Then click "New", select "Force authenticate", enter the name as "AdminAuthenticate", and select "CorporateAuthProxyAdminRealm (LOCAL)" from the drop-down in the Realm section, as shown below:

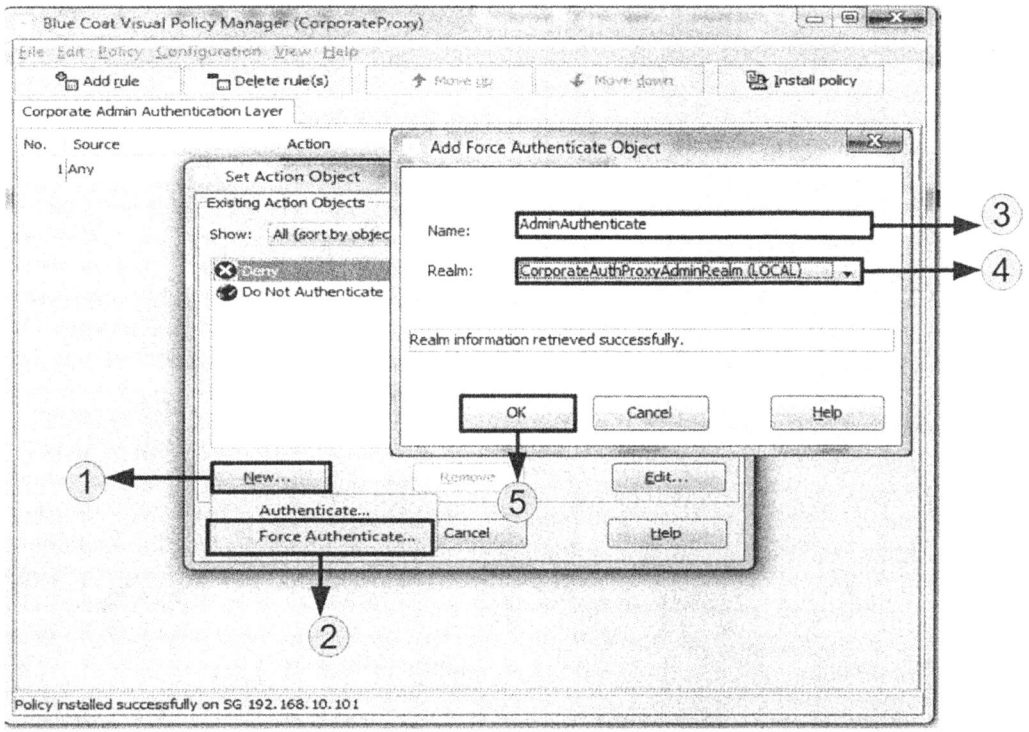

Figure 6:14 Adding the Force Authenticate Object

And click "OK" to confirm. Then you are back to the "Set Action Object" screen. The object that you have added will always be selected so that you can confirm it by clicking "OK".

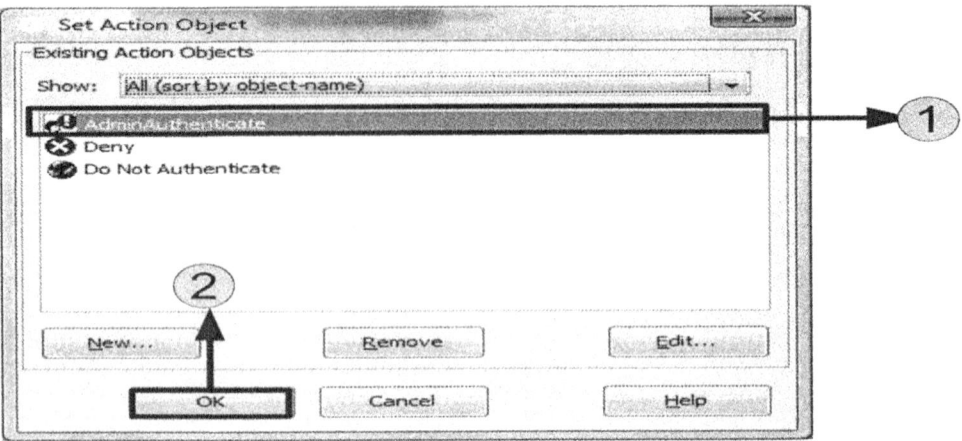

Figure 6:15 Adding the AdminAuthenticate Action object

The rule should look as follows:

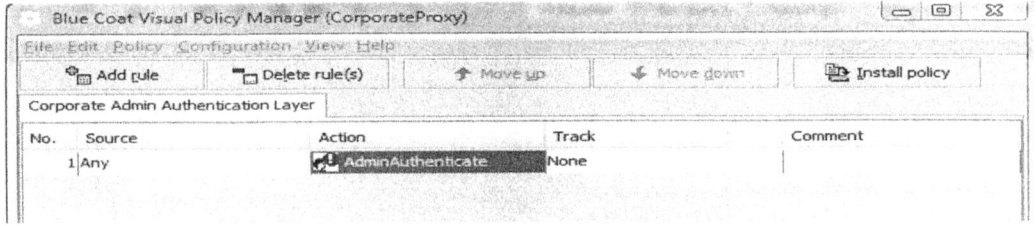

Figure 6:16 VPM Policy with Admin Authentication Layer

8. Now you have created Authentication layer. Now you need to create the Admin Access Layer (Authorization). This defines what the user should perform after authenticating. Click "Policy", select "Add Admin Access Layer", and name the layer as "Corporate Admin Access Layer" and confirm "OK", as shown below:

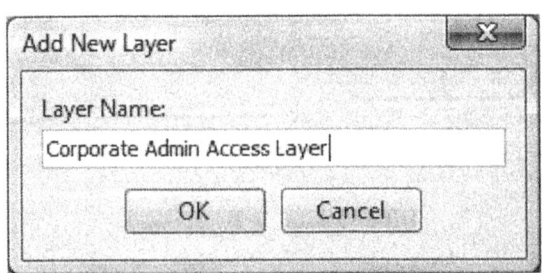

Figure 6:17 Adding the Admin Access Layer

9. Now right-click on the source, select "Set", click the "New" button, select "User", enter the username as "Jane" in the "User:" field, and click "OK" to confirm the change, as shown below:

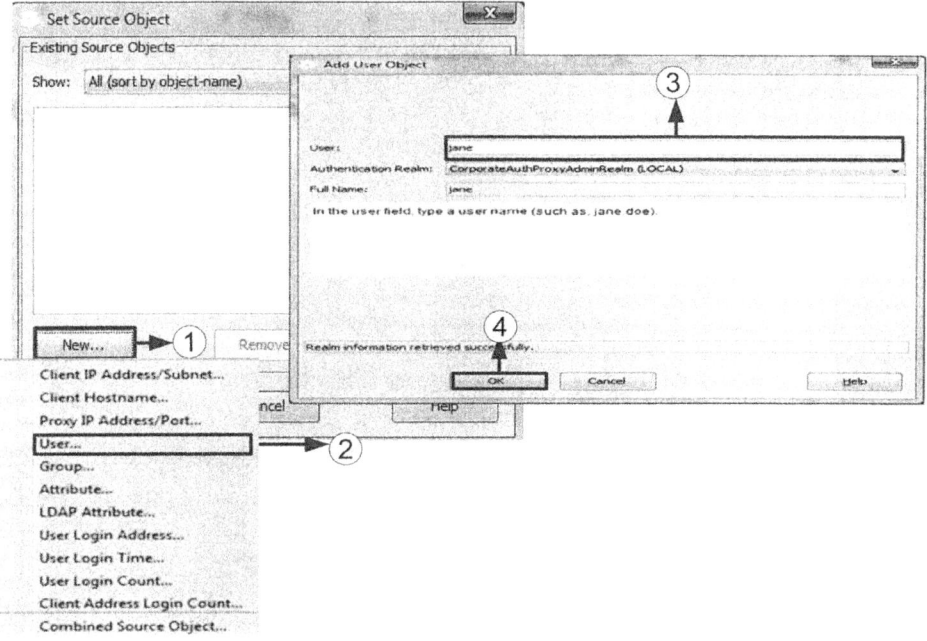

Figure 6:18 Adding admin user Jane to the Source column

And confirm OK in the "Add user object", and then confirm OK in the "Set Source Object" to the "Set Source Object" window.

10. Then right-click on the "Action" column and select the "Allow Read-only Access" option as shown below:

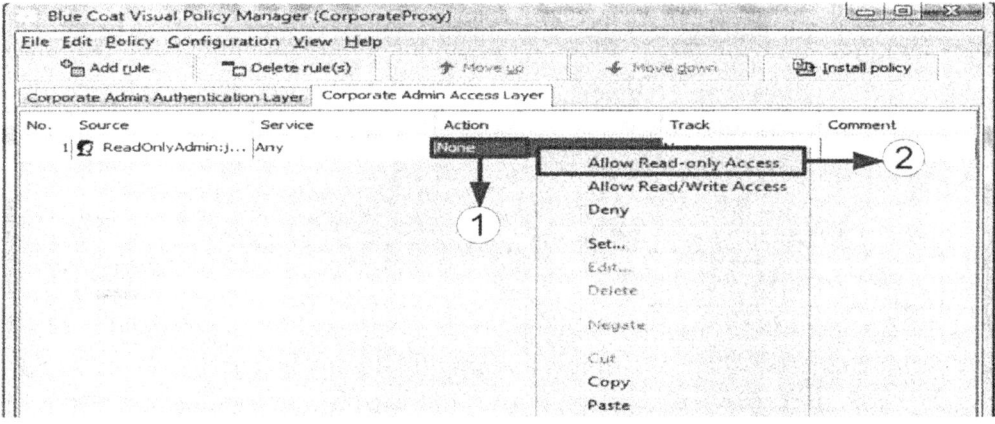

Figure 6:19 Adding the Read-Only Access object to the Action column

Add one rule by right-clicking on "No" column. Then click "Add Rule" from the toolbar as shown in Step 9 and do the same to add the user "james. But for users "katty" and "jack", choose "Allow Read/Write Access" in the Action column. The final rule set should be as shown below:

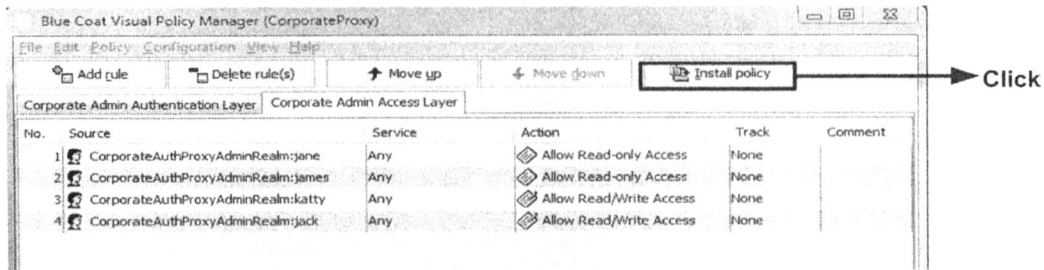

Figure 6:20 Installing the VPM policy

Then click the "Install Policy" button on the top of the VPM as shown in the figure above. If the polices are created correctly, you will see the following pop-up:

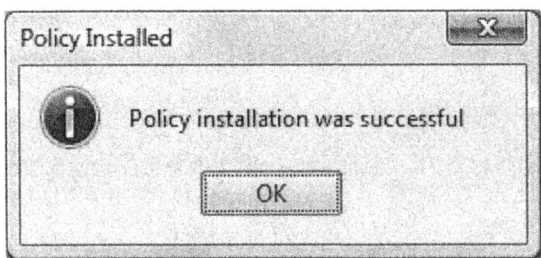

Figure 6:21 Output of Policy installation

So you have successfully created ReadOnly administrators and ReadWrite administrators. You can check whether you have configured them correctly by logging out of the Management console and logging in with the account Jane, James, Katty, or Jack with the corresponding username and password, or if the administrator concerned created the password, ask them to log in to the Management console. You could also check the access by logging with the SSH console using the administrator accounts that you created.

VPM Dashboard

Let's take a quick overview about how you can use the VPM dashboard for creating policies, rules, objects, etc. in the simple and easy GUI-driven interface, in which all the options are straightforward and you could use VPM with less effort. The figure shows the layout of the VPM dashboard:

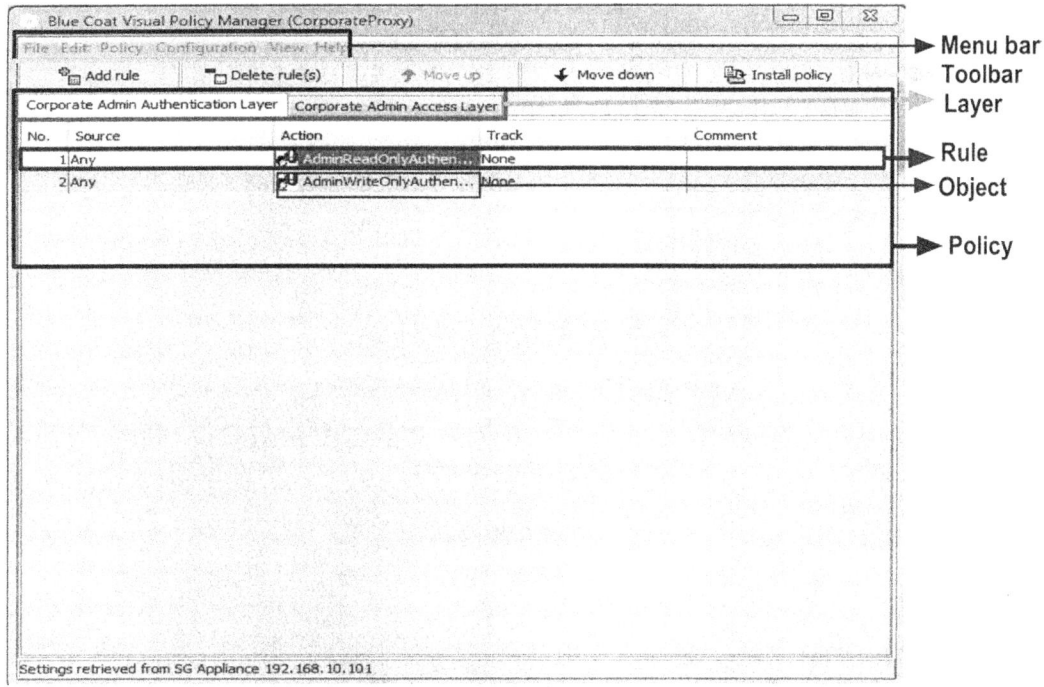

Figure 6:22 VPM policy and its components

The above figure clearly explains how different options and menus are distributed in the VPM and lets you see each option one by one:

1. Menu bar:

In the Menu bar you have File, Edit, Policy, Configuration, View, and Help.

a. File option:

When you click the File option, you will see the menu as shown below:

> File | Edit Policy Configuration View Help
> Install Policy on SG Appliance
> Revert to Existing Policy on SG Appliance
>
> Exit

Figure 6:23 Installing the VPM policy via the Menu Bar

1. **Install the policy on the SG Appliance.** After configuring the policy you click this option "Install the policy on the SG Appliance", then the policy is installed in BlueCoat Proxy SG.

2. **Revert to the existing Policy on the SG Appliance:** Let's say you have made some changes and want to revert back to make sure the Proxy SG runs with the old policy, you could click this option.

3. **Exit:** Click the "Exit" button to exit off the VPM dashboard.

b. Edit option:

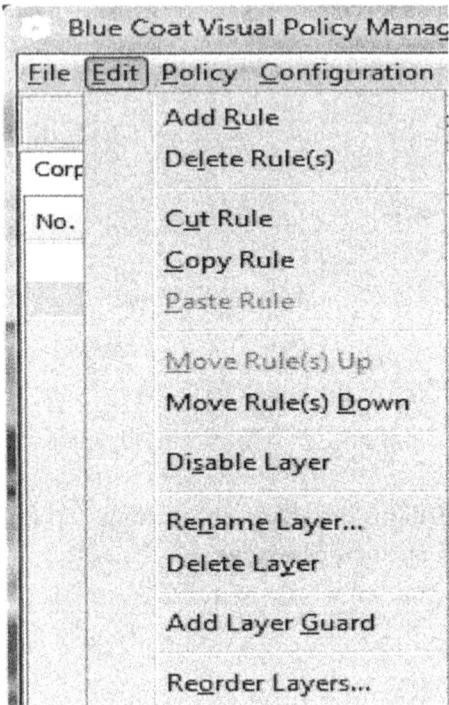

Figure 6:24 Edit options in Menu Bar

Add, Delete, Cut, and Copy Rule: These options are pretty self-explanatory; they are used for adding a new rule, deleting an existing one, but cut and copy works the same way in operations,   you could do that the cut and copy only for the same types of layer not for different layers. In the earlier example we could not cut or copy from Admin Authentication Layer to the Admin Access Layer; we could only cut and copy from the Admin Authentication layer to a another Admin Authentication Layer or within that Admin Authentication Layer.

Move Rule(s) Up and Move Rule(s) Down: If you want to move the rules up and down within the same layer, just highlight the entire layer and use these options where you need to.

Disable Layer: If you want to disable a layer, just select the layer and click this option. By so doing, that particular layer is not complied by BlueCoat. We could use this for testing. The disabled layer will in red as shown below:

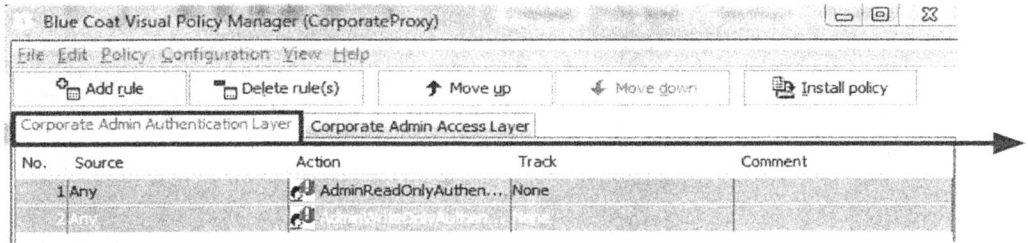

Figure 6:25 Disabling Layer in the VPM

You can enable it again by clicking the layer and this time when you go to Edit, you will find the "Enable Rule" option.

Rename/Delete Layer: Just select the corresponding layer and click "Rename" if you want to rename any layer or Delete to delete a layer. (You can revert by going to File → Revert to Existing Policy on SG.)

Add Layer Guard: The layer guard feature allows you to set a condition by which the whole layer is evaluated or not. This is used to save system resources where large and complex rules are used.

Reorder Layers: You can reorder the layers by moving either up or down. Just select the layer and click either "Move Up" or "Move Down" to reorder layer and you will have a screen like shown below:

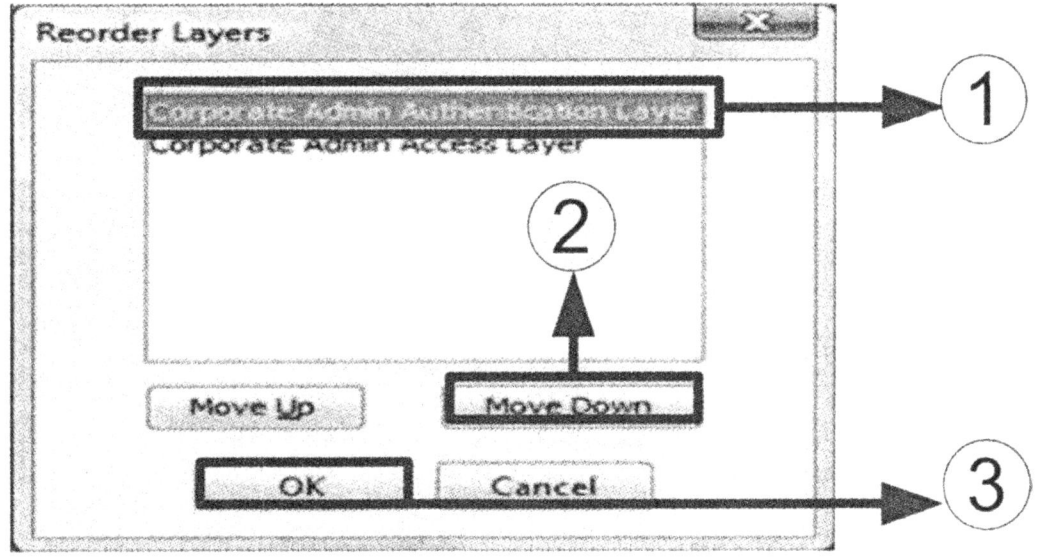

Figure 6:26 Reordering layers in VPM

If you want to move "Corporate Admin Authentication Layer" below, select and click the "Move Down" button and confirm it by clicking "OK". You will then have the VPM layer as shown below:

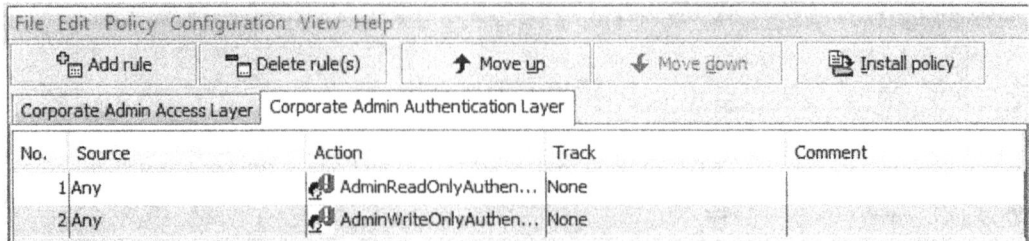

Figure 6:27 Reordered Policy in VPM

c. Policy:

When you click the Policy option, you will see the screen below:

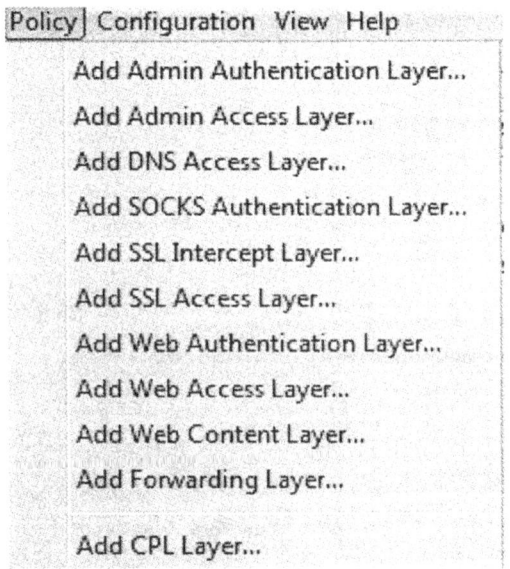

Figure 6:28 Policy option in Menu Bar

We will briefly describe the layer of each function:

Admin Authentication Layer: the authentication mechanism to authenticate administrators.

Admin Access Layer: determines the tasks that can be performed by administrators.

DNS Access layer: handles DNS requests.

SOCKS Authentication Layer: the method of authentication used for accessing the proxy through SOCKS.

SSL Intercept Layer: This layer defines which encrypted traffic should be intercepted or tunneled.

SSL Access Layer: SSL Access layer defines the actions and conditions for the traffic.

Web Authentication Layer: authenticates the users accessing the proxy.

Web Access Layer: Defines actions and conditions for users accessing the proxy.

Web Content Layer → Defines caching methods and scanning methods for objects.

Forwarding Layer: defines hosts that should be tunneled.

CPL Layer → We could write CPL codes directly in VPM.

d. Configuration:

When you click "Configuration", you will see the following configuration:

Set DNS Lookup Restrictions: This option is only used in Transparent deployment, when you trust a particular server, and when DNS request has no valid entry you just allow it, this is achieved by making Proxy SG not performing a DNS lookup, to do this you could add all the domains or IP address to avoid DNS lookup.

Set Reverse DNS Lookup Restrictions: This is same as the "Set DNS Lookup Restrictions", but applies for a subnet range. Once a subnet is added to the list, the ProxySG will not perform a reverse lookup of addresses on that subnet during policy evaluation.

Set Group Log order: The Group Log Order object allows you to create the order in which the group data appears in the access logs.

Edit Categories: You can only add or edit the local categories that you created. This is a separate file store and maintained, if you edit it just appends to the category that you created in either the Local, Forward, or Central file, not physically, but logically.

The options "Set DNS Lookup Restrictions" and "Set Reverse DNS Lookup Restrictions" are the used to override the global options for the DNS lookup feature.

e. View:

Generated CPL: You can see the generated CPL for the current VPM policy that is installed.

Current SG Appliance VPM Policy Files: Here you can see the complete complied Policy files that the BlueCoat Proxy SG will use to inspect traffic.

Object Occurrences: If you want to know the occurrences of objects in the whole VPM, you can use this. It is mainly used for troubleshooting, so that duplicate entries can be removed.

All Objects: This is the one where all objects are stored, which includes static objects, configurable objects, and user-defined objects. So objects are found in all parts of the column in the all the layers and rules such as Source object, Destination object, Service object, Time object, Action object, and Track object.

f. Help

The "Help topics" menu helps you to use the Help options for documentation purposes.

2. Toolbar

A Toolbar is a quick place you can used when configuring rules or Layers. As you see in the figure, we "Add Rule", "Delete Rule", "Move up", "Move down" and "Install Policy"; all these options are available in the Menu bar also—they both allows us to serve the same purpose of configuring the policy. This becomes handy when using the Toolbar to configure rules and layers, as it is easier to navigate. It's all about the user's experience in using either the toolbar or the menu bar and which they are comfortable.

POLICY EVALUATION ORDER:

Now we shall discuss how the policy is evaluated and in what order the policy is complied and enforced in the BlueCoat Proxy SG. We saw what rules, layers, and objects are, and we saw different types of each. The Policy is enforced in BlueCoat Proxy SG, combining all the rules and layers together. This means that all layers which are similar are combined together starting from left to right. For example, in your policy if you have two "Web Access Layers" and two "Admin Authentication Layers", then from left to right policy combines similar layers; that is, both "Web Access Layers" are combined together and both "Admin Authentication Layers" are combined together. The combined layers then combine their rules, just by appending (for understanding) to the end of the first "Web Access Layer" that is found in the leftmost side, then rules are executed from top to bottom. For example, if there are any two similar layers, for e.g. the "Web Access Layer snamed as "First Web Access layer" and "Second Web Access Layer", in which first layer

"First Web Access Layer"appears on the left side and then "Second Web Access Layer" on the right side. The "First Web Access layer" has three rules and the "Second Web Access Layer" has five layers, so applying the principles all together, you will get only one "Web Access Layer" after combining them from left to right, so the first three rules will be in top and then the 5 rules from "Second Web Access Layer" appends after the third rule, and altogether there will be eight rules. So now the rules are executed from top to bottom. This is shown in the figure below:

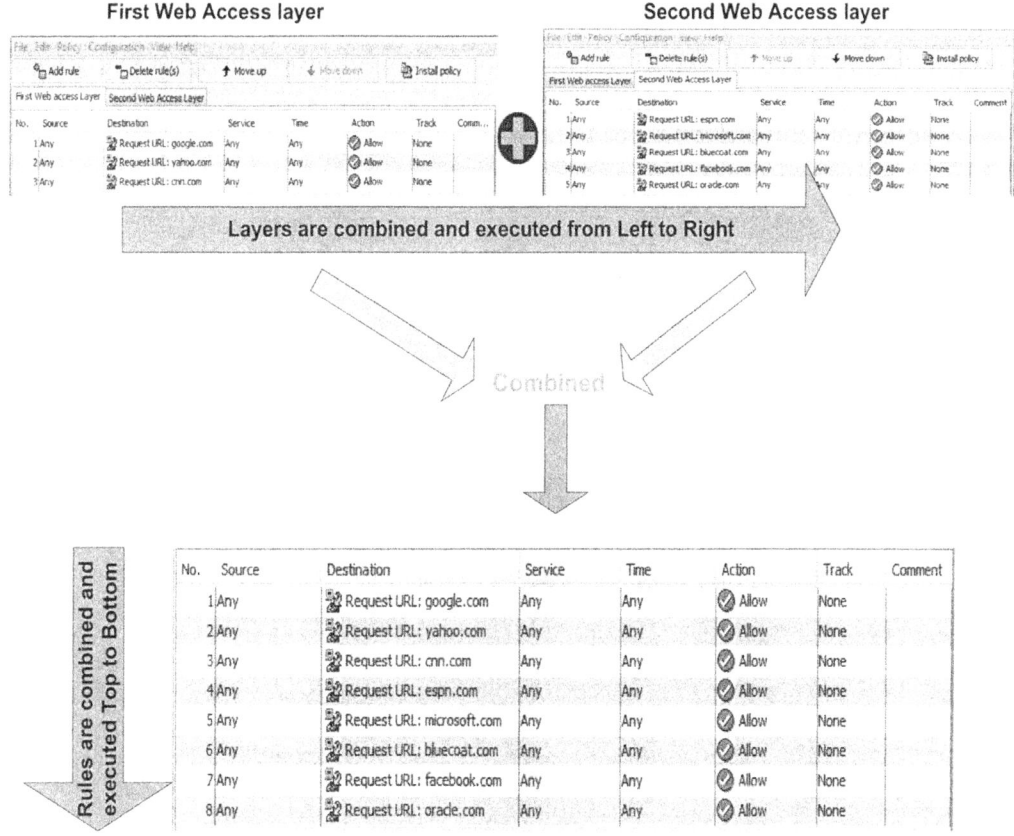

Figure 6:29 Policy execution in Proxy SG

In the above figure in the top portion we see that the layers are executed left to right, and rules are from top to bottom. The above figure in the bottom portion is represented in a logical way and made pictorial in a simple way for easy understanding. But the real order of execution is that all similar layers get combined and the leftmost layer gets executed first (First Access Web Layer) by executing the rules from top to bottom; then it moves to the next layer (Second Web Access Layer) and executes the rules from top to bottom; and then it moves to the next "Web Access Layer" if available until it executes all the "Web Access Layers" in the VPM policy. So the execution moves from layer to layer.

In the figure, we showed an easier way to logically think of how the policy is executed, so the rules are not actually appended to each other from layers.

So here the next question is: when you have different types of layers, which one gets executed first? Say you have an Admin Access Layer, a Web Access Layer, a Web Content Layer, an SSL Access Layer, a DNS Layer, etc. in our VPM policy. Which layer gets executed first? You now know that similar layers are combined together and that rules get executed starting from the leftmost one until all the similar layers get executed. Is the Web Access Layer executed first or is SSL Access Layer, Web Content Layer, DNS Layer, or Admin Access Layer first? It doesn't matter in the VPM; you could create any layer and it could be in any order. But BlueCoat Proxy SG executes in the following order:

1. Admin Authentication Layer
2. Admin Access Layer
3. DNS Access Layer
4. SOCKS Authentication Layer
5. SSL Intercept Layer
6. SSL Access Layer
7. Web Authentication Layer
8. Web Access Layer

9. Forwarding Layer

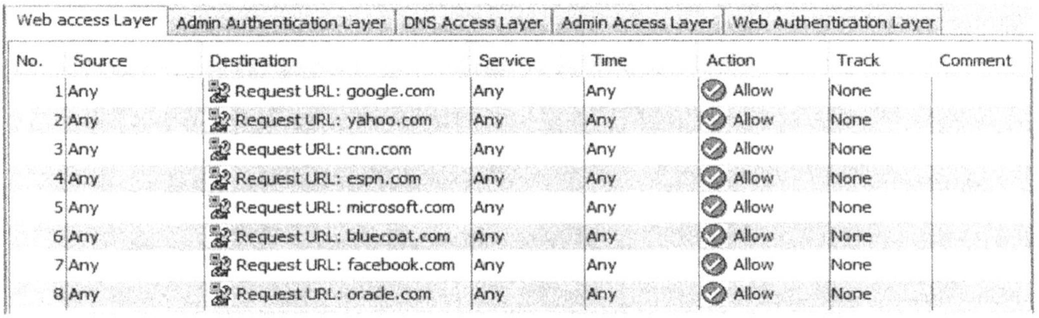

No.	Source	Destination	Service	Time	Action	Track	Comment
1	Any	Request URL: google.com	Any	Any	Allow	None	
2	Any	Request URL: yahoo.com	Any	Any	Allow	None	
3	Any	Request URL: cnn.com	Any	Any	Allow	None	
4	Any	Request URL: espn.com	Any	Any	Allow	None	
5	Any	Request URL: microsoft.com	Any	Any	Allow	None	
6	Any	Request URL: bluecoat.com	Any	Any	Allow	None	
7	Any	Request URL: facebook.com	Any	Any	Allow	None	
8	Any	Request URL: oracle.com	Any	Any	Allow	None	

Tabs: Web access Layer | Admin Authentication Layer | DNS Access Layer | Admin Access Layer | Web Authentication Layer

Figure 6:30 Different Layers in the VPM

Let's say that in the figure above, when the Proxy SG compiles the policies, applying the order as in the table, the first layer executed is the Admin Authentication Layer, then the Admin Access Layer, then the DNS Access Layer, then the Web Authentication Layer, and finally the Web Access Layer. The order of layout in the VPM doesn't really matter; it is when the policy gets complied into CPL code by the Proxy SG that the different layer of rule execution comes into the picture. As shown in the figure above, if you have similar layers, they combine and follow the layered execution order as per in the table, and the rules gets executed from top to bottom for each layer. The figure below shows the policy execution schema for BlueCoat Proxy SG.

Policy Evaluation Order

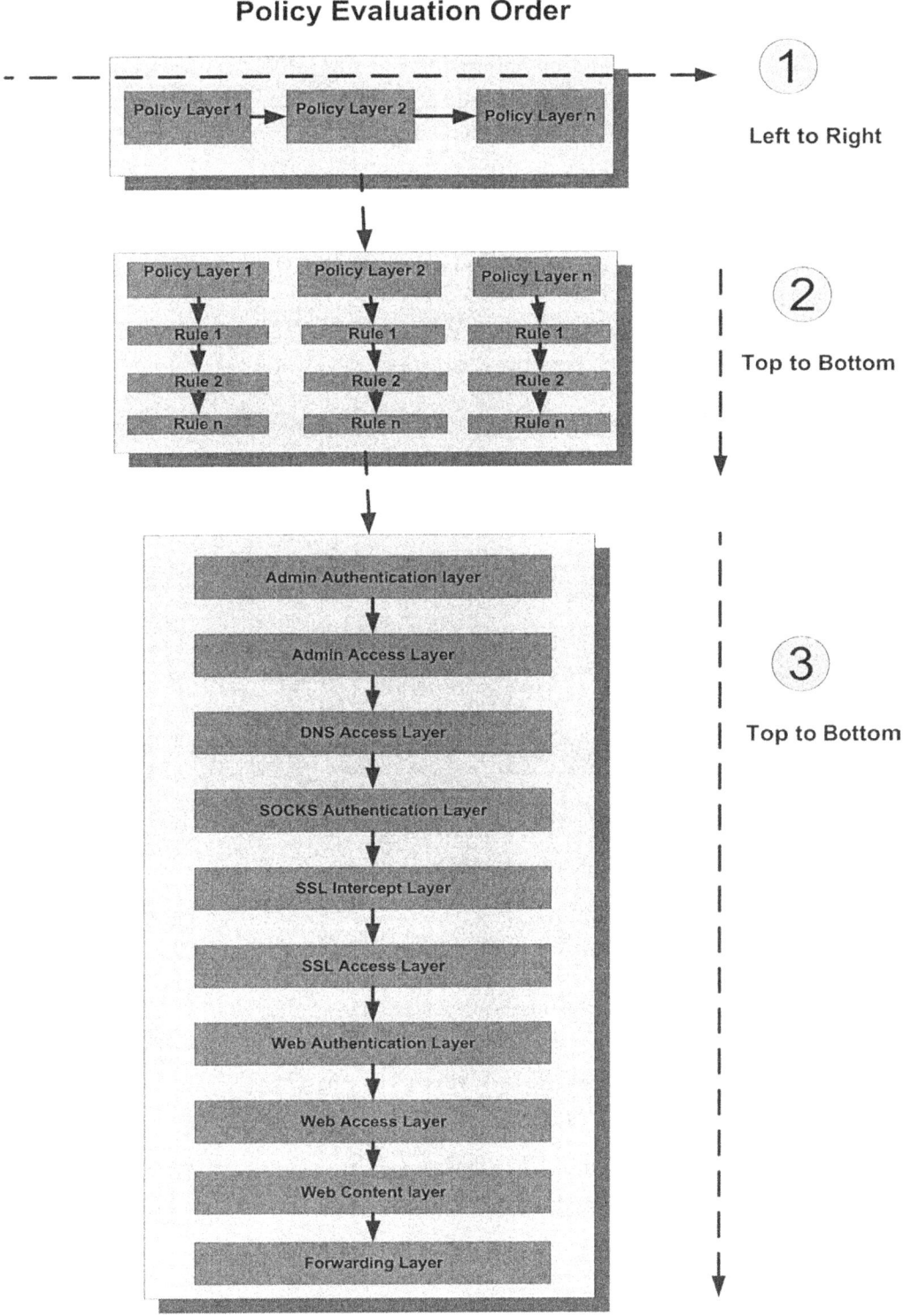

Figure 6:31 Policy evaluation Order in Proxy SG

POLICY TRANSLATION AND VPM OBJECTS:

Now you have a solid understanding of how the BlueCoat Proxy SG works. Here we will see how the business process gets converted into real policies in Blue Coat and how the VPM objects that composes of rules and layers and appropriate actions that are triggered for the users request.

We can illustrate policy translation as follows: the all employees in a corporation should be denied access to all gambling sites on the Internet, during the office hours of 9 a.m. to 6 p.m., and their manager should be notified via email. In the figure below, we show mapping between business processes and the VPM policy.

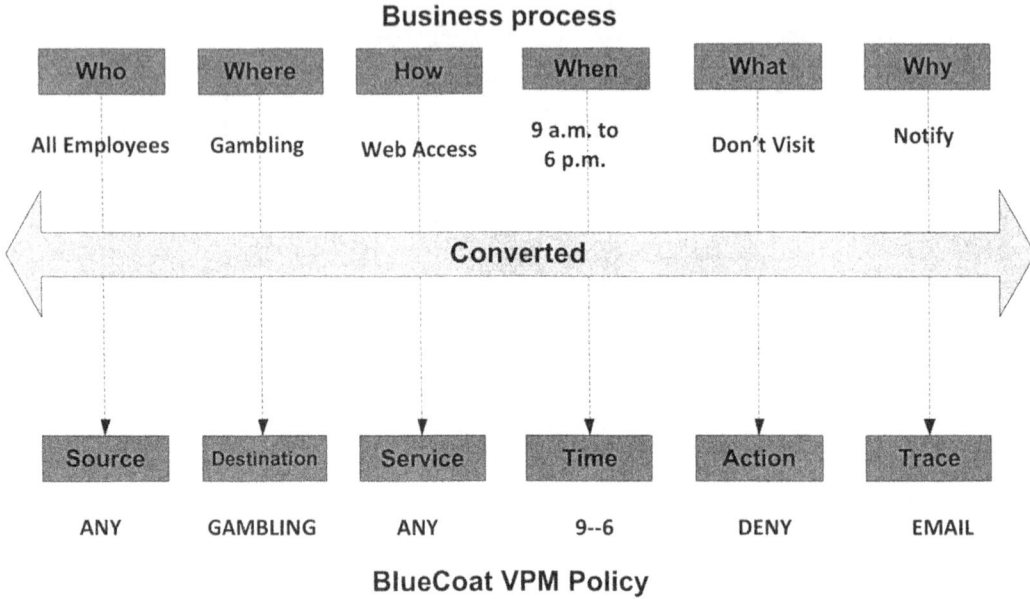

Figure 6:32 Access List built for Business Process

The above figure explains how the business process gets converted into VPM policies. We will discuss how to create the Web Access Layer and apply the categories shortly. While you created the administrator access, you saw how to use different VPM objects like the source, destination, service, and action fields. Each field areavailable VPM objects and we could easily implement the policies in BlueCoat Proxy SG.

So the VPM objects are classified into two types:

1. Trigger objects:

The trigger object represents the business process "Who, Where, How, and When," and the corresponding VPM objects are "Source, Destination, Service, and Time". If all the objects are matched for a policy then there is a trigger for the traffic. Now whatever should be done with this request, the Action Object takes care of it.

2. Action objects:

The action object represents the business process "What and Why," and the corresponding VPM objects are "Action and Track". Once the trigger is encountered, whatever action the Proxy should do with the request, allow or deny it, the Action VPM object takes care of it. And after "Allow" or "Deny" it does log the request, or send an SNMP trap, or send a notification email. Such actions are taken care by the "Track" VPM object.

So now that you have all the required knowledge about the objects, rules, layers, and policy and have seen how to create administration access, we will show to create web content filtering for users, and different caching options available through VPM.

WEB CONTENT FILTERING:

We have discussed in detail about Web content filtering in the chapter "Content Filtering and WebPulse." Now in this chapter we will discuss how to create policies for users based upon categories, and how to enforce policies of the network for users and implement security policies.

IN VPM, first you have created the administration layers for administration authentication and authorization; now you will add the Web Access layer for users to allow and deny access to web.

Let's say there is a company that allows certain departments particular types of access. For example, the finance department is the only team that will have access to all financial-related sites and categories, the IT team is the only team that will have access to all IT-related sites and categories, and the Sales team only will have access to their Sales-related sites and categories.

This is just an example of how the policies and business processes will vary from company to company. To summarize, we will allow the following categories to the respective departments:

Sales Department: Business/Economy and Real Estate

Finance Department : Financial Services and Brokerage/Trading

IT Team: Computers/Internet and Web Applications

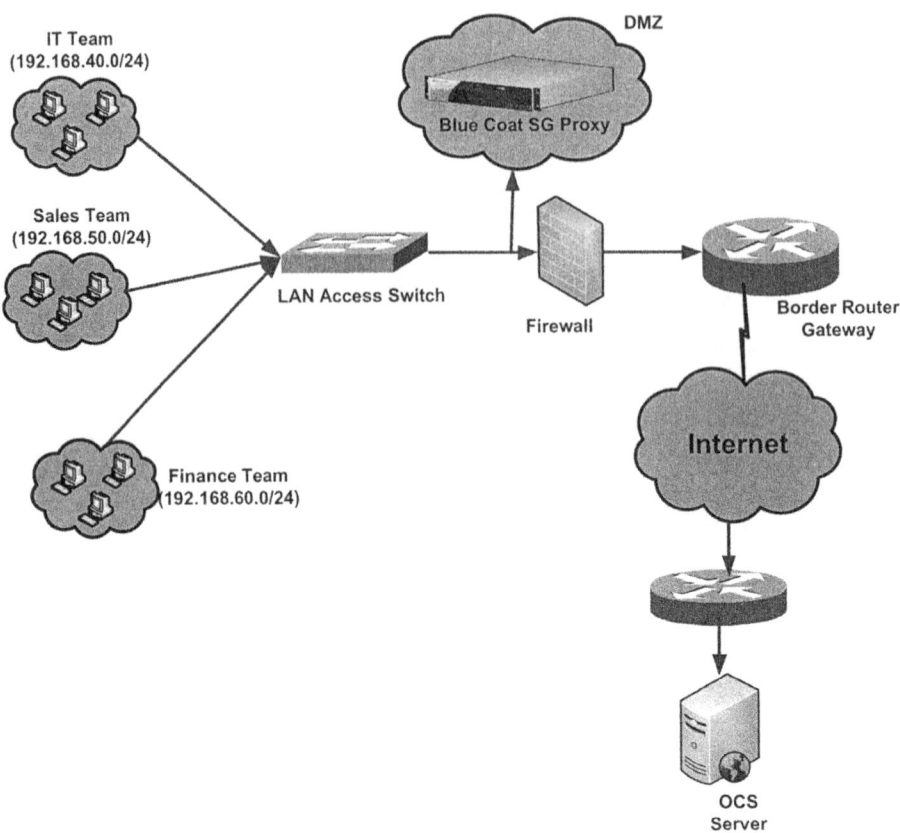

Figure 6:33 Example for VPM policy for a sample network

You have created policies based upon the subnet information for each team, so the source will be its IP address, and the corresponding team will access the Internet from that particular IP address range.

1. Launch the VPM by going to the Management Console → Policy → Visual Policy Manager → "Launch" button, then click Policy → "Add Web Access Layer" and name it is as "Corporate Web Access Layer" as shown below:

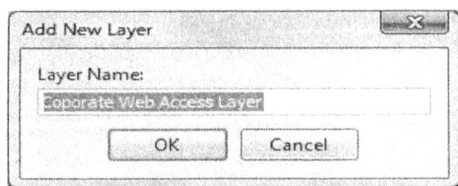

Figure 6:34 Adding Web Access Layer

2. First you will add the IT team policies. Right-click on "Source" in the rule of the "Corporate Web Access Layer" and click "Set". Then click the "New" button and click "Client IP Address/Subnet" and enter the IT team subnet as shown below:

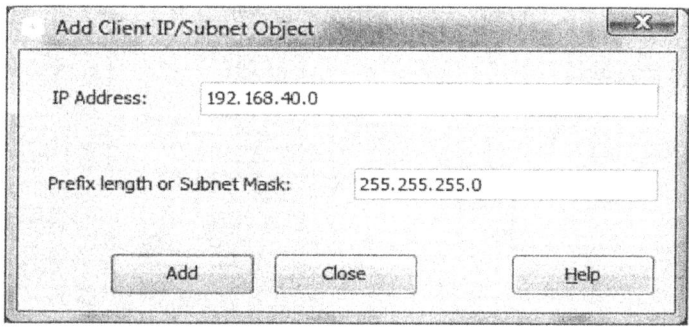

Figure 6:35 Adding Client IP/Subnet Object

And confirm the changes by clicking the "Add" button. Then click "Close" since you are creating only one object now, and confirm "OK" in the "Set Source Object" window.

3. The destination field is where you add objects where the users are allowed to go. Right-click on the destination object and click "Set". Then click the "New" button and select the option "Request URL category" and enter the name "IT Team". Then expand the "BlueCoat" tree; this is the place where you will find all the categories which will be defined for policies. In the chapter "Content filtering and WebPulse," you learned to configure the BCWF. Once it is properly configured, you will see the option "BlueCoat" here, which contains all the 83 categories, and each category will have a list of all the sites in it. Now you need to allow access to the Computers/Internet and Web Applications categories, so select the check box of each category as shown below:

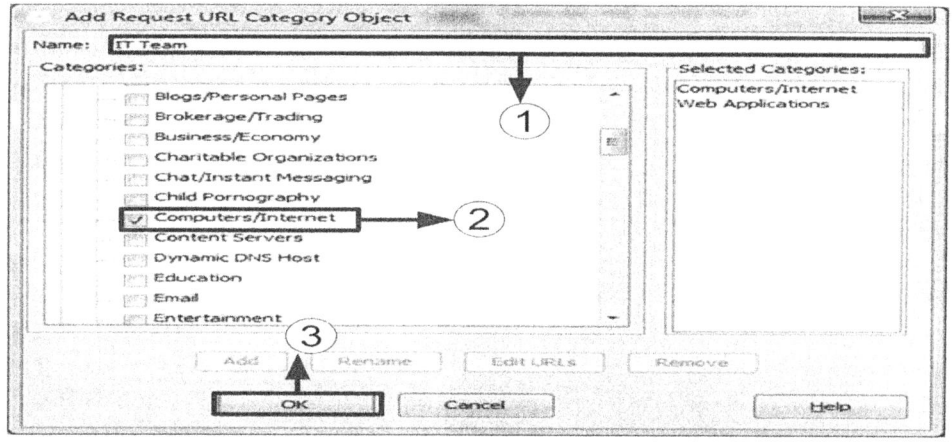

Figure 6:36 Adding Request URL Category Object for allowing access to the IT Team group

And confirm OK to the "Add Request URL Category Object" and confirm OK to the "Set Destination Object". In the above object, we also noticed an option called "Policy". This is a local database category that was created using the Local, Forward, or Central file, when we discussed the manual local database. If you want use this local database, it is done same way as when you created the categories in the above figure. Just select the required database by checking the box and confirm OK.

4. Let the Service column be "Any", which means that this applies to all traffic: FTP, HTTP, HTTPS, MMS, RTSP, etc. This implies that any service hosted on these categories will be allowed, provide a corresponding "Service port" is created on the proxy to listen. And regarding the "Time" object, let it be "Any", since you will allow access to these business-approved sites all the time for these departments.

5. Now to create the "Action" object, right-click on the "Action" column and "Allow", and do the same for "Sales Team" and "Finance Team" by adding the rule and clicking the "Install Policy" button. The final policy will be as shown below:

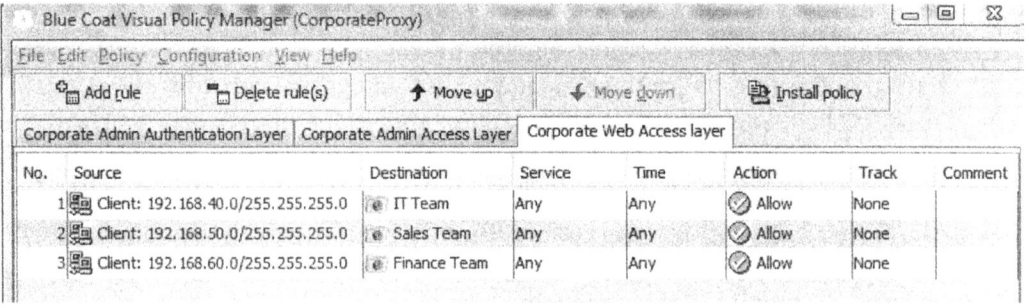

Figure 6:37 Web Access Layer for allowed policies

Imagine that some users are trying to access the internet other than the six categories; then what happens? Are the requests Allowed or Denied? It depends: if your global policy is "Deny", then all the requests that don't match the policies above will be denied. You can check the global policy in Management Console by going to Configuration → Policy Options. "Deny" should be selected.

DENY ACTION:

In the above section you have used the global deny option. The other way to deny the request is to add a "Denied" statement in the VPM Web Access Layer policy. Both ways have one disadvantage: when the user goes to a site, he gets a general "Denied" statement with no additional information given, such as which category denied the user, so that he could know that the site he is trying accessing is correctly categorized or mis-categorized. For example, when a user from the Sales team tries going to http://www.microsoft.com, as per the policy you built, the user might see an the following error message:

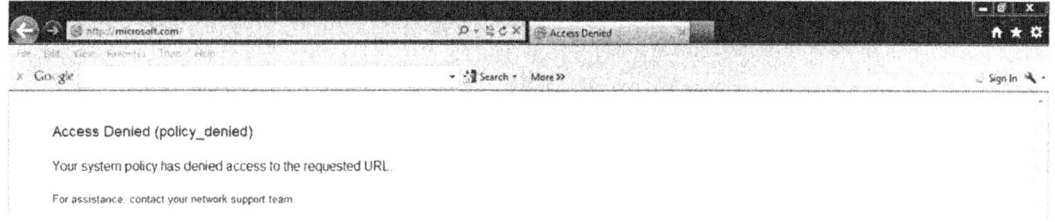

Figure 6:38 Blocked Page of user access

 This is just a example so you will get how policies work. In real-world situations, you need to allow http://www.microsoft.com for users, because they need to update the software and the OS, though of course you could use SCCM to centrally upgrade.

To get around this, you could add a policy that explicitly denies all access for that department from the subnet they are trying to access.

1. So Launch the VPM and go to "Corporate Web Access Layer", and click the "rule No:1" and click "Add Rule" and an empty rule is created as shown below:

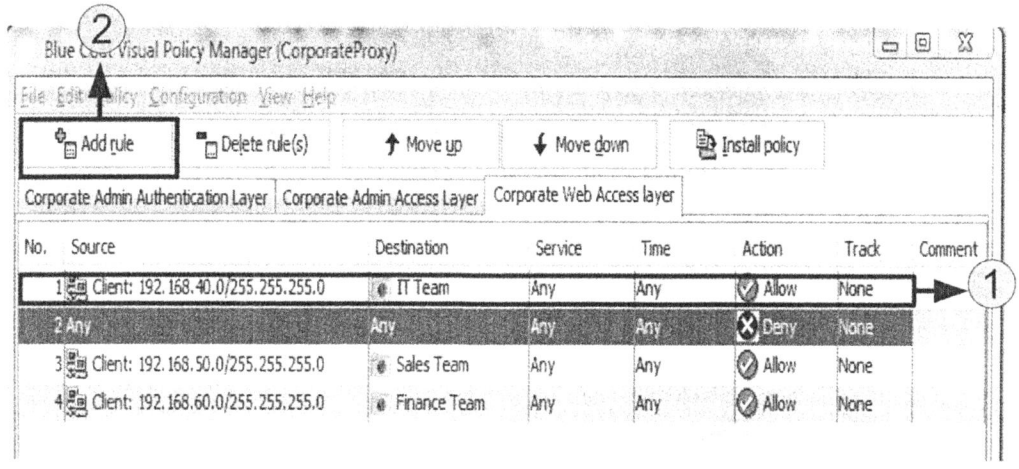

Figure 6:39 Adding a New Rule

2. Then right-click on the Source and add the IT Team subnet that you already created as 192.168.40.0/255.255.255.0, and on destination column right-click and select the "Set" option. Select "Request Category" and in the "Name field"write the name as "Block IT Team". Select all categories except Computers/Internet and Web Applications as shown below:

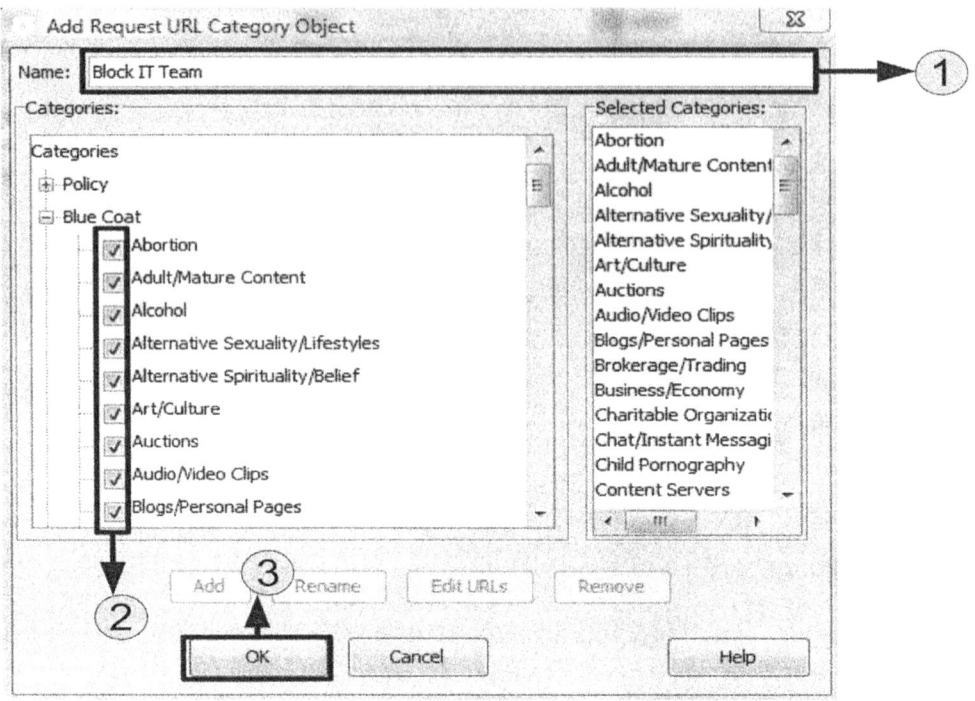

Figure 6:40 Adding Request URL Category Object for blocking IT Teamusers group

And confirm "OK", and click "OK" to the "Request URL Category Object".

3. Let the Service and Time objects be "Any", In the Action column, right click and select "Deny (Content Filter)". If you use the "Deny" option instead of "Deny (Content Filter)", as you can see in the option, it still gives a generic message as you saw in figure 6:38. The "Deny (Content Filter)" object gives the reason for the category that denied the user access to the requested content and describes that the request was denied because it belongs to a category blocked by corporate policy.

Do the same for the Sales team and the Finance team by creating a rule after the "Allow" rule. Select all the categories except the one used by the corresponding team.The final policy will be as follows:

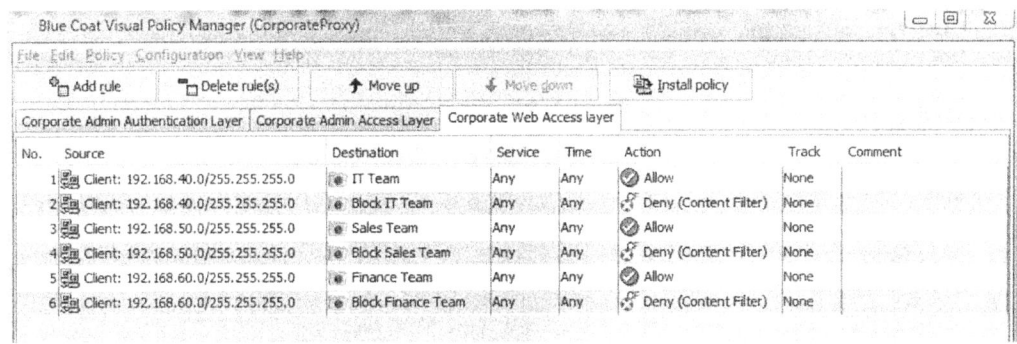

Figure 6:41 Web Access Policy for both Allowed and Denied content

Now if the Sales Team tries accessing http://www.microsoft.com, they will get the following error message with the category that denied them:

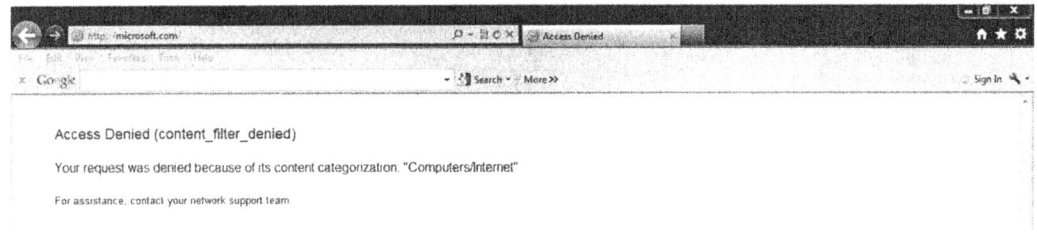

Figure 6:42 Blocked page with category displayed

COMBINED OBJECTS:

Combined objects are used when there are more objects that need to be added to rules. Their main purpose is that they reduce the number of rules and multiple conditions can be used to match a request. The simple way to explain Let's say you want to allow access to http://www.google.com and http://www.foxnews.com for the entire company. (This can also be achieved by using a static local database, which we saw in the chapter "Content Filtering and WebPulse").

To add the sites, please follow the steps shown below:

1. 1. Launch VPM by going to Configuration → Policy → Visual Policy Manager and clicking the "Launch" button. Go to the layer "Corporate Web Access Layer" and click the first rule . Click "Add Rule" and move the new rule above rule 1 by selecting rule 2 and click the "Move Up" button in the toolbar.

2. Let the source be "Any". In the destination field, right-click and select "Set". Click "New" and select "Combined Destination object" at the very bottom of the menu. Enter the name as "Allowed News Sites" and again click the "New" button. Select the "Request URL" option and enter google.com in the URL portion as shown below:

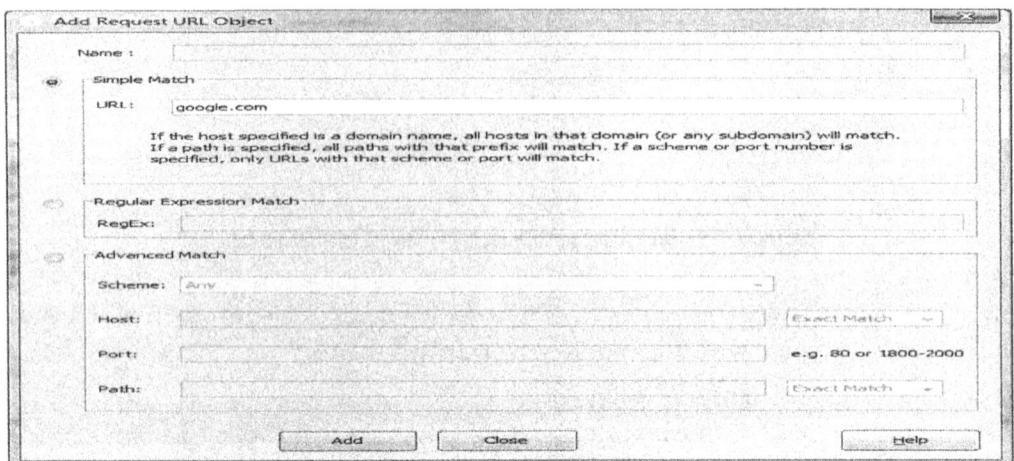

Figure 6:43 Adding Request URL object for google.com

And confirm by clicking "Add". Then again add in "Add Request URL object", enter foxnews.com next to the URL section as you did for google.com and click the "Add" button. Then click the "Close" button to come out of the "Add Request URL object" window.

Then you will see a screen similar to the one shown below:

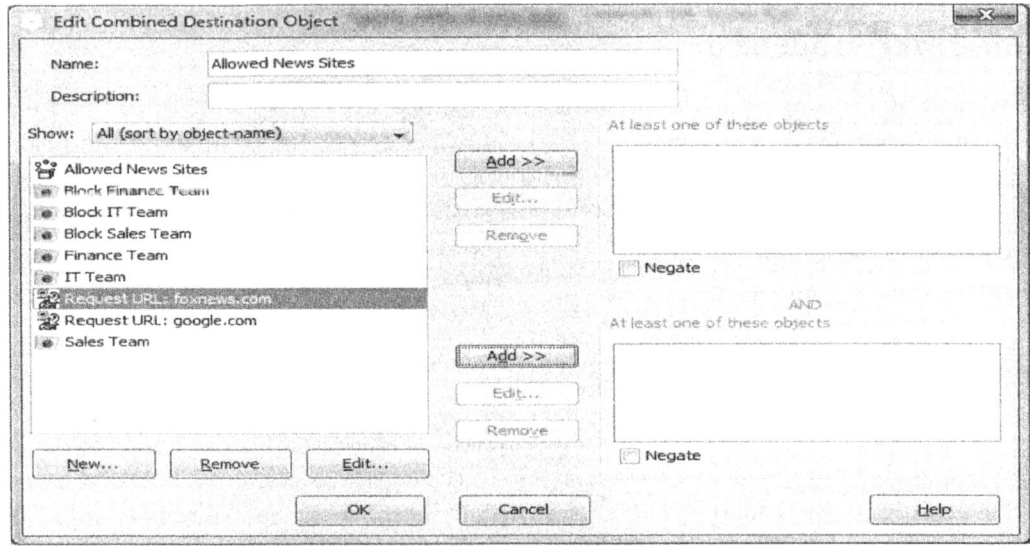

Figure 6:44 Adding Combined Destination object "Allowed News Sites"

3. Now you need to add the rule to, so select the "Request URL" object for cnn.com and click the "Add" button as shown below:

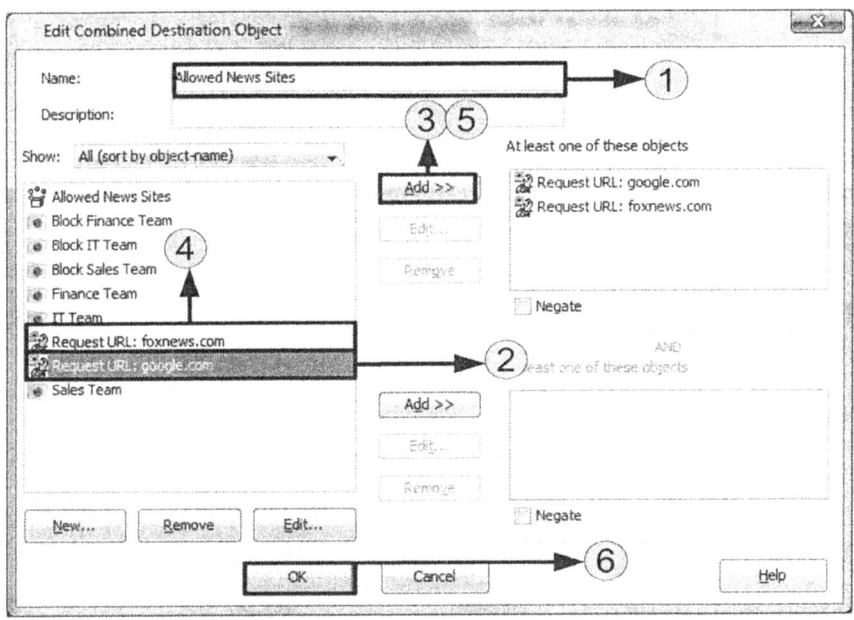

Figure 6:45 Moving Objects for Destination Objects

And confirm by clicking "OK". Then click "OK" in the "Set Destination Object" window.

4. Let the "Service" and "Time" be "Any". Right-click on "Action" and set it as "Allow", then install the policy by clicking the "Install Policy" button. The final rule set should be as shown below:

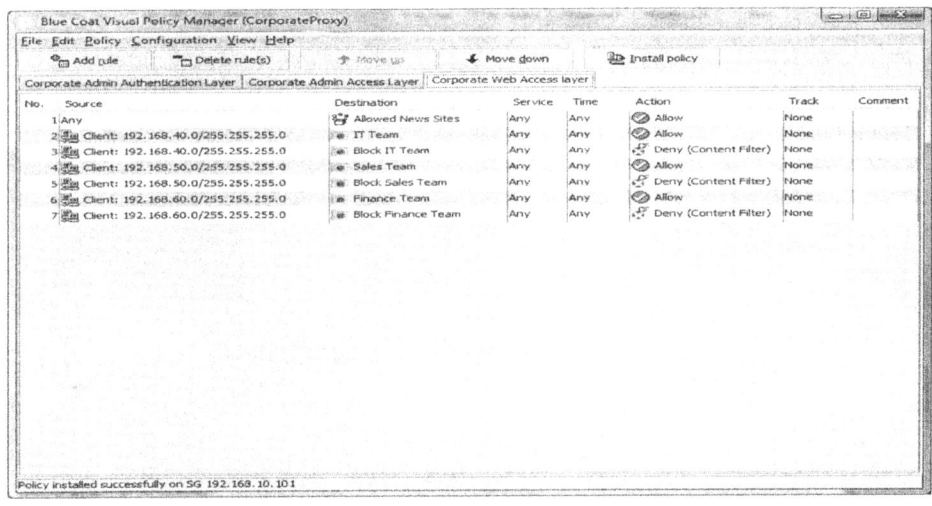

Figure 6:46 Web Access Layer with Allowed News Site combined object

DENY AND FORCE DENY:

You know how the policy gets executed. Let's say you want to deny access to a site, such as http://www.google.com, but you want to explicitly deny access to http://video.google.com. Now you will create a rule to explicitly deny it, by following the following procedure:

1. Launch VPM by going to Configuration → Policy → Visual Policy Manager" and clicking the "Launch" button. Go to "Corporate Web Access Layer" and select Rule 1 and click the "Add rule" button, and move the rule using the "Move Up" button in the toolbar. The reason you should have the denied rule at the top of the rule set is that you first deny access to video.google.com and then allow all sub-domains in google.com.

2. Let the Source be "Any" in the destination. Right-click and select "Set". Click the "New" button and select "Request URL". Enter video.google.com in the URL portion and click the "Add" button. Then click the "Close" button in the "Request URL object". Select the "Request URL" object and click "OK" as shown below:

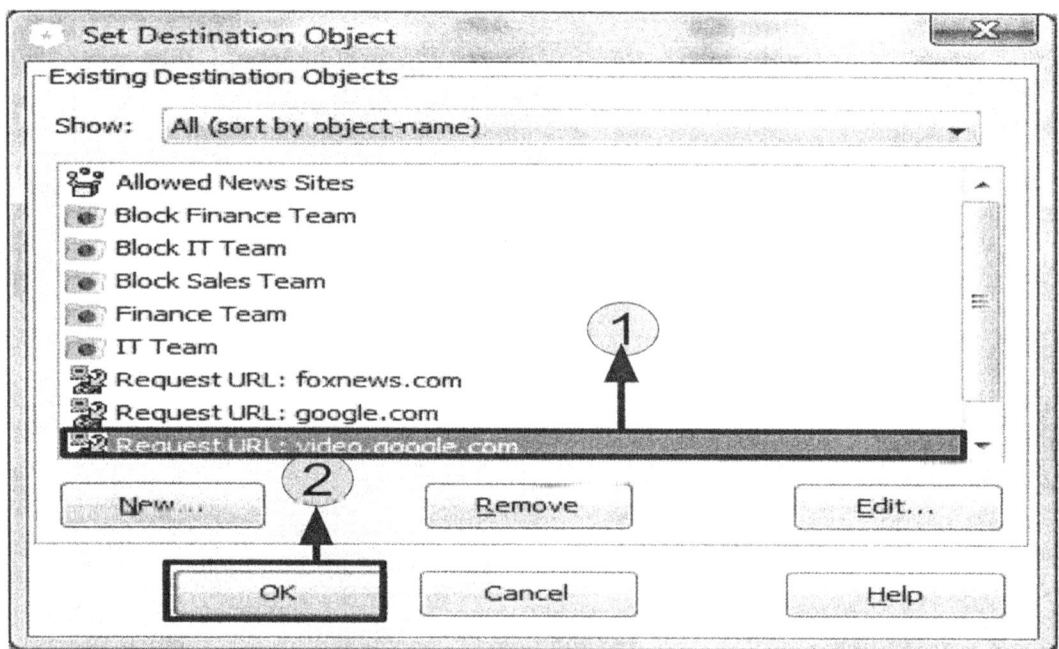

Figure 6:47 Destination object for Deny Action

3. Let the Service and Time object be "Any". By default the Action is "Deny" when we add a rule, so leave and install the policy by clicking the "Install Policy" button. The final policy should be as shown below:

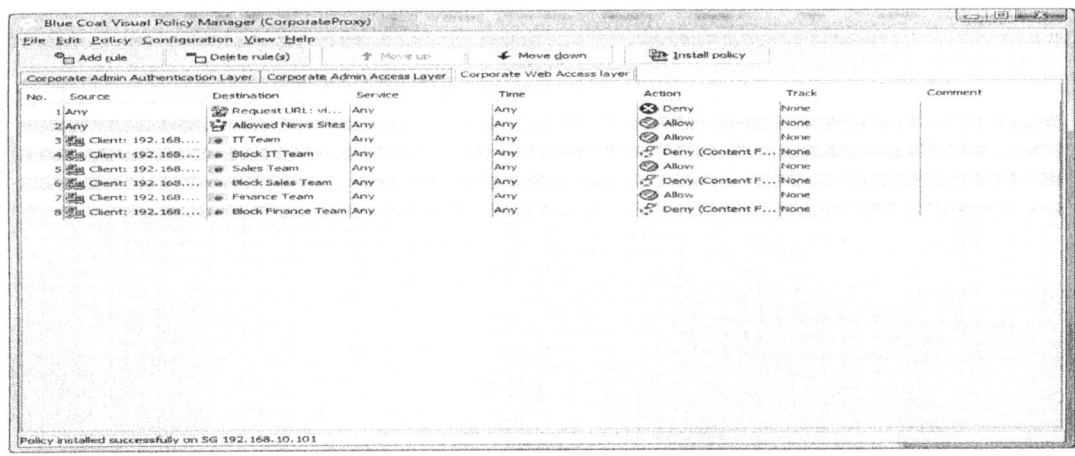

Figure 6:48 Web Access Layer VPM Policy with Deny Action

Now try accessing http://video.google.com. It should be denied as shown below:

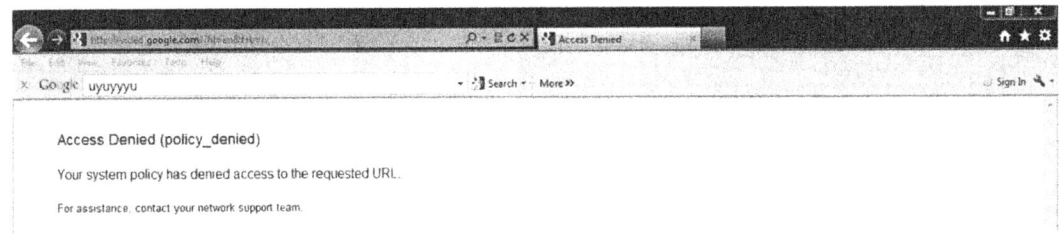

Figure 6:49 Blocked page for Deny rule

This is how to block access to a site. If there are multiple sites, you can use the local database or use the Combined objects as seen in the previous section. There is one problem with the "Deny" object: say that in the layer "Corporate Web Access Layer" you deny access. Suppose you allow video.google.com in a different Web Access Layer. Then what happens? Here we will show the difference between "Deny" and "Force Deny". Let's create a new "Web Access Layer" and allow access to video.google.com and see what happens.

Please follow the steps as shown below:

1. In the VPM, add one more "Web Access Layer" by clicking "Policy" in the menu bar, selecting "Web Access Layer", and naming it "Testing Web Access Layer".
2. Let the source be "Any", right-click on the destination. Select "Set", select "video.google.com", and click "OK" as shown below:

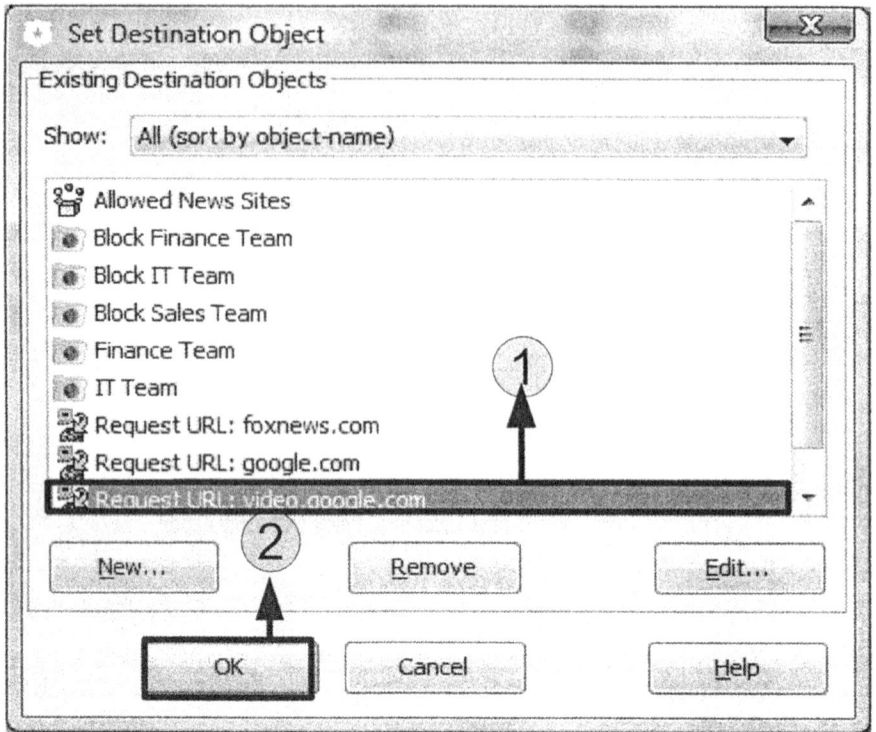

Figure 6:50 Destination object for Testing Web Access Layer

3. Let the Service and Time objects be "Any". Right-click on "Action", select "Allow", and install the policy by clicking the "Install Policy" button. The final policy will be as shown below:

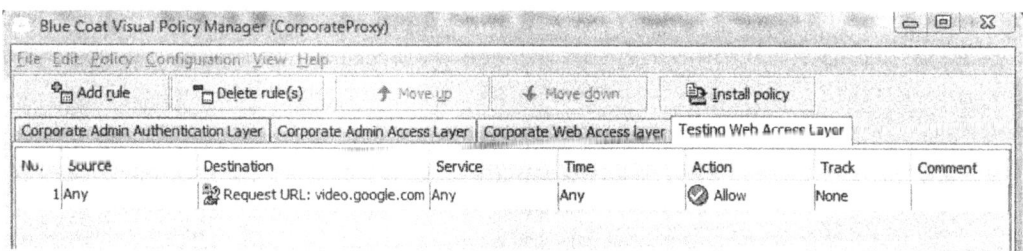

Figure 6:51 Testing Web Access layer

Now test whether access to the site "video.google.com" will be allowed. Surprised? Yes, this is the problem with the "Deny" object: you have to make sure that access is not allowed anywhere in the VPM. To get around this problem, use the "Force Deny" object, which will deny access, and the execution of the policy will not move further when it matches the request. Whereas for the "Deny" object, though it finds a match, it will execute the other rules in the VPM, and a decision is made on the last match for the request.

So use the "Force Deny" object in the VPM you created above, and follow the steps as shown below:

1. Go to the "Corporate Web Access Layer". Right-click on "Action" and click "Set". Then scroll down in the "Set Action Object", select the "Force Deny" object, and click "OK" as shown below:

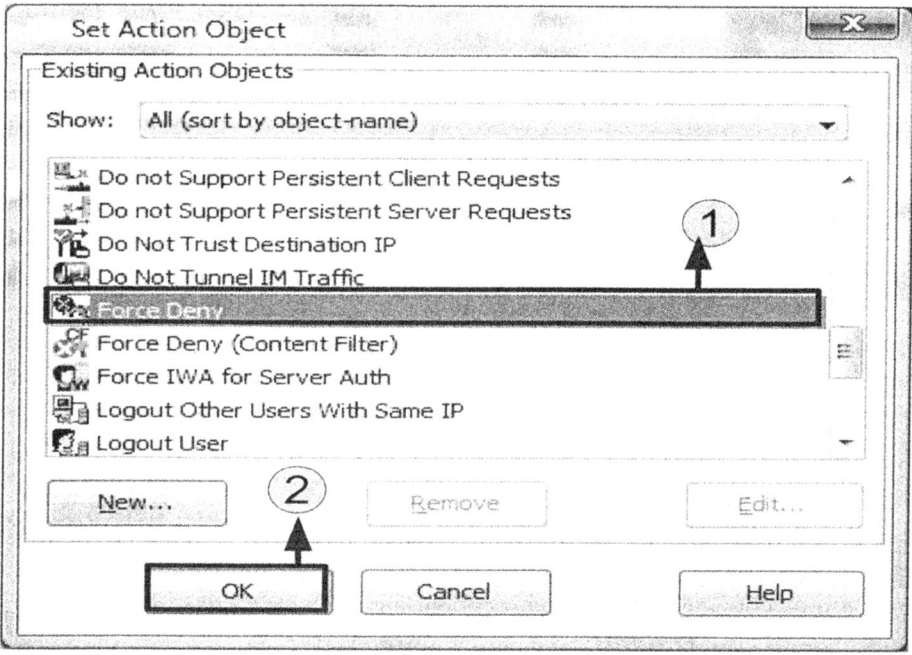

Figure 6:52 Force Deny Object for the Action column

2. Now install the policy by clicking the "Install Policy" button on the toolbar. The final VPM should look like the figure shown below:

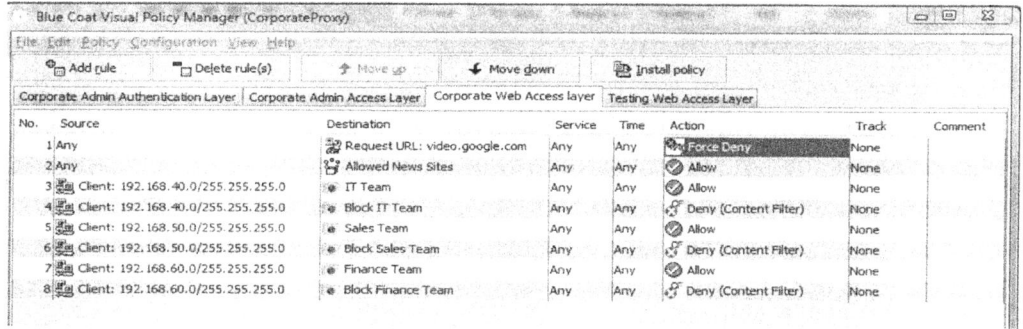

Figure 6:53 VPM Policy with Force Deny

Please make sure that there is an allow rule for videos.google.
com in the "Testing Web Access Layer."

3. Now test the site by using IE. You will be denied access to video.google.com.

So now you have seen the difference between "Deny" and "Force Deny". The same concept will apply to "Deny (Content Filter)" and "Force Deny (Content Filter)" objects as well, if you use content filtering BCWF for users URL access.

Local Database

In the section "Combined objects" we showed how to add multiple sites and allow access to them, but in a real world situation you wouldn't do it. This was just to demonstrate how "Combined objects" works. Say you have hundreds of URLs that need to be allowed or denied. You won't use this method of combined objects but instead you will use a local database. The other advantage of using a local database is that several proxies can be configured in the download path directed to the web server and you can maintain local database file for all the proxies. For this you will use a web Server like IIS or Apache. But here we use the "Central File" for the local database for simplicity of explanation; it is the same concept—just the throw the code in a webserver and it works the same. In the chapter "Content Filtering and WebPulse," we explain how to create a local database. Here we will show how use the local database in the VPM.

1. Please add the following in the local database by going to Configuration → Policy → Policy Files → Policy Files. In the "Install Central File from" section in the drop-down, select "Text Editor" and just paste the code as given below:

    define category Allowed_News_Sites_Localdatabase

    google.com

    foxnews.com

    end

    define category Denied_Sites_Localdatabase

    video.google.com

    end

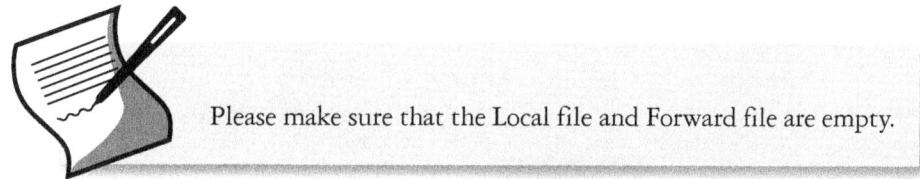

Please make sure that the Local file and Forward file are empty.

2. Now go to the VPM in the "Corporate Web Access Layer". On the first rule, right-click on the destination and select "Set". Click "New" and select "Request URL category". Name the object as "Blocked Sites", expand the "Policy" tree under the categories, and check the box next to "Denied_Sites_Localdatabase" as shown below:

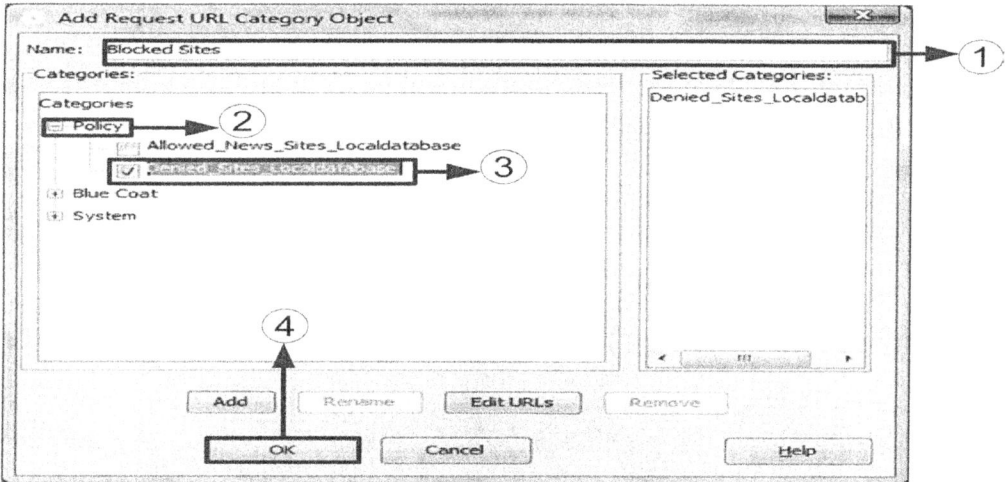

Figure 6:54 Creating Request URL category for Blocked Sites

And confirm by clicking "OK" to the "Add Request URL Category Object" and "OK" to the "Set Destination Object".

3. Then install the policy by clicking the "Install Policy" button in the toolbar. The final policy will be as shown below:

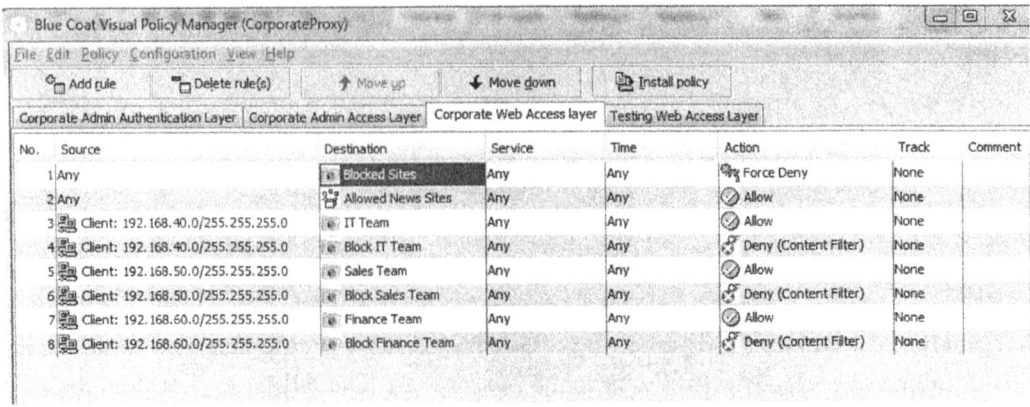

Figure 6:55 VPM Policy for Request URL category Blocked Sites

Now try accessing the site video.google.com; it will be blocked. Follow the same steps for allowing access to google.com and foxnews.com. Here you have used the "Allowed_ News_Sites_Localdatabase" local database. So rule 2 should be added with a new "Request URL category" in the destination field and named as "Allowed Sites". The Allowed_News_Sites_Localdatabase should be selected and theninstall the policy, and the final VPM policy should be as follows:

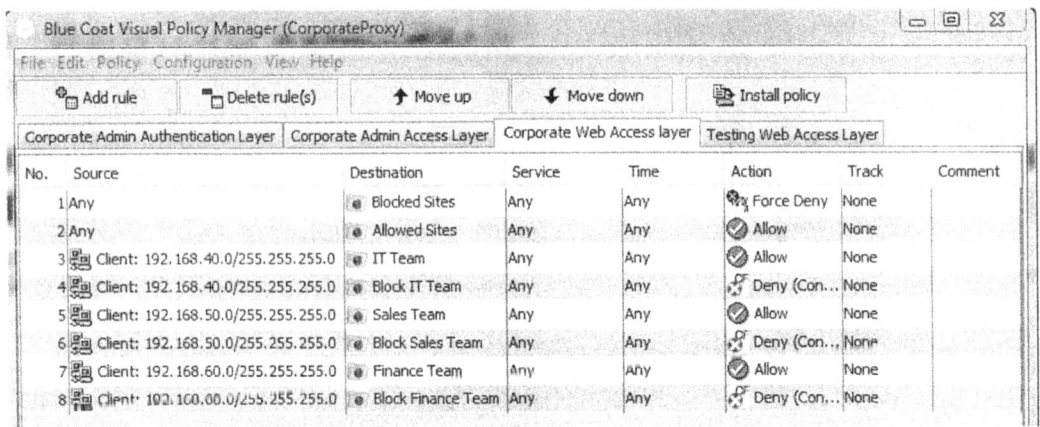

Figure 6:56 VPM Policy for Request URL category Allowed Sites

Caching configuration

We have discussed caching in detail in the "Caching and Optimization Techniques" chapter. BlueCoat uses its own caching algorithm for serving cache objects, but if you want to override this, you can use different caching options that are available in the VPM.

There are many reasons to override the default behavior. One of the major reasons is that certain web servers do not work well with the proxies. Other reasons are that certain sites shouldn't be cached, and the users always needs access fresh content that is not from the cache, such as with stock trading where the contents are dynamic, where the data should always be fresh because the trading sites are very dynamic and change every second.

So there are three situations to use the cache options in with the web, and these are all configured with the "Web Content Layer" and are as follows:

1. Always Verify

If you want the BlueCoat Proxy to always check the content before serving it to the clients, use the "Always Verify" caching option. If a client makes a request and if the destination is set as "Always Verify", the Proxy SG doesn't look even if it has a copy in the cache; instead, it will send a "If-Modified-Since" request to the OCS and check whether the content is fresh or stale. So for every request to that destination, always the freshness is checked. To configure this, follow the steps below:

1. Launch the VPM. Click "Policy" in the Menu bar, select "Web Content Layer", and name as "Corporate Web Cache Layer".

2. Right-click on the destination. Click "Set", then add the "Request URL" object as "scottrade.com", Scottrade.com is an well know example for stock trading market.

3. Right-click on the "Action" object and click "Set". Choose the static object "Always Verify" in the list and install the policy. The final VPM policy should look as follows:

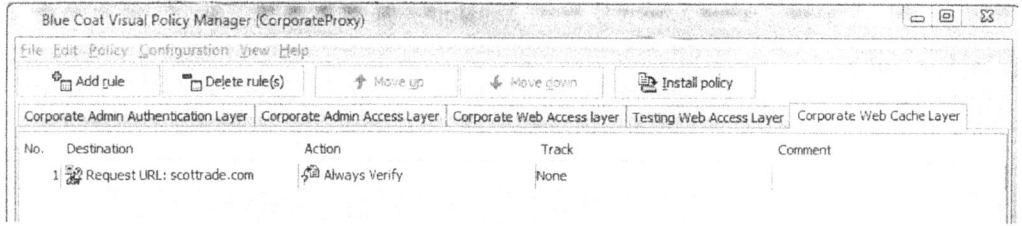

Figure 6:57 Caching VPM Policy

2. Do not cache

If you don't want to cache certain objects, use the caching feature as "Do not cache". When this option is used, the server response is not cached and the previous cache is deleted. The reason for using this caching option is used when certain specific defined content should not be cached, as it is unique to each client who is accessing it. To configure the option, please follow the steps below:

1. Launch the VPM, and go to the "Corporate Web Cache Layer" that you created in the VPM. Click "Add Rule".

2. In the destination column you could add the domain "yahoo.com". This is just an example; you could add any site that you don't want to cache. Add the site yahoo. com as a "Request URL" object.

3. Right click on the "Action" object, click "Set", choose the static object "Do Not Cache" in the list, and install the policy. The final VPM policy should look as follows:

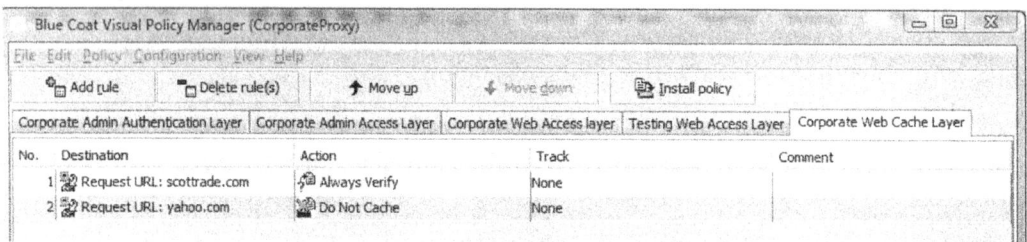

Figure 6:58 Do not cache VPM Policy

3. Force Cache

The "Force Cache" object is used where you need BlueCoat to "Force Cache" the request, so that all the users view the content from the cache. You can use this object where certain static videos need to be force-cached, because users frequently visit the sites and the videos changes very rarely. This could be applied for certain sites where the standard document is hosted and should be accessed by all the users. To configure this option, please follow the steps below:

1. Launch the VPM, and go to the "Corporate Web Cache Layer" that you created in the VPM. Click "Add Rule".

2. In the destination, you can put "nsa.gov"—this is just an example; you can add any site that you don't want to cache. Add the site yahoo.com as a "Request URL" object.

3. Right-click on the "Action" object and click "Set". Choose the static object "Force Cache" in the list and install the policy. The final VPM policy should look as follows:

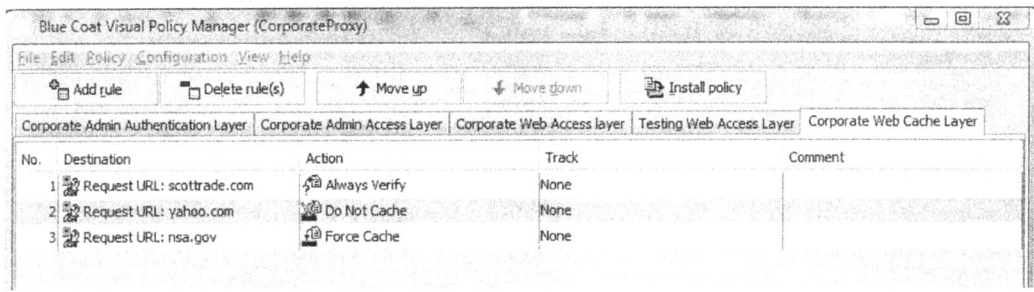

Figure 6:59 Force Cache VPM Policy

In all the three examples, instead of using the "Request URL", you could create a static local database, and add the URL that needs to be used for caching options for "Always Verify", "Do not Cache", and "Force Cache".

Test Yourself

1. When you create policies on VPM, what is the complied code of policies called?

   a. VPM
   b. Perl script
   c. C objects
   d. CPL

2. What is the default policy evaluation order in BlueCoat Proxy SG?

   a. VPM → Local → Central → Forward
   b. Forward → Local → Central → VPM
   c. Forward → VPM → Central → Local
   d. Central → Local → VPM → Forward

3. What is the maximum number of users that can be created in a database, and what is the maximum number of databases that can be created?

   a. 1 database with 10,000 users
   b. 50 databases with each database containing a maximum of 10,000 users

    c. 50 databases with each database containing 1,000 users

    d. We can only create administration accounts and not users.

4. In your VPM policy for the Proxy SG, you only have two layers. From the left, the first layer is the Web Access Layer and next to it on its right is Forwarding Layer. When the Proxy SG complies the policy and executes, which layer is executed and checked first irrespective of the traffic it is inspecting?

    a. First the Forwarding Layer and then the Web Access Layer

    b. The policy is not correct; the Admin Access Layer and the Admin Interception Layer also need to be in every policy.

    c. First the Web Access Layer and then the Forwarding Layer

    d. Only the Web Access Layer is evaluated and the Forward Layer is ignored.

5. What is the difference between a "deny" and "force deny" policy? (Choose two.)

    a. When a Deny object executes the policy, if the condition is matched then it doesn't evaluate other policies in other layers.

    b. When a Force Deny object executes the policy, if the condition is matched then it doesn't evaluate other policies in other layers even if there is match.

    c. When a Force Deny object executes the policy, if the condition is matched then it doesn't evaluate other policies in other layers unless there is match.

    d. When a Deny object executes the policy, if the condition is matched then it will still evaluate the rest of the policy.

6. In your VPM policy you have two Web Access layers. On the first layer you block access to http://www.cisco.com with a "Deny" object, and in the second layer you have allowed http://www.cisco.com. There is a Global policy set to "Deny" in the policy options. Will your Proxy SG allow access to http://www.cisco.com?

    a. Access http://www.cisco.com will be allowed.

    b. Access to http://www.cisco.com will be denied.

    c. The Global Policy is Deny, so access to http://www.cisco.com or any other sites will be denied.

    d. Global Policy is Deny, so access to http://www.cisco.com will be denied.

7. In your VPM policy, you have two Web Access layers. On the first layer you allow access to www.weather.com and in the second layer you have denied www.weather.com using a "Deny" object and there is global policy set to "Allow" in the policy options. Will your Proxy SG will allow access to www.weather.com?

    a. Access to www.weather.com will be denied.

    b. The Global Policy is "Allow"; access to www.weather.com will be denied.

   c. The Global Policy is Allow; access to www.weather.com will be allowed and any other site which matches the "Deny" statement will be allowed unless there is a "Force Deny".

   d. The Global Policy is Allow; access to www.weather.com will be allowed and all sites will be allowed.

8. In your company you have 10 GB Internet pipe. You always want fresh objects from the site and you don't want any cached content from the Proxy SG, since there is more bandwidth and you not are much concerned about bandwidth. What options could help you fulfill such a requirement?

   a. Do not cache

   b. Always Verify

   c. Force cache

   d. No VPM or CPL policy

9. What is the flow in which the policy layers and rules are executed?

   a. Policy layers right to left and rules top to bottom

   b. Policy layers top to bottom and rules top to bottom

   c. Policy layers top to bottom and rules left to right

   d. Policy layers left to right and rules top to bottom

10. What is the Policy file that BlueCoat could use when Proxy SG has performance issue (bugs in SGOS) and filters issue (new emerging viruses, worms, etc.)?

   a. Central policy file

   b. Local policy file

   c. Forward policy file

   d. CPL file

C H A P T E R   7

....

AUTHENTICATION

Authentication is the process of determining whether someone in fact who he or she is declared to be. Authentication is a very important piece in identifying the users in the network and assigning required privileges to them. It also ensures that legitimate users access the Corporate Internet and it is very helpful in situations where hacking or virus outbreak happens. Only with valid authentication to the internet, which makes harder for the attack to take place, since authentication adds a level of security. Authentication can be used to run Internet reports on users to find any Internet activity which doesn't comply with corporate security standards.

Authentication can be achieved in many ways, based on username/password (local and remote), tokens (RSA Secur ID), Single-Sign-On (SSO), guest authentication, etc. The simplest means of authentication is integrating with LDAP, local database, IWA, or Radius. The most efficient way of all is integrating with LDAP since it is very efficient in cases of creating groups and managing a large number of users. If you have other authentication mechanisms in your corporation, moving to LDAP is a better choice and the other authentication mechanisms still works well like IWA, Radius, and the local database. But as the number of users grow, scalability and performance will be problem.

In BlueCoat, authentication can be achieved in three different ways:

1. Authentication for managing the BlueCoat Proxy SG:

Authentication should be used for administrators who log in to the Proxy SG to configure and manage the box. This can be achieved by creating local accounts in the Proxy SG as we showed in the VPM chapter, or you could integrate Proxy SG with LDAP. So by using authentication, you can grant users access to the box based on their roles of Read-only or Read-write. The other form of authentication, besides CLI and the management console, is via the serial console and the front panel. Serial console is the first step of connection and of configuring a new Proxy SG and only (Out-of_Band) OOB connection available to the Proxy SG, so you can configure a password to protect it. The front panel can be configured with a password to avoid a physical security threat to the box. In the chapter "Visual Policy Manager (VPM)," we saw how to create an administrator account with Read-only and Read-write permissions.

2. Authentication for accessing Proxy SG services:

The Proxy SG nc be configured for authentication for users who access the Internet, intranet, and extranet services proxied by the Proxy SG. All users accessing the Proxy SG should authenticated, especially when using Internet web services, FTP, and video streaming, as these are very critical applications and many security issues are involved in the applications. If you authenticate, you will have the logs for authenticated users, which helps track users' activity and have complete visibility of the network. Usually user authentication for services can be integrated with LDAP, IW, RADIUS, SSO, Oracle Coreid, CA Siteminder, using certificates, etc.

3. Authentication for the OCS:

The OCSs are the peer servers which the user is trying to access. If the OCS needs authentication of the user to access the content, it sends a challenge to the user and the proxy just forwards it back and forth between the user and the OCS. Here it acts as the relay, and remember that the Proxy SG has no control over the remote OCS server as it is not owned by the Proxy or the corporation using it. An example is , email, username, and password for Hotmail accounts, as you don't have control of Microsoft email services.

AUTHORIZATION:

Before we start discussing the different types of authentication, you should know what authorization is in BlueCoat, since you will build user policies, configure authentication servers, user groups in Proxy SG based upon this.

Once the user is authenticated, what resources is the user is allowed to access and for how long? These requirements are fulfilled by configuring authorization in BlueCoat Proxy SG. Authorization can be achieved by configuring groups so that each user is assigned as a part of the group, so when you create policies, you assign groups for the authorization for users. For example, you built policies in the last chapter where you allowed access to users based on IP addresses. Say you want to allow access based on usernames. To achieve this, you should create groups and assign them to users, so if a user needs access to certain BCWF categories or certain sites, the Proxy SG will use the source field as the "Group" and check that the group is configured for the user; if yes, it allows access.

AUTHENTICATION IN BLUECOAT:

We saw the three ways that authentication could be performed by the BlueCoat Proxy SG. Let's describe each authentication in detail now.

1. Authentication for managing the BlueCoat Proxy SG:

This type of authentication is used to change the settings of configuration on the BlueCoat Proxy SG itself. The purpose of configuring this type of authentication is to secure the BlueCoat Proxy SG from unauthorized access, so that only administrators and authorized persons are allowed to configure and manage the BlueCoat Proxy SG.

There are four main ways to configure and manage the BlueCoat Proxy SG:

1. Using the Serial console
2. Using the LCD panel
3. Using the remote CLI shell
4. Using the GUI console

1. Using the Serial console:

You should configure authentication for the serial console, since anyone with physical access to the box could connect their laptop to the BlueCoat Proxy SG and change the configuration. To protect gaainst this unauthorized access, configure authentication to access the serial port. Since serial interface is OOB, you cannot configure VPM or CPL to access it, you need to configure it with the OOB connection. You may recall that we showed in the chapter "Configuring Blue Coat Proxy SG" how to use terminal services like Putty to connect to a console. We need to connect to the console of the Proxy SG and follow the steps as shown below:

Press "Enter" three times to activate the serial console.
    Welcome to the SG Appliance Serial Console
    Version: SGOS 5.5.5.1, Release id: 63141
------------------------ MENU ----------------------------
1) Command Line Interface
2) Setup Console

Enter option:
Welcome to the Blue Coat ProxySG 510 configuration wizard.

This appliance's serial number: 3107104015

You can get field help by entering a question mark ? in the fields.

You can move backwards through the steps by pressing the UP arrow.

You can exit the wizard without saving your entries by pressing ESC.

Step 1: How do you plan to configure this appliance?

    a) Through a manual setup

    b) Through a Director-managed setup

      Your choice: [a] **a**

Step 2: Which solution would you like to implement?

    a) Acceleration

    b) Other solution

      Your choice: [b] **b**

Welcome to the SG Appliance Setup Console

---------------------- (page 1 of 4) ----------------------

Press <ESC> at any time to return to the main menu

Setup mode: Manual

DIRECTIONS:

Please enter the IP addresses for the SG Appliance.

    The following interfaces are available for configuration:

        1. Interface 0:0 (link)

        2. Interface 1:0 (no link)

        3. Bridge passthru-2 (WAN: no link, LAN: no link)

Enter interface number to configure [1]: **1**

Is the IP address to be configured on a non-native VLAN? (Y/N) [No] No

IP address [192.168.10.101]:

IP subnet mask [255.255.255.0]:

IP gateway [192.168.10 1]:

DNS server [4.2.2.2]:

You have entered the following IP addresses:

IP address: 192.168.10.101

IP subnet mask: 255.255.255.0

IP gateway: 192.168.10.1

DNS server: 4.2.2.2

Would you like to change any of them? Y/N [No]

---------------------- (page 2 of 4) ----------------------

Press <ESC> at any time to return to the main menu

DIRECTIONS:

The console username, password, and enable password are special administrative credentials which can be used to log in to the command line interface or web management interface.
Would you like to change the console user account now? Y/N [No] **No**

DIRECTIONS:

When the serial port is secured, access via the serial port must be authenticated. A setup password is required to gain access to the Setup Console and administrative credentials are required to access the command line interface.

Do you want to secure the serial port? Y/N [Yes] **Yes**

Enter setup password: "Enter the password"
Verify setup password: "Enter the password"

WARNING:

If you continue and enable the secure serial port it will not be possible to enter the setup console without the setup password. If the setup password is lost, assistance from Blue Coat Systems will be required and all system configuration may be lost. It is recommended that this password be stored in a physically secure location. Access to the CLI on the serial port will challenge for credentials.

To enable the secure serial port, re-enter the setup password:"Enter the password"

--------------------- (page 3 of 4) ---------------------
Press <ESC> at any time to return to the main menu

DIRECTIONS:

The console username and password are special: they can be used to log in to the CLI or Web Management interface even in circumstances where this is denied by VPM or CPL policy. This makes the console account useful in emergencies, as a way to log in when policy is broken, but it may also create a security hole. To close the security hole, we recommend that you restrict the use of the console account to specific workstations, identified by their IP address. This dialog allows you to add one IP address to the list of workstations that are authorized to use the console account. (This same list is also used to restrict which workstations can use SSH with RSA authentication.) Additional workstations may be configured later, from the command line interface or the web interface. WARNING: The console account can currently be used to log in from any workstation.

Would you like to restrict access to an authorized workstation? Y/N [Yes] No

-------------------- (page 4 of 4) --------------------

DIRECTIONS:

The SG Appliance has been successfully configured to use IP address: "192.168.10.101" You can connect to the command line interface or webinterface to perform additional management tasks. To connect to the command line interface, open the following location from your SSH application: 192.168.10.101 To connect to the webmanagement interface, go to the following location with your web browser:

https://192.168.10.101:8082/

To confirm access to the console server, unplug the console and reconnect and check you will be getting a prompt as shown below:

Press "enter" three times to activate the serial console

    Welcome to the SG Appliance Serial Console
    Version: SGOS 5.5.5.1, Release id: 63141
------------------------ MENU ----------------------------
    1) Command Line Interface
    2) Setup Console

Enter option:2
Enter setup password:"Enter the console password that you created"
Welcome to the Blue Coat ProxySG 510 configuration wizard.
This appliance's serial number: 3107104015

    You can get field help by entering a question mark ? in the fields.
    You can move backwards through the steps by pressing the UP arrow.
    You can exit the wizard without saving your entries by pressing ESC.

Step 1: How do you plan to configure this appliance?
    a) Through a manual setup
    b) Through a Director-managed setup
       Your choice: [a]

If you forget the console password, you will need to contact the BlueCoat Support team to unlock it. Sometimes you could even lose the configuration of the Proxy SG as well. So please these write down and store them in a safe place and remember it.

2. LCD panel authentication:

You also need to protect the LCA panel by configuring authentication in it. If you provide authentication to the LCD panel, you are protecting device from physical access. We explained in the chapter "Configuring Blue Coat Proxy SG," how to use the LCD panel to configure the initial settings like the IP address, subnet, gateway, etc. So here we will show how to configure a pin for the LCD panel which will be used as an authentication mechanism for anyone who wants to change or update the settings of the SGOS via the LCD panel.

Log in to the Proxy SG via SSH, and go to Enable mode and follow the steps as shown below to configure the LCA panel pin:

CorporateProxy>**en**

Enable Password:

CorporateProxy#**conf t**

Enter configuration commands, one per line. End with CTRL-Z.

CorporateProxy#(config front-panel)**exit**

CorporateProxy#(config)**security front-panel-pin** 1234

If you want the front panel pin to be in a hashed format then use the following command to setup.

CorporateProxy#(config)**security hashed-front-panel-pin** 1234

So the next time you try accessing the front panel, you will be authenticated, and you should enter the the password you configured as shown above.

3. Remote CLI Shell

We have already discussed about CLI access to the Proxy SG in the previous chapter and you can configure the management serviceseither using a remote shell (SSH/Telnet) or using the Management console GUI. Always make sure to only allow remote CLI via SSH and not via Telnet, since SSH is encrypted and secure, while telnet is in plain text and is not secure since anyone running a packet sniffer could capture the password in the wire. By default, in all new Proxy SG versions telnet is not included in menu options, as you can see from figure 1 below:

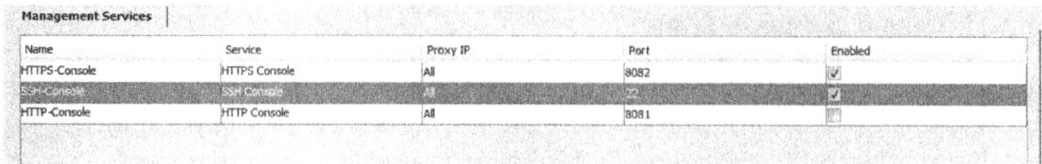

Figure 7:1: Management Services console

If you need to check or change any settings for the remote CLI, log in to the management console and go to Configuration → Services → Management Services. Click on the SSH-Console and click "Edit" under the "Management Services". You will see a screen as shown below:

Figure 7.2: Editing Management Services console

If you want to change the default port of SSH to any other random port, click the line under "Listeners", change the port, and apply the change by clicking "OK" and click "Apply", confirming the change.

This is just an information to show that you could enable Telnet option as a remote CLI, but please do not enable this, as it will cause a potential security issue for the Proxy SG. To enable telnet remote CLI, log in to the management console and go to Configuration → Services → Management Services. Click "New" under the "Management Services" and enter the details as shown below and apply the change:

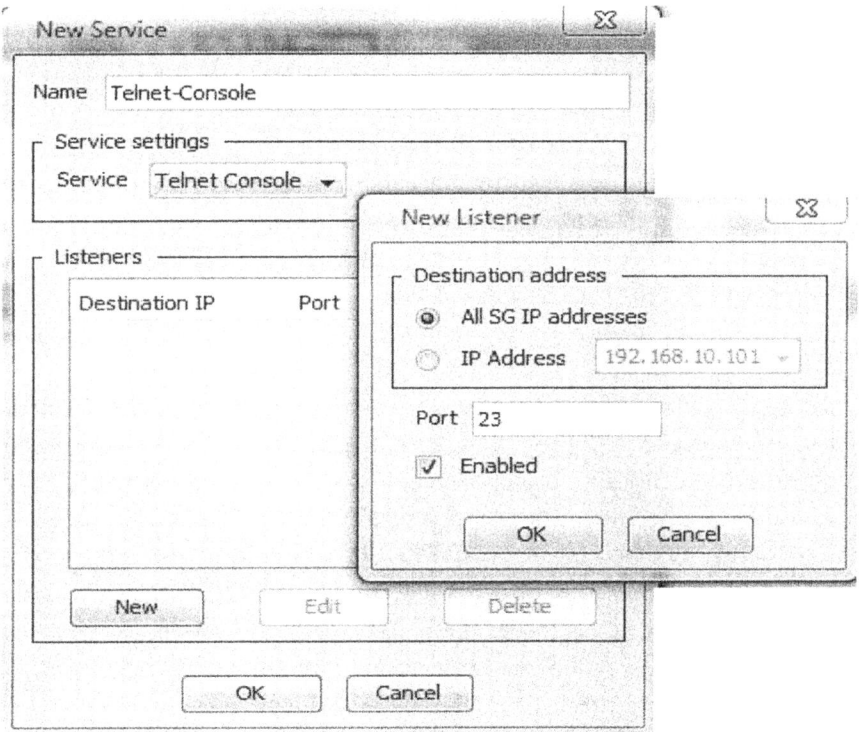

Figure 7:3: Editing Telnet Management Services console

4. Using GUI console:

The GUI console as you are already aware of it, is also known as the management console which we use to log in via a browser and connect using port 8082 for accessing HTTPS console access. There are two options here of accessing the management console, either via HTTP or HTTPS. But by default, only HTTPS is enabled, because it is encrypted and secure. Please don't use HTTP as it is in clear text and it creates a security hole in the Proxy SG. You can access the settings by logging in to the management console and going to Configuration → Services → Management Services. Under "Management Services" you change the settings as per your environment, as shown below:

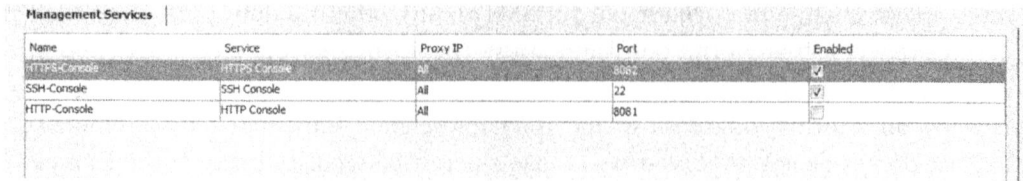

| Management Services | | | | |
Name	Service	Proxy IP	Port	Enabled
HTTPS-Console	HTTPS Console	All	8082	☑
SSH-Console	SSH Console	All	22	☑
HTTP-Console	HTTP Console	All	8081	☐

Figure 7.4: Management Services console

The above figure shows that HTTP is not enabled by default. You can change the port of HTTPS to other ports other than 8082, but please do not change any port that the proxy is enabled to listen to for proxy services. For example, do not change it to 443, as you know you will be using this service for intercepting HTTPS user traffic. Though the port 8082 is an HTTPS traffic it is intended for management access to the Proxy SG GUI interface and not for user's proxy access or intercepting SSL traffic. Be careful when changing such default settings; in most situations leave them to the default and it should be good.

2. Authentication for OCS:

You need know this first before we start discussing the proxy authentication of user traffic, as it uses the same principle. The authentication for OCS means that the peer web server wants to authenticate the user before allowing access to its resources. A very easy example is when you are trying accessing your email via Hotmail, Gmail, Yahoo Mail etc. You will be authenticated before allowing access to your inbox. The same principle applies to all your internal web servers as well, where you authenticate all the users before allowing access to the resources in the server. So what is the role of Proxy SG in these types of requests/responses? The Proxy SG has no major role in this; it just forwards the requests and responses back and forth between the user and the OCS server. Let's show an example of how authentication works when a user tries accessing an OCS server where authentication is involved; this transaction is between user and OCS, and no proxy is involved. Let's imagine a user from home tries accessing a web server where authentication is involved before allowing access to web resources, as shown below.

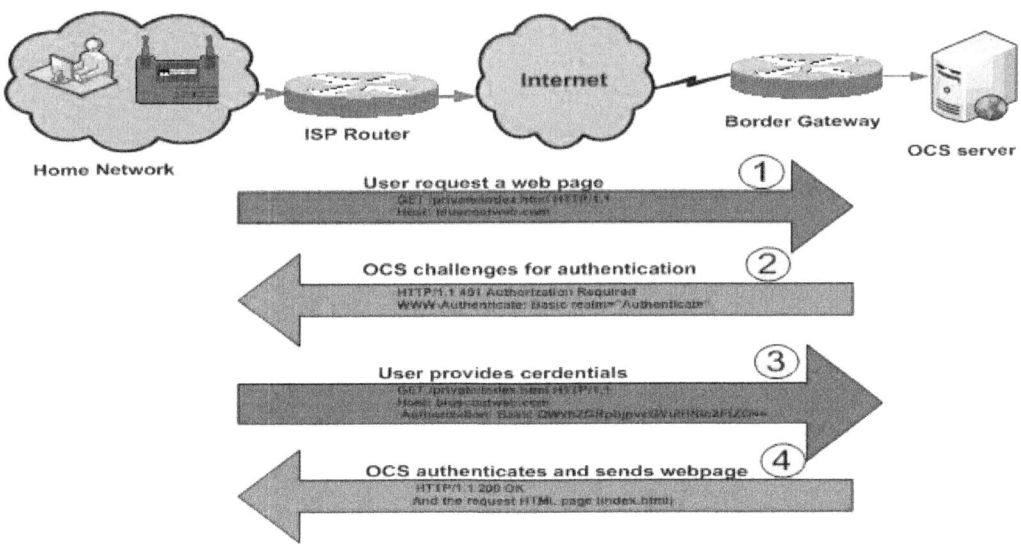

Figure 7.5: Authentication from OCS

As we see in the above figure, the when the user tries accessing a web page that needs authentication, it sends an HTTP 401 (Authorized Required) response and a WWW-Authenticate header, and the user responds with an "Authorization" with the credentials back to the OCS. So this is the way the web server authenticates the user. The key concept you should know here is that the OCS requires an HTTP 401 message, which basically notifies the user that it needs authentication to be allowed access to the resources.

USER AGENT:

In this chapter we will be talking about the user agent, which is a term used for browsers, such as Internet Explorer, Mozilla, Firefox, Opera, Safari, etc. In short, all the browsersyou can call as User Agent(UA). A user will always try to access a UA, which is browser to surf the web.

3. Authentication for accessing Proxy SG services:

Now we will discuss how to authenticate users trying to access the Internet via Proxy SG. Say your organization needs to authenticate the users before allowing them to access the Internet. It could track user access and do auditing in terms of when the user has violated its Internet polices. By performing authentication, you know only authorized persons can access the Internet, and unauthorized persons can be blocked since they needs authentication. Thus you are implementing security policies in the organization.

You already know that the BlueCoat Proxy SG can be deployed in two different ways:

1. Explicit deployment
2. Transparent deployment

In the same way, there are two types authentication modes that can be implemented:

1. Explicit Authentication
2. Transparent Authentication

1. Explicit authentication:

As the name states, explicit authentication is used for explicit deployment, meaning where the browsers are explicitly pointed to the Proxy SG in the settings. So when using this type of authentication, the UA clearly knows that it is talking to a proxy. And when the proxy authenticates the UA, the UA knows how to handle such requests. In explicit authentication, the Proxy SG sends an HTTP 407 (Proxy-Authenticate) message response, and in turn the UA will return the username password in the "Proxy Authorization" header. The flow of this is shown in the following figure:

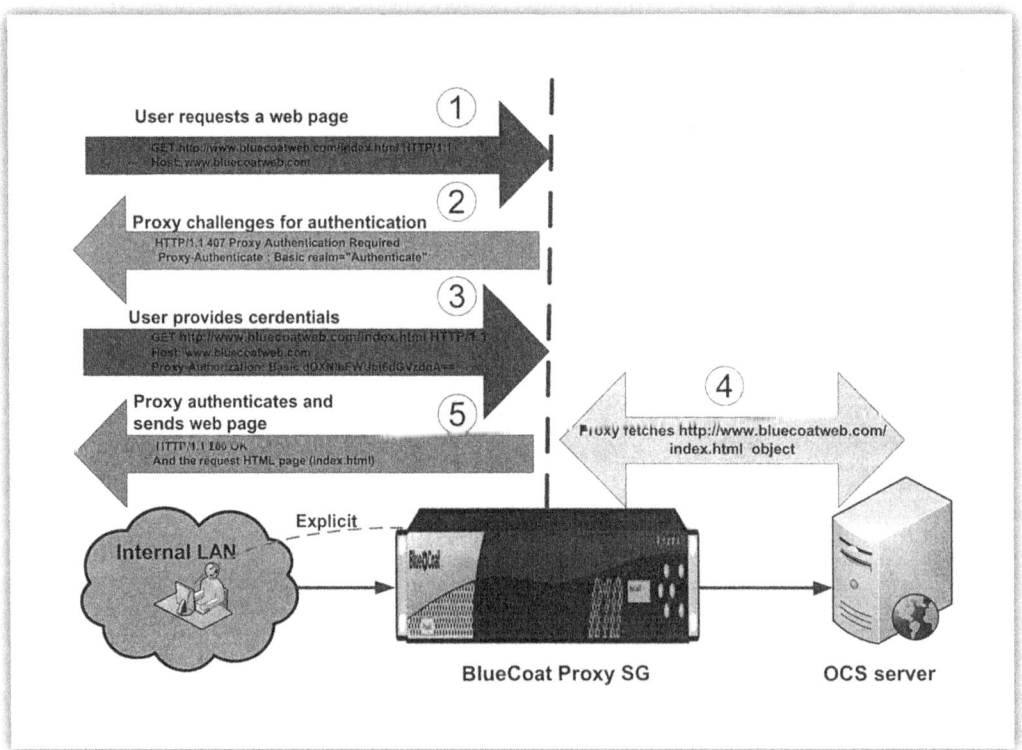

Figure 7.6: Explicit Authentication

You should also observe the difference between a GET request when using explicit proxy to access the OCS server and when accessing OCS server directly without using proxy.

GET /private/index.html HTTP/1.1 → Direct OCS access without proxy (Refer figure 7:6)

GET http://www.bluecoatweb.com/index.html HTTP/1.1 → Accessing OCS in explicit mode

2. Transparent authentication:

In transparent authentication the user sends a request, the same as in the case of "Authentication for OCS". The browser assumes that it is talking to the OCS server and does not know that there is a Proxy in the transit. The packet flow will be the same as that of "Authenticate for OCS" for the GET request. When the Proxy SG wants to authenticate such traffic, it cannot send "HTTP/1.1 407 Proxy Authentication Required"; because when the browser or UA receives such request, it will drop and ignore the traffic. The reason is that the UA initiates the traffic assuming it is talking to a OCS server, and it expects a reply from that OCS server; when it encounters "HTTP/1.1 407 Proxy Authentication Required", which is only used for explicit authentication, the UA will drop the traffic. To overcome this issue, you need to authenticate the URL that the UA is trying to access by impersonating the UA or tricking UA and making the UA believe it is been challenged by the OCS. This can be achieved by sending a "HTTP/1.1 401 response" back to the UA and making it authenticate. This is explained and shown below:

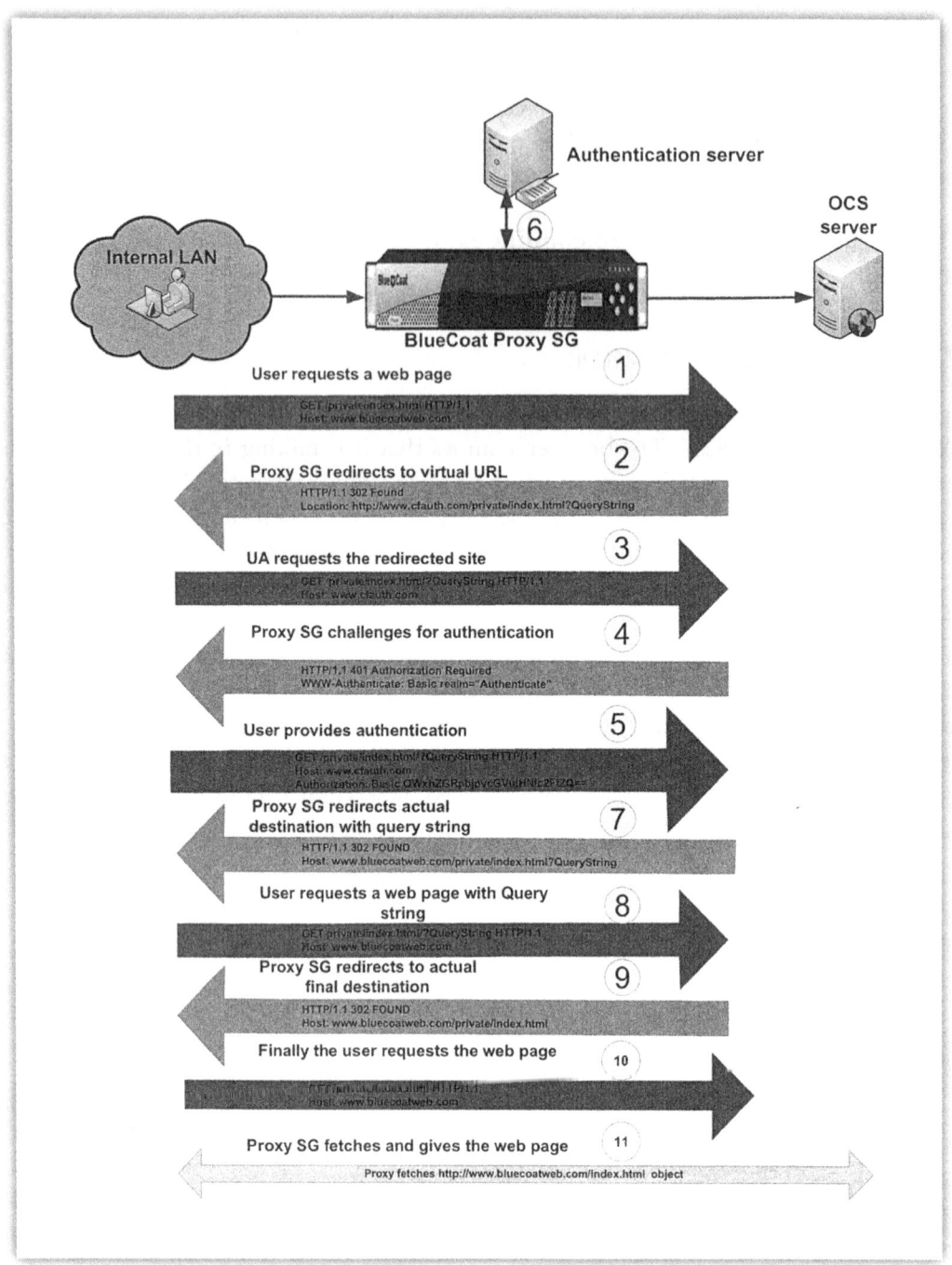

Figure 7.7: Transparent Authentication

The flow of the request is described as below:

1. The UA makes a request to http://www.bluecoatweb.com/private/index.html and then the Proxy SG, which is deployed in transparent mode, intercepts the traffic.

2. The Proxy SG checks its policy and finds that the traffic needs to be authenticated, so it sends a redirect 302 (Temporarily Moved) request back to the UA, saying the site http://www.bluecoatweb.com/private/index.html has temporarily been moved to http://www.cfauth.com/private/index.html. The URL www.cfauth.com is called a virtual URL. This could be any domain that is resolvable in the network and unused. By default, BlueCoat is configured by default with this domain www.cfauth.com, which resolves to 216.52.23.29. This domain is not a real website; it is just used for redirection and considered a virtual URL. If you don't want to use this URL you can also buy your own domain and use it in your corpration only for the virtual URL. Otherwise you can use internal domain space for the virtual URL, for example virtualdomain.corporation.com. And always make sure that this domain name is not used by any applications and it is resolved by your internal DNS server.

You should also note http://www.cfauth.com/private/index.html?QueryString , in the URL "?QueryString", this is actual a sort of encoding mechanism that BlueCoat uses, encoding is that each user will get a unique for each request and it looks like "fa2f357e162142 0=1D1D84AE00000005+H1Jw". The encoding that is used is Base 64 encoding and encoding is generated based upon the absolute URI. The reason you use a query string is it identifies and separates the request by using this as an ID. Imagine same user opens two browsers and request the same website, one way the Proxy SG differentiates is via the source port numbers, as it will be different for each request, but we know one TCP connection will pull two objects, which means it uses the same port number, so only by using the Query string it could identify each specific request and the BlueCoat Proxy SG knows that it only encoded the request and knows how to decode it and knows the difference in between each request.

3. The UA now makes a GET request "**GET /private/index.html/?QueryString HTTP/1.1**" to the **host** www.cfauth.com. This is the place where the Proxy SG tricks the UA that the destination site is been redirected.

4. At this stage, the BlueCoat Proxy SG sends an authentication request with HTTP/1.1 401 Authorization Required back to the UA, challenging the UA for credentials. So now the browser will trust the request since it gave HTTP/1.1 401 and not HTTP/1.1 407.

5. The user sends the credentials in a Base 64 format back to the BlueCoat Proxy SG to the virtual URL which the Proxy SG redirected.

6. The BlueCoat Proxy SG sends back a redirect 302 and confirms that the authentication passed through to the actual URL that the UA requested and the query string is appended to the UA request, because that is the GET request which the UA requested in step 5.

7. Now the UA again initiates a request which was sent in step 6 to the Proxy SG (**GET private/index.html/?QueryString HTTP/1.1**).

8. Now the Proxy SG redirects the UA to the actual request which you requested in Step 1, http://www.bluecoatweb.com/private/index.html.

9. And now the UA makes a request of the web page, the same as in the Step 1.

10. The Proxy SG fetches the request from the OCS server and gives it back to the UA.

Transparent Authentication using cookie surrogate

In the above scenario, we saw how the user was authenticated in a transparent authentication. Always remember to authenticate the user using the virtual URL http://www.cfauth.com or any domain or the proxy hostname (which should be resolvable in DNS). As shown in the above example, the user is authenticated for http://www.bluecoatweb.com. What happens if the user wants to visit a new site such as http://www.microsoft.com? The process repeats and the user is prompted for authentication because it is a new domain and has never been authenticated. In contrast, if the user is authenticated for bluecoatweb.com and tries going to any sub-domain such as download.bluecoatweb.com, the user will not be prompted for authentication, as the browser cache will handle it by giving the credentials without prompting the user; this still requires the browser settings. So to handle the repeated authentication process, you will authenticate the user against a common virtual URL, which is an index and front-end of all sites visited by the user.

If authentication is done with a virtual URL, and if the credentials are cached in the browser, then the user is not prompted for authentication every time he or she goes to any new site. But here is the limitation: the caching depends upon browser settings; in the most cases it is feasible and advisable to cache credentials, and this approach will not work in real world deployment. It is just a theory in the IT world. Then how can one-time authentciation be achieved? Cookies. Yes, this is the best way to authenticate the user. The Proxy SG gives a cookie and this cookie is stored in the user's browser. When the user goes to any site, the Proxy SG requests the cookie for the virtual URL. Yes, the cookie is delivered for the virtual URL http://www.cfauth.com or any domain or proxy hostname, so for every request that is redirected for a new site that is visited by the user is redirected to the virtual URL, the browser will automatically deliver the cookies for the virtual URL, and the Proxy SG evaluates the cookie and allows access if the cookies are valid.

So are cookies the only solution? No, we have one more means authentication called the IP surrogate authentication. This is where the user credentials are tied with the IP address of the user machine, as after an initial authentication, all the requests that comes from the user are evaluated by the Proxy SG based on the IP address of the user. This solution is useful when in certain cases, the browser doesn't accept cookies.

First we will show how authentication can be achieved by using a virtual URL and a cookie that is tied to the user's browser for the first time the user tries accessing the Internet. All later Internet requests are handled by the cookie between the browser and the Proxy SG.

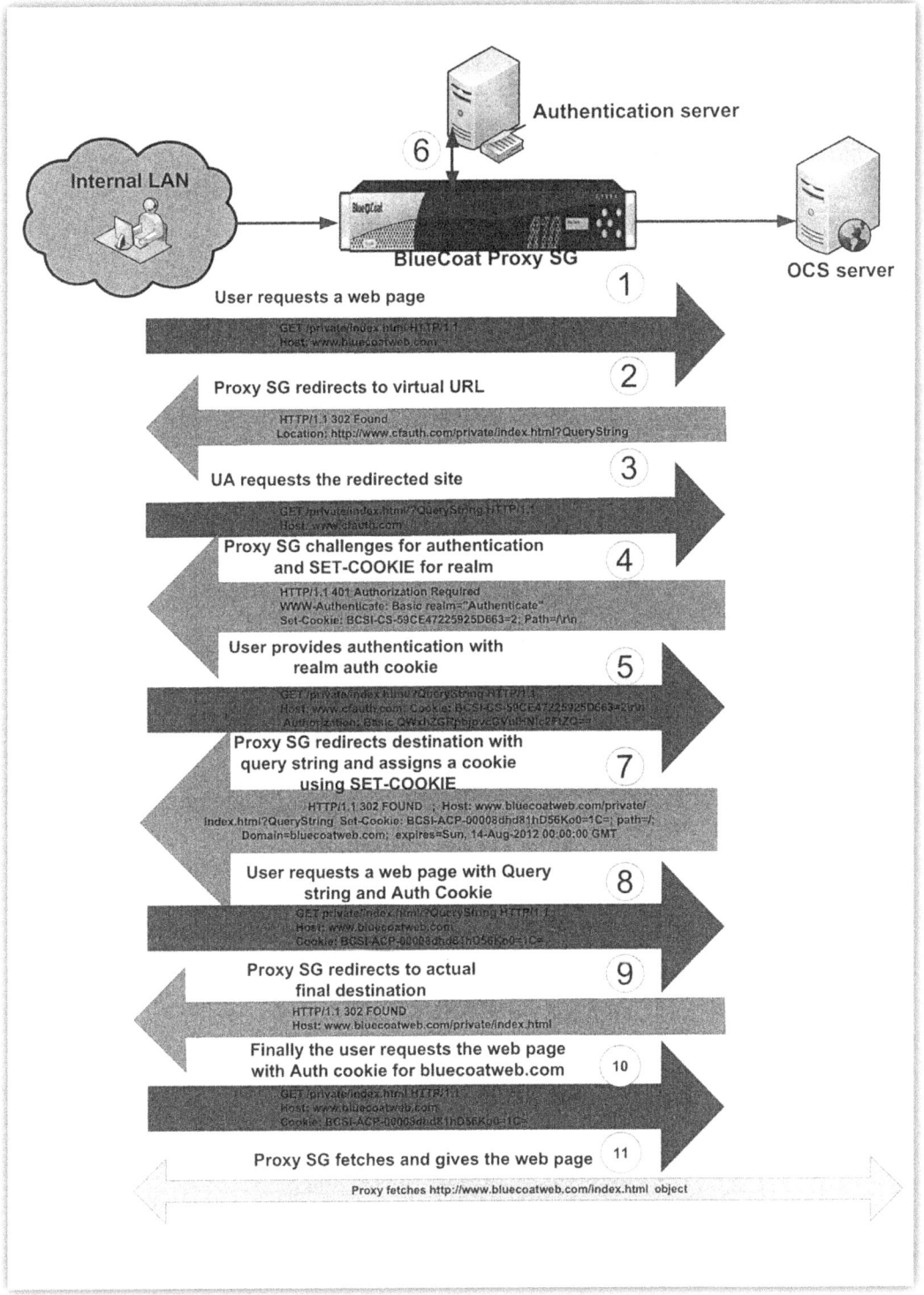

Figure 7.8: Transparent Authentication using cookie surrogate for single domain

As we see in the above figure, the first time the user gets authenticated, the Proxy SG gives a cookie for the virtual URL realm http://www.cfauth.com, and then domain-based cookies are assigned for the website the user visits. In our above example, the user tries going to http://www.bluecoatweb.com. The BlueCoat Proxy SG assigns an authentication cookie for that domain, and all later requests are allowed, since every time the user goes to any subdomain in http://bluecoatweb.com, the browser automatically forwards the request to the BlueCoat Proxy SG for http://bluecoatweb.com, and the Proxy SG verifies the cookie and allows access to the site.

What happens when the user tries accessing www.bluecoat.com a different domain? It is the same process, but the user is not prompted for authentication this time, An authentication cookie is assigned to bluecoat.com, and every time the user tries going to any sub-domain in bluecoat.com, the browser automatically forwards the request to the BlueCoat Proxy SG for bluecoat.com and the Proxy SG verifies the cookie and allows access to the site. The flow is shown in the figure below.

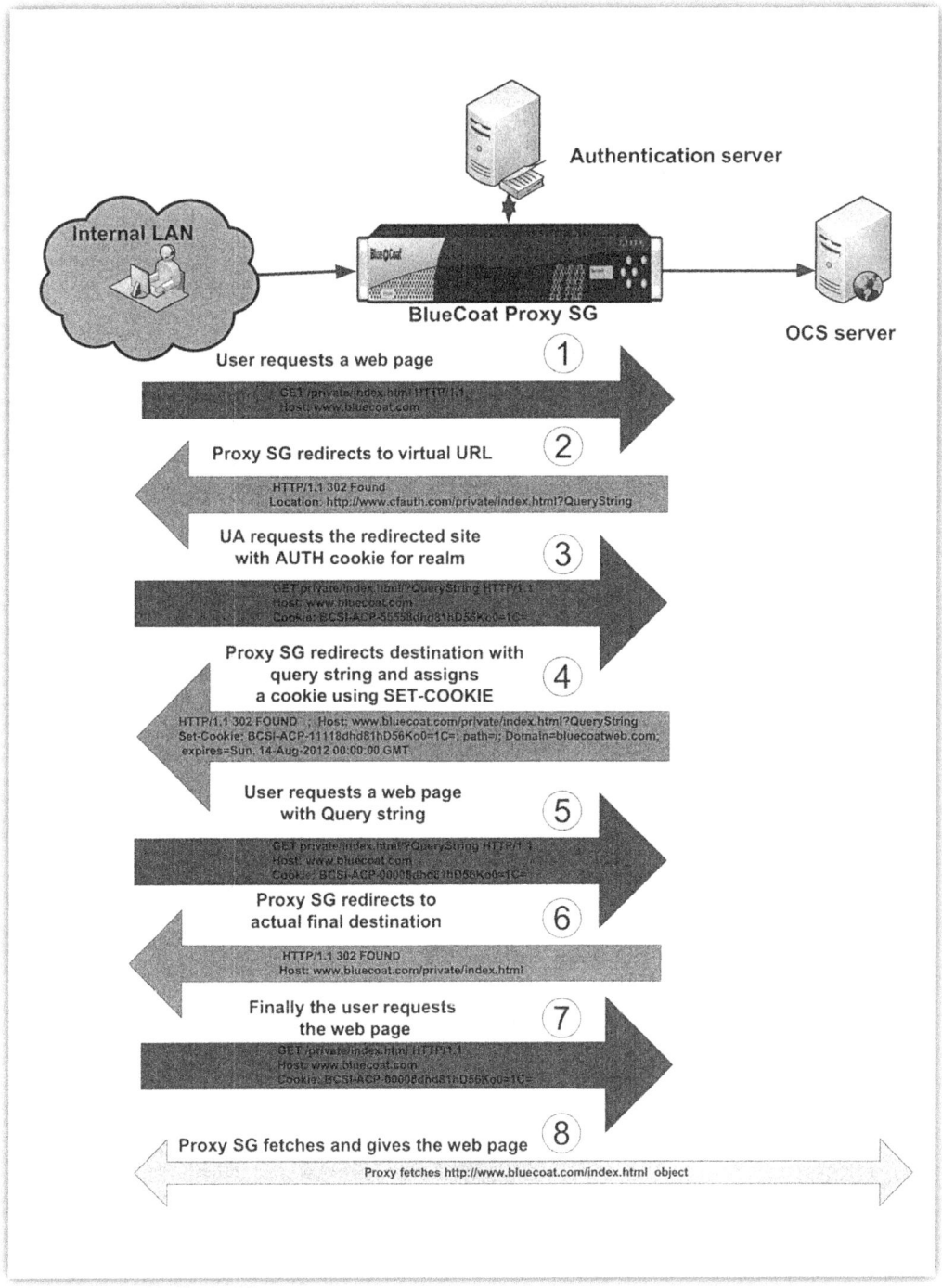

Figure 7.9: Transparent Authentication using a cookie surrogate for multiple domain

TRANSPARENT AUTHENTICATION USING AN IP SURROGATE

The other way to authenticate users is by using an IP surrogate. Instead of assigning a cookie to the user browser, the Proxy SG after the initial authentication will remember the user for all further transactions using the client IP address. Here no cookie is involved; only the client IP address needs to be known to the Proxy SG, then the Proxy SG evaluates the request and allows or denies based on the policies. Using an IP surrogate is not a good security practice, as the most easiest way to hack any system is spoofing the IP. So it is not a really advisable method. The main problem with the IP surrogate is that it cannot be used in a NAT environment, because the IP which is seen by the Proxy SG is a NAT IP and not a client IP address. The flow is shown in the figure below.

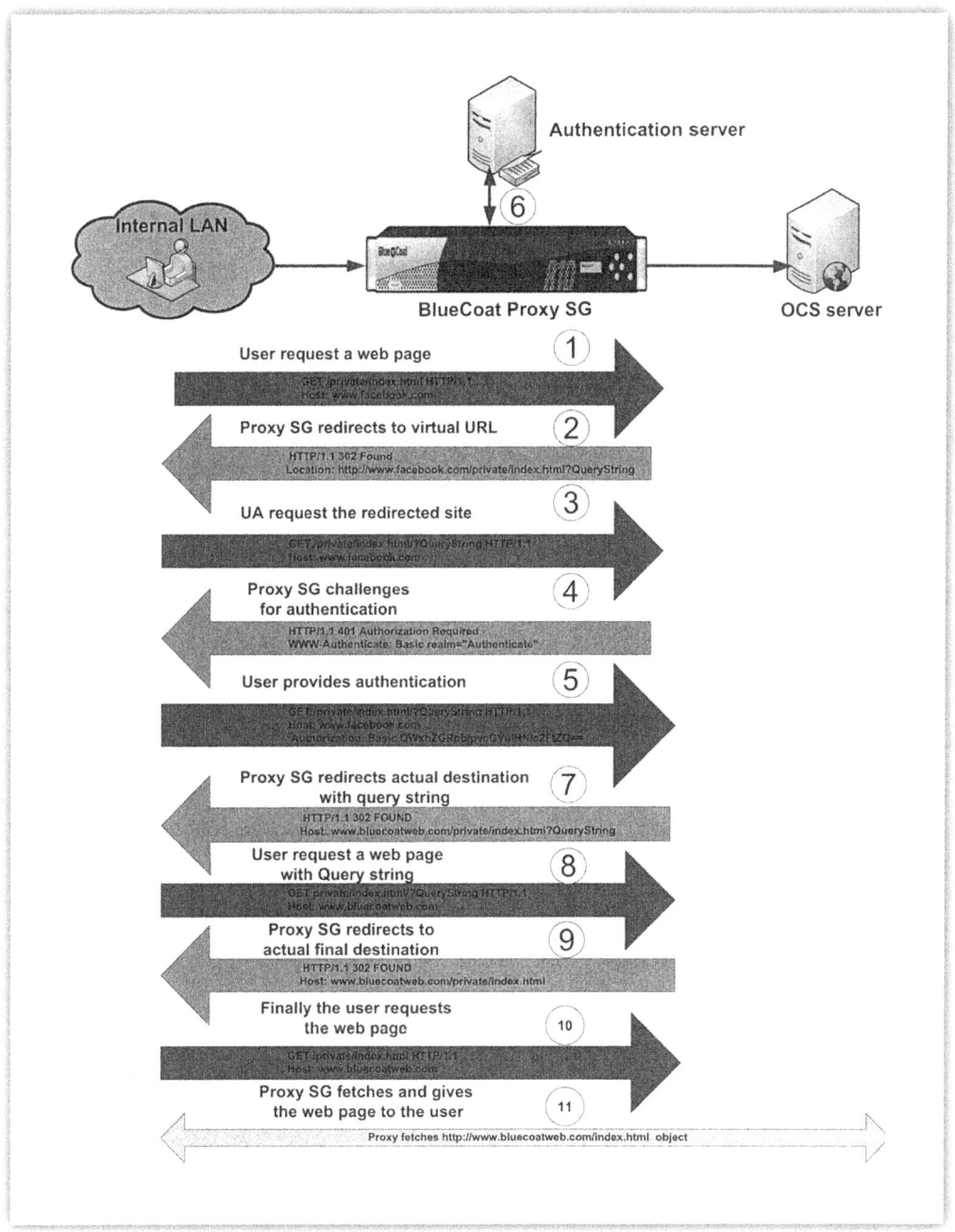

Figure 7.10: Transparent Authentication using an IP surrogate

Once the user is being authenticated, an IP surrogate is created in the Proxy SG and so all the rest of the access that the user tries accessing is not authenticated since a TTL value is associated with the IP address of the user-agent (browser), until the TTL value is not expired the user is not prompted for authentication and there are no redirects for every request all the transaction is authenticated by the Proxy SG by using the client IP. In the client which has been authenticated for the first time, until the TTL dies, any user that is using the machine will be able to access the Internet because the authentication is checked with the IP address and the TTL is valid. This is one of the major security problem with IP surrogates.

Enabling Cookie/IP authentication for Transparent proxy

To enable the cookie or IP authentication for the transparent-based proxy, log in to the BlueCoat Proxy SG via the management console and go to Configuration → Authentication → Transparent Proxy. In the Transparent Proxy options tab, you can select the method either as Cookie or IP, based upon your requirements, as shown below:

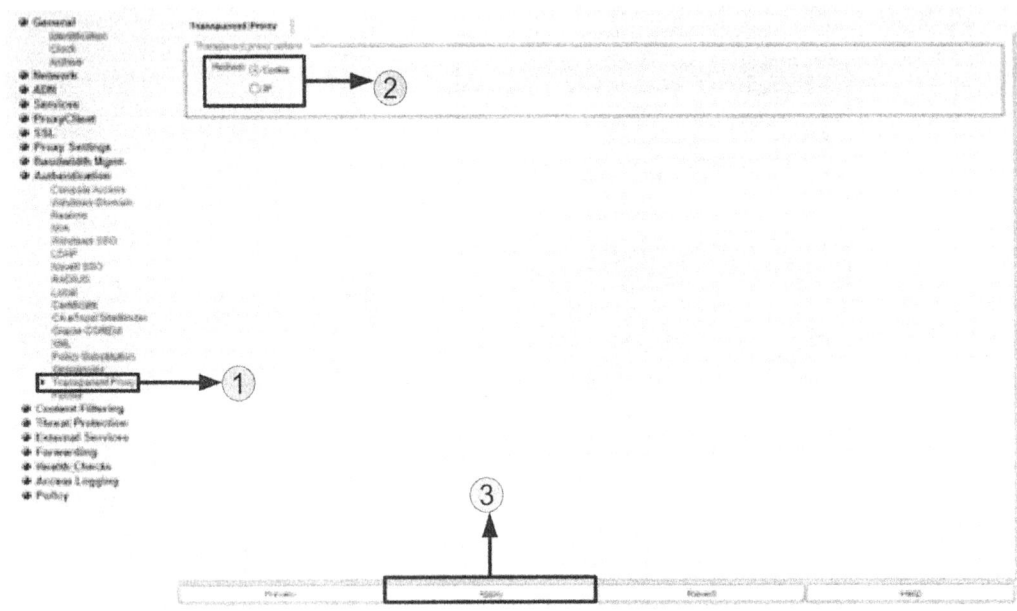

Figure 7.11: Enabling Cookie/IP authentication for Transparent proxy

About LDAP

LDAP, which stands for Lightweight Directory Access Protocol, is an Internet standard protocol used by applications to access information in a directory. Here, "Directory" is a generalized term for database-stored information about the network or user objects with access or security attributes. Examples: Microsoft SAM database, Novell NDS database, NIS/NIS+ database. LDAP is client/server model that runs directly over TCP. LDAP servers provide the directory service, and LDAP clients use the directory service to access entries and attributes.

In LDAP, directory entries are arranged in a hierarchical tree-like structure, starting at the root and then branching down into individual entries. At the top level of the hierarchy, entries represent larger organizations. Under these larger organizations in the hierarchy might be entries for smaller organizations. The hierarchy might end with entries for individual people or resources.

The example that we use in this chapter for LDAP structure, are shown below:

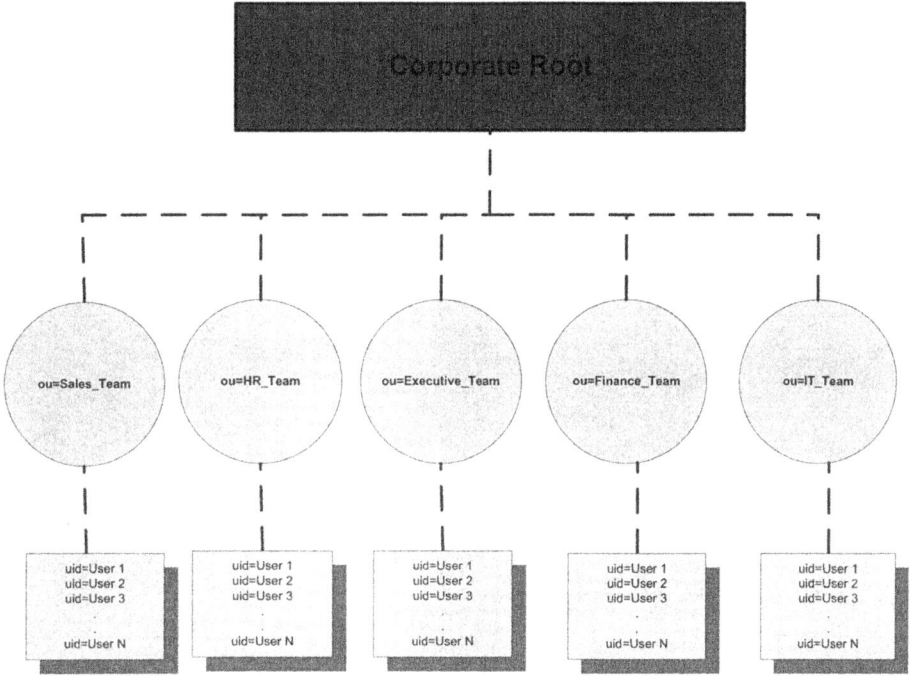

Figure 7.12: LDAP tree structure

Configuring authentication servers

Proxy SG can be integrated with many authentication servers, such as LDAP, Novell/ Windows SSO, RADIUS, IWA, SiteMinder, etc. In this chapter we will show how to configure LDAP. You should already be familiar with the concepts of LDAP about the tree, domain, forest, and naming convention. Here we will show how to configure the Microsoft LDAP with different attributes by following the steps as shown below:

1. Log in to the management console and go to Configuration → Authentication → LDAP → LDAP Realms tab. Click "New" to add a new realm and enter the details as shown below:

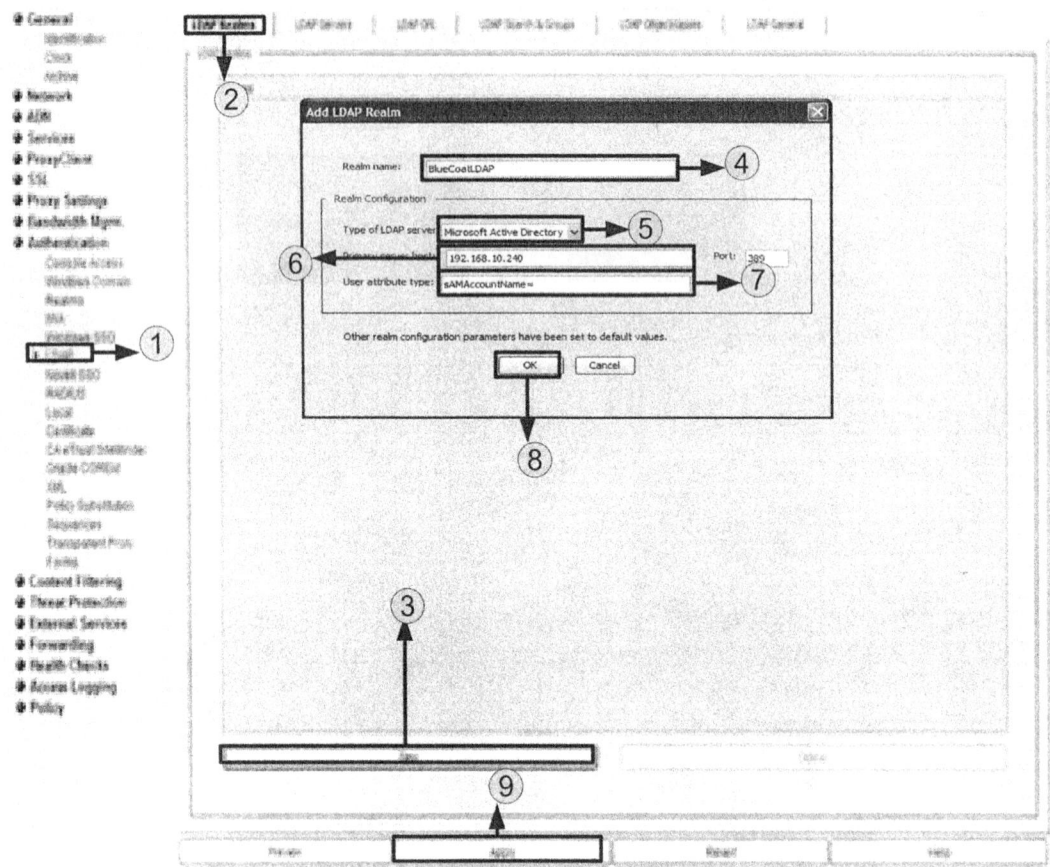

Figure 7 13: Adding LDAP realm

2. If you have any alternate hosts for the LDAP, enabling SSL and timeout values can be configured in the tab LDAP servers as shown in the screen below.

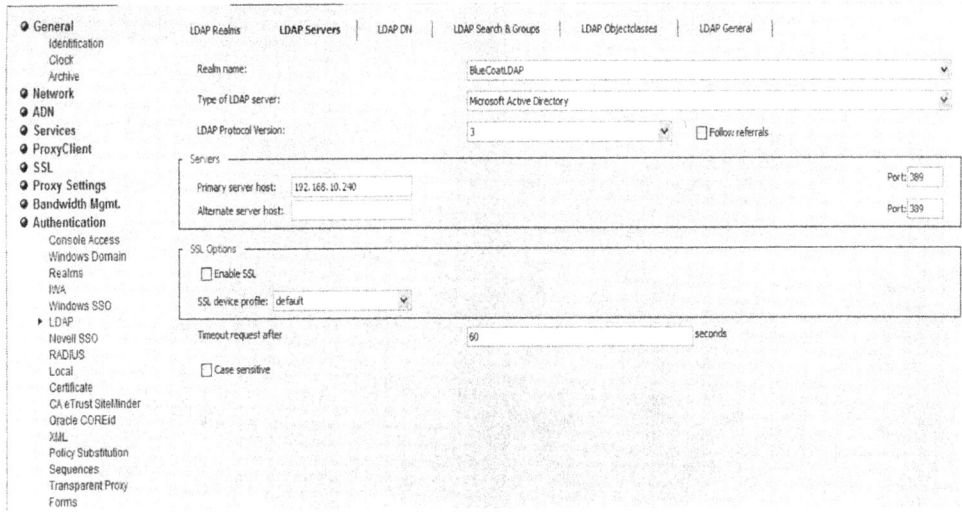

Figure 7.14: LDAP server settings

3. If you need to add the LDAP Base DN and user attribute type, go to the LDAP DN tab and enter the details as shown below:

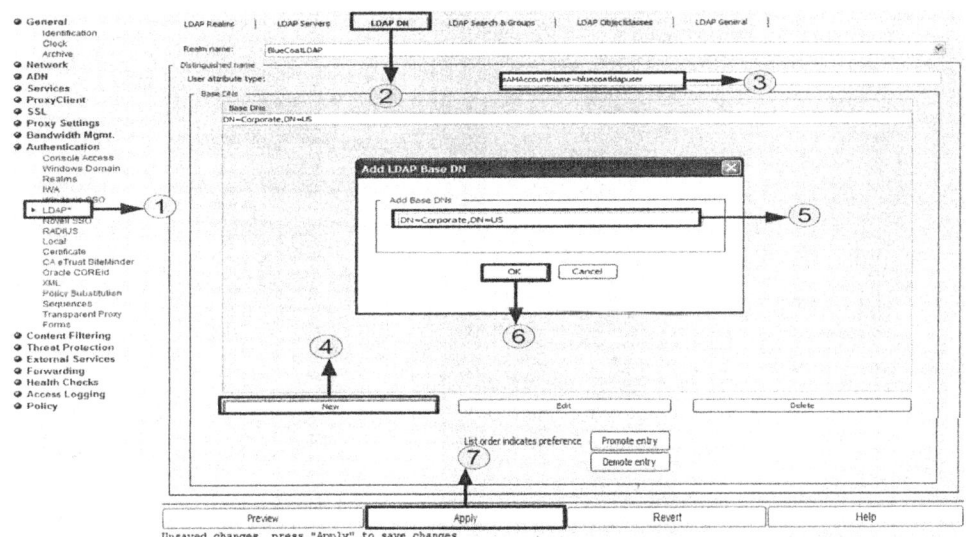

Figure 7.15: Configuring the LDAP DN

4. If you need to configure the LDAP Search & Groups, you can specify the settings here in the "LDAP Search & Groups section". If you have allowed an anonymous

search then you can move to the other configuration and leave all the page config as defaults, as shown below:

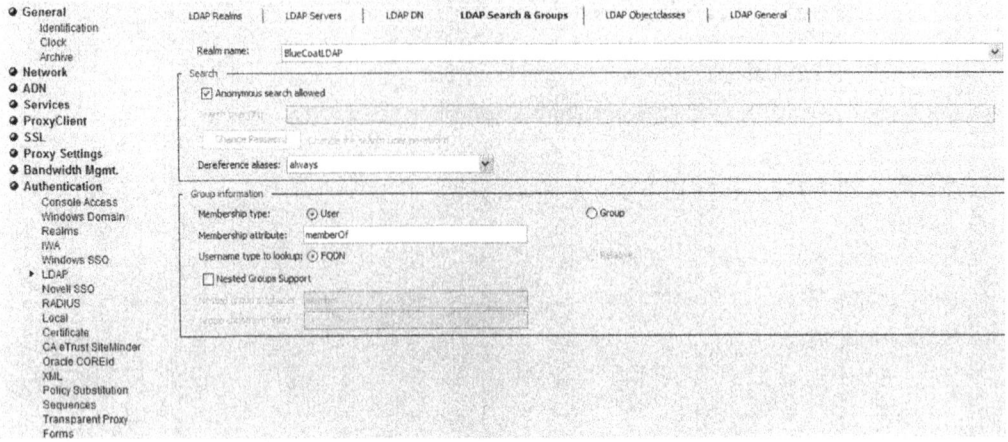

Figure 7 16: Configuring LDAP Search and Groups

5. If you have object classes for containers, users, and groups, you can create object classes here in the "LDAP Objectclasses". Otherwise leave other settings to the defaults as shown below:

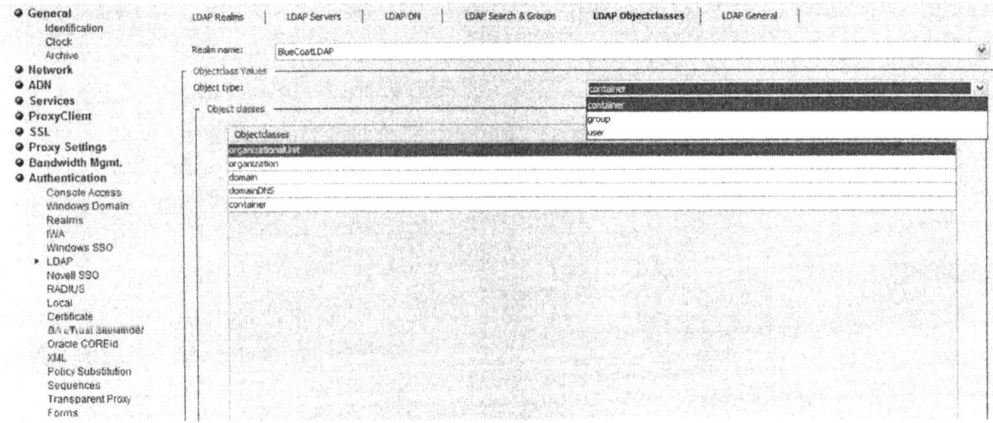

Figure 7.17: Configuring LDAP Object Classes

6. If you want to configure timeouts for re-authentication, configure inactivity timeout, and persistent cookies, configure different virtual URLs for authentication, do this here in the LDAP general tab, as shown below:

The default timeout for the credentials refresh time and for inactivity timeout is 15 minutes, but you can configure any time value as per your requirements.

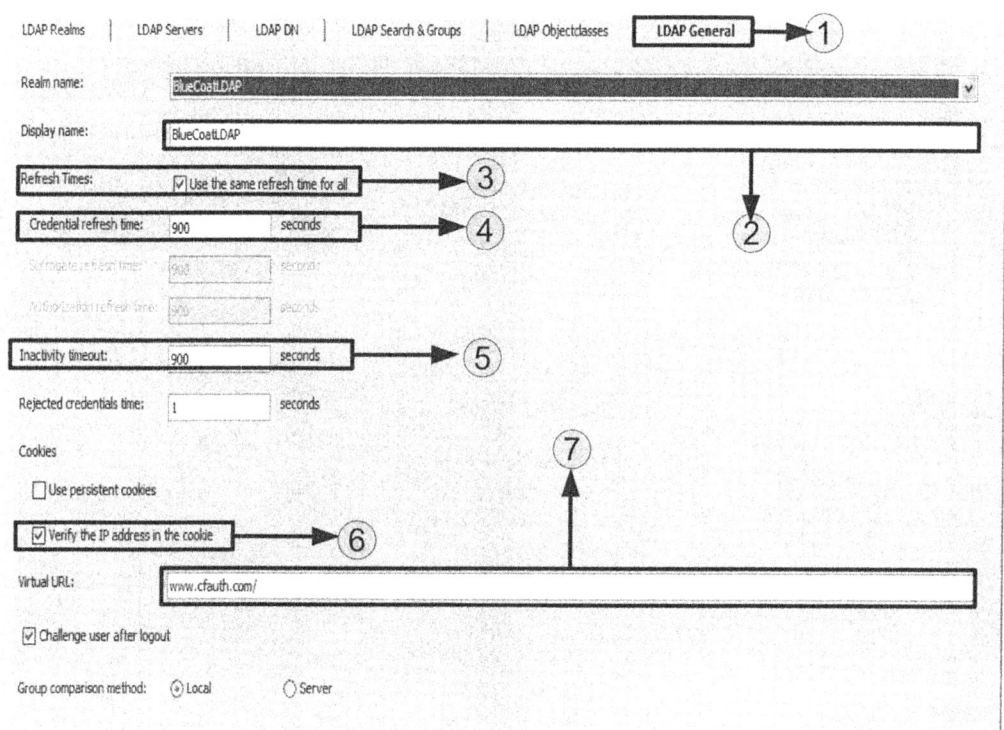

Figure 7.18: Configuring LDAP General settings

CONFIGURING THE VPM

Once you have configured the LDAP settings, you'll need to configure the VPM policies for authenticating and allowing users to access the Internet via BlueCoat proxy.. As you may recall, in "Chapter 6 – Visual Policy Manager," we created a policy based on the IP to access the Internet. In a similar way, you could allow users access based on groups or users. Using groups is the most efficient way of handling the user policy. We could create groups in the LDAP such as the Finance Team, the Sales Team, and the IT Team, and add all the users to their corresponding groups. Instead of using the IP address for allowing access, we add these groups in the Web Access layer and allow access to the users. So when a user from the Sales Team needs to access the Internet, he or she will be authenticated and only allowed access to the Business Economy and Real Estate categories; all the other categories will be denied. The same concept will be applied to the Finance and IT teams accessing the allowed categories.

To configure access based on users and groups, launch the VPM and go to "Corporate Web Access Layer", as discussed in the Chapter 6. Go to Rule 3 and right-click on the Source column. Click "Set", then click New" → Group and select the "Authentication Realm" as "BlueCoatLDAP". Click the "Browse" button, and a LDAP browser will pop up as shown below:

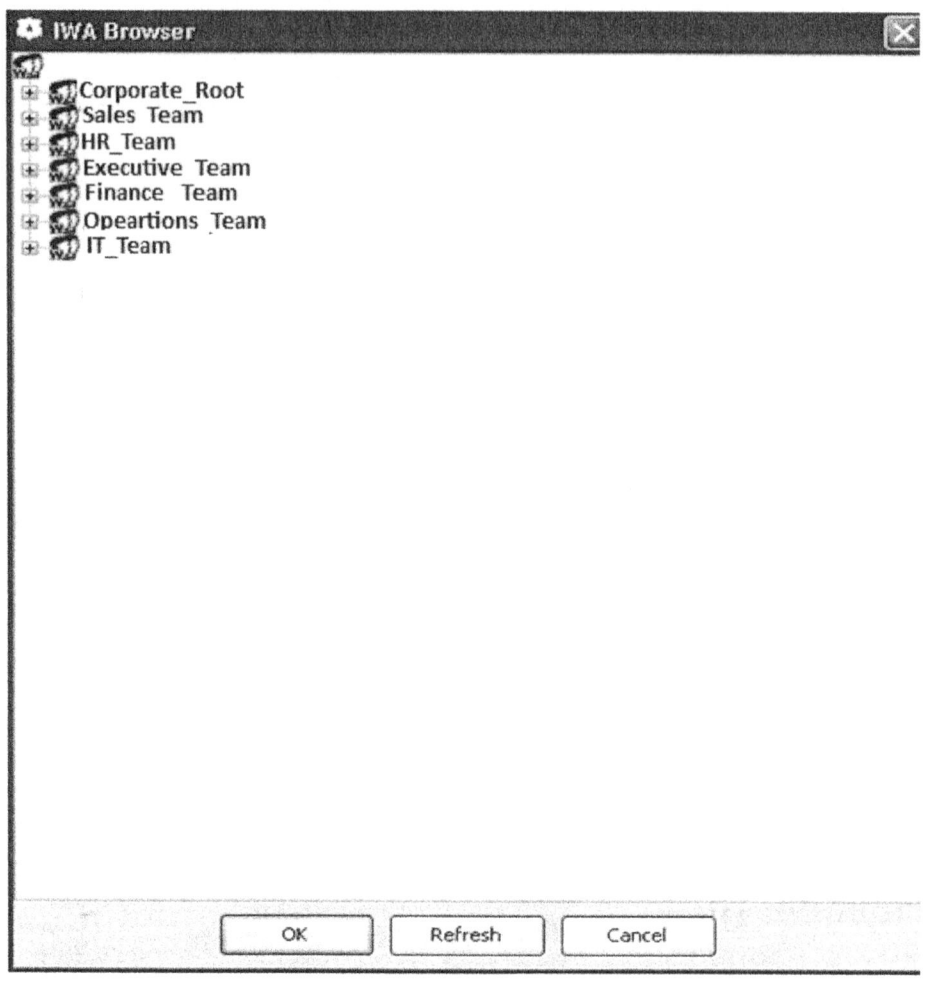

Figure 7.19: LDAP/IWA browser

Select the IT_Team LDAP group and click "OK" to confirm the change and install the policy. Repeat the same step for Rule 4 for the IT_Team. Do the same for all the rules in the policy for the corresponding LDAP group and users for the Sales and Finance teams, and install the policy. So when user now goes to any Internet sites, he or she will be prompted for Username/Password using HTTP basic authentication mechanism. Now the user should provide the LDAP credentials used for the email, file server, etc. So now we could track all users in the company based on their usernames; this is more secured than the IP-based authentication.

The above configuration is based on the LDAP group. If we want to create the user-based access, we can do that as well. Say the CEO of the company needs access to all the websites; we can add his username and destination as "Any" and allow access. To do this, follow the same procedure above, but instead of selecting the "Group", select the "User" option and in the LDAP browser expand the "Executive_Team" LDAP group and select the username for the CEO and apply the changes. So now the CEO will have access to all the sites through BlueCoat.

 Please make sure the rule for the CEO Internet access is above all others; that is, it should be the Rule 1.

Test Yourself

1. What are the Out-of-Band (OOB) and physical ways of protecting the BlueCoat Proxy SG? (Choose two.)

   a. Using the Serial Console
   b. Using the LCD panel
   c. Using the remote CLI shell
   d. Using the GUI console

2. When a user is trying to authenticate a password-protected resource in the web server, what HTTP code does the user get while the web server is trying to authenticate the browser?

   a. HTTP 302 code
   b. HTTP 200 code
   c. HTTP 401 code
   d. HTTP 403 code

3. When a user is trying to access http://www.yahoo.com without using a proxy, directly connecting from his home, how will the GET request be from the user? (No proxy setting is configured.)

   a. GET index.html HTTP/1.1
   b. GET www.yahoo.com/index.html HTTP/1.1

c. GET index.html

d. GET http://www.yahoo.com/index.html

4. When a user is trying to access http://www.bluecoat.com using a BlueCoat Proxy SG and the user's browser is explicitly pointed to the proxy, how will the GET request be from the browser?

a. GET index.html

b. GET www.bluecoat.com /index.html HTTP/1.1

c. GET index.html HTTP/1.1

d. GET http://www.bluecoat.com/index.html HTTP/1.1

5. When a user is trying to authenticate a password-protected resource in the web server, what HTTP code does the user get while the web server denies access to the website?

a. HTTP 302 code

b. HTTP 403 code

c. HTTP 401 code

d. HTTP 200 code

6. For a one-time authentication and cookie-based authentication, what is the very essential requirement for designing the Proxy-based authentication method?

a. The IP address of the proxy

b. A cookie for the browser

c. A virtual URL

d. Policies

7. When you configure a proxy-based authentication, what will the HTTP header for the HTTP code and authenticate attribute field looks like when sent from the proxy to the browser?

a. HTTP 401 and Proxy Authorization

b. HTTP 407 and Proxy Authenticate

c. HTTP 401 and Proxy Authenticate

d. HTTP 407 and Proxy Authorization

8. You are deploying BlueCoat websecurity solutions for a company and the requirement is that you need to configure an authentication policy for all the users and allow access to all sites in the Internet. You created the first layer as the Web Access Layer and configured an Allow All policy. Then the next layer you created was the Web Authentication policy through VPM. So when the user tries to go to the Internet, will the user be prompted for authentication?

a. Yes, the user will be prompted for authentication.

b. No, the user will not be prompted for authentication.

c. The access is an Allow All policy; the user will not be prompted.

d. The Allow All policy cannot be used with the Web Authentication policy.

9. When the web server is configured to authenticate users, what will the HTTP header for the HTTP code and the authenticate attribute field look like, when sent from the proxy to the browser?

a. HTTP 401 and Web Authorization

b. HTTP 407 and Proxy Authenticate

c. HTTP 401 and WWW-Authenticate

d. HTTP 407 and Proxy Authorization

CHAPTER 8

WEB CACHE COMMUNICATION PROTOCOL (WCCP)

In this chapter we will discuss the Web Cache Communication Protocol (WCCP), which is one of the very important redirection protocols used in transparent deployment of the Proxy SG. We will show how to configure the BlueCoat and show commands that should be executed in the Cisco router and switch for enabling the WCCP protocol.

WHAT IS WCCP?

The WCCP is a Cisco-developed content-routing protocol, introduced in 1997, that allows WCCP-supported Cisco firewalls, routers, and switches to transparently redirect traffic to a cache engine such as a ProxySG appliance. It is widely used in a transparent deployment where the users don't need to configure any settings in their browsers and there is few network changes that should be done, in order to redirect the traffic to the Proxy SG. WCCP has two versions: version 1 and version 2. BlueCoat recommends using WCCP V2, and we will explain the difference in features of both. In chapter 1 we have given details about transparent deployment, and here we will discuss all the features of the WCCP.

INTRODUCTION TO BLUECOAT WEB SECURITY

The advantages of using WCCP:

1. Scalability:

WCCP protocol can support 32 BlueCoat Proxy SG or cache engines and 32 routers or switches for traffic distribution. It provides liner scalability, which means you can expand the infrastructure by adding more BlueCoat. If the existing infrastructure is overloaded, then you can add BlueCoat and expand linearly and increase web traffic computation.

2. Load balancing:

In addition to traffic redirection, the WCCP protocol load balances traffic to all Proxy SGs. When we say it load balances, it may be equally the traffic could be distributedor unequally depending upon the weights configured in WCCP. For example you could send more traffic to the high-end Proxy SG and less traffic to the low-end Proxy SG. It uses different methods like hash assignment and mask assignment which we will discuss in detail later in this chapter.

WCCP V2 uses three techniques to perform load balancing:

a. Hot Spot handling:

WCCP V2 allows an individual hash bucket to be distributed across all the cache engines. Before WCCP v2, information from one hash bucket always went to one cache engine.

b. Dynamic load balancing:

WCCP V2 allows the set of hash buckets assigned to a cache engine to be adjusted in the router, so that the load can be moved from an overloaded or overwhelmed Proxy SG to other cluster members that have available capacity.

c. Security:

All WCCP groups including both router, switch, and BlueCoat Proxy SG are password protected with MD5 authentication. You can configure the WCCP-enabled devices to restrict access to certain proxies, and to the hosts that connect to it using the ACL.

In Chapter 2 we discussed how the design of the transparent deployment is and the redirection of the traffic from the routers and various information regarding transparent proxies. Now we will discuss how WCCP works and various factors that make up its protocol. We will start discussing service groups, service group types, and service group addressing.

What is a service group?

As the name states, a service group is a group of devices or a group which unites WCCP enabled devices (routers, switches, and firewalls) with the Proxy SG in a transparent deployment. Here, service refers to the protocols that are combined together, such as a group of devices which work together for redirection of services like FTP, HTTP, RTSP, MMS, RTMP, etc.

For simplicity we will just use the term router in this chapter, which means it is and equivalent of being either switches and firewalls. If there are any explicit difference between all these devices, we will mention the device separately.

So every service group that you has a service number which is configured on both routers and the Proxy SG. The number range is between 0 and 99. The router and Proxy SG can have multiple groups and work for the transparent redirection.

1. Router with multiple service groups with BlueCoat SG.

In the diagram below, we see how multiple service groups are configured on the router, which redirects traffic to the proxies in different DMZs. When the router receives the traffic, it checks the destination port for where the traffic to be redirected: either DMZ1 or DMZ2. The service groups configured on the router are service group 80 and service group 90. Service 80 has services configured as 80, 443, and 8080 and service 90 is configured as 554, 1755, and 1935. If the destination port is for 80, 443, and 8080, then the traffic is redirected to the DMZ 1 proxies, which intercept the traffic and forward it back to the WCCP-enabled router. If the destination port is for 554, 1755, and 1935, then the traffic is redirected to the DMZ 2 proxies, which intercept the traffic and forward it back to the WCCP-enabled router.

From here, the WCCP-enabled router forwards the traffic to the firewall (WCCP-enabled router default gateway). From there, the traffic reaches the OCS server, the packet comes back to the firewall, and WCCP forwards the traffic to the proxies which intercepted it. Why? Does the router does WCCP again? The answer is no. Remember that the proxy initiates the connection to the OCS after the initial WCCP from the router. The proxy checks the object, caches it, and sends it back to its default gateway, which may be the same WCCP router or a different router.

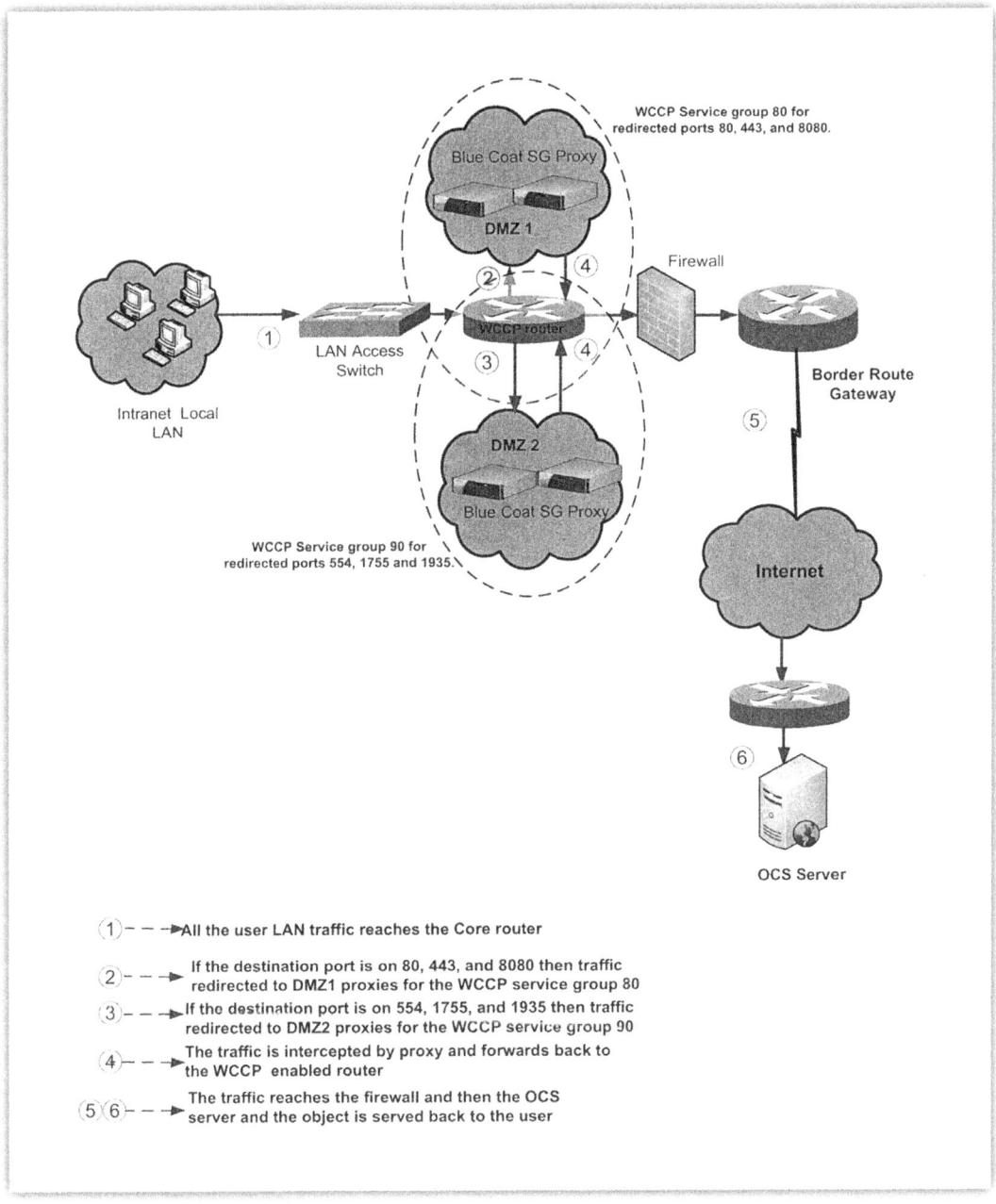

WCCP Service group 80 for
redirected ports 80, 443, and 8080.

Blue Coat SG Proxy

DMZ 1

Firewall

WCCP router

LAN Access
Switch

Border Route
Gateway

Intranet Local
LAN

DMZ 2

Blue Coat SG Proxy

Internet

WCCP Service group 90 for
redirected ports 554, 1755 and 1935.

OCS Server

(1)- - -►All the user LAN traffic reaches the Core router

(2)- - -► If the destination port is on 80, 443, and 8080 then traffic
redirected to DMZ1 proxies for the WCCP service group 80

(3)- - -►If the destination port is on 554, 1755, and 1935 then traffic
redirected to DMZ2 proxies for the WCCP service group 90

(4)- - -► The traffic is intercepted by proxy and forwards back to
the WCCP enabled router

(5)(6)- - -► The traffic reaches the firewall and then the OCS
server and the object is served back to the user

Figure 8:1 WCCP router with multiple service groups

257

2. BlueCoat SG with multiple service groups with router

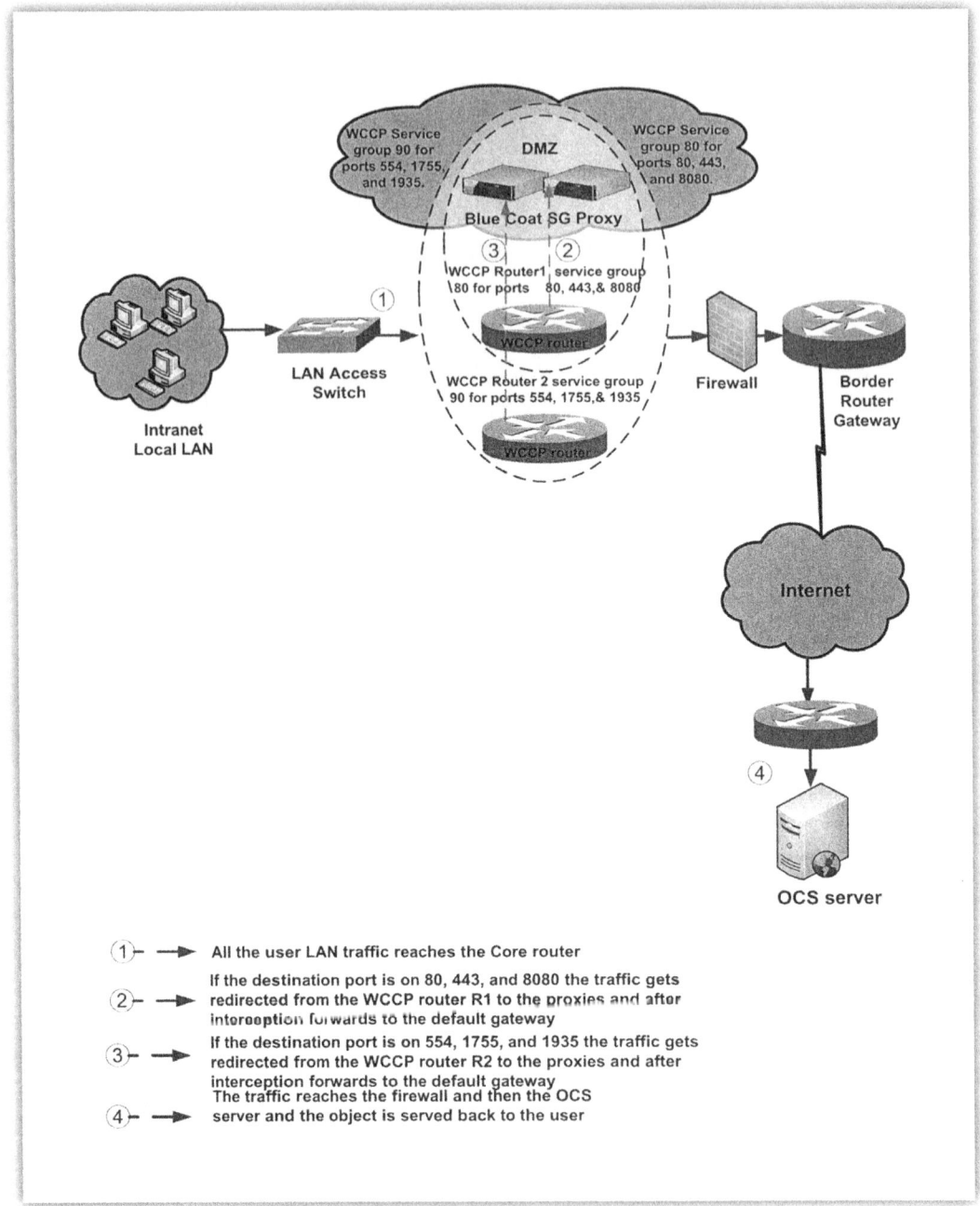

Figure 8:.2: BlueCoat SG with multiple service groups with router

Here the BlueCoat can have multiple groups configured and can unite with multiple routers also. This example shows the different functionality of WCCP and its service group. Here the user traffic reaches the LAN access switch which has PBR (Policy-Based

Routing) configured. So when the destination traffic is for 80, 443, and 8080, the traffic is forwarded to the Router 1, which has service group 80 configured. Here it gets redirected using WCCP to the proxy farm or pool, and proxies intercept the traffic. After the interception of the traffic is done by the proxy, it forwards the traffic back to the default gateway that is configured, which could be either Router 1 or Router 2. The flow of the traffic will be the same for the traffic 554, 1755, and 1935 as well.

SERVICE GROUP TYPES:

The service group type defines what type of traffic the routers in the group should redirect, and how to handle the redirected traffic. WCCPv1 supports the redirection of HTTP (TCP port 80) traffic only. WCCPv2 supports the redirection of packets such as multimedia, FTP, and HTTPS.

There are two types of service group types:

a. Well-known service groups:

Currently WCCP has only one well-known service groups, which is the web cache on port 80. The reason is that the router and Proxy SG understand the characteristics of the service or protocol.

b. Dynamic service groups:

All the other services that needs to be negotiated between the router and Proxy SG should be known. The reason is simple: certain protocols support both UDP and TCP; the Proxy SG for some services doesn't support et UDP portion. For example, for RTSP, both TCP and UDP are supported by the Proxy SG, but for H.323, the UDP portion is not supported by the Proxy SG. So this information should be shared by both the WCCP master and peers to understand the functionality and support for the services that should be forwarded.

Service group IP addressing:

There are two ways that the Proxy SG and routers can be configured with IP addresses for them to talk to each other:

1. Unicast:

In unicast IP addressing, the Proxy SG should be configured with IP addresses of all the routers to which the Proxy SG that needs to be participated in WCCP. So when a router is removed and then changed with a new IP address, the same change should then be reflected to all the Proxy SGs that are there in the service group.

2. Multicast:

In multicast addressing, the Proxy SG and routers in the same service group should communicate using a single IP address in the multicast range of 224.0.0.0 to 239.255.255.255. In multicast addressing, the router and ProxySG that there in the part of the service group should be less than one hop apart. If it is more than one hop, then IP multicast routing must also be enabled on the intervening routers that are in the path.

Before moving to the packet, let's first understand what GRE is.

GRE, which stands for Generic Routing Encapsulation, is a tunneling protocol developed by Cisco Systems that can encapsulate a wide variety of network layer protocols inside virtual point-to-point links over an IP internetwork. GRE tunnels are designed to be completely stateless, such that each tunnel end-point does not keep any information about the state or availability of the remote tunnel end-point.

How does the actual redirection take place?

So far we have seen the traffic redirection, but here we will see how the actual traffic gets redirected. So when the user traffic reaches the core router where WCCP is enabled, this is the router that is responsible for redirection. As we know, WCCP is used in the transparent environment, the redirection in the router looks for the destination field, that is both the IP address of the destination and the destination port that is for the OCS server; then it forwards the packet that is based upon the ACL and service groups configured on the router. To redirect traffic to the router is based on one of the following two methods:

1. GRE redirection
2. L2 redirection

Remember that each of these methods has a forwarding method and return method. A forwarding method is when the traffic is sent from the router to the Proxy SG, and the return method is when the traffic is sent from the Proxy SG to the router. Each redirection has to be based on one of the following two methods:

1. GRE forwarding and return method
2. L2 forwarding and return method

1. GRE forwarding and return method

GRE forwarding, once the WCCP-enabled router receives the packet from the user, encapsulates the packet with another header, with the source as the IP address of the router and the destination as destination address of the Proxy SG. When Proxy SG receives the packet, it strips the outside header that the router added and gets the original packet which the user sent during the request. In transparent deployment when using WCCP or PBR the packet that is sent by the user is not changed in transit(except in the NAT environments), so the original characteristics of the request by the user is not changed and most of the TCP protocols expect the same as well. After the decapsulation, the Proxy SG inspects the packet based upon the policies. If the request is allowed, then it checks in the cache; if not available, it has to fetch the object from the OCS server. In both situations, the return method comes in play. The Proxy SG again does the GRE encapsulation with the source as the IP address of the Proxy SG and the destination as the router IP address.

a. For Cached data

The figure below explains the packet flow for the traffic for WCCP using GRE forwarding and return methods. Lets explain the step-by-step procedure of how the redirection works.

1. The user tries accessing http://www.cnn.com. The user IP address is 192.168.10.10 (source port random, e.g., 10000). The machine does a DNS query and gets a reply from the DNS server for http://www.cnn.com and the IP is 157.166.226.25. So the destination IP is 157.166.226.25 (destination port is 80) and the client machine forwards the request to its default gateway.

2. The network routers should route the traffic to the core router (WCCP enabled router), which does a traffic inspection and the finds destination port is 80. So the WCCP enabled router encapsulates the packet with WCCP GRE headers as source as the router interface (WCCP enabled interface) which is E0/1 192.168.20.254 and the destination as Eth 0:0 192.168.20.250(BlueCoat WCCP IP address), here the original packet which is still retained by the router, and forwards the packet to the BlueCoat Proxy SG.

3. The BlueCoat Proxy SG decapsulates WCCP GRE headers of the packet by stripping the outside GRE header. It checks the HTTP GET request and finds it is for http://www.cnn.com, so it checks the policy and finds it is allowed. The Proxy then checks whether the request is there in the cache and finds the objects for http://www.cnn.com in the cache.

4. The BlueCoat Proxy SG now acts as http://www.cnn.com, by setting the source IP as 157.166.226.25 (Source port as 80) and the destination as the user's IP address 192.168.10.10 (destination port is 10000), and encapsulates with WCCP GRE headers with the source IP address as the BlueCoat Proxy SG WCCP interface Eth 0:0 192.168.20.250 and the router interface E0/1 192.168.20.254 and returns the packet to the WCCP router.

5. The router decapsulates WCCP GRE headers, checks the destination as 192.168.10.10, and forwards the request to the internal network, which gets routed to the user machine. Users views the http://www.cnn.com page as if the request came from the real OCS server, which is http://www.cnn.com.

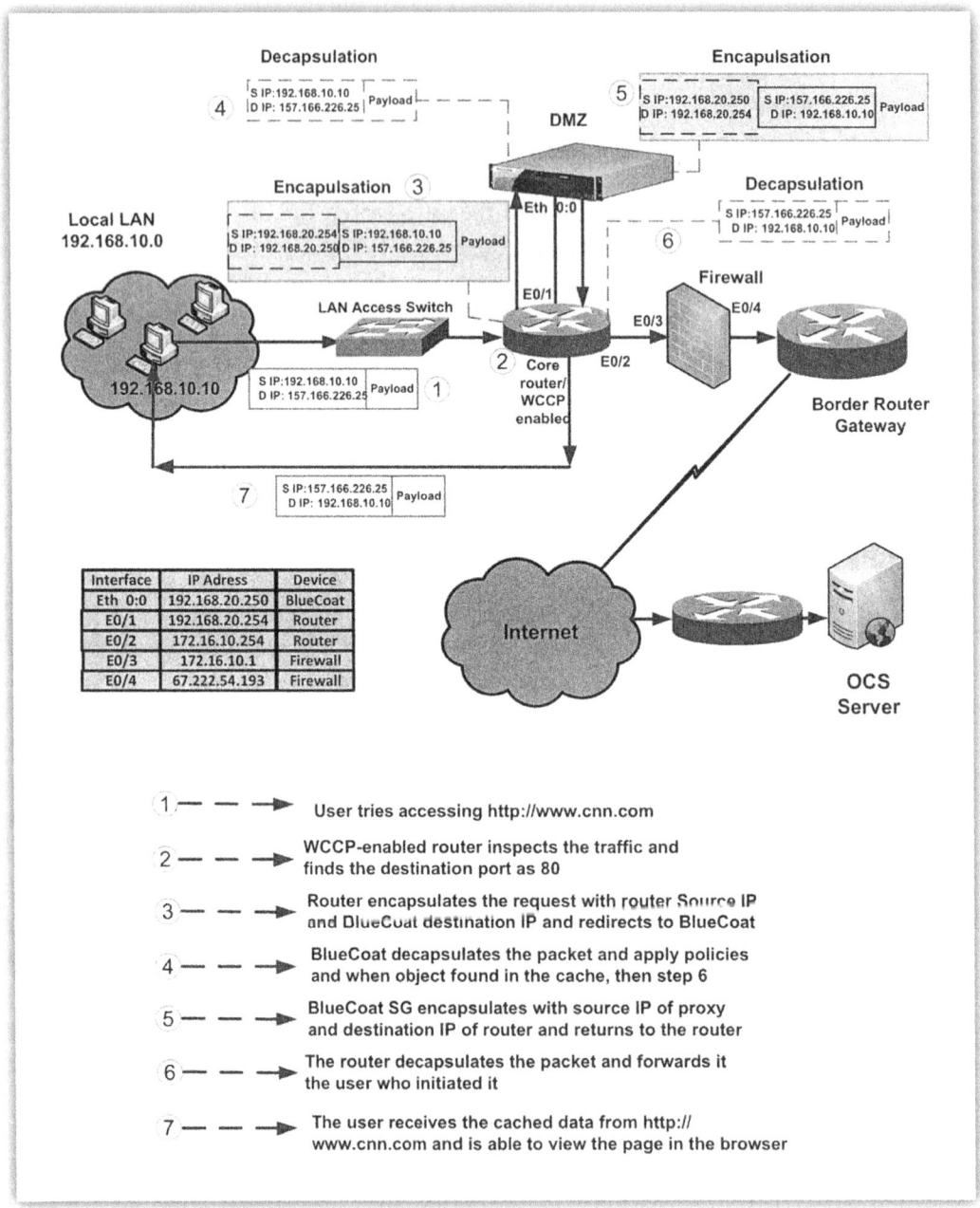

Figure 8.3: GRE forwarding and return method for cached data

For an easy-to-understand explanation, we have used just one BlueCoat Proxy SG; in reality there are several proxies in the farm.

b. For non-cached data

Here we see the user request an object which cannot be found in the cache, so the BlueCoat Proxy SG initiates a connection to the OCS server, and then the packet is delivered back to the client. Here we used the example of the user trying to access http://www.cnn.com, but this time the object is not in the cache. The packet flow is described below:

1. The user tries accessing http://www.cnn.com. The user's IP address is 192.168.10.10 (source port random, e.g., 20000). The machine does a DNS query and gets a reply from the DNS server for http://www.cnn.com. The IP is 157.166.226.25, so the destination IP is 157.166.226.25 (destination port is 80). Then the machine forwards the request to its default gateway.

2. The network routers should route the traffic to core router (WCCP-enabled router), which does a traffic inspection and finds that the destination port is 80. So the WCCP-enabled router encapsulates the packet with additional header source as the router interface (WCCP-enabled interface) which is E0/1 192.168.20.254 and the destination as Eth 0:0 192.168.20.250(BlueCoat WCCP IP address), here the original packet which is still retained by the router, and forwards the packet to the BlueCoat Proxy SG.

3. The BlueCoat Proxy SG decapsulates the packet by stripping the outside header, checks the HTTP GET request, and finds that it is for http://www.cnn.com. It then checks the policy and the site is allowed, so the Proxy checks whether the request is there in the cache, and cannot find the object for http://www.cnn.com in the cache.

4. The BlueCoat Proxy SG now initiates a new connection to the OCS server with the source IP address as 192.168.20.250 (random source port is 25000) and destination as 157.166.226.25 (destination port is 80). It then encapsulates the packet with the WCCP GRE headers with the source as the WCCP interface of the BlueCoat Proxy SG as Eth 0:0 192.168.20.250 and destination as 157.166.226.25 (destination port is 80) and returns the GRE traffic to the WCCP-enabled router.

5. The router decapsulates the WCCP GRE header and checks the destination as http://www.cnn.com with IP address 157.166.226.25. Then it forwards the request to its default outbound gateway, which is firewall to the interface E0/3 IP address 172.16.10.1.

6. The firewall checks its access list and finds that all outbound traffic for destination port 80 is allowed (unless there is a denied ACL). Then it does a NAT by changing

the source IP with its (firewall) IP address 67.222.54.193 (from 192.168.20.250 to 67.222.54.193), and source port again is changed to a random port which is chosen by the firewall (source port 35000), and forwards the traffic to the Internet gateway.

7. The traffic gets routed to the Internet and it reaches the OCS server. The OCS server (http://www.cnn.com) processes the traffic and returns the object to the actual user who requested it. Now the source IP will be the IP of the OCS server (source port is 80), and destination IP is the NAT IP of the firewall (destination port is 35000). The packet gets routed and reaches back your firewall, since the traffic is already an established connection, the firewall does the NAT by changing the destination IP to the BlueCoat SG destination IP 192.168.20.250 (destination port is 25000) and forwards the request back to the core router.

8. The router checks the packet, but now the destination port is 25000. So WCCP will not be used to redirect the packet to the BlueCoat, because as we know, the WCCP is enabled for ports 80 and 443. Now the router uses its own routing table to determine how to reach the BlueCoat Proxy SG. Since both are there in the same subnet and directly connected, it just forwards the traffic to the BlueCoat Proxy SG.

9. The BlueCoat Proxy SG inspects the traffic.It now knows that the connection was established by the BlueCoat Proxy SG by checking the connection table. Now it maps the IP address setting by changing the source IP address to 157.166.226.25 (http://www.cnn.com) and the destination IP to 192.168.10.10 (destination port is 20000).

10. 10. The traffic gets routed to the internal network with the intranet routers and reaches the destination, which is the user with IP address 192.168.10.10 who initiated the connection. The user is now able to view the http://www.cnn.com page which he requested.

In the above packet flow you can notice that there is a NAT that is taking place in the firewall. This is one type of design or architecture that you could use, in situations only the firewall should do the NAT to the public IP address for the internal network. We can design without using NAT on a firewall and this can be performed two different ways.

a. Proxy having only one Public IP address:

In this scenario, there is only one IP address for the Proxy SG, and it is configured as the public address. So both WCCP redirection and forwarding are done via this public IP address, and all the traffic is initiated by the public IP of the Proxy SG. But still the BlueCoat Proxy SG should be behind the firewall. The only flow change is that the firewall does not do the NAT from internal IP addresses to external IP address.

b. Proxy having one private and one public IP address:

In this scenario there are two IP addresses. Blue Coat Proxy SG can either configured be as a separate interface or can be configured as a sub-interface. But configuring IP address as separate interface is better because this will make more bandwidth space for traffic and for separating the internal traffic from the external traffic. So the internal interface should be used for the WCCP between the router and BlueCoat Proxy SG. If the   BlueCoat Proxy SG needs to fetch objects from the Internet, the packets gets translated to the other interface which is configured as the public IP address. Translating the packet directly to the public IP address, though there are two interfaces, is done by configuring the routes in the Proxy SG. That is, all the internal network routes should point to the internal default gateway (explicit route), and the BlueCoat Proxy SG default route should point to the Internet router. So the exiting interface, which is public IP, will be the source IP of the packet.

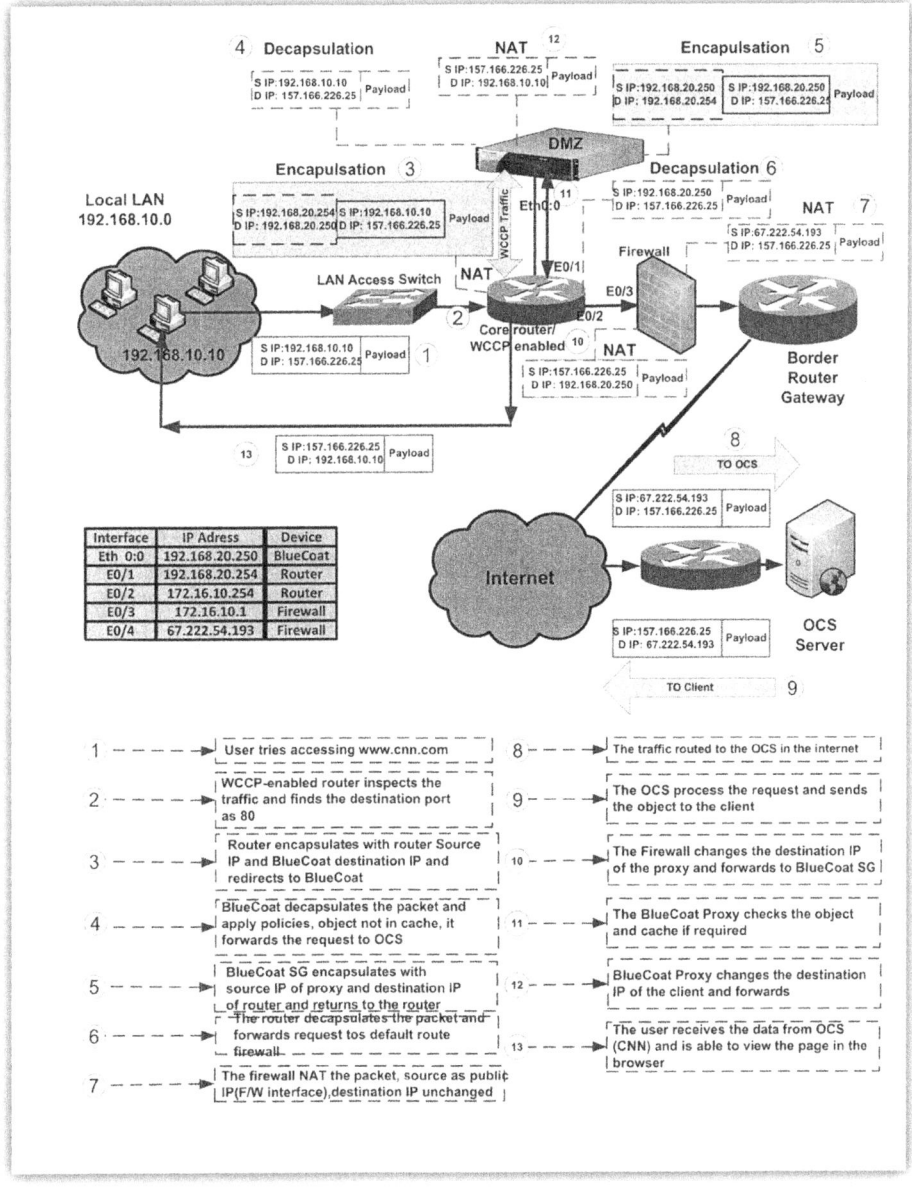

Figure 8.4: WCCP for fetching object from OCS with Firewall NAT

2. L2 forwarding and return method

As the name indicates in the L2 forwarding and return method occurs at the Layer2 of the TCP/IP which is used for the redirect methods. Here the L2 is the MAC address information of the packet, is changed as compared to the GRE redirection the forward and return takes place in the IP layer or L3 layer of the TCP/IP. Here no encapsulation or decapsulation takes place; only a rewrite takes place in the L2 layer for the destination MAC address. So the WCCP-enabled router intercepts the traffic and if it is on port 80, it forwards the traffic to the Proxy SG by rewriting the destination MAC with the Proxy SG MAC address; and when returning the packet, the Proxy SG rewrites the destination MAC address of the WCCP-enabled router. The main constraint is that the Proxy SG and WCCP router should be in the same L2 broadcast domain; that is, not more than one hop apart. The main advantage of using L2 redirection is that it is faster than GRE redirection, because it happens at the L2 layer that takes on the hardware levelof the TCP/IP; but GRE redirection takes place in Layer 3 of TCP/IP, which is the software level of the operating system.

The figure below explains the packet flow for the traffic for WCCP using the L2 forwarding and return methods. Let's explain the step-by-step procedure of how the redirection works.

1. The user tries accessing http://www.cnn.com. The user IP address is 192.168.10.10 (source port random, e.g., 5000). The machine does a DNS query and gets a reply from the DNS server for http://www.cnn.com and the IP is 157.166.226.25. So the destination IP is 157.166.226.25 (destination port is 80), and the machine forwards the requestto its default gateway.

2. The network routers should route the traffic to the core router (WCCP-enabled router), which does a traffic inspection and finds that the destination port is 80. The WCCP-enabled router rewrites the destination MAC address of the Proxy SG interface Eth 0:0 as 98:76:54:32:10:cd, and the source MAC address (01:23:45:67:89:ab) will be the WCCP-enabled router interface E0/1. Here still the original charactertics of the packet which is still retained by the router (Source IP 192.168.10.10 and destination IP 157.166.226.25), and forwards the packet to the BlueCoat Proxy SG.

3. The BlueCoat Proxy SG strips the MAC information from the request, checks the HTTP GET request, and finds that it is for http://www.cnn.com. It checks the policy and finds this site is allowed, so the Proxy checks whether the request is there in the cache, and finds the objects for http://www.cnn.com in the cache.

4. The BlueCoat Proxy SG now acts as http://www.cnn.com with the source IP as 157.166.226.25 (source port is 80) and the destination is user IP address 192.168.10.10 (destination port is 5000). Proxy SG rewrites the destination MAC address of the WCCP-enabled router of the interface E0/1, and the source MAC address as its own MAC address of the interface Eth 0:0, and returns the packet to the WCCP router.

5. The router strips the MAC addresses and checks the destination as 192.168.10.10, and forwards request to the internal network, which gets routed to the user's machine. The user views the http://www.cnn.com page as if the request has come from the real OCS server, which is http://www.cnn.com.

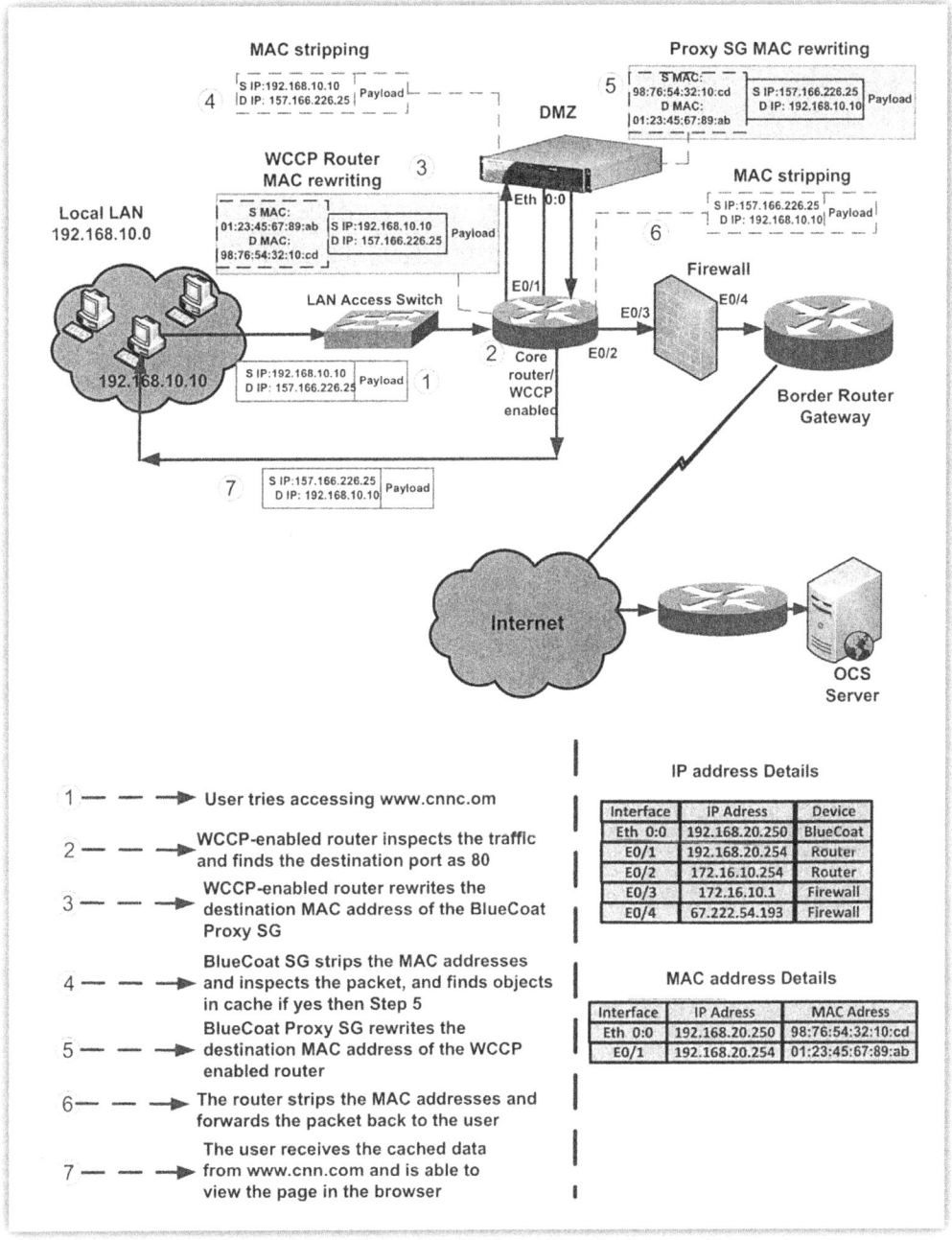

Figure 8.5: WCCP with L2 forwarding and return method

As we know in networking, if the devices are in the same L2 broadcast domain, the sending device gives a MAC broadcast ff:ff:ff:ff:ff:ff to find the destination MAC of the receiver, and the destination MAC replies to the ARP broadcast. From this is point, the sending device knows the port from which the receiving device is connected and MAC rewriting happens for all the traffic that is destined for that receiving device. The same principle is applied to L2 redirection. Instead of looking for an IP lookup to find the peer destination device, it checks the destination port of the traffic and sends traffic to the interface where WCCP is enabled (in routers there can be multiple interfaces). This means for our example above that our router interface E0/1 is configured as the WCCP interface. Imagine there is one more interface configured in the router, for example E0/3 on the router with the IP address 192.168.20.253. The L2 redirection only looks for the interface on the WCCP-enabled interface; in this case it is E0/1. Though   E0/3 is in same subnet, the router will not send to that interface; the L2 layer is checked and always given priority and is the only way to reach the BlueCoat SG.

Non-cached objects

The same logic applies for objects that are not cached in the Proxy SG, as we saw in the GRE redirection for the non-cached objects. The redirect happens only at the L2 layer both for forwarding and returning the packet. Still the traffic initiation from the Proxy SG source IP will have its own IP address and the destination the OCS server, and the MAC layer source is Proxy SG MAC address and destination MAC address is WCCP enabled router or any other router/firewall which is configured as the default gateway. So all the return packets after it fetched the object from the OCS server when it reaches back the WCCP enabled router, it looks at the destination as a different port other than port 80, and delivers the packet to the BlueCoat Proxy SG.

If the BlueCoat Proxy SG has only one interface, and if it has an internal network address space (in our example, it is 192.168.20.250), then the source IP is 192.168.20.250 and the destination will be the OCS server. But there should be NAT translation which changes the internal address to the external address. Usually this is done by the firewall, so that the source IP 192.168.20.250 is changed to an external IP, which gets routed through the Internet and reaches the OCS server and return packet reaches back to our firewall, which does the NAT(change back to Proxy internal IP address), and the router receives the traffic from the firewall and forwards back to the Proxy SG. The Proxy SG processes the return packet and sends back the request to the client who initiated it, with the OCS server as the source IP and the client as the destination IP address.

If the BlueCoat Proxy SG has two interfaces, usually the WCCP-enabled interface receives the traffic using the L2 method, and the other external interface with a public address or configured gateway that it can reach via the exiting interface will be the source IP address. If the source IP address from the Proxy SG is not an external public address, then again a NAT is required from the firewall.

ROUTER AFFINITY:

As you know exactly how the traffic gets forwarded and returned using WCCP, and always consider you only need to use the forwarding method and don't want to use the returning method, you need to have router affinity. So by default, the BlueCoat Proxy SG uses the routing table lookup for the intercepted traffic, and the configured return method (L2 or GRE) to return the bypassed traffic (forwarded and non-intercepted traffic) to the WCCP device that redirected it. By enabling router affinity, intercepted traffic and/or bypassed traffic are forwarded by the configured the return method (GRE or L2) from the Proxy SG to the WCCP device that redirected it, bypassing the route lookup table.

Router affinity is very useful in the following two situations:

1. Routing policies that may prevent your client/server-bound traffic from reaching its destination, because the return traffic is given back to the router which should know how to reach those devices. Enabling router affinity simplifies the ProxySG configuration process by eliminating the need to replicate these policies on the ProxySG.
2. When there are multiple home routers or when our WCCP-enabled router is multiple hops away from the ProxySG, because this ensures that the traffic is always returned to the same WCCP router that redirected it.

By default, the ProxySG appliance will use a routing table lookup when responding to a client or when connecting to the upstream/OCS.

Load-Balancing Methods

You now a have clear understanding of how WCCP works with the BlueCoat Proxy SG and WCCP-enabled devices like routers, switches, and firewalls. You know that the WCCP master, which is the router, switch, or firewall, which does the actual redirection, does WCCP peer or cache is one or more BlueCoat devices. The question is, which BlueCoat Proxy SG receives the traffic? To answer this question, the load-balancing methods come into picture. Load balancing is the way in which WCCP knows how to balance traffic across multiple WCCP peers. The load balancing could be of two types:

1. Equal load balancing:

In equal load balancing, the WCCP-enabled device evenly load balances to the multiple Proxy SGs, so that each Proxy SG has an equivalent amount of traffic it is processing. That way, no Proxy SG gets overwhelmed, since traffic gets evenly distributed to it. When one of the Proxy SGs fail, the WCCP master removes the peer from its table, recalculates the load-balancing method again, and passes traffic evenly to the available Proxy SG.

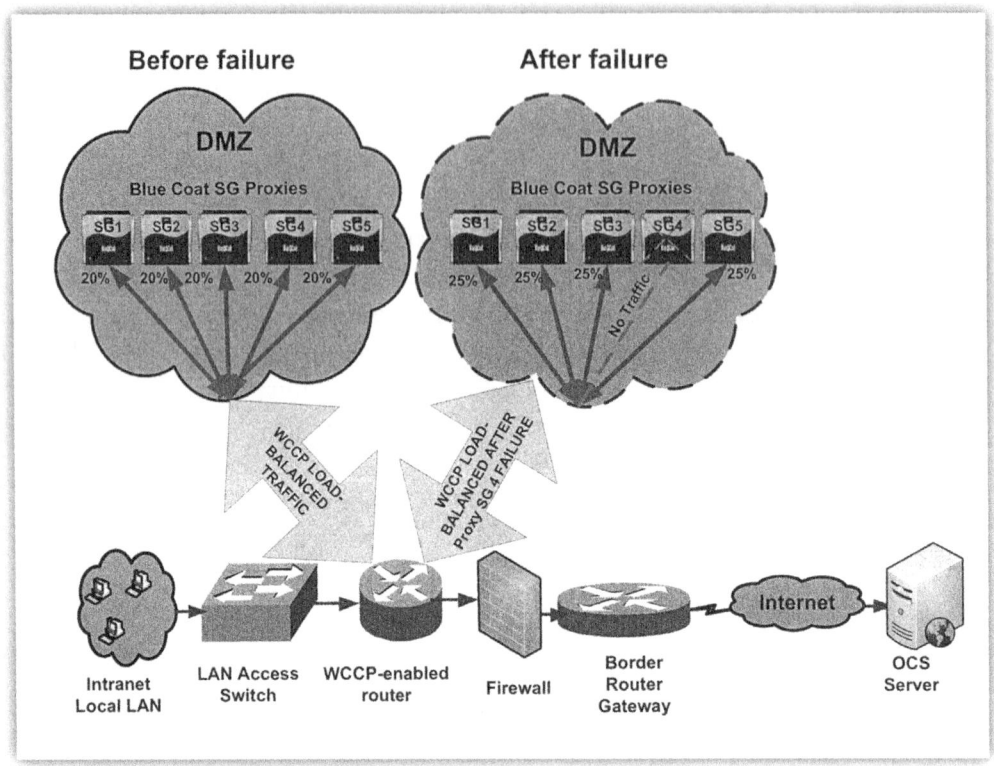

Figure 8.6: WCCP equal load balancing

2. Unequal load balancing

Let say that you have different proxies with different platforms, like SG 810, SG 8100, and SG 9000. Different platforms have different load-handling capacities, so you cannot evenly load balance since the platform cannot withstand the load. Since due to the platform limitations of processing, at these types of situations you use weights to load balance. Say you have three 8100s and two 810s with the following weights:

Proxies SG1 8100, SG2 8100, and SG3 8100 weigh 100 each.
Proxies SG4 810 and SG 810 weight 50 each.

The total weight is 400 (sum of all Proxy SG weights). Proxies SG1, SG2, and SG3 will receive 3/4 of the traffic (sum of Proxy SG 8100 weights/total weight), and SG4 and SG5 will receive 1/4 of the traffic (sum of Proxy SG 810 weights/total weight).

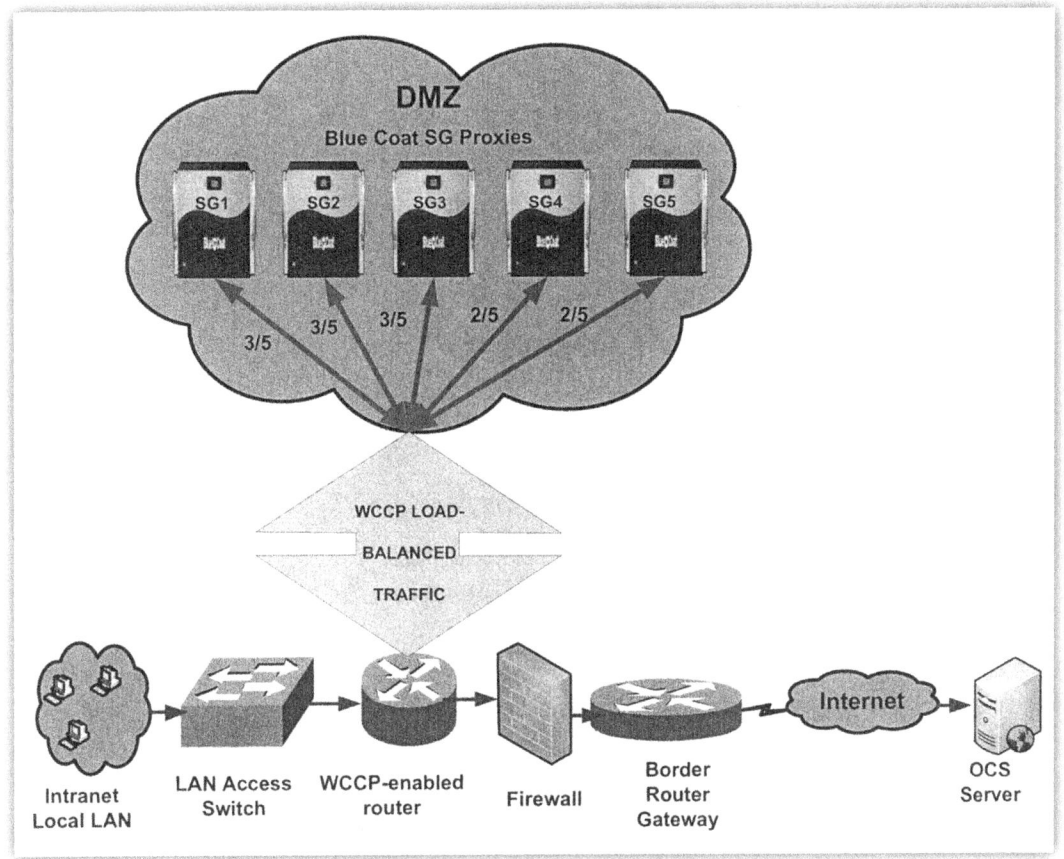

Figure 8.7: WCCP unequal load balancing

LOAD-BALANCING ALGORITHM

Before explaining the load-balancing algorithm, you need to first understand a key concept called a "designated cache", which will be explained below.

What is a "Designated cache"?

When a service group is formed between the BlueCoat Proxy SG and the router, ProxySG with the lowest IP address automatically becomes the designated cache and the designated cache defines the router how to redirect traffic should be distributed between the members of the Proxy SG.

So what exactly does the Proxy SG tell the router about redirection? The Proxy SG that is the elected designated cache tells the assignment types and settings to the router or the firewall. These assignment types and settings are defined in the Proxy SG service group. So the assignment settings are not defined in the router, but in the Proxy SG. That is the reason the Proxy SG informs the router about the assignment settings.

> When there is only one Proxy SG, then that will be the designated cache in WCCP.

The Proxy SG supports two assignment types or load-balancing algorithms, also called distribution algorithms:

1. Hash Assignment

A hash function is a transformation that takes a variable-size input m and returns a fixed-size string. These fixed-size strings are unique and cannot be repeated for variable inputs. As we are aware, different hashing functions are available, such as MD5, SHA-1, etc. In a similar way, the router uses XOR (exclusive function) as a hash function. It computes hash on the values such as source IP, destination IP, source port, and destination port of the packet. It is a combination of any of the four address/port fields that is fed into the XOR hash function; the resulting output will be in a range between o and 256 bucket value. Then the Proxy SG calculates how many other Proxy SGs there are in a service group and divides the 256 bucket value by the number of proxies in the same service group. It then gives a portion of 256 bucket hash table to all the Proxy SGs in the same service group and all the assignment to the router.

There are two Proxy SGs with IP addresses 192.168.10.101 and 192.168.10.102 The lowest IP Proxy (SG1) 192.168.10.101 is the designated cache, which does the calculation of 256/2 = 128 and splits the 0–127 and 128–256 range. 256 is the total hash length and 2 is the number of proxies used. Then this information is communicated to the Proxy (SG2) and the WCCP-enabled router. The clients 192.168.20.10 and 192.168.20.11 try accessing http://www.bluecoatweb.com (67.222.54.193) and the traffic is intercepted by WCCP enabled routers. Now the router does the XOR function with the Source IP, destination IP, source port, destination port, for both the client request and the hashed bucket value is 100 for 192.168.20.11 and hashed bucket value is 200 for 192.168.20.10. The router now knows which proxy to redirect the traffic to, so the traffic 192.168.20.11 goes to SG1 (0–127) based upon the hash value, and the traffic 192.168.20.10 goes to SG2 (128–256) as shown in figure below.

When the hashed value is generated, the input is fed with the source IP, destination IP, source port,and destination port, but there could be any combination of these. This means you could select only the source IP and source port, or the destination IP and destination port. Usually the selection isn't based on the destination IP and/or port, because this would cause a hot spot on the router. For example, if you choose this destination IP and/or port, then all the users requests for http://www.google.com generates the same hash bucket, and one proxy gets overloaded. Usually the best practice is to use the source port and source IP, in which case the traffic is evenly distributed to all the proxies.

The default setting is the hash assignment for the service group in the Proxy SG.

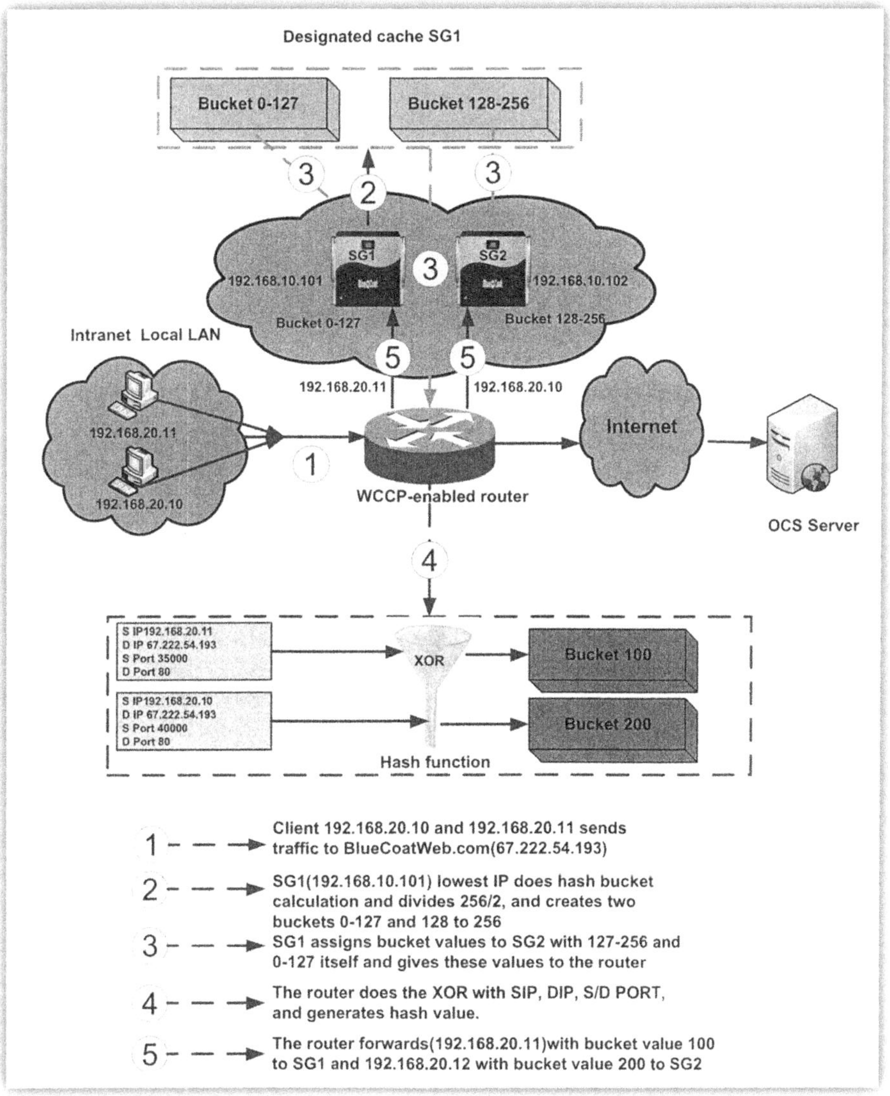

Figure 8.8: Hash assignment in WCCP

2. Mask assignment

The second assignment type is the mask assignment. Unlike the hash assignment, it uses the AND operation. With the mask assignment, the source IP address, destination IP address, source port, and destination port are concatenated together and AND with a 96-bit mask to yield a value. Then the resulting 96-bit value is compared to a list of mask/value pairs. Each mask/value pair is associated with a bucket, and each bucket is in turn assigned to all Proxy SGs. The bucket range is from 0–64. So if there are two proxies, 64/2 (number of proxies), the first Proxy gets a range 0–31 and the second Proxy SG gets a range 32–64.

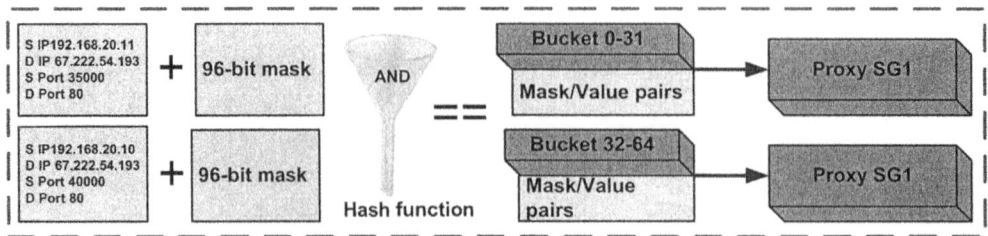

Figure 8.9: Mask assignment in WCCP

It is the same logic and traffic flow as we explained for hash assignment. The only difference is that the mask assignment uses the AND operation, as shown in the above figure.

Configuring WCCP in BlueCoat SG

We have explained all the options and features that are available in WCCP. To configure WCCP in BlueCoat Proxy SG, follow the steps as shown below:

1. Log in to the Proxy SG via https://192.168.10.101:8082 and go to Management Console → Network → WCCP. Enable the WCCP and click "New" to add new groups as shown below:

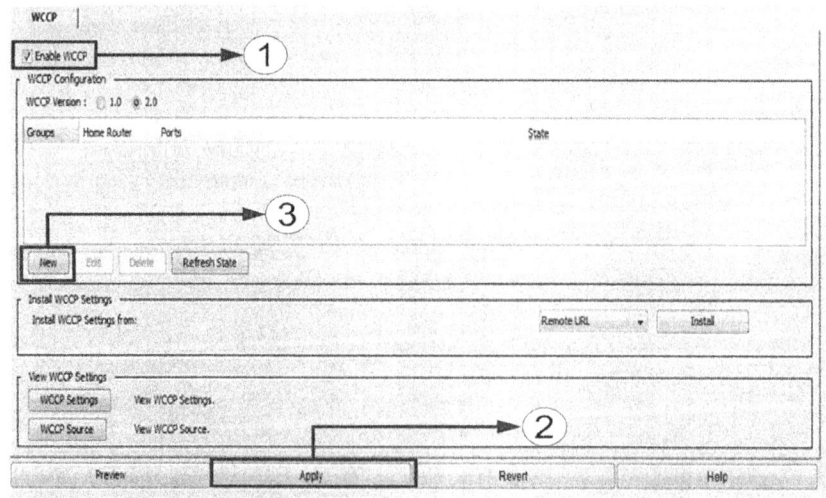

Figure 8.10: Enabling WCCP in Proxy SG

2. Then you'll need to create a service group number and enter the WCCP password that is used for authentication between the Proxy SG and the WCCP-enabled router, as shown below:

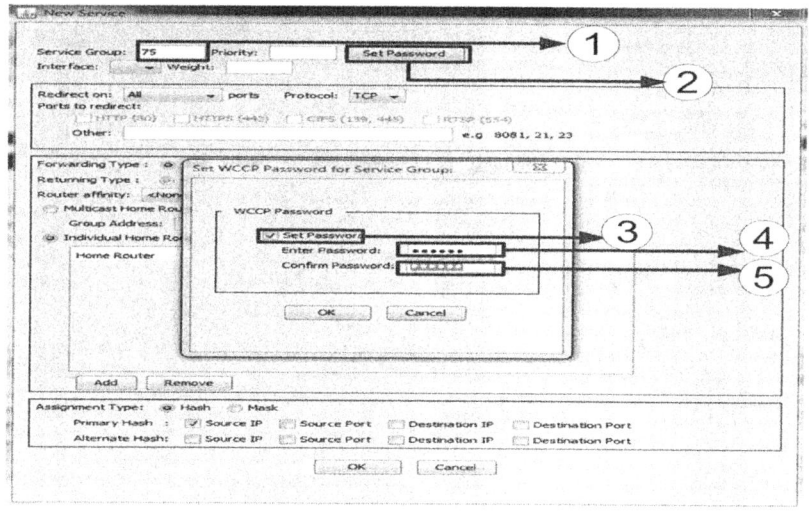

Figure 8.11: Adding WCCP service group password in the Proxy SG

3. You need to define the interface through which the Proxy SG will be listening for WCCP traffic. Then we need to define all the services that should be intercepted (HTTP, HTTPS, RTSP, MMS, RTMP)by the Proxy SG. We should define the forwarding type as GRE and define the WCCP router or also called the home router, as all these are shown in the figure below.

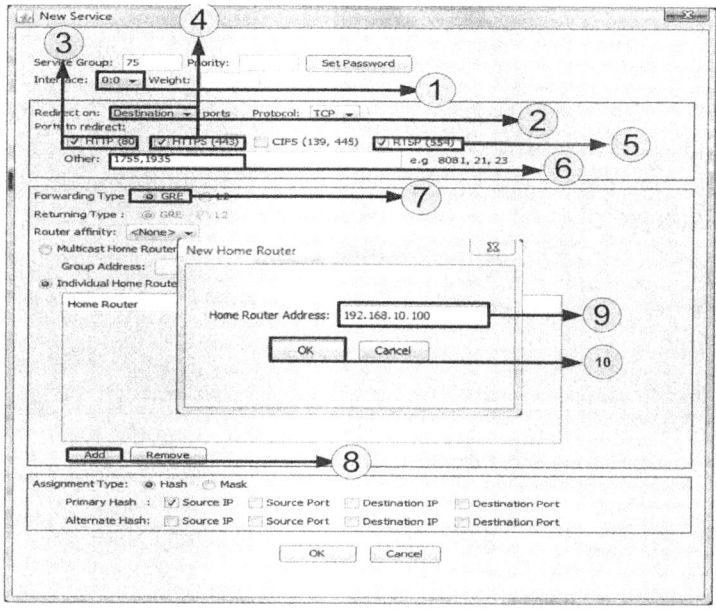

Figure 8.12: Configuring the WCCP service in the Proxy SG

4. You can select the assignment methods (Hash or Mask) and the different attributes like the Source IP, Source port, Destination IP and Destination port to it, as shown in the figure below you have selected only the Source IP as the "Primary Hash" as an example to demonstrate.

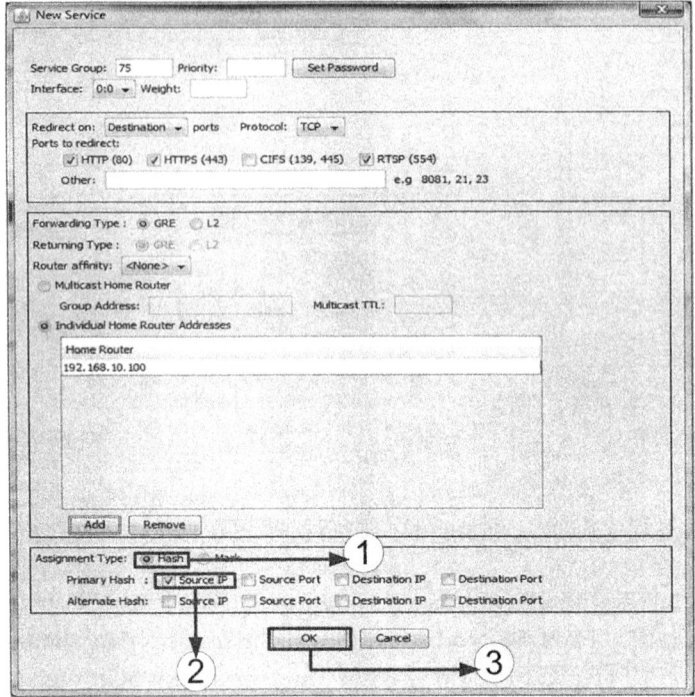

Figure 8.13: Hash assignment for the WCCP service in the Proxy SG

5. Then you need to "Apply" the change in the main screen. The Proxy SG and the WCCP-enabled router will start communicating by sending a hello packet. For example, the Proxy SG sends a "WCCP2_HERE_I_AM" message. In turn, the router with the same service group as the Proxy SG will send back a "WCCP2_I_SEE_YOU" message. While it is negotiating, you will monitor the state changes as shown below:

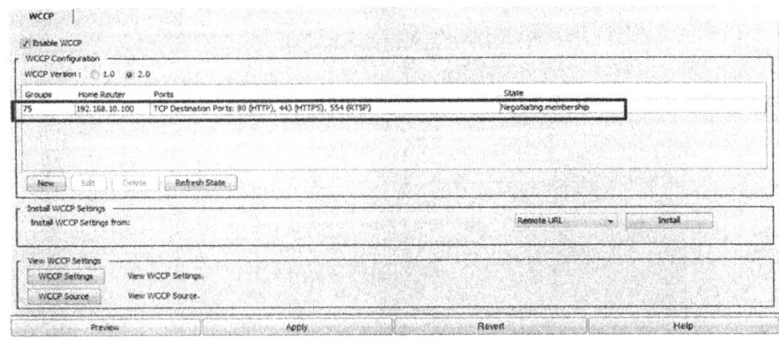

Figure 8.14: WCCP membership negotiation in the Proxy SG

Once the negotiation is done, the state will be "Ready", as shown below:

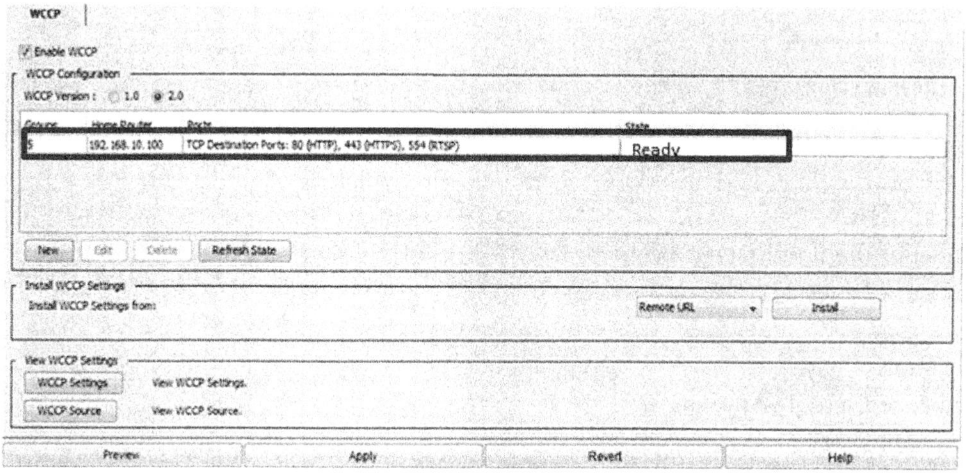

Figure 8.15: WCCP peer establishment in Proxy SG

6. Using the CLI, you can view the state changes, configuration, negotiation as shown below, to do login to the CLI using SSH via Putty and the run the commands:

a. sh wccp configuration

CorporateProxy#sh wccp configuration
;WCCP Configuration
;Version 1.3
State: Enabled

Version: 2
Service-group: 75
Password: ******
Priority: 0
Protocol: TCP
Ports-to-redirect: 80 443 554 1755 1935 (destination)
Interface: 0:0
Weight: 0 on 0:0
Assignment-type: Hash   Primary
hash: source-ip   Alternate-hash:
Forwarding-type: GRE
Returning-type: GRE
Home-routers: 192.168.10.100
Multicast-ttl: 1

Router-affinity: None

b. show wccp status

CorporateProxy#show wccp status
;WCCP Status
;Version 1.3
Number of GRE redirected packets: 14
Number of Layer 2 redirected packets: 0
Service group: 75
State: Ready
Number of Here_I_Am sent: 277
Number of I_See_You received: 277
Number of Redirect_Assign sent: 1
Router IP: 192.168.10.100
Cache IP: 192.168.10.101

In addition, ` run the statistics command CorporateProxy#sh wccp statistics, which will show the statistics in detail.

Test Yourself:

. . . .

1. What are the devices in Cisco that support WCCP?

    a. Router
    b. Firewall
    c. Switch
    d. All the above

2. What are the well-known service groups in WCCP?

    a. 80 and 443
    b. 80
    c. 21, 80, and 443
    d. All the ports

3. As a BlueCoat engineer you are designing Internet Web gateway using BlueCoat Proxy SG solution, what ports will you include in the WCCP services for accessing web, multimedia, and streaming services?

    a. 80, 443, 554, 1755, and 1935
    b. 80, 443, 554, and 1935

   c. 53, 80, 443, 1755, and 1935

   d. 80, 443, and 554

4. Which will consume less overhead both in the router and the Proxy SG when enabling WCCP, using either GRE or L2 methods?

   a. GRE

   b. L2

5. In your network, you have four BlueCoat Proxy SGs, and all are configured with service group 50. Proxy SG1 IP is 10.10.10.100, Proxy SG2 IP is 10.10.10.50, Proxy SG3 IP is 10.10.10.200, Proxy SG4 IP is 10.10.10.99, and the WCCP-enabled firewall IP is 10.10.10.1. Which is the designated cache?

   a. Proxy SG1 10.10.10.100

   b. Proxy SG4 10.10.10.99

   c. Proxy SG 2 10.10.10.50

   d. Firewall IP 10.10.10.1

6. What is the algorithm and bucket output value used by the hash and mask assignments?

   a. Hash uses a XOR operation with 256 bucket value, and mask uses AND with 128 bucket value.

   b. Hash uses an OR operation with 256 bucket value, and mask uses AND with 64 bucket value.

   c. Hash uses a AND operation with 256 bucket value, and mask uses OR with 64 bucket value.

   d. Hash uses a XOR operation with 256 bucket value, and mask uses AND with 64 bucket value.

7. In your network, you want all returned packets to be redirected to the WCCP-enabled devices, and you don't want the BlueCoat Proxy SG to send the return packet directly to the client by using a routable table in the Proxy SG. What feature will help you do this?

   a. Router affinity

   b. Designated cache

   c. L2 return method

   d. GRE return method

8. You are configuring WCCP in BlueCoat and you have decided to use the hash assignment. You have selected the primary hash as the destination IP, and users start accessing the Internet. You see a hotspot on one Proxy SG. What is the cause of it?

    a.   More traffic is sent to one Proxy SG if the hash assignment is used.

    b.   The ash assignment will consume more CPU.

    c.   If users are accessing the same destination, then one Proxy SG will be overloaded.

    d.   The router and BlueCoat have miscalculated the hash assignment; the boxes need to be rebooted.

9. You have three proxies. Two are Proxy SG 810 and one is Proxy SG 8100. You have configured weights on the WCCP. Both Proxy SG 810s have a weight of 50, and Proxy SG 8100 has a weight of 100. What is the amount of traffic received by each Proxy SG?

    a.   Both Proxy SG 810s will receive ¼ of the traffic, and Proxy SG 8100 will receive ½ of the traffic .

    b.   Each Proxy SG 810 will receive ¼ of the traffic, and Proxy SG 8100 will receive ½ of the traffic.

    c.   All proxies will receive equal traffic

    d.   Proxy SG 8100 will receive ¼ of the traffic and each Proxy SG 810 will receive ½ of the traffic .

CHAPTER 9

....

PROXY ANTIVIRUS

PROXY ANTIVIRUS

Introduction

The BlueCoat Proxy AV (Antivirus) is a security product that can be integrated with the BlueCoat Proxy SG to provide malware protection at the border gateway. Since it provides protection at the gateway, your internal network is safe from all security threats that are there on the Web. So by intergrating Proxy AV with the Proxy SG in the network, it adds one more layer of defense from the hackers and thus becomes the state-of-art for the best security design and practices.

What is BlueCoat Proxy AV?

BlueCoat Proxy AV is a hardware platform that is manufactured and distributed to all BlueCoat customers. BlueCoat has a hardened Windows OS in it. While the base OS begin Windows, there are different antivirus or malware-scanning engines running in it. The BlueCoat Proxy AV though has Windows OS, has six different flavors of antivirus or malware-scanning engines built into it: a

1. Kaspersky
2. Sophos
3. McAfee
4. Panda

5. AhnLab
6. TrendMicro (Only in Europe and not for sales now)

The customer has a wide variety of choices from which to pick his or her the preferred vendor. For instance, if you want MacAfee, you will be getting a BlueCoat Proxy AV appliance with Windows in it and McAfee's malware engine on top of it. The same model applies to all the malware engine vendors. Usually, the decision in an organization is proposed by the security team, based upon their environment.

What protocols and content can the BlueCoat AV scan?

BlueCoat can scan only HTTP and FTP objects, as these are not limited to the BlueCoat AV technology. But the communication between Proxy SG and the OCSbecomes infinite. For example, for streaming media, the content for a live stream is not known, so the proxy has to completely download the video before sending the object for scanning. This is not actually possible, since as you know, a live stream may be infinite and it will cause a huge delay in the network for end users.

The Proxy SG can scan protocols like

1. HTTP Objects;
2. HTTPS connections terminated at a ProxySG;
3. FTP objects (uploads and downloads); and
4. transparent FTP responses.

The Proxy SG doesn't support the following protocols:

1. HTTPS connections tunneled through a Blue Coat client-side ProxySG
2. Live HTTP streams (e.g., HTTP radio streams)
3. Streaming content (e.g., RTSP or MMS)

The above are the supported and non-supported protocols. The different content types or file extensions that are supported by ICAP are many, but we will name a few popular ones that we know of: .exe, .bat, .com, .zip, .wmv, .rtf, .rar, .dll, .doc, .mpeg, .mp3, .jpeg, .jpg, .js, .vbs, and .pdf. The complete list will be shown when you configure the VPM policies for the scanning file extensions. The Proxy AV can scan HTTP MIME types such as application/pdf, application/hta, application/x-javascript, audio/wav, audio/mpeg, image/jpeg, and image/gif, to name a few.

This is the most frequently asked question regarding ICAP? And from the ICAP forum the answer is below:

"ICAP/1.0 has been designed to encapsulate HTTP messages. By translating other protocols first to HTTP and then encapsulating them into ICAP, some vendors have found a way to also use ICAP for other protocols such as FTP; in this case implementation remains interoperable with other ICAP services. ICAP has also been used to encapsulate messages of other protocols natively (without translating to HTTP first); those implementations are usually not standard implementations and are not interoperable with other solutions.".

What is Malware?

Malware, which is short for malicious software, is any program, code, or file that is dangerous and harmful to a computer. Malware is designed to gain unauthorized access, deny legitimate operation, data theft, setting backdoor, replicates itself and any other abusive behavior that can be done to the system. Malware is the biggest threat on the Internet to corporations, governments, school and colleges, home users, etc. Since its main purpose is to abuse and/or destroy the computer system, it has caused a lot of damage to users and to the computing industry. So malware is used as a very broad term, but there are different types of malware:

1. Adware
2. Backdoors
3. Crimeware
4. Dialers
5. Downloadesr
6. Exploits
7. MMC
8. Ransomware
9. Rootkits
10. Spyware
11. Trojan horses
12. Viruses
13. Worms
14. URL injectors

ICAP PROTOCOL

As you know, the BlueCoat Proxy SG is integrated with the BlueCoat AV, which provides scanning of objects for users request and responses. But what protocol is involved? And how does the Proxy SG communicate with the Proxy AV? It is via a protocol known as ICAP. ICAP stands for Internet Content Adaptation Protocol, and it is open standard, which is a lightweight HTTPbased Remote Procedure Call(RPC) protocol, which is used for virus scanning and content filtering for objects and user requests.

ICAP protocol was introduced b Peter Danzig and John Schuster, and later Don Gillies took over the project in 2000 and enhanced the protocol to allow pipelined ICAP servers and to support all three encapsulations of HTTP allowed by HTTP 1.1. As per in RFC specification of HTTP, the protocol can be encapsulated three times. This is somewhat similar to a GRE header that we saw in the WCCP chapter. The main goal of ICAP is to off-load specific Internet-based content to dedicated servers, thereby freeing up resources and standardizing the way in which features are implemented. So in BlueCoat's architecture, the scanning of objects is off-loaded from the Proxy SG and that task is given to the Proxy AV, thereby improving the performance and security of objects. By off-loading, the scanning of objects from the Proxy SG is made to perform more efficiently than the scanning engine that is built inside the Proxy SG. A study from the ICAP engineers revealed that a webserver performing only language translation is inherently more efficient than any standard webserver performing many additional tasks. So we take the same principle and apply it to the BlueCoat Proxy environment and provide the best of the security services to all our customers.

ICAP is not only used for scanning objects in the Proxy AV, but can also be used for off-box web filtering and it is supported for Websense. But the questions becomes, why do on-box BCWF in the Proxy SG? The answer is that it is much faster in terms of round-trip and processing time to perform the local database lookup for URL filtering rather than to use a remote database for URL filtering.

ICAP mainly serves for adaptation. Adaptation refers to the content manipulation of the client requests and responses. ICAP works on port 1344, and the secure ICAP works on port 11344. So when the proxy receives the request, it checks the policy for whether the site is allowed or denied, If the site is allowed, it checks whether the object is in the cache or not. If it is not available in the cache, Prosy SG sends all the requests and responses from the server to the ICAP by encapsulating the packet.

Note: In ICAP terms, the Proxy SG is called the ICAP client (the one which sends request to scan), and the Proxy AV is called the ICAP server (the one which scans the objects).

Scanning modes in ICAP

To scan objects, ICAP uses two types of modes:

1. REQMOD mode
2. RESPMOD mode

1. REQMOD mode:

The REQMOD (Response Modification Service) mode, is the modification of the request, is what also known as adaptation of the services used by the client. All the requests initiated by the client are scanned using the REQMOD mode That is, when the Proxy SG

(ICAP Client) receives the request, it checks the policy for whether the request is allowed or blocked. If allowed, it then forwards the client request to the Proxy AV (ICAP server) for scanning. The Proxy AV scans with its antivirus signatures, and if the packet is free from malware then Proxy AV doesn't not modifies the scanned packet and forwards to the Proxy SG. The Proxy SG fetches the object from the OCS, then RESPMOD mode is used to scan the responses from the OCS server, which is described below. The main reason to use REQMOD to check the outbound web requests, so for instance the client doesn't uploads a malware file to the Internet using the Webmail (Hotmail, Gmail, Yahoomail) or some infected computers sends all data using Keyloggers, through PUT or POST methods.. So if you scan, you can make sure that you are in compliance with the security standards and that you don't pose a threat to the Internet and others users. The main reason to use REQMOD for avoiding data leak, such that the internal users is blocked from corporate data theft. Usually the best way is to integrate with DLP (Data Leak Prevention) technology and scan all the client requests.

The Proxy SG will make a REQMOD ICAP RPC call like "**REQMOD icap:// ProxyAVIP/ ICAP/1.0\r\n**" inside the ICAP header, which is similar to the HTTP GET request (**GET http://www.test.com   HTTP/1.1 \r\n**"). After scanning, Proxy AV, if there is no malware found in the object, returns "**ICAP/1.0 204 No modifications needed\r\n**". This is similar to WCCP, as shown in the figure 9:1 below:

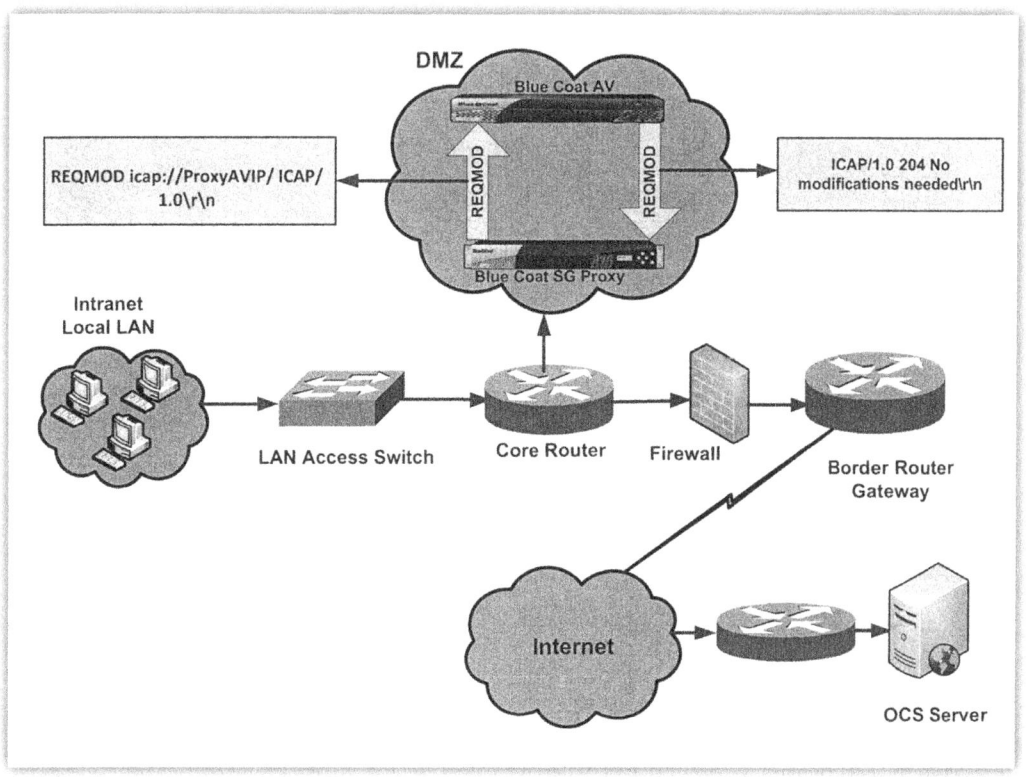

Figure 9.1 REQMOD mode ICAP scanning

2. RESPMOD mode:

The RESPMOD (Response Modification) mode inspects all the inbound traffic or return traffic. As we saw with the REQMOD mode, after the client request gets scanned and when the object is fetched from the OCS, the object is first fully downloaded by the Proxy SG. While the Proxy SG cannot download the object, the scanning cannot begin. Once the object is completely downloaded, the Proxy SG (ICAP client) encapsulates it and sends it to the ICAP server (Proxy AV) for scanning. The Proxy AV scans it and if clean, sends back the object without modifying it. The Proxy SG checks if it is cacheable; if the object is cacheable then it is cached in the Proxy SG and delivered to the client. All further requests for the same object are not scanned; the Proxy SG delivers it to any client who requests it, if the policy states that it is allowed.

The Proxy SG will make a RESPMOD ICAP RPC call like "**RESPMOD icap://ProxyAVIP/ ICAP/1.0\r\n**" inside the ICAP header, which is similar to the HTTP GET request (**GET http://www.test.com HTTP/1.1 \r\n**"). If after scanning, the Proxy AV detects a malware in the object, it returns "**ICAP/1.0 200 OK \r \n**". This is similar to the figure below:

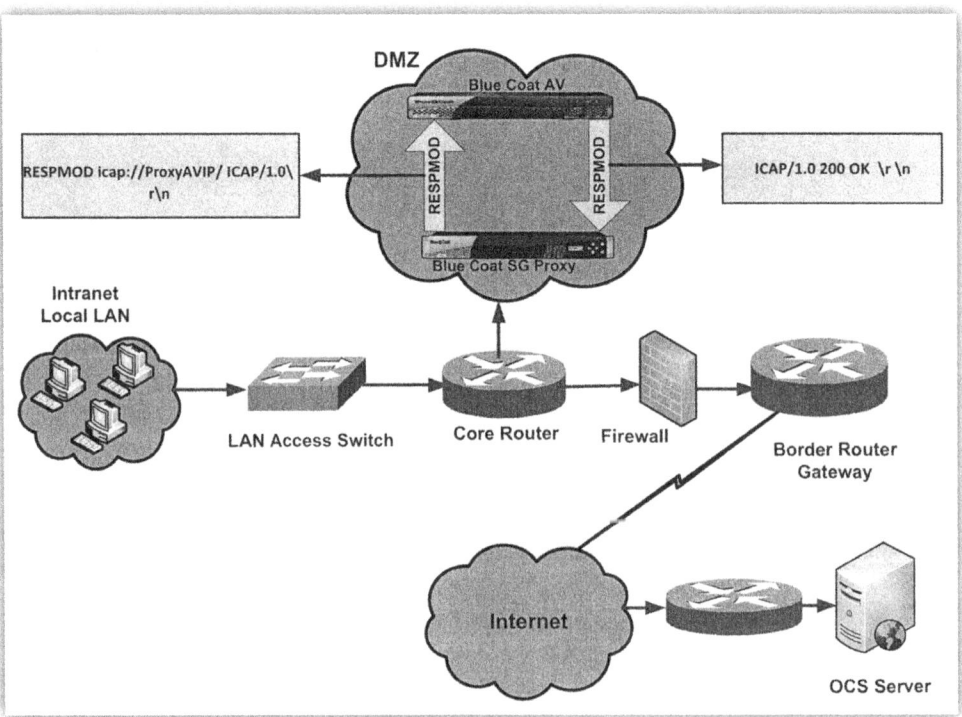

Figure 9.2: RESPMOD mode ICAP scanning

The actual ICAP header is shown in figure 9:3 below; for simplicity, only the transaction that happens between Proxy SG and Proxy AV is shown. The other components, such as the firewall, router, and internal LAN remain the same. The encapsulation is slightly different from the GRE, as we saw in the Chapter 8 ; it is as follows:

1. When the client (192.168.10.10) tries to access to http:/www.facebook.com (69.171.224.42), the BlueCoat Proxy SG receives the request, and if the policy is allowed and the object not in the cache, it fetches the object from the OCS server.
2. Proxy SG then creates a new ICAP request with Source IP as the Proxy SG IP (192.168.10.101) and the destination (192.168.10.120) of the Proxy AV IP, with source port a random port > 1024, say 16000 that is selected by the Proxy SG and the destination port as 1344.

    It also encapsulates an ICAP header over the HTTP header with the client IP filled in the field X-Client-IP as 192.168.10.10 and the X-Server-IP as 69.171.224.42. The X-Client-IP and X-Server-IP are in the application layer and not in the IP or TCP layer. That is how it differs from GRE, which you can see in thebelow figure.

3. The Proxy SG forwards the packet to the Proxy AV for scanning. The Proxy AV scans the packet with its signatures and replies to the Proxy SG based on two conditions:
    a. If the object is clean, then Proxy AV sends ICAP 204 code (No modifications) on the ICAP application header to the Proxy SG, with the source IP as 192.168.10.120, source port as 1344, destination IP as 192.168.10.101, and destination port as 16000.
    b. If the object is infected, then it sends ICAP 200 code (No Modifications) on the ICAP application header to the Proxy SG, with the source IP as 192.168.10.120, source port as 1344, destination IP as 192.168.10.101, and destination port as 18000.

An ICAP server wants to change the header of an encapsulated HTTP message but does not want to change the body. A 204 (No content or No modification) ICAP response does not allow to modify the data. A 200 (Modified) ICAP response does allow the Proxy AV to change the data.

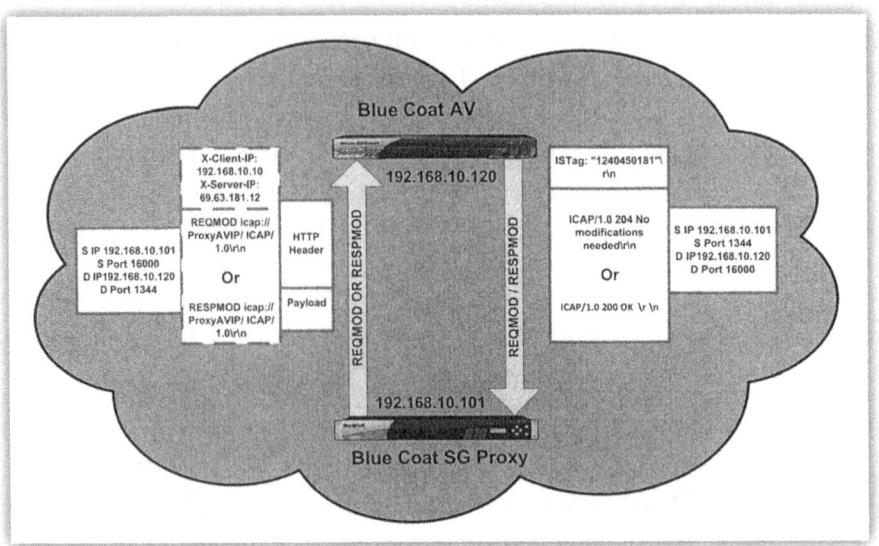

Figure 9.3: REQMOD and RESPMOD ICAP traffic flow

IS TAG

In the above figure, notice that in the response header there is attribute called IS Tag. IS Tag is service-specific cookie that is given to the ICAP client by the ICAP server, to represent the current ICAP service state of the ICAP server. For example, when the Proxy SG forwards an object for scanning by the Proxy AV, if it is clean you will get ICAP 204 code and then the Proxy SG will cache the result, stating that the cache is clean. Imagine that after a while, the Proxy AV software gets updated with the new signature. Now all the contents that are cache by the Proxy SG need to revalidated with the new Proxy AV software, because now there are new signatures. So now the Proxy AV notifies its new ISTag cookie, and if the Proxy SG (ICAP client) sees a new ISTag number other than the old one, it will rescan all the objects that is stored in the Proxy SG.

ISTag is just is a 32-byte integer value you can find in the ICAP header and it will looks as follows:

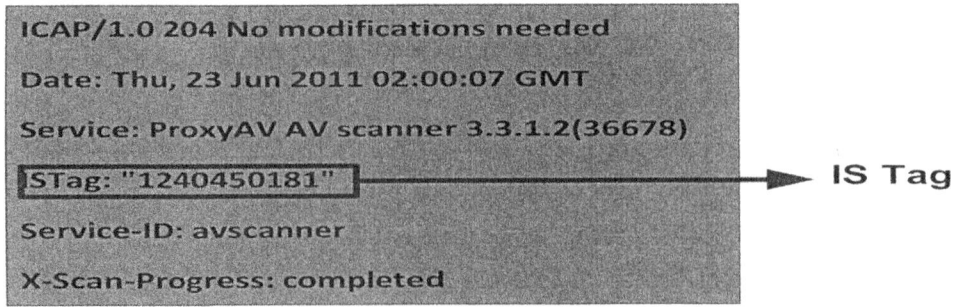

Figure 9.4 : IS Tag

IS Tag can change into any number at random, and it doesn't mean it has to increment all the time, even it could decrement, the only difference is that the change in the IS Tag number is noticed by the Proxy SG, and it remembers the current and the old IS Tag numbers.

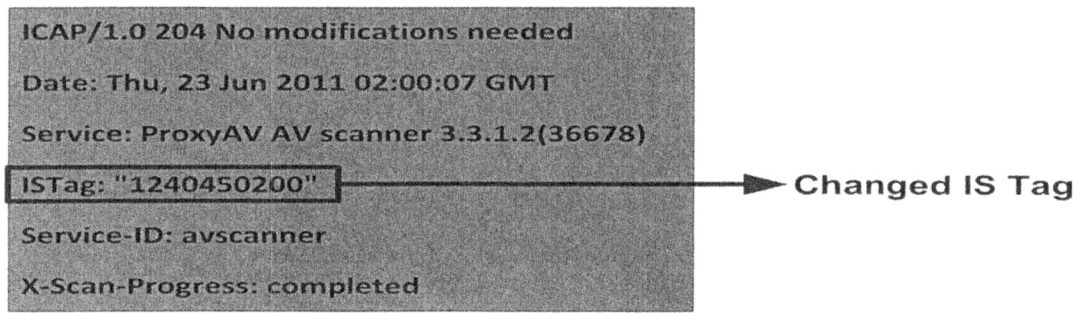

ICAP/1.0 204 No modifications needed

Date: Thu, 23 Jun 2011 02:00:07 GMT

Service: ProxyAV AV scanner 3.3.1.2(36678)

ISTag: "1240450200" ➤ **Changed IS Tag**

Service-ID: avscanner

X-Scan-Progress: completed

Figure 9.5: Modified IS Tag

PROXY AV DEPLOYMENT

In this section we will discuss the various types of deployment that you can integrate both Proxy SG and Proxy AV in different methods. It all depends on the business requirements and financial budget of the corporation for doing this. Before we go into different architecture models where Proxy SG and Proxy AV can be deployed, we should consider and understand three main concepts:

1. Security: If either Proxy SG or Proxy AV goes down, what is the impact on security? Malware scanning and Proxy Policy enforcement will be still performed?
2. Scalability: How is the load distributed for the traffic in both Proxy SG and Proxy AV?
3. High Availability: When a failover happens, is my network redundant ?

There are four types of deployment that can be used to integrate Proxy SG and Proxy AV and they are as follows:

1. One Proxy SG and One Proxy AV

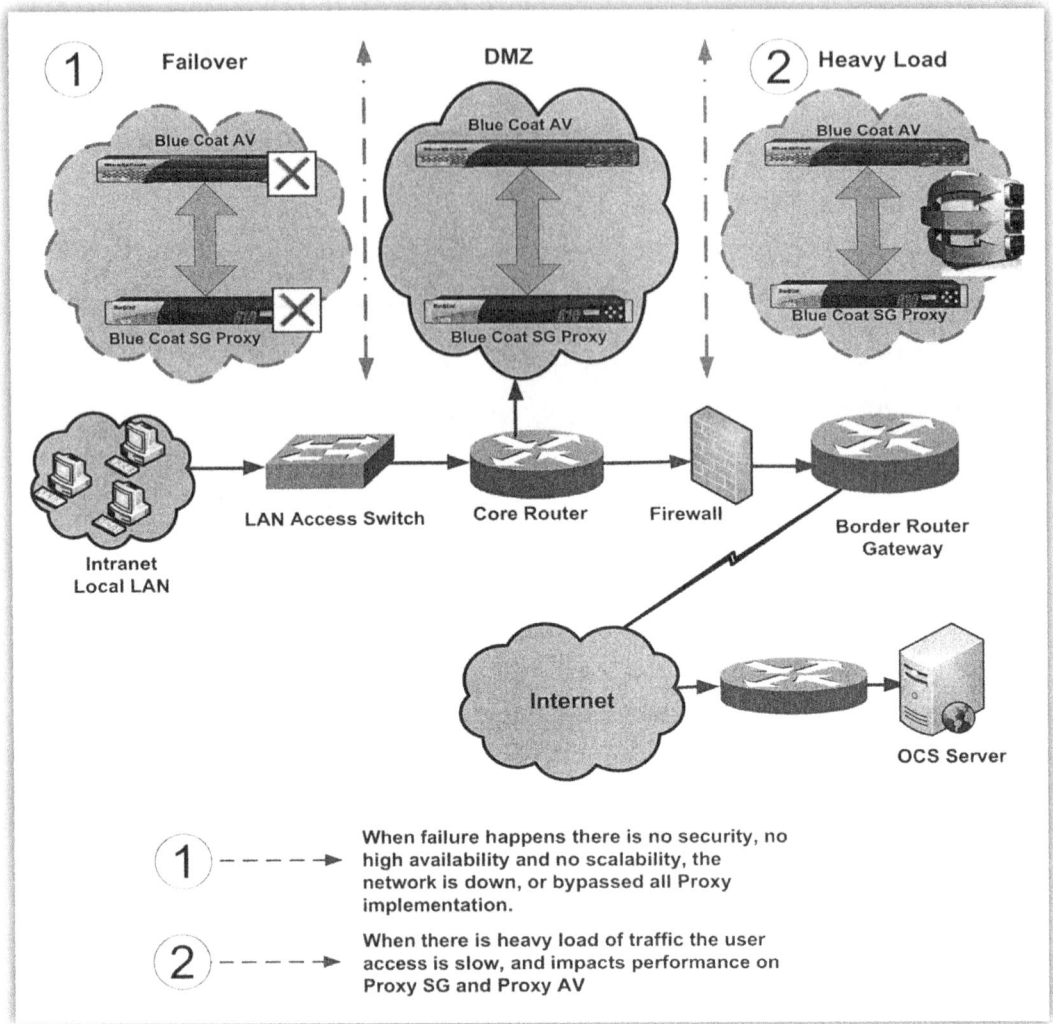

Figure 9.6: One Proxy SG and One Proxy AV deployment

As we see in the above figure, when the proxy devices are either down or under heavy loads, this introduces performance issues, bad user experience on the web, bypassed security, business downtime, etc. So this design is not suitable for large and critical environments.

2. Multiple Proxy SGs and One Proxy AV

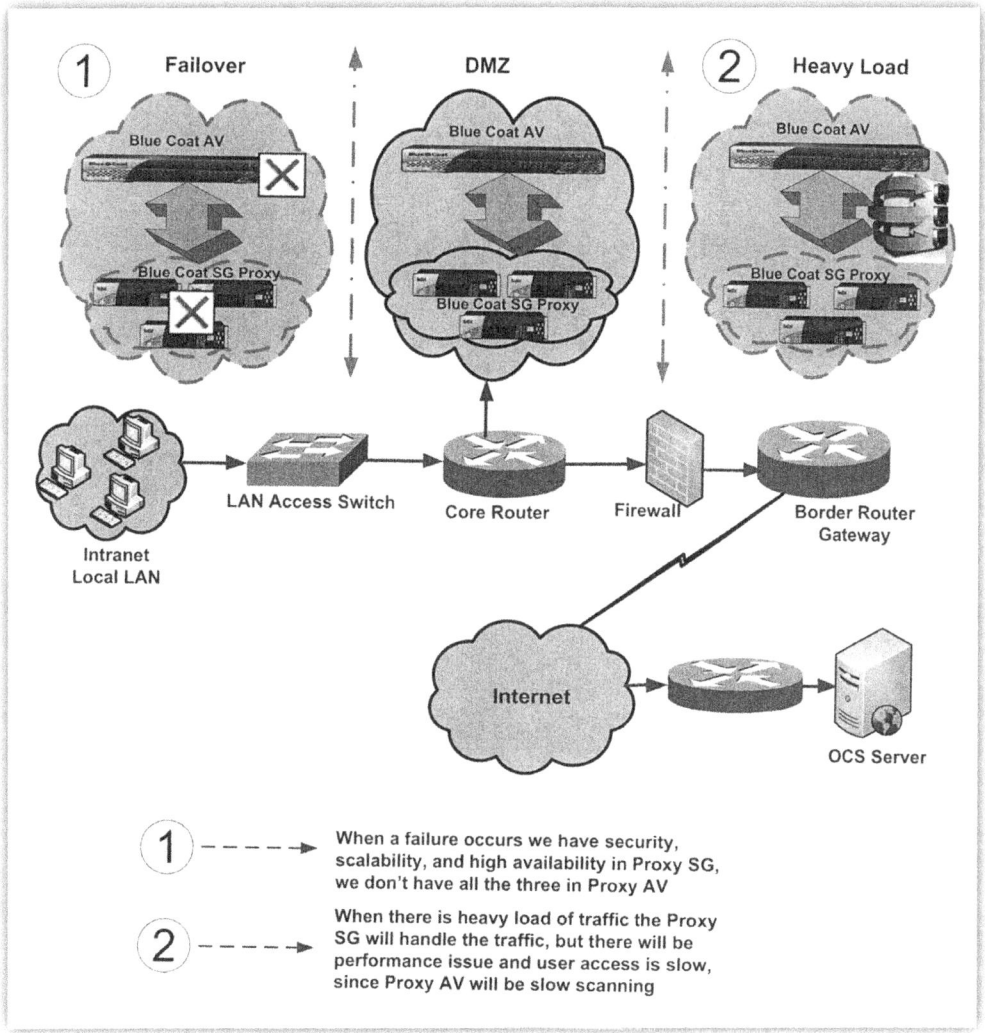

Figure 9:7 Multiple Proxy SGs and One Proxy AV deployment

As shown in the above figure, on failure all the three Proxy SG, security, scalability, and high availability is not achieved and the whole internet access goes down. If only one Proxy SG goes down, while the other Proxy SG shares the load of the failed Proxy SG and but all the three factors security, scalability and hih availability impacts the Proxy AV. In failure situation, you cannot do malware scanning, and a security hole will be created in your network. During heavy traffic load the Proxy SG will perform with same performance ; but the Proxy AV is overloaded, and in total the network performance, user's experience, and business impact will be seen. This is suitable for a medium-sized organization.

3. Multiple Proxy AVs and One Proxy SG

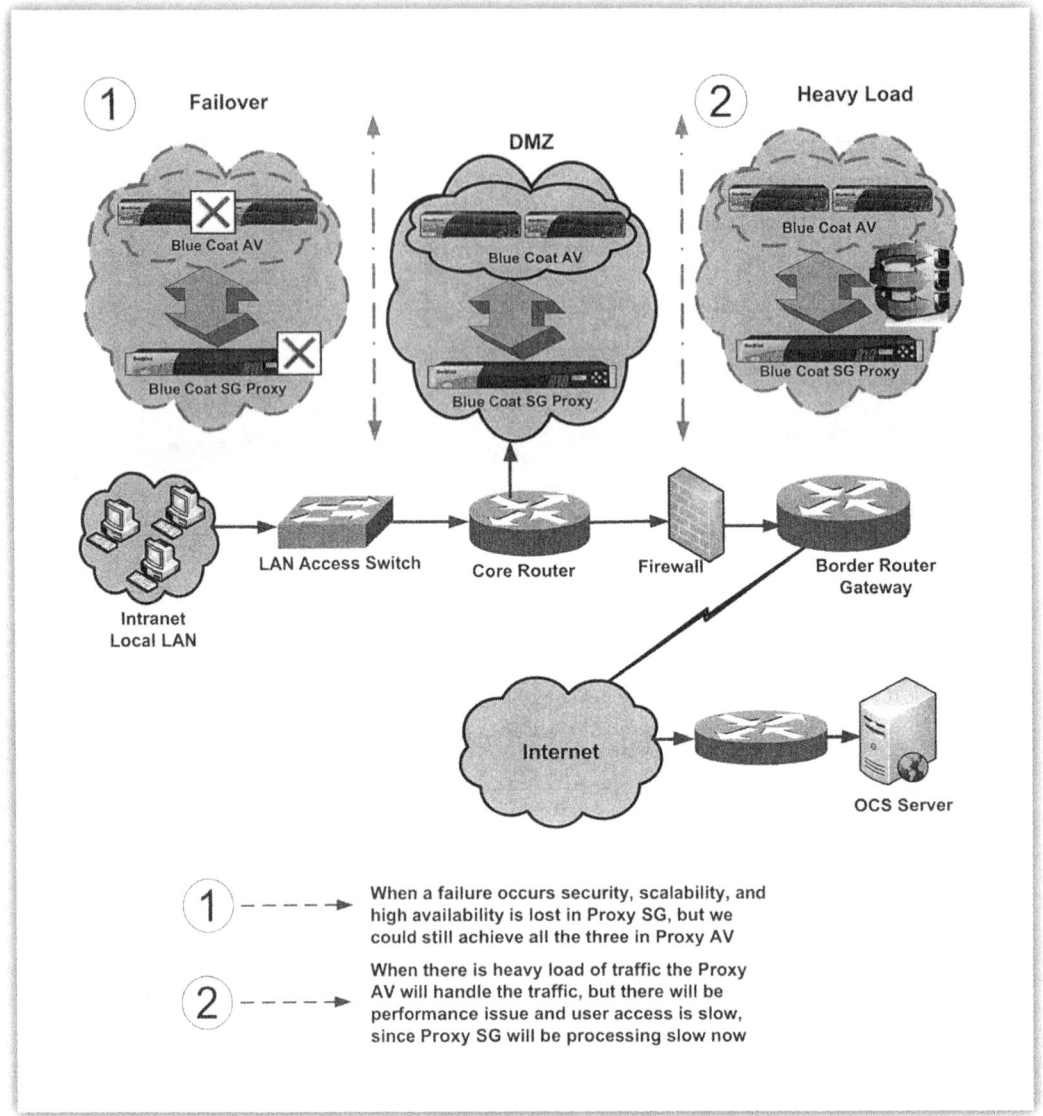

Figure 9:8 Multiple Proxy AVs and One Proxy SG deployment

As you can see in the above figure, when there is a failure in Proxy SG, all the traffic should be bypassed from the Proxy SG since there is no interceptor for the traffic, and all the features—security, scalability, and high availability—cannot be implemented. Though you can achieve all the three features security, scalability and high availability in Proxy AV, but still this design is like the first deployment (One Proxy SG and One Proxy AV), since the primary and important is the traffic interception which is done only by Proxy SG, which is down and not functioning. Eventually the network's internet access for the users is down.

4. Multiple Proxy SGs and Multiple Proxy AVs

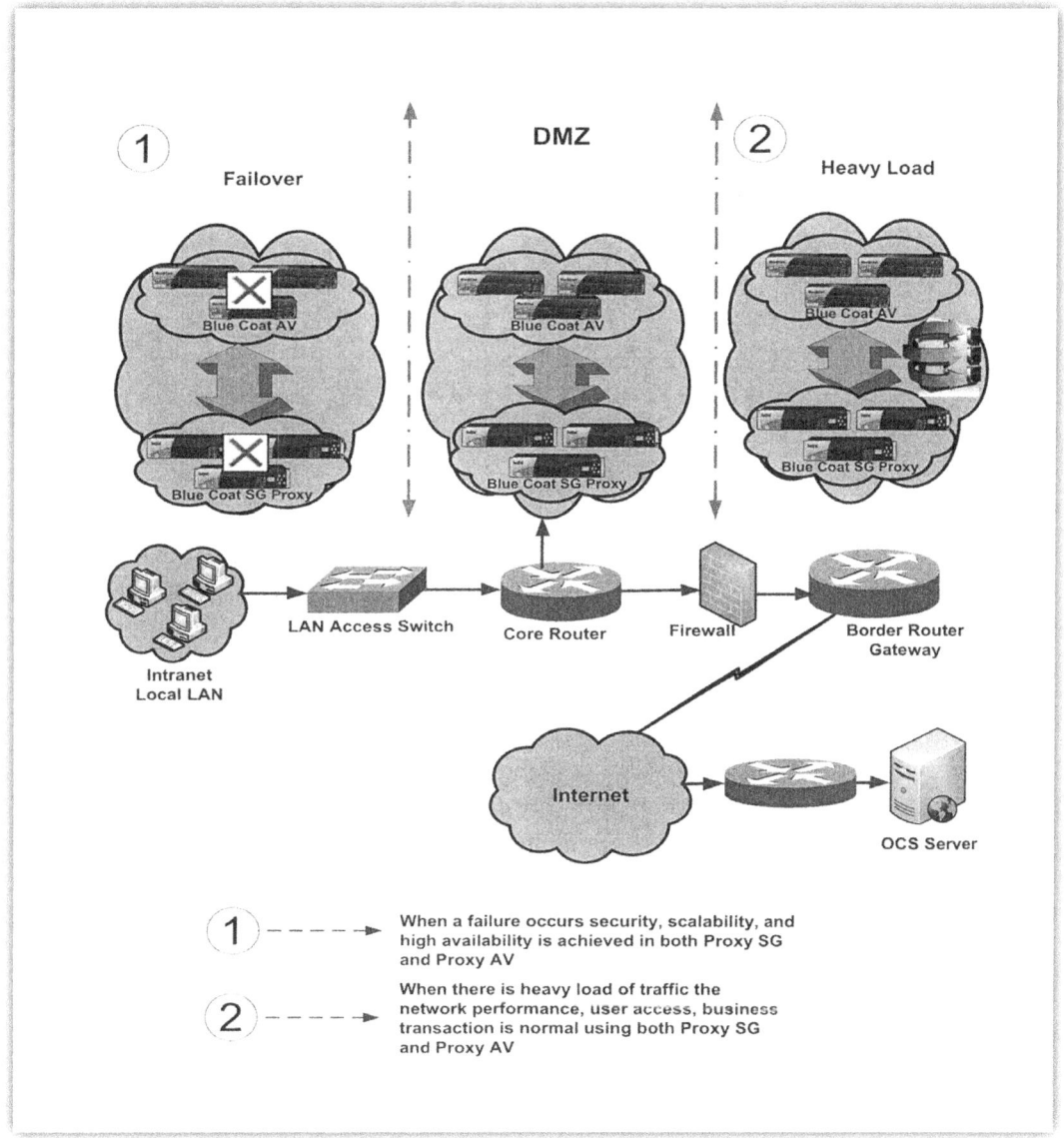

Figure 9:9 Multiple Proxy SG and Multiple Proxy AV deployment

As shown in the above figure, this is the state-of-the-art design, since with either Proxy SG or Proxy AV failure, security, high availability, and scalability can still be achieved. When the load of the traffic increases in the network, the performance and user's experience is normal and there is no business impact.

Initial Configuration of BlueCoat Proxy AV

In this section, we will show how to initially setup a BlueCoat Proxy AV, by connecting to a console and configuring the initial parameters like the IP address, its default gateway, the DNS, the administrator account, etc.

This is done the same way you configured the Proxy SG, as we have shown in the chapter "Configuring Blue Coat Proxy SG" under the section "Serial Console." You will see a similar screen below, after connecting the console to the computer.

Copyright (c) 1997-2010, Blue Coat Systems, Inc.

Welcome to the ProxyAV Appliance Setup Console
---------------------- (page 1 of 4) ----------------------
 Press <ESC> at any time to return to the main menu

DIRECTIONS:

This setup console is used to assign IP addresses to the Proxy AV Appliance. After assigning the IP addresses you can connect to the command line interface or web interface to perform additional management tasks.

IP address [0.0.0.0]:192.168.10.120 → **Enter the IP address of the Proxy AV**
IP subnet mask [0.0.0.0]:255.255.255.0 → **Enter the subnet mask of the Proxy AV**
IP gateway [0.0.0.0]:192.168.10.100 → **Enter the default gateway of the Proxy AV**
DNS server [0.0.0.0]:192.168.10.50 → **Enter the DNS server**

You have entered the following IP addresses:

IP address: 192.168.10.120
IP subnet mask: 255.255.255.0
IP gateway: 192.168.10.100
DNS server: 192.168.10.50

Would you like to change any of them? Y/N [No]:**No**

Would you like to change Ethernet Adapter Media Type? Y/N [No]:**Yes**
Press <ESC> at any time to return to the main menu

DIRECTIONS:

By default, the ProxyAV automatically detects the link settings. This option allows you to manually specify the Ethernet media adapter type. To change the configuration, select an option from the menu.

```
----------------------- MENU ----------------------------

1) Auto
2) 10 Mbit/Half
3) 10 Mbit/Full
4) 100 Mbit/Half
5) 100 Mbit/Full
6) 1000 Mbit/Full
---------------------------------------------------------
```

Enter option [1]:1 → **Confirm it is set to "Auto"**
-------------------- (page 2 of 4) --------------------
 Press <ESC> at any time to return to the main menu

DIRECTIONS:

The console username, password and enable password are special administrative credentials which can be used to log in to the command line interface or web management interface.

Would you like to change the console user account now? Y/N [No]:**Yes**

Enter console username [admin]: → **Just Press Enter, the username is "admin"**
Enter console password: → **Enter the password**
Verify console password: → **Enter the same password to confirm it.**
Enter enable password: → **Enter the enable password**
Verify enable password: → **Enter the same password to confirm it.**
Do you want to secure the serial port? Y/N [Yes]:**No**
-------------------- (page 3 of 4) --------------------
Press <ESC> at any time to return to the main menu

DIRECTIONS:

WARNING: The console account can currently be used to log in from any workstation.
    This dialog allows you to define the only IP address that is authorized to use the console account.
    Additional workstations may be configured later, from the webinterface. By accepting default value, you will delete any IP address restrictions.

Would you like to restrict access to an authorized workstation? Y/N [Yes]:**No**

-------------------- (page 4 of 4) --------------------

DIRECTIONS:

The ProxyAV Appliance has been successfully configured to use IP address: "192.168.10.120" You can connect to the command line interface or webinterface to perform additional management tasks.

To connect to the webmanagement interface, go to the following location with your web browser: **https://192.168.10.120:8082/**

---------------- CONFIGURATION COMPLETE ------------------

ProxyAV is updating settings. Please wait.

....

Press "Enter" three times to activate the serial console.
After the initial configuration, you can launch the browser and log in to the Proxy AV via **https://192.168.10.120:8082/**. You will get a screen as shown below:

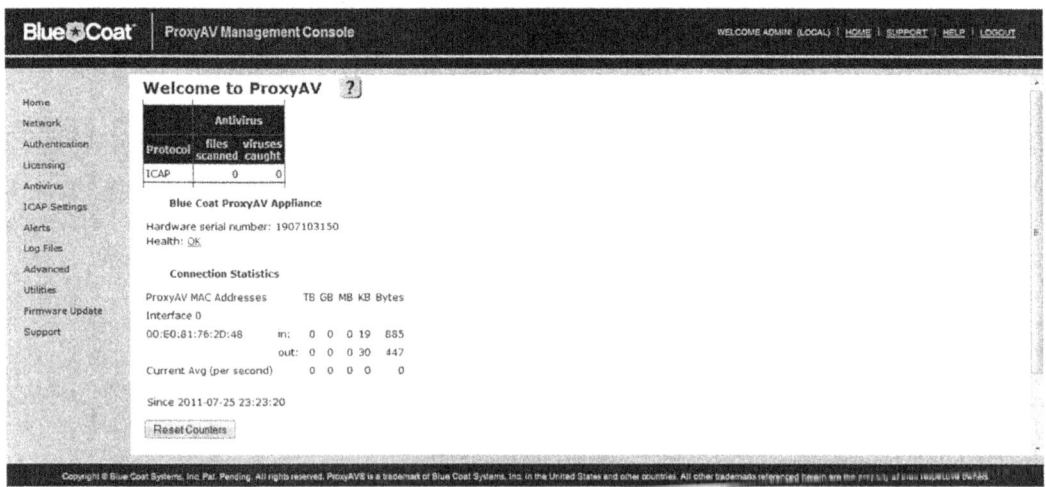

Figure 9:10 Initial screen of the Proxy AV

In our example below we will be showing how to configure Proxy AV and integrate it with Proxy SG. In this chapter we will using two Proxy AVs that are integrated with Proxy SG and we will be defining proxy groups. The design for your configuration will be as shown below:

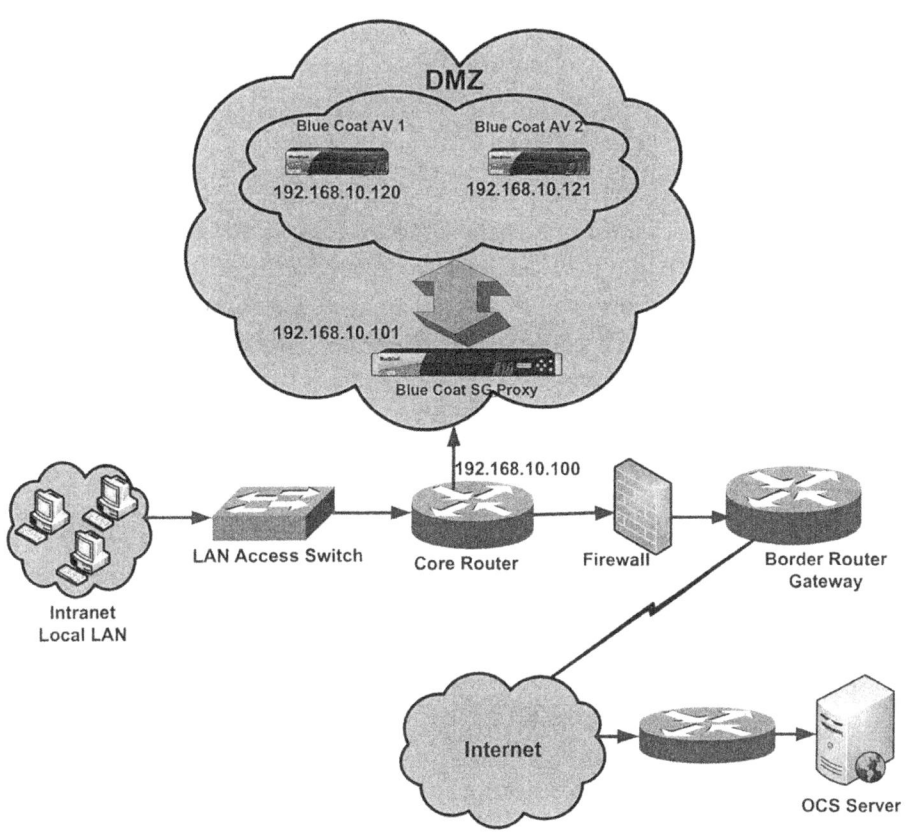

Figure 9:11 Proxy example diagram for our configuration

So as per in the above figure, we have configured the BlueCoat AV1, and now we need to do the initial configuration. Please follow the same steps that you used to configure BlueCoat AV1, to configure BlueCoat AV2 with the following details:

BlueCoat AV2

IP address: 192.168.10.121

Subnet Mask: 255.255.255.0

Default Gateway: 192.168.10.100

DNS Server: 192.168.10.50

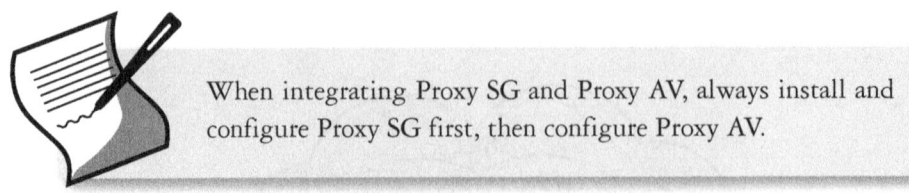

When integrating Proxy SG and Proxy AV, always install and configure Proxy SG first, then configure Proxy AV.

Before integrating the Proxy SG and Proxy AV, you need register the Proxy AV with BlueCoat, apply the license, and upgrade the BlueCoat Proxy AV to the latest version if BlueCoat doesn't ships with the new version. To do upgrading the Proxy AV you need to make sure your network allows the Proxy AV to access the internet directly without using the Proxy SG or Proxy AV could access the internet only via the Proxy SG, and these are explained as shown below:

1. Without the Proxy SG:

If in your network you have the Proxy AV directly accessing to the Internet, then you don't need to add the Proxy setting in the BlueCoat Proxy AV. This means that if the firewall allows Proxy AV connections, you can apply licenses, update AV signatures, etc.

2. With Proxy SG:

If the firewall is configured so that only Proxy SG can make connections to the Internet, then you need to configure the Proxy setting in the Proxy AV so that you can access the BlueCoat license portal, update the AV database, upgrade firmware and the OS, etc. To do this, log in to the BlueCoat Proxy AV via the browser using the IP address of the Proxy AV https://192.168.10.120:8082, or if you have a DNS name configured for the Proxy AV you could use the domain name,for example https://proxyav1.mycorporate.com:8082, and click the option "Network" on the left-hand side of the screen. You will see a screen as shown below:

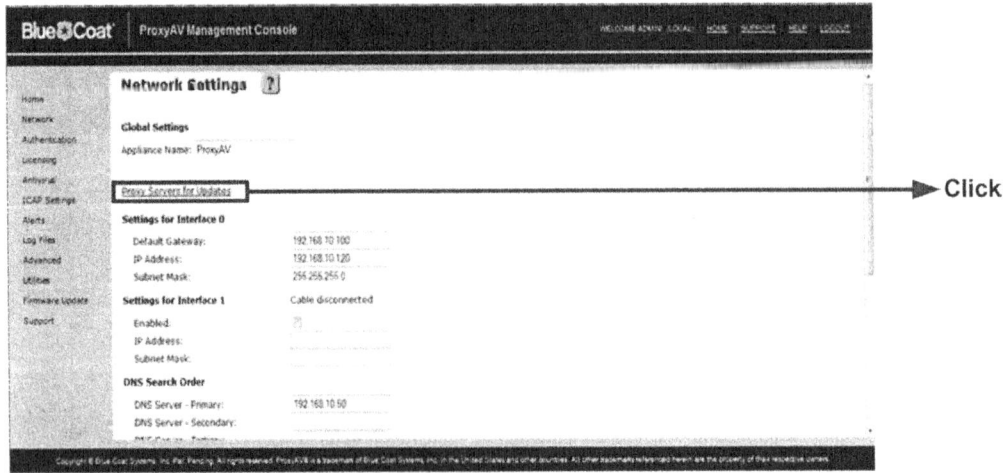

Figure 9:12 Network settings screen

And click the Proxy Servers for Updates link as shown in the above figure.

You will get a Proxy Setting screen as shown below:

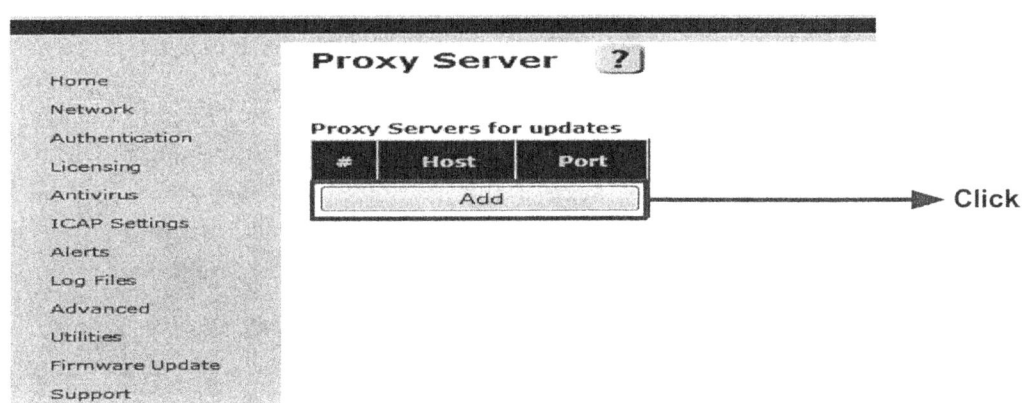

Figure 9:13 Proxy server settings screen

Click the "Add" button and enter the proxy setting as shown below and confirm it by clicking the "Add" button.

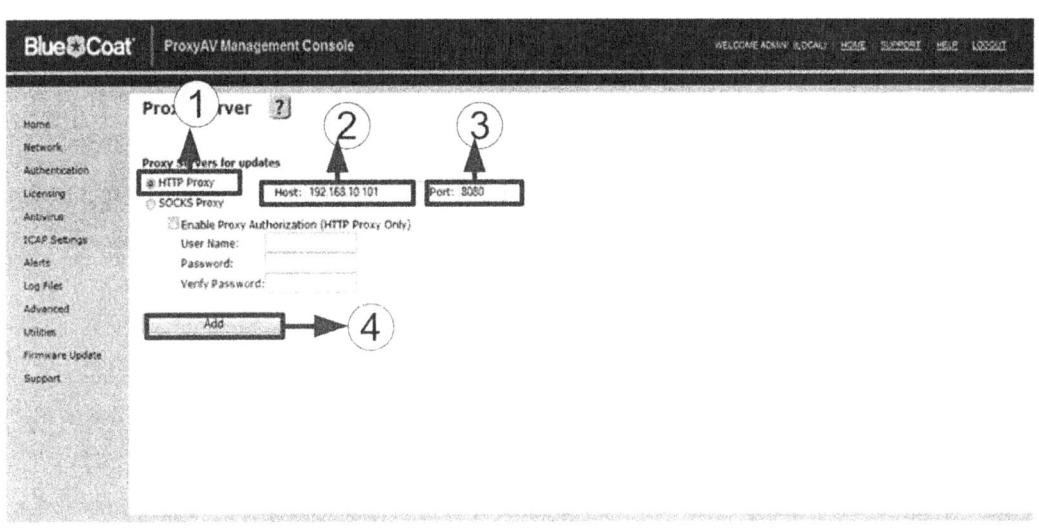

Figure 9:14 Adding Proxy server details

Figure 9:14 Adding Proxy server details

The above setting will confirm that the Proxy AV can access the Internet using only the Proxy SG. Do the same for the other Proxy AV 192.168.10.121.

Adding Proxy AV in VPM policies

Once you have done the initial configuration and have added the necessary proxy settings in the Proxy AV, you'll need to add the Proxy AV IP in the VPM policies so that you can first license the Proxy AV and upgrade if it if necessary. Then we will show you how to integrate the Proxy AV and Proxy SG and configure VPM policies.

Log in to the Proxy SG via the management console and go to Configuration → Policy → Visual Policy Manager. Click "Launch" and go to the "**Corporate Web Access Layer**" that you created in the chapter "Visual Policy Manager." Add a rule by clicking on Rule 1 and move the rule all the way to the top. Right-click on the "Source" column and select "Set". Select "Combined Source Object" and name it as "Proxy AV". Add the two Proxy AVs using the "Client IP/Subnet Object" by clicking "New", and then move to the selected object as shown below:

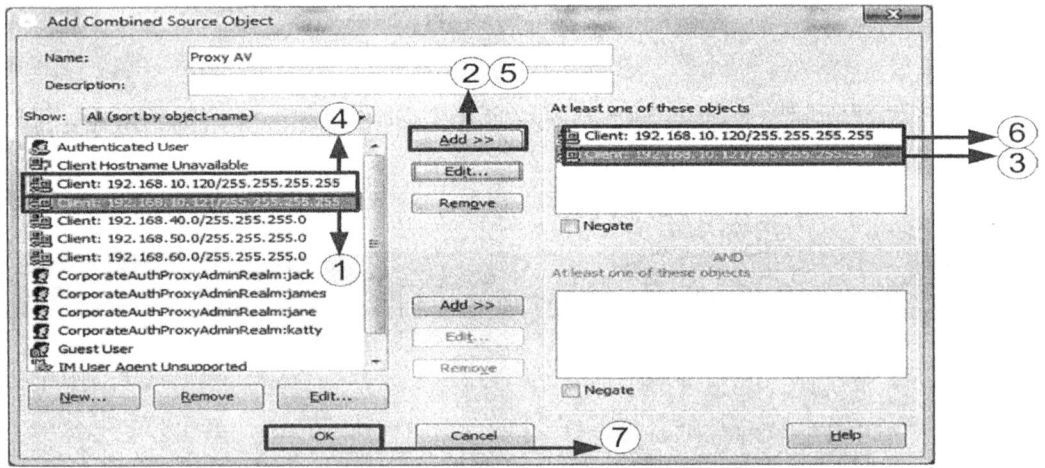

Figure 9:15 Adding Proxy AV combined objects in Proxy SG

And confirm it by clicking "OK", on the "Add Combined Source Object" box, and then click "OK" in the "Set Source Objects", and change the Action as "Allow" and install the policy. The final policy will look as shown below:

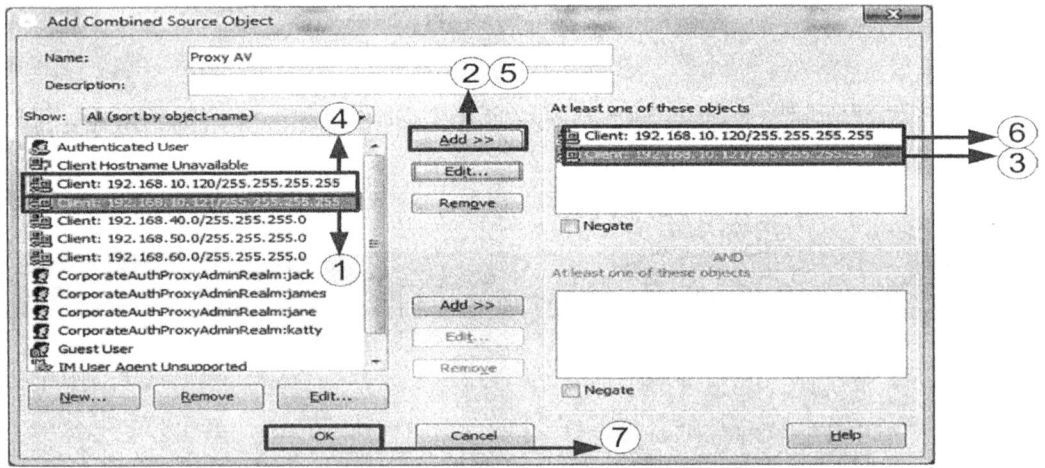

Figure 9:16 Web access layer for allowing Proxy AV traffic

Update the license and upgrade the Proxy AV

Now you need to update the license and upgrade the firmware if needed, so that after this you can proceed to integrate the Proxy SG with the Proxy AV. Log in to the Proxy AV via the management console https://192.168.10.120:8082, and go to "Licensing" as shown below:

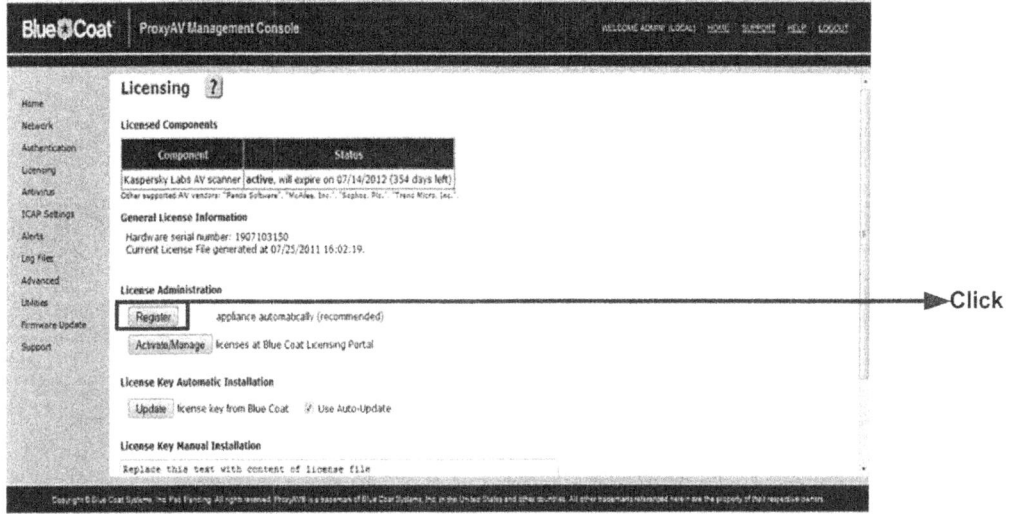

Figure 9:17 Licensing Portal in Proxy AV

If you want to register the BlueCoat Proxy AV box, click the "Register" button as shown in the above figure, and enter the details as shown below:

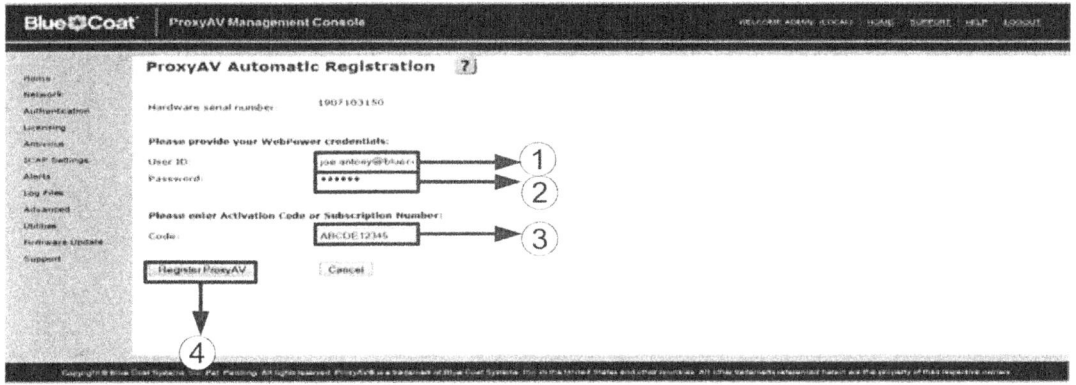

Figure 9:18 Licensing Portal in Proxy AV

Enter all the details for accessing the WebPower account as shown above. The activation code is the code that the BlueCoat sales team would have sent you by email. WebPower account is created when you purchase the appliance. If you don't have it, please contact the sales team and they will help you to get one. Otherwise you can license it using the

BlueCoat Licensing Portal. To do this, click the "Activate/Manage" button as shown in the figure above, which takes you to the BlueCoat Licensing Portal, as shown below:

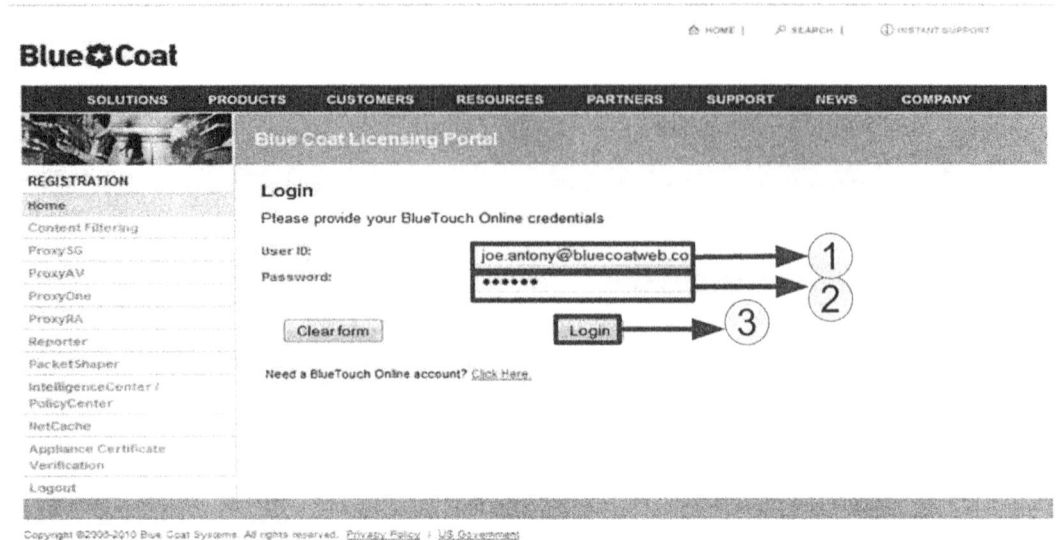

Figure 9:19 BlueCoat Licensing Portal for Web Power account

Log in by entering the WebPower account as shown above. After authentication you will see a screen as shown below:

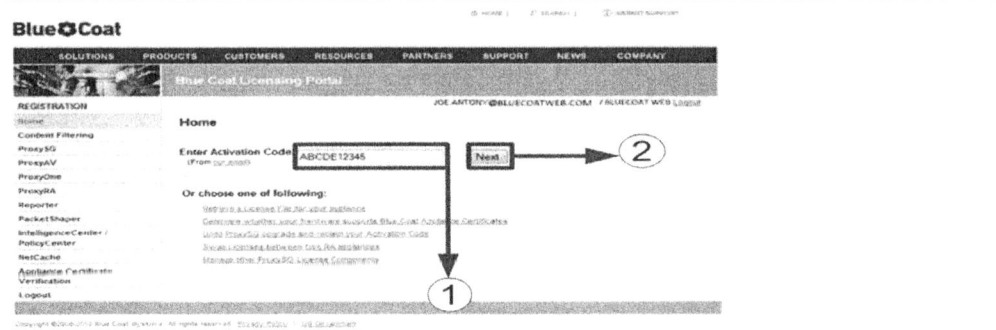

Figure 9:20 License activation code for the Proxy AV

Now you need to enter your activation code, which was emailed to you by the sales team. Once you enter the right activation code, you will get a screen as shown below, where you enter the Proxy AV serial number and the activation code one more time.

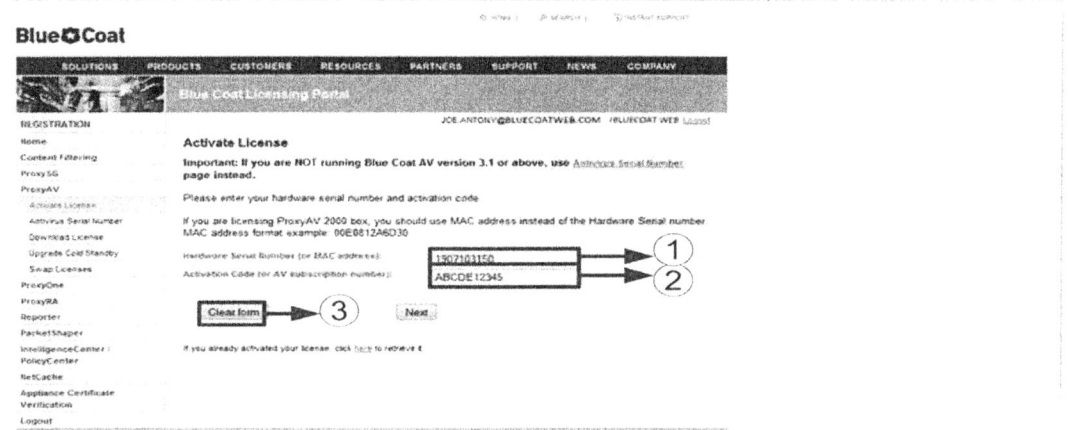

Figure 9:21 Serial number and License activation code for the Proxy AV

Both options shown above figure 9:18 and figure 9:19, "Register" and "Activate/ Manage", are the same, it will redirect you to login page of the portal.So we need WebPower account, activation code, serial number, to login successfully and you will get an agreement page as shown below:

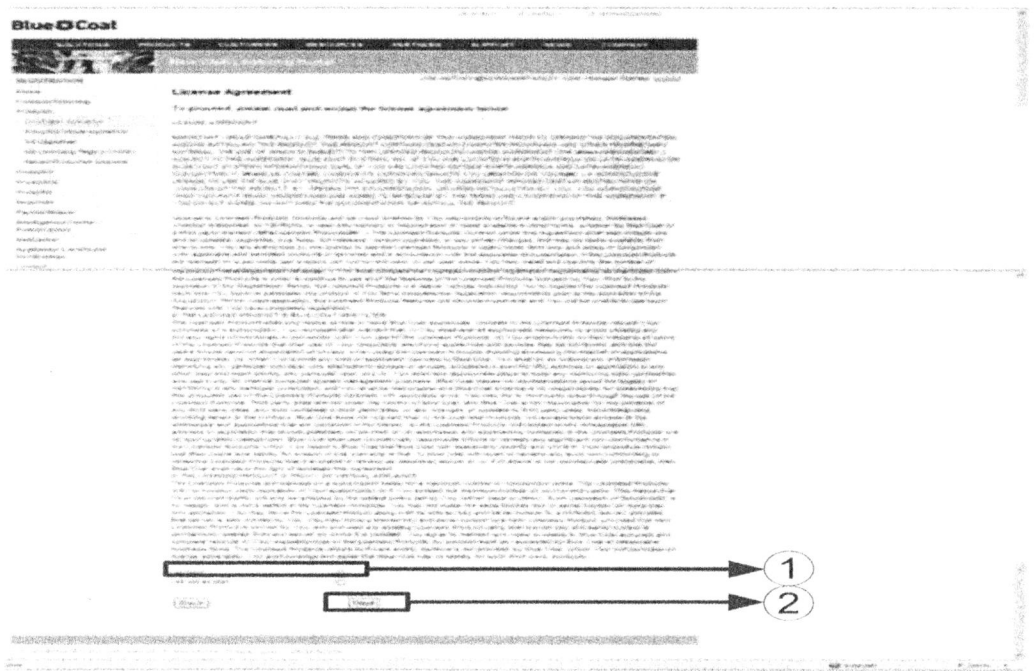

Figure 9:22 License Agreement for the Proxy AV product

Then it will take about two minutes for the license to sync their database, and after that you get will get a confirmation that the license has been created, as shown below:

Figure 9:23 Activation confirmation

Then you can return to the Proxy AV console management screen and in the "Licensing" page click the "Update" button under "License Key Automatic Installation". The license will get updates from the BlueCoat portal and will be installed in the appliance as shown below:

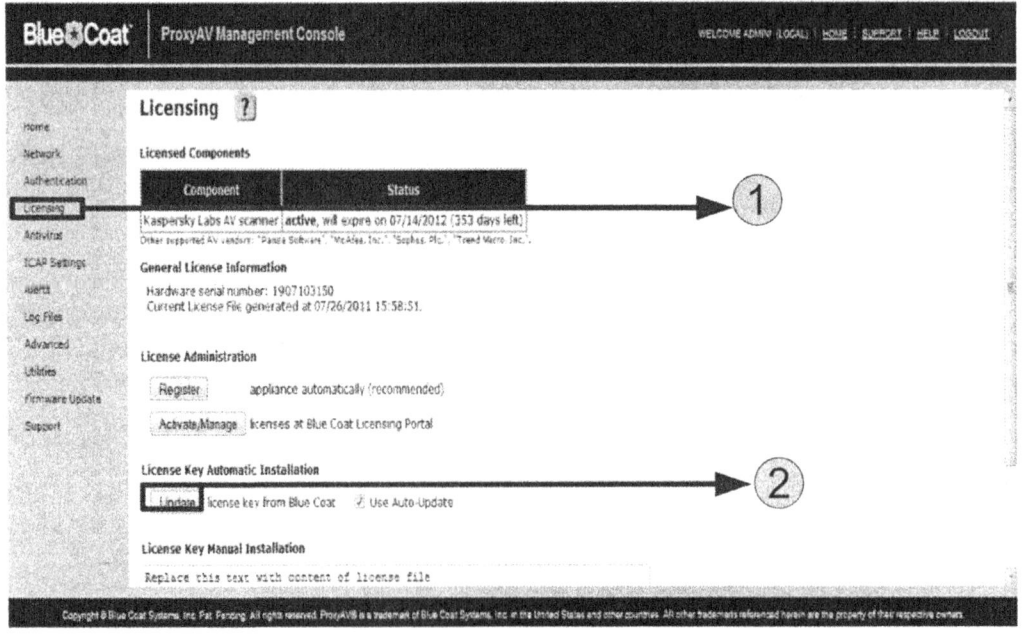

Figure 9:24 Updating License in the Proxy AV

Antivirus signature and firmware update

Once the license is updated, you can then update the antivirus database and update the firmware easily, so that we havethe latest AV signatures and the OS.

1. Antivirus Signature update

You can update the latest antivirus database by logging in to the management console of the Proxy AV via https://IPaddressof ProxyAV:8082. Go to "Antivirus" on the left panel, check the "Force update" checkbox, and click the "Update" button under the Action column as shown below. The antivirus signatures will be updated.

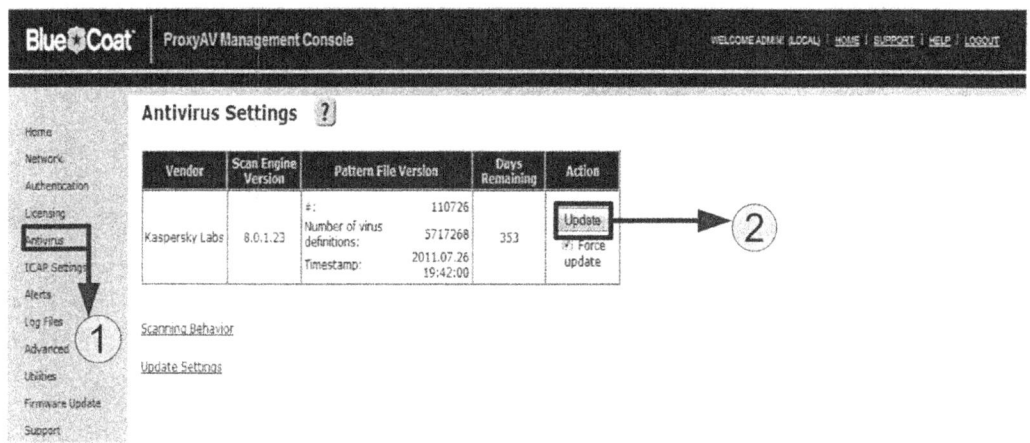

Figure 9:25 Proxy AV Antivirus Signature update

2. Firmware update

You can update the firmware of the Proxy AV, which is similar to an OS upgrade of the servers. Usually the newly shipped Proxy AV has the latest code, but in times wen you are planning to use the other, unused Proxy AV for while which you want to put in production, then a firmware update is required. It is one very easy step: after logging into the Proxy AV, go to the "Firmware Update" menu on the left and click the "Update Now" button at the bottom of the screen. Then the firmware of the Proxy AV will be updated within five minutes and the Proxy AV willreboot once the firmware is updated, as shown below:

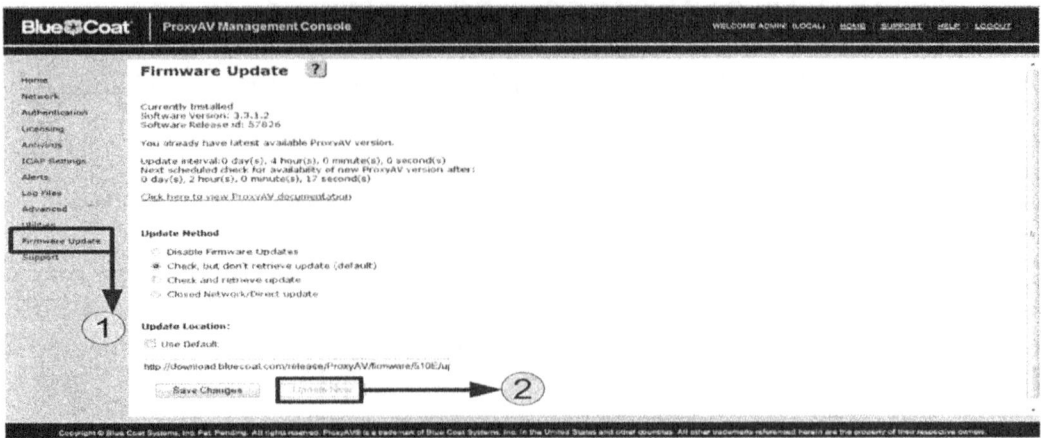

Figure 9:26 Proxy AV Firmware update

Integrating Proxy SG and Proxy AV

In this section we will show how to integrate the Proxy SG and Proxy AV. As we already stated, first configure the Proxy SG and put it in the network, then configure the Proxy AV. This is the method that you should follow, which makes the implementation and configuration faster and more efficient. To integrate the Proxy SG and Proxy AV, please follow the steps as shown below:

1. Log in to the Proxy SG management console and go to "External Services" → "ICAP" and go to the "ICAP Services" tab. Click "New" and enter the name as "av1requestmode". This is a user-defined mode, so enter any name that is convenient, as shown below:

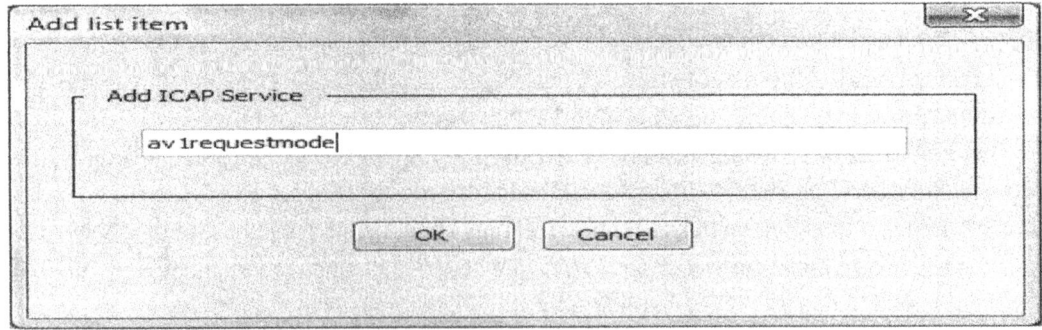

Figure 9:27 Adding ICAP Request mode service

And click "OK" to confirm it and click "Apply" in the main menu to apply the changes.

2. The ICAP service is created. The ICAP service "av1requestmode" is selected by default once you commit the change. In the ICAP services tab, under "Service", select "av1requestmode" and click "Edit". You will see the screen below; enter the details as shown:

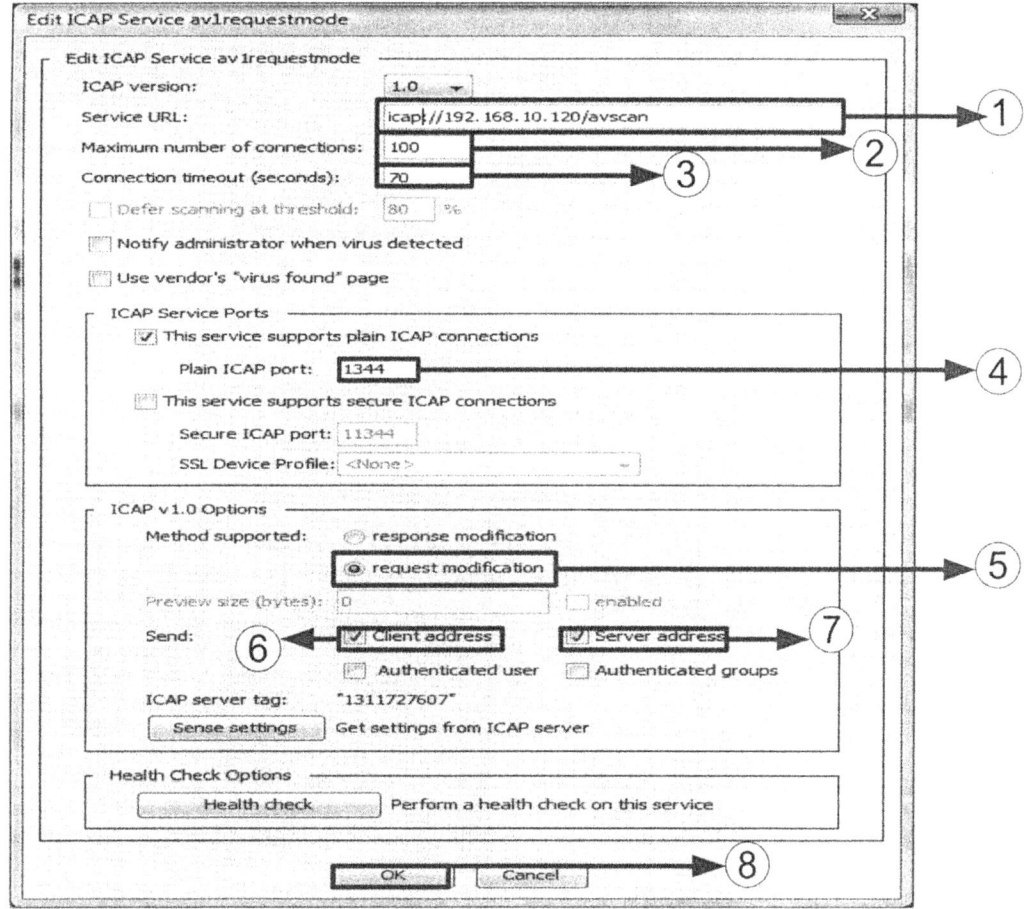

Figure 9:28 Configuring ICAP Request mode ICAP service for Proxy AV1

We will explain only the fields that we entered, as these are the important options that are required for the initial understanding of integrating the Proxy SG and Proxy AV.

a. **Service URL:** This is the URL of the Proxy AV1 IP address. This is the one that is used by the Proxy SG to communicate to the Proxy AV. You can notice that after the IP address in the ICAP address, you will find a "avscan" in the path. This is the path found in the Proxy AV; this is the default name. To find where the option is in the Proxy AV, log in to Proxy AV management console and go to ICAP settings as shown below:

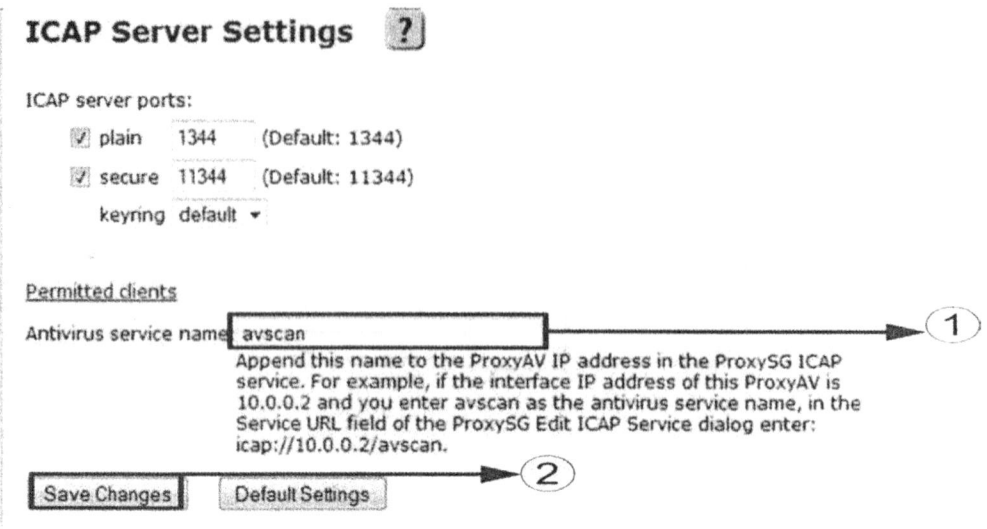

Figure 9:29 ICAP server scan URL setting

b. **Maximum number of connections:** The connections value represents the maximum number of connections that the Proxy AV supports. We use Proxy AV810 in all our example is the maximum number of connection is 100. Always check with the Proxy AV manual for the maximum number of connections that it can support. The list below shows the number of connections for the different models.

	Proxy AV 400	ProxyAV 510	ProxyAV 810	ProxyAV 2000
Default	50	50	100	100
Maximum	120	120	1200	1200

Table 9:1

c. **Connection timeout:** The time Proxy SG waits for Proxy AV to reply. The default is 70 seconds, and the range is 1 to 65535 seconds. Optimize according to your requirements; large files needs more time so 70 seconds is too low.

d. **ICAP service ports:** The default port is 1344 which is a plain ICAP service, and not encrypted traffic between the Proxy SG and Proxy AV.

e. **Request Modification:** We know there are two modes for ICAP, REQMOD, and RESPMOD, so here we are configuring REQMOD. If both modes are needed, each mode will need to be configured separately; this will be shown in the next section.

f. **Client Address and Server address:** The Proxy SG sends the details of the client and the server address of the request.

3. So you have created REQMOD for the Proxy AV1, and now you have to create RESPMOD for the Proxy AV1 by following the same steps. In the SG management console, go to "External Services" → "ICAP" and go to the "ICAP Services" tab. Click "New" and enter the name as "av1respondmode". This is a user-defined mode, so enter any name that is convenient, as shown below:

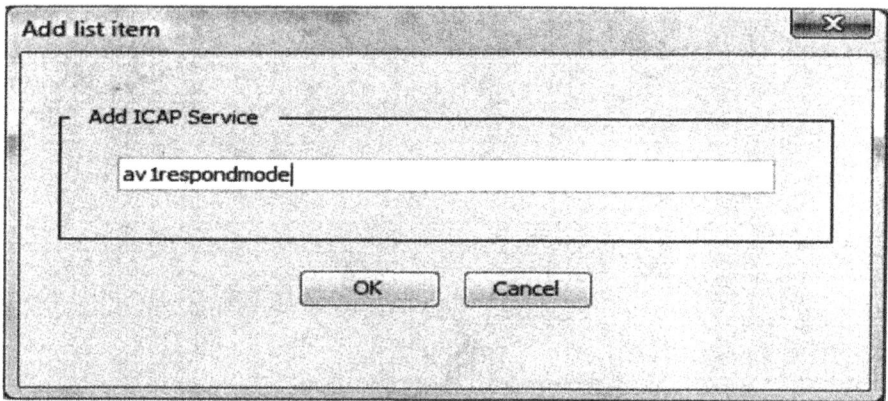

Figure 9:30 Adding ICAP Respond mode service

And click "OK" to confirm it and "click "Apply" in the main menu to apply the change.

4. The ICAP service is created. The ICAP service "av1respondmode" is selected in the ICAP services tab, under "Service", select "av1respondmode" and click "Edit". You will see a screen below; enter the details as shown:

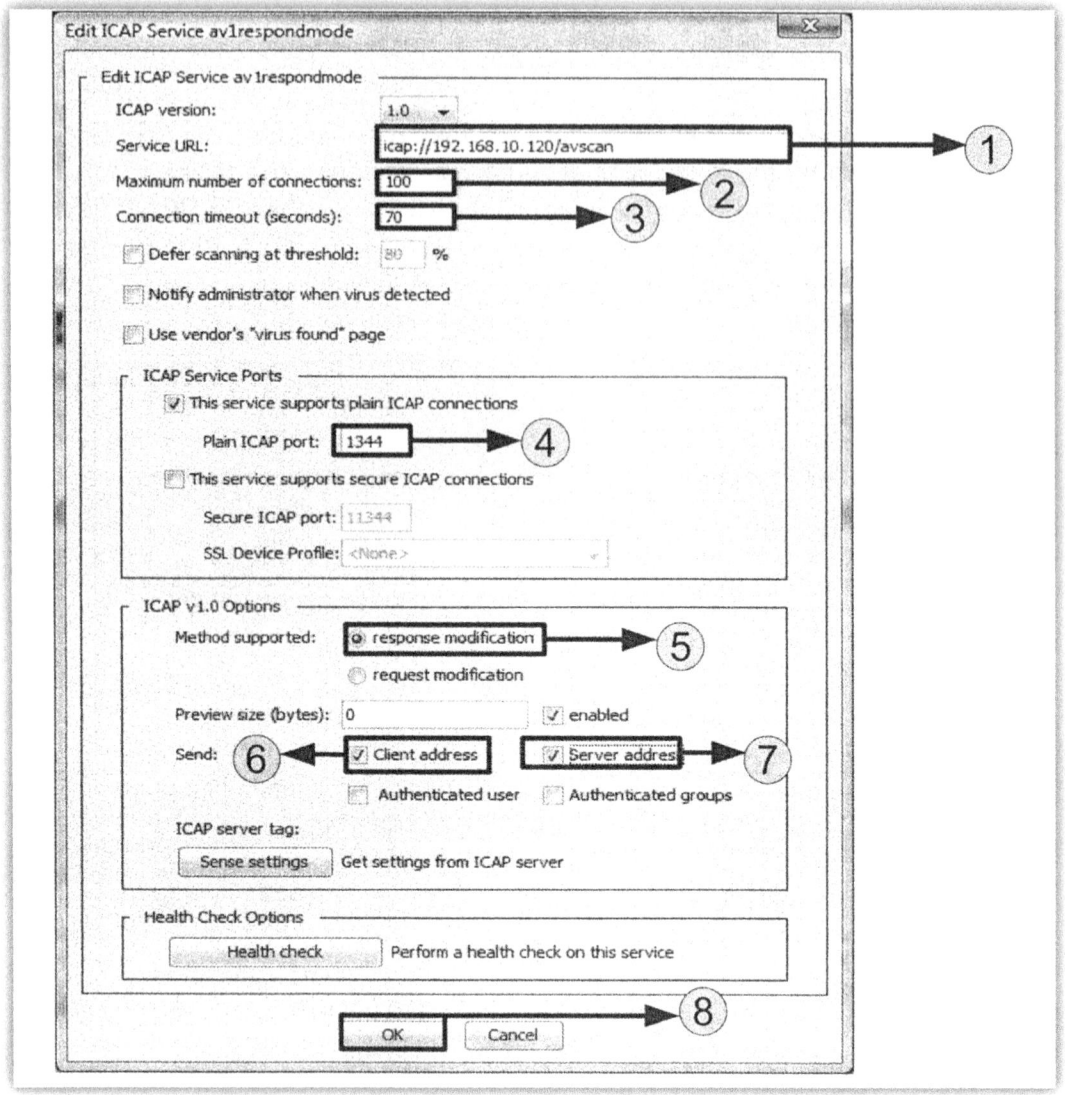

Figure 9:31 Configuring ICAP Response mode ICAP service for Proxy AV1

All the settings are the same as in "av1requestmode", except here you select "response modification" for RESPMOD. As you can see there we have enabled an additional option in the above figure ICAP v1.0 Options as "Preview size bytes" is 0. This is used when blocking response headers based on file extensions on your VPM policies. So when this option is selected, only response headers are sent to the Proxy AV, unless the Proxy AV requests more data for the object.

5. Follow the same steps 1 through 4 for the Proxy AV2, and make sure the ICAP URL is icap://192.168.10.121/avscan. For REQMOD, create an ICAP service as "av2requestmode" and "av2respondmode" accordingly. The final ICAP services should be as shown below:

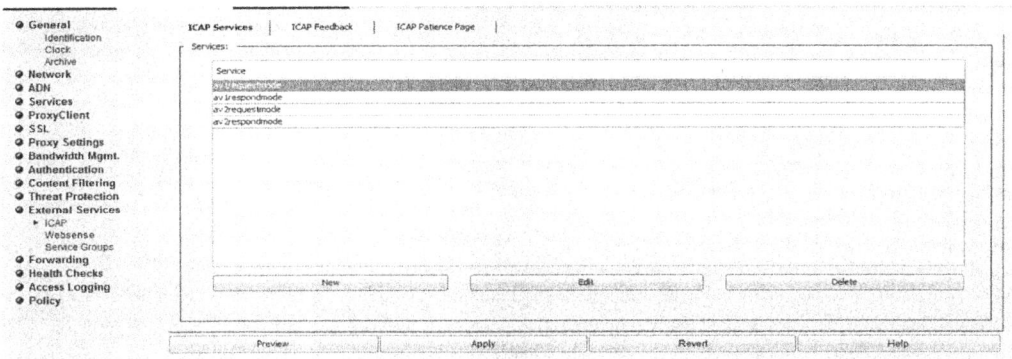

Figure 9:32 ICAP services for both Proxy AV1 and Proxy AV2

Figure 9:32 ICAP services for both Proxy AV1 and Proxy AV2

6. You need to create service groups for the four ICAP services that we created in the above figure. The reason is that it is easy for you to map the policies in the VPM by using service groups. So you should create two service groups: one for the REQMOD and one for the RESPMOD. Ideally the REQMOD group will have "av1requestmode" and "av2requestmode", and RESPMOD will have "av1responsemode" and "av2responsemode".

To create service groups go to Configuration → External services → "Service Groups" and click "New". Enter the name as "proxyavrequestgroup", confirm "OK", and "Apply" the changes as shown below:

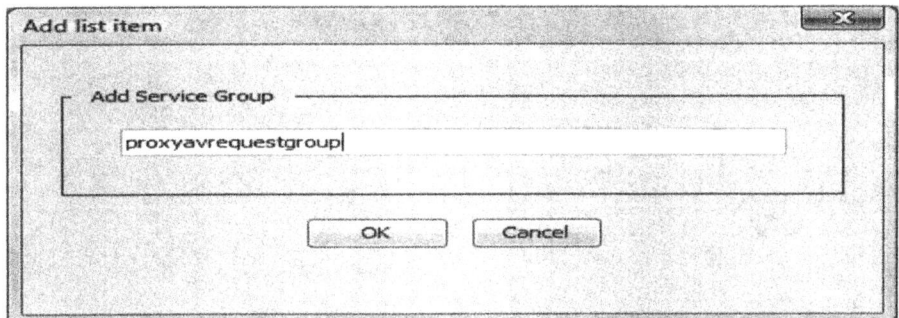

Figure 9:33 Creating the Proxy AV group for proxyavrequestgroup

Then select the service group that you created and select "Edit". Click "New" and select both the "av1requestmode" and "av2requestmode" from the "List ICAP services" option by using the Ctrl key, and click "OK" as shown below:

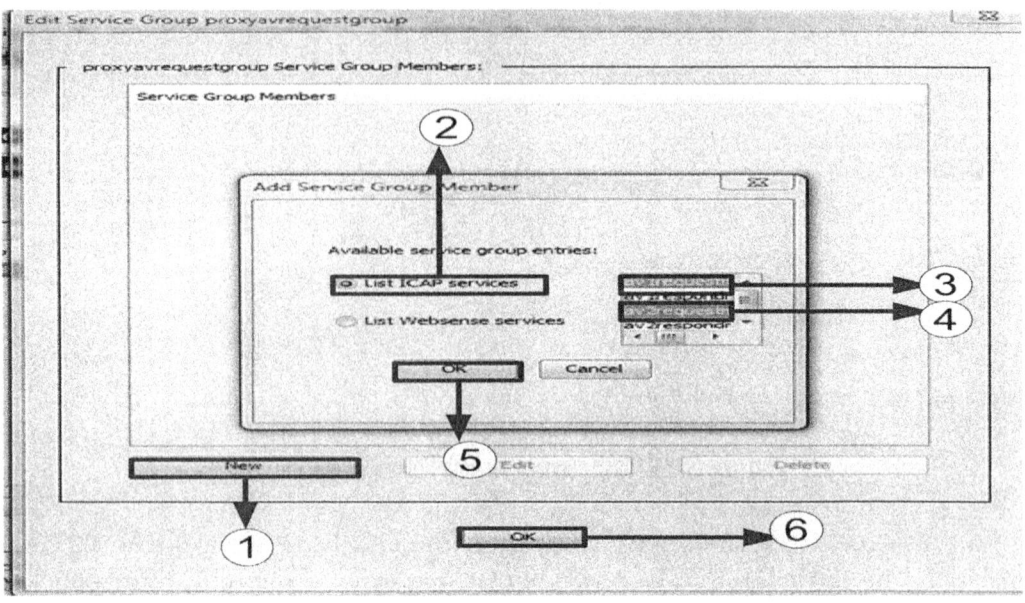

Figure 9:34 Adding Proxy AV1 and Proxy AV2 requests ICAP service to "proxyavrequestgroup" group

And both ICAP services will be added. Click "OK" to confirm the changes, as shown below:

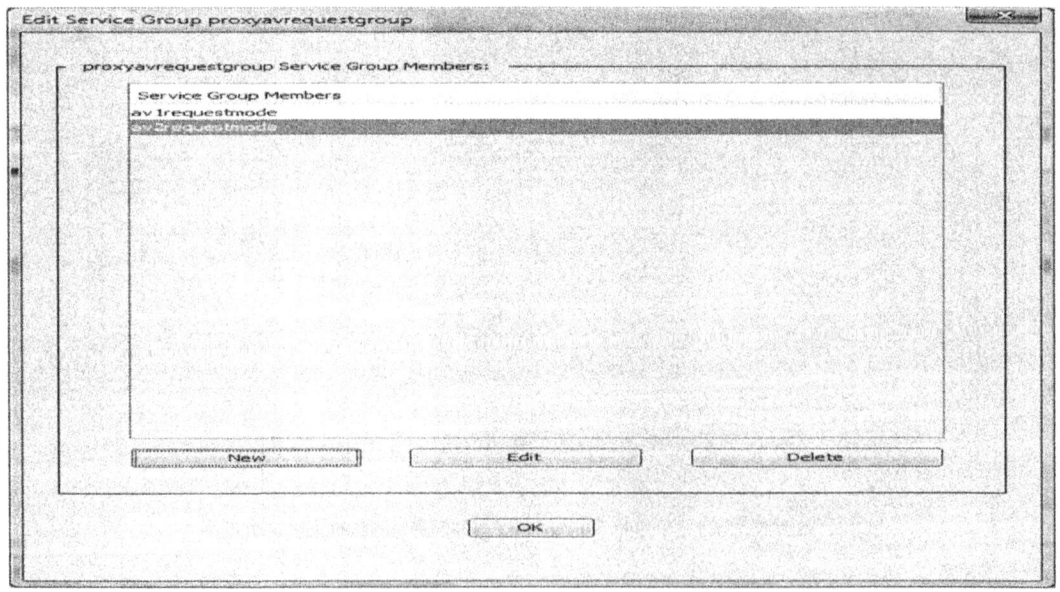

Figure 9:35 The "proxyavrequestgroup" group

Follow the same steps and create a service group called "proxyavresponsegroup". Add "av1respondmode" and "av2respondmode" ICAP services to it. The final service group should be as shown below:

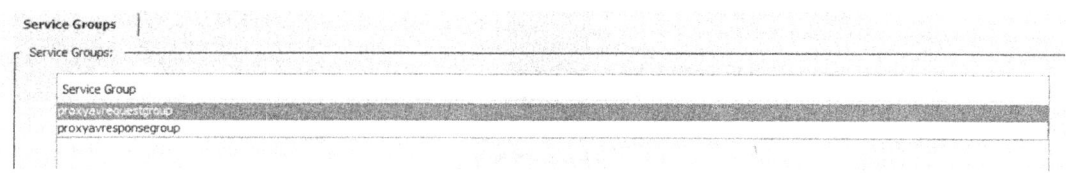

Figure 9:36 The service group for Request and Response mode

7. Creating RESPMOD ICAP VPM policy.

Now launch the VPM and go to the management console. Go to Configuration → Policy → Visual Policy manager and click the "Launch" button. Add a "Web Content Layer" by clicking "Policy" and then select "Add Web Content Layer" and name the layer as "Corporate AV scanning". Select the destination and right-click on the column and select "Set". Click "New" and select "Request URL category" and name it as "Scan allowed category". Expand the Policy tree and select "Allowed_News_Sites_Localdatabase". Then expand the Blue Coat category and only select the categories that are allowed in the VPM policies.

Remember that when we created the different VPM policies in the "Visual Policy Manager" chapter, we created three different teams with two allowed categories for each team and an allowed local database. Like the earlier example in chapter 6, these are the lists of categories you are going to scan; since all the other categories are blocked by the BCWF, there is no need for adding those categories.

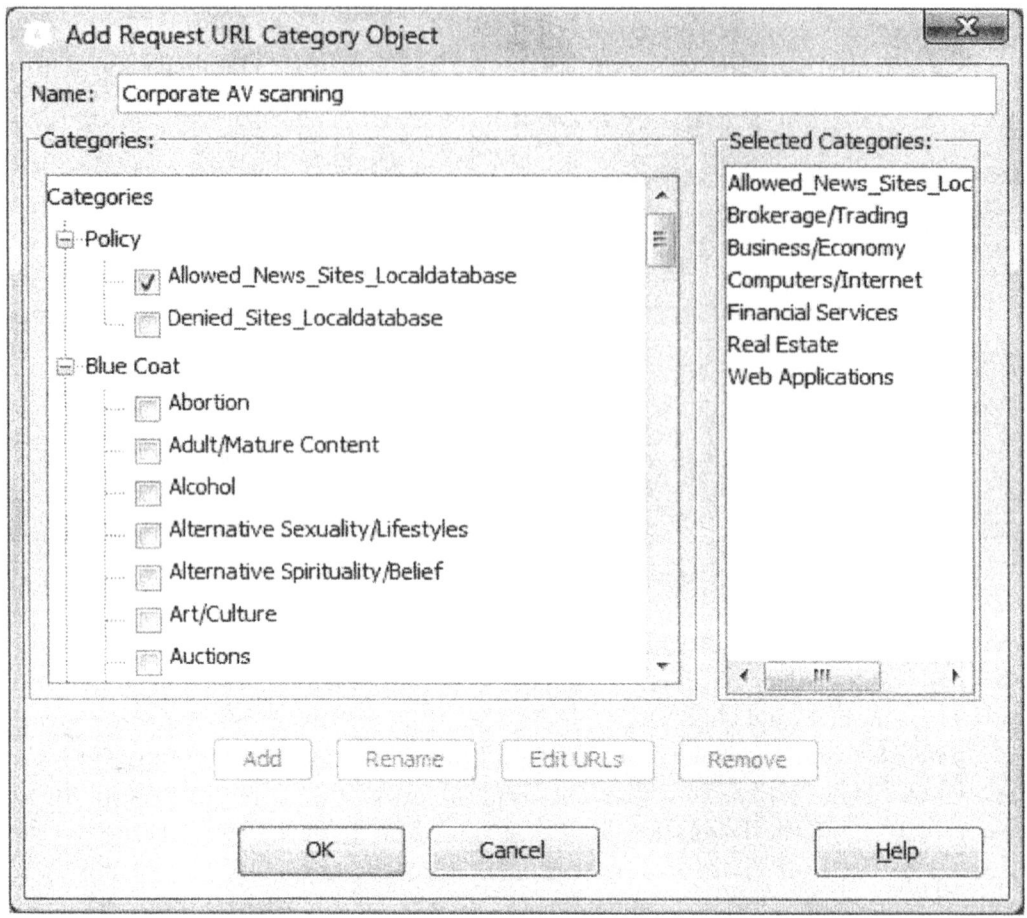

Figure 9:37 Adding the URL category object for AV scanning

Then go to the "Action" column, right-click and select "Set". Click "New" in the "Set Action object". Select "Set ICAP Request Service" and enter the name "ProxyAVResponseScanning". Under "Use ICAP request service", select the option "Always use plain ICAP connections". Move the "proxyavresponsegroup", the group that you created from the "Available services:", to "Selected failover sequence". Leave the rest of the options as is and click "OK" to confirm. Select the create ICAP request service object and click "OK" in the "Set Action object" to add in the "Action" column as shown below:

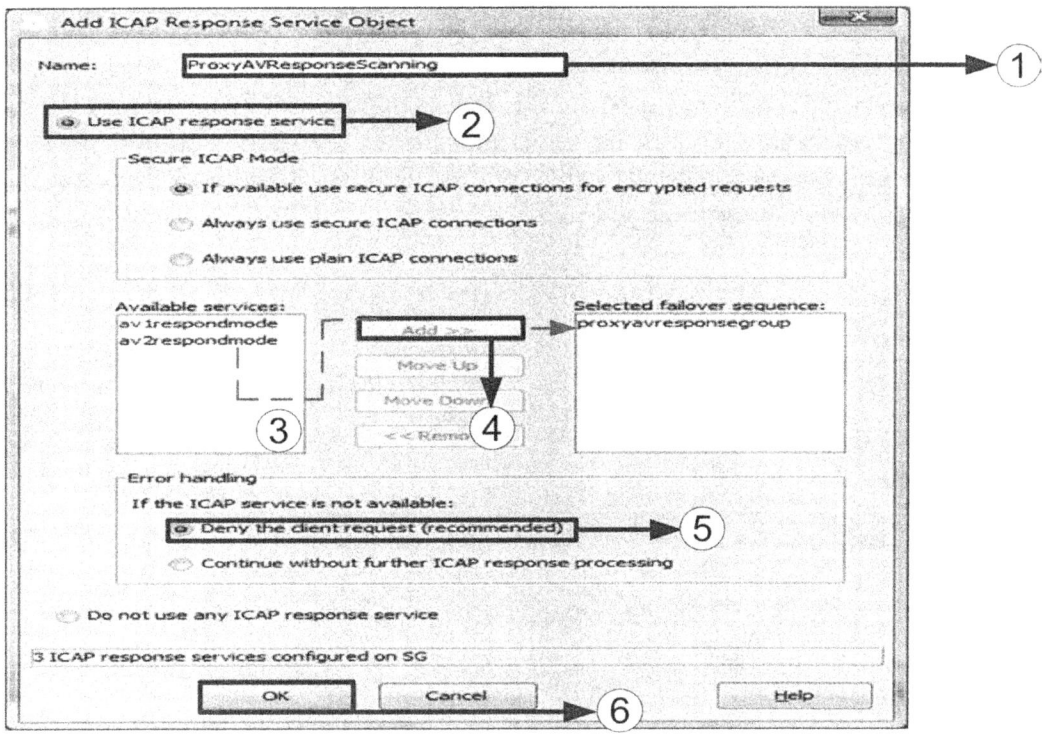

Figure 9:38 Creating the ICAP Response Service Object for scanning

As you see in the above figure, in the error handling section, the default option "Deny the client request (recommended)" is selected. This means when the Proxy SG cannot reach the Proxy AV in any circumstances via ICAP service, all the users access are denied. So if you don't want to deny users when the Proxy AV is not reachable or down, you can select "Continue without further ICAP request processing". It all depends upon your business requirements.

8. We are just showing the next rule as an example of different options we have for scanning. The first rule that you created for scanning is for the categories. That means that all responses are scanned for the file extension. But if you want to have an exception so that you don't have to scan .txt or PDF files because they are not so harmful, and you want to save the Proxy AV load, then you can ignore it.

You could also configure policies based on file extensions rather than using categories. You could add all the extensions that are considered potentially harmful for the corporation. Here we have added just two extensions to show how to implement the policies. Always consult your security team and discuss how to implement the best practices.

Now add a new rule below the one that you have created by clicking "Add Rule" in the toolbar. Select the destination and right-click the column. Select "Set", click "New", select "FileExtension", and   as "Corporate File Extension Blocked". Then add the extension txt or pdf by selecting it on the left panel and clicking the "Add" button to move to the "File Extension" section.Now the extensions .pdf and .txt would have moved to the right panel under "File Extension" and then click "OK" to confirm it, as shown below.

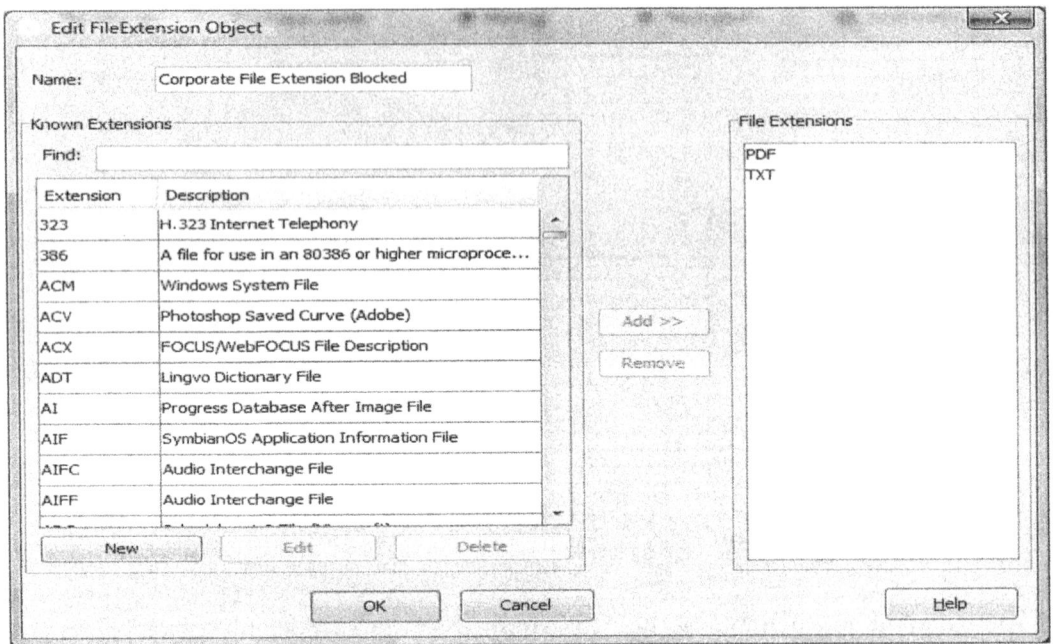

Figure 9:39 Creating File Extension

Then go to the "Action" column and right-click on column. Select "Set" and click "New" in the Set Action object. Select "Set ICAP Request Service" and enter the name "DoNotResponseScanning". Select the option "Do not use any ICAP response service" at the bottom of the object, and click "OK" to confirm. Select the created ICAP request service object" and click "OK" in the "Set Action object" box to add in the "Action" column as shown below:

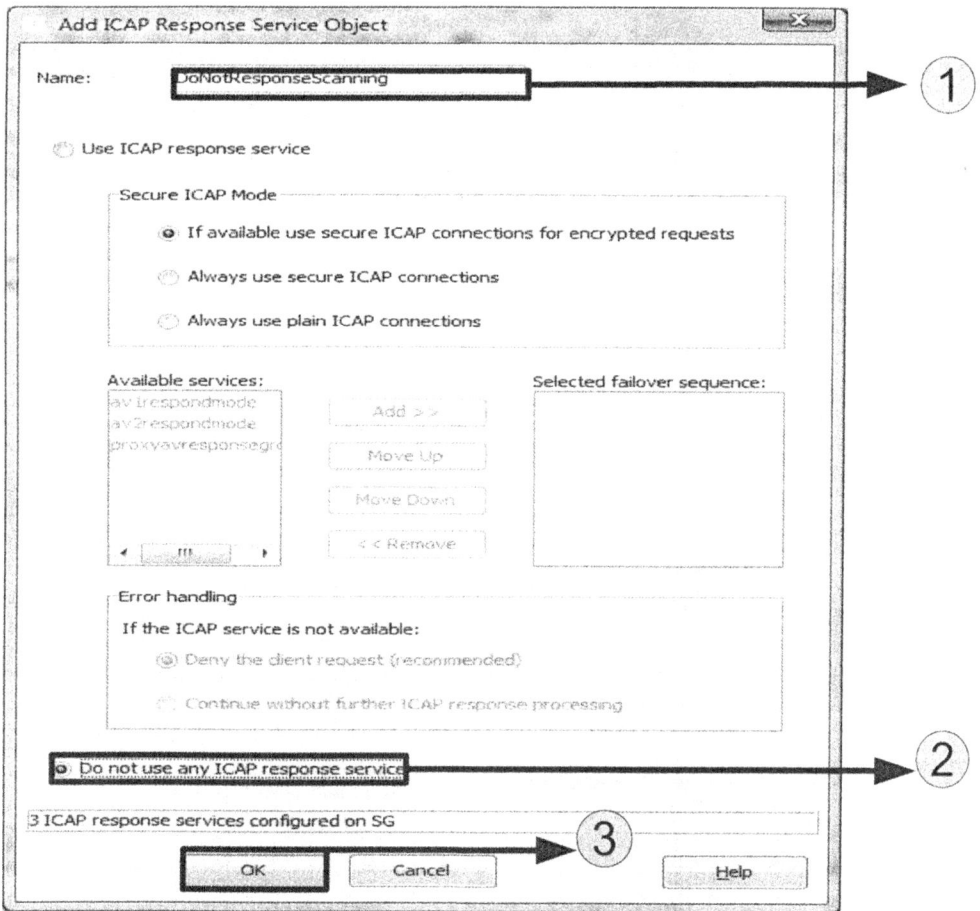

Figure 9:40 Adding ICAP Response Service Object for not scanning

9. Creating REQMOD ICAP VPM policy

Now add a new rule below the one that you have created by clicking "Add Rule" in the toolbar. Leave the destination as "Any" and go to the "Action" column. Right-click on the "Action" column and select "Set". Click "New" in the Set Action object. Select "Set ICAP Request Service" and enter the name "ProxyAVRequestScanning". Under "Use ICAP request service", select the option "Always use plain ICAP connections" and move the "proxyavrequestgroup", the group that we created from the "Available services:", to "Selected failover sequence". Leave the rest of the options as is and click "OK" to confirm. Select the created ICAP request service object and click "OK" in the "Set Action object" box to add the in the "Action" column as shown below:

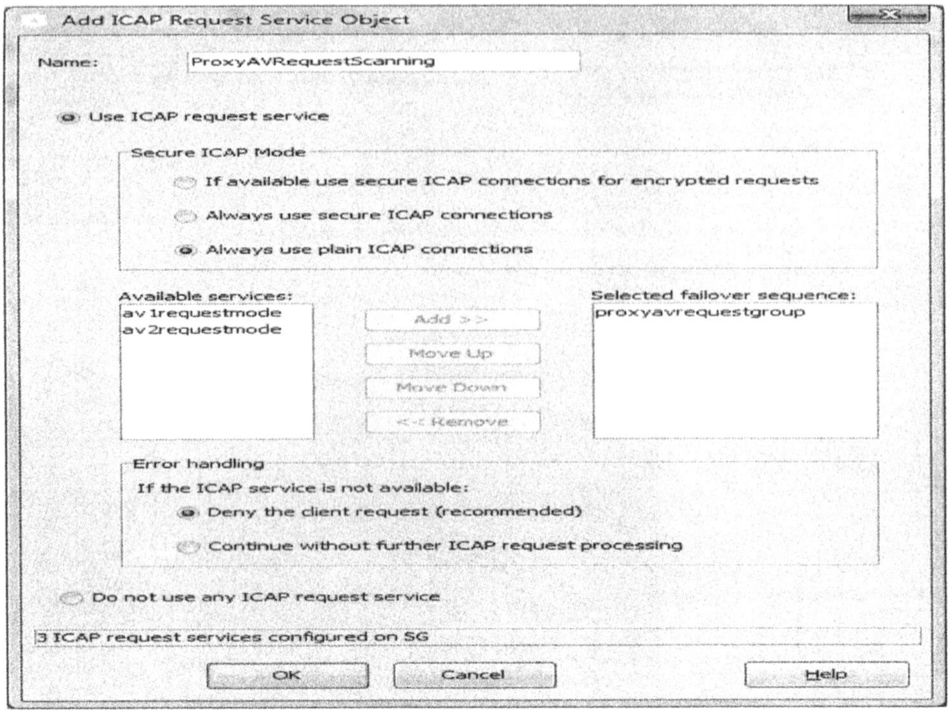

Figure 9:41 Adding ICAP Request Service Object for scanning

As you see in the above figure, in the error handling section, the default option "Deny the client request (recommended)" is selected. This means when the Proxy SG cannot reach Proxy AV in any circumstances via ICAP service, all user access is denied. So if you don't want to deny the users access when the ICAP servers are not reachable or down , you can select "Continue without further ICAP request processing". It all depends upon your business requirements.

Install the policy by click the "Install policy" button.

The final policy should look as shown below:

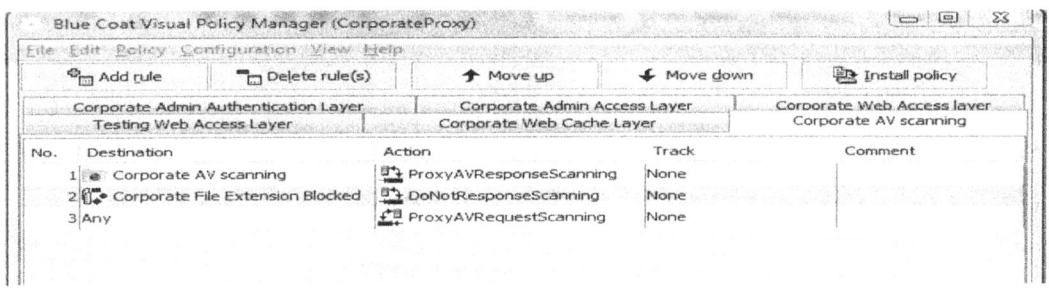

Figure 9:42 VPM for AV scanning

We are explaining with just one proxy for easy understanding. These are the same steps you will need to follow if you have two or more proxies.

Testing the Proxy AV

1. Testing the RESPMOD

Now you need to test the Proxy AV functionally for RESPMOD after you have integrated Proxy AV with Proxy SG. The best method is to go to the site http://www.eicar.org/. EICAR is the European Institute for Computer Antivirus Research where files are tested which are not real malware files but some random strings and characters such as "X5O!P%@AP[4\PZX54(P^)7CC)7}$EICAR-STANDARD-ANTIVIRUS-TEST-FILE!$H+H* , which all AV engines thinks are viruss and blocks. This is the official approved security site where all the antivirus vendors in the world do their testing for their AV engines. Once at the site, click the "Download" button, and under the section "Download area using the standard protocol http", choose any of the four files such as "eicar.com, eicar.com.txt, eicar_com.zip or eicarcom2.zip" and you will get a blocked page as shown below.

Virus was detected in the content (virus_detected)

Content contained "EICAR-Test-File" virus. Details: Virus: EICAR-Test-File; File: eicar.com; Sub File: Memory region; Vendor: Kaspersky Labs; Engine error code: 0x00000000; Engine version: 8.0.1.23; Pattern version: 110728.222300.5738626; Pattern date: 2011.07.28 22:23:00

For assistance, contact your network support team

Figure 9:43 Blocked page message from Proxy AV for user access

The above page confirms that the Proxy AV is working fine and that it is correctly integrated with the Proxy SG. Alternatively, you can use the following links below to access the test virus files if you cannot find the download file on the website.

http://www.eicar.org/download/eicar.com
http://www.eicar.org/download/eicar.com.txt
http://www.eicar.org/download/eicar_com.zip
http://www.eicar.org/download/eicarcom2.zip

2. Testing the REQMOD

Now you can test the REQMOD by trying to upload a infected file. downloading the file from EICAR, save it to the desktop, and try uploading it to your web email like Yahoo, Gmail, or Hotmail; you will be blocked. Alternatively, you can use the Jquery plugin available at http://aquantum-demo.appspot.com/file-upload. Please use only a test from EICAR.

When you try saving the file from EICAR, if desktop AV is running on your machine, it will not allow you to save the file; so create a exception in your desktop AV and then try saving it.

Scanning file types

As we have shown in the previous section about scanning or not scanning file types based on extensions, in Proxy SG you can only define rules in the VPM or CPL the file types that should be sent to Proxy AV. Only in Proxy AV we have options to scan or block, or not scan. To configure blocked file types, log in to the Proxy AV to the management console via https://Proxyavip:8082, and go to Antivirus and click "Scanning Behavior". Click "Policies for file types" and select the file the Proxy AV should scan or block or not block based upon your requirements, as shown below:

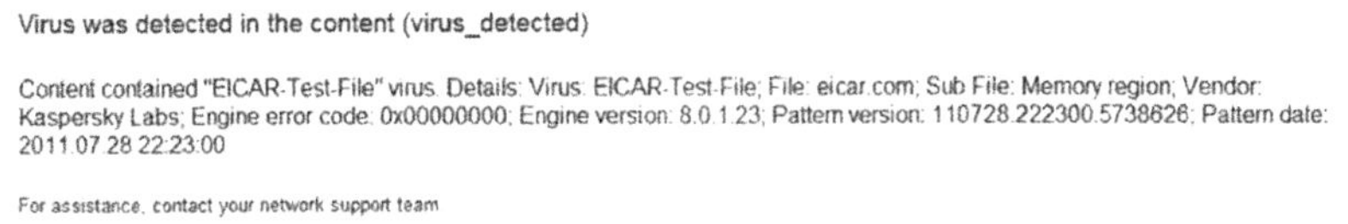

Virus was detected in the content (virus_detected)

Content contained "EICAR-Test-File" virus. Details: Virus: EICAR-Test-File; File: eicar.com; Sub File: Memory region; Vendor: Kaspersky Labs; Engine error code: 0x00000000; Engine version: 8.0.1.23; Pattern version: 110728.222300.5738826; Pattern date: 2011.07.28 22:23:00

For assistance, contact your network support team

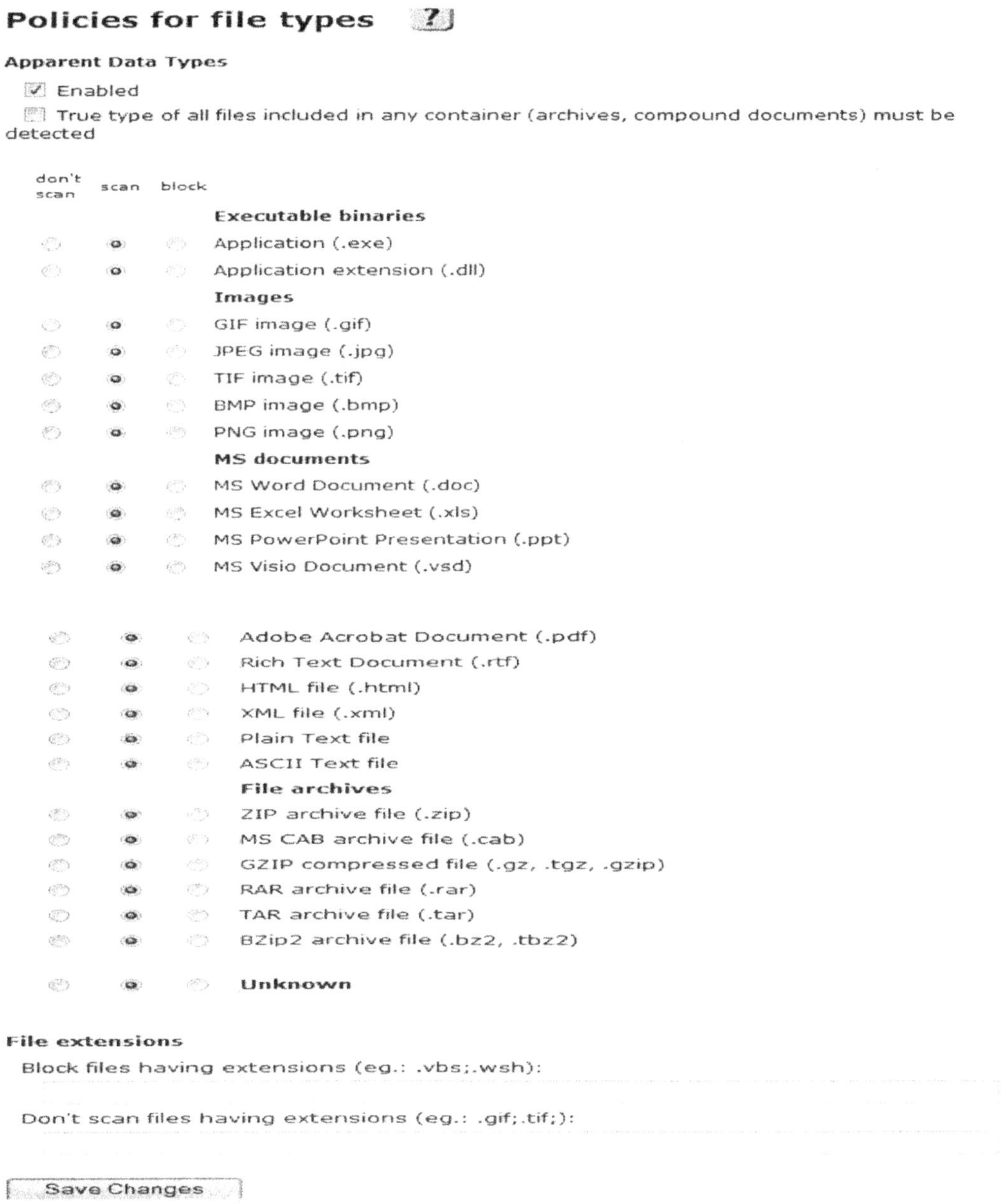

Policies for file types ?

Apparent Data Types

☑ Enabled

☐ True type of all files included in any container (archives, compound documents) must be detected

don't scan	scan	block	
			Executable binaries
○	⊙	○	Application (.exe)
○	⊙	○	Application extension (.dll)
			Images
○	⊙	○	GIF image (.gif)
○	⊙	○	JPEG image (.jpg)
○	⊙	○	TIF image (.tif)
○	⊙	○	BMP image (.bmp)
○	⊙	○	PNG image (.png)
			MS documents
○	⊙	○	MS Word Document (.doc)
○	⊙	○	MS Excel Worksheet (.xls)
○	⊙	○	MS PowerPoint Presentation (.ppt)
○	⊙	○	MS Visio Document (.vsd)
○	⊙	○	Adobe Acrobat Document (.pdf)
○	⊙	○	Rich Text Document (.rtf)
○	⊙	○	HTML file (.html)
○	⊙	○	XML file (.xml)
○	⊙	○	Plain Text file
○	⊙	○	ASCII Text file
			File archives
○	⊙	○	ZIP archive file (.zip)
○	⊙	○	MS CAB archive file (.cab)
○	⊙	○	GZIP compressed file (.gz, .tgz, .gzip)
○	⊙	○	RAR archive file (.rar)
○	⊙	○	TAR archive file (.tar)
○	⊙	○	BZip2 archive file (.bz2, .tbz2)
○	⊙	○	**Unknown**

File extensions

Block files having extensions (eg.: .vbs;.wsh):

Don't scan files having extensions (eg.: .gif;.tif;):

[Save Changes]

Figure 9:44 Various scanning file types in Proxy AV

Deferred Scanning

As you know, the Proxy SG should first download the object completely; only then can it send it to the Proxy AV for scanning. But for infinite streams such as flash videos where their no content length defined, so the streams will consume all the ICAP connection, by making the ICAP service cannot scan another further objects and later the Proxy AV remains fail- open. Deferred scanning helps you detect and defer unnecessary ICAP connections until the full object has been downloaded. So when the ICAP connection is deferred, the connection to Proxy AV is closed but the object gets downloaded; once it is downloaded completely, the ICAP request is restarted queued ahead of new requests. Remember that the old connections are deferred only when the threshold is reached. This setting can be found by going to the Proxy SG Configuration → External services → ICAP and editing any of the four ICAP services that you created, as shown below:

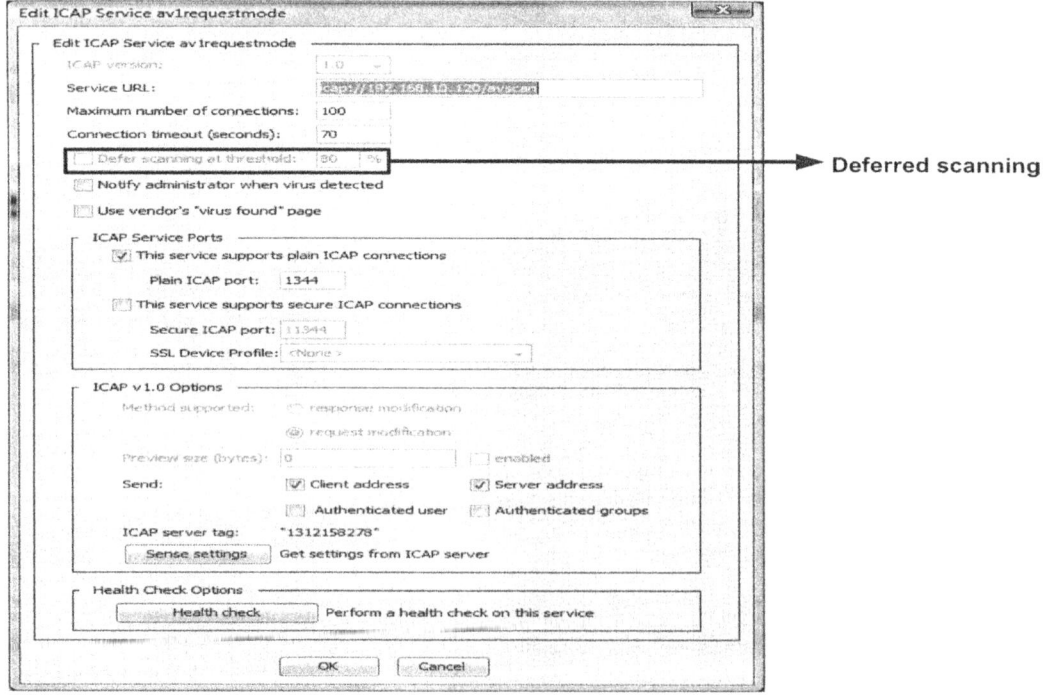

Figure 9:45 Deferred Scanning

ICTM (Intelligent Connection Traffic Monitoring)

Intelligent Connection Traffic Monitoring (ICTM) allows the ProxyAV to drop download connections that are taking longer than the normal amount of time to complete. This makes the Proxy AV available for other objects. One example is the stock ticker which polls every minute forthe updated stocks information and thus creates infinite stream. If the critical threshold is reached, the ProxyAV terminates the oldest and slowest connections, so the maximum connections threshold is maintained.

Log in to the Proxy AV management console and go to Advanced. Click Intelligent Connection Traffic Monitoring (ICTM) and by default the option is enabled, as shown below.

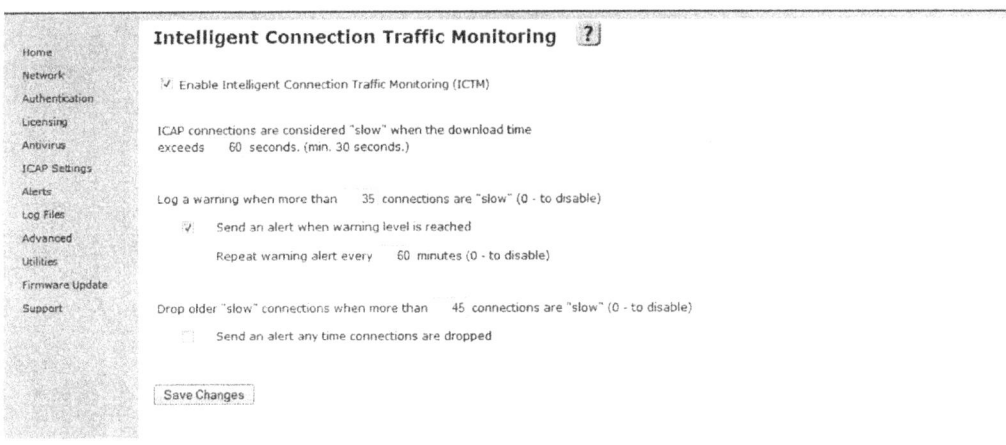

Figure 9:46 ICTM (Intelligent Connection Traffic Monitoring)

You can tweak the settings as per your requirements. Usually the default settings shown work for most environments. As shown above, 60 seconds is the maximum time before the Proxy AV assumes that connection is a slow download. When the slow connections reach 45 seconds, they are dropped by the Proxy AV.

Test Yourself

1. What protocols can the ICAP scan? (Choose two.)

   a. HTTP
   b. MMS
   c. FTP
   d. Telnet

2. You have planned to implement BlueCoat solutions in your company. You have decided to use BlueCoat DLP for identifying data theft and to scan all inbound traffic via BlueCoat Proxy AV (Sophos). Which mode will you use for integrating BlueCoat DLP and Proxy SG, and which mode will you use to integrate BlueCoat Proxy AV (Sophos)?

   a. BlueCoat DLP in REQMOD and BlueCoat Proxy AV in RESPMOD

b. BlueCoat DLP in RESPMOD and BlueCoat Proxy AV in REQMOD

c. BlueCoat DLP in REQMOD and BlueCoat Proxy AV in REQMOD

d. BlueCoat DLP in RESPMOD and BlueCoat Proxy AV in RESPMOD

3. IS Tag is the mechanism that is given by the ICAP server (BlueCoat Proxy AV) about the current service state to the ICAP client (BlueCoat Proxy SG). If a current IS Tag is 1, then the Proxy AV updates its signature database and notifies the Proxy SG about its state and sends an IS Tag 0. Now there is a change in the IS Tag, so the Proxy should rescan all the objects in the cache with the new signature from the Proxy AV. Does the rescan will happen, because the value of the IS Tag has decremented from 1 to 0?

a. Yes

b. No

4. If an ICAP request or response should be made from a Proxy SG to a Proxy AV, what will be the URL protocol format?

a. http://proxyavip:8082/avscan

b. https://proxyavip:8082/avscan

c. icap://proxyavip:8082/avscan

d. icap://proxyavip/avscan

5. In your company, your network has an Internet pipe of 2 MB. Downloading certain large files takes long time, and you are very concerned about large downloads because they will consume your Proxy AV connections. What is the feature that the Proxy AV uses to remove slow connections?

a. Deferred scanning

b. ICTM

c. Data trickling

d. d. This solution cannot be implemented.

6. You have implemented BlueCoat Proxy AV solutions in your company. Now you want to test both REQMOD and RESPMOD mode. What is the best method that all the security professionals use for testing Proxy AV scanning engine functionality for detecting malware?

a. Download a virus for RESPMOD, and upload a virus for REQMOD.

b. Wait until Proxy AV catches some virus and later you can check in the logs.

c. Test via http://www.eicar.org.

d. Install a Trojan file in Proxy AV and check whether it can detect the malware.

7. What is the default port does secure ICAP works?

    a. Port 11344
    b. Port 1344
    c. Port 443
    d. Port 211344

8. What is the feature in Proxy AV that will defer unnecessary ICAP connections until the full object has been downloaded?

    a. IS Tag
    b. ICTM
    c. Data trickling
    d. Deferred scanning

9. Which is the best method of deployment of implementing Proxy AV solutions in your network in terms of achieving better security, performance, and high availability?

    a. One Proxy SG and any Proxy AVs
    b. Many Proxy SGs and many Proxy AVs
    c. Many Proxy AGs and one Proxy AV
    d. One Proxy SG and one Proxy AV

10. Let's imagine you have 4 Proxy AVs in your network and all fail at one time. Which network security technology will help at these times of outage?

    a. IDS
    b. Desktop AV
    c. IPS
    d. Firewall

CHAPTER 10

BLUECOAT REPORTER

BLUECOAT REPORTER

In the chapter 1, "Introduction to BlueCoat," we briefly described the BlueCoat reporter. Let's recapture the information that we introduced there. Blue Coat® Reporter provides an intelligent dashboard to have complete visibility of the user's activity on the web. This helps an organization to meet its audit compliance, security best practices, monitoring the network for suspicious activites, and thus providing efficient bandwidth management. Both Proxy SGand Proxy Client can forward the access logs to the Blue Coat® Reporter, which processes the raw log files and gives reports about the traffic access in the network.

Blue Coat® Reporter is software that can be installed on Windows or Linux servers. Blue Coat® Reporter processes by log lines, so if the network traffic and the access logs are huge, you will need to get a license, depending upon the data. Usually, retaining 6 months of data is the security best practice and fulfills the compliance. You can log all the access requests and supports different log formats that are used in protocols like HTTP, HTTPS, CIFS, Endpoint mapper, FTP, Instant Messaging, telnet, Windows Media, Real Media/Quick Time, HTTPS Reverse/Forward proxy, SOCKS, Flash, Peer to Peer, and MAPI.

The key benefits of using Blue Coat® Reporter:

1. It gives complete visibility of the network web traffic and users' surfing habits.
2. It provides a dashboard which gives an quick overview of the network.
3. It enables a visibility of the web traffic performance, security threats, bandwidth management, streaming traffic levels, top domains accessed/blocked, etc.

4. Blue Coat® Reporter uses custom databases so that large access log files can be compressed and stored.
5. Real-time logs can be fed into the Blue Coat® Reporter for analysis.
6. It can integrate with SIEM tools like ArcSight and forward logs, for log correlation.
7. It provides role-based access to the reports and dashboard to different teams in the organization.
8. You can have predefined reports and easy custom report creation for all data trends.

BLUECOAT REPORTER NETWORK ARCHITECTURE:

Below is the BlueCoat Reporter network architecture for a very large enterprise. You can see from the size of the organization, the Proxy SG is distributed across the region and around the globe, forwarding the logs to the centralized BlueCoat Reporter for the log consolidation. The BlueCoat Reporter collects all the logs, generates a database, and stores all the original log files in the same format in which they were received.

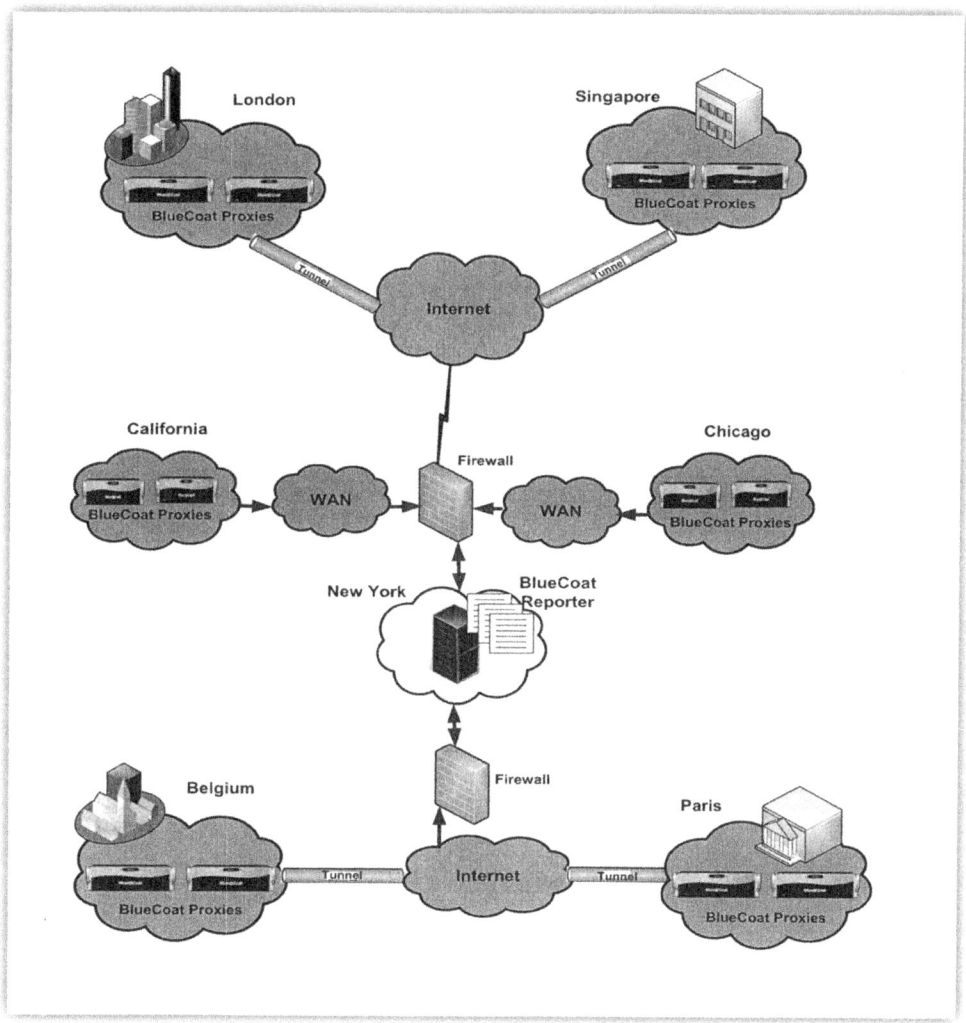

Figure 10:1 BlueCoat Reporter deployment

BlueCoat Reporter Internal Architecture

The BlueCoat Reporter is software that is installed on Windows or Linux servers. Like other reporting software, it doesn't use any external databases like Oracle, My SQL, or SQL server to maintain and store the logs, generate the database, and run reports. BlueCoat Reporter has its own database, which is a proprietary database called the BlueCoat Reporter Database. Because it has its own database, there are no administrator skills required to install a third-party database and then install BlueCoat Reporter on top of it. The internal architecture consists of a Log Processor, Log Parser, Log Reader, PVC, Memory Buffer, Database, and Web Interface as shown below:

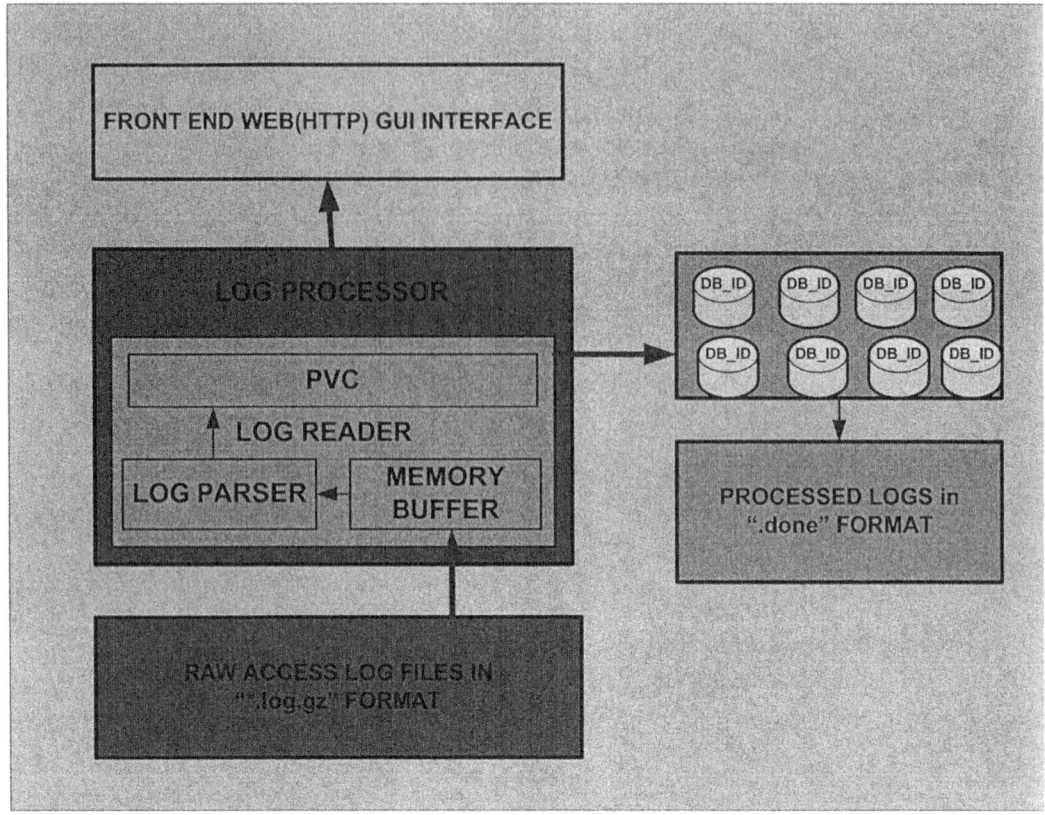

Figure 10:2 BlueCoat Reporter internal architecture

We will describe each component as follows:

1. Raw Logs:

The raw logs are fed into the log processor. The logs are sent from the BlueCoat Proxy SG. Their format can be either .gz or .log. The actual format is .log, but if the file is big and you need to shrink it, you can compress it by using .gz in BlueCoat Proxy SG. The raw logs come from different proxies from several locations. Usually the BlueCoat Proxy SG sends the logs to the BlueCoat Reporter via FTP, HTTP,or BlueCoat customized client.

2. Memory Buffer:

The memory buffer is a temporary storage of data that's being transferred to and from the BlueCoat Reporter server.

3. Log Parser:

The log parser will parse the fields in the logs sent by the BlueCoat Proxy SG. The fields are client IP, server IP, bytes transferred, UA, etc. The whole list can be found in the Proxy SG. You add only the fields that are required for your environment. There are almost a hundred fields available. Selecting all of them increases the on the Proxy SG and also increases the size of the log file. You should select the optimal fields that are required for you. After the log parser parses the fields, it converts them to a format which the log reader can understand.

4. Log Reader:

The log reader reads access log data into memory once when the log parser has converted it to a readable format which it can understand.

PVC(Page View Combiner) is a subcomponent of the log reader that combines multiple HTTP requests that are associated with a single web page into a single log line. For example, as we know, when a user tries accessing http://www.cnn.com, client pulls information from several URL, and the PVC combines all this information and makes it a single log line entry. All the bytes that are there from several URLs are also combined and one total byte is recorded.

5. Log Processor:

The log reader feeds the log into the memory and the log processor generates and populates the databases with the log data. It creates all the pointers, maps, and tables which are combined together form of a database. This database is called the BlueCoat Reporter database.

6. Database:

The database resides in a separate directory as chunks, and each of these has a DB_ID associated with it. So the database knows where each single log record is located, as it has mapping and locations of all the DB_ID.

7. Processed logs:

Once the logs get processed, you can change the file format from .log.gz to the ".done" extension, so that the log data is separate from the raw logs and you can easily identify them by using the extension.

8. Front-end web interface:

The front-end web interface is used to log in and configure the BlueCoat Reporter. Here you can view the dashboard for all the events that are happening in the network, generate reports, configure various options for the tools, etc.

Types of logs in BlueCoat

In BlueCoat Proxy SG, there are different types of logs that you can use for diagnostic and troubleshooting purposes. They are as follows:

1. Access logging:

Access logging is used for logging all users' access traffic, so that you can know about users' Internet access and use tools like BlueCoat Reporter to collect logs from all BlueCoat Proxy SG and consolidate the reports. In this chapter we will be discussing access logs.

2. Event logging:

Event logging is used for logging system events such as BlueCoat Proxy SG errors, administrator changes, policy installation, service failure, etc. These can be forwarded to syslog servers for storing all the event logs in the central server.

3. Policy traces:

Policy traces are used to evaluate the user traffic against a CPL policy (VPM, Central file, Local file, and Forward file). Policy tracing allows you to see how a request is evaluated by a policy line-by-line.

4. Core images:

Core images are logged to disk when a system is restarted. They are used by the BlueCoat support team for diagnosing the problem by dumping all the RAM content into the system disk.

5. Snapshots:

Snapshots are used to take a snapshot or system view for configured times of various system statistics like the CPU, RAM, sysinfo, health checks, etc.

BlueCoat Reporter installation

In this section we will show how to install BlueCoat Reporter on a Windows server. It can also be installed on a Linux server, but we will show only the installation on Windows, which is quite easy to do and helps to understand the different configuration options available in BlueCoat Reporter. The following is the installation procedure:

1. Download the Reporter software for the BTO website; download the version that is specific to the OS (Windows or Linux) as shown below:

Products >> Reporter >> Reporter9.2 Releases

Figure 10:3 BlueCoat Reporter software download from BlueTouch

Figure 10:3 BlueCoat Reporter software download from BlueTouch

2. Double-click the software icon and you will get the installation screen as shown below, then click "Next".

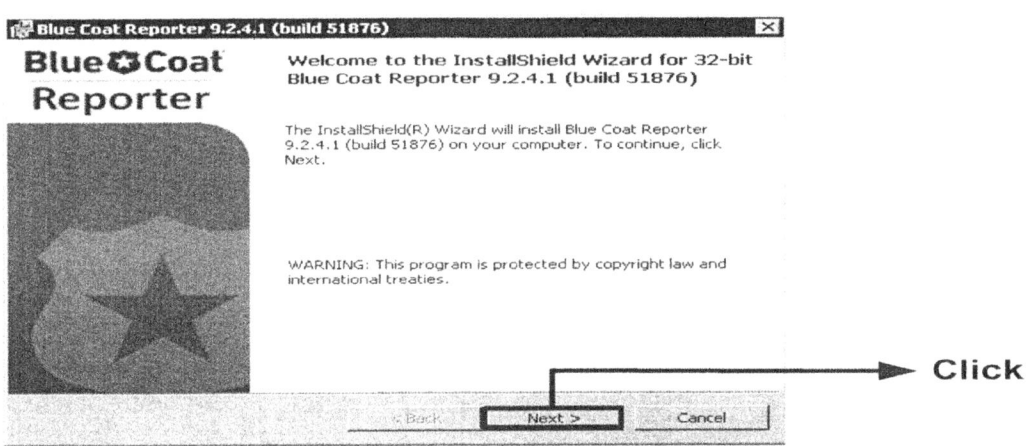

Figure 10:4 BlueCoat Reporter installation wizard

3. Then accept the license agreement as shown below:

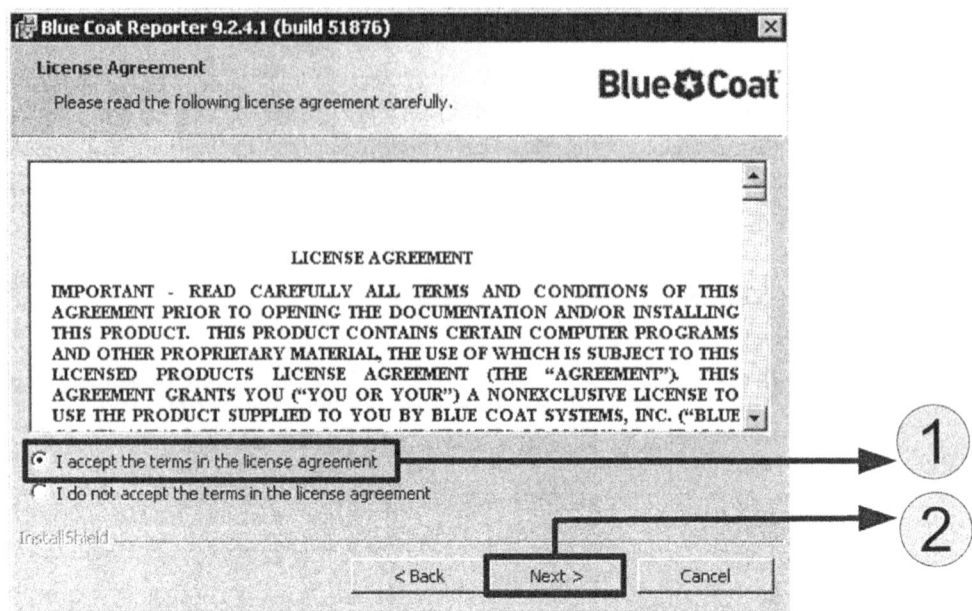

Figure 10:5 BlueCoat Reporter license agreement

4. 4. Then read the information page and click "Next".

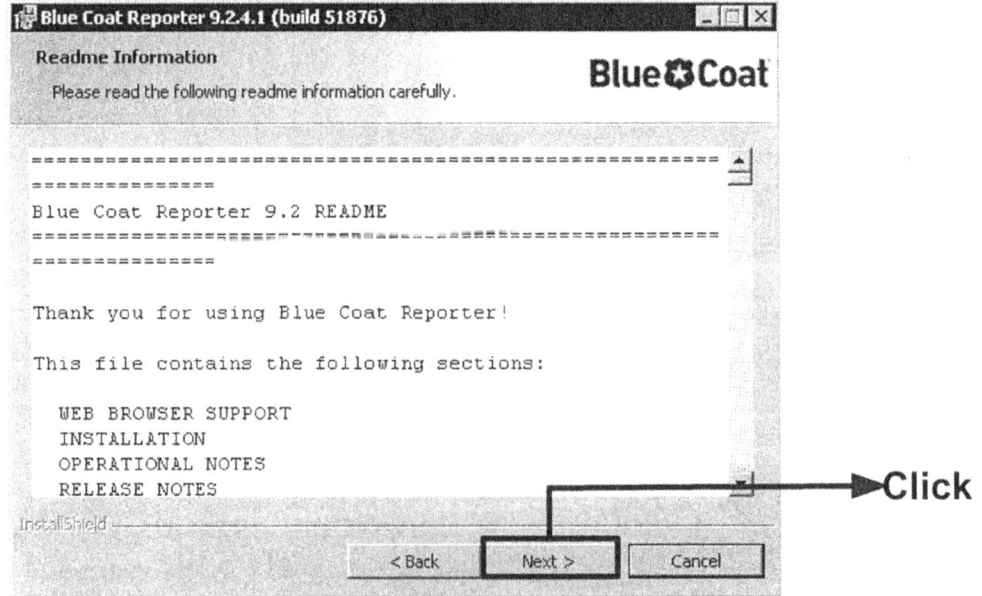

Figure 10:6 BlueCoat Reporter README information

5. Now chose the installation path. Select any directory where the BlueCoat Reporter could be installed. If you want to use the default, then click "Next", as shown below:

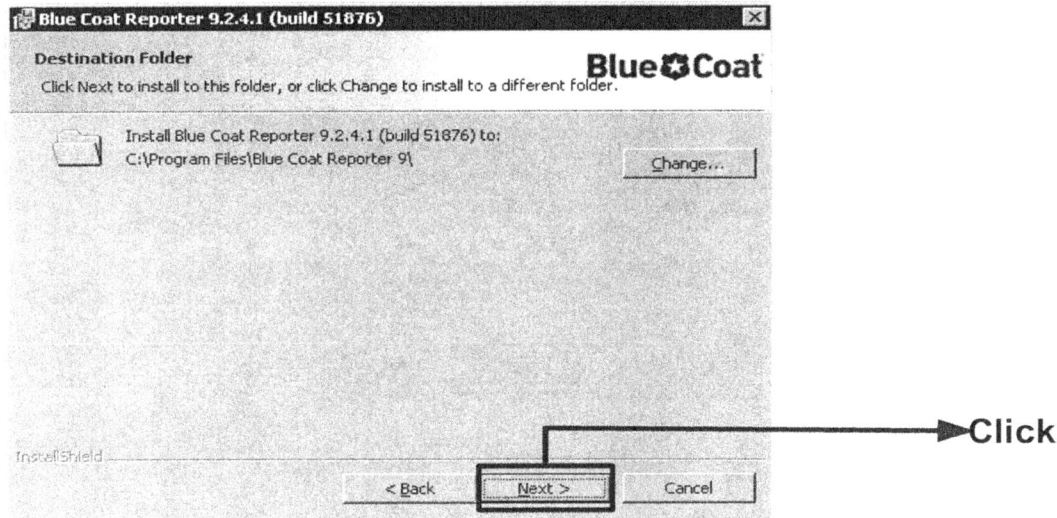

Figure 10:7 BlueCoat Reporter software path

6. In this page the BlueCoat Reporter collects system information like the OS, CPU, disk storage, and RAM and sends it to BlueCoat via HTTPS for the BlueCoat Improvement Program. Click "Next" as shown below:

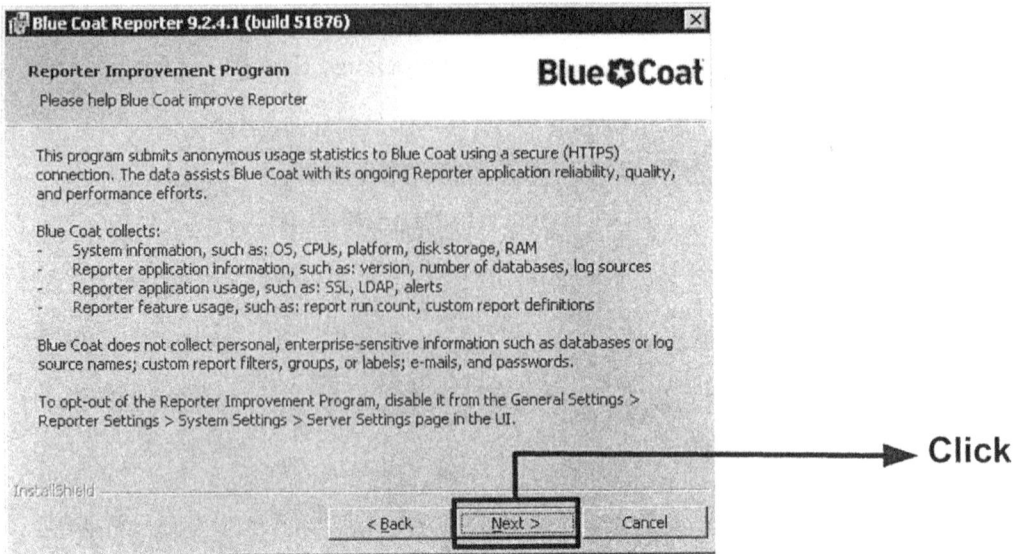

Figure 10:8 BlueCoat Reporter Improvement Program

7. Now enter the administrator user name and password and the license information (for this please contact the BlueCoat sales team and they will provide a key), as shown below:

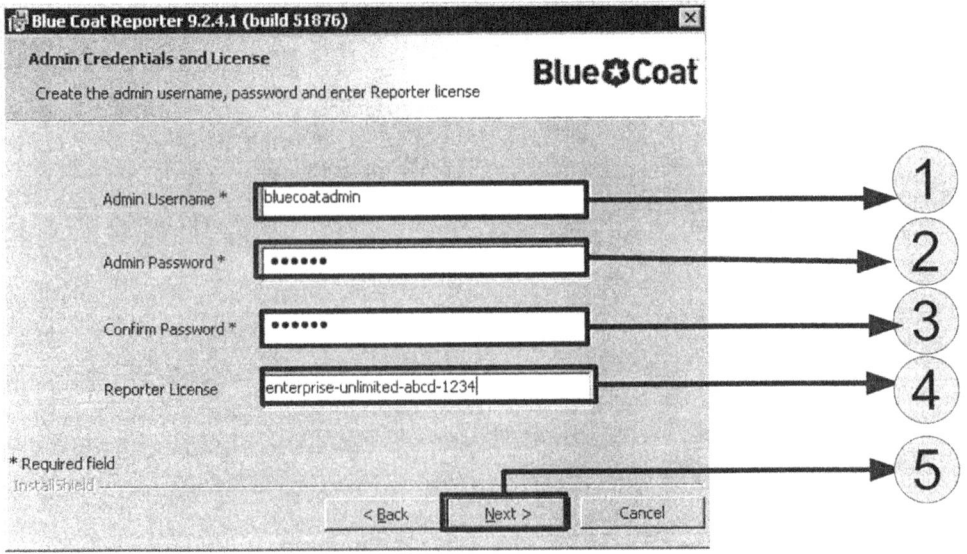

Figure 10:9 BlueCoat Reporter administrator account and license page

8. Then click the "Install" button for installation of the BlueCoat Reporter software:

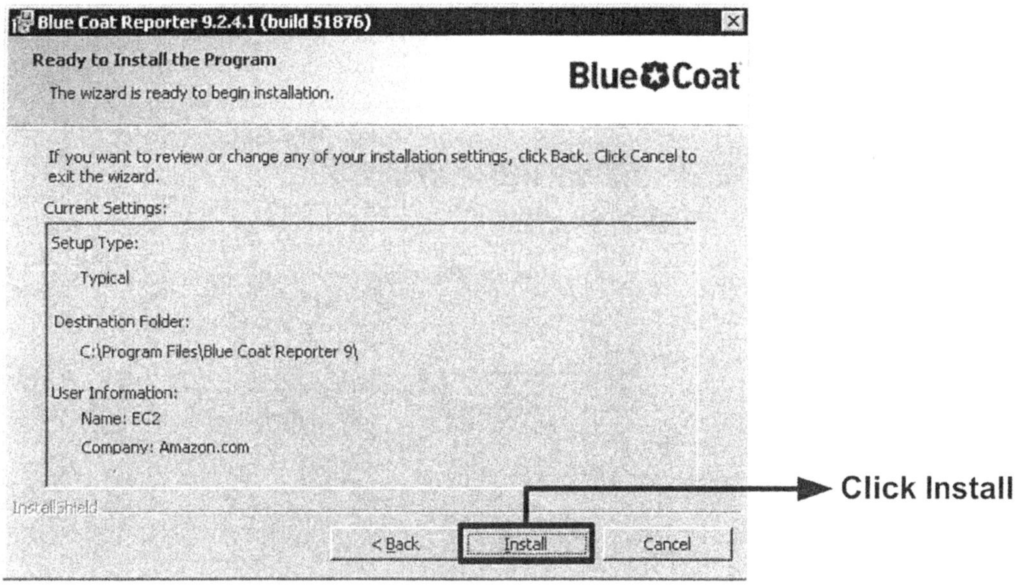

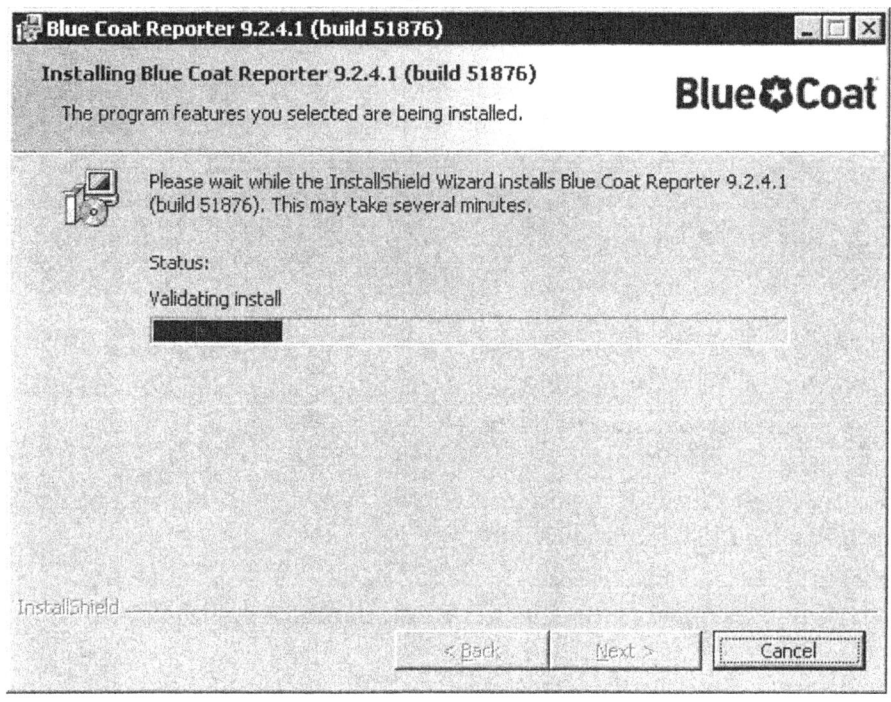

Figure 10:10 BlueCoat Reporter setup completion wizard

Wait for some time until the software gets installed:

Figure 10:11 BlueCoat Reporter installation status

9. Then confirm the installation by clicking the "Finish" button and log in to the BlueCoat Reporter tool http://127.0.0.1:8081 locally on that system, or use an IP address of the BlueCoat Reporter with the port 8081 as shown below:

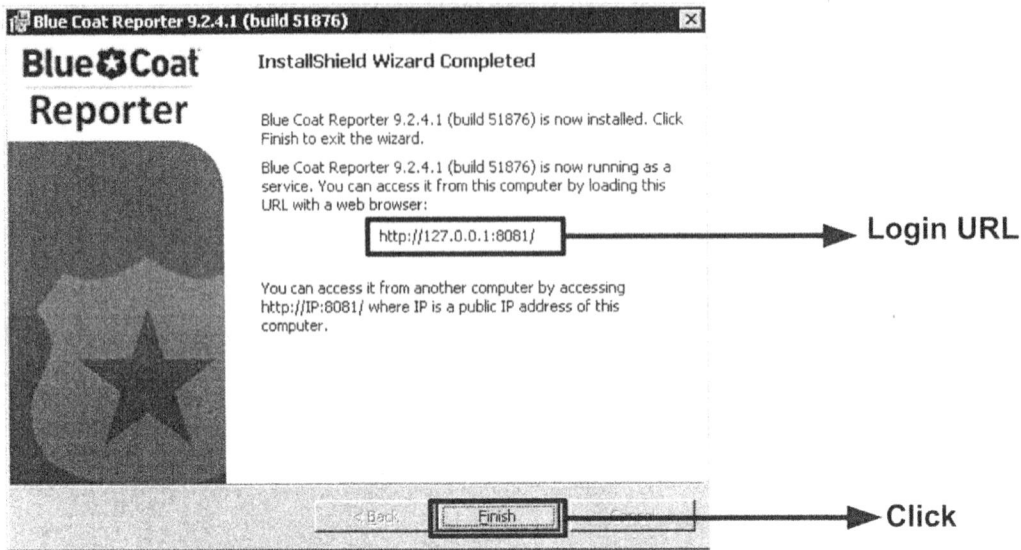

Figure 10:12 BlueCoat Reporter installation completion wizard

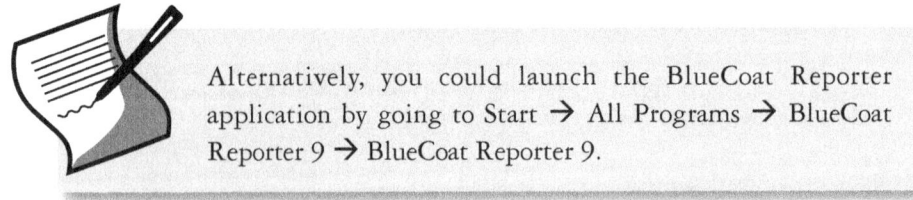

Alternatively, you could launch the BlueCoat Reporter application by going to Start → All Programs → BlueCoat Reporter 9 → BlueCoat Reporter 9.

10. Install a FTP server where the BlueCoat Reporter application is installed, because the using the FTP all the BlueCoat Proxy SG will communicate to the BlueCoat Reporter server and uploads the access logs.

If you are installing a BlueCoat Reporter server on a Windows 2008 machine, you can use one of the following URL for installation:
http://technet.microsoft.com/en-us/library/cc732769%28WS.10%29.aspx
http://technet.microsoft.com/en-us/library/dd722761%28WS.10%29.aspx

If you are installing BlueCoat Reporter server on a Windows 2003 machine, you can use one of the following URL for installation:
http://support.microsoft.com/kb/323384
http://www.microsoft.com/technet/prodtechnol/WindowsServer2003/Library/IIS/31c2427c-c0a5-49fa-9e03-823f34fba3e8.mspx?mfr=true

Configuring the BlueCoat Proxy for access logs

Now you need to configure the BlueCoat Proxy SG for enabling the access logs, FTP settings, adding log formats, uploading schedules, etc. To configure all these settings, please follow the instructions as shown below:

1. Log in to the BlueCoat Proxy SG via the management console https://192.168.10.101:8082 and go to Configuration → Access Logging → General. Click "Enable Access Logging" and "Apply" the change. By default the access log is disabled, so first you need to enable it, as shown below:

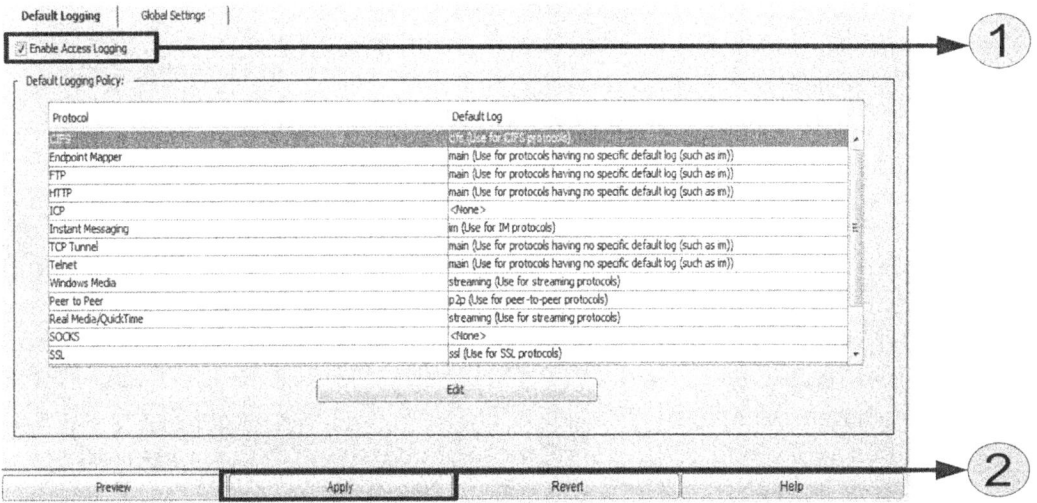

Figure 10:13 Enabling access logging

Go to Configuration → Access Logging → General → Global Settings tab and let all the Global settings be the default, "Limit total system access logging to" will define the max of the log file size, and conditions such as "Stop logging" or "Delete oldest log entries" when once after the threshold is meet and all these options could be found as shown below:

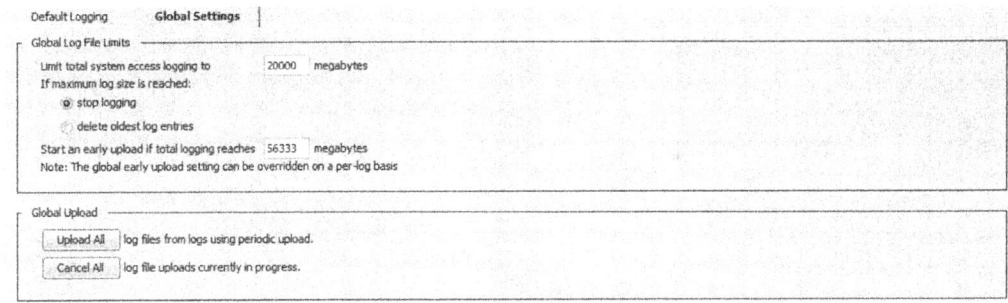

Figure 10:14 Proxy SG access log Global setting

2. By default BlueCoat has different log files for each protocol, such as the "main" logs for HTTP traffic; and there are different logs for other protocols, such as CIFS, SSL, MAPI, Streaming, and P2P, as shown below:

Go to Configuration → Access Logging → Logs → Logs tab.

Name	Format
main	bcreportermain_v1
im	im
streaming	streaming
p2p	p2p
ssl	bcreporterssl_v1
cifs	cifs
mapi	mapi

Figure 10:15 Proxy SG log format

As you can see, the corresponding format for all the log files, such as the main log file, uses the log format bcreportermain_v1. A log format is a group of log field codes, such as IP address, port numbers, UA, time, URL, bytes transferred, etc. You will use all the defaults that are there in the system.

3. After you have enabled the access log, all the HTTP traffic is logged into the "main" log file. You'll need to set the FTP server options so that the BlueCoat Proxy SG will send all the access logs to the FTP server that is running in the BlueCoat Reporter application. To do this, please configure the settings as shown below:

Go to Configuration → Access Logging → Logs → Upload Client, as shown below:

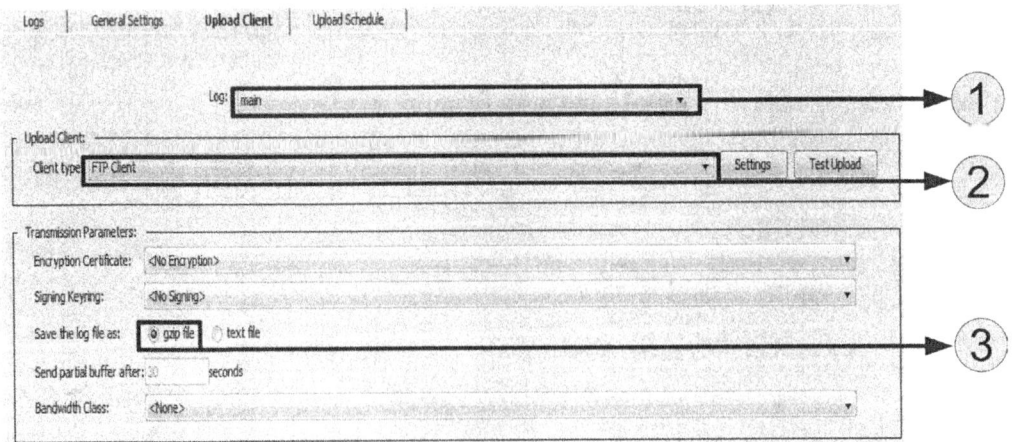

Figure 10:16 Configuring upload client on Proxy SG

Figure 10:16 Configuring upload client on Proxy SG

As shown in the above figure, all the log files are GZIP so that the data is compressed and can be sent to the BlueCoat Reporter with minimum bandwidth. Then click the "Settings" button shown in the above figure and configure all the FTP settings for the BlueCoat Proxy SG to send all the logs to the BlueCoat Reporter server, such as the IP address of the BlueCoat Reporter FTP server, and the path in the FTP server, the password for the FTP server, as shown below:

There are other ways for the Proxy SG to send all the access logs to the BlueCoat Reporter via Custom client, HTTP client, Websense client, and BlueCoat Reporter client. We are just showing FTP client because it is easy to setup and manage.

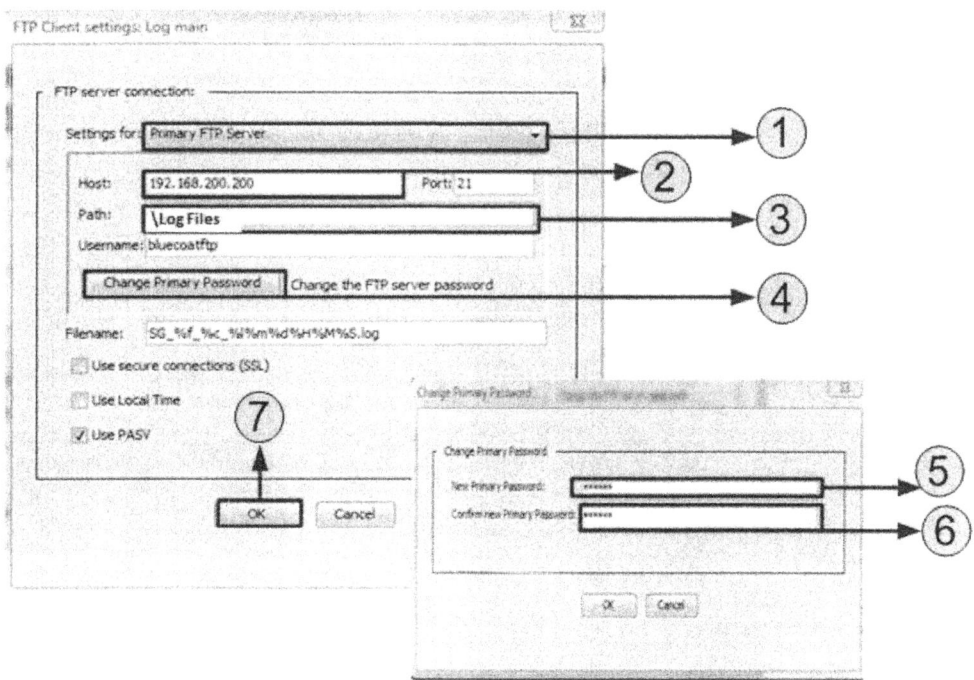

Figure 10:17 FTP settings for upload client on Proxy SG

4. By default the BlueCoat Proxy SG will send all the logs at 2:00 a.m.. You can tweak the setting for sending at any time, or you can continuously send data so that you can monitor the logs in real time and as shown in the settings below:

Go to Configuration → Access Logging → Logs → Upload Schedule.

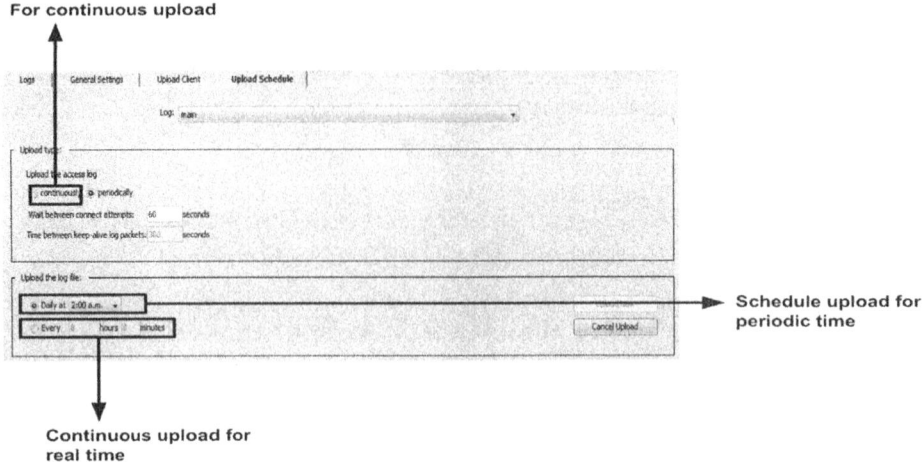

Figure 10:18 Upload schedule for access log on Proxy SG

5. As you know, there are many fields and much information in the HTTP header that could be logged in. There are almost 100 fields that the BlueCoat SG could log in, but for the best performance you need to log only the required headers in the logs. The fields that the "main" log file contains are shown in the figure below.

To view the fields, go to Configuration → Access Logging → Formats, select "main", and click the "Edit/View" button as shown below:

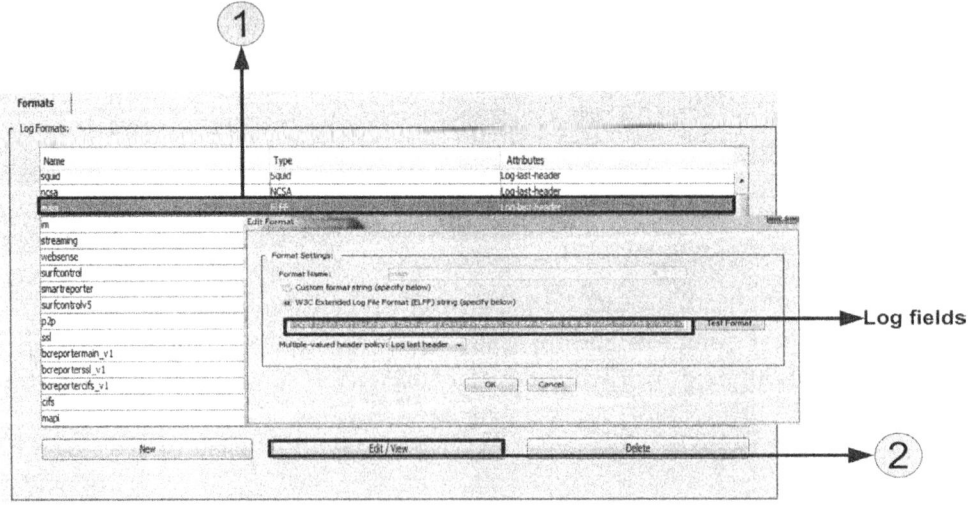

Figure 10:19 Viewing log fields on Proxy SG

The log fields in the "main" format are "date time time-taken c-ip cs-username cs-auth-group x-exception-id sc-filter-result cs-categories cs(Referer) sc-status s-action cs-method rs(Content-Type) cs-uri-scheme cs-host cs-uri-port cs-uri-path cs-uri-query cs-uri-extension cs(User-Agent) s-ip sc-bytes cs-bytes x-virus-id:" and each field are explained below:

Log field	Description
date	GMT Date in YYYY-MM-DD format
time	GMT time in HH:MM:SS format
time-taken	Time taken (in milliseconds) to process the request
c-ip	IP address of the client
cs-username	Relative username of a client authenticated to the proxy (i.e., not fully distinguished)
cs-auth-group	One group that an authenticated user belongs to. If a user belongs to multiple groups, the group logged is determined by the Group Log Order configuration specified in VPM. If the Group Log Order is not specified, an arbitrary group is logged. Note that only groups referenced by Policy are considered.
x-exception-id	Identifier of the exception resolved (empty if the transaction has not been terminated)
sc-filter-result	Deprecated content-filtering result: Denied, Proxied, or Observed
cs-categories	All content categories of the request URL
cs (Referer)	Request header: Referer
sc-status	Protocol status code from appliance to client
s-action	What type of action did the Appliance take to process this request; possible values include ALLOWED, DENIED, FAILED, SERVER_ERROR
cs-method	Request method used from client to appliance
rs (Content-Type)	Response header: Content-Type
cs-uri-scheme	Scheme from the log URL.
cs-host	Hostname from the client's request URL. If URL rewrite policies are used, this field's value is derived from the 'log' URL.
cs-uri-port	Port from the 'log' URL
cs-uri-path	Path from the 'log' URL. Does not include query.
cs-uri-query	Query from the 'log' URL
cs-uri-extension	Document extension from the 'log' URL

cs(User-Agent)	Request header: User-Agent
s-ip	IP address of the appliance on which the client established its connection
sc-bytes	Number of bytes sent from appliance to client
cs-bytes	Number of bytes sent from client to appliance
x-virus-id	Identifier of a virus if one was detected

Table 10:1 Log Fields Description

Creating databases in the BlueCoat Reporter

You have installed the BlueCoat Reporter application and configured in the Proxy SG what is required for sending all access logs to the BlueCoat Reporter. You have also installed the FTP server using IIS in the BlueCoat Reporter server. Now you have to create a database in the BlueCoat server which will collect all the data from various proxies and process and store it in the Reporter server. To configure the database, please follow the steps as shown below:

1. Log in to the BlueCoat Reporter server either by (a) using RDP and going to Start → All Programs → BlueCoat Reporter 9, and the application will open in an IE browser with the URL http://127.0.01:8081/; or (b) log in remotely by using the IP address of the Reporter server using the port 8081, as http://192.168.200.200:8081. You will get a message stating that the database has not been not created. Click "OK" and then click "New" to create a new database, as shown below:

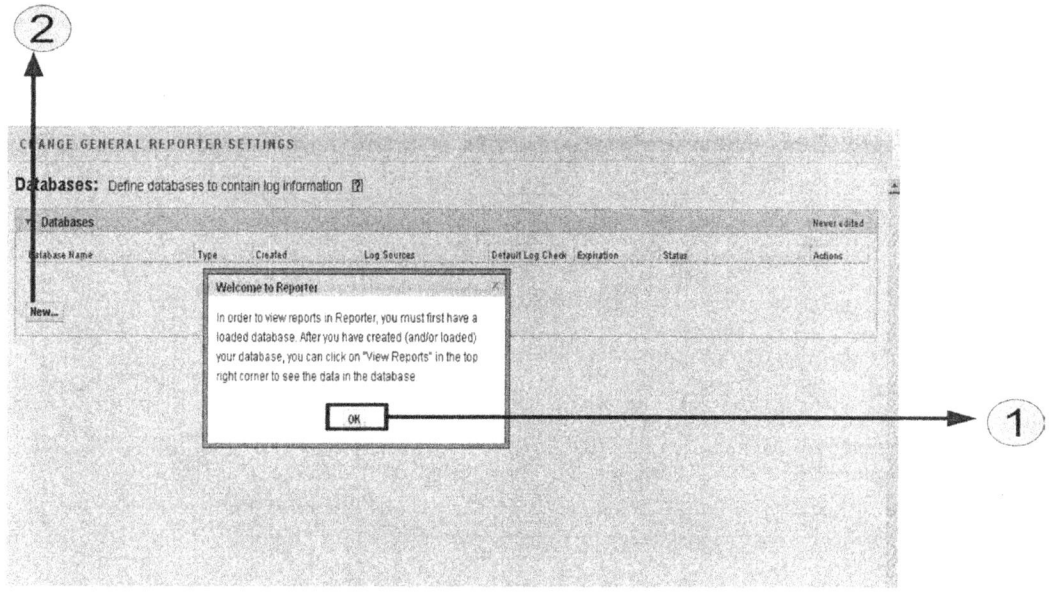

Figure 10:20 Creating a new database in BlueCoat Reporter

2. Then you will see the "Create New Database" wizard. Enter the name of the database as "CorporateBlueCoatReporter" or any user-defined name and click "Next".

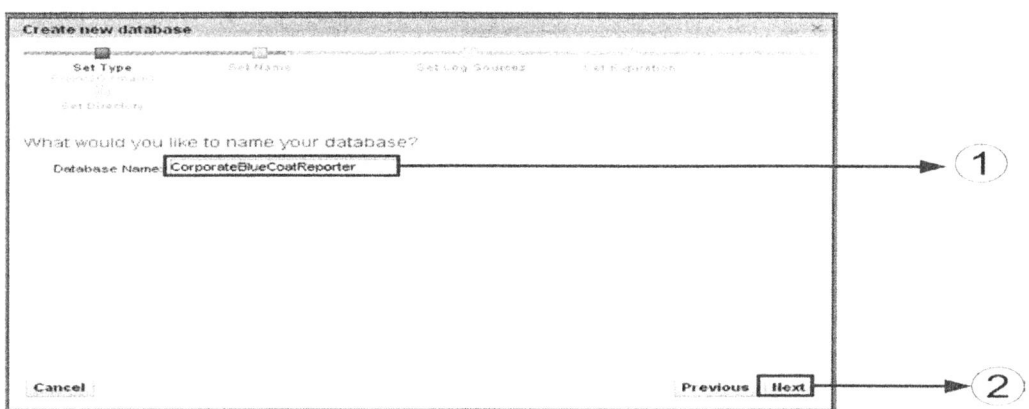

Figure 10:21 Defining the database name in BlueCoat Reporter

3. Then you will need to create the "Log source". This is the place where all the logs are uploaded it could in any directory or file shares, i.e. all the BlueCoat Proxy SG uses FTP and uploads to some directory on the BlueCoat Reporter server. Here we define that the path where it can reside on the server and the configuration is shown below:

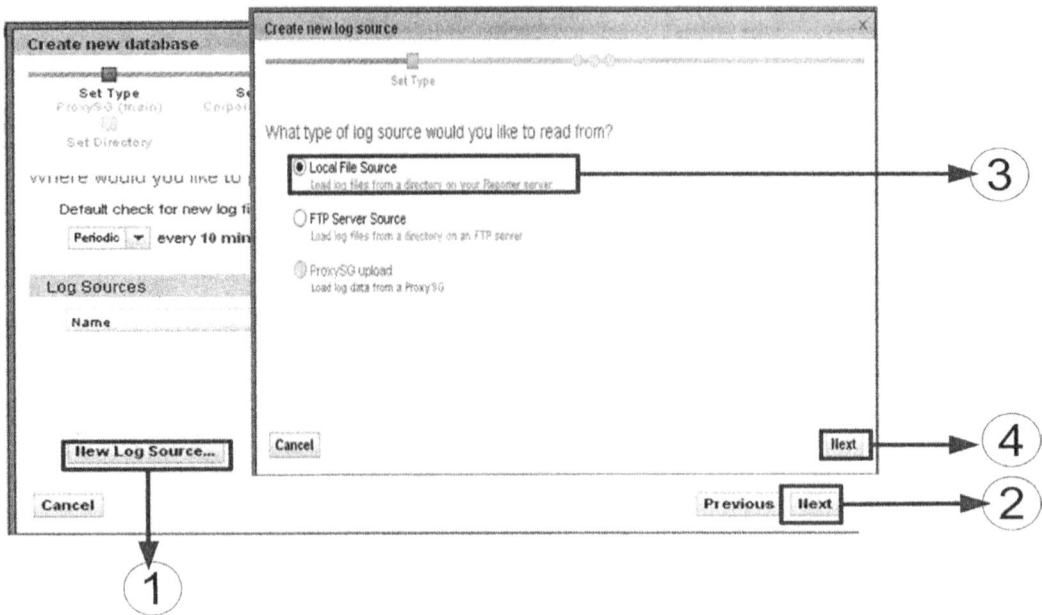

Figure 10:22 Defining the Log source options in BlueCoat Reporter

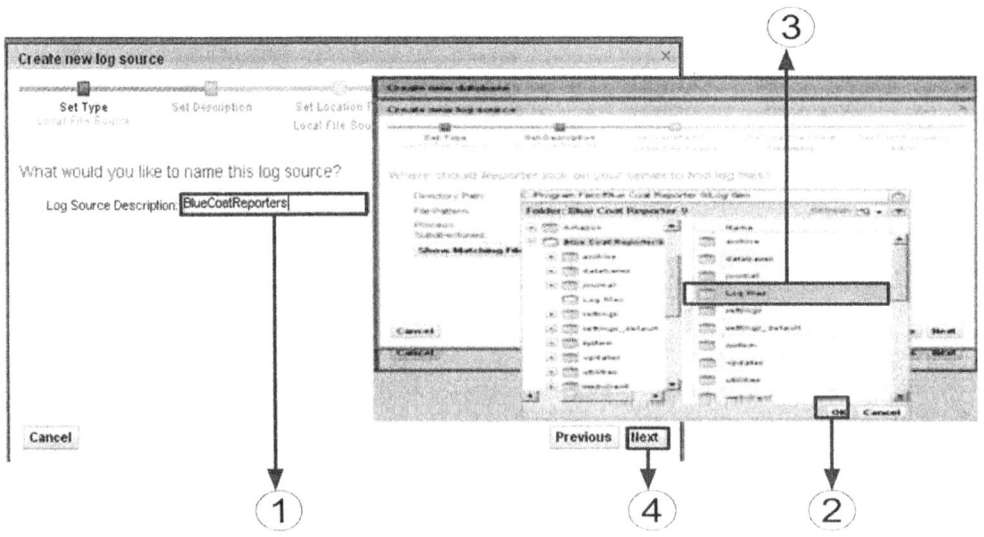

Figure 10:23 Selecting the log source path in BlueCoat Reporter

As shown in the above figure, enter the Log Source Description as "BlueCoatReporters" and select the path where the FTP server is listening for all logs from all the proxies. As an example, choose the path as "C:/Program Files/Blue Coat Reporter 9/Log Files". Usually it should be the D drive or any other drive, as the C: primary drive is not used for logging all log requests. Here we just show this as an example for easy understanding.

4. Once the Log Source is confirmed in the above step, it shows the directory path. All the files in that directory with .log and .log.gz are loaded into the Reporter server for generating the database. Then once you click "Next", you can "Set Log File Check Frequency", which by default is every 10 minutes. In other words, that reporter server looks for new logs in this directory for every 10 minutes; if you want to set up a custom schedule you can, here you leave as the defaults.

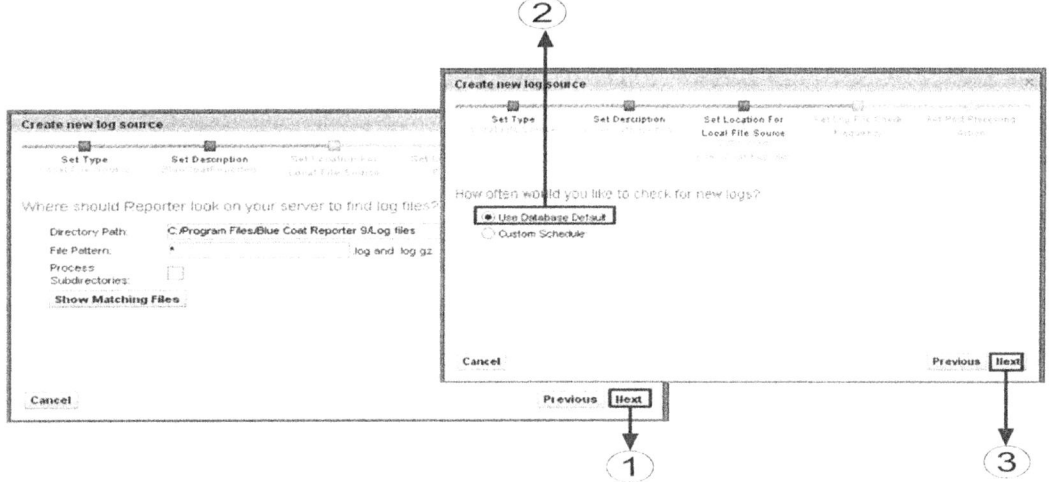

Figure 10:24 Defining Log File check frequency interval in BlueCoat Reporter

5. Once the log file is processed, rename all the log files to the .done extension so that you know the difference between which log files have been processed by BlueCoat Reporter and the raw log file that need to be processed. Processed log files have the extension ".done". Click "Done" in the "Set Post Processing Action" screen. Then once you confirm that the settings are correct, click "Next" in the "Set Log Source" screen as shown below:

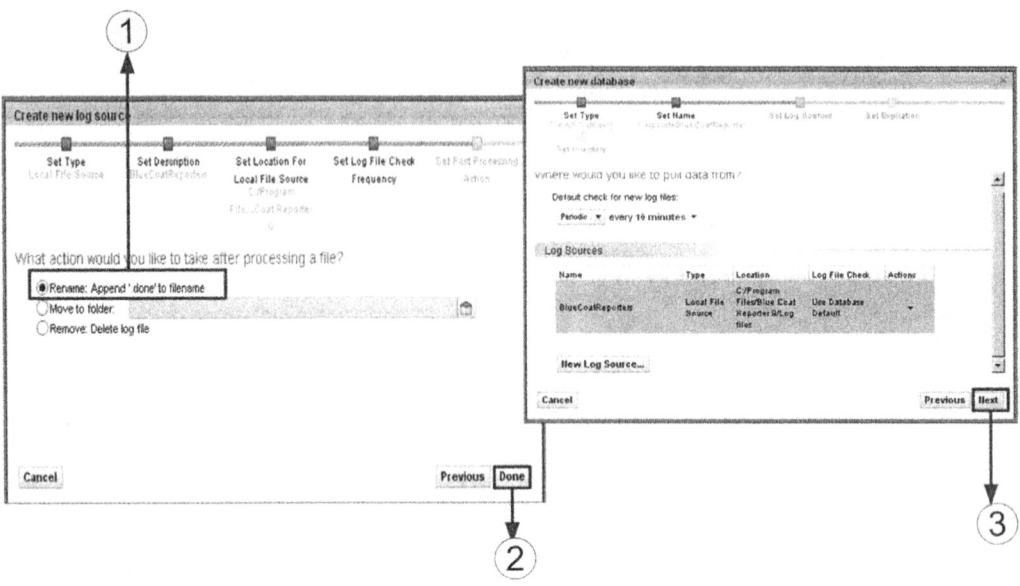

Figure 10:25 Defining Post processing Action in BlueCoat Reporter

6. In the "Set Expiration" page, you can set how often the BlueCoat Reporter database will expire. The default is 30 days; this means you have log reports for only 30 days. If you want to find some data beyond 30 days, you cannot do it. Most security standards recommend having the logs for 180 days and here you have configured for 180 days. Then click "Next" button, and the next configuration is the "Set Directory" page where you could configure where you want the actual BlueCoat Reporter database to be. This is different from the "Log Source File"; here the database is the one that is generated after processing the raw log files. You can configure the archive folder for the BlueCoat Reporter to be storing all the archive-generated reports. Leave all these setting as defaults and click "Done" as shown below.

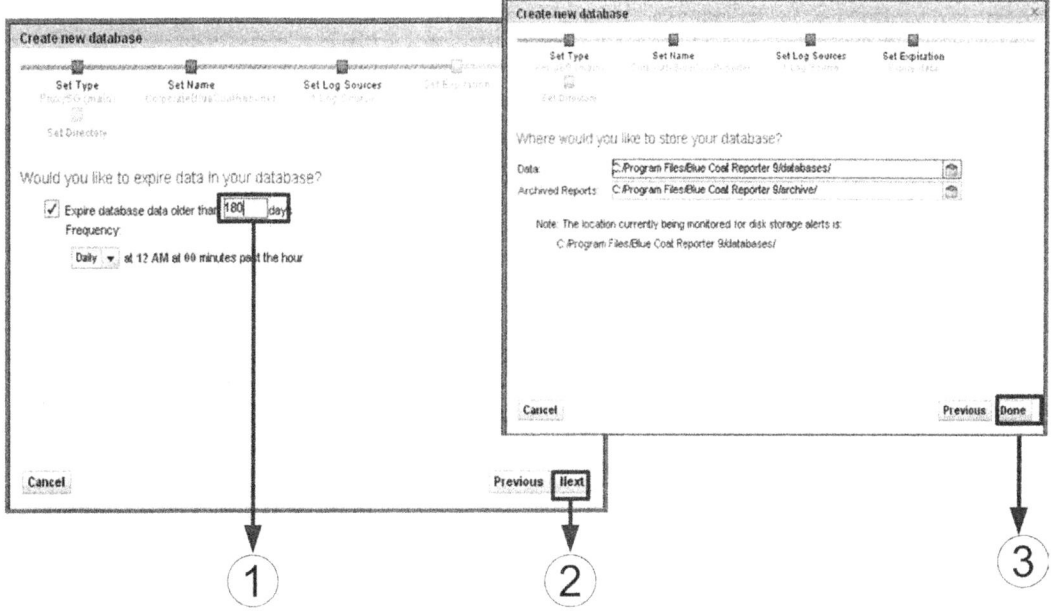

Figure 10:26 Defining Expiration in BlueCoat Reporter

Now the BlueCoat Reporter creates a new database with all the settings that you configured in the above steps, as shown below:

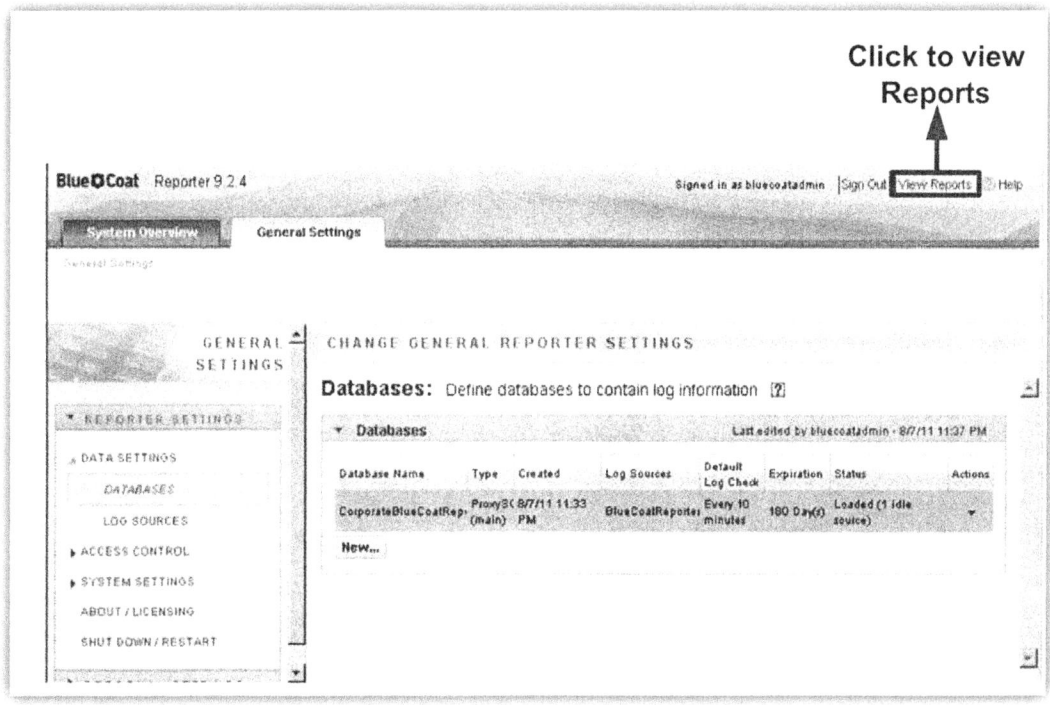

Figure 10:27 Viewing Reports in BlueCoat Reporter

7. After you have created the database, initially the source directory where all the logs get collected and the Reported Dashboard are empty, because the BlueCoat Proxy SG has not yet uploaded the log files. If you remember refer figure 10:18 you configured the upload time as 2:00 a.m. If you want to force upload, you can do it by going to Configuration → Access Logging → Logs → Upload Schedule, selecting "main" as the log, and hitting the "Upload Now" button at the bottom of the screen. All the collected logs are uploaded to the BlueCoat Reporter.

You can see the empty log directory and empty BlueCoat Reporter Dashboard in the figure below:

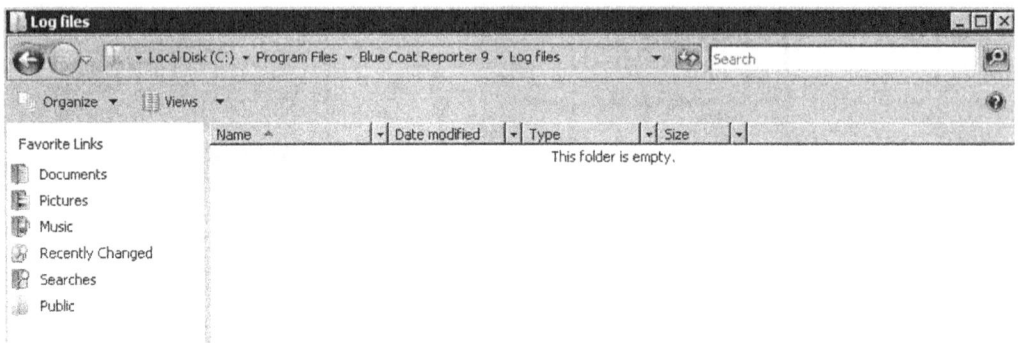

Figure 10:28 Log Source folder before log uploads in BlueCoat Reporter

Figure 10:29 Dashboard in BlueCoat Reporter

To view the DashBoard, click the "View Reports" button at the right top corner of the screen, as shown in the above figure.

Log source and Dashboard

Once all the proxies have started to forward the logs to the BlueCoat Reporter, you will have all the logs in the source directory, as shown below:

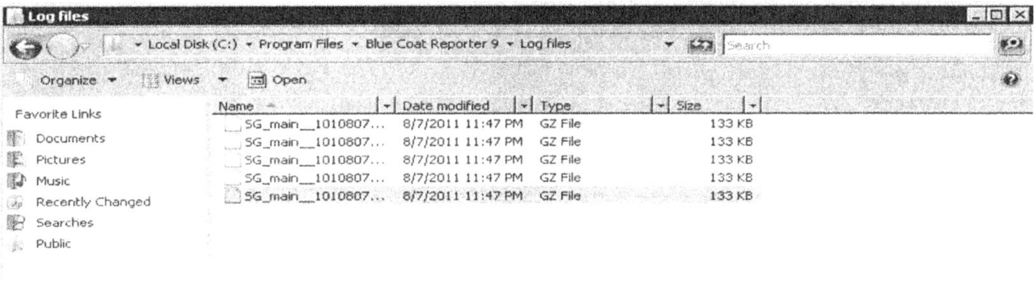

Figure 10:30 Log Source folder after log uploads in BlueCoat Reporter

And once the logs get uploaded, BlueCoat Reporter will look into the source directory for new logs every 10 minutes; that is the default time you defined when you created the database. The logs get processed by the BlueCoat Reporter Engine and the database is created. The processed log file is renamed as *.log.gz.done and moved to a different directory or kept in the same directory where it fetched the source. This is based upon the settings you configured while creating the database. In this case, for simplicity, we retain in the same folder, as shown in the figure below:

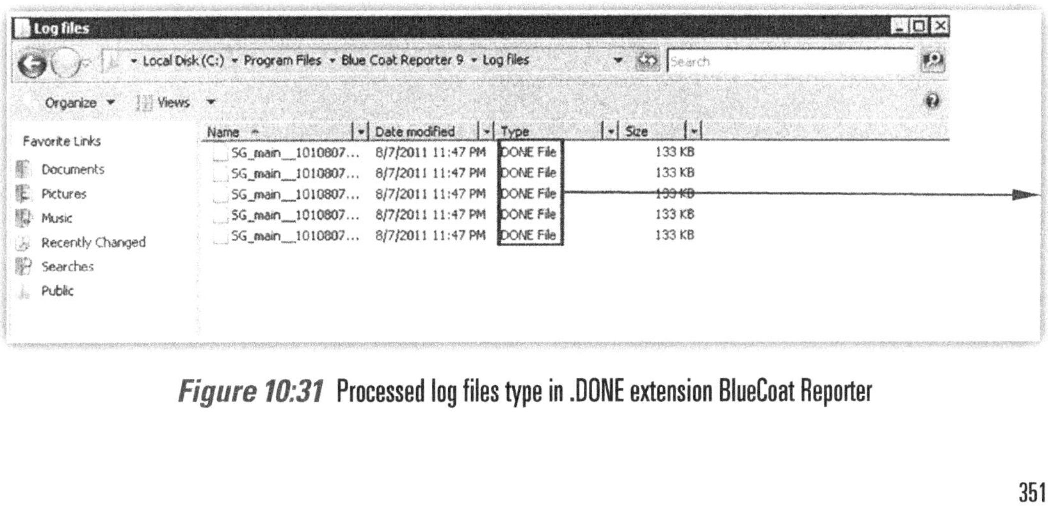

Figure 10:31 Processed log files type in .DONE extension BlueCoat Reporter

Now the dashboard has all the data that has been populated and will look similar to the figure below:

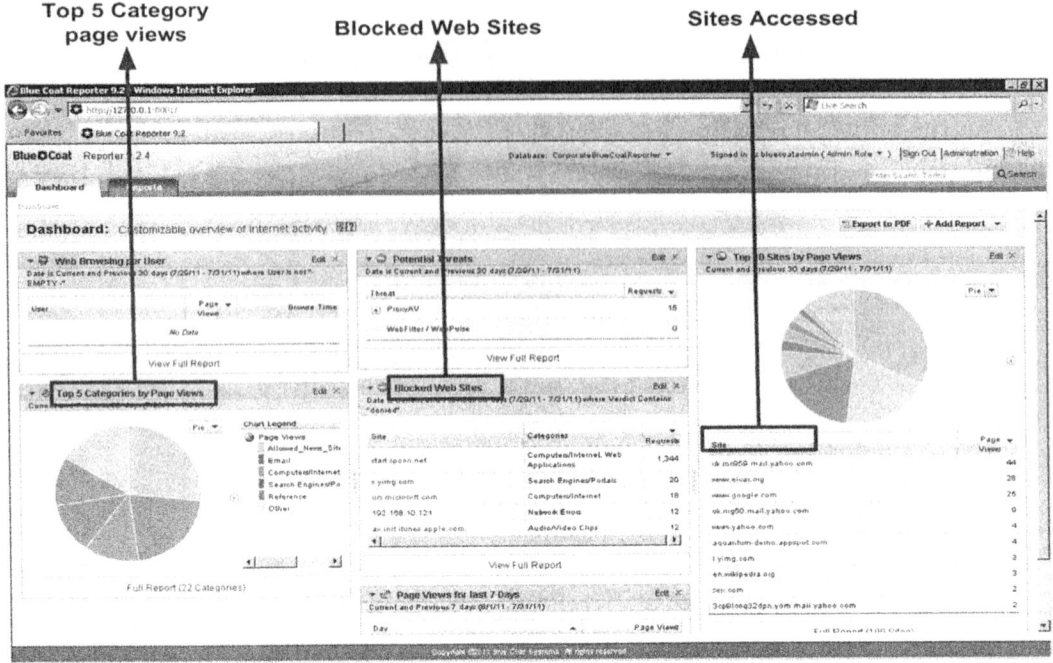

Figure 10:32 Dashboard with reports in BlueCoat Reporter

This is the default dashboard that is generated with predefined reports. You can also see the different data that has been populated by the BlueCoat Reporter and shows the different statistics based the top ten lists of data that is available.

You can add your own custom reports that will help you to analyze the user's traffic pattern. For example, if you want to know the report of your network which client IP address that has been maximum malware detected and blocked by the Proxy AV, you can create a custom group as shown below:

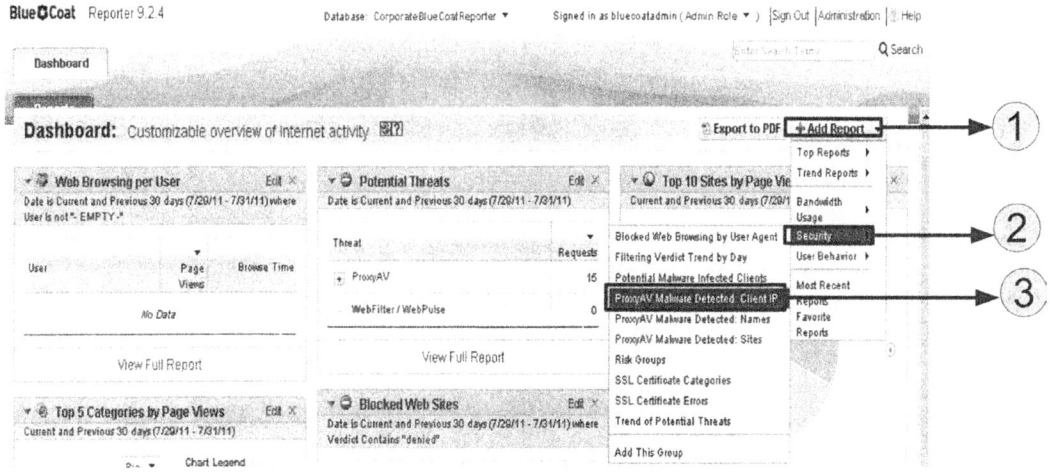

Figure 10:33 Adding new Internet activity view in BlueCoat Reporter Dashboard

And once the custom report "ProxyAV Malware Detected: Client IP" is created, we will have the report at the bottom of the dashboard page with the client IP address and details as shown below:

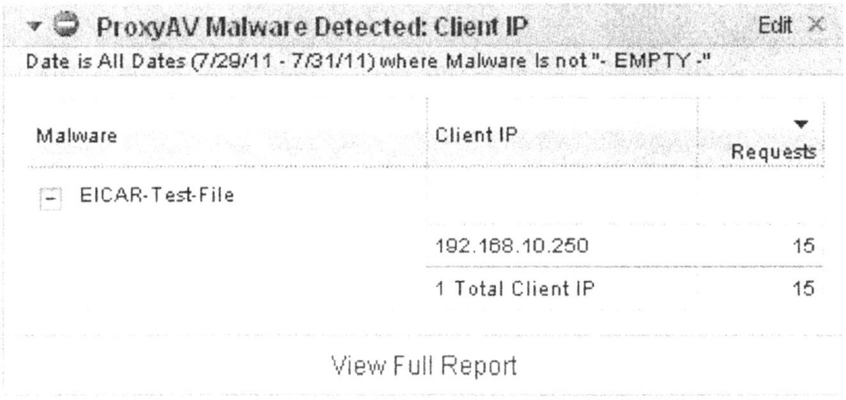

Figure 10:34 Proxy AV Malware Detected: Client IP BlueCoat Reporter Dashboard

GENERATING REPORTS:

Reports can be generated in the BlueCoat Reporter either as CSV or PDF files. If you want to find more details about a particular user's surfing habits or if you want to generate Internet reports to your higher management or to law enforcement, then you will be generating Internet reports for your tasks. Here you will be generating a report for the IP address 192.168.10.250,and all information regarding the sites visited.

To generate an Internet report, click the "Reports" tab in the Dashboard page and follow the steps below:

1. Click on the "Reports" tab and then click "New Reports", as shown below:

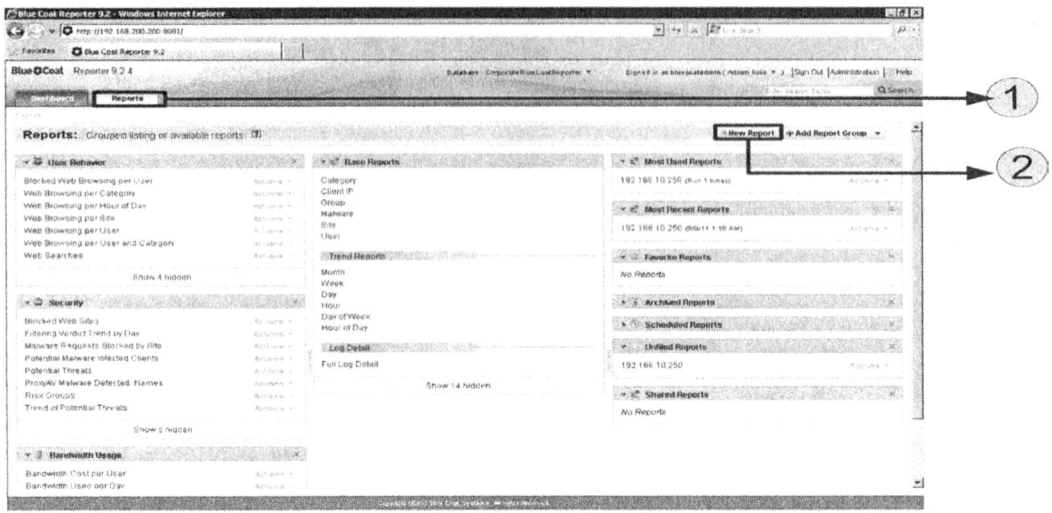

Figure 10:35 Generating Internet reports in BlueCoat Reporter

2. Now enter the name of the report (the name is user-defined) as "IP – 192.168.10.250". For "Summarize by", select "Site", and click "Next", as shown below:

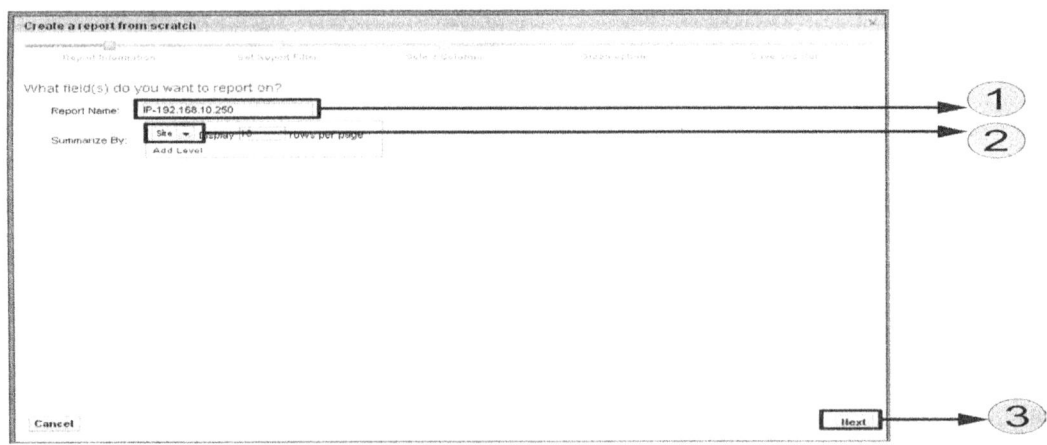

Figure 10:36 Defining report name in BlueCoat Reporter

3. Then select the dates for which you have to run the report. You could run the report based on a certain time interval, for example from June 1st to July 31st,

2011. Here you are running reports for all dates. Once the dates are selected, click "Next" as shown below:

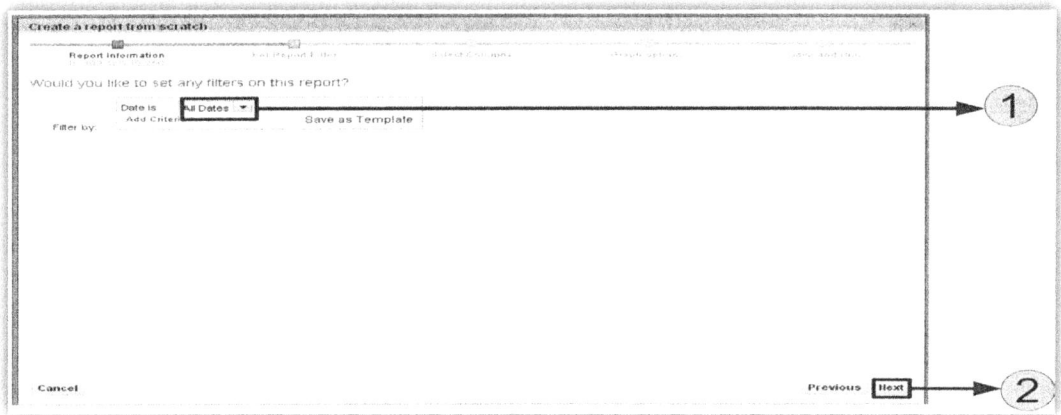

Figure 10:37 Defining dates for the report in BlueCoat Reporter

4. Then in the "Select Columns" page, the columns that appears in the report are shown. These are the main fields for which the data is generated. By default all the required columns are selected. If you want to add additional columns, select them in the "Display the following:" menu as shown below:

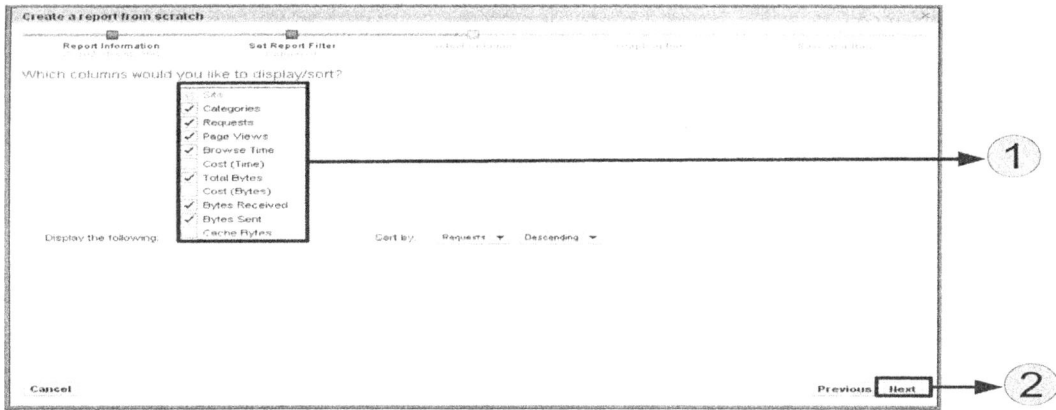

Figure 10:38 Defining columns for the report in BlueCoat Reporter

5. The "Graph Options" page will help to generate the reports based on graphs, by default the displayed format is "Pie". Graphs can be generated as either area, bar, line, column, or scatter graphs. Click "Next" as shown below:

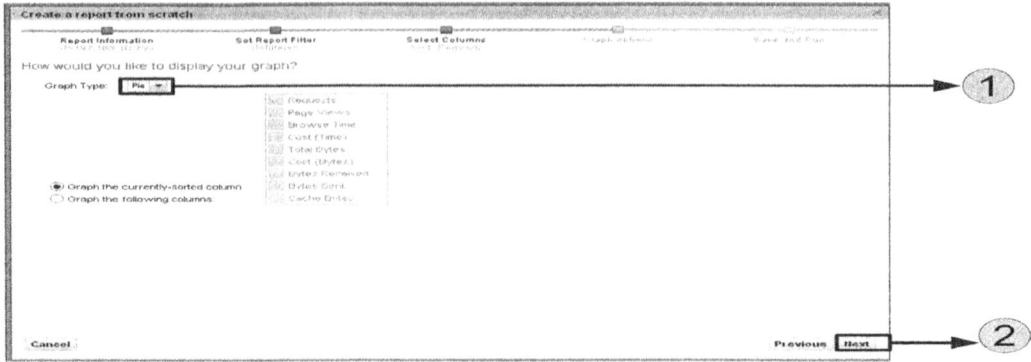

Figure 10:39 Defining graph type for the report in BlueCoat Reporter

6. Then in the "Save and Run" page, click "Run Report". The report will start to be generated.

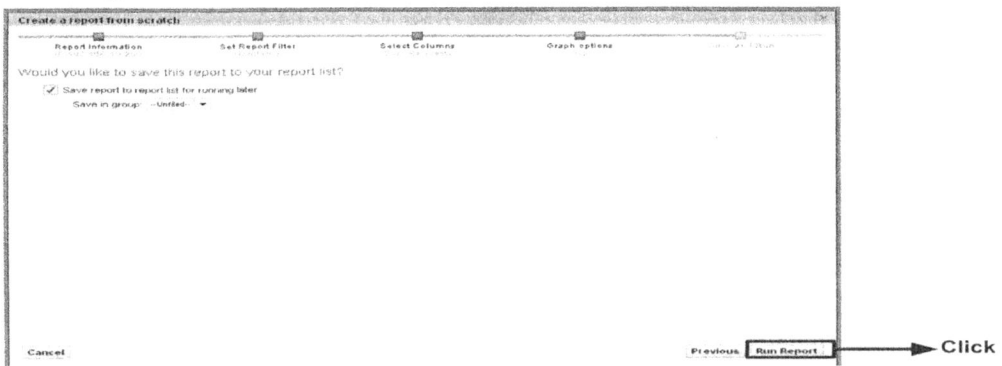

Figure 10:40 Running report in BlueCoat Reporter

7. Then the report is generated with sites visited, and each site's categories, the browse time, the bytes sent and received, etc. As you can see in the figure below, a graph has also been generated based upon the requests. You can save the Internet reports in either CSV or PDF format, by clicking the "Download" button on the top of the screen and the save the file to your system.

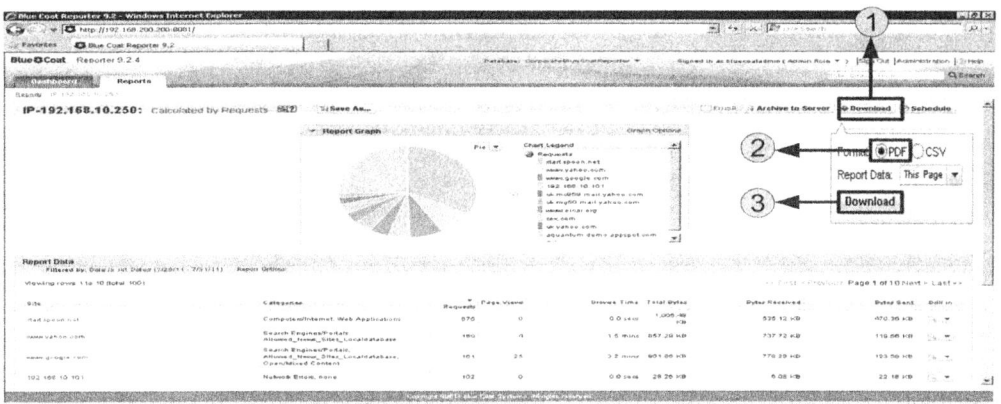

Figure 10:41 Downloading Internet report in PDF format

For the above report to work properly and prevent Reporter from disregarding some log lines, the Reporter's main databases require these fields:

1. cs-host
2. sc-status
3. cs-uri-scheme

For the PVC to operate correctly, Reporter requires these additional fields:

1. cs (Referer) or x-cs (Referer)-uri
2. x-exception-id or sc-filter-result (x-exception-id preferred)
3. sc-filter-category, cs-category, or cs-categories

Test Yourself

1. What are the types of log that is been forwarded to the BlueCoat Reporter by the Proxy SG?

   a. Event log
   b. Access log
   c. Policy Trace
   d. Core files

2. Can BlueCoat Reporter be integrated with third-party SIEM tools like Arcsight, Symantec, IBM, etc.?

   a. Yes
   b. No

3. What is the database that the BlueCoat Reporter uses?

   a. MySQL
   b. Cassandra
   c. BlueCoat Database
   d. Oracle

4. On which operating system can the BlueCoat Reporter canbe installed?

   a. Linux
   b. Solaris
   c. Unix
   d. Windows

5. If the BlueCoat Reporter is down and the access log in the Proxy SG has reached its space limit, what are two decisions that could be made by the Proxy SG?

   a. Expand more space in the hard disk.
   b. Stop logging.
   c. Delete oldest log entries.
   d. Reboot the proxy SG.

6. What happens to the logs once the Proxy SG has been uploaded to the BlueCoat Reporter successfully?

   a. Have a copy of the logs in Proxy SG after uploading
   b. Compress the file and archive in the Proxy SG
   c. Wait till the log reaches the maximum limit and then delete it.
   d. Once uploaded, then the Proxy SG deletes it.

7. To encrypt the access logs, could they be sent on the Internet via a VPN connection to the BlueCoat Reporter?

   a. Yes, they could be sent on the Internet via a VPN connection.
   b. b. They could only be sent through the intranet.
   c. The BlueCoat Reporter should be in the same subnet as the Proxy SG.
   d. Access logs should not be encrypted.

8. Could you install BlueCoat Reporter software on a SAN drive rather than a physical drive for better performance?

   a. Yes
   a. No

CHAPTER 11

....

K9 WEB PROTECTION

K9 WEB PROTECTION

We have introduced K9 web protection in Chapter 1, "Introduction to BlueCoat." Let's review it again here. Blue Coat® K9 Web Protection is a free product for home users, which is mostly an Internet filter and parental control software for your home Windows or Mac computer. It enables parents to monitor and control what sites their children access and enables them to block offensive or potentially dangerous sites. K9 Web Protection also uses the same best-of-breed Web-filtering technology, WebPulse service, to update the database continuously and protect it from all the new threats.

The key benefits of using Blue Coat® K9 Web protection include:

1. The web filter is same as BCWF and has 81 categories, for parents to control internet access to their children while web surfing and protecting from them visiting potential dangerous sites.
2. It is integrated with the WebPulse cloud service so that a DRTR real-time site categorization is done.
3. It is free parental control software that is offered by Blue Coat® to protect kids from visiting bad sites.
4. K9 web protection software can be installed in both Windows and Mac machines.
5. K9 uses enhanced anti-tampering technology, which makes it much harder for children to break and circumvent the system.

6. It also provides "Safe Search" for all major and popular search engines, such as Google, Yahoo, MSN Bing, etc.
7. Users can log all the activities, generate reports, and monitor the surfing habits of their children.
8. K9 provides efficient caching for the web browser, which reduces Internet traffic since frequently visited objects are cached.
9. K9 Web protection can be installed on the IPhone, iPod, and iPad.

K9 web protection was developed mainly for the kids who access the Internet and not exposed to any adult content or download any malicious content which will infect the computer. It also helps home computer newbie users to computers, who are protected by the K9 web protection, which is the same as the BCWF filtering database that we saw in the chapter "Content Filtering and WebPulse," but K9 is installed in the computer rather than the BlueCoat Proxy SG.

Before moving to the technical details, the survey from BlueCoat K9Web protection tells how important K9 Web protection is and explained below :

- Pornography is a $57-billion-a-year industry. In comparison, the combined revenues of all teams in the NBA, NHL, MLB, and NFL is $12 billion, and the combined revenues of ABC, CBS, and NBC is a mere $6.2 billion. (Sources: Internet Filter Review, Economic Values of Professional Sport Franchises in the United States)
- One in four youth have unwanted exposure to inappropriate pictures each year. (Source: The Internet Keep Safe Coalition)
- Nine of ten kids aged 8-16 have viewed pornography on the Internet, often in the process of doing homework. (Source: London School of Economics January 2002)
- Students were most at risk for cybersex compulsions due to a combination of increased access to computers, more private leisure time, and developmental stage characterized by increased sexual awareness and experimentation. Both computer classes and colleges might need to recognize this increased vulnerability and institute new primary prevention strategies. (Source: Sexual Addiction and Compulsion: The Journal of Treatment and Prevention, March, 2000 (available by subscription)
- "Cyber-sex is the crack cocaine of sexual addiction," Jennifer P. Schneider, M.D., Ph.D. (Source: The New "Elephant in the Living Room" Effects of Compulsive Cybersex Behaviors on the Spouse, from the book Sex and the Internet, 2002)
- "Cyber-sex reinforces and normalizes sexual disorders" (Source: Robert Weiss, Sexual Recovery Institute)
- One in five children ages 10-17 have received a sexual solicitation over the Internet (Source: Online Victimization: A Report on the Nation's Youth, sponsored by the National Center for Missing and Exploited Children. See also UNH Study Finds Many Youth Exposed to Sexual Solicitation, Pornography and Harassment on Internet, 19 March, 2001.)

- 74% of commercial pornography sites display free porn images on the homepage. (Sources: <u>Child-Proofing on the World Wide Web: A Survey of Adult Webservers, 2001, Jurimetrics (abstract)</u>, Summarized in Youth and the Internet (Chapter 3, <u>The Adult Online Entertainment Industry</u>), National Research Council, 2002.)
- 45% of 1,000 surveyed teens admitted parents are the biggest influence in deciding whether or not to have sex.
- 88% of teens say it would be easier to postpone sex if they could have more open, honest conversations with their parents.
- Two-thirds of U.S. teenagers who have had sexual relations wish they had waited longer. (Source: National Campaign to Prevent Teen Pregnancy, September 2003. <u>Brief</u> | <u>Full survey</u>)

System requirements for installing BlueCoat K9 protection

BlueCoat K9 Web protection can be installed on either Windows or Mac machines. In this chapter we will discuss the installation on a Windows machine only. The installation wizards are different in MAC desktops with different GUI interface, but all the other options will be the same as for the Windows machine.

Hardware requirement:

- Processor: 233 MHz or faster Pentium-compatible CPU
- Memory: At least 64 megabytes (MB) of RAM
- Hard disk: 25 MB free space

Operating System requirement:

- Microsoft Windows Vista or Windows Vista Service Pack 1
- Windows XP, Service Pack 2 or later required
- Windows 2000, Service Pack 5 required

Web Browser requirement:

- Windows Internet Explorer version 6 and later
- Firefox version 2 and later
- Safari version 2 and later

Registration with BlueCoat K9 Web Protection

First you will need a license for BlueCoat K9 Web Protection. The license is absolutely free for anyone. All that's needed is a valid email address, and the license will be emailed to you. So that you could use nexttime of installation K9 web protection with the same license. The license is only for one computer, so if you have multiple computers you will need a license for each individual computer. To obtain the license, follow the steps as shown below:

1. Open the IE browser and go to http://www1.k9webprotection.com/get-k9-web-protection-free.
2. Fill in all the details for the license request ,as shown below:

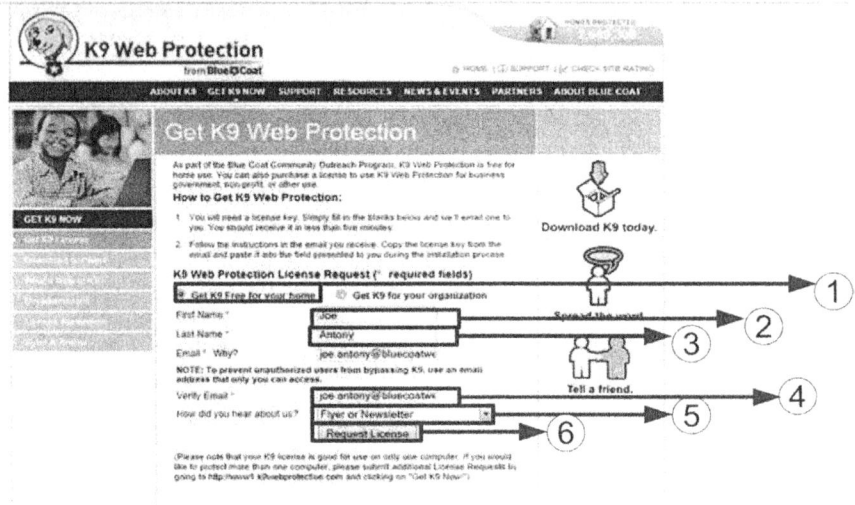

Figure 11.1 Registration and license request for K9 Web Protection

3. You will receive an email within 10 minutes, which has the license and download information.

Installing BlueCoat K9 protection

Now we will show how to install the K9 web protection. The installation procedure is very simple and easy. The key point is that when you create the password for the administrator console of K9 web protection, make sure it complicated, since if it easy the kids to decipher the password and misuse the Internet for bad purposes. Chose a very complicated password, write it down, and keep it in safe place so that only you know where it is. Please don't lose the password—it is very hard to break in: as K9 web protection is a security software, it is built against all the password attacks.

Follow the steps below to install K9 web protection:

1. Open the email that the K9 web protection sent once you registered with a valid email address, and click the download link as shown below:

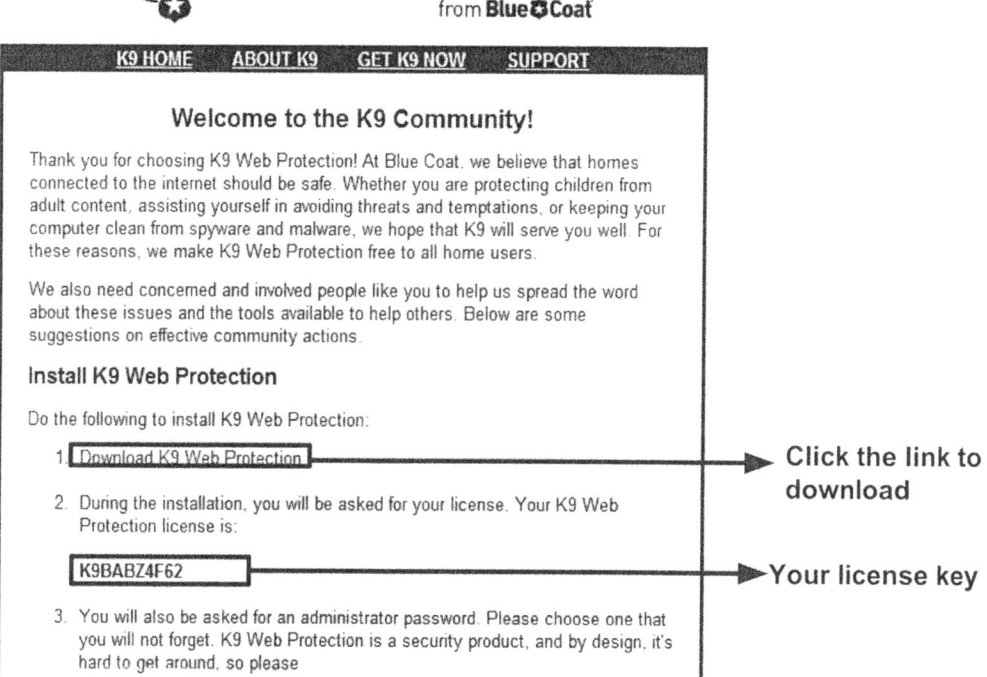

Figure 11.2 Software download and license key email from K9 Web Protection

2. You will be redirected to the web page shown below. Click the Windows icon to download for the Windows operating system and save it on the desktop:

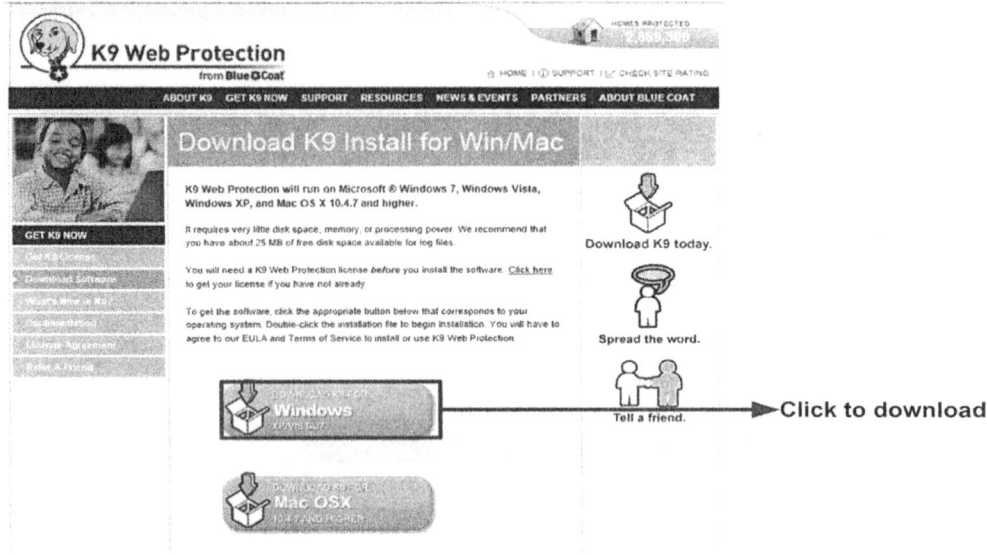

Figure 11.3 Software download for K9 Web Protection

3. 3. Then run the K9 web protection software that you downloaded and saved on the desktop by double-clicking the icon "k9-webprotection". You will see a setup wizard as shown below. Click "Next".

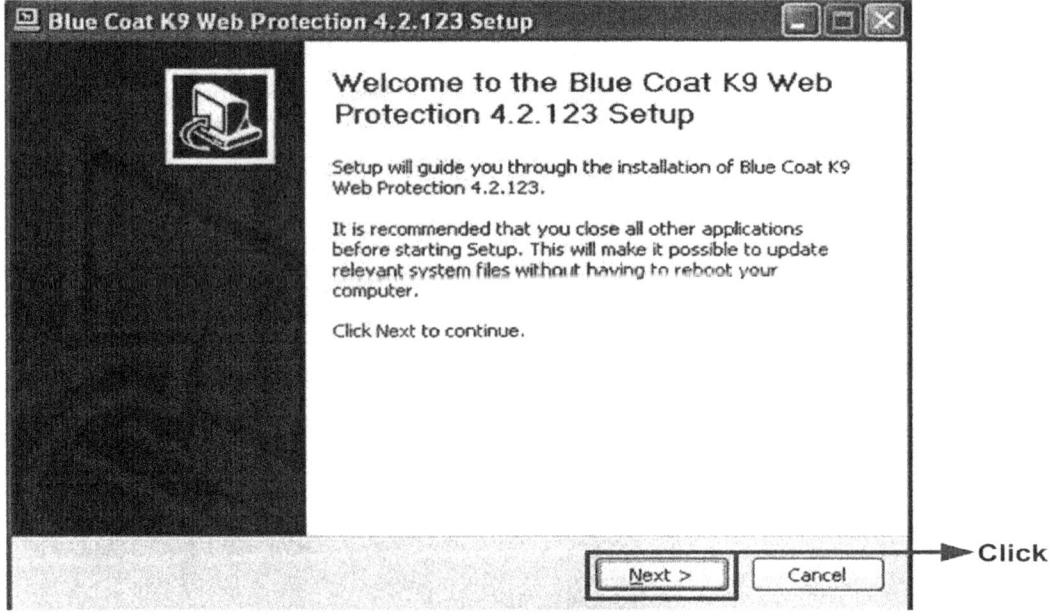

Figure 11.4 Installation setup for K9 Web Protection

4. Then accept the "End-User License and Service Agreement" by clicking the "I Agree" button as shown below:

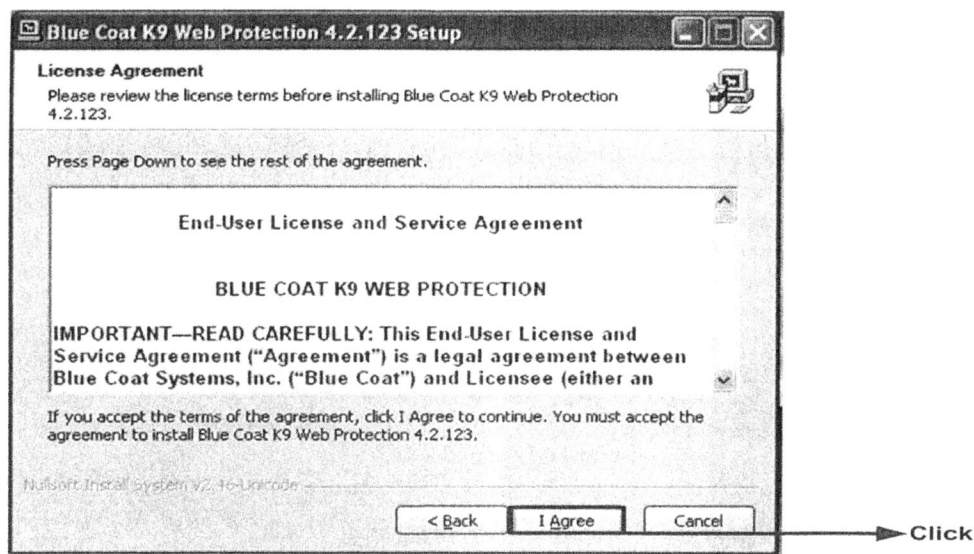

Figure 11.5 License Agreement for BlueCoat K9 Web Protection

5. The next step is to enter the license key that was emailed by the K9 protection team as is shown in the figure 11:1and then enter the password for administrating the K9 management console. Please choose a strong password for maximum security and click the "Install" button as shown below:

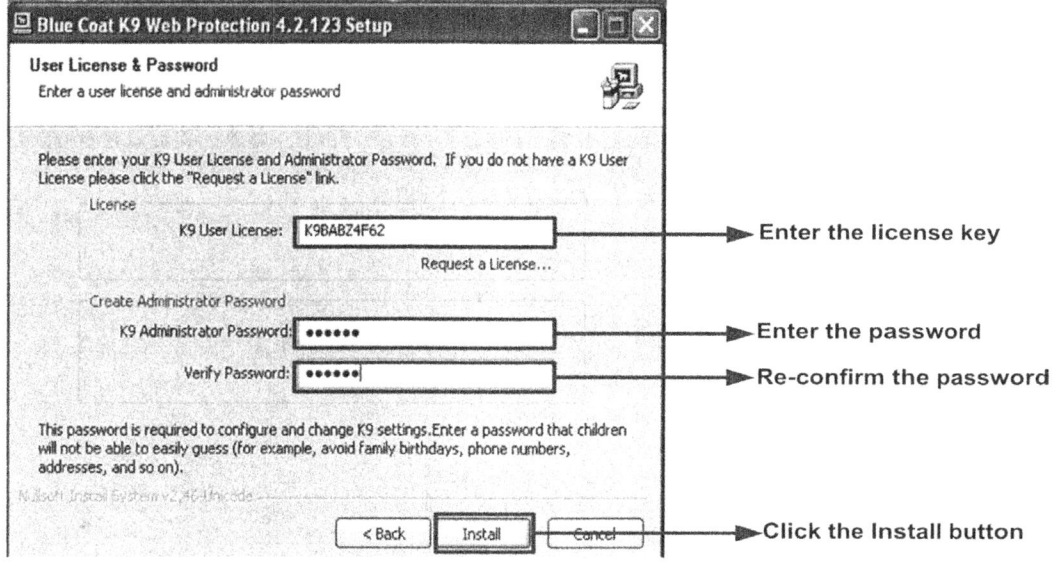

Figure 11.6 License key and Administration account for BlueCoat K9 Web Protection

6. When the BlueCoat K9 web protection gets installed, it will prompt you to re-boot. Confirm the installation by clicking the "Finish" button and the computer will reboot, as shown below:

Figure 11.7 Installation finish setup for BlueCoat K9 Web Protection

Administrating and configuring the BlueCoat K9 Web Protection

In this section we will show how to administer and configure BlueCoat K9 web protection to tweak the setting per your requirements. It is a very simple GUI-driven interface which allows you configure policies with minimum effort and protects the system from all malicious sites.

The first step is to log in to the administrator console of the K9 web protection. Please follow the steps as shown below:

1. Go to Start --> [All] Programs --> Blue Coat K9 Web Protection --> Blue Coat K9 Web Protection Admin to open he K9 Web protection interface. A web page will open in the default browser that you configured, as shown below:

Figure 11.8 Launching BlueCoat K9 Web Protection

As you can see in the above figure, the BlueCoat K9 Web protection runs on port 2372, which is the administrator port where K9 Web protection runs.

2. One you hit the "Setup" icon, you will get a password page where you can enter the password to log in to the administrator console. This is the same password you created when installing K9 web protection, as shown below:

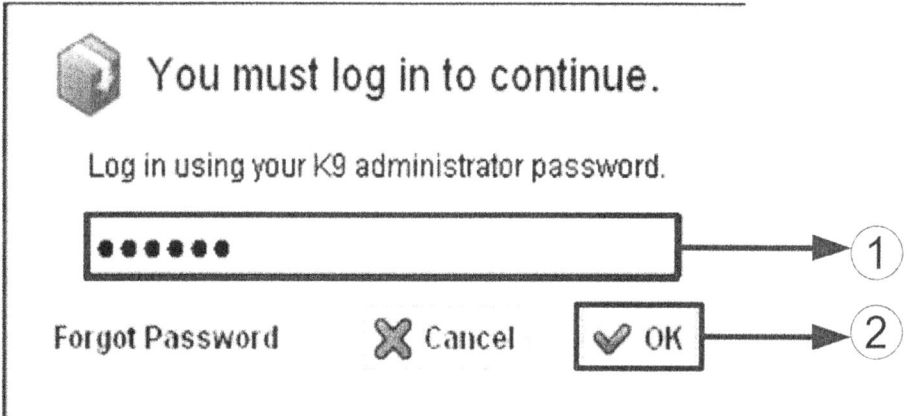

Figure 11.9 Administration credentials for BlueCoat K9 Web Protection application

Once when you have entered the correct credentials, you will see the administrator page as shown below:

Figure 11.10 Administration Portal for BlueCoat K9 Web Protection application

In this section we will discuss the different options that you can configure in the K9 web protection for our yown requirements. Each options is described below:

1. Configuring the Web categories:

After you have entered the credentials, you will see the "Web Categories to Block" page with the "Default" as the protection mode. In the center of the page, you will find all the main categories that are blocked. These are the categories that are grouped for the "Default" mode as shown below:

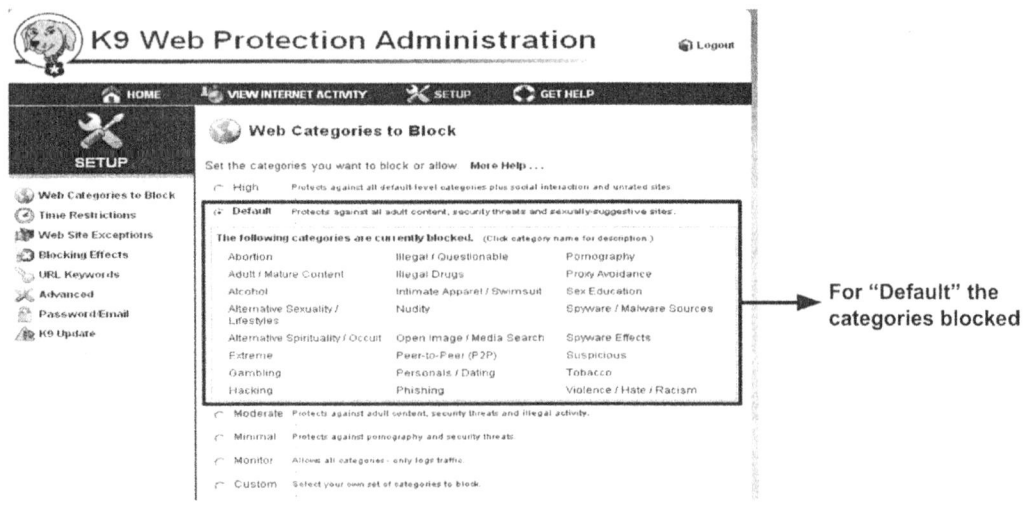

Figure 11.11 Default blocked categories for BlueCoat K9 Web Protection

You can check each mode for the list of categories that are blocked. There are High, Moderate, Minimal, Monitor, and Custom modes. You can check each of the mode and see which categories are blocked; for example, click "High" and check the list of categories that are blocked, as shown below:

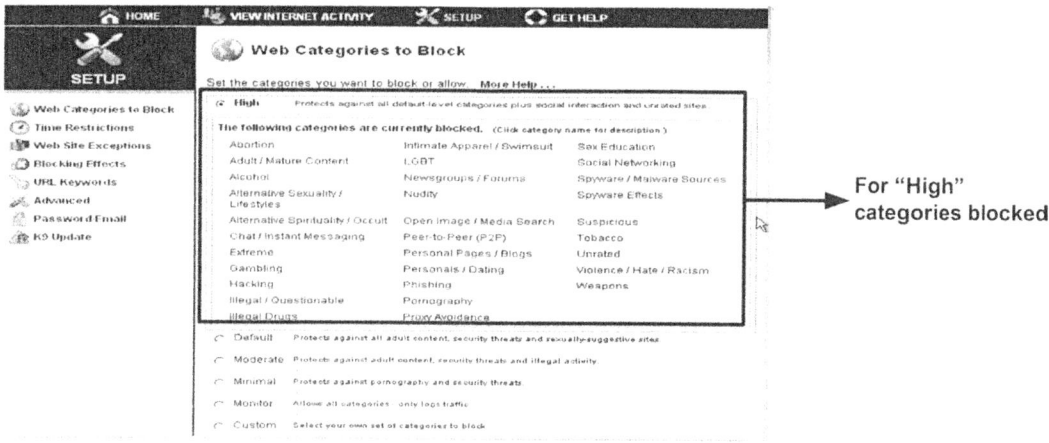

Figure 11.12 The "High" mode blocked categories for BlueCoat K9 Web Protection

If the whole list doesn't have the group of categories that you want, then you can create a "Custom" category by clicking the "Custom" option at the bottom of the screen, selecting the categories that you want to block, and clicking "Save" to save the changes, as shown below:

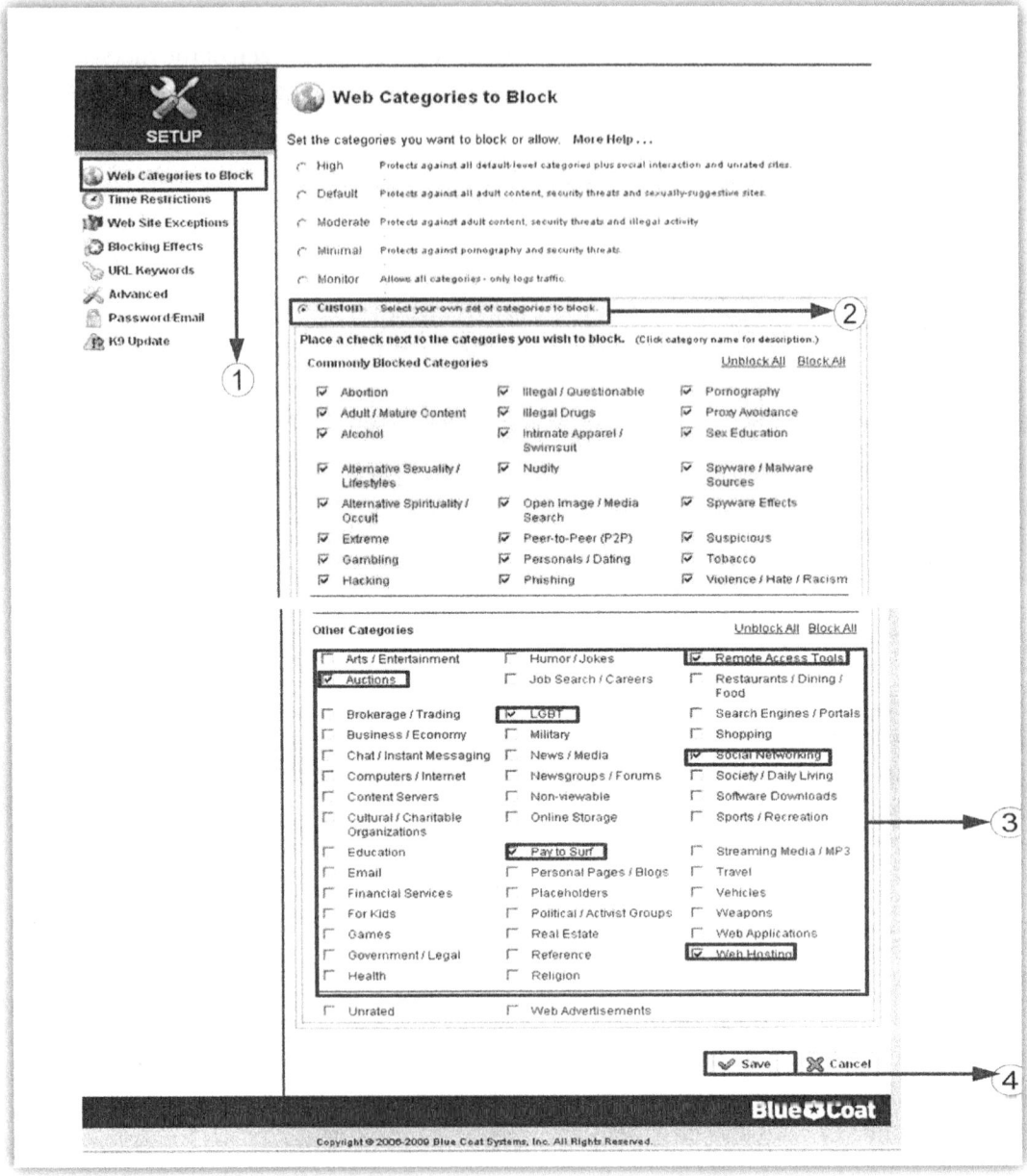

Figure 11.13 Configuring custom categories for BlueCoat K9 Web Protection

2. Time restrictions:

The time restrictions are used to allow or block Internet access based upon time values. This is a very useful option because you can control the access based upon time values. There is also a feature called "Night Guard" in K9 web protection, which blocks Internet access completely for certain time period. Say for example that you want to block all

Internet access from 10:00 p.m. to 7:00 a.m. to make sure that your kids don't try to access malicious content during the night when you are asleep. There are also custom-configured options which allows you to add the time frame from Sunday to Saturday the whole week schedule and fine tune in such a way only for certain hours the Internet is available which makes a complete control to the Internet for the kids. To configure this option, log in to the administrator console and "Time restrictions" on the left panel. The default is "Unrestricted". Here you could change to the "Night Guard" feature as shown below:

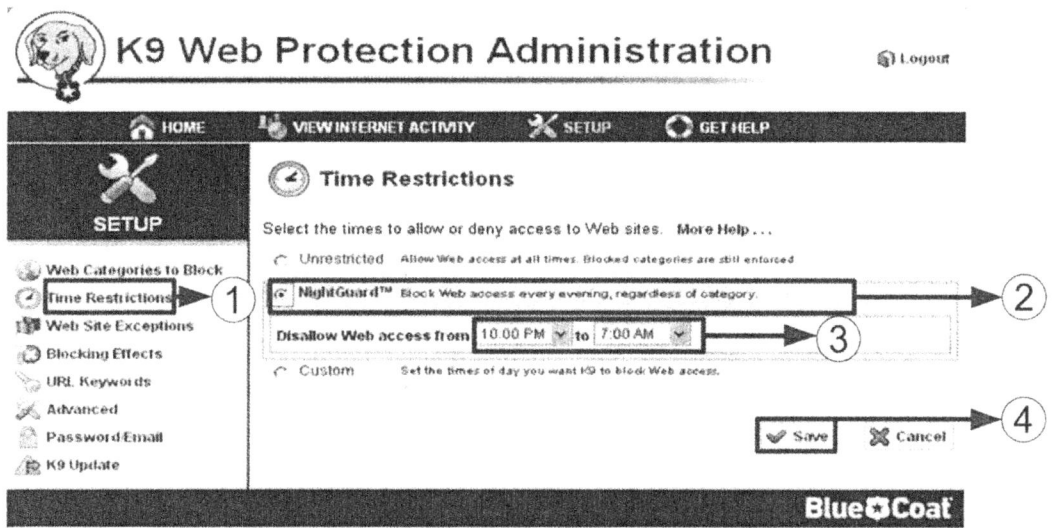

Figure 11.14 Night Guard options for BlueCoat K9 Web Protection

To allow custom access for certain hours in a day and for the whole week, use the "Custom" option and select the different time frames that you need and right-click on the timestamps, and select "Allow Web Access" or "Deny Web Access" as shown below. The light red color shows the different time frames that have been selected.

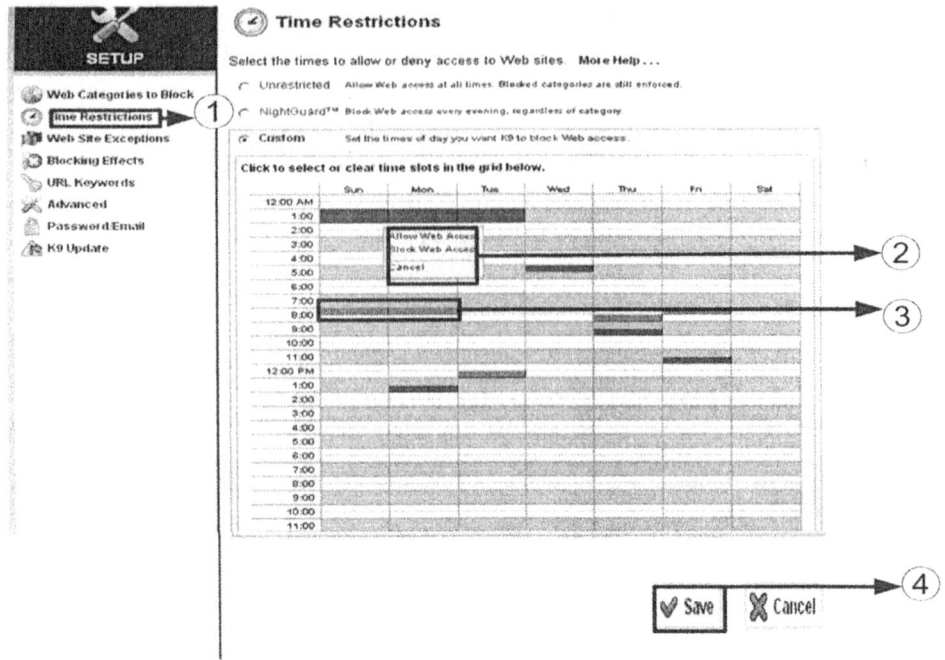

Figure 11.15 Custom time restrictions configuration for BlueCoat K9 Web Protection

3. Website exceptions:

You can allow or block certain websites that you need to access based upon your requirements. Though whole categories are allowed or denied, you can create exceptions based upon our requirements. This is similar to the exception rule that you created in the BlueCoat Proxy SG. To do this, log in to the administration console, and go to "Web Site Exceptions" on the left panel. Enter the sites in the "Web Site to Add:" section and click the "Add to list" button to add. Click "Save" to confirm the changes, as shown below:

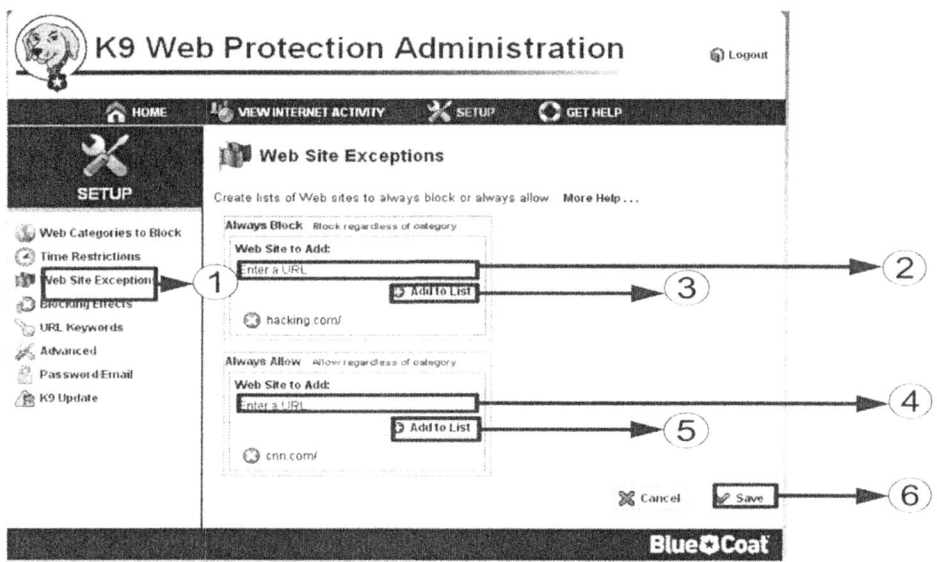

Figure 11.16 Website Exception configuration for BlueCoat K9 Web Protection

4. Blocking effects:

When a site gets blocked, there are three that can take effect:

a. Barked when Blocked
a. Show Admin Options
a. Enable Timeout

All the three options cn be configured by logging in to the administrator console and going to "Blocking Effects" on the left panel. You will the screen shown below:

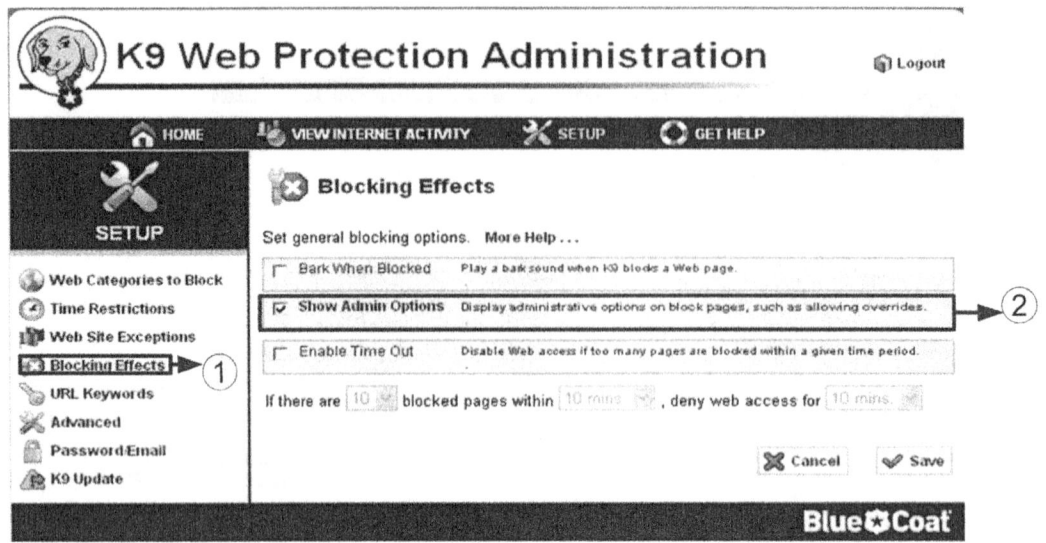

Figure 11.17 Blocking effects in BlueCoat K9 Web Protection

a. Barked when Blocked:

When a site gets blocked or denied, it will sound a barking dog. This will helps the parents to hear the audio of barking when the site is blocked and aware that the kids or users try to accessing some content which is not appropriate. For this to work, make sure the speakers are always "ON" and on high volume, so the sound reaches the whole home.

b. Show Admin Options:

This is the default option that is selected. When a site gets denied, you can simply override it by using the admin credentials for a certain amount of time or permanently. You can also allow the entire category that blocked that particular site for a certain amount of time or permanently. To do this you will need admin access—the one you used to log in to the administrator K9 web protection console. Usually this is done when the owner or the admin who is accessing the web needs complete access and wants to make sure they are protected by the web filtering system as well.

When a user accessing IE tries accessing the website www.proxy.org, he will get a denied page as shown below. There are admin options to override this block, as also shown in the figure below.

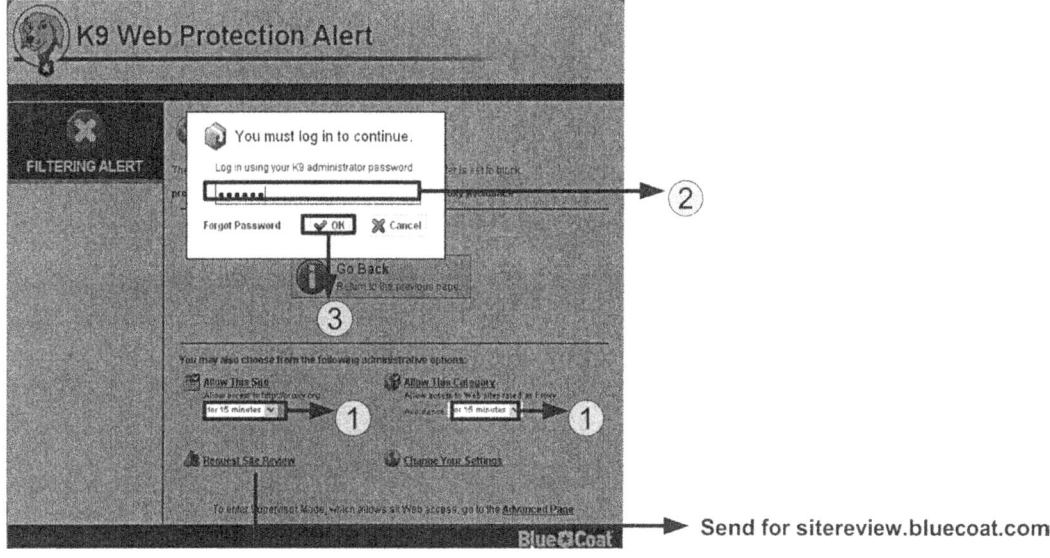

Send for sitereview.bluecoat.com

Figure 11.18 Overriding blocking effects in BlueCoat K9 Web Protection

c. Enable Timeout:

This option is used when a certain request to the site gets blocked and the user keeps trying repeatedly for a certain length time. Say a user tries accessing a malicious site 10 times within 10 minutes. You will find that such a request can block that site for a specific amount of time or permanently. The settings are shown in the following figure:

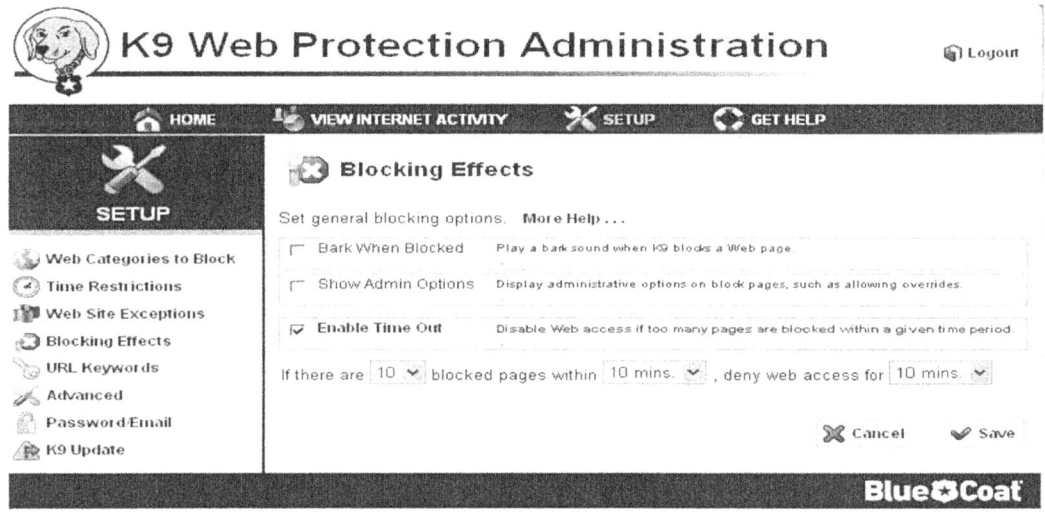

Figure 11.19 Timeouts for blocked pages in BlueCoat K9 Web Protection

5. URL Keywords

Certain keywords can be blocked in the URL. It is similar to a Regex(Regular expressions) operations that you want to block. This applies to both allowed and denied categories. To configure URL keywords, log in to the administrator console and go to "URL keywords" in the left panel. Add the keyword in the "Keyword to Add:" section and click "Add to List" to add to the list and "Save" to confirm the changes, as shown below:

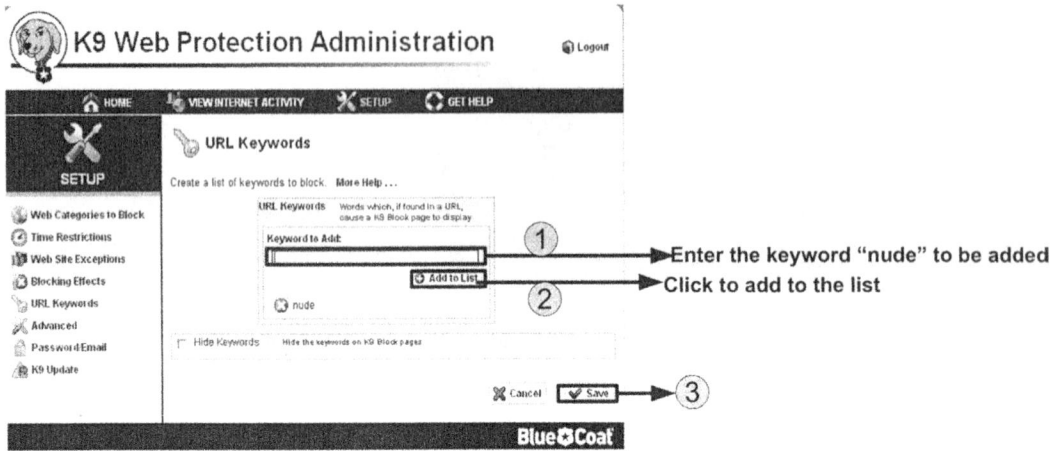

Figure 11.20 Blocking URL based on keywords in BlueCoat K9 Web Protection

Advanced Options:

There are a few advanced options that can be configured on the K9 web protection. Each option is discussed below:

1. Update to Beta:

If you want to update the K9 web protection with the new beta version you could use, usually don't enable this option because the beta version could be unstable and cause problems. Always download the stable version. The default setting for this option is disabled, as shown below:

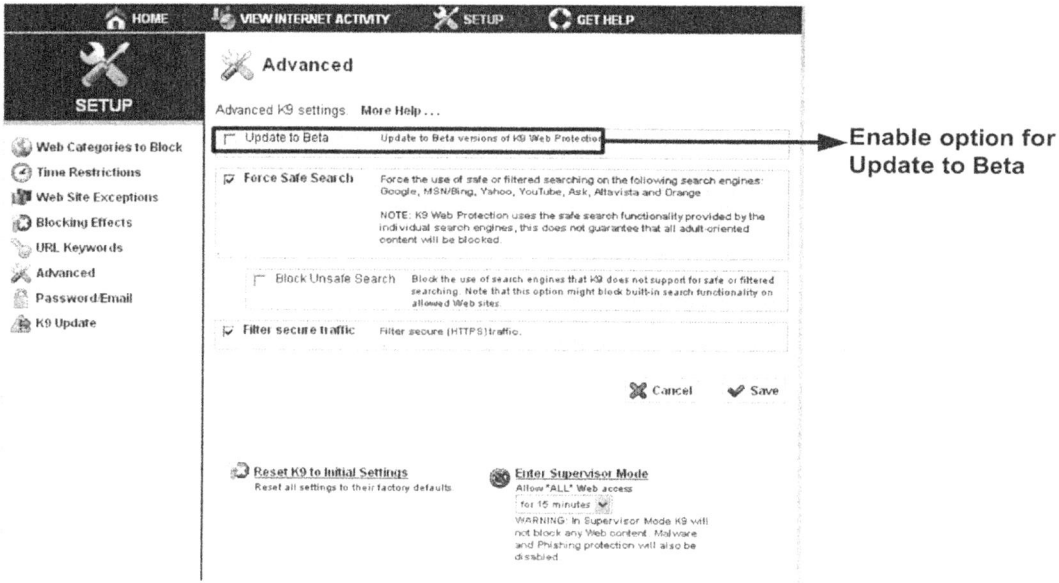

Figure 11.21 Beta update in BlueCoat K9 Web Protection

2. Force Safe Search

The Force Safe Search will enable the browser only to search engines that support strict search filters, and the filters themselves are based upon the capabilities of the search engine. For example, if a user tries searching for a keyword "porn", the search engine web page will typically display Safe search ON, Family filter ON, Safe search strict, or another engine-specific message.

The list of search engines that the K9 Web protection is enabled are as follows:

- A9
- Altavista
- MSN/Live
- Google
- Yahoo
- Ask
- Orange.co.uk

By default the Force Safe Search option is enabled.

Block Unsafe Search:

When Block Unsafe Search is disabled, the K9 web protection will prevent the use of a search engine that does not support safe search. If a user on your computer attempts to use a search engine that does not support safe search, the access will be blocked.

> Blue Coat recommends you enable both options. If you enable safe search but disable block unsafe search, users can get search results from unsupported search engines.

By default, "Block Unsafe Search" is disabled; enable the configuration for both options and save changes as shown below:

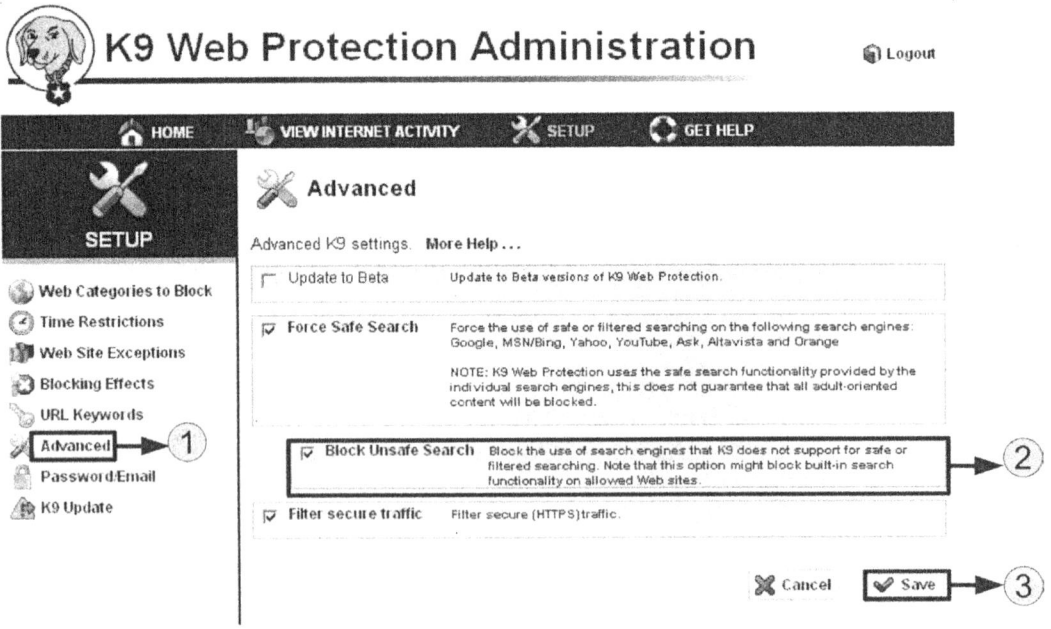

Figure 11.22 Block Unsafe Search BlueCoat K9 Web Protection

3. Filtering Secure Traffic

K9 Web Protection enables you to filter Hypertext Transfer Protocol Secure (HTTPS) protocol. HTTPS is referred to as a secure protocol because it uses encryption to prevent third parties from intercepting and reading the traffic between two entities, such as with online banking. By default Filtering Secure Traffic is enabled, as shown in the figure below:

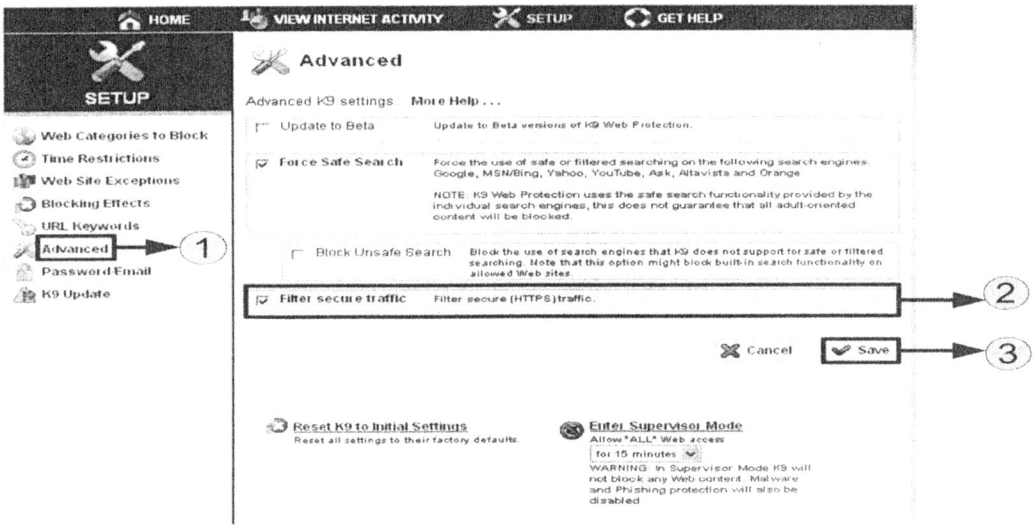

Figure 11.23 Filtering Secure Traffic in BlueCoat K9 Web Protection

4. Supervisor Mode

Supervisor Mode enables anyone using the computer to browse the Internet without any restrictions for a maximum of one hour. Before enabling Supervisor Mode make sure no one uses computer to access Internet, while the computer is unattended.

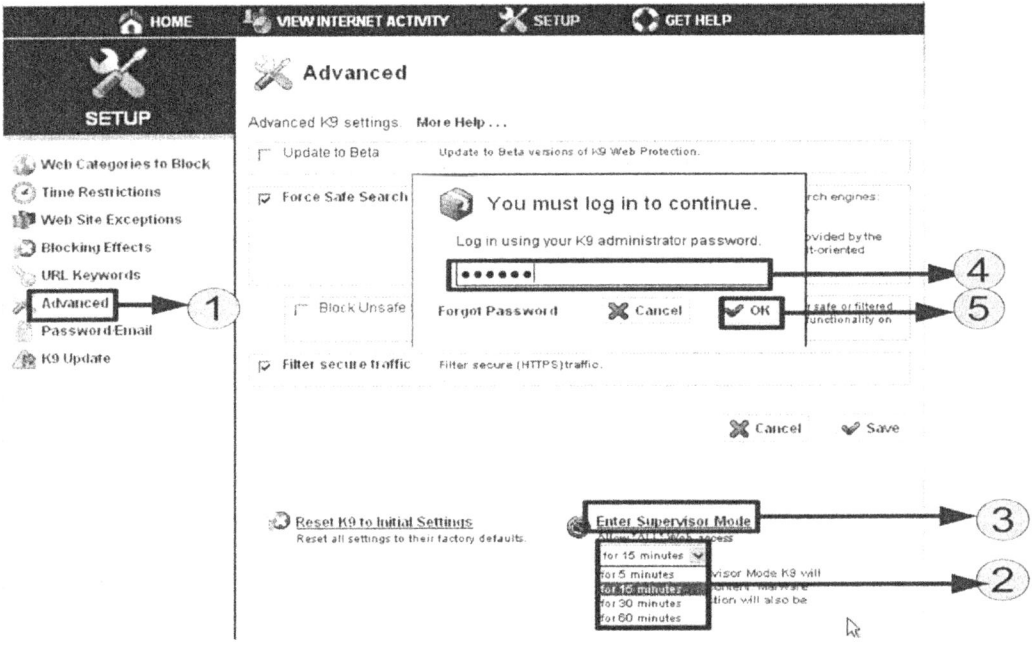

Figure 11.24 Supervisor Mode in BlueCoat K9 Web Protection

5. Reset to Initial Settings:

If the K9 Web Protection software is not functioning like you expected or if you believe someone has misconfigured or tampered with certain administrator settings, you can return K9 Web Protection to its original settings. The following option in the Advanced page below shows hows to reset to initial settings:

Figure 11.25 Resetting to Initial Settings

Internet activity:

If you want to review or monitor the Internet logs, K9 web protection provides an Internet activity tool, where you can monitor based on category, and URL requests. You can also view all the Admin events for all the activity changes that were made in the K9 web protection software. From any screen in the K9 web protection, click the option called "View Internet Activity" and you will get a screen of "View Activity Summary" as shown below:

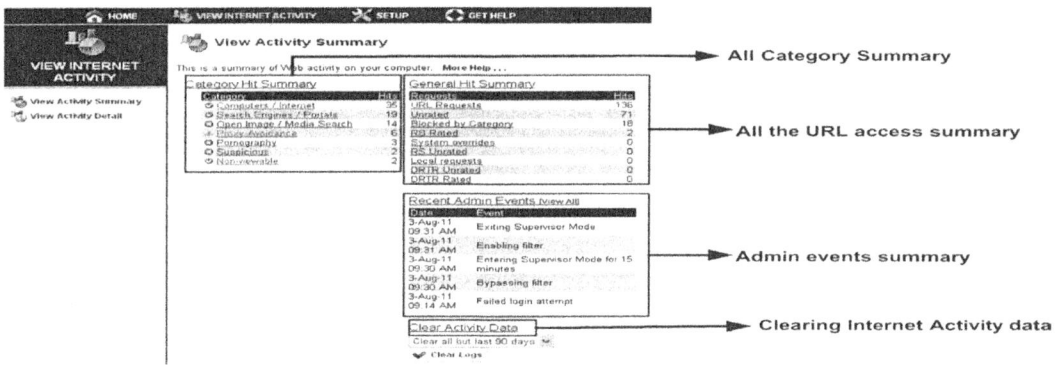

Figure 11.26 Viewing Internet activity summary

If you want view a detailed Internet activity, click the "View Activity Detail" in the above figure, and you will see all the logs and events that are either in days or month, as shown below:

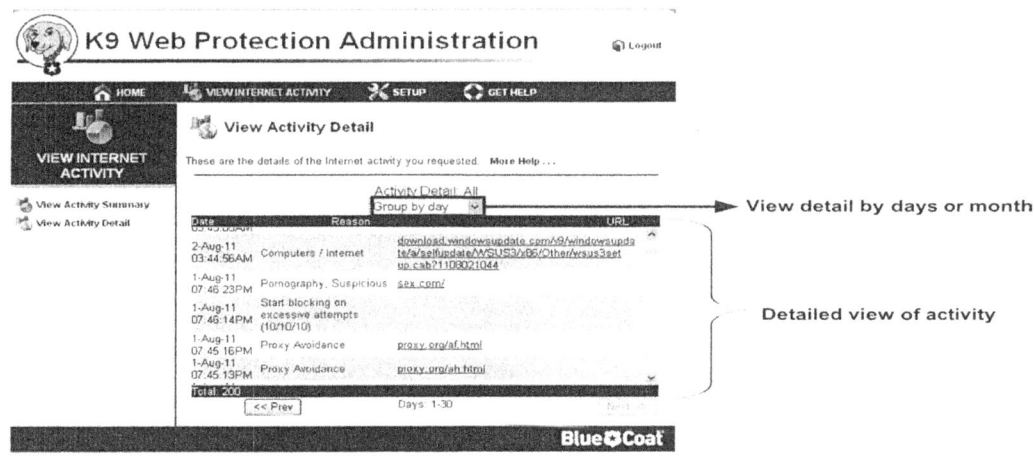

Figure 11.27 Viewing Internet activity detail

K9 Software update

If you want to update your K9 web protection to the latest software, use the "K9 Update" option, which will upgrade your software to the new version of K9 Web protection. When a new version of K9 web protection is available, it will show in the "K9 Update" page as shown below:

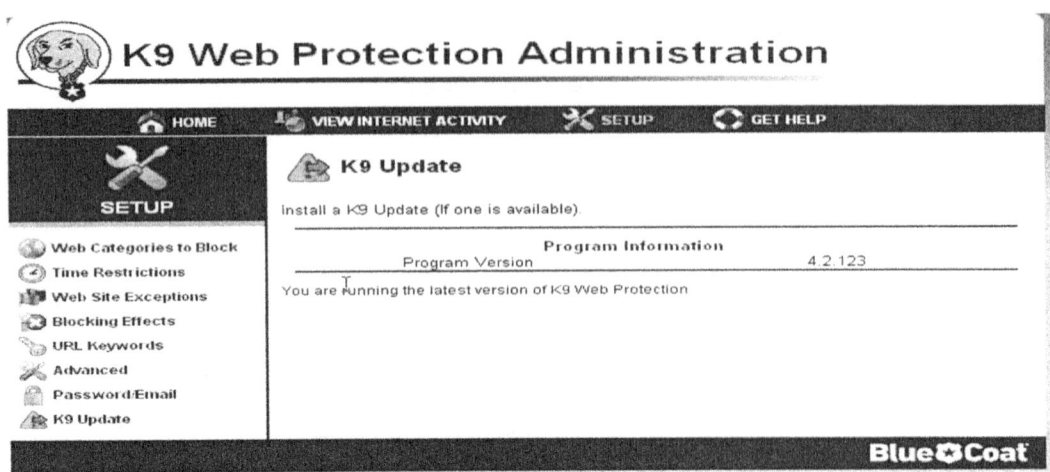

Figure 11.27 K9 update page for latest software

Figure 11.28 K9 update page for latest software

Right now there is no new software available and you are running the latest K9 web protection software.

Test Yourself

1. What is BlueCoat K9 web protection?

   a. A web browser
   b. A content-filtering database
   c. A security tool
   d. A security tool that contains content filtering

2. Can BlueCoat K9 web protection software be installed on MAC desktops, IPhones, iPods, and iPads?

   a. Yes
   b. No

3. If you want to block Internet access every nighttime for kids, what feature is available for this in BlueCoat K9 web protection?

   a. Supervisor mode
   b. Force Safe search
   c. Night Guard
   d. Blocking effects

4. Does the BlueCoat K9 web protection have the same filtering database as BCWF that is installed in BlueCoat Proxy SG?

   a. No, they are different.
   b. Yes, they are the same.
   c. Yes, they are the same and also contain the IWF database.
   d. Only certain categories are included.

5. If the "Block Unsafe Search" option is disabled in "Force Safe Search", what happens when the user accessing a search engine that is not supported by BlueCoat K9 web protection?

   a. The search engine is blocked.
   b. K9 Web protection redirects to the allowed search engine.
   c. c. The search engine is allowed.
   d. K9 Web protection enforces safe search for all search engines.

6. You are using a computer in which BlueCoat K9 web protection is installed. You have been blocked by certain website but you want to temporarily un-block it. What is the best way to override access?

   a. Supervisor mode
   b. Timeout options
   c. Night Guard
   d. Blocking effects using Admin options

7. You are using a computer in which BlueCoat K9 web protection is installed. You want to permanently unblock all sites for one hour. What is the best way to override access?

   a. Supervisor mode
   b. Timeout options
   c. Blocking effects using Admin options
   d. Night Guard

8. If you are a parent and always busy working and arranging the home and the kids are on the computer surfing the Internet and you next close to them, as you are in different room, what is the best way to be notified when the kids try accessing blocked sites?

   a. a. Email alerts
   b. Barking effect
   c. SMS to your phone
   d. View logs

9. Someone has made some hacked or changed your settings in BlueCoat K9 web protection software. What is the easiest way to recover the original settings?

    a. Reboot the computer
    b. Reinstall the software
    c. Reset to initial settings
    d. Change the administrator password

CHAPTER 12

··

TROUBLESHOOTING AND MAINTENANCE

TROUBLESHOOTING AND MAINTENANCE

In this chapter we will show how to troubleshoot BlueCoat Proxy SG, BlueCoat Proxy AV, and BlueCoat Reporter when configuring or installing these devices. We will cover all the skills required to fix problems when certain issues pop up or certain services are not functioning.

Troubleshooting Proxy SG:

In this section we will show how to troubleshoot the Proxy SG when a problems arises. Certain tools are built-in and a few tools are open source, which you can download and install in your desktop and use for troubleshooting.

1. Ping and Traceroute:

These are the basic networking commands used to check if the OCS is up and running fine. It is just a layer 3 testing of whether you are able to reach the device on the Internet or intranet and whether all traffic is routable. To use ping and traceroute, log in to the SSH console using PUTTY and type in the commands (shown in bold in the command prompt) as shown below:

Ping command:

CorporateProxy#**ping** www.bluecoatweb.com

Type escape sequence to abort.

Sending 5, 64-byte ICMP Echos to www.bluecoatweb.com, timeout is 2 seconds:

!!!!!

Success rate is 100% (5/5), round-trip min/avg/max = 100/102/110 ms

Number of duplicate packets received = 0

CorporateProxy#

In the above command, if the route, link, and interfaces are good, then you will get output as "Success rate is 100% (5/5)", as shown above. 5/5 means there is no packet drop. If you get other values, either there is a packet drop or some security device like the firewall or ACL enabled is blocking the request. But if you get 0/0, it means that either the link is down, there is some networking problem, or again the firewall is blocking the request. The best way to check is always ping the domain like http://www.google.com or http://www.yahoo.com, as they don't block ICMP traffic and also make sure that the outbound ICMP is allowed in your firewall.

Traceroute command:

The traceroute command is used for checking the network path between your Proxy SG and the OCS server. Here you can get the complete throughput of the path.

CorporateProxy#**traceroute** www.google.com

---------------------------------Output begin----------------------------------

Type escape sequence to abort.

Tracing the route to www.google.com

1 192.168.10.1 0 0 0

2 * * *

3 gig-0-3-0-17-nycmnyf-rtr2.nyc.rr.com 9 10 8

4 gig-5-1-0-nycmnyrdc-rtr1.nyc.rr.com 10 10 10

5 24-29-148-66.nyc.rr.com 12 11 9

6 107.14.19.24 10 12 10

7 ae-4-0.cr0.dca20.tbone.rr.com 24 16 15

8 107.14.19.135 16 15 ae-1-0.pr0.dca10.tbone.rr.com 15

9 74.125.49.181 39 39 41

10 216.239.48.108 85 216.239.48.112 17 120

11 209.85.248.73 26 209.85.248.75 23 209.85.248.73 25

12 209.85.254.237 24 209.85.254.239 25 209.85.254.233 25

13 216.239.46.78 32 64.233.174.182 28 216.239.47.34 24

14 qw-in-f103.1e100.net 25 24 25

----------------------------------Output End----------------------------------

2. HTTP commands:

You can use the HTTP test commands to check whether the proxy works in Layer 3 through Layer 7 and whether all functions are supported for the HTTP stack. Just type in the command "test http get www.google.com" as shown below:

CorporateProxy#**test http get www.google.com**

---------------------------------Output begin---------------------------------
Type escape sequence to abort.

Executing HTTP get test

* HTTP request header sent:

GET HTTP://www.google.com/ HTTP/1.0

Host: www.google.com

User-Agent: HTTP_TEST_CLIENT

* HTTP response header recv'd:

HTTP/1.1 200 OK   <--------------------------Note--------------------------- >

Date: Wed, 10 Aug 2011 23:58:54 GMT

Expires: -1

Cache-Control: private, max-age=0

Content-Type: text/html; charset=ISO-8859-1

Server: gws

X-XSS-Protection: 1; mode=block

Connection: close

Set-Cookie: PREF=ID=904a1817e8e536a1:FF=0:TM=1313020734:LM=13130207 34:S=HUmYYRUddHHy_bjA; expires=Fri, 09-Aug-2013 23:58:54 GMT; path=/; domain=.google.com

Set-Cookie: NID=49=naJ7DV1ouiGIyaDthdI189iVN8qN5QbvIJQpYPsBTKZh5
DP UGvqGseca8xKCLC1gfKMO880zdyJRLABDcjbkVZ9VI7Im56aTwEk6urR79
UWcQCuOxx8KsQSg_fpeEFyg; expires=Thu, 09-Feb-2012 23:58:54 GMT; path=/;
domain=.google.com; HttpOnly
Measured throughput rate is 76.75 Kbytes/sec
HTTP get test passed

-----------------------------------Output End-----------------------------------

As you see in the output line as marked as **"Note 1"** in the line "HTTP/1.1 200 OK"
which means that you are able to reach the OCS server, since a 200(OK) response means web
page found from the OCS server. Alternatively you could get 301 (Moved Permanently
redirection) or 302 (Found), which will confirm that the HTTP stack of the proxy is
working. You will get 301 when you just type in "test http get google.com" instead of
"test http get www.google.com"; that is, when you remove www from the google.com,
which will do a redirect. Try it!!!

3. Restarting the BlueCoat Proxy SG:

In situations were you need to reboot the BlueCoat Proxy SG when the Proxy SG gets hung
or not responsive, you will need to do a soft reboot. Follow the steps below to restart:

Using GUI:

Log in to the management console of the BlueCoat Proxy SG via https://
ipaddressoftheproxy:8082 and go to Maintenance à System and Disks à Tasks and click
the "Restart Now" button as shown below:

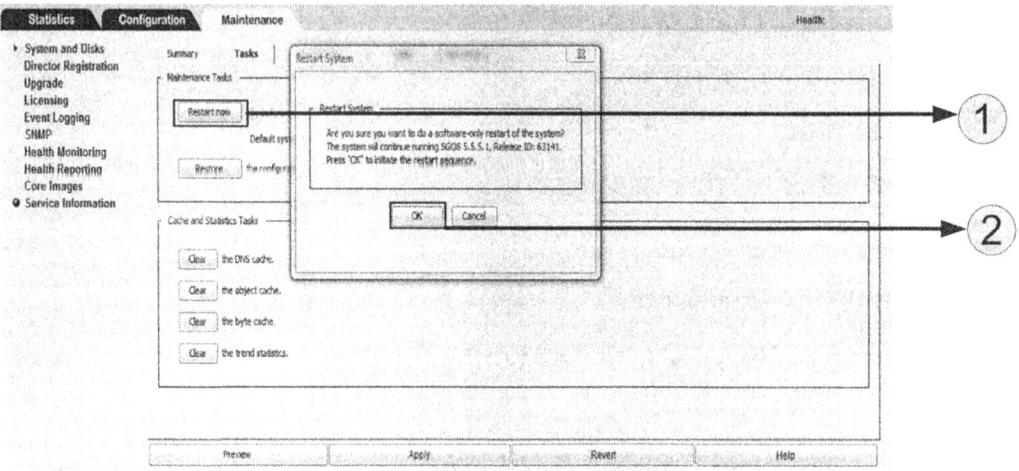

Figure 12.1 Restarting the BlueCoat Proxy SG

Then the BlueCoat Proxy SG gets rebooted. After the reboot, you can log in to the system via the GUI or CLI.

Using CLI:

In certain situations the Proxy SG management GUI hangs, and looking into the GUI becomes impossible. At that time you could use the CLI via the SSH console or the terminal console connection and run the command as shown below:

   CorporateProxy#**restart regular**

4. Backing up the BlueCoat Proxy SG

You need to back up the configuration of the BlueCoat Proxy S, since when the Proxy SG crashes and the configuration the system is lost, you will need to restore it. You can back up the configuration by using the Management Console. Just follow the steps below:

   Log in to the Proxy SG management console and go to Configuration à General à Archive à Archive Storage. Under the "Local Save" section, expand the tree Save Archive as "Configuration -expanded" and save as shown below:

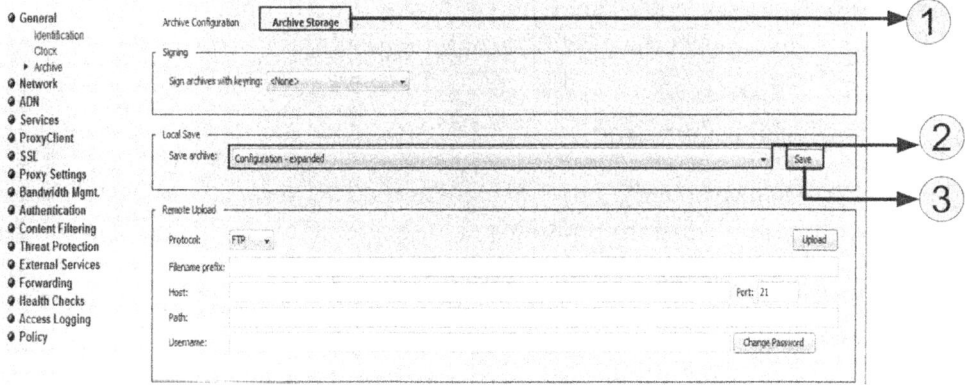

Figure 12.2 Backing up the BlueCoat Proxy SG

Once you hit the "Save" button as shown in the above figure, a windows pop-up will ask where you need to save the file. Save it as a .txt (Text File).

5. Restoring the backup in Proxy SG

If you need to restore the configuration in the Proxy SG, you will need to change the hash password and encrypted password in the saved backup file. As these are generated based upon the private keys that are present in the BlueCoat Proxy SG box. Since after the crash the keys are deleted and now a new key is being generated by the BlueCoat Proxy SG, so when you import the old configuration which contains encrypted keys that can only be decrypted by the old private key of the BlueCoat Proxy SGand now it is lost. So for this reason to use the old configuration with the new private key we will make all the passwords in simple text and import it. Follow the steps below to change the encrypted keys:

Remove all the words with "hashed-", or "encrypted-", and enter the real password instead of the encrypted password. To do this, open the saved Proxy SG back-up file in a text editor like notepad.

If you see entries like the following,

security hashed-enable-password "1GamH$AB7sR2Rx2mfN7qWLYm.yp/"

security hashed-password "1W91GNc$sRx3zQlVS9.X.kM9vnAbh/"

If the real password is "test123" then change the above encrypted password to "test123", and remember to use the quotes, as shown below:

security enable-password "test123"

security password "test123"

Do the above steps for all the entries that you see in the configuration file,where you find "hashed-", or "encrypted-" and remove it and then add the real password with the quotes.

After the above modification, you will need to upload the file. Log in to the Proxy SG and go to Configuration à General à Archive à Archive Configuration. Under the "Install Configuration" section, click "Local File" in the "Install Configuration from" option. Click "Install" and upload the modified configuration file.

6. Generating the Core file:

There are situations where the Proxy SG spikes its CPU several times a day, box crashes frequently, there are hardware problems or disk problems, etc. BlueCoat support will request that you generate a full core image file and upload it to BlueCoat. A Full Core file contains the entire contents from the RAM which is copied to the hard disk and saving it. Without a full core dump, the RAM content will get erased after the reboot. To save the content and to know the exact problem that caused the issue, you do a full core dump. If a Proxy SG is having some problem, first make sure that the "Full Core" is enabled; by default only the "Context only" mode is enabled. To enable Full Core, log in to the management console and go to Maintenance → Core Images and select "Full" as the option and "Apply" the changes as shown below:

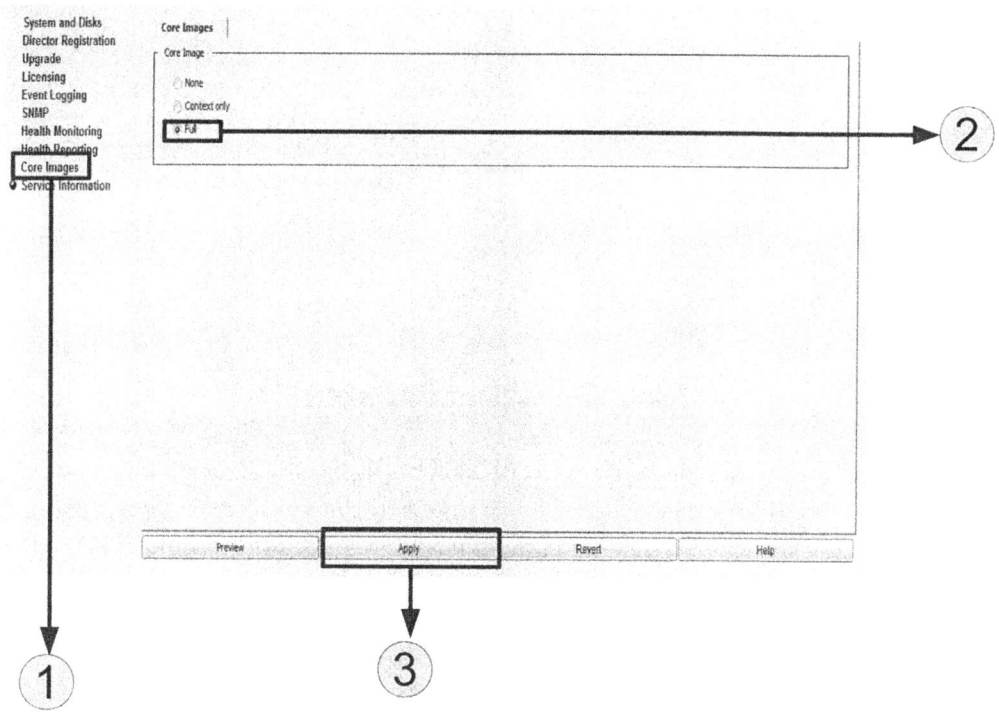

Figure 12.3 Generating Core files in Proxy SG

Let's imagine that a problem occurs and the BlueCoat CPU is spiking and the Internet access to the users is slow and responsive. You have enabled the Full Core option as shown in above figure. Now you have to go to the CLI using SSH or use serial connection and type the following command:

CorporateProxy#**restart abrupt**

Then the system will starting dumping all the RAM contents into the disk. This will take 10 to 15 minutes; it depends on the BlueCoat Proxy SG hardware, because the bigger the hardware the RAM size also increases, so it will take more time to dump the files with large RAM to the hard disk.

Once the system restarts, you can check whether the core dump went fine by going to the following URL: https://192.168.10.101:8082/CM/Core_image. You will see the file that is generated for the Full Core if it is generated, as shown below:

ProxySG Appliance Core Image Statistics

Version 10.0

System cores:

Time	Version	Hardware Exception	Software Exception	Page Fault Address	Process		
Thursday August 11 2011 01:55:08	5.5.5.1.63141	0x0	0x6001a	0x0	Process "CLI_Worker_1" in "kernel_shim.dll" at .text+0xcc3	Details; Minicontext (37888); Context (60864540); Full (1076737440)	Delete
Thursday August 11 2011 00:49:28	5.5.5.1.63141	0x0	0x60019	0x0	Process "CAG_Maintenance" in "kernel_shim.dll" at .text+0xcc3	Details; Minicontext (37888);	Delete
Thursday August 11 2011 00:43:49	5.5.5.1.63141	0x0	0x60019	0x0	Process "CAG_Maintenance" in "kernel_shim.dll" at .text+0xcc3	Details; Minicontext (37888);	Delete
Thursday June 16 2011 00:57:22	4.2.7.1.32941	0x0	0x4803d	0x0	Process "CLI_Worker_0" in "ce_admin.dll" at .text+0x62ff	Details; Minicontext (37888);	Delete
Wednesday June 1 2011 02:16:03	5.2.3.3.32845	0x0	0x4803d	0x0	Process "CLI_Worker_0" in "ce_admin.dll" at .text+0x678b	Details; Minicontext (37888);	Delete

➤ Full Core file

Figure 12.4 Core image Statistics Proxy SG

Now you need to upload the core file to BlueCoat support. The easiet way to do this, if the Proxy SG has an Internet connection, is to go to the management console via GUI and go to Maintenance → Send Information → Send Service Information. Then enter the service request number which BlueCoat support would have given you when you opened a ticket in the "Service Request Number:" column, select the contexts to be uploaded, and send the information to BlueCoat as shown below:

Please wait during the process of a full core dump, do not reset the power of the BlueCoat Proxy SG manually, if it takes more time. Else the Full Core dump is not created, and makes sure the process itself is a little time-consuming.

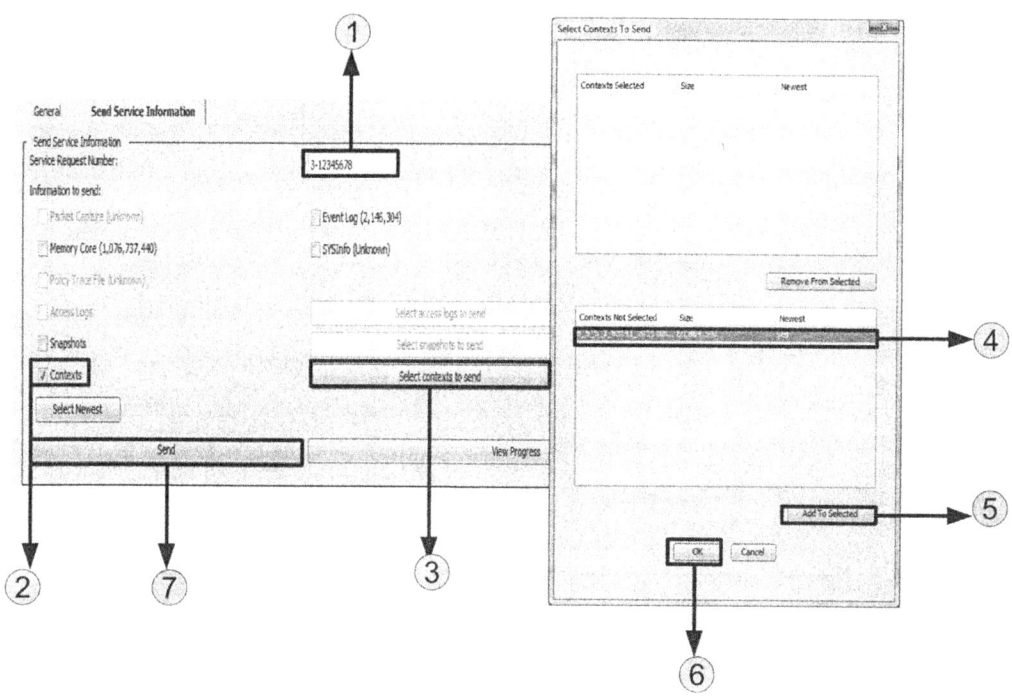

Figure 12.5 Uploading Core Images

7. Packet capture

The packet is the one of the most important concepts when troubleshooting Proxy SG. The packet capture will capture all the raw data that is transferred in the wire to the Proxy SG, which you can collect it as a PCAP format, which you can download from the Proxy SG and open the file with tools like WireShark for analyzing the data. To take the packet capture, go to the management console and go to Maintenance → Packet Captures. Click "Start capture" and make sure the "Capture filter" is empty (this will make a wide-open packet capture). Once the data is captured, click "Stop capture" and then click "Download capture" and open the PCAp file in Wireshark. Then you can analyze the data, which is the PCAP format, and see the frames of the packet and understand exactly what is happening in the data transfer between client/servers and the Proxy SG.

If you want to troubleshoot with certain specific filters, in order to avoid the buffer of the BlueCoat Proxy SG being filled, then you will use filters. The maximum data that can be captured is 100 MB in any Proxy SG. So the different filters you can use with the PCAP file are the following formats:

ip host 192.168.10.140 ----------------------------------- > For specific IP address, either
client or server

port 80 --- > For specific port number to
be captured

ip host 192.168.10.140 and ip host 192.168.10.141 ------ > For two specific IP addresses

An example is shown below of how to apply the filter and take the packet capture:

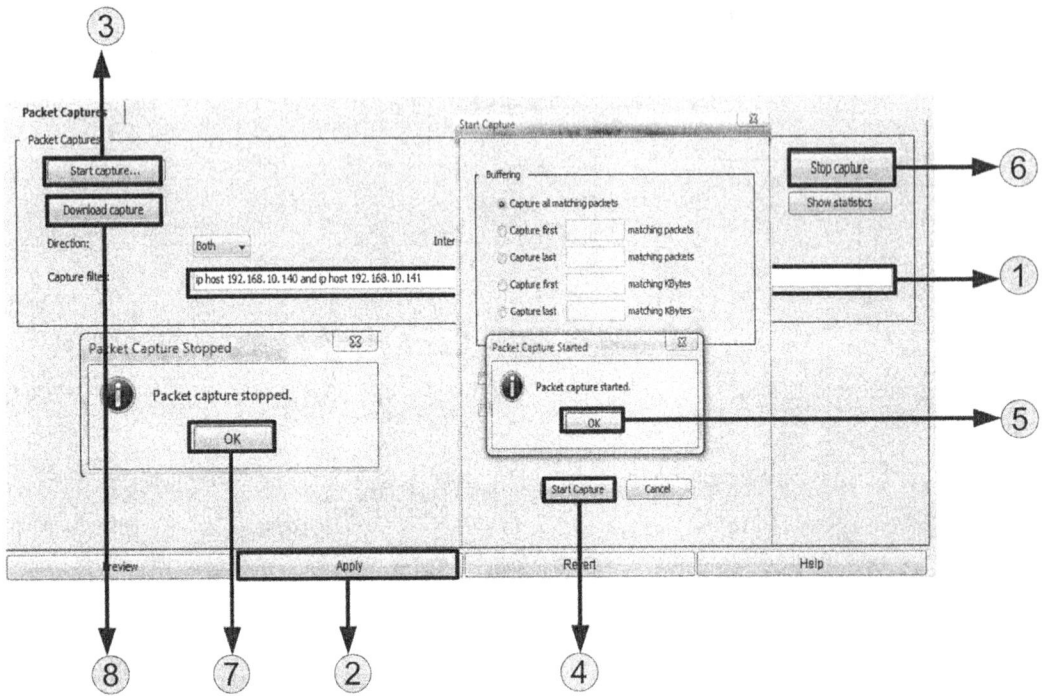

Figure 12.6 Packet Capture in Proxy SG

8. Policy Trace

The important troubleshooting tool in the Proxy SG is the policy trace, is used to troubleshoot users' access to websites. A policy trace is an application trace that evaluates the VPM and local, central, and forward policies that you built and shows the order of execution of each layer. When there is match for allowed or denied user access, this is shown in the policy trace. You can understand which layer in the policy is blocking the user access and add or delete the appropriate policy to allow access for the user.

Delete or disable the "Web Authentication layer", that we built in the Chapter 7, as it makes us to easily understand the policy trace., For some readers who have not included the layer in the policy just ignore the disabling of "Web Authentication layer".

To enable the the policy trace, please follow the steps below:

1. Add the policy trace to the VPM policy that you created earlier in this book. Launch the VPM and go to Policy → "Add Web access layer" and name the layer "Corporate Policy Trace".

2. On the source column, add the IP address of the user for whom you want to run a trace. Right-click the source and click "Set" → "New" → "Client IP Address/Subnet". Enter the IP address, such as 192.168.10.250/255.255.255.255, and click "OK" to confirm it.

3. Then leave the destination as "Any" unless you want to track a specific destination. Let the service column be "Any" and the time be "Any". Right-click on the "Action" column and click "Delete". Now the action should now be "None".

4. Now right-click on the "Track" column, and click "Set" and click "New". Select " Trace", and in the "Add Trace Object", enter the name "CorporateTrace" (it is user-defined). Then select "Verbose tracing" for the "Trace Level", select the check box for "Trace File", enter "trace.htm" next to it, and click "OK" as shown below:

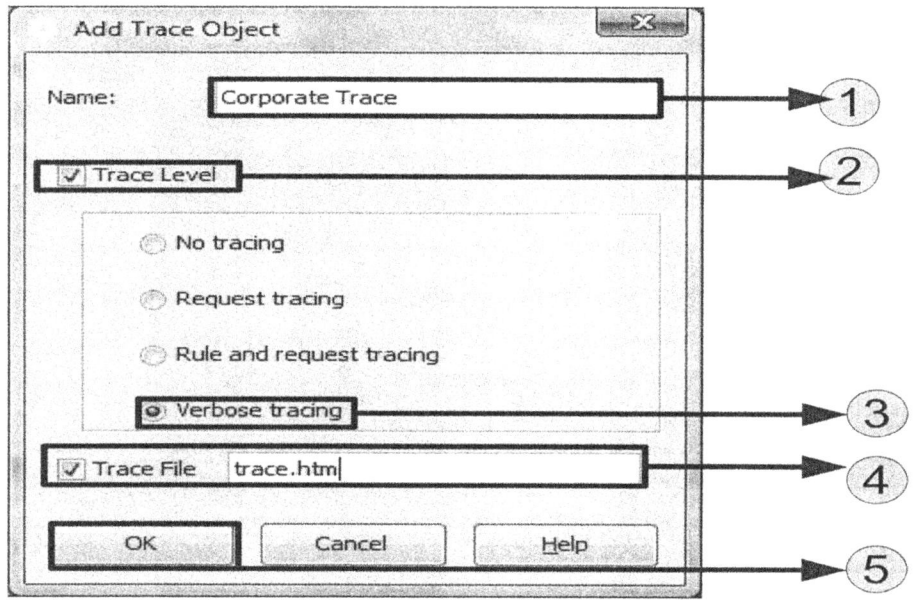

Figure 12.7 Adding a Policy Trace object

Now install the policy by clicking the "Install Policy" button in the toolbar. The final policy should look as shown below:

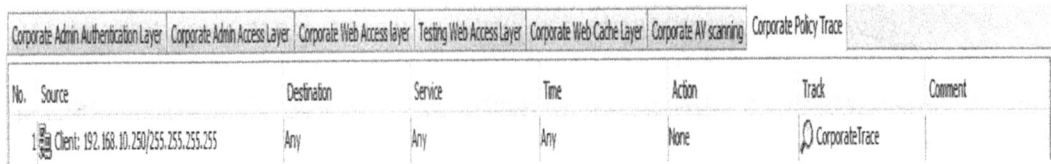

Figure 12.8 VPM policy for Policy Traces

Now to run and check the policy trace, go to https://192.168.10.101:8082/Policy/ and request the user to go to the site that is blocked, such as http://en.wikipedia.org, and you will have policy trace for the request. Then click the "trace.htm" link as shown below:

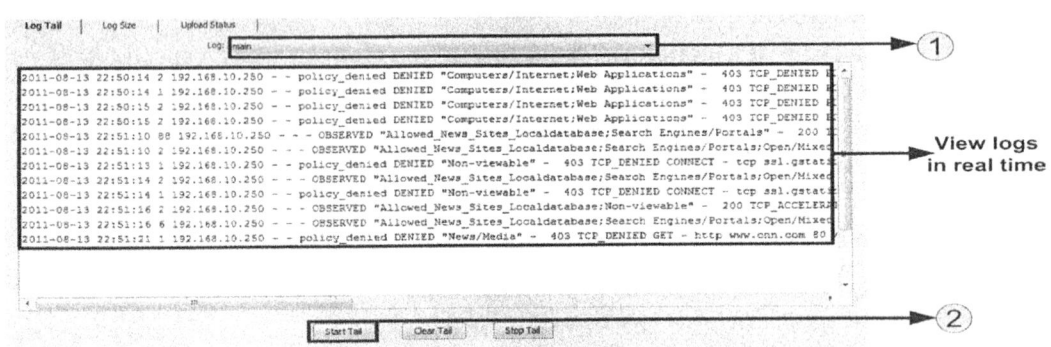

Figure 12.9 Viewing Policy Traces

Now you will examine the trace execution output as shown below:

start transaction ------------------   {1}
    CPL Evaluation Trace: transaction ID=15622
        <Proxy>   {2}
    miss : category=Denied_Sites_Localdatabase
    miss : category=(Allowed_News_Sites_Localdatabase, AV_Scan) {3}
    miss : client.address=192.168.40.0/24
    miss : client.address=192.168.40.0/24
    miss : client.address=192.168.50.0/24
    miss : client.address=192.168.50.0/24
    miss : client.address=192.168.60.0/24
    miss : client.address=192.168.60.0/24
        <Proxy> {2}
    miss : url.domain=//video.google.com/

```
    <Cache>   {2}
  miss :  url.domain=//scottrade.com/
  miss :  url.domain=//yahoo.com/
  miss :  url.domain=//nsa.gov/
    <Cache>  {2}
  miss :  category=(Allowed_News_Sites_Localdatabase, AV_Scan, Brokerage/
Trading, Business/Economy, Computers/Internet, "Financial Services", "Real
Estate", "Web Applications") {4}
  miss :  condition="Corporate File Extension Blocked"
  MATCH:  request.icap_service(proxyavrequestgroup)     request.icap_service.
secure_connection[proxyavrequestgroup](no)
    <Proxy>  {2}
 MATCH:  client.address=192.168.10.250 trace.request(yes) trace.rules(all) trace.
destination(trace.htm)
  connection:  service.name=HTTP  client.address=192.168.10.250  proxy.
port=8080
 time: 2011-08-13 21:24:01 UTC
 GET http://en.wikipedia.org/  {5}
User-Agent: Mozilla/5.0 (compatible; MSIE 9.0; Windows NT 6.0; WOW64;
Trident/5.0) [6]
 user: unauthenticated   {7}
 DENIED: Default secure policy mode  {8}
  url.category: Reference@Blue Coat  {9}
 DSCP client outbound: 65
 DSCP server outbound: 65
```

stop transaction -------------------- {1}

{1} Start/Stop markers

A Start/Stop marker shows the beginning and end of a policy transaction. A transaction can be Web, FTP, SOCKS, etc. In this trace it is a web transaction. For every object that is accessed, a transaction is generated (HTML page, images, java script etc.).

{2} Layer markers

A layer marker is created when a new layer is evaluated in the policy. As you can see in the policy trace, only "<Proxy>" and "<Cache>" layers are created. And as you know, when you created the policy, you had admin layers. Those are not generated here; only <Proxy> and <Cache> layers will be created. These are the most popular layers.

The <Proxy> is created for the Web Access Layer, Web Authentication Layer, and the SOCKS Layer.

The <Cache> is created for the Web content Layer.

The <SSL> is created for the SSL Intercept and SSL Access layer.

So when these layers are evaluated and the corresponding and appropriate marker is created.

Note: Do not get mixed up the terms by the CPL layer naming convention for policies, with the policy trace.

[3] A miss condition

When troubleshooting, always search for the match condition and then the miss condition. This tells you that the access to http://www.en.wikipedia.org is evaluated against the rule and misses all the local databases as shown in the above policy trace: "miss : category=(Allowed_News_Sites_Localdatabase, AV_Scan)".

The same is for [4] the miss condition of all the allowed categoies in the policy "miss : category=(Allowed_News_Sites_Localdatabase, AV_Scan, Brokerage/Trading, Business/Economy, Computers/Internet, "Financial Services", "Real Estate", "Web Applications")".

[5] The user request

This is the actual request that the user tried accessing the site with, which is a GET request to http://en.wikipedia.org/. You will get an output as http:// for regular web connection, ssl:// for an intercepted SSL connection, and tcp:// for a tunneled connection.

[6] User-agent

A user-agent is the client that is used by the user to access the site. In this example, the user uses Internet Explorer 9 "User-Agent: Mozilla/5.0 (compatible; MSIE 9.0; Windows NT 6.0; WOW64; Trident/5.0)" to access the site http://en.wikipedia.org.

[7] User authentication

The user's request is unauthenticated, which means that no authentication is set. If there were authentication, you would have the trace as "user: name="cn=david,cn=corporate,d c=proxyauth,dc=com" realm=CorporateLDAP".

[8] Matched policy

In your policy you didn't use any force deny; and you are blocked by the Global Deny rule, and we could confirm in the policy trace as it shows "DENIED: Default secure policy mode".

[9] Actual category

This line shows the actual category that the request matched, that is http://en.wikipedia. org is "url.category: Reference@Blue Coat " BCWF Reference category.

So always make sure when you troubleshoot to look for the "match" keyword in the policy so you know where the request matches. A match may be allowed or denied; in the example http://en.wikipedia.org, it is denied. It will help you to trouble-shoot faster and save time..

9. Access Logging

You can view all the transactions that are taking place at a quick glance by viewing the access log in real time, while the logs still been forwarded to the reporter server. To view the access log in real time, go to the management console and go to Statistics →Access Logging, and in the "Log Tail" section select "Main" as the Log query and click "Start Tail" as shown below:

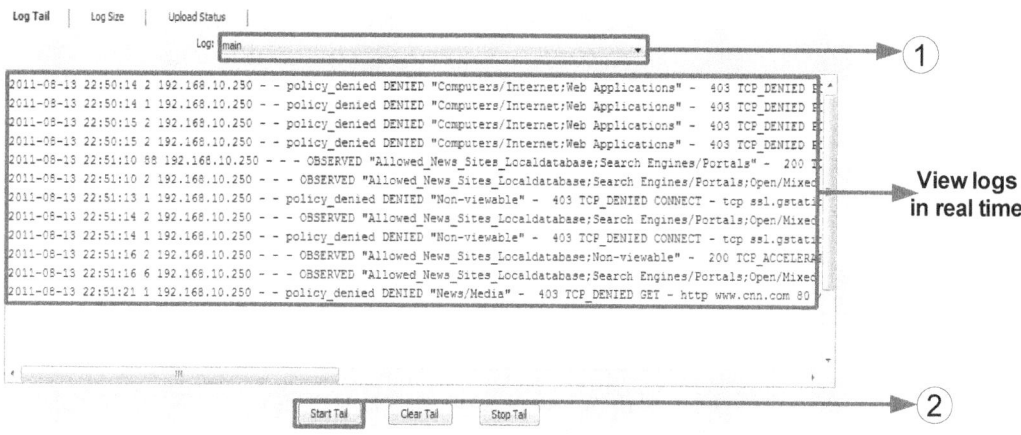

Figure 12.9 Viewing the Access Log in Proxy SG

10. Use Fiddler

Fiddler is a great web-debugging tool which is used by most web developers. You can download it from http://www.fiddler2.com/fiddler2/ and follow all the instructions to install it in the system. It is integrated with IE and Firefox, so as a BlueCoat Engineer, when you troubleshoot you can launch the tool and try accessing the problem website. You will get all the information regarding the different objects that have been accessed, the request and response headers, the time frame for accessing each object, the different HTTP codes (e.g., 200, 302, 307, or 403), the cache directive values, etc. The documentation and videos online are free for everyone. The documentation can be viewed at http://www.developer.com/lang/jscript/article.php/3631066 or http://msdn.microsoft.com/en-us/library/Bb250446.aspx. There is free online video which is a great value which shows how to use tool and you could have great understanding about the tool. You could view all the training videos at http://www.fiddler2.com/Fiddler/help/video/default.asp.

11. Health check

You can check the health of all the services you created, such DNS servers, ICAP servers, forwarding settings, authentication realm, etc. By default, every 10 seconds all the services that you manually created are monitored by the BlueCoat Proxy SG. Remember that these services are all the services that you created; remember the DNS settings you configured in Chapter 4, the ICAP settings in Chapter 8, the Authentication settings in Chapter 7, and DRTR settings that you created in Chapter 5. To view the "Health Check" go to Statistics → Health Checks → Health Checks as shown below:

Health Checks									
Current Time: 2011-08-15 19:10:51		Last Boot: 2011-08-15 18:56:09			Since Boot: 14.7min				
	Status		Last check			Since last transition			
Name ▲	State	When	Time (ms)	Duration	#Checks	Avg (ms)	Min (ms)	Max (ms)	
4.2.2.1	OK	19:10:45	12	13.8 min	82	75	11	5,023	→ DNS Server Health Check
hs.4.2.2.2	OK	19:10:45	13	13.8 min	82	103	11	4,537	
Prr.rating_service	OK	19:05:13	258	.	5	258	44	496	→ DRTR Health Check
icap.av.1requestmode	OK	19:10:48	5	12.8 min	77	76	5	4,926	
icap.av.1respondmode	OK	19:10:49	12	12.8 min	77	80	11	4,710	
icap.av.2requestmode	OK	19:10:42	5	12.9 min	77	35	5	1,913	
icap.av.2respondmode	OK	19:10:43	13	12.8 min	76	137	12	9,171	→ ICAP Health Check
icap.proxyav.requestgroup	OK	19:10:48	5	12.8 min	154	55	5	4,926	
icap.proxyav.responsegroup	OK	19:10:49	12	12.8 min	153	108	11	9,171	

Figure 12.10 Monitoring Health Check in Proxy SG

You have created an additional internal DNS server; this will also appear in the "Health check" menu, the internal DNS server hasbeen removed and the output only shows the public open DNS, for easier understanding.

> You have created an additional internal DNS server; this will also appear in the "Health check" menu, the internal DNS server hasbeen removed and the output only shows the public open DNS, for easier understanding.

12. CPU and disk usage

The CPU and disk usage can be monitored while troubleshooting. To check the CPU usage, go to the Management Console → Maintenance → Service Information → Summary as shown below:

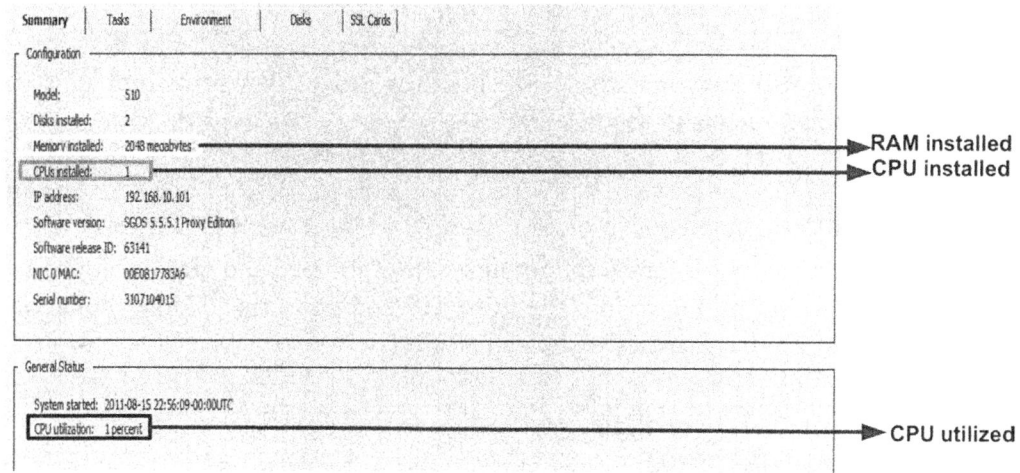

Figure 12.11 CPU and disk summary in Proxy SG

To check the disk status, go to the Management Console → Maintenance → Service Information → Disks as shown below:

Summary | Tasks | Environment | Disks | SSL Cards

Disks Installed

Disk	Status	Capacity	Vendor	Product	Revision	Serial Number
1	Present	320.1 GB	SEAGATE	ST3320620AS	3.AAD	[illegible]
2	Present	320.1 GB	SEAGATE	ST3320620AS	3.AAD	9QF4ZHXP

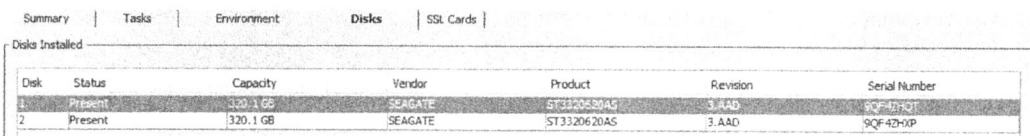

Figure 12.12 Disk summary in Proxy SG

To check the CPU, RAM, and interface usage, go to Statistics → Health Monitoring → General as shown below:

General

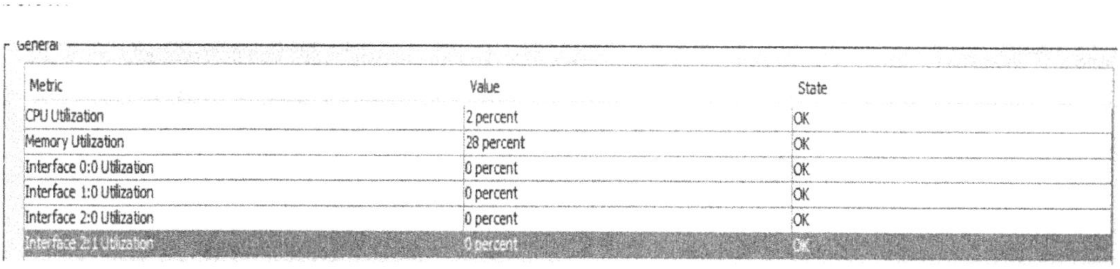

Metric	Value	State
CPU Utilization	2 percent	OK
Memory Utilization	28 percent	OK
Interface 0:0 Utilization	0 percent	OK
Interface 1:0 Utilization	0 percent	OK
Interface 2:0 Utilization	0 percent	OK
Interface 2:1 Utilization	0 percent	OK

Figure 12.13 Health monitoring of CPU, Memory, and Interface in Proxy SG

Troubleshooting Proxy AV:

In this section we will show how to troubleshoot the Proxy AV when a problems arises, with built-in tools which is in the PROXY AV.

1. Scan status:

If you want a quick review to know the amount of files scanned and viruses caught and to know the interface status, log in into the Proxy AV and go to the "Home" menu on the left. You will see all the statistics as shown below:

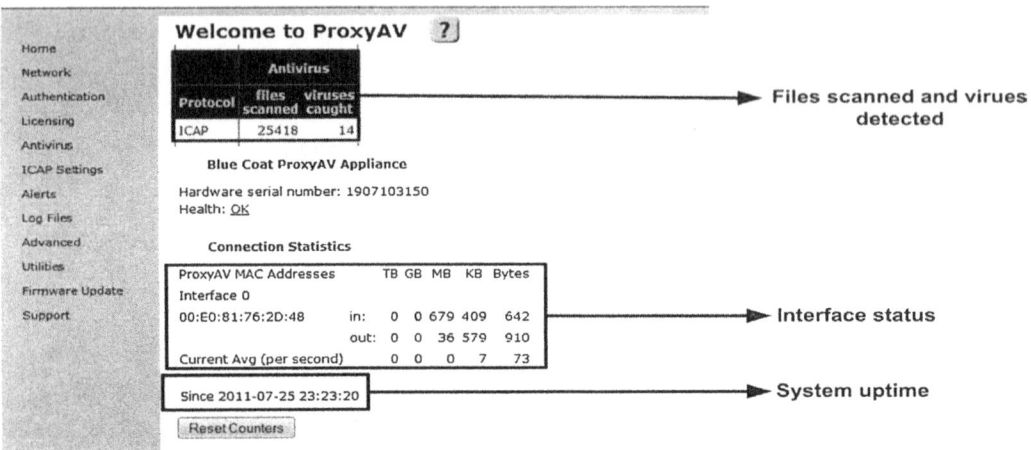

Figure 12.14 Overview of system statistics in Proxy AV

2. Network tools

If you want to use the ping utility or check for the ARP table, use the GUI management console of the Proxy AV. Always remember that you don't have the CLI interface for the Proxy AV; you only have the GUI management console.

To view the ARP table, in the Proxy AV management console, go to Advanced → ARP Table and you can view the ARP table as shown below:

ARP Table ?

IP	MAC	Interface	Flags
192.168.10.250	00:1D:BA:03:04:8D	Interface 0	
192.168.10.101	00:E0:81:77:83:A6	Interface 0	
192.168.10.1	C0:C1:C0:EE:6B:29	Interface 0	

Clear Arp Table   Clear Arp Table (incl. Static)

	: : : : :	Interface 0 ▾	Add

Figure 12.15 ARP table in Proxy AV

To use the Ping tool, in Proxy AV management console, go to Advanced PING utility and enter the IP address of the device for which you want check the connectivity, as shown below:

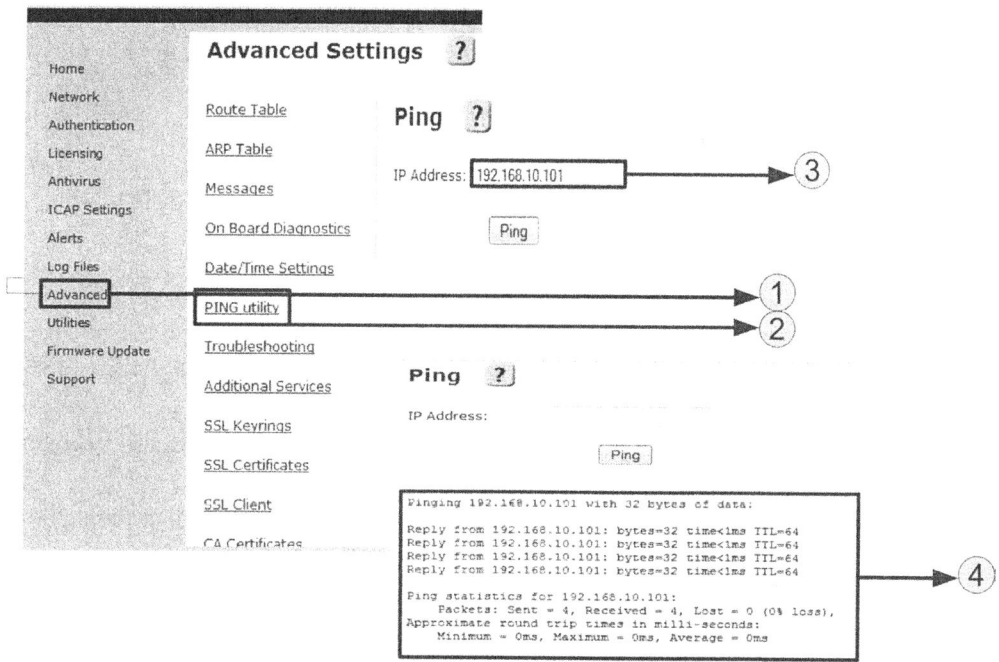

Figure 12.16 Ping Utility in Proxy AV

3. Detailed access logs statistics

You can view the access log statistics in detail regarding the time of access, the client IP address, whether the scan was clean or infected, the URI of the request, etc. To view the detailed access log statistics, go to Advanced → Detailed Stats, click the "Requests history" link, and you will find the statistics as shown below:

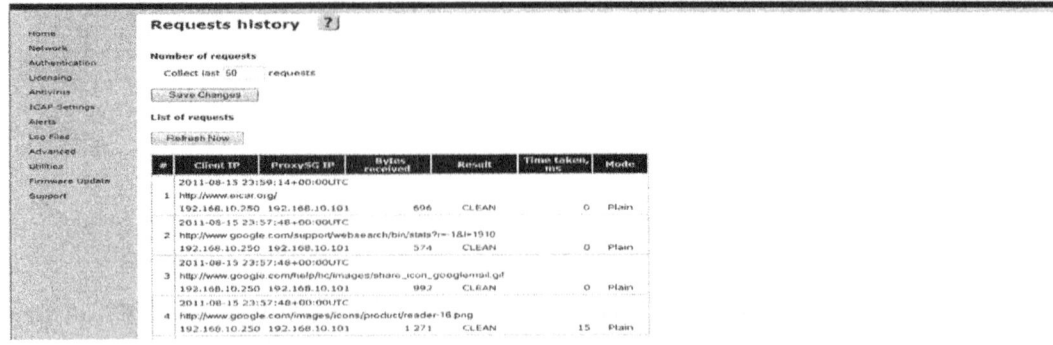

Figure 12.17 Detailed log statistics in Proxy AV

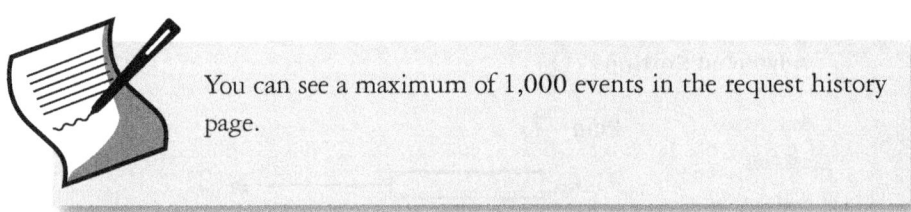

You can see a maximum of 1,000 events in the request history page.

4. Uploading Troubleshooting information

If you have a problem with Proxy AV like CPU, driver problems, or any hardware problem, in a similar way that you generated the core file for the Proxy SG, in the Proxy AV you can gather detailed debugging information and upload it to the BlueCoat Engineering team and allow them to analyze the files. To enable and upload the debug information, go to the management console, enable all the options for logging the debugs, enter the service request number which BlueCoat support would have given when opening a case. and upload the information as shown below:

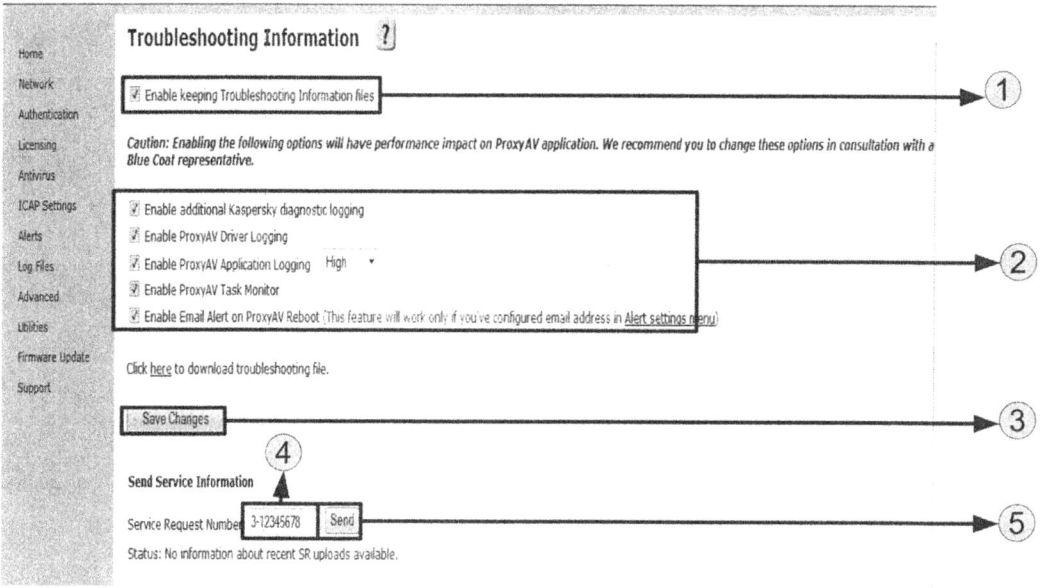

Figure 12.18 Uploading troubleshooting information to the BlueCoat team from Proxy AV

5. ICAP scanning problems

All the ICAP file scanning failures, such as timeout, file too big, and decompression errors, are logged in the AlertLogFile.log. When the AlertLogFile.log reaches 1 MB, it is renamed to "alert LogFile_YYYY_MM_DD_N.log" format and the AlertLogFile log starts over. When the total of the AlertLogFile log files reaches 35 MB, the ProxyAV begins deleting the oldest alert logs. To view the alert log files, go to Log Files and under the Log Files section you will see the Alert log files. All the names start with AlertLogFile*.log as shown below:

Log Files

File Name		
AlertErrors.log	The file contained no data	
boot.log	View log file in browser	Delete
2007-08-30-19-ProxyAV_Access.log	View log file in browser	Delete
2007-11-20-16-ProxyAV_Access.log	View log file in browser	Delete
AlertLogFile.log	View log file in browser	Delete
AlertLogFile_2010_07_28_1.log	View log file in browser	Delete
diagnosticS.log	View log file in browser	Delete
diagnosticT.log	View log file in browser	Delete

→ **Alert Log Files**

Figure 12.19 Alert Log files in Proxy AV

6. Boot and Diagnostic Logs

The boot log records all reboots of the machine, which can be used for troubleshooting the cause of the reboot. The diagnostic logs are used for debugging the Proxy AV for thread counts, scanning queue length, and periodic dumps of internal system information. These all will be used by the BlueCoat support team to diagnose the problems. There are two main diagnostic logs that can be analyze:

diagnosticS.log: This file can be used for analyzing the thread counts for Proxy AV scanning, the number of active threads, and scanning queue length.

diagnosticT.log: BlueCoat Proxy AV periodically dumps all internal information, so that you can analyze information regarding CPU, RAM, disk, processors, etc.

To view the information of boot.log, diagnosticS.log, and diagnosticT.log, go to the management console → Log Files. In the Log Files, section you can find log files as shown below:

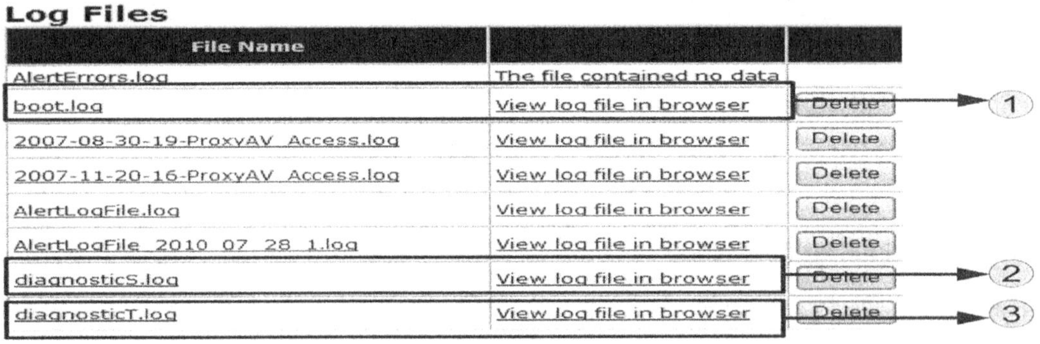

Figure 12.20 Boot Log and Diagnostic log files in Proxy AV

7. Rebooting/Reloading Proxy AV

If you want to reboot the Proxy AV at times when it gets hanged, so that we could produce diagnostics information about the cause. log After the reboot log into the management console of the Proxy AV and go to Utilities. There are several options there for the reboot, and each one is explained below:

Reload the AV Engine

The ProxyAV reloads its current AV engine by stopping and restarting it. This reboot is quick and reloads only the AV engine. When reloading the AV engine, the Proxy AV temporarily interrupts the TCP/IP traffic until the reload is complete.

Refresh Engine and Signatures

The Proxy AV refreshes the AV engine and the signature DAT files for processing the ICAP traffic with fresh codes. This is similar to reloading the AV engine, but here the signature also gets reloaded. When reloading the AV engine and signatures temporarily interrupt the TCP/IP traffic until the reload is complete.

Reload Drivers

The ProxyAV reloads its drivers. This reboot is faster and reloads only its drivers. This option should be used if you performed a configuration change that does not appear to be in effect. On reloading the drivers temporarily interrupts the TCP/IP traffic until the reload is complete.

Soft Reboot

This is a physical reboot of the Proxy AV, and a new entry in the boot.log occurs. The soft reboot temporarily interrupts the TCP/IP traffic until the reboot is complete.

Diagnostics

This Diagnostics reload will create a large and detailed log file that provides information for troubleshooting certain network configurations. This process is intensive and affects performance. This option should be performed when the BlueCoat support team requests you to do it and creates the internal diagnostics.

All of the above five reload options can be done via the management console by going to Utilities → Utilities, and you will the all the options as shown below:

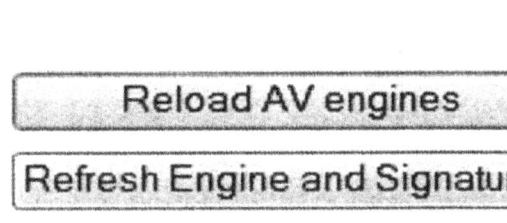

Figure 12.21 Rebooting/Reloading Proxy AV

8. Restoring the backup in Proxy AV

figuration",and click the "here" link and save the file in the local system as shown below:

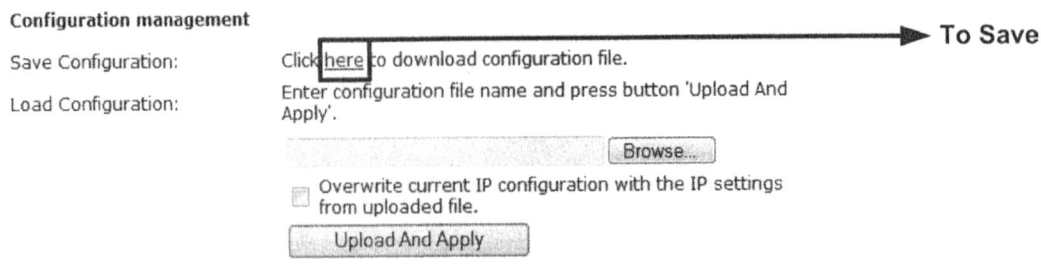

Configuration management

Save Configuration: Click here to download configuration file.

Load Configuration: Enter configuration file name and press button 'Upload And Apply'.

Browse...

☐ Overwrite current IP configuration with the IP settings from uploaded file.

Upload And Apply

To Save

Figure 12.22 Back up the configuration in Proxy AV

To restore the saved configuration, go to management console → Utilities → Configuration Management. Click the "Browse" button and choose the file from the local system where it is saved, and click the "Upload and Apply" button as shown below:

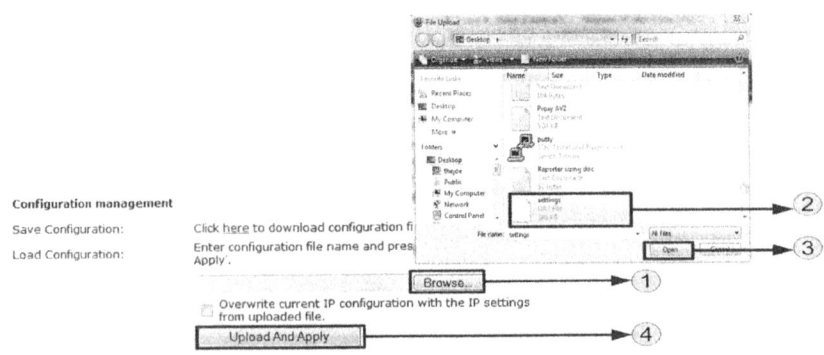

Figure 12.23 Restoring the backup in Proxy AV

Figure 12.23 Restoring the backup in Proxy AV

Troubleshooting BlueCoat Reporter:

In this section we will show how to troubleshoot and view the diagnostic information in BlueCoat Reporter. The other networking commands, system maintenance commands, are Windows or Linux dependent where the BlueCoat Reporter is installed. You should be well aware of using ping, traceroute commands, system disk size, patching the OS, etc. on both Windows and Linux OS.

To view, diagnostic and administration of the BlueCoat Reporter–can be done by first navigating to the "Administration" menu, after log in to the BlueCoat Reporter server using browser and go to http://ip addressofthereporter:8081/ , then click "Administration" at the top right corner of the BlueCoat Reporter portal as shown below:

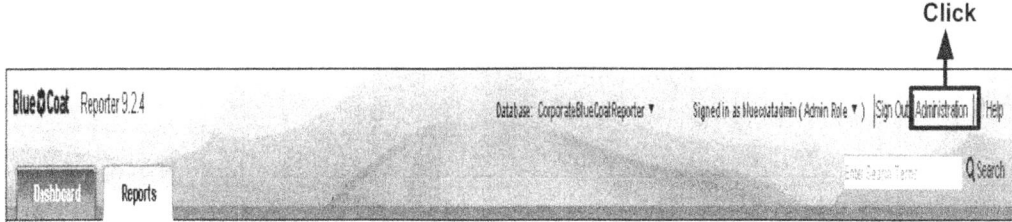

Figure 12.24 Administration tool in BlueCoat Reporter

Once you are in the "Administration" utility, you can view licenses, event logs, configuration, and diagnostics in the BlueCoat Reporter software. All this information is in this administration portal or utility.

1. System overview

You can view the system information regarding the CPU installed, disk storage, memory, OS type, license type, reporter version, and BlueCoat Reporter administration port. To view all this information, go to Administration → System Overview → System Diagnostics as shown below:

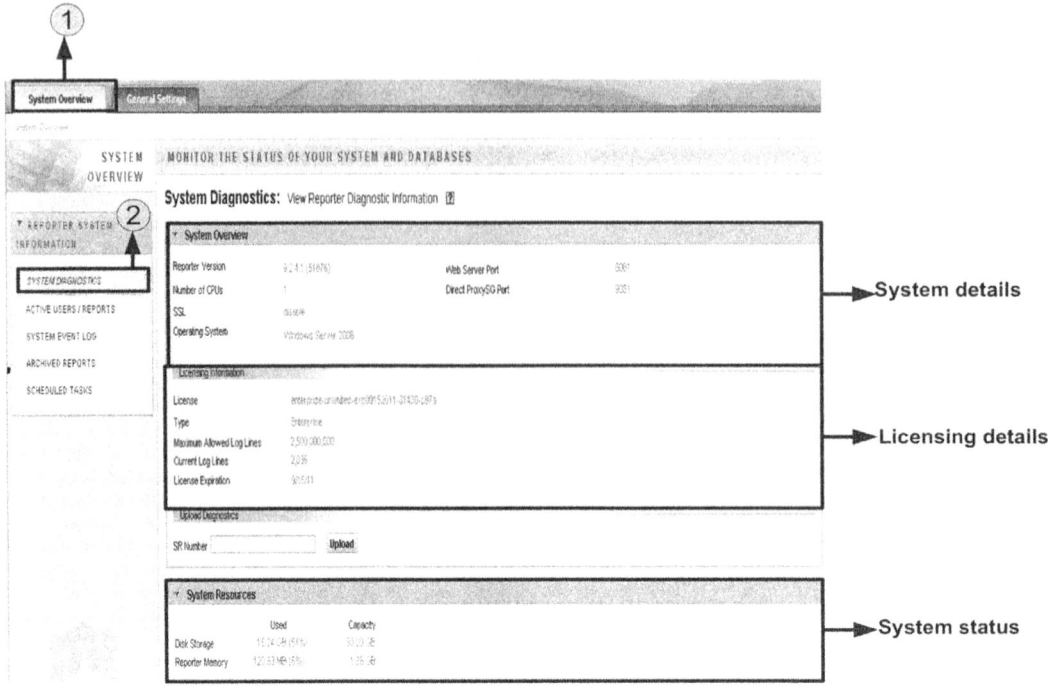

Figure 12.25 System Overview in BlueCoat Reporter

2. Uploading System Diagnostics

At times if there is some problem with the BlueCoat Reporter software, a general server hardware problem, a BlueCoat Reporter database problem, memory leaks, etc., you will need to send to the BlueCoat support team so they can evaluate and provide you the recommendation to follow to fix the problem . This is the same concept that we discussed when you uploaded the core file from the Proxy SG, debug files from Proxy AV. Go to Administration → System Overview → System Diagnostics → System Overview section and enter the service request number which was given by the BlueCost support team when you opened, the case as shown below:

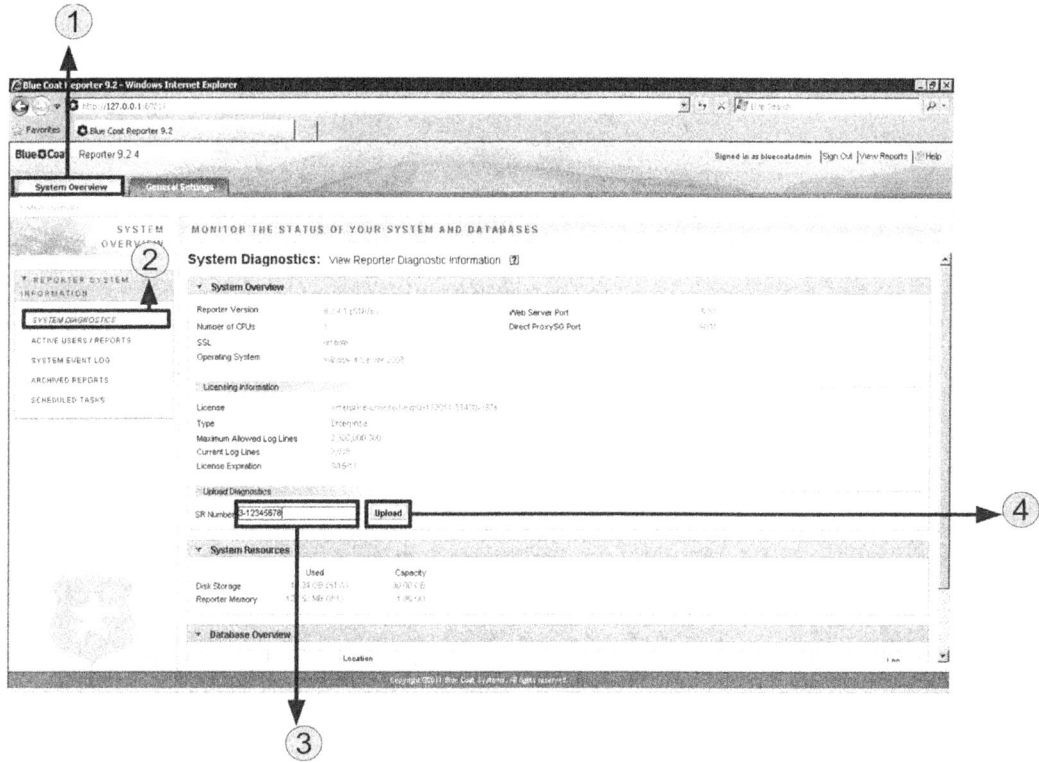

PH Uploading System Diagnostics in BlueCoat Reporter

Database Overview

If you want to view the BlueCoat Reporter database disk usage, bytes processed, lines processed, memory disk, etc., go to Administration → System Overview → System Diagnostics →Database overview section, and you can view the status of the BlueCoat Reporter as shown below:

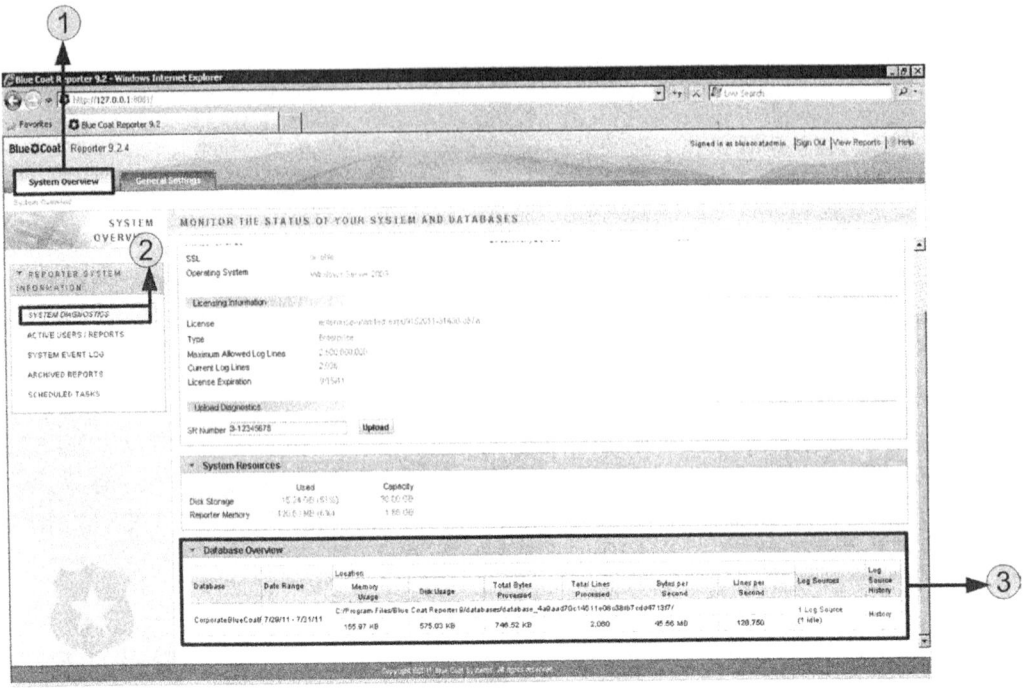

Figure 12.27 Database Overview in BlueCoat Reporter

Event logs

If you want to review the event log of the BlueCoat Reporter while you are troubleshooting to check all the administration actions, system event information, database logs, deleted logs, expired logs that all are recorded here in the vent log., This gives an information about the complete system activities.

Go to Administration → System Overview → System Event log → and you can view the event log as shown below:

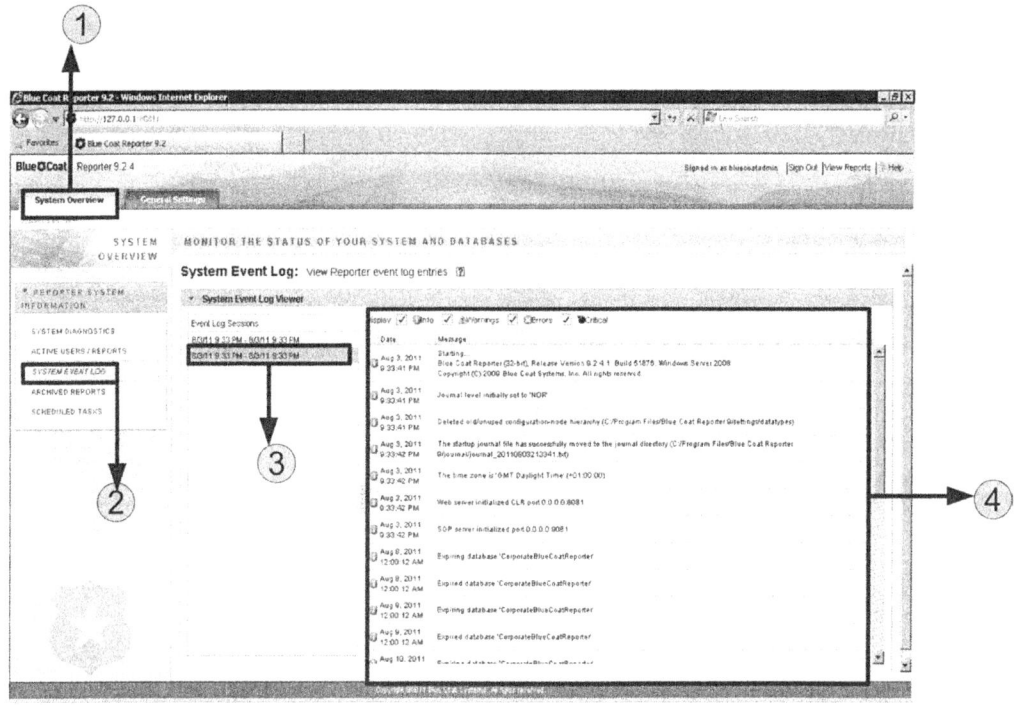

Figure 12.28 Viewing event log in BlueCoat Reporter

5. Loading and Unloading the database

If you want to work on the BlueCoat Reporter server for maintenance that requires in certain situationswe can unload the database. One instance is that if you apply patches to your Windows server and you need to unload the database first, after the patch is applied you need to load the database back again to the BlueCoat Reporter. To do this, go to General Settings →Reporter Settings →Data Settings → Databases and follow the steps as shown below:

When the database is unloaded, any administrator who is connected to the BlueCoat Reporter web portal will not able to run reports or perform queries.

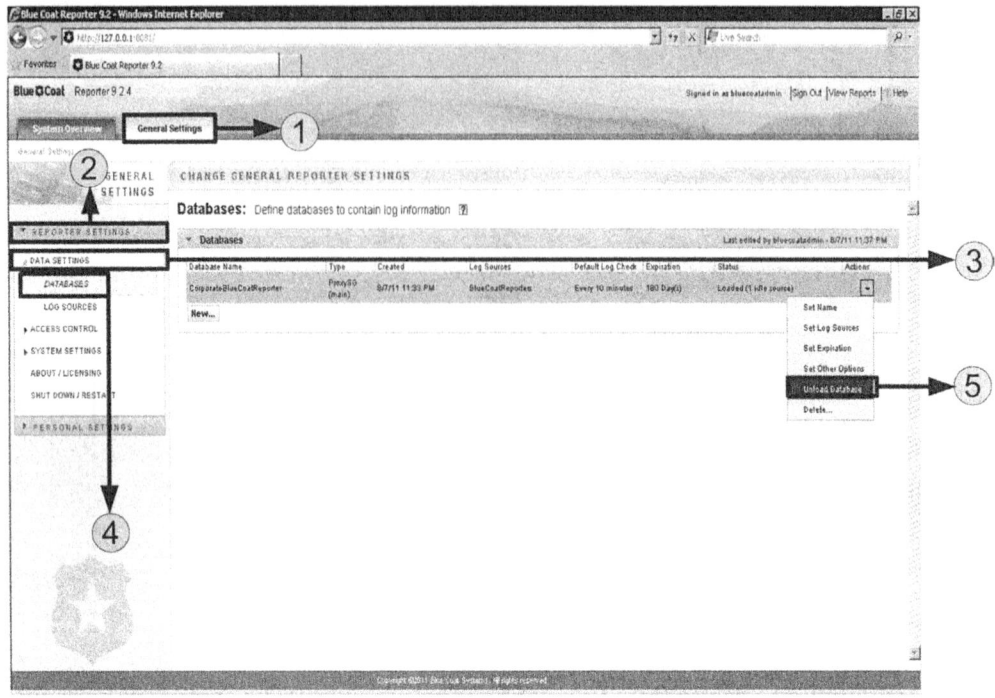

Figure 12.29 Loading and Unloading database in BlueCoat Reporter

Once you have unloaded the database, after the maintenance work you can load the database it by following the same steps as shown in the above figure, and at Step 5 you will have the option at this time to "Load Database".

6. Starting and Stopping Log source

If you want do some maintenance work on the BlueCoat Reporter server disks, you will need to stop the log source until some maintenance is completed. Once the maintenance is completed, you can start the logs sources, and all the BlueCoat Proxy SGs will start sending the logs back to the BlueCoat Reporter server. To do this, go to General Settings → Reporter Settings → Data Settings → Log Sources and follow the steps as shown below:

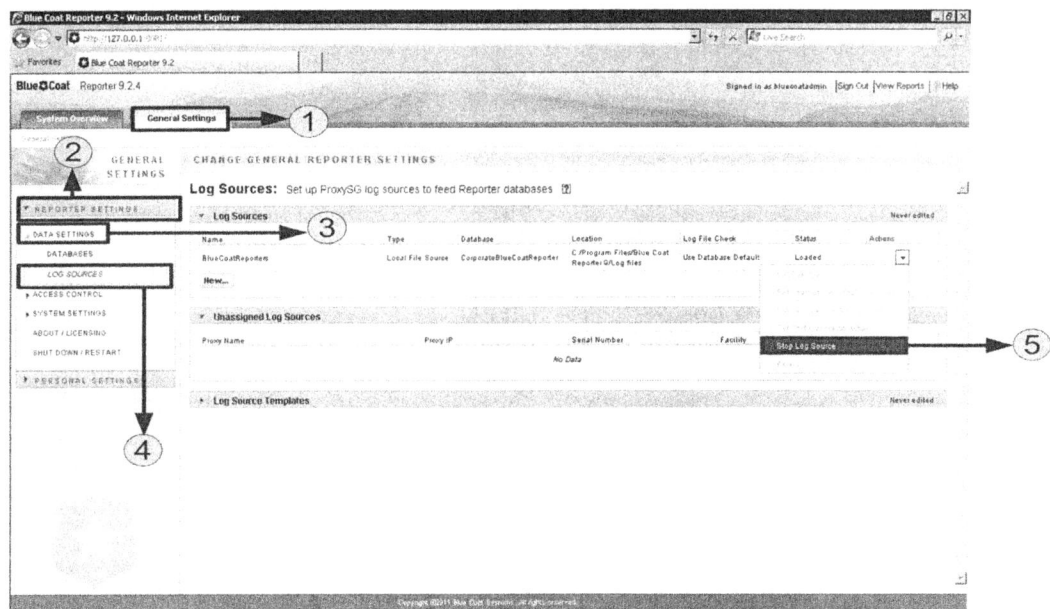

Figure 12.30 Starting and Stopping Log source in BlueCoat Reporter

> While you turn off the log source, all the BlueCoat Proxy SGs which need to send the logs will wait until the Reporter server log source is back. In the case that the log file size reaches its limit, then appropriate action is performed according to the setting that you configured such as delete old log files, if yes, then the log files are lost. So make sure that the maintenance work is scheduled for off-peak hours and performed quickly.

Once you have stopped the log source, after the maintenance work you can load it by following the same steps as shown in the above figure, and at Step 5 you will have an option to "Start LogSource".

7. Restarting/Shutting down the Reporter Server

If you need to restart or shut down the BlueCoat Reporter server for maintenance, go to 6button for restarting it or hit the "Shut Down Reporter" button to shut down the Reporter server completely.

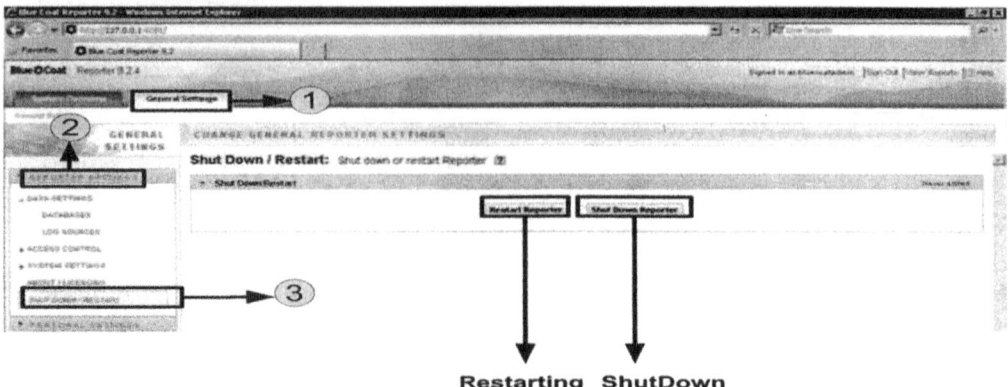

Figure 12.31 Restarting/Shutdown BlueCoat Reporter

Test Yourself

· ·

1. While you are troubleshooting the BlueCoat Proxy SG, you run ping, traceroute, and "test http get" command for the domain http://www.google.com to check if the Proxy SG is reachable through the Internet. None of the three commands give positive results. What can you conclude is the problem, based on the results?

   a. A internal or external firewall is blocking the traffic.
   b. The Internet link is down.
   c. The DNS server is not responding.
   d. All the above.

2. When running a "test http get" command, what are the HTTP codes that confirm that the Proxy SG web engine is working properly and the OCS server is reachable and responding?

   a. HTTP codes 200, 301, 302, 307, and 400
   b. HTTP codes 200, 301, 302, and 307
   c. HTTP codes 200, 301, 500, and 502
   d. d. HTTP codes 200, 307, and 503

3. In your data center, one of the BlueCoat Proxy 8100 SGs crashed and has hardware problems. BlueCoat support team has did a RMA of new box, you have back-up all the config from the old box, and now you have to apply the config to the new BlueCoat Proxy 8100 SG, as you know you need change and remove all the keywords "hashed-" and "encrypted-" and add the plain text password.

What is the main reason for performing this step of modifying the passwords before uploading the config file?

a. Because the private keys used in both boxes are different, the new box cannot decrypt the encrypted password of the configuration which was signed by a different private key.

b. b. The hashed password and encrypted password were removed, because the Proxy SG can easily upload the file without decrypting it.

c. The different Proxy SGs use different encryption algorithms, and removing the cipher keys makes the Proxy SG understand the config and password since it is easily readable.

d. The encrypted password are one-time generated so that each time when you have upload you have to change the cipher text to clear text and upload the config file.

4. **What different CLI options are available in the BlueCoat Proxy AV?**

a. No CLI options are available for Proxy AV.

b. b. SSH is the only available CLI option.

c. CLI is only available via serial connection and not via remote connection.

d. CLI is available via SSH and serial connection.

5. **What is the difference between the Alert Log file and Diagnostic log files?**

a. The Alert Log file contains ICAP failures; Diagnostic log files contain both internal information and ICAP failures.

b. The Alert Log file contains ICAP failures; Diagnostic log files contain internal information.

c. The Alert Log file contains ICAP failures and scanning queue length; Diagnostic log files contain internal information.

d. d. The Alert Log file contains ICAP failures and the CPU spikes that caused the ICAP failures; Diagnostic log files contain internal information.

6. **What happens when you "Shut Down Reporter" service in a BlueCoat Reporter server?**

a. Both the Windows OS and Reporter service get shut down.

b. The BlueCoat Reporter completely shuts down all services, including log source and report generation, but doesn't reboot or shut down the Windows OS.

c. Only the Reporter service, but reports can still be run from the Reporter server.

d. The Reporter service gets shut down, but the log source is opened so that all BlueCoat Proxy SGs can forward the logs, and the database is not generated.

7. **What are the steps that should be followed to generate a core file in BlueCoat Proxy SG?**

    a. Go to Maintenance → Core Images and change the menu option to "Full". "Apply" the changes, then go to CLI and restart the Proxy SG using the command "**restart abrupt**".

    b. Go to Maintenance → Core Images and change to the menu option "Full". "Apply" the changes, then go to CLI and restart the Proxy SG using the command "**restart regular**".

    c. Go to Maintenance → Core Images and change to the menu option "Full". "Apply" the changes, then power down the Proxy SG manually and power it on again.

    d. Go to Maintenance → Core Images and change to the menu option "Full". "Apply" the changes and wait for the Proxy SG to crash and reboot by itself.

8. **In ICAP scanning, while you are troubleshooting the Request History stats, you see a request such as the following:**

http://www.hacking.com/index.html Scanning, 1024 bytes, 23 ms, **Secure**

What does "Secure" mean in the above line?

    a. The Proxy AV is scanning HTTPS traffic.
    b. The ICAP scanning service is in "Secure mode".
    c. The Proxy AV is scanning a tunneled service.
    d. The Proxy AV is protected from the attacks of the payload from http://www.hacking.com.

9. **You have enabled a policy trace for the source IP address 192.168.10.250 as the client address on the Proxy SG with IP 192.168.10.101. When an administrator logs in to the Proxy SG from the machine 192.168.10.250 for which the policy trace is running, what information can you find in the policy trace, to evaluate it is a administration policy is log in?**

    a. The <Admin> marker is created in the policy trace and will have the access URL of CONNECT tcp://192.168.10.101:8082/

    b. The <Proxy> marker is created in the policy trace.

    c. There is only the access URL of "CONNECT tcp://192.168.10.101:8082/".

    d. No information is created regarding the administration access in the policy trace.

QUESTION AND ANSWERS

Chapter 1: Introduction to Proxies:

Answers:

1. If you have the world's best FireWall in your network and it could also do proxy and AV scanning, do you still need BlueCoat in your network?

The answer is a, Yes, because you don't want to load more resources in the firewall and make it a single point of failure. Though it provides proxy, what about caching, bandwidth management, URL filtering etc.?

2. How many websites are being rated per day by BlueCoat BCWF?

The answer is c. 7 Billion. WebPulse can categories and rate 7 billion sites per day.

3. Is BlueCoat Reporter?

a. A software product. It runs on Windows and Linux servers.

4 . Which is not a Secure Web gateway solution product?

d. Blue Coat® IntelligenceCenter Appliance. Blue Coat IntelligenceCenter provides powerful application performance monitoring for PacketShaper appliances deployed across your entire system.

5. What is K9 web protection?

b. A software product. It is installed on Windows and Mac systems, which will support browsers like IE, Firefox, and Safari as well as the IPad and IPhone.

6. Which of the following products that BlueCoat Director cannot manage?

a.,c. d., as BlueCoat Director can only manage BlueCoat Proxy SG.

7. Is BCWF installed on Proxy Client?

a. Yes, BCWF is installed on both BlueCoat Proxy SG and BlueCoat Proxy Client, and both contribute to the WebPulse cloud.

8.
Which company has the best products for both Secure Web Gateway and WAN optimization and is rated as the as number one product in the industry in Gartner?

c. BlueCoat is the only company that has the best products for both Secure Web Gateway and WAN optimization and is rated as the as as number one product in the industry.

9.Which application does the BlueCoat ProxySG does not provide complete proxy functionality(Application level) and can only do a TCP tunnel?

a. Blackberry. BlueCoat can only have application-level intelligence for HTTP, SSL, CIFS, SOCKS, EndPoint Mapper, FTP, Yahoo IM, MSN IM, AOL IM, DNS Proxy, HTTPS reverse Proxy, MMS, and Telnet. All the other non-standard applications or protocols could only be TCP tunneled in a proxy.

10. What protocol could be Antivirus and DLP integrated with BlueCoat Proxy SG?

d. ICAP. ICAP (Internet Content Adaptation Protocol) is a lightweight HTTP-like protocol which is used to integrate Antivirus and DLP with Proxy SG.

Chapter 2: Caching and Optimization

Answers:

1. If you are using BlueCoat Proxy SG as a caching engine for your organization, which is the best decision you could conclude that the cache engine is working at best performance based on Cache Hit and Cache Miss?

b. More Cache Hits. If there are more cache hits, it means there are lots of objects cached for the repeated user request.

2. If John started watching a video at 10:00 AM, and Sam wants to watch the video and requested the video at 10:10 AM, how much of the video is stored in the cache ?

d. 10 minutes, it is the temporary time difference between the first request and second request of the similar object.

3. The ARC(Adaptive Replacement cache) always constantly balances between two algorthims (Chose Two)

a, d.

4. Does MACH5 (Multiprotocol Accelerated Caching Hierarchy) provides encryption feature?

b. MACH5 (Multiprotocol Accelerated Caching Hierarchy) is a framework providing a multilayered approach to accelerate application. SSL can be used to provide encryption while still accelerating the traffic, but encryption is not a built-in feature of MACH-5.

5. In web and proxy terminology which of the following is not an object?

d. a user-agent is an HTTP header attribute on a user's request. All the other three are called objects, which will fetched from the OCS.

6. How does Asynchronous Adaptive Refresh (AAR) feature works in BlueCoat?

c. Without the user's request, all the cached objects are automatically refreshed based on their rate of change and their popularity.

7. With object pipelining how many objects are requested for one TCP connection?

a. 2. With one TCP connection, two objects can be requested, and pipelining is only supported in HTTP 1.1 and not in HTTP 1.0.

8. If you are deploying MACH 5 solution in your company, you want make sure that the web traffic used by different groups in the organization is controlled such IT team uses 25 % of the web traffic, 25% by the Sales and Marketing team for web traffic, and Senior management uses the rest 50% of the web traffic. Which MACH 5 feature will you implement to achieve this?

b. Bandwidth management. Bandwidth management is the process or technique of measuring, controlling, and monitoring the network traffic on a link to avoid throttling of thethe link, which would result in network congestion and poor performance of the network.

9. What are the compression/decompression methods supported by Proxy SG?

a., c. GZIP and Deflate are the compression/decompression methods supported by Proxy SG. But GZIP is considered more efficient than the Deflate algorithm.

Chapter 3: BlueCoat Proxy SG deployment

Answers:

1. Which the most challenging deployment for BlueCoat Engineers?

a. Transparent deployment. This is because the client web browse is not aware that is talking to a Proxy, when we introduce advanced concepts like authentication, web filtering, and networking, it becomes a real challenge for the BlueCoat engineers to implement it.

2. In transparent mode if a user is try accessing a website www.bluecoatweb.com , what will be source IP, destination IP and GET request when originating from the user?

c. The source IP will be the user machine IP address, destination will be the IP of http://www.bluecoatweb.com, and the GET request will be index.html HTTP/1.1, since the user browser thinks it is talking to the OCS server directly.

3. You have customer who wants to deploy BlueCoat Proxy SG solution, all the nodes in the company are not managed by the Domain Controller, they allow external DNS queries in the internal network, what is the best deployment method you would recommend for this customer?

b. Transparent proxy, because all the nodes are not managed by Domain Controller so you cannot manage the browser settings of all these nodes, and the client can able to resolve the DNS query, which is idle setup for Transparent deployment.

4. If you decided to use Transparent deployment for a large network, which is the most efficient and reliable method of implementing the solution?

d. Virtually inline method, because the Proxy SG is not the default gateway or in bridge mode, which will be a single point of failure in the network. The Inline method is only suitable for small networks.

5. In which method we point all the client computers default gateway to the BlueCoat Proxy SG?

b. Transparent—BlueCoat Proxy SG default router mode, which is the best security implementation by making all client computers point to a security gateway as the default gateway.

6. In explicit mode if a user is try accessing a website www.bluecoatweb.com , what will be source IP, destination IP and GET request when originating from the user?

a. Source IP: User's machine IP: Destination IP: Proxy IP; GET request: "**GET http:// www.bluecoatweb.com/index.html HTTP/1.1**", because in explicit deployment the Proxy SG will do the DNS lookup.

7. As a BlueCoat Engineer a customer wants to implement BlueCoat solution for Internet access to the users, and the customer doesn't wants to buy any extra hardware like L4 switch or router and doesn't wants to change any network design,to implement Blue-Coat Proxy SG, which BlueCoat Proxy SG method will you recommend to the customer.

b. Explicit proxy. For explicit deployment you don't need any network change or need to buy any extra hardware like an L4 switch, router, or any WCCP-enabled devices.

8. You work for a BlueCoat consulting firm, a customer has 4 web servers which needs to be hosted in the Internet, the customer wants the servers to be protected, load balanced, should have caching have caching feature, all the traffic should scanned with AV and should be handle heavy amount of traffic, which is the BlueCoat deployment mode you would recommend.

c. Reverse proxy.

9. What are the features of BlueCoat Proxy SG reverse proxy deployment method over the traditional load balancers?

a. Security, scalability, virus scanning, performance, and caching.

10. You are consulting for a BlueCoat customer, who has high volume of Internet traffic in the network, wants to implement BlueCoat web security solution, such as high caching of data, separating the users from directly accessing the Proxy SG, masquerade the network traffic few times, wants to separate internal and external cache data, which deployment could you recommend.

d. Forwarding proxy.

Chapter 4: Configuring Blue Coat Proxy SG.

Answers:

1. Which serial console cable do you use to connect to the BlueCoat Proxy SG and configure the initial settings?

d. Null modem cable. Always make sure you use this type of cable. The settings are as follows:

* Bits per second (bps): 9600

* Data bit: 8

* Parity: None

* Stop bits: 1

* Flow control: None

2. What are the different ways the settings can be configured on a BlueCoat Proxy SG?

a. Serial console, LCD panel, SSH, and HTTPS GUI .You can also configure Porxy SG using via Telnet and HTTP, but these methods are not used by default because of security issues.

3. When viewing the rear portion of the Proxy SG, you see an Ethernet naming convention as 1:0, what does it infer?

b. Adapter 1: Interface 0; it is always adapter:interface.

4. There are two gateways 10.10.10.100 and 10.10.10.200 configured in the Proxy SG with Group ID as 5 and weight as 5, what would be traffic between Proxy SG and the two gateways?

a. The traffic is load balanced between the two gateways 10.10.10.100 and 10.10.10.200 from the Proxy SG.

5. There are four gateways configured in the Proxy SG Gateway 1, Gateway 2, Gateway 3 with Group 5 and weight 100 and Gateway 4 with Group 10 and weight 50, when does Gateway 4 will activate in processing traffic.

c. When all Gateway 1, Gateway 2, and Gateway 3 are down, then the traffic is failover happens to Gateway 4, when any of the three gateways are up within 20 seconds, then it is failover to Group 5.

6. You have Internet facing Proxy SG and you have configured only two Primary DNS servers 4.2.2.2 and 8.8.8.8 in the same order and no Alternate DNS servers configured, and 4.2.2.2 DNS server is down and failed to respond DNS queries, will the users in your network will be able to access the Internet?

d. No. The Internet will be down, if the first DNS server in the Primary is down then it will not failover to the second DNS in the Primary, it will only failover if there is a DNS server configured in the Alternate.

7. What is the default time zone in the Proxy SG?

c. UTC

8. You have configured DNS imputing in the proxy as corporate.com. The user try accessing an internal website as http://perks, how does Proxy SG will apply DNS imputing to it.

b. The Proxy SG will append .corporate.com to the user's request as perks.corporate. com and will query the DNS server for the IP address.

9. In the interface setting you configure the interface as "Bypass transparent intercep-

tion", how does the BlueCoat Proxy will handle the explicit traffic?

a. The Proxy SG will bridge or forward all inbound traffic on this interface for transparent connections, not for explicit connections.

Chapter 5: Content Filtering and Web Pulse

Answers:

1. If you consider performance which one will you recommend to your customer between On-box content filtering or Off-box filtering solutions.

a., because the network round-trip time is saved and the queries cannot be tapped in a wire.

2. Which is the state-of-art design in the content filtering solutions provided by Blue-Coat?

c., BlueCoat web security gateway is a state-of-art design for content-filtering solutions provided by BlueCoat.

3. BlueCoat offers a hybrid content filtering solutions, which is a combination of On-Box content filtering and Off-Box content filtering, what is the technology that is called as On-Box and the Off-Box content filtering solution?

b. On-Box is BCWF and Off-Box is WebPulse DRTR Threat Protection

4. You are a Blue Coat customer and you would like to participate, contribute check content filtering database, by recommendation for categorizing the domain names, which is the online site portal which BlueCoat offers this service?

a. http://sitereview.bluecoat.com

5. What is the WebPulse service points provided by BlueCoat?

d. sp.cwfservice.net, which global DNS domain name which will resolve to an IP address based upon the region that is closest to the BlueCoat Proxy SG.

6. Which of the following content filtering combination is feasible for installing in a BlueCoat Proxy SG?

c. BCWF +IWF + Local database. Only one vendor content filtering can exist and it can be with IWF and the local database.

7. Which is the best design for the local database could resides so that all BlueCoat Proxy SG in the network could download it?

b. Create the local database in a web server or FTP server so that all Proxy SGs can download it.

8. Which database does the BCWF gets the daily update from the WebPulse cloud?

a. BUFF database. The external database is queried for unrated sites.

9. Does the information regarding the Private Networks and Private Domain from the BlueCoat Proxy SG are sent to the WebPulse cloud?

b. No. Refer to table 5.3 for the list of information sent to the WebPulse cloud. Any private information is not forwarded, and if the customer feels that certain information is private, he or she can customize using via the policies.

10. Could a domain be in multiple categories in BCWF?

a. Yes

Chapter 6: Visual Policy Manager (VPM)

Answers:

1. When you create policies on VPM, what is complied code of policies called?

d. CPL. If you write policies in VPM, they are complied into CPL; but instead of writing CPL directly you use the GUI tool which automatically generates it.

2. What is the default policy evaluation order in BlueCoat Proxy SG?

a. VPM → Local → Central → Forward. The order is configurable.

3. What is the maximum number of users could be created in a database and how many maximum databases could we create?

b. 50 databases with each database containing a maximum of 10,000 users.

4. In your VPM policy for the Proxy SG you only have two layers from the left the first layer is Web Access Layer and next to on it's right is Forwarding Layer, when the Proxy SG complies the policy and executes, which layer is executed and checked first irrespective of the traffic it is inspecting?

c. First Web Access Layer and then Forwarding Layer. There could be one admin to manage the box, but due to security and auditing reasons, additional admin accounts are created.

5. What is the difference between deny and force deny policy? (Chose Two)

b., d. A Force Deny object will execute the policy and if the condition is matched then it doesn't evaluate other policies in other layers, even if there is match. But a Deny object will execute the policy and if the condition is matched, it will still evaluate the rest of the policy.

6. In your VPM policy you have two Web Access layer, on the first layer you block access to www.cisco.com with a "Deny" object and in the second layer you have allowed www.cisco.com and we have global policy set to "Deny" in the policy options. Will your Proxy SG will allow access to www.cisco.com ?

a. You can access http://www.cisco.com. When a policy is finally allowed by the last layer and the last policy it evaluated, then Global Deny will not come into consideration.

7. In your VPM policy you have two Web Access layer, on the first layer you allow access to www.weather.com and in the second layer you have denied www.weather.com using a "Deny" object and we have global policy set to "Allow" in the policy options. Will your Proxy SG will allow access to www.weather.com ?

c. Global Policy is Allow. Access to http://**www.weather.com** is allowed and any other site which matched the "Deny" statement will be allowed unless there is "Force Deny".

8. In your company you have 10 GB Internet pipe and you always want fresh objects from the site and you don't want any cached content from the Proxy SG, since there is huge bandwidth and you not are much concerned about bandwidth, what options could help you design such a requirement?

b. Always Verify. If you use "Do not cache", the server response is not cached and the previous cache is deleted.

9. What is the flow in which the policy layers and rules are executed?

d. Policy layers left to right and rules top to bottom

10. What is the Policy file that BlueCoat could use when Proxy SG for performance (bugs in SGOS) and filters(new emerging virus, worms, etc..)?

a. Central policy file. The default location is https://download.bluecoat.com/release/SG4/files/CentralPolicy.txt.

Chapter 7: Authentication

1. What are the Out-of-Band and physical way of protecting the BlueCoat Proxy SG. (Choose two)

a., b. The other two methods are through the network.

2. When a user is trying to authenticate a password protected resource in the web server, what is the HTTP code does the user gets while the web server is try authenticating the browser?

c. The 401 HTTP code is generated by web server when authenticating the web browser.

3. When a user is try accessing www.yahoo.com, without using a proxy, directly connected from his home, how does the GET request will be from the user. (No proxy setting configured)

a. It should be the GET request, and the version of the HTTP protocol also should be in the client request.

4. When a user is try accessing www.bluecoat.com using a BlueCoat proxy SG and the user's browser is explicitly pointed to the proxy, how does the GET request will be from the browser.

d. and not b., since the request should follow the RFC specification as **scheme://domain:port/path?query_string#fragment_id** .

5. When a user is trying to authenticate a password protected resource in the web server, what is the HTTP code does the user gets while the web server denied access to the website?

b. When the user credentials are not valid, then the user will get an HTTP 403 message.

6. For one time authentication and cookie based authentication what is the very essential requirement for designing the Proxy-based authentication method.

c. Virtual URL

7. When we configure a proxy based authentication what will be HTTP header for the HTTP code and authenticate attribute field looks like, when sent from the proxy to the browser.

d. HTTP 407 and Proxy Authorization

8. You are deploying BlueCoat Web security solutions for a company and the require-

ment is that you need to configure authentication policy for all the users and allow access to all the sites in the Internet. You created the first layer as Web Access Layer and configured Allow all policy, then the next layer you created the Web Authentication policy through VPM. So when the user is trying to go to Internet, will the user will be prompted for authentication?

a. Yes. The user will be prompted for authentication, since the policy gets executed from left to right, though the first layer is Web Access Layer, the Web Authentication gets executed first.

9. When web server is configured to authenticate users what will be HTTP header for the HTTP code and authenticate attribute field looks like, when sent from the proxy to the browser.

c. HTTP 401 and WWW-Authenticate

Chapter 8: WCCP

Answers:

1. What are devices in Cisco supports WCCP?

d. All the above

2. What is the well-know service groups in WCCP?

b. 80. There is only one well-known port in WCCP, because the router and Proxy SG should understand the characteristics of the service or protocol.

3. If you BlueCoat engineer and designing and Internet Web gateway using BlueCoat Proxy SG solution, what are the ports will you include in the WCCP services for accessing web, multi-media and streaming services?

a. 80, 443, 554, 1755, and 1935, it the HTTP, HTTPS, MMS, RTSP, and RTMP ports that should be included in the WCCP service group.

4. Which will consume less overhead both in the router and Proxy SG when enabling WCCP either using GRE or L2 methods?

b. L2, because it happens at Layer 2, while GRE happens at Layer 3.

5. In your network you have four BlueCoat Proxy SG and all configured with service group 50, and Proxy SG1 IP is 10.10.10.100, Proxy SG2 IP is 10.10.10.50, Proxy SG3 IP is 10.10.10.200 and Proxy SG4 IP is 10.10.10.99, and the WCCP enabled FireWall IP as 10.10.10.1. Which is the designated cache?

c. Proxy SG 2 10.10.10.50. When a service group is formed between the BlueCoat Proxy SG and the router, the ProxySG with the lowest IP address automatically becomes the designated cache is the one that defines the router how to redirect traffic

6. What is the algorithm and bucket output value used by hash and mask assignment?

d. Hash uses XOR operation with 256 bit bucket value and mask uses AND with 64 bit bucket value.

7. In your network you want all returned packet to be redirected to the WCCP enabled devices and don't want the BlueCoat Proxy SG to send the return packet directly to the client by using a routable table in the Proxy SG. What feature will help you do this?

a. Router affinity

8. You are configuring WCCP in a BlueCoat and you have decided to use hash assignment and you have selected the Primary hash as Destination IP, and users start accessing the Internet and you see a hotspot on one Proxy SG what is the cause of it?

c. If most users are accessing http://www.google.com, then any one of the Proxy SG will be overloaded because the request is to the same destination. Selecting the destination port will also not help, so you have to be very careful in selecting the hash attribute.

9. You have three proxies, two are Proxy SG 810 and one is Proxy SG 8100, and you have configured weights on the WCCP, both Proxy SG 810 has a weight of 50 and Proxy SG 8100 has a weight of 100, what is the amount of traffic received by each Proxy SG?

b. Each Proxy SG 810 will receive ¼ traffic and Proxy SG 8100 will receive ½ traffic. The total weight is 200, so each Proxy SG 810 should receive 50/200, which is ¼, and Proxy SG 8100 should receive 100/200, which is ½.

Chapter Proxy Antivirus
Answers:

1. What are the protocols could the ICAP can scan? (Chose Two)

a.,c. ICAP/1.0 has been designed to encapsulate HTTP messages. By translating other protocols first to HTTP and then encapsulating them into ICAP, some vendors have found a way to also use ICAP for other protocols such as FTP; in this case implementation remains interoperable with other ICAP services. ICAP has also been used to encapsulate messages of other protocols natively (without translating to HTTP first); those implementations are usually not standard implementations and are not interoperable with other solutions.

2. You have planned to implement BlueCoat solutions in your company, you have decided to use BlueCoat DLP for identifying data theft and to scan all inbound traffic via BlueCoat Proxy AV (Sophos), which mode will you use for intergrating BlueCoat DLP and Proxy SG and which mode will you use to integrate BlueCoat Proxy AV(Sophos)?

a. For BlueCoat DLP it is the REQMOD mode and BlueCoat Proxy AV it is the RESP-MOD mode.

3. ISTag is the mechanism that is given by the ICAP server(BlueCoat Proxy AV) about the current service state to the ICAP client(BlueCoat Proxy SG), so an current ISTag is 1, then the Proxy AV updates it's signature database and notifies the Proxy SG about it's state and sends an ISTag 0, now there is a change in the ISTag, so the Proxy should re-scan all the objects in the cache with the new signature from the Proxy AV. Will this re-scan will take place, because the value of the ISTag have decremented from 1 to 0?

a. Yes. It could be any number; 0 is a number.

4. If an ICAP request or response should be made from a Proxy SG to Proxy AV, what will be the URL protocol format?

d. icap://proxyavip/avscan. The ICAP request by default are made to port 1344.

5. In your company your network has a Internet pipe of 2 MB, and when downloading certain large files takes time and you are much concerned about large downloads because it will consume your Proxy AV connections. What is the feature that the Proxy AV uses to remove slow connections?

b. Intelligent Connection Traffic Monitoring (ICTM) allows the ProxyAV to drop download connections that are taking longer than a normal amount of time to complete.

6. You have implemented BlueCoat Proxy AV solutions in your company, now you want to test both REQMOD and RESPMOD mode. What is the best method does all the security professional uses for testing Proxy AV scanning engine functionality for detecting malware?

c. Test via http://www.eicar.org.

7. What does the port secure ICAP works?

a. Port 11344

8. What is the feature in Proxy AV that will deferred unnecessarily ICAP connections until the full object has been downloaded?

d. Deferred scanning

9. Which is the best deployment of implementing Proxy AV solutions in your network in terms of security, performance, and redundancy ?

b. Many Proxy SGs and many Proxy AVs

10. Let's imagine you have 4 Proxy AV in your network and all failed at one time, which network security technology will help at these times of outage?

c. IPS can stop all malwares in real time in the network, so it should help you in addition to the Proxy AV scanning.

Chapter 10: BlueCoat Reporter

Answers:

1. What are the log that is been forwarded to the BlueCoat Reporter by the Proxy SG?

b. Access log. The event log can be forwarded to a syslog server; policy traces and core files can be sent to BlueCoat support for analysis when there is a problem.

2. Can we intergrate BlueCoat Reporter with third party SIEM tools like Arcsight, Symantec, IBM, etc..

a. Yes.

3. What is the database does the BlueCoat Reporter uses?

c. BlueCoat Database; it is the BlueCoat proprietary database.

4. What are operating system could the BlueCoat Reporter could be installed?

a., d.

5. If the BlueCoat Reporter is down and the access log limit in the Proxy SG reached it's limit of space, what are two decisions that could be made by the Proxy SG?

b., c. The limit is based upon the hardware platform you use. You can check the limit by logging into the Management Console → Configuration → Access Logging → Global Settings and look under the section "If maximum log size is reached:".

6. What happens to the logs when once the Proxy SG has uploaded to the BlueCoat Reporter successfully?

d. Once uploaded, then delete it.

7. To encrypt the access logs could we send it in the Internet via a VPN connection to the BlueCoat Reporter .

a. Yes, you can use VPN to do it, or in BlueCoat Proxy SG you have the option of encrypting the access log.

8. Could we install BlueCoat Reporter software on SAN drive rather than a physical drive for better performance?

a. Yes. For high performance it is recommended to install it on a SAN drive so the R/W access is faster via a fibre channel.

Chapter 11: K9 Web Protection

Answers:

1. What is K9 web protection?

d. Security tool that contains content filtering

2. Does BlueCoat K9 web protection software could be installed on MAC books, IPhone, iPod, and iPad?

a. Yes.

3. If we want to block Internet access every night time for kids, what is the feature that is available in BlueCoat K9 web protection called?

c. Night Guard. It turns off Internet access between 10:00 p.m. and 7:00 a.m. by default, when enabled. The time range could be modified to custom time interval.

4. Is the BlueCoat K9 web protection has the same filtering database as BCWF that is installed in BlueCoat Proxy SG?

b. Yes, they are the same.

5. If the "Block Unsafe search" option is disabled in "Force Safe Search", what happens when the user using a search engine that is not supported by BlueCoat K9 web protection?

c. It is allowed.

6. You are using the computer in which BlueCoat K9 web protection is installed and you are been blocked by certain website, but you want to temporarily to unblock it, what is the best way to override access?

d. Blocking effects using Admin options

7. You are using the computer in which BlueCoat K9 web protection is installed and you want to permanently unblock all sites for 1 hour, what is the best way to override access?

a. Supervisor mode. At maximum you could block for one hour.

8. If you are a parent and always busy working and arranging the home and the kids are on the computer surfing the Internet and you next close to them, as you are in different room, what is the best way to notify when the kids try accessing the blocked site?

b. Barking effect

9. Someone has made some hacked or changed your settings in BlueCoat K9 web protection software what is the easiest way to recover to the original settings?

c. Reset to initial settings

Chapter 12: Trouble-shooting and Maintenance

Answers:

1. While you are trouble-shooting the BlueCoat Proxy SG you run ping, traceroute and test http get command for the domain www.google.com to check the Proxy SG is reachable through the Internet and none of the three commands gave no positive results. What is the problem you could conclude based on the results?

d. All the above, even DNS is working, you will get no positive results, it means not the Proxy SG or Internet or firewall is down, the Proxy SG is not able to do a lookup. Try running a ping, traceroute, and test HTTP GET with the IP address of http://www.google.com.

2. When running a test http get command what are HTTP codes that confirms that the Proxy SG web engine is working properly and the OCS server is reachable and responding.

b. HTTP codes 200, 301, 302, and 307. All others are related to bad requests and error messages.

3. In your data center one of the BlueCoat Proxy 8100 SG crashed and has hardware problems, and BlueCoat support have did a RMA of new box, you have back-up all the config from the old box, and now you have to apply the config to the new BlueCoat Proxy 8100 SG, as you know you need change the remove all the keywords "hashed-" and "encrypted-" and add the plain text password, what is the main reason of performing this step of modifying the passwords before uploading the config file?

a. This change applies even if the Proxy SG crashes and you lose all the information or if you do a factory reset which deletes all the config and keys, and try uploading the same config in the same crashed or reset proxy, because now you have a private being generated.

4. What are different CLI options are available in the BlueCoat Proxy AV?

c. Always remember that there is no CLI available via a remote shell for the Proxy AV.

5. What is the difference between the Alert Log file and Diagnostic log files?

b. The Alert Log file contains ICAP failures and the Diagnostic log file contains internal information, scanning queue length, Proxy AV scanning, number of active threads, CPU, memory, etc.

6. What happens when we "Shut Down Reporter" service in a BlueCoat Reporter server?

d. The Reporter service gets shut down, but the log source is opened so that all Blue-Coat Proxy SGs can forward the logs, but the database is not generated. The reason you have still the FTP service running in the Reporter server, which is a Windows server component, if you want to shut down for the Reporter server not to listen to any logs, you need to turn-off the FTP server also.

7. What are the steps that should be followed to generate a core file in BlueCoat Proxy SG?

a. Make sure you run the restart abrupt command; an automatic reboot or manual reboot will not generate the core file.

8. In ICAP scanning while you are trouble-shooting the Request History stats and you see a request such as follows:

http://www.hacking.com/index.html Scanning, 1024 bytes, 23 ms, **Secure**

What does "Secure" means in the above line?

b. the Proxy AV scanning the traffic is in Secure ICAP mode, as could confirm the traffic sent from the Proxy SG to the Proxy either in ICAP or ICAPS mode. ICAPS is used in secure environment where the data shouldn't be tapped with packet sniffers.

9. You have enabled policy trace for a source IP address 192.168.10.250 a on Proxy SG with IP 192.168.10.101, so when an administrator logs in to the Proxy SG from the machine 192.168.10.250 for which policy trace is running, what are the information could we find in the policy trace, to evaluate it is a administration login?

c. You will have only the access URL as "CONNECT tcp://192.168.10.101:8082/", and you can evaluate it is a administration traffic because it is the Proxy IP on port 8082 which is administration port.

APPENDIX A:

The different Proxy SG model that was discussed in Chapter 1 is the legacy models and will not be in sale from next year. The new models of Proxy SG are shown below:

Older Proxy SG models are SG 210, SG 510, SG 810, and SG 8100. The newer generations of Proxy SG models are SG 300, SG 600, SG 900 and SG 9000.

Always check with the sales team with different sub-models in each of the Proxy SG which in turn has different RAM size, Hard Disk space, bandwidth speed etc... For e.g. in SG 900 model we have SG 900-10, SG 900-20, 900-30 and SG 900-45. Each of the sub models, the pricing is different based on the computation power of the proxy.

Blue Coat ProxySG Appliances	
Blue Coat ProxySG Series: Full Proxy Edition	
Blue Coat ProxySG 300 Full Proxy Edition	**Blue Coat ProxySG 600 Full Proxy Edition**
• 30 to Unlimited User License Capacity • 1x250GB SATA Disk Drives • 2GB - 4GB RAM	• 500 to Unlimited User License Capacity • 1x250GB SATA to 2x250GB SATA Disk Drives • 4GB RAM
Blue Coat ProxySG 900 Full Proxy Edition	**Blue Coat ProxySG 9000 Full Proxy Edition**
• 3500 to Unlimited User License Capacity • 2x500GB SAS to 4x1TB SAS Disk Drives • 6 GB RAM - 16 GB RAM	• 3500 - Unlimited User License Capacity • 2x500GB SAS to 4x1TB SAS Disk Drives • 6 GB RAM - 16 GB RAM

INDEX

Access logging 332, 399
Action object 187, 201
Adapters 94
Adaptive Refresh 55
Adaptive Replacement Cache (ARC) 33
Admin Access Layer 194
Admin Authentication Layer 194
Administrator accounts 182
Advanced locality principle 31
Allowing 129
Alternate DNS servers 111
Always verify 217
Anti-virus scanning 2
Anti-virus signature updates 305
Asynchronous Adaptive Refresh 55
Authentication 223
Authentication servers 244
Authenticate-401 120
Authentication 3
Authorization 224
Background mode 158
Bandwidth management 47
Barked when blocked 373
BCWF categories 137-146
BCWF database 147
Belady's Algorithm 30
Blocking 129
Blue Coat® Director 14
Blue Coat® K9 Web Protection 12, 359
Blue Coat® Proxy Client 10
Blue Coat® Reporter 13, 327
BlueCoat 3

BlueCoat AV Appliance 6
BlueCoat AV Product family 8
BlueCoat Product Suite 4
BlueCoat Proxy SG Appliance 5
BlueCoat Proxy SG Family 6
Bluecoat SG Proxy Deployment 55
BlueCoat WebFilter(BCWF) 8,9, 137
Boot logs 406
BUFF 155
Bypassing proxy services 123
Byte Caching 45
Cache Hit 20
Cache miss 21
Caching 19
Caching algorithm 24
Central file 177
Child proxy 71
Chrome 68
Client Connector 16
Clock 36
Combined objects 207
Competitive ratio 29
Compression 49
Compression/Decompression Browser 51
Compression/Decompression 50, 51
Configurable objects 181
Configuration Mode 84
Configuration tab 88
Connection timeout 308
Console services 117
Content Filtering 127
Content Policy File (CPL) 175

Content-Filtering Categories 128
Content-Filtering Databases 128
Content-filtering vendors 131
Cookie surrogate 237
Core file 391
Core Images 332
CPL file 176
CPL Layer 195
Custom DNS Group list 114
Custom-built local DB 134
Default gateway 102
Deferred scanning 322
Delete Layer 193
Deny 210
Deny action 204
Designated cache 270
Detect Protocol 121
Diagnostic logs
Dictionary Compression 45
DLP 3
DLP 3
DNS 109
DNS Access layer 195
DNS imputing 114
DNS Lookup Restrictions 195
Do not cache 217
Down arrow buttons 87
Downstream proxy 71
DRTR 151
Duplex 96
Dynamic Categorization 151
Dynamic content 50
Dynamic Load Balancing 254
Edit Mode 85
Edit option 192
Eicar 319
Enable ADN 121
Enter button 85
Equal Load Balancing 268
Error answer 110
Event logging 332, 412
Explicit Authentication 233
Explicit Proxy 16
Explicit proxy deployment 66

Extended Time-Based Expiration 36
External Database 155
Failover 106
Fiddler 399
File extension 316
File option 191
File types 320
Firefox 67
FirmWare updates 305
First in First Out (FIFO) 35
Force Authenticate Object 187
Force cache 217
Force deny 210
Force Safe Search 377
Forward File 177
Forward Proxy Deployment 71
Forwarding Layer 195
Full answer 110
Fundamental locality principle 31
Generated CPL 196
Generating reports 353
Global denied access 180
GRE 259
GRE Forwarding 260
GRE Redirection 259
Group Log order 195
Hash Assignment 271
Health check 400
Hit Rate 23
Hot Spot Handling 254
HTTP commands 387
HTTP method 50
Hybrid 135
ICAP Protocol 283
ICAP service ports 308
Inline deployment 57
Intelligent Connection Traffic Monitoring
    (ICTM) 322
Internal proxy 71
Internet activity 380
Internet Explorer 67
Intranet proxy 71
Invalidation 23
IP forwarding 65

IP routing 102
IP surrogate 237
IPSec VPN 16
IS-TAG 288
IWF 132,164
IWF database 164
K9 Software updates 381
L2 Forwarding 265
L2 Redirection 259
Latency 23
Layer 181
Layer Guard 193
LCD Panel 83, 229
LDAP 243
LDAP DN 246
LDAP Object Classes 247
LDAP Realm 245
LDAP Search and Groups 247
LDAP/IWA Browser 249
Least-Frequently Used (LFU) 32
Least-Recently Used (LRU or Last Used) 30
Left arrow buttons 87
Link Settings 97
Listener 122
Load Balancing 104, 254
Local Database 132, 166, 214
Local file 109, 176
Local Realm 184
Log Parser 331
Log Processor 331
Log Reader 331
Log source 351, 414
MACH 5 5, 38
Maintenance tab 88
Malware 283
Malware feedback 160
Man in the Middle 69
Management console 88
Mask Assignment 272
Master Rating Database (MRD) 155
Memory Buffer 330
Menu bar 191
Menu button 86
Most-Recently Used (MRU) 31

Multicast 258
Network interfaces 94
Network tools 402
Night Guard 371
None 151
Non-recursive queries 110
NTP 93
Object 39, 181
Object caching 41
Object Occurrences 196
Object pipelining 41
Off-Box filtering 134
Off-line algorithm 26
On-Box filtering 132
On-line algorithm 24
Packet capture 393
Paging 20
Partial answer 110
Pending 151
Ping 385
Pipelining 42
Point-to-Point method 52
Policy 182
Policy Evaluation Options 179
Policy Evaluation Order 196
Policy Traces 332, 394
Primary DNS Server 110
Private Domains 115
Private Networks 115
Proactive Threat Detection 160
Processed logs 331
Protocol optimization 48
Proxied application 2
Proxy 1,
Proxy AV 281
Proxy AV Deployment 289
Proxy Chaining 158
Proxy Chaining 16
Proxy products 17
Proxy Services 117,118
Proxy SG default router 64
Pseudo-LRU 32
Random Replacement 34
Raw logs 330

Real-time mode 151

Recursive queries 113

Redirection 259

Reload drivers 407

Remote CLI 230

Remote URL 108

Rename Layer 193

Reorder layers 193

Replacement Policy or Algorithm 23

REQMOD 284

Request Modification 308

RESPMOD 286

Retrieval Cost 23

Return method 260, 265

Reverse DNS Lookup Restrictions 195

Reverse Proxy Deployment 69

Right arrow buttons 87

Router Affinity 268

Rule 181

Safari 68

Scalability 254

Scan status 402

Second chance 35

Second Chance Replacement (SCR) algorithm 35

Security 254

Serial Console 77, 225

Service Group 120

Service Group 255, 258

Simple Time-Based 36

Sliding time-based expiration 37

Snapshots 332

SOCKS Authentication Layer 195

SOCKS Gateway 158

Speed 96

SSL Access Layer 195

SSL Intercept Layer 195

SSL optimization 55

Static content 50

Static routes 107

Statistics tab 88

Status Mode 83

Storage Cost 23

Supervisor Mode 379

TCP handshake 44

Text Editor 109, 178

Threat Pulse 15

Time 91

Time restrictions 370

Time zone 91

Toolbar 196

Traceroute 385

Transparent Authentication 234

Transparent Bridging 63

Transparent interception 95

Transparent Layer 4 switch 58

Transparent proxy deployment 56

Transparent WCCP 61

Trigger Objects 200

Unavailable 151

Unequal Load Balancing 269

Unicast 258

Unlicensed 151

Unsafe search 378

Up arrow buttons 87

URL filtering 3

URL keywords 376

User Agent 233

Virtual inline deployment 57

Visual Policy Manager(VPM) 175

VLAN 98

VLAN ID 98

VPM dashboard 190

VPM files 178

WCCP 253

Web Access Layer 195

Web Authentication Layer 195

Web Categories 370

Web Content Layer 195

WebPulse 150

WebPulse cloud service 160

WebPulse service points 160

Website exceptions 372

X-Client IP 287

CPSIA information can be obtained at www.ICGtesting.com
Printed in the USA
LVOW03s1524190514

386429LV00007B/224/P

9 780615 582931